HANDBOOKS

O'AHU

ROBERT NILSEN

O'AHU

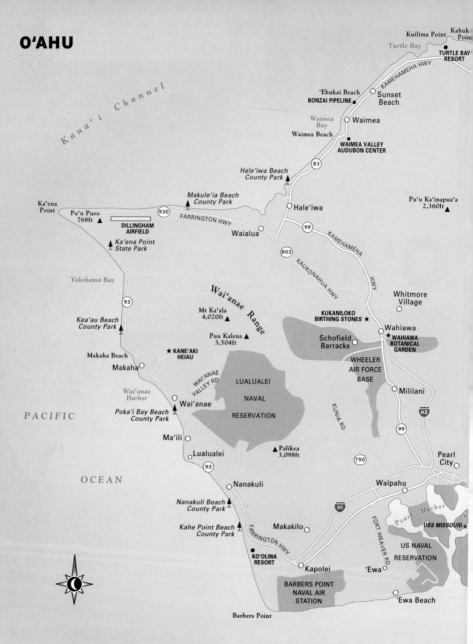

Kuilima Point
Kahuku Point
Turtle Bay
TURTLE BAY RESORT

Kaua'i Channel

'Ehukai Beach
BONZAI PIPELINE ■
Sunset Beach

Waimea Bay
Waimea
Waimea Beach
■ **WAIMEA VALLEY AUDUBON CENTER**

Hale'iwa Beach County Park ▲

83

Makule'ia Beach County Park

Ka'ena Point
Pu'u Pueo 768ft ▲
DILLINGHAM AIRFIELD

930

FARRINGTON HWY

Hale'iwa

Pu'u Ka'inapua'a 2,360ft ▲

Waialua

99

803

▲ Ka'ena Point State Park

Yokohama Bay

93

Wai'anae Range

Mt Ka'ala 4,020ft ▲

Puu Kalena 3,504ft ▲

KAUKONAHUA HWY

KAMEHAMEHA HWY

Whitmore Village

KUKANILOKO BIRTHING STONES ★

Schofield Barracks

Wahiawa
★ **WAHIAWA BOTANICAL GARDEN**

Kea'au Beach County Park ▲

★ **KANE'AKI HEIAU**

Makaha Beach

Makaha

WHEELER AIR FORCE BASE

WAI'ANAE VALLEY RD

LUALUALEI NAVAL RESERVATION

Mililani

H2

Wai'anae Harbor

Wai'anae

Poka'i Bay Beach County Park ▲

Ma'ili

KUNA RD

99

PACIFIC

Lualualei

93

▲ Palikea 3,098ft

750

Pearl City

OCEAN

Nanakuli

Nanakuli Beach County Park ▲

Waipahu

Pearl Harbor

USS MISSOURI ★

Kahe Point Beach County Park ▲

Makakilo

FARRINGTON HWY

H1

FORT WEAVER RD

US NAVAL RESERVATION

■ **KO'OLINA RESORT**

Kapolei

'Ewa

BARBERS POINT NAVAL AIR STATION

'Ewa Beach

Barbers Point

Mamala Bay

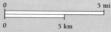

0   5 mi

0   5 km

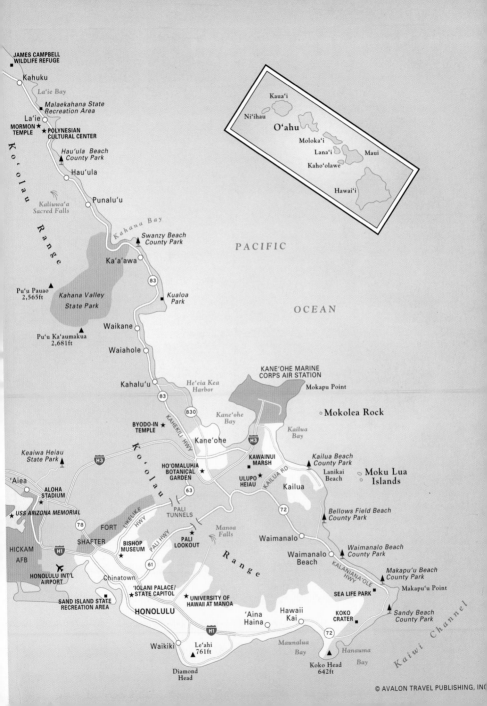

JAMES CAMPBELL
WILDLIFE REFUGE

Kahuku

La'ie Bay

Malaekahana State
Recreation Area

La'ie
MORMON ★
TEMPLE
★ POLYNESIAN
CULTURAL CENTER

Hau'ula Beach
County Park

Hau'ula

Ko'olau Range

Punalu'u

Kaliuwa'a
Sacred Falls

Kahana Bay

Swanzy Beach
County Park

Ka'a'awa

Pu'u Pauao
2,565ft

Kahana Valley
State Park

Kualoa
Park

83

Waikane

Pu'u Ka'aumakua
2,681ft

Waiahole

PACIFIC

OCEAN

Kahalu'u

83

He'eia Kea
Harbor

830

KANE'OHE MARINE
CORPS AIR STATION

Mokapu Point

Mokolea Rock

BYODO-IN
TEMPLE

KAHEKILI HWY

Kane'ohe
Bay

Kailua
Bay

Kane'ohe

H3

Keaiwa Heiau
State Park

H3

HO'OMALUHIA
BOTANICAL
GARDEN

KAWAINUI
MARSH

Kailua Beach
County Park

Lanikai
Beach

Moku Lua
Islands

'Aiea

ALOHA
STADIUM

ULUPO
HEIAU

Ko'olau

63

Kailua

KAILUA RD

USS ARIZONA MEMORIAL

78

FORT
SHAFTER

LIKELIKE HWY

PALI
TUNNELS

72

Bellows Field Beach
County Park

HICKAM
AFB

H1

BISHOP
MUSEUM

PALI HWY

Manoa
Falls

PALI
LOOKOUT

Range

Waimanalo

HONOLULU INT'L
AIRPORT

Chinatown

61

Waimanalo
Beach

Waimanalo Beach
County Park

SAND ISLAND STATE
RECREATION AREA

'IOLANI PALACE/
STATE CAPITOL

★ UNIVERSITY OF
HAWAII AT MANOA

KALANIANA'OLE HWY

Makapu'u Beach
County Park

HONOLULU

'Aina
Haina

Hawaii
Kai

SEA LIFE
PARK

Makapu'u Point

Waikiki

H1

Le'ahi
761ft

KOKO
CRATER

72

Sandy Beach
County Park

Diamond
Head

Maunalua
Bay

Koko Head
642ft

Hanauma
Bay

Kaiwi Channel

© AVALON TRAVEL PUBLISHING, INC.

Kaua'i

Ni'ihau

O'ahu

Moloka'i

Lana'i

Maui

Kaho'olawe

Hawai'i

DISCOVER O'AHU

It is the destiny of certain places to be imbued with an inexplicable magnetism, a power that draws people whose visions and desires combine at just the right moment to create a dynamism so strong that it becomes history. The result for these "certain places" is greatness . . . and O'ahu is one of these. Aside from the original Polynesian settlers, O'ahu has drawn adventurers, traders, missionaries, businesspeople, large numbers of immigrants, and a multitude of sun seekers to its shores, who together have created a melting pot society like few places on earth.

It is difficult to separate O'ahu from its vibrant metropolis, Honolulu, whose massive political, economic, and social muscle dominates the entire state, let alone its home island. But to look at Honolulu *as* O'ahu is to look only upon the face of a great sculpture, ignoring the beauty and subtleties of the whole.

The island is much more than the big city of Honolulu. First and foremost there is Waikiki, the town's most famous beach, a strand of

Byodo-In Temple at the Valley of the Temples

soft sand that has drawn water worshippers for well over a century. The name Waikiki conjures up images of gentle surf, palm trees swaying, and a golden moon rising romantically over a white-sand beach. Most first-time and return visitors spend at least a few days on O'ahu, usually in Waikiki. For many, Waikiki is their first exposure to the American tropics, and its reality does not disappoint.

For others, O'ahu means surfing. While the other Hawaiian Islands also have their premier surfing spots and there are plenty of great waves in other countries, O'ahu's North Shore has, arguably, the best surfing in the world. Waimea Bay, Banzai Pipeline, Sunset Beach, and others all have their mystique; each one contributed to the halcyon days of the 1960s when surfing became a lifestyle – and that way of life is still vibrant for many along the North Shore.

Far earlier than surfing enthusiasts, others had their eye on this island. The military saw O'ahu as a great place for anchorage, and over time it became the most important Pacific naval port for

Plumeria

the United States Navy. The army and air force arrived as well, and as the island came to be viewed as an unsinkable battleship, the state became the most militarized in the union. However, this militarization didn't keep the dogs of war from its doorstep. It was the bombing of Pearl Harbor and the sinking of the USS *Arizona* that caused the country to declare war against Japan, and it was on the deck of the USS *Missouri* that the Japanese finally surrendered. These two "bookends" to that war lie within a gunshot distance of each other in the now calm waters of Pearl Harbor. World War II had an indelible effect on the country, and O'ahu proudly preserves a great number of the commemorative sites and memorials from the Pacific theater of that war.

O'ahu is partly a tropical garden, bathed by soft showers and sunshine, swaying with a gentle but firm rhythm. You can experience this feeling all over the island, even in pockets of downtown Honolulu and Waikiki. With such a large population and so much activity, O'ahu still has a fair amount of unspoiled natural areas. The

The traditional double-hulled sailing vessel *Hokule'a* is emblematic of a vibrant Hawaiian cultural renewal.

island has a mountainous interior, an indescribably rugged *pali* facing the trade winds to the east, large tracts set aside as natural preserves for indigenous flora and fauna, undeveloped coastal zones, and lush rainforests. With all this, there's still room for a healthy agricultural sector. While sugar is now gone, the interior plateau's fields of pineapple and gardens of organic fruits and vegetables contribute to the city's larder.

O'ahu has a brash side – the confidence of a major American city perched on the Pacific Basin whose music is a pounding staccato jackhammer, a droning bulldozer, and the mechanical screech of the ever-present building crane. Even with its deep history and the resurgence of its cultural past, O'ahu looks inexorably forward to meet the demands of the coming day.

People are amazed at the diversity of experiences the island has to offer. Besides the obvious (and endless) beach activities, there are museums, botanical gardens, a fine zoo and excellent aquarium, nightclubs, extravagant shows, free entertainment, theaters, sporting

Ma'ili Beach County Park is one of several fine camping sites on O'ahu.
© ROBERT NILSEN

events, a major university, historical sights galore, an exotic cosmo-politan atmosphere, and backcountry hiking — all easily accessible via terrific public transportation. Finally, to sweeten the pot, O'ahu can be the least expensive of the Hawaiian Islands to visit.

O'ahu is called the "Gathering Place," and to itself it has indeed gathered the noble memories of old Hawaii, the vibrancy of a bright-eyed fledgling state, and the brawny power so necessary for the future. On this amazing piece of land adrift in the great ocean, 900,000 people live and over seven times that number visit yearly. O'ahu has garnered strength and maturity, and as time passes, it remains strong as one of those certain places of greatness.

The site of competitions for decades, Makaha Beach produces some of the best surfing waves on the island.

Contents

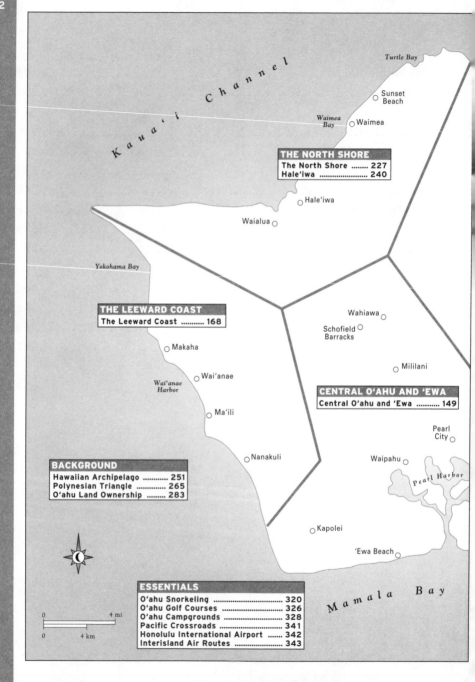

Kaua'i Channel

Turtle Bay

○ Sunset Beach

Waimea Bay ○ Waimea

THE NORTH SHORE

○ Hale'iwa

Waialua ○

Yokohama Bay

THE LEEWARD COAST

Wahiawa ○

Schofield ○ Barracks

○ Makaha

○ Wai'anae

Wai'anae Harbor

○ Mililani

CENTRAL O'AHU AND 'EWA

○ Ma'ili

Pearl City ○

BACKGROUND

○ Nanakuli

Waipahu ○

Pearl Harbor

○ Kapolei

'Ewa Beach ○

ESSENTIALS

Mamala Bay

0   4 mi
0   4 km

MAP CONTENTS

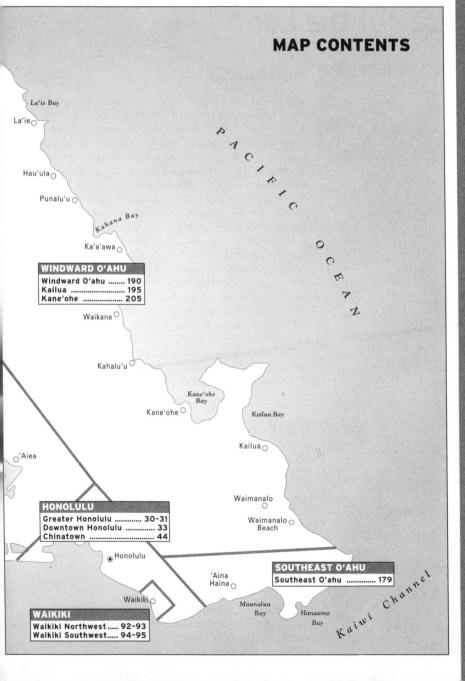

P A C I F I C   O C E A N

La'ie Bay
La'ie

Hau'ula

Punalu'u

Kahana Bay

Ka'a'awa

Waikane

Kahalu'u

Kane'ohe Bay

Kane'ohe

Kailua Bay

Kailua

'Aiea

Waimanalo

Waimanalo Beach

Honolulu

'Aina Haina

Waikiki

Maunalua Bay

Hanauma Bay

Kaiwi Channel

Lay of the Land

HONOLULU

In Honolulu, you'll find a delightful mixture of exotic and ordinary, of quaintly historic and future-shock new. The center is ʻIolani Palace, heralded by the gilded statue of Kamehameha I; within easy walking distance is the State Capitol and attendant government buildings. Chrome and glass skyscrapers holding the offices of Hawaii's economical mighty shade small stone and wooden missionary structures from the 19th century. Down at the harbor, Aloha Tower greets passenger ships that still make port. The nearby streets of Chinatown exude the strong and distinctive flavor of transplanted Asia, and the Bishop Museum boasts *the* best Polynesian cultural and anthropological collection in the world. Behind the city rises the Koʻolau Range. Between it and the city you'll find the University of Hawaiʻi; Punchbowl, an old crater cradling the National Cemetery of the Pacific; the Royal Mausoleum, the final resting place of Hawaiian royalty; and Queen Emma Summer Palace, a Victorian home of gentility and lace. A place of ancient battle, where Kamehameha I sealed his dominance over this island kingdom, the Nuʻuanu Pali Lookout is now just a hauntingly beautiful spot, where the mountain drops suddenly to the coastal plain of Windward Oʻahu.

WAIKIKI

Ah! Everyone knows this magical name. This town within a town and world-famous beach, once the haunt of Hawaiian *aliʻi* and wealthy *kamaʻaina* families, is now a booming center of hotels, condos, and other lodgings which provide rooms for more than 60,000 visitors every day. If you placed a $20 bill on the ground, it would barely cover the cost of the land beneath it.

This hyperactive area will delight and disgust you, excite and overwhelm you, but never bore you. Waikiki gives you the feeling that you've arrived *someplace*. Besides lolling on the beach and walking the gauntlet of restaurants, hotels, malls, and street merchants, you can visit the Waikiki Aquarium or Honolulu Zoo. Then, ever-present Diamond Head, that monolith of frozen lava so symbolic of Hawaii, is easily reached by a few minutes' drive and a short hike to its summit.

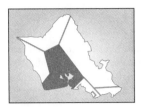

CENTRAL O'AHU AND 'EWA

You can't help noticing the huge military presence around Pearl Harbor, and it becomes clear why Hawaii is considered the most militarized state in the country. The major attraction here, which shouldn't be missed, is the USS *Arizona* Memorial, but the nearby USS *Bowfin* submarine and the USS *Missouri* are also worthy stops you should make.

Pearl Harbor is ringed by rather ordinary communities, the suburbs of Honolulu. Because of its topography and climate, it was a mainstay of the sugar industry until quite recently and remains a player in the pineapple industry. In Waipahu, Hawaii's Plantation Village gives you a glimpse of what life was like for those living and working in the ever-present plantations. Dominating huge areas of this central plain are the broad and beautiful Schofield Barracks Army base and Wheeler Air Force Base. Although much of 'Ewa is still rather undeveloped, some is being transformed into huge new suburban communities and a fashionable resort area.

LEEWARD COAST

The western edge of the island is the Wai'anae Coast. The towns of Ma'ili, Wai'anae, and Makaha are considered some of the last domains of the locals on O'ahu. This coastal area has escaped mass development so far, and it's one of the few places on the island where ordinary people can afford to live near the beach. World-class surfing beaches along this coast are preferred by many of the best-known surfers from Hawaii. Many work as lifeguards in the beach parks, and here offers is a perfect chance to mingle with the people and soak up some of the last real *aloha* left on O'ahu.

SOUTHEAST O'AHU

Head eastward around the bulge of Diamond Head and, passing exclusive residential areas, you quickly find a string of unimpressive beaches. The next bulge in the shoreline is Koko Head, below which lies Hanauma Bay, a nature preserve renowned for magnificent family-class snorkeling. Koko Crater is just inland, and within its encircling arms lies the little-visited Koko Crater Botanical Garden, which specializes in dry land plants. Below Makapu'u Point, the easternmost tip of the island, is Sea Life Park, an extravaganza of the deep. From here, it's hard to believe the city's just a dozen miles back.

WINDWARD O'AHU

On the Windward side, Kailua and Kane'ohe, and to a lesser extent, the sleepy village of Waimanalo, have become suburban bedroom communities for Honolulu. Resplendent with beaches, this area remains relatively uncrowded. The beaches are excellent, with beach parks and camping spots one after another, and the winds make this side of the island perfect for sailboarding. Inland of downtown Kailua is Ulupo Heiau, an ancient Hawaiian temple; inland of Kane'ohe a Buddha rests calmly in Byodo-In Temple. Just up the coastal highway comes Waiahole, O'ahu's outback, where tiny farms and taro patches dot the valleys and local folks move with the slow beat of bygone days. Then follows a quick succession of beaches, many rarely visited by more than a passing fisherman, and small communities. At the north end, in neat-as-a-pin La'ie, the Polynesian Cultural Center, Brigham Young University, and the stark white Mormon temple welcome visitors.

NORTH SHORE

The North Shore is famous for magnificent surf. From Hale'iwa to Sunset Beach, world-class surfers come here to be challenged by the liquid thunder of Banzai Pipeline, Waimea Bay, and other well-known surf breaks. Art shops, boutiques, and restaurants are concentrated in Hale'iwa, the main North Shore town, but secluded hideaways line these sun-drenched miles. To the west of the former sugar town of Waialua lies the long and nearly unvisited Mokule'ia Beach and Dillingham Airfield, where you can take a glider ride or a more thrilling parachute jump. Where the road ends, a rugged trail continues to Ka'ena Point, renowned for some of the most monstrous surf on the North Shore.

Planning Your Trip

WHEN TO GO

In Hawaii, the prime tourist season starts two weeks before Christmas and lasts until Easter. It picks up again with summer vacation in early June and ends once more in late August. Everything is usually much more heavily booked then, and prices are inflated. Hotel, airline, and car reservations are a must at those times of year. You can generally save considerably and it will be a lot less hassle if you go in the "off-season"—September to early December and mid-April (after Easter) until late May. Recently, the drop in numbers of tourists during the off-season has not been as substantial as in years past, indicating the increasing popularity of the islands all year round, but you'll still find the prices better and the beaches, trails, activities, and even restaurants less crowded. The local people will be happier to see you, too.

The average visitor to Hawaii spends 6–8 days on his or her vacation, most often on one island but sometimes split between two. The majority of visitors to Oʻahu stay in Waikiki, and there is so much to see and do there that you could conceivably spend your entire vacation without leaving the area. But don't just stay put. Get out of town and see the rest of the island. Oʻahu is small enough that driving anywhere and back can be a leisurely day. At a minimum, spend a full morning or more in each of the major areas of the island. So close to Waikiki, downtown Honolulu is an easy drive and holds many interesting cultural and historical sights for the visitor. A full day of sightseeing is recommended, but two would not be overkill for those who desire to delve a bit deeper into this city's treasures. The historical sites of Pearl Harbor and Central Oʻahu mostly revolve around World War II. Take a day to learn what so drastically shaped our country during the middle part of this last century. A morning or afternoon at Hanauma Bay or other fine snorkeling sites should not be missed, and this can be coupled with other exploration in the Southeast corner of the island. Take a day for a drive up the Windward Coast to try out some of the best beaches the island has to offer. The North Shore can easily captivate you for another day, particularly during winter when local surfers try their skill against the monster waves. So many people miss the Leeward Coast, but it too has wonderful scenery and a cultural site or two. Take a drive up this lovely coast and give it a day, not forgetting to spend a few hours hiking out to Kaʻena Point at its very tip. Shopping in Waikiki alone can easily occupy a full day. Then there are the activities, many of which are half-day or full-day affairs. Remember that some activities should not be coupled with others on the same day, like scuba diving and a helicopter ride. Leave them for different days to allow your body to adjust to the elevation changes. Soon you're at a week or more, and there is still much more to explore. If you spend less than a week on Oʻahu you may feel like you just didn't give yourself enough time. For the ancient Hawaiians, Oʻahu was the Gathering Place, and it remains so for many visitors today.

WHAT TO TAKE

It's a snap to pack for a visit to Oʻahu. Everything is on your side. The weather is moderate and uniform on the whole, and the style of dress is delightfully casual. The rule of thumb is to pack lightly: few items, and light clothing both in color and weight. If you forget something at home, it won't be a disaster. You can buy everything you'll need in Hawaii.

Even for those who have traveled to warmer climates previously, a few points are worthy of note. While shorts and T-shirts or short-sleeve shirts and blouses might be your usual daily wear, jeans or other long pants and closed-toe shoes are best and sometimes required, if you plan on taking a horseback ride or other adventure tour. Remember to bring a billed or brimmed hat for the rain and sun, and if you forget, inexpensive baseball caps and straw or woven hats are found easily throughout the island. For men, an aloha shirt or other collared shirt and slacks is as fancy as you might expect to get. Sport coats are hardly seen anymore, even for dinner at the classiest restaurants. For women, an informal dress will suffice for most any occasion. By and large, "resort casual" is as dressy as you'll need to be in Hawaii.

Tropical rain showers can happen at any time, so you might consider a fold-up umbrella. Nighttime winter temperatures may drop into the lower 60s or upper 50s, so be sure to have a sweater and long pants along.

Dressing your feet is hardly a problem. You'll most often wear zori (rubber thongs) for going to and from the beach, leather sandals for strolling and dining, and jogging shoes for hiking and sightseeing. Teva and other types of outdoor strap sandals are good for general sightseeing and beach and water wear, plus they're great in the rain. Some people prefer *tabi,* a type of rubberized slipper, for crossing streams or wet trails. If you plan on heavy-duty hiking, you'll definitely want your hiking boots: the lightweight version is usually sufficient. Lava, especially 'a'a, is murderous on soles. Most backcountry trails are rugged and muddy, and you'll need those good old lug soles for traction and laces for ankle support. If you plan moderate hikes, jogging shoes should do.

Two specialty items that you might consider bringing along are binoculars and snorkel gear. A pair of binoculars really enhances sightseeing—great for viewing birds and sweeping panoramas, and almost a necessity if you're going whale-watching. Flippers, mask, and snorkel can easily be bought or rented in Hawaii but don't weigh much or take up much space in your luggage. They'll save you a few dollars in rental fees, and you'll have them when you want them.

Explore Oʻahu

OʻAHU AT ITS BEST

Oʻahu, the Gathering Place, is where many visitors first experience the wonders of Hawaii. While Waikiki is not a tropical paradise of grass shacks, swaying palms, and deserted beaches, it does have warm inviting water, a great moonlit shore, and a plethora of wonderful food and varied entertainment. Waikiki is the tourist center of the island, and it will certainly captivate those who reach its sun-splashed shore, but visitors are advised to look beyond it to explore the rest of the island. While you can "do" the island in a few days, give it a week or more. You may be surprised by how rich and varied it really is. The following seven-day tour will give you a good introduction to the island, while leaving plenty of time for your own interests.

Day 1

Fly in, pick up your rental car, and head for your hotel. Honolulu is a big city, so be prepared for traffic; it's manageable, so go with the flow and watch for signs. If you are a first-time visitor, head straight to your hotel and settle in. Get your bearings, then head to the beach. There is nothing like a soothing plunge in warm tropical water after a long flight to the islands. So as not to overdo on the sun, spend the heat of the day shopping, visiting the **Honolulu Zoo,** or seeing the **Waikiki Aquarium.** If you want more exercise, head to **Diamond Head,** where a short hike to the summit opens up a superb panoramic view over the Waikiki strip. As you head back to your hotel, look for a place to eat and then let your ears direct you to where the music is happening.

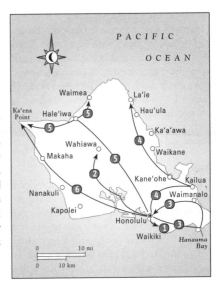

Day 2

Make your pilgrimage to **Pearl Harbor** this morning. Start early, as the USS *Arizona* is one of the most visited attractions in the state. Make a day of it and see the USS *Bowfin* submarine, the USS *Missouri* battleship, and the Pacific Aviation Museum on Ford Island. From here, head up to **Wahiawa** for a look at the Tropic Lightning Museum and additional military history. On the way up, make a detour to **Hawaii's Plantation Village,** where you get a glimpse of what life was like for the immigrants who came to Hawaii to work the plantations and better their lives. As this open-air museum offers tours only for a few hours through the midday, don't dally.

Day 3

Today, turn your sights east. One of the state's top snorkeling spots is **Hanauma Bay,** and it's only a short distance from Waikiki. Go early as this, too, is a very popular tourist site. A few hours in the water should be enough, so head back up and continue along the coast. Drive out past Makapuʻu Point and head up to Waimanalo. Return to town via the Pali Highway to complete the "Circle Route." Once back in town, spend the afternoon at one or more of the historical sights of downtown Honolulu. ʻIolani Palace or the Mission Houses Museum are good places to start. Leave a little time for Chinatown and plan on having dinner there.

Day 4

Explore the rest of Windward Oʻahu today. Head to **Kailua** and make your first stop at Ulupo Heiau before carrying on to the beach for time of the water windsurfing or kayaking. Turn north and make a side trip to see Byodo-In, a replica Japanese Buddhist temple. Across from Chinaman's Hat is the Kualoa Ranch, where many and varied outdoor activities await. Drive slowly north along this verdant coast and stop in **Laʻie** to see the Mormon Temple. In late afternoon, head to the Polynesian Cultural Center for a walk through its "villages" and for dinner and evening entertainment.

Day 5

Today the **North Shore** beckons. If it's winter, go just to look. The waves can truly be awe-inspiring in their size and force. In the summer, when the sea calms, it's much easier to get in the water for some fine swimming or snorkeling. Bring your snorkel gear, as **Shark's Cove** is a good site for exploring the underwater realm.

Before making a stop at the **art galleries of Haleʻiwa,** turn uphill to **Puʻu O Mahuka Heiau,** where you not only can ponder the importance of this ancient Hawaiian religious site, but you also have a wonderful panoramic view of the entire west end of the North Shore. Save time for a little excitement and head for Dillingham Airfield for a **glider ride** or—if you have the guts—a **parachute jump.** Haleʻiwa has some good restaurants, so dine there before heading back over the hill.

Day 6

Many people miss the drier **Leeward side,** but it, too, has fine scenery. Head all the way to the end of the road first and work your way back down the coast. For those who enjoy the great outdoors, set aside several hours for a hike to **Kaʻena Point,** where you will encounter one of the best-preserved coastal beach dune environments left in the state. At midday, make your way up Makaha Valley and visit **Kaneʻaki Heiau,** the island's best-preserved *heiau.* However, don't go on Monday as the *heiau* is closed. This coast has many fine beaches, so as you head back down the highway, look for a good spot to try the water. **Pokaʻi Bay** is one of the best, usually calm even when the rest of the coast is getting waves.

Day 7

Today is for relaxing, last-minute shopping, and a quick dip in the ocean before packing up and heading home.

A BOTANICAL ODYSSEY

O'ahu has plenty of botanical diversity, both natural and landscaped, and the beauty of this tropical island hits you immediately when you arrive. Some of the gems are listed below in this botanical tour of the island.

Day 1

Head first to **Foster Botanical Garden,** the primary site of the city's botanical garden system. Within the confines of this rather small enclave, you are greeted by massive trees, a variety of ferns, showy flowers, and medicinal plants from the tropical areas of the world. A number of these plants are rare and endangered, so this garden is an important repository of tropical flora. When you've satisfied yourself here, make your way inland to the much larger but less manicured **Lyon Arboretum,** a research facility and arm of the University of Hawai'i. This arboretum has an impressive collection of native and imported plants and maintains horticultural and ethnobotanical sections. As a treat to yourself, stop by the **Moanalua Gardens** for a stroll under the large and truly impressive collection of expansive monkeypod trees.

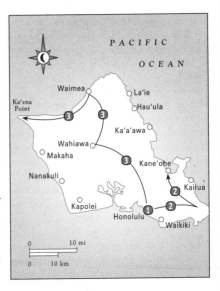

Day 2

Drive out east today and make your first stop at the **Koko Crater Botanical Garden.** A part of the city's botanical garden system, this section focuses on arid region plants and others that thrive in this dry environment. For more color and greenery, head up the coast to the **Ho'omaluhia Botanical Garden** in Kane'ohe. An area of much rain, here you see plants that thrive in a much wetter environment. Split into sections by regions of the world, this large garden is more like a park than anything else. For another look at wet climate plants, head to the much more petite **Ha'iku Garden.** Located in a natural bowl depression, this garden is a wonderland of green with a pond at its center.

Day 3

Head over the Leilehua Plateau to the North Shore today, but stop first in Wahiawa, where you will find the **Wahiawa Botanical Garden.** Also part of the city's botanical garden system, this garden features mostly trees from around the world, although flowering plants and vines are also part of this ravine environment. Make a short stop at the commercial Dole Pineapple Plantation, where various manicured gardens showcase hibiscus, bromeliads, *ti,* and native flora. Your next stop is the **Waimea Valley Audubon Center,** well known for its variety of native plants and its collections of endangered species. Many flowers and flowering plants are labeled. The garden collects, preserves, and propagates rare species. You should still have plenty of energy left for the last stop today, which will require a hike of several hours. Head to the end of the road and hike to **Ka'ena Point,** a natural preserve of rare and endangered beach and dune plants and flowers.

DEEP SEA TO DIAMOND HEAD

Oʻahu, with the huge metropolitan center of Honolulu, is not an adventure wasteland, as some might suspect. On the contrary, there are many adventure activities; the following tour is a sampling of what the island has to offer. You can choose among tour operators for the type of activity that best fits your desires and physical abilities. Most organized tours can be reserved in advance; some must be. You may need to make some arrangements before you arrive on the island or on the day you fly in. Contact numbers for tour operators are listed in the chapters that follow.

Day 1

Start the day by **snorkeling** at Hanauma Bay, the best-known snorkel spot on the island. Go *early* to avoid the throngs of people who also want to see what beauty underwater Hanauma Bay has to offer. While there are many very good snorkel sites on the island, this is a favorite for visitors and residents alike. Float in the aquamarine waters over a jumble of coral and survey the array of colorful fish that make this sunken crater their watery home.

Reward yourself after snorkeling with an afternoon **hike** up to the rim of Diamond Head. This famous tuff cone overlooks Waikiki, so from the top you have a great view over this tourist enclave and much of eastern Honolulu. As it's close to Waikiki, getting there, the hike itself, and getting back should take not much more than two hours. While not overly strenuous, it's still a hike, so go prepared with water, a hat, and binoculars.

Day 2

Start today with a **helicopter tour** around the Koʻolau Mountain range. While this flight doesn't take in the Leeward Coast, it does give you a bird's-eye view of the majority of the island and offers up the "lay of the land" for further exploration. Count on at least two hours for transportation to the heliport, the flight, and your transportation back. This leaves much of the rest of the day, which you can spend enjoyably learning how to **surf** at Waikiki. Most often, the waves at Waikiki are gentle and just right for beginners, so it's usually perfect for a first-time surf lesson.

Because there is plenty of time this afternoon, add to your water activity with an **underwater tour.** You've seen the fish and the coral, so this is your opportunity to go deep. Atlantis Submarine tours off Waikiki take eager visitors to a number of underwater wrecks and artificial reefs in the bay. These trips leave from the Hilton hotel pier and run about one hour, with one-half hour below the waves. It's amazing how the color changes from yellow to blue as you drop in depth, and the type and number of fish differ as you move into deeper water. Be your own Captain Nemo and take the dive.

Day 3

Head to the Windward side today and reserve the morning for a **kayak trip** from Lanikai Beach to nearby coastal sites and the several islands just offshore. With generally calm and shallow water and the near-constant and gentle trade winds, this area is one of the premier sites on the island for skimming the water in a "sit-upon" kayak. Rental kayaks often go by the hour, so you can take as much time as you like or, better yet, sign up for a four-hour kayak tour, which will not only show you wonderful spots but give you an ecological lesson as well.

In the afternoon, head up the coast to the Kualoa Ranch for a **horseback ride.** While there are a number of stables on O'ahu, this one leads group rides through the beauty of the east shore, into its deep valleys, and along its deeply scarred *pali*.

Day 4

Today is another day of adventure in the sky. Start out with a **parasail** ride. Both Kewalo Basin and Hawaii Kai have companies that offer these tours, but whichever you choose, you'll have the wind in your hair and marvelous views of the sea and land below. It's amazingly quiet once you get in the air, so you can concentrate on the scenery. These rides are fairly short, so consider renting and riding a **Jet Ski,** which most parasail companies also offer.

Make your way to distant Dillingham Airfield in the afternoon for a **parachute jump.** This North Shore airstrip is the only place in the state that offers this heart-pounding adventure. No experience is necessary. All jumps are tandem, so you'll be attached to an expert for the jump. For many visitors, this will be the most exhilarating activity of their vacation, but if jumping out of an airplane is not within your comfort zone, try a more sedate **glider flight.** Head to the other end of the airstrip to be taken on a motorless glide over

this picturesque coast. While not without thrills, a glider ride is not nearly as much of a daredevil activity as parachuting.

Day 5

Reserve today for a half- or full-day **deep sea fishing** trip. While expensive if you charter the entire boat, search for one that offers shared rides. Most boats leave from the Kewalo Basin in Honolulu, but there are a few that head out from Wai'anae and Hale'iwa. The waters around O'ahu offer some great fishing and, with luck, you will have an exciting day reeling in a big one.

Day 6

There are many fine **scuba** locations on O'ahu, and any of the island's several scuba companies would be eager to line you up for a trip to one or more. You don't have to be certified to join a scuba tour, as introductory trips give you the basics to make a safe easy dive. So, make the plunge, but be sure that you haven't been up in a plane or helicopter during the previous 24 hours.

Where you were below the surface this morning, skim across the water this afternoon. Look for an **outrigger canoe** ride at Waikiki Beach. After paddling out to meet incoming waves, you turn the canoe and "surf" the waves coming into shore.

Day 7

Today is your day for a short trip on two wheels. Take an organized **bicycle ride** down a paved mountain road with overviews of downtown Honolulu and a short hike to a waterfall. For the more athletic, a mountain biking downhill tour can also be arranged. This trip runs until mid-afternoon, so rest until your late afternoon sail. A **sunset sail,** skimming the breezy waters off Waikiki and Diamond Head, will be a memorable and romantic last adventure for your time on O'ahu.

O'AHU: PAST AND PRESENT

While it may be its beaches and world-class waves that draw most visitors to O'ahu today, the island has many significant historical and cultural points of interest. This island has, for centuries, had a sizeable population and vibrant agricultural base and since the mid-1800s has been its seat of power. Few of the ancient Hawaiian sites are more than long-forgotten rubble, but many of the more recent points of interest remain.

Day 1

Being the capital and longtime seat of power, Honolulu has the lion's share of historical sites on the island of O'ahu. Start your day at the center: tour **'Iolani Palace,** the only "real" royal palace in the country. Built by King Kalakaua, the palace was used only for a few short years by him and his sister and successor, Queen Lili'uokalani, before the revolution of 1893. Directly mountainside of the palace is the state capitol building and to the front of the palace is the statue of King Kamehameha I and Ali'iolani, the old State Judiciary Building. When finished there, head down King Street to Kawaiaha'o Church, the first permanent Christian church on the island, still very much in use. Step next door to tour the Mission Houses Museum, the headquarters and home site of the early Protestant missionaries to the islands. Far more than their numbers would indicate, the early missionaries had a huge impact on the Hawaiian nation. Finally, explore the Hawaii Maritime Center to learn about the island's strong connection to the sea from early days to the present.

Day 2

Walk a little farther afield today and head to **Chinatown.** Of all the large immigrant communities in Hawaii, the Chinese were the first after the Americans. Chinatown is a multicultural enclave, a few square blocks of Asia in Hawaii. If the day and your timing are right, follow along on one of the excellent tours given by the Chinese Chamber of Commerce or the Hawaii Heritage Center. After exploring the streets of Chinatown, head to the **Bishop Museum,** an excellent anthropological museum of Hawaii and Polynesia. From the museum, make a quick stop at the Royal Mausoleum to pay your respects to the Hawaiian royalty interred there before continuing up Nu'uanu Valley to Queen Emma Summer Palace, a royal country estate. At the top end of the Nu'uanu Valley, the forces of King Kamehameha I and those of Kalanikupule, ruler of O'ahu, met in a decisive battle in the late 1700s. With the defeat of Kalanikupule and the later capitulation of Kahekili, King of Kaua'i, King Kamehameha brought the Hawaiian Islands together under his control, effectively creating a unified nation.

Day 3

Today, head to the Windward side. First stop is at **Ulupo Heiau,** which overlooks Kawainui Marsh above Kailua. Ulupo Heiau is one of the few well-preserved religious sites on this side of the island. At this large and well-constructed *heiau* you can sense the importance of religious ceremony and tradition for the old Hawaiians. After the Chinese, the Japanese were the next large group of Asian immigrants to Hawaii. They built **Byodo-In Temple** in the Valley of the Temples, just up the road. Spend a little time there in the serenity of this Buddhist temple before heading up to La'ie and the **Polynesian Cultural Center,** where you'll see portrayed the "roots" of Hawaiian culture.

Day 4

This will be a day of some driving. In Waipahu, on the north edge of Pearl Harbor is **Hawaii's Plantation Village.** This outdoor village and its indoor display galleries present in some detail the immigrant experience in Hawaii, life on the plantations for these communities, and way they contributed to the growing nation—and later, state—of Hawaii. From there, head up to the Leilehua Plateau for a quick stop at **Kukaniloko Birthing Stones.** It was here, as one of only two such places in the islands, that royal women came to birth their babies in order to accord them the highest status among their ranks. It is, indeed, one of the most sacred of ancient Hawaiian sites. Continue on to the North Shore and turn east to Waimea. On the cliff edge overlooking this luxuriant valley is **Pu'u O Mahuka Heiau,** the largest *heiau* on the island. An ancient site of human sacri-

fice and a place of ceremony for the gods, it is now an excellent spot from which to view the North Shore coastline. If there is time enough left in the day, take the long drive around to the Wai'anae coast and proceed up the Makaha Valley to the smaller and partially reconstructed Kane'aki Heiau, the best place on the island to get a sense of what an ancient religious site actually looked like in centuries past. As this *heiau* is only open for a few short hours during the midday, it may be best to leave this for another day if you are running short on time.

Day 5

The Japanese attack on the military installations of Hawaii, particularly the ships at anchor in **Pearl Harbor,** abruptly and dramatically sent the country into a state of war. A number of sites at Pearl Harbor bear witness to those days and commemorate those who lost their lives that day. Make your first stop at the USS *Arizona* memorial for an introduction to what transpired on that fateful morning of December 7, 1941. Next down the line is the refurbished USS *Bowfin* submarine, where you can learn of life under the sea. Across the water sits the USS *Missouri,* on whose deck the U.S. military command took the surrender of the Japanese forces to end World War II. Along the airfield behind this great battleship is the newer Pacific Aviation Museum. There is plenty here to see, so take your time and let the seriousness of these museums and memorials hit home.

A GOLFER'S PARADISE

O'ahu has some three dozen golf courses, most of which are open to the public; each has its unique charms and characteristics. Below—in alphabetical order—are a few suggestions for a fun and varied golf experience for your time on the island.

The **Ala Wai Golf Course** is flat but presents some challenge by being mounded and finishing up with a narrow last fairway and green that parallels the Ala Wai Canal. This municipal course, surrounded by city, is the most convenient to Waikiki, is fairly priced, and is said to be one of the busiest in the country with over 500 starts a day.

One of the newest courses on the island, **Coral Creek Golf Course** is getting rave reviews for its layout and its use of coral rock outcrops and water features. It is beautiful and playable, but tough. Looking for an easy, walkable course?

Look no farther than the municipal, nine-hole **Kahuku Golf Course,** a wonderful but spartan seaside links course that may be surprisingly challenging if the trade winds are blowing. Located in a very rural setting on the north end of the Windward Coast, this is the least expensive course on the island.

Kapolei Golf Course is favored by many resident golfers. It's challenging and scenic, with plenty of water and countless bunkers, and is an appropriate challenge for golfers of all skill levels.

Ko'olau Golf Course on the Windward side is often called the most difficult course in the country. With a slope rating of 162 from the back tees, it's no wonder! Carved from the forest and incorporating several deep ravines, this course is a challenge to good players but perhaps beyond the ability of beginners. Backed up against the serrated *pali,* the scenery inland is awe-inspiring, while the distant views of the ocean are uplifting.

Of the several military courses on the island open to the general public, **Leilehua Golf Course** is a good choice. It is located on the central plateau, with fairways bordered by mature trees. This is one of the best bargains on the island, and a very playable course.

Tucked into the steep forested hillside of the Windward Coast, **Luana Hills Country Club** is often regarded as the prettiest course on the island. Its undulating terrain also makes it a tough but rewarding course.

As a resort course, the **Makaha Resort Golf Club** stands out as one of the best. Tucked into a quiet valley under tall volcanic walls, it's a beauty with distant views of the blue ocean. Its location is distinctly rural, so you may have to contend with peacocks on the fairway. Golfers in the know rate this course tough but fair.

Established in 1898, the nine-hole, semiprivate **Moanalua Golf Club** is the oldest golf course on the island. While it's not a difficult course, playing it will establish a bond with those golfers who drove their way to seeing golf as one of the prime tourist activities in the state.

Arguably the best course on the island, the **Turtle Bay Arnold Palmer Course** is set along the rough north coast and built around a natural wetland. This links-style course has a first-rate layout and is eminently playable, but it presents the challenges of sand, water, and wind. This is the most expensive course on the island.

Overlooking Pearl Harbor, with the Ko'olau Mountains in the background, the **Waikele Golf Course** not only has great scenery, but it also is one of the favorite courses for residents and visitors alike for its rolling fairways and tricky greens.

HONOLULU

Honolulu is the most exotic city in the United States. It's not any one attribute that makes this so; it's a combination of things. Honolulu's like an ancient Hawaiian goddess who can change her form at will. At one moment you see a black-eyed beauty, swaying provocatively to a deep and basic rhythm, and in the next a high-tech scion of the computer age sitting straight-backed behind a polished desk. The city is the terminus of "manifest destiny," the end of America's relentless westward drive, until no more horizons were left. Other Mainland cities are undoubtedly more historic, cultural, and perhaps, to some, more beautiful than Honolulu, but none come close to having all of these features in the same overwhelming combination. The city's face, although blemished by high-rises and pocked by heavy industry, is eternally lovely. The Ko'olau

Mountains form the background tapestry from which the city emerges; the surf gently foams along Waikiki; the sun hisses fire-red as it drops into the sea; and Diamond Head beckons with a promise of tropical romance.

In the center of the city, skyscrapers rise as silent, unshakable witnesses to Honolulu's economic strength. In glass and steel offices, businesspeople wearing conservative three-piece uniforms are clones of any found on Wall Street. Below, a fantasia of people live and work. In nooks and crannies is an amazing array of arts, shops, and cuisines. In a flash of festival the streets become China, Japan, Portugal, New England, old Hawaii, or the Philippines.

New England churches, a royal Hawaiian palace, bandstands, tall-masted ships, and the narrow streets of Chinatown illustrate Honolulu's

© ROBERT NILSEN

HIGHLIGHTS

(**'Iolani Palace:** As the only true royal residence in the United States, this is a must for all those who have an interest in Hawaiian history and culture (page 32).

(**Mission Houses Museum:** The best example of early missionary architecture in the islands. It was from such humble origins as this that the West made its heavy impact on the Hawaiian nation (page 37).

(**Hawaii Maritime Center:** This museum does a wonderful job showing various ways the surrounding sea has affected the island nation of Hawaii (page 40).

(**Chinatown:** Its life and activity is a window on the diverse community that makes up Hawaiian society (page 43).

(**Queen Emma Summer Palace:** This simple royal residence shines a light on the then-rural yet stately life of Hawaiian royalty (page 47).

(**Nu'uanu Pali Lookout:** This is the best vantage point from which to see the lower expanse of Windward O'ahu (page 48).

(**Bishop Museum:** This is by far the best museum of Polynesian artifacts in the state. It is a must-see for anyone with an interest in cultural aspects of the Hawaiians (page 53).

(**Hawaii State Art Museum:** This is a great place to see a broad range of art by Hawaiian residents (page 55).

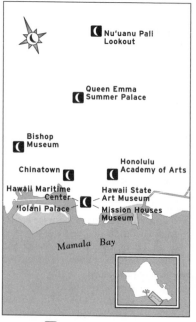

LOOK FOR (TO FIND RECOMMENDED SIGHTS, ACTIVITIES, DINING, AND LODGING.

(**Honolulu Academy of Arts:** The foremost repository of world art in the state (page 55).

history. And what a history! You can visit places where in a mere twinkle of time past, red-plumed warriors were driven to their deaths over an impossibly steep *pali,* or where the skies were alive with screaming Zeros strafing and bombing the only American city threatened by foreign attack between the War of 1812 and the September 11, 2001, terrorist attacks. In hallowed grounds throughout the city lie the bodies of fallen warriors. Some are entombed in a mangled steel sepulcher below the waves, others from three wars

rest in a natural bowl of bereavement and silence. And a nearby royal mausoleum holds the remains of those who were "old Hawaii."

Honolulu is the pumping heart of Hawaii. It is by far the largest city in the state. The state government and university are here, as are the state's principal transportation centers. It is the economic center of the state, and Hawaii's largest companies have their headquarters toe to toe in the downtown business district. Although Honolulu also has the muscle and might of Pearl

Harbor and adjacent military bases, it is home to botanical parks, a fine aquarium and zoo, a floating maritime museum, and the world's foremost museum on Polynesia. Art flourishes like flowers, as do professional and amateur entertainment, festivals, and local and world-class sporting events. But the city isn't all good, clean fun. Like large metropolitan areas everywhere, it has its seedier side. Yet somehow this blending and collision of East and West, this hodgepodge of emotionally charged history, this American city superimposed on a unique Pacific setting works well in Honolulu, the "Sheltered Bay" of humanity and its dreams.

PLANNING YOUR TIME

The best way to see Honolulu is to start from the middle and fan out on foot to visit the inner city. You can "do" downtown in one day, but the sights of greater Honolulu require a few days to see and would be best to do by car. It's a matter of opinion where the center of downtown Honolulu actually is, but the King Kamehameha statue in front of Ali'iolani Hale is about as central as you can get, and a perfect landmark from which to start.

If arriving by car, park in one of the lots in the downtown area and walk; if coming by trolley or bus from Waikiki, get off at or near the State Capitol building and walk from there. Start early, as there is plenty to see.

You can easily spend one full day in downtown Honolulu, Chinatown, and the harbor area. Plan at least one more day for the outlying sights, and an additional day or two if you care to see more than the palace and a couple of the museums, or do any hiking. Remember that many of the sights, like the palace, Mission Houses Museum, and art museums are closed on Mondays, so you must leave these for later in the week.

The State Foundation on Culture and the Arts has produced walking-tour brochures for the capitol district, and for the Chinatown and the financial district.

PARKING AND TRANSPORTATION IN DOWNTOWN HONOLULU

If you're staying in Waikiki, leave your rental car in the hotel garage and take TheBus nos. 2, 19, 20, 42, or B for downtown sightseeing. If you can't bear to leave your car behind, head for Aloha Tower. In front of Aloha Tower is Irwin Park, and to its side is a pay parking lot open 24 hours. The rate is $2 with validation for up to three hours 7:15 A.M.-3 P.M. and $3 for each 30 minutes after that. Non-validated parking is $3 for the first hour, $3 for each subsequent 30 minutes. After 3 P.M. weekdays and all day on weekends, the rate is a flat $2. Similar rates are charged at another lot just east of the Maritime Museum near Piers 5 and 6. You should have plenty of time for the local harborfront attractions, well within walking distance, and you may also have time to go as far as Chinatown. A handful of pay parking structures can also be found in the business district directly inland of Aloha Tower, as well as the municipal lot east of city hall.

For various sights outside the downtown area, your rental car is fine. Some shuttles running out to the Arizona Memorial are more expensive than TheBus but so convenient they're worth the extra few coins. The Waikiki Trolley conducts a Honolulu City Line circle route (red line) that runs through the downtown area between Waikiki and the Bishop Museum. The trolley departs daily at 45-minute intervals 9:10 A.M.-5:37 P.M. from the DFS Galleria. You can get off and on at any of the two dozen stops along the way or ride along for the entire two-hour trip for $25 adults or $12 children for the entire day. The stops in downtown Honolulu going west are at the Honolulu Academy of the Arts, State Capitol, and Foster Botanical Gardens; going east, stops include Hilo Hattie, Aloha Tower Marketplace, the King Kamehameha statues, Ward Centers, and Ala Moana Shopping Center.

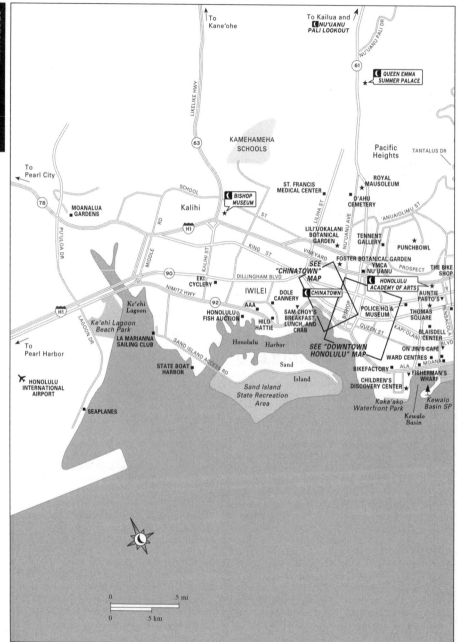

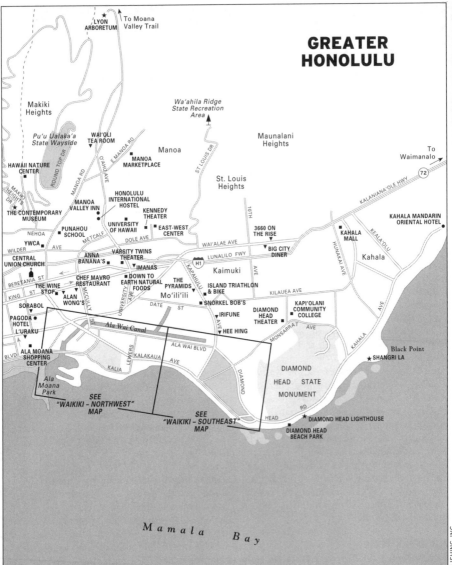

GREATER HONOLULU

LYON ARBORETUM
To Moana Valley Trail

Makiki Heights

Pu'u Ualaka'a State Wayside

WAI'OLI TEA ROOM

Wa'ahila Ridge State Recreation Area

Maunalani Heights

To Waimanalo

Manoa

MANOA MARKETPLACE

St. Louis Heights

KALANIANA'OLE HWY

72

HAWAII NATURE CENTER

HONOLULU INTERNATIONAL HOSTEL

MANOA VALLEY INN

KAHALA MANDARIN ORIENTAL HOTEL

THE CONTEMPORARY MUSEUM

KENNEDY THEATER

UNIVERSITY OF HAWAII

EAST-WEST CENTER

3660 ON THE RISE

KAHALA MALL

PUNAHOU SCHOOL

DOLE AVE

WAI'ALAE AVE

Kahala

NEHOA

METCALF

YWCA

WILDER   AVE

ANNA BANANA'S

VARSITY TWINS THEATER

LUNALILO FWY

BIG CITY DINER

CENTRAL UNION CHURCH

H1

Kaimuki

BERETANIA   ST

IMANAS

CHEF MAVRO RESTAURANT

DOWN TO EARTH NATURAL FOODS

THE PYRAMIDS

ISLAND TRIATHLON & BIKE

KILAUEA AVE

THE WINE STOP

KING   ST

ALAN WONG'S

Mo'ili'ili

SNORKEL BOB'S

KAPI'OLANI COMMUNITY COLLEGE

SOROBOL

DATE   ST

IRIFUNE

DIAMOND HEAD THEATER

PAGODA HOTEL

Ala Wai Canal

HEE HING

L'URAKU

ALA MOANA SHOPPING CENTER

ALA WAI BLVD

BLVD

KALAKAUA   AVE

Black Point

SHANGRI LA

Ala Moana Park

KALIA

LEWERS

DIAMOND HEAD STATE MONUMENT

SEE "WAIKIKI – NORTHWEST" MAP

SEE "WAIKIKI – SOUTHEAST" MAP

HEAD   RD

DIAMOND HEAD LIGHTHOUSE

DIAMOND HEAD BEACH PARK

M a m a l a   B a y

ROUND TOP DR

MANOA RD

OAHU AVE

E MANOA RD

ST. LOUIS DR

10TH

HUNAKAI AVE

KEALA OLU

KAPAHULU

MONSARRAT   AVE

KAHALA   AVE

DIAMOND   HEAD   RD

Sights

THE CAPITOL DISTRICT
King Kamehameha I Statue

The statue of King Kamehameha I is near the junction of King and Mililani Streets. Running off at an angle is Merchant Street, the oldest thoroughfare in Honolulu, and you might say it's "the beginning of the road to modernity." The statue is much more symbolic of Kamehameha's strength as a ruler and unifier of the Hawaiian Islands than as a replica of the man himself. Of the few drawings of Kamehameha that have been preserved, none is necessarily a good likeness. Kamehameha was a magnificent leader and statesman, but by all accounts not very good-looking. This statue is one of four. The original, lost at sea near the Falkland Islands en route from Paris where it was bronzed, was later recovered, but not before insurance money was used to cast this second one. The original now stands in the tiny town of Kapa'au, in the Kohala District of the Big Island, not far from where Kamehameha was born; although they supposedly came from the same mold, they somehow seem quite different. The third stands in Washington, D.C., dedicated when Hawaii became a state. The Honolulu statue was dedicated in 1883, as part of King David Kalakaua's coronation ceremony. Its black and gold colors are striking, but it is most magnificent on June 11, King Kamehameha Day, when 18-foot lei are draped around the neck and the outstretched arms. More recently, a fourth similar but not exact replica was cast and erected below the county government office building in Hilo on the Big Island.

Ali'iolani Hale

Behind Kamehameha stands **Ali'iolani Hale** (Chief Onto Heaven), now the State Judiciary Building. This handsome structure, designed by an Australian architect and begun in 1872, was originally commissioned by Kamehameha V as a palace but was redesigned as a general court building. It looks much grander than 'Iolani Palace across the way. Kamehameha V died before it was finished, and it was officially dedicated by King Kalakaua in 1874. Less than 20 years later, on January 17, 1893, at this "hall of justice," the first proclamation by the Members of the Committee of Safety was read, stating that the sovereign nation of Hawaii was no more, and that the islands would be ruled by a provisional government. On the ground floor of this building, the **Judiciary History Center** (808/539-4999, www.judiciaryhistorycenter.org, open 8 A.M.–4 P.M.) offers free exhibits weekdays; docents are available for groups by appointment. This center portrays aspects of Hawaiian law from the traditional *kapu* system through the introduction of Western legal codes to the present legal system. In addition, the center theater shows a 10-minute video on land law in Hawaii, there's a refurbished courtroom from the territorial period, and a special exhibition presents aspects of martial law instituted following the bombing of Pearl Harbor during World War II. Upstairs are the state Supreme Court and justice's chambers.

Next door to the east is the **Territorial Office Building,** which is home to several state department offices, and on the west side is the downtown **post office.** To their rear are the old **U.S. Customs and Court House** and **Kapuaiwa Hale,** the family courts building. These buildings, plus **Hale 'Auhau,** which stands across the street from Kapuaiwa Hale, are all from the monarchy and territorial periods. Numerous other structures, particularly those along or near Merchant Street to the west, are also from this prestatehood time. Toward the water from Hale 'Auhau are newer government office buildings, including Ke'elikolani Building, the Prince Kuhio Federal Building, and Ka'ahumanu Hale.

◖ 'Iolani Palace

As you enter the 11-acre parklike palace grounds, notice the emblem of Hawaii in the

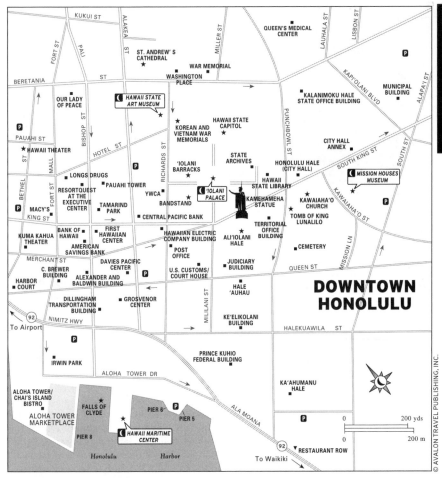

© AVALON TRAVEL PUBLISHING, INC.

center of the large iron gates. They're often draped with simple lei of fragrant *maile*. The quiet grounds are a favorite strolling and relaxing place for many government workers, especially in the shade of a huge banyan, purportedly planted by Kalakaua's wife, Kapi'olani. The building, with its glass and ironwork imported from San Francisco and its Corinthian columns, is the only true royal palace in America. (Queen Emma Summer Palace in Nu'uanu Valley and Hulihe'e Palace at Kailua-Kona on the Big Island, while

royal residences, were never the seat of power.) 'Iolani (Royal Hawk) Palace, begun in late 1879 under orders of King Kalakaua, was completed in December 1882 at a cost of $350,000. It was the first electrified building in Honolulu, having electricity even before the White House in Washington D.C., and it had a direct phone line to the Royal Boat House, located near where the Aloha Tower stands today.

Through the first floor of this palace runs a broad hallway with a grand stairway that

© ROBERT NILSEN

Now open to the public for guided tours, 'Iolani Palace was once the seat of power for the Hawaiian monarchy, and home to King Kalakaua and Queen Lili'uokalani.

leads to the second story. On the east side of the building is the large and opulent Throne Room, the scene of formal meetings and major royal functions. On the west side are the smaller Blue Room, an informal reception area, and the dining room. The upstairs level was the private residence of the king and his family. It also has a wide hallway and on each side are bedrooms, sitting rooms, a music room, and office. The basement held servants' quarters, the kitchen, and offices of certain government officials.

Non-Hawaiian Island residents of the day thought it a frivolous waste of money, but here poignant scenes and profound changes rocked the Hawaiian Islands. After nine years as king, Kalakaua built a Coronation Stand that originally stood directly in front of the palace but was later moved to the left where you see it today. In a belated ceremony, Kalakaua raised a crown to his head and placed one on his queen, Kapi'olani. During the ceremony, 8,000 Hawaiians cheered, while Honolulu's foreign, tax-paying businessmen boycotted. On August 12, 1898, after only two Hawaiian monarchs, Kalakaua and Lili'uokalani (his sister), had resided in the palace, the American flag was raised up the flagpole following a successful coup that marked Hawaii's official recognition by the United States as a territory. During this ceremony, loyal Hawaiian subjects wept bitter tears, while the businessmen of Honolulu cheered wildly. On the far side of the approach path is a raised earthen platform, the original site of the royal mausoleum, which was later moved out along the Pali Highway.

Kalakaua, later in his rule, was forced to sign a new constitution that greatly reduced his own power to little more than figurehead status. He traveled to San Francisco in 1891, where he died. His body was returned to Honolulu and lay in state in the palace. His sister, Lili'uokalani, succeeded him; she attempted to change this constitution and gain the old power of Hawaii's sovereigns, but the businessmen revolted and the monarchy fell. 'Iolani Palace then became the main executive building for the provisional government, with the House of Representatives meeting in the throne room and the Senate in the dining room. It served in this capacity until 1968. It has since been elevated to a state monument and National Historical Landmark.

'Iolani Palace (808/522-0832, www.iolani palace.org) is open for 90-minute guided tours, starting every 20 minutes Tues.–Sat. 9–11:15 A.M.; $20 adults, $15 *kama'aina* and military, $5 children 5–12, with no children under five admitted. Self-guided, 50-minute audio tours are also offered on the same days 11:45 A.M.–3 P.M.; $12 adults, $5 children. These tours are popular, so make reservations at least a day in advance. The palace is open 10 A.M.–2 P.M. on the first Sunday of every month for free admission to *kama'aina*. The **'Iolani Palace Gallery,** in the basement of the palace, is also open to visitors on a self-guided basis. This gallery contains the Hawaiian crown jewels and other royal accoutrements. No reservations are needed to view this site, which is open 9 A.M.–4:30 P.M. on days the palace is open. The cost of viewing the galleries is $6 adults, $5 *kama'aina,* and $3 children 5–12. Tickets are sold at a window at the 'Iolani Barracks, behind the Royal Bandstand, open Tues.–Sat. 8 A.M.–4 P.M. Also in the barracks, the palace gift and book shop is open Tues.–Sat. 8:30 A.M.–4 P.M. and on *kama'aina* Sundays.

Palace Grounds

Kalakaua, known as the "Merrie Monarch," was credited with saving the hula. He also hired Henry Berger, first Royal Hawaiian Bandmaster, and together they wrote "Hawai'i Pono'i," the state anthem. Many concerts were given from the Coronation Stand, which became known as the **Royal Bandstand.** Behind it is **'Iolani Barracks** (Hale Koa), built in 1870 to house the Royal Household Guards. When the monarchy of Hawaii fell to provisional government forces in 1893, only one of these soldiers was wounded in the nearly bloodless confrontation. The barracks were moved to the pres-

ent site in 1965 from nearby land on which the State Capitol was erected.

To the right behind the palace are the **State Archives** (808/586-0329, open Mon.–Fri. 9 A.M.–4 P.M.). This modern building, dating from 1953, holds records, documents, and vintage photos. A treasure trove to scholars and those tracing their genealogy, it is worth a visit by the general public to view the old photos on display. Next door is the **Hawaii State Library** (808/586-3500, www.librarieshawaii.org, open Mon. and Wed. 10 A.M.–5 P.M., Tues., Fri., Sat. 9 A.M.–5 P.M., Thurs. 9 A.M.–8 P.M.), housing the main branch of this statewide system. Some of the original money to build the library was put up by Andrew Carnegie.

Washington Place

Lili'uokalani was deposed and placed under house arrest in one room on the second floor of 'Iolani Palace for nine months. Later, after much intrigue that included a visit to Washington, D.C. to plead her case and an aborted counterrevolution, she sadly accepted her fate and moved to nearby Washington Place. This solid-looking structure fronts Beretania Street and was originally the home of sea captain John Dominis. It was inherited by his son John Owen Dominis, who married a lovely young Hawaiian aristocrat, Lydia Kapa'akea, who became Queen Lili'uokalani. She lived in her husband's home, proud but powerless, until her death in 1917. Washington Place was the official residence of governors of Hawaii until 2003, when a new governor's mansion was built behind it, allowing Washington Place (808/586-0248, www.hawaii.gov/gov/washington_place) to be used for state functions. Free 45-minute tours are offered Mon.–Fri. for up to a dozen people, but tours require a 48-hour prior arrangement.

To the right of Washington Place is the eternal flame **War Memorial.** Erected in 1974, this memorial replaced an older one and is dedicated to the people who perished in World War II. An approach walk and benches are provided for quiet meditation. Partially sunk into the ground on the west side of the State Capitol building and across from the Hawaii State Art Museum are the **Korean and Vietnam War Memorials,** which consist of piled black granite blocks inscribed with the names of soldiers lost during those conflicts.

Hawaii State Capitol

Directly behind 'Iolani Palace is the magnificent Hawaii State Capitol, built in 1969 for $25 million. The building is a metaphor for Hawaii: the pillars surrounding it are palms, the reflecting pool is the sea, and the cone-shaped rooms of the Legislature represent the volcanoes of Hawaii. It's lined with rich koa wood from the Big Island and is further graced with woven hangings and murals, with two gigantic, four-ton replicas of the State Seal hanging at both entrances. The inner courtyard has a 600,000-tile mosaic, *Aquarius,* rendered by island artist Tadashi Sato. Standing at the *mauka* entrance to the building is a poignant sculpture of *Father Damien,* while the statue *The Spirit of Lili'uokalani* fronts the building on the ocean side. The State Legislature is in session for 60 working days starting on the third Wednesday in January. The legislative session opens with dancing, music, and festivities, and the public is invited. Peek inside, then take the elevator to the fifth floor for outstanding views of the city.

Across Punchbowl Street to the east is the Kalanimoku Hale state office building and to its front at the corner of S. King Street stands **Honolulu Hale,** Honolulu City Hall. Built in 1928, with annex additions in 1951, this office building is open weekdays during normal business hours and houses the office of the mayor, the city council, and a few city departments. It too has a courtyard where music, art, and other public events are held. To the east, between Kapi'olani and Alapai Streets, is the newer Honolulu Municipal Building.

Cathedrals

To the left of Washington Place is **St. Andrew's Cathedral** (224 Queen Emma Square, open Mon.–Fri. 6 A.M.–6 P.M.). Construction started in 1867 as an Anglican church but wasn't re-ally finished until 1958. Many of its stones and ornaments were shipped from England, and its stained-glass windows, especially the large contemporary-style window on the narthex end, and bell tower are of particular interest. Hawaii's monarchs worshiped here, and the church is still very much in use. A free guided tour is offered following the 10 A.M. Sunday service.

A few steps away at Bishop and N. Beretania Streets is the **Cathedral of Our Lady of Peace.** Constructed in 1843 of plastered coral blocks, it has fine painted glass windows. This structure was Hawaii's first Roman Catholic church, and although the building has gone through numerous renovations, it has remained in continuous use. As it's quiet inside, you may be tempted to pop in for a midday escape from the hectic and boisterous streets outside.

Kawaiaha'o Church

This church, so influential in Hawaii's history, is the most enduring symbol of the original missionary work in the islands. A sign welcomes you and bids the blessing, "Grace and peace to you from God our Father." Hawaiian-language services are given here every Sunday, along with English-language services. The church was constructed 1837–1842 according to plans drawn up by Hiram Bingham, its minister, and is the oldest permanent church structure in Honolulu. Before this, at least four grass shacks of increasing size stood here. One was destroyed by a sailor who was reprimanded by Reverend Bingham for attending services while drunk; the old sea dog returned the next day and burned the church to the ground. Kawaiaha'o (Water of Hao) Church is constructed from more than 14,000 coral blocks quarried from offshore reefs. In 1843, following Restoration Day, when the British returned the Hawaiian Islands to sovereignty after a brief period of imperialism by a renegade captain, King Kamehameha III uttered here in a thanksgiving ceremony the profound words that were destined to become Hawaii's motto, *"Ua mau ke ea o ka 'aina i ka pono"* ("The life of the land is preserved in righteousness").

Other noteworthy ceremonies held at the

© ROBERT NILSEN

Kawaiaha'o Church

church were the marriage of King Liholiho and his wife Queen Emma, who bore the last child born to a Hawaiian monarch. Unfortunately, little Prince Albert died at the age of four. On June 19, 1856, Lunalilo, the first king elected to the throne, took his oath of office in the church. A bachelor who died childless, he always felt scorned by living members of the Kamehameha clan and refused to be buried with them at the Royal Mausoleum in Nu'uanu Valley; he is buried in a tomb at the front of the church. Buried along with him is his father, Charles Kana'ina, and nearby lies the grave of his mother, Miriam Kekauluohi. In the graveyard at the rear of the church lies Henry Berger and many members of the Parker, Green, Brown, and Cooke families, early missionaries to the islands. In fact, the names on the headstones here read like a veritable who's who of early missionaries, and most are recognizable as important and influential people in 19th-century Hawaiian history. Queen Lili'uokalani's body lay in state in the church before it was taken to the Royal Mausoleum. A jubilation

service was held in the church when Hawaii became a state in 1959. Kawaiaha'o holds beautiful Christmas services with a strong Polynesian and Hawaiian flavor. Hidden away in a corner of the grounds is an unobtrusive adobe building, remains of a schoolhouse built in 1835 to educate Hawaiian children.

◖ MISSION HOUSES MUSEUM

The days when tall ships with tattered sails crewed by rough seamen bore God-fearing missionary families dedicated to Christianizing the savage islands are alive in the halls and buildings of the Mission Houses Museum (553 S. King St., 808/531-0481, www.missionhouses.org), now a registered National Historical Landmark. Set behind Kawaiaha'o Church, the complex includes two main houses, a printing house annex, a research library, and a fine gift shop. It's operated by the nonprofit Hawaiian Mission Children's Society, whose members serve as guides and hosts. Many are direct descendants or spouses

© ROBERT NILSEN

Mission Houses Museum

of descendants of the Congregationalist missionaries who built these structures. One-hour guided tours are offered Tues.–Sat. at 11 A.M. and 2:45 P.M.; admission is $10 adults, $8 *kama'aina,* military, and seniors, $6 students six through college age.

Construction

If you think that precut modular housing is a new concept, think again. The first structure you enter is the **Frame House,** the oldest wooden structure in Hawaii. Precut in Boston, it came along with the first missionary packet in 1819. Since the interior frame was left behind and didn't arrive until Christmas Day, 1820, the missionary families lived in thatched huts until it was erected. Finally the Chamberlain family occupied it in 1821. Many missionary families used it over the years, with as many as four households occupying this small structure at the same time. This is where the Christianizing of Hawaii truly began. This structure was renovated in 1996, and most artifacts and furniture are from the 1820–1860 period, with some reproductions.

The missionaries, being New Englanders, first dug a cellar. The Hawaiians were suspicious of the strange hole, convinced that the missionaries planned to store guns and arms in this "fort." Although assured to the contrary, King Liholiho, anxious to save face and prove his omnipotence, had a cellar dug near his home twice as deep and large. This satisfied everyone.

Notice the different styles, sizes, and colors of bricks used in the structures. Most of the ships of the day carried bricks as ballast. After unloading cargo, the captains either donated or sold the bricks to the missionaries, who incorporated them into the buildings. A common local material was coral stone—pulverized coral was burned with lime to make a crude cement, which was then used to bind cut-coral blocks. The pit used for this purpose is still discernible on the grounds.

Kitchen

The natives were intrigued with the missionaries, whom they called "long necks" because of their high collars. The missionaries, on the other hand, were a little more wary of their "charges." The low fence around the complex was symbolic as well as utilitarian. The missionaries were obsessed with keeping their children away from Hawaiian children, who at first ran around naked and played many games with overt sexual overtones. Almost every evening a small cadre of Hawaiians would assemble to peer into the kitchen to watch the women cook, which they found exceedingly strange because their *kapu* said that men did the cooking. In the kitchen, actually an attached cookhouse, the wood-burning stove kept breaking down. More often than not, the women used the fireplace with its built-in oven. About once a week, they fired up the oven to make traditional New England staples like bread, pies, cakes, and puddings. The missionaries were dependent on the Hawaiians to bring them fresh water. Notice a large porous stone through which they would filter the water to remove dirt, mud, and sometimes brackishness.

The Hawaiians were even more amazed when the entire family sat down to dinner, a tremendous deviation from their beliefs that separated men and women when eating. When the missionaries assembled to dine or meet at the "long table," the Hawaiians silently stood at the open door to watch the evening soap opera. The unnerved missionaries eventually closed the door and cut two windows into the wall, which they could leave opened but draped. The long table took on further significance. The one you see is a replica. When different missionaries left the islands, they, like people today, wanted a souvenir. For some odd reason, they elected to saw a bit off the long table. As years went by, the table got shorter and shorter until it was useless.

Residents

The house was made a duplex in 1824 and turned into a home for one family in 1851. Although many families lived in it, two of the best known were the Binghams and the Judds. Much of the furniture here was theirs. Judd, a member of the third missionary company, assumed the duties of physician to all the missionaries and islanders. He often prescribed alcohol of different sorts to the missionary families for a wide variety of ailments; many records remain of these prescriptions, but not one record of complaints from his patients. The Binghams and Judds got along very well and entertained each other and visitors, most often in the Judds' parlor because they were a little better off. The women would often congregate here to do their sewing, which was in great demand, especially by members of the royal household. Until the missionary women taught island girls to sew, providing clothing for Hawaii's royalty was a tiresome and time-consuming obligation.

The missionaries were self-sufficient and had the unbounded energy of youth, as the average age was only 25. The husbands often built furniture for their families. Reverend Bingham, a good craftsman, was pressed by Queen Ka'ahumanu to build her a rocking chair after she became enamored of one made for Mrs. Bingham. The queen weighed almost 400 pounds, so building her a suitable chair was no small feat! Still, the queen could only use it in her later years when she'd lost a considerable amount of weight. After she died, the Binghams asked for it to be returned, and it sits in their section of the house. Compare Bingham's chair to another in the Judds' bedroom, jury-rigged by a young missionary husband from a captain's chair. An understatement, found later in his diary, confirmed that the young man was not a carpenter.

When you enter the Judds' bedroom, note how small it is and consider that two adults and five children slept here. As soon as the children were old enough, they were sent back to the Mainland for schooling, no doubt to relieve some of the congestion. Also notice that the windows were fixed, in the New England style, and imagine how close it must have been in these rooms. The Binghams' bedroom is also small and not as well furnished. Bingham's shaving kit remains and is inscribed with "The Sandwich Isles." In the bedroom of Mary Ward, a missionary woman who never married, the roof was raised to accommodate her canopy bed.

Another famous family that lived in the complex was the Cookes. When the missionary board withdrew its support, the Cookes petitioned them to buy the duplex, which was granted. Shortly thereafter, Mr. Cooke, who had been a teacher, formed a partnership with one Mr. Castle, and from that time forward Castle and Cooke grew to become one of Hawaii's oldest and most powerful corporations.

Chamberlain House

The largest building in the compound is the coral-block Chamberlain House. This barn-like structure was completed in 1831 and used as a warehouse and living quarters for Levi Chamberlain's family. Chamberlain was the accountant and business agent for the mission, so goods for all mission stations in the islands were stored in most of the structure, while the family occupied three modest rooms. This building went through extensive renovation inside and out in 2002.

Printing House

The missionaries decided almost immediately that the best way to convert the natives was to speak to them in their own language and to create a written Hawaiian language they would teach in school. To this end, they created the Hawaiian alphabet, consisting of 12 letters, with five vowels and seven consonants. In addition, to disseminate the doctrines of Christianity, they needed books, and therefore a printing press. On the grounds still stands the Printing House, built in 1841 but first used as annex bedrooms of the Frame House by the Hall family. The original printing house, built in 1823, was located across the street and no longer exists. In the Printing House is a replica of the Ramage press brought from New England, first operated by Elisha Loomis. He returned to the Mainland when he was 28 and soon died of tuberculosis, but not before he had earned the distinction of being the first printer west of the Rockies. Here were printed biblical tracts, textbooks, and anything the king or passing captains were willing to pay to have printed. Although it took eight hours of hard work to set up one page to be printed, it is estimated that in the 20 years the press operated under the missionaries, more than seven million pages were produced.

Gift Shop

While you're on the grounds, be sure to visit the bookstore and gift shop; open Tues.–Sat. 10 A.M.–4 P.M. It's small but has an excellent collection of Hawaiiana, some inexpensive but quality items, and outstanding Ni'ihau shell-work, considered the finest in Hawaii. The shelves hold tasteful items like wood carvings, bread boards, tapa bookmarks, hats, weavings, chimes, flags of old Hawaii, and stuffed pillows with classic Hawaiian quilt motifs, as well as a good collection of Hawaiian dolls, for kids and adults. Between the bookstore and the research library are restrooms.

Special Programs

Along with other programs, the museum hosts a Kama'aina Day program, with volunteers dressed in fashions of the period, who assume the roles of missionaries in 1830s Honolulu. Feel free to interact and ask questions, but remember that they stay in character, so the answers may surprise you. This program is usually offered on the last Saturday of the month; regular admission except for *kama'aina,* who get in for half price. Other special programs are also offered, like a candlelight Christmas affair, crafts and quilt fairs, and quilt classes. For anyone wanting to delve into the history of the mission, the reference library is open Tues.–Fri. 10 A.M.–4 P.M.

HONOLULU HARBOR AREA
C Hawaii Maritime Center

The development of this center was a wonderful concept whose time finally came. It's amazing that a state and former nation, whose discovery and birth are so intimately tied to the exploration, navigation, and exploitation of the sea, had never had a center dedicated exclusively to these profoundly important aspects of its heritage. Now, the Hawaii Maritime Center (808/536-6373, www.bishopmuseum.org/

© ROBERT NILSEN

Part of the Hawaii Maritime Center exhibit, the four-masted *Falls of Clyde* reflects a time when trade and travel to Hawaii were all done by sail.

exhibits/hmc/hmc.html, open every day except Christmas 8:30 A.M.–5 P.M., $7.50 adults or $4.50 children 4–12) at Pier 7, across from the Aloha Tower Marketplace in Honolulu Harbor, is exactly that. Open since 1989, the center consists of three attractions: the Maritime Center building with displays of Hawaii's past; the classic fully rigged, four-masted *Falls of Clyde* floating museum; and the reproduction of a Hawaiian sailing canoe, the *Hokule'a,* which has sailed back in time using ancient navigational methods to retrace the steps of Hawaii's Polynesian explorers. Take TheBus no. 19 or 20 or the Waikiki Trolley from Waikiki; if you're driving, there is $5 validated parking. Admission includes a taped tour that guides you through the museum. Don't just walk past or save this for last because it explains the exhibits and gives insight into what you're seeing. Also, stop in at the gift shop for a collectible of Hawaii's past.

The main building of the center is the two-story museum. Upon entering you find a glass case filled with trophies and memorabilia from the days of King Kalakaua. His words have a sadly prophetic ring. "Remember who you are. Be gracious, but never forget from whence you came for this is where your heart is. This is the cradle of your life." Notice the phones installed throughout Honolulu in 1887, a few years before California had electricity. Kalakaua had previously installed telephones between his boathouse and the palace in 1878, just two years after Bell's invention. The bottom floor of the center recalls ancient fishing methods and the traditional division of land and sea resources among the people. Another fascinating display traces the development of surfing through the ages, from original boards—more like seagoing canoes at 18 feet long—to the modern debut of the fiberglass board. You can spot a vintage album of *Surfin' Safari* by the Beach Boys.

Here, too, is a land-surfing sled used for games during the Makahiki Festival. Trails to accommodate it were up to one mile long. Built on steep hills, they were paved in stone, layered with earth, and topped with slippery grass. Once launched there was no stopping until the bottom. Yeeee! One corner of the museum is dedicated to tattooing, Polynesian and Western. It shows traditional tattoos worn by both men and women, and then how the Western style became more popular because Hawaii was a main berth for sailors, who sported these living souvenirs from around the world. Mail buoys sound uninteresting, but these tidbits of old Hawaiiana are fascinating, and the tradition is still alive today. Passing ships, mainly from Peru and Ecuador, still radio Honolulu Harbor that they are dropping one of these gaily painted metal cans. Someone, anyone, who hears the message fetches it. Inside are little gifts for the finder, who takes the enclosed mail and sends it on its way.

The second floor is dedicated to the discovery of Hawaii, both by the Polynesians and Westerners. Through ledgers, histories, and artifacts, it traces original discovery, Western discovery, the death of Captain Cook, and the role of the sea otter pelt, which brought the first whalers and traders after sandalwood. The whaling section is dripping with blood and human drama. Look at the old harpoons and vintage film footage. Yes, film footage, and photos. A remarkable display is of scrimshaw from the whaling days. Sailors would be at sea 5–7 years and had untold hours to create beauty in dismal conditions. Suspended from the ceiling are replicas of double-hulled sailing canoes and one of only two fully restored skeletons of the humpback whale (this one is in diving position). One corner is a replica of H. Hackfeld and Co., a whaling supply store of the era. The rear of the second floor shows steamships that cruised between Hawaii, Japan, and the East Coast; a nature exhibit of weather, marinelife, and volcanoes; and an auditorium with a video on the *Hokule'a*.

Behind the museum is the seafood Pier Seven Restaurant and an area called Kalakaua Park, a garden and observation area perfect for lunch. Eighty-one steps lead to the "crow's nest" and "widow's walk," with great views of the harbor and city.

Falls of Clyde

This is the last fully rigged, four-masted ship afloat on any of the world's oceans; it has been designated as a National Historic Landmark. It was saved from being scrapped in 1963 by a Seattle bank attempting to recoup some money on a bad debt. The people of Hawaii learned of its fate and spontaneously raised money to have the ship towed back to Honolulu Harbor. The *Falls of Clyde* was always a worker, never a pleasure craft. It served the Matson Navigation Company as a cargo and passenger liner from 1898 to 1920. Built in Glasgow, Scotland, in 1878, it was converted in 1906 to a sail-driven tanker; a motor aboard was used mainly to move the rigging around. After 1920, it was dismantled and towed to Alaska, becoming little more than a floating oil depot for fishing boats. Since 1968, the *Falls of Clyde* has been a floating museum, sailing the imaginations of children and grownups to times past, and in this capacity has performed perhaps its greatest duty.

Hokule'a

The newest and perhaps most dynamic feature of the center is the *Hokule'a*. This authentic re-creation of a traditional double-hulled sailing canoe captured the attention of the world when in 1976 it made a 6,000-mile round-trip voyage to Tahiti. It was piloted by Mau Piailug, a Caroline Islander, who used only ancient navigational techniques to guide it successfully on its voyage. This attempt to relive these ancient voyages as closely as possible included eating traditional provisions only—poi, coconuts, dried fish, and bananas. Toward the end of the voyage, some canned food had to be broken out!

Modern materials such as plywood and fiberglass were used, but by consulting many petroglyphs and old drawings of these original craft, the design and lines were kept as authentic as possible. The sails, made from heavy cotton, were the distinctive crab-claw type. In trial runs to work out the kinks and choose the crew, it almost sank in the treacherous channel between O'ahu and Kaua'i and had to be towed in by the Coast Guard. But the *Hokule'a* performed admirably during the actual voyage. The experiment was a resounding technical success, but it was marred by bad feelings between crew members. Both landlubber and sea dog found it impossible to work as a team on the first voyage, thereby mocking the canoe's name, Star of Gladness. The tension was compounded by the close quarters of more than a dozen men living on an open deck only nine feet wide by 40 feet long. The remarkable navigator Piailug refused to return to Hawaii with the craft and instead sailed back to his native island. Since then, the *Hokule'a* has made six more voyages, including one to distant Rapa Nui, logging more than 90,000 miles, with many ethnically mixed crews who have gotten along admirably.

The *Hokule'a*, owned by the Hawaii Maritime Center but sailed by the Polynesian Voyaging Society, makes Pier 7 its home berth when not at sea. This canoe has been joined by another, the *Hawai'iloa*, which also has made a long trip to Polynesia and back. When not at sea, it too is docked at the Hawaii Maritime Center. For more information about the Polynesian Voyaging Society, check its website (www.pvs-hawaii.org).

Aloha Tower

Next door to the Hawaiian Maritime Center, at Pier 9, is the Aloha Tower, a beacon of hospitality welcoming people to Hawaii for eight decades. When this endearing and enduring tourist cliché was built in 1926 for $160,000, the 184-foot, 10-story tower was the tallest structure on O'ahu. As such, this landmark emblazoned with the greeting and departing word, Aloha, and with clocks embedded in all four walls, became the symbol of Hawaii. Before the days of air transport, ocean liners would pull up to the pier to disembark passengers, and on these "Boat Days," festive well-wishers from throughout the city would gather to greet and lei the arriving passengers. The Royal Hawaiian Band would even turn out to welcome the guests ashore. Almost a recreation of days past, similar "Boat Days" ac-

tivities are held at the pier when cruise ships arrive for a stop in the islands.

Aloha Tower was originally connected to surrounding buildings. Visitors to the islands entered the huge ground-floor U.S. Customs rooms, which at one time processed droves of passengers coming to find a new life. Today, crowds come to find bargains at the adjacent Aloha Tower Marketplace. When refurbished in 1994, the tower's attached buildings were removed, making the tower stand out with more prominence. Only a few harbormasters on the top floor oversee the comings and goings of cargo ships. The observation area is reached by elevator (open free of charge daily 9 A.M.– 5 P.M.), which has the dubious distinction of being one of the first elevators in Hawaii. The elevator is a bit like a wheezy old man, huffing and puffing, but it still gets you to the top. Once atop the tower, you get the most remarkable view of the harbor and the city. A highrise project planned for next door would surely have ruined the view, and due to good sense and citizens with clout, this ill-considered idea thankfully met a timely end. A remarkable feature of the vista is the reflections of the city and the harbor in many of the steel and reflective glass high-rises inland. It's as if a huge mural were painted on them.

◖ CHINATOWN

Chinatown has seen ups and downs in the last 150 years, ever since Chinese laborers were lured from Guangdong Province to work as contract laborers on the pineapple and sugar plantations. They didn't need a fortune cookie to tell them there was no future in plantation work, so within a decade of their arrival they had established themselves as merchants, mostly in small retail businesses and restaurants. Chinatown is roughly an area contained by Vineyard Boulevard and Nimitz Highway on the north and south and Bethel Avenue and River Street on the east and west. Twice this area has been flattened by fire, once in 1886 and again in 1900. The 1900 fire was deliberately set to burn out rats that had brought bubonic plague to the city. The fire got out of

HONOLULU

© AVALON TRAVEL PUBLISHING, INC.

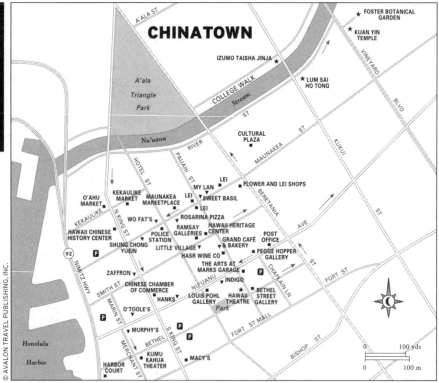

CHINATOWN

control and burned down virtually the whole district. Some contended that the fire was allowed to engulf the district in order to destroy the growing economic strength of the Chinese. Chinatown reached its heyday in the 1930s, when it thrived with tourists coming and going from the main port, which was then at the foot of Nu'uanu Avenue.

Today, Chinatown is a mixed bag of upbeat modernization and run-down sleazy storefronts. Although still strongly Chinese, there are Japanese, Laotians, Vietnamese, Filipinos, and Koreans doing business here as well. The entire district takes only minutes to walk and is a world apart from "tourist" O'ahu. This is Asia come to life: meat markets with hanging ducks and a host of ethnic Asian foods with their strange aromatic spices all in a few blocks.

Incredible shops, down-and-outers, tattoo parlors, lei and flower shops, Buddhist temples, shopkeepers, businesspeople, and hookers all can be found in this quarter. This is a different Honolulu, a Pacific port and immigrant enclave, crusty and exciting.

Chinatown is relatively safe, especially during the daytime, but at night, particularly along infamous Hotel Street, you have to be careful. To help ease potential problems, a Honolulu Police Department downtown substation is located at Hotel and Maunakea Streets. But it's not all down and dirty here. On the periphery of Chinatown there are many new upscale bars and restaurants and even a few art galleries. The art community is doing its part to help revitalize the area with the **First Friday** event, a self-guided gallery walk, held

© ROBERT NILSEN

Izumo Taisha Jinja

on the first Friday evening of each month 5–9 P.M., where art galleries and other venues stay open late to let guests soak up the art scene, partake of refreshments, and enjoy some entertainment. Pick up a copy of the *Gallery Walk, Restaurant & Parking Guide* to help you navigate the area.

Limited-time street **parking** is available, but finding a spot is not always easy. You'll have a better chance finding space in municipal and private parking structures and lots. Several are conveniently located along or near Bethel Street like Macy's Garage, Chinatown Gateway Garage across from Macy's, and the Harbor Court Garage.

Chinatown Sights

Look for the pagoda roof of the **Wo Fat Restaurant** on the corner of Hotel and Maunakea Streets. Started in 1886 by Wo Fat, a baker, this was the oldest chop suey house in Honolulu until its closure around 2005. Nonetheless, it's still a good landmark

for starting your tour of this historical and cultural enclave.

The **Hawaii Theatre** (808/528-0506), a Chinatown landmark since about 1922, has been renovated inside and once again is open to the public for performances and tours. One-hour tours of this historic building are given Tuesday at 11 A.M., and the $5 charge goes into the fund to refurbish the building's exterior.

If you want to clear your head from the hustle and bustle, visit the **Kuan Yin Temple** (open daily 8:30 A.M.–2 P.M.) where the Bodhisattva of Mercy is always praised with some sweet-smelling incense. If that's not enough to awaken your spiritual inner self, visit the **Izumo Taisha Jinja,** a Japanese Shinto shrine. All the accoutrements of a shrine are here— roof, thick coiled rope, bell, and prayer box. This one houses a male deity. You can tell by the cross on the top. There's a ferroconcrete example of a *torii* gate. If you've never visited a Japanese Shinto shrine, have a look here, but be respectful and follow the rules. Or peek into the **Lum Sai Ho Tong** across the street from the Shinto shrine on River Street. This Chinese family association building with a small and basic Taoist shrine on the second floor is usually open until about 2 P.M.

Along both banks of the river are pedestrian malls with benches and tables that are always filled with old-timers playing checkers, dominoes, or Go. On one side of the river is a statue of Dr. Sun Yat-Sen, the main driving force behind the Republic of China, and Dr. Jose Rizal, a Filipino writer and revolutionary opposed to the Spanish occupation of the Philippine Islands.

Across the river is **'A'ala Triangle Park,** often used by young kids to practice their moves at the skateboard park and by derelicts and down-and-outers looking for a place to hang out.

Walking Tours

You can easily do Chinatown on your own, but for another view and some extremely knowledgeable guides, try the **Chinese Chamber of Commerce** (808/533-3181) tour, which has been operating as a community service for almost 30 years. A guide will show you around Chinatown for only $10. This tour is offered Monday at 9:30 A.M. and starts from the chamber office at 42 N. King Street, second floor. Or try the **Hawaii Heritage Center** (808/521-2749) Chinatown Historical and Cultural Walking Tour, which starts at 1140 Smith St., Friday at 9:30 A.M. The two-hour tours are $10 per person. An excellent source of general information on Chinatown is the **Hawaii Chinese History Center** (111 N. King St., 4th Floor, 808/536-5948, open Tues.–Fri. 10 A.M.–1 P.M.).

Another walking tour, one that goes beyond the confines of Chinatown to take in historical structures and old edifices in the rest of downtown Honolulu, is that given by the **American Institute of Architects (AIA)** (808/545-4242, www.aiahonolulu.org). This Architectural Walking Tour starts from its office at 119 Merchant Street, Suite 402, Saturday at 9 A.M., returning about 11:30 A.M. The price is $10

per person, with a minimum of four persons, and reservations and prepayment by credit card are necessary.

PALI HIGHWAY

Cutting across O'ahu from Honolulu to Kailua on the windward coast is Route 61, better known as the Pali Highway. Before getting to the famous Nu'uanu Pali Lookout at the very crest of the Ko'olau Mountains, you can spend a full and enjoyable day sightseeing. Stop en route at Punchbowl's National Memorial Cemetery, followed by an optional side trip to the summit of Tantalus for a breathtaking view of the city. Pu'u 'Ualaka'a State Wayside, also known as Round Top, is where Honolulu lies at your feet. Numerous hiking trails cross or start from Tantalus Drive as it circles its way up and then back down as Makiki Heights Drive.

A short distance up the Pali Highway through this posh valley community are Temple Emmanuel, the Dai Jingu Temple, a Baptist college, a Catholic church, and several other churches and temples. It almost seems as though these sects were vying to get farther up the hill to be just a little closer to heaven. A sign, past Queen Emma Summer Palace, points you off to Nu'uanu Pali Drive. Take it! This few-minutes' jog off the Pali Highway (which it rejoins) takes you through some wonderful scenery. Immediately the road is canopied with trees, and in less than half a mile there's a bubbling little waterfall and a pool. The homes in here are grand, and the entire area has a park-like feel. One of the nicest little roads you can take while looking around, this side trip wastes no time at all.

Royal Mausoleum

Take the H-1 freeway to Vineyard Boulevard (exit 22), cross the Pali Highway to Nu'uanu Avenue, and follow it inland to the Royal Mausoleum State Monument (open weekdays 8 A.M.–4:30 P.M.). This small chapel was built in 1865 by Kamehameha IV to hold the bodies of most of the royal family who died after 1825. Their bodies were originally interred elsewhere but were later moved to this site. This small cross-shape building at one time held 18 royal bodies but became overcrowded, so they were moved again to three underground crypts within this three-acre site. Moving the bodies allowed the former mausoleum to become a chapel, which it remains to this day. Of the eight Hawaiian monarchs, only King Kamehameha I and King William Lunalilo are buried elsewhere—King Kamehameha I somewhere on the Big Island and Lunalilo at Kawaiaha'o Church. Few tourists visit this serene place, but for Hawaiians, this is a spot of great *mana*. and cultural importance.

Across Nu'uanu Avenue and down just a bit is the O'ahu Cemetery. Founded in 1844, it holds the graves of some of the oldest and best-known island families.

◖ Queen Emma Summer Palace

Called Hanaiakamalama, this summer home is more the simple hideaway of a well-to-do family than a grand palace. The 3,000-square-foot interior has only two bedrooms and no fa-

cilities for guests. John George Lewis put the house on the property in 1848. He purchased the land for $800 from a previous owner by the name of Henry Pierce. The simple square home, with a front lanai, was resold to John Young II, Queen Emma's uncle, in 1850. The exterior has a strong New England flavor, and indeed the house was prefabricated in Boston, but it definitely has a neoclassical flourish with its tall, round Doric columns. When Young died, Emma inherited the property and spent many relaxing days here, away from the heat of Honolulu, with her husband King Kamehameha IV. The huge rear room was added in 1869 for a visit by the Duke of Edinburgh. Emma used the home little after 1872, and following her death in 1885 it fell into disrepair.

Rescued from demolition by the Daughters of Hawaii in 1913, the palace (2913 Pali Hwy., 808/595-3167, www.daughtersofhawaii.org., open daily 9 A.M.–4 P.M., except for major holidays, $6 adults, $4 seniors and *kama'aina*, $1 youth 5–17) was refurbished and has operated as a museum since 1915. In the 1970s,

Queen Emma Summer Palace

the Summer Palace was added to the National Register of Historic Sites. Although it's just off the Pali Highway, the one and only sign comes up quickly, and many visitors pass it by. If you pass the entranceway to the Oʻahu Country Club just across the road, you've gone too far.

As you enter, notice the tall *kahili*, symbols of noble rank in the entranceway, along with *lau hala* mats on the floor, which at one time were an unsurpassed specialty of Hawaii. Today they must be imported from Fiji or Samoa. The walls are hung with paintings of many of Hawaii's kings and queens, and in every room are distinctive Hawaiian artifacts and royal memorabilia, such as magnificent feather capes, fans, and tapa hangings. Many of the furnishings belonged to Queen Emma, but some were from other royal family members.

The furnishings have a very strong British influence. The Hawaiian nobility of the time were enamored with the British. King Kamehameha IV traveled to England when he was 15 years old; he met Queen Victoria, and the two became good friends. Emma and Kamehameha IV had the last child born to a Hawaiian king and queen on May 20, 1858. Named Prince Albert after Queen Victoria's consort, he was much loved but died when he was only four years old on August 27, 1862. His father followed him to the grave in little more than a year. The king's brother, Lot Kamehameha, a bachelor, took the throne but died very shortly thereafter, marking the end of the Kamehameha line; after that, Hawaii elected its kings. Prince Albert's canoe-shaped cradle is here, made in Germany by Wilhelm Fisher from four different kinds of Hawaiian wood. His tiny shirts, pants, and boots are still laid out, and there's a lock of his hair, as well as one from Queen Emma. The royal bedroom (originally the dining room) displays a queen-size bed, covered with an exquisite bedspread or quilt that is changed periodically. In the Cloak Room, originally built as the bedroom but later used as the dining room, is a fine example of a royal feather cloak.

Throughout the house, there's vintage Victorian furniture, a piano built in London by Collard and Collard, and even a stereopticon given as a gift from Napoleon III. A royal cabinet made in Berlin holds porcelains, plates, and cups. After Queen Emma died, it stood in Charles R. Bishop's drawing room but was later returned. In the cellar of the house were the servants' quarters, and the original cookhouse once stood to the side where the paved patio is today. Queen Emma once owned 65 acres of the surrounding land. The two acres that remain are beautifully manicured, and the house is surrounded by shrubbery and trees, many dating from when the royal couple lived here. Restrooms are around back, as is the gift shop, which is open the same hours as the palace. Managed by the Daughters of Hawaii, it's small but packed with excellent items like greeting cards, books, beverage trays (reproductions of the early Matson Line menus), little Hawaiian quilt pillows, T-shirts with the Queen Emma Summer Palace logo, and Niʻihau shellwork, the finest in Hawaii.

◖ Nuʻuanu Pali Lookout

This is one of those extra-benefit places where you get a magnificent view without any effort at all. Merely drive up the Pali Highway to the well-marked turnout and park. The lookout closes at 8 P.M. and opens at 4 A.M., so you can come for sunrise or the night lights of Windward Oʻahu in the distance. Rip-offs happen, so take all valuables with you when getting out of the car. Before you, if the weather is accommodating, an unimpeded view of Windward Oʻahu lies at your feet. Nuʻuanu Pali (Cool Heights) lives up to its name; the winds here are chilly and extremely strong, and they funnel right through this notch in the mountain ridge. You may need a jacket or windbreaker. On a particularly windy day just after a good rainfall, various waterfalls tumbling off the *pali* will actually be blown uphill! Several roads, punched over and through the *pali* over the years, are engineering marvels. Originally a footpath, later expanded to a horse trail, the famous "carriage road" built in 1898 was truly amazing. Honolulu native John Wilson built it for only $37,500, using 200 laborers and plenty of dynamite. Droves of people come here, many in huge buses, and they all go to the railing to have a peek. By walking down the old road built in 1932 that goes off to the right, you actually get private and better views, and the wind is quieter.

Nu'uanu Pali figures prominently in Hawaii's legend history. It's said—but not without academic skepticism—that Kamehameha the Great pursued the last remaining defenders of O'ahu to these cliffs in one of the final battles fought to consolidate his power over all of the islands in 1795. If you use your imagination, you can easily feel the utter despair and courage of these vanquished warriors as they were driven ever closer to the edge. Mercy was neither shown nor expected. Some jumped to their deaths rather than surrender, while others fought until they were pushed over. The estimated number of casualties varies considerably, from a few hundred to a few thousand, and some believe the battle never happened at all. Compounding the controversy are stories of the warriors' families, who searched the cliffs below for years and supposedly found bones of their kinsmen, which they buried. An annual commemoration is held here for this pivotal event in Hawaii's history.

PUNCHBOWL, NATIONAL CEMETERY OF THE PACIFIC

One sure sign that you have entered a place of honor is the hushed and quiet nature that everyone adopts without having to be told. It's like this the moment you enter this shrine. The Hawaiian name, Puowaina (Hill of Sacrifice), couldn't have been more prophetic. Punchbowl is the almost perfectly round crater of an extinct volcano. It holds the bodies of more than 46,000 men and women who fell fighting for the United States, from World War II to Vietnam, and a few notable individuals who served the country in other ways. At one time, Punchbowl was a bastion of heavy cannon and artillery trained on Honolulu Harbor to defend it from hostile naval forces.

© ROBERT NILSEN

The statue Columbia honors those who have given their lives for their country at Punchbowl, National Cemetery of the Pacific.

Before that, it had been a place where some Hawaiian royalty were secretly buried to protect their *mana*. In 1943, Hawaii bequeathed it to the federal government as a memorial; it was dedicated in 1949, when the remains of an unknown serviceman killed during the attack on Pearl Harbor were the first interred. One of the more recent to be buried here was astronaut Ellison Onizuka, who died in 1986 aboard the *Challenger* space shuttle. To attest to its sacredness and the importance of those who lie buried here, more than five million visitors stop here yearly to pay their respects, making this the most visited site in the state. In addition, the annual Easter sunrise service held here draws thousands.

As you enter the main gate, a flagpole with the Stars and Stripes unfurled is framed in the center of a long sweeping lawn. A roadway lined with monkeypod trees adds depth, as it leads to the steps of a marble, altarlike monument in the distance. The field is dotted with trees, including eight banyans, a special tree and symbolic number for the many Buddhists buried here, and plumeria and rainbow shower trees, often planted in Hawaiian graveyards because they produce flowers year-round as perennial offerings from the living to the dead when they can't personally attend the grave. All are equal here: the famous, like Ernie Pyle, the stalwart who earned the Congressional Medal of Honor, and the unknown who died alone and unheralded on muddy battlefields in godforsaken jungles.

Like a pilgrim, you climb the steps to the monument, where on both sides marble slabs seem to whisper the names of 28,778 servicemen, all MIAs whose bodies were never found or those who were buried at sea, but whose spirits are honored here. The first slabs on the right are for the victims of Vietnam, and on the left are those from World War II; time is already weathering the marble. Their names stand together, as they fought and died—men, boys, lieutenants, captains, private soldiers, infantrymen, sailors—from everywhere in America. "In proud memory . . . this memorial has been erected by the United States of America." At the monument, built in 1966, is a chapel, and in the middle is a statue of a woman, a woman of peace, a heroic woman of liberty. Around her on the walls are etched maps and battles of the Pacific War whose names still evoke passion: Pearl Harbor, Wake, Coral Sea, Midway, Iwo Jima, the Gilbert Islands, Okinawa. Many of the visitors are Japanese. Many of Hawaii's war dead are also Japanese. Many years ago we battled each other with hatred and malice. Today, on bright afternoons we come together with saddened hearts to pay reverence to the dead.

To the right just after you enter is the cemetery office (808/532-3720, www.cem.va.gov/cem/cems/nchp/nmcp.asp, open weekdays 8 A.M.–4:30 P.M.), with a general information kiosk, historical information, brochures, and restrooms. The cemetery is open free of charge 8 A.M.–5:30 P.M. Sept. 30–March 1 and until 6:30 P.M. March 2–Sept. 29, except for Memorial Day when there is a special memorial ceremony and the grounds are open 7 A.M.–7 P.M. You are free to enter and look around as you wish. Don't leave valuables in your car. Roberts

Hawaii (808/954-8652 or 866/898-2519) offers the Stars and Stripes tour, which includes a walking tour of the National Cemetery led by a member of the American Legion as part of an all-day tour, for $68 adults and $58 children 4-11 years old. Polynesian Adventure Tours (800/622-3011) and E Noa Tours (800/824-8804) also include the National Cemetery as a stop on a longer Pearl Harbor tour.

To get to Punchbowl take the H-1 freeway to Route 61, the Pali Highway, and exit at 21B. Immediately get to the right, where a sign points you to Punchbowl. You'll make some fancy zigzags through a residential area, but it's well marked and you'll come to Puowaina Drive, which leads you to the main gate. Take note of landmarks going in, because as odd as it sounds, no signs lead you back out, and it's easy to get lost.

UNIVERSITY OF HAWAI'I

Established in 1907, the University of Hawai'i at Manoa (www.hawaii.edu) is the main campus of a 10-branch university system. The Manoa campus teaches about 20,000 students in undergraduate and graduate programs and, like the rest of the state, is a multicultural and multiracial establishment. The Manoa campus lies in Manoa Valley, one of the loveliest residential areas on O'ahu. To get there, follow the H-1 freeway to exit 24B (University Avenue). Follow University Avenue to Dole Avenue, and make a right onto campus. Stop immediately at one of the parking lots and get a parking map! Parking restrictions are strictly enforced, and this map not only helps to get you around but also saves you from fines or having your car towed. Parking is a flat $3 for visitors each time you use the lot, so think about taking TheBus no. 4, which services this area quite well from Waikiki.

Two six-week summer sessions beginning in late May and early July are offered to bona fide students of accredited universities at the University of Hawai'i at Manoa, including courses in Hawaiian language and history and Pacific Island studies. For information, catalog, and enrollment, contact the Outreach College

(University of Hawai'i, 2440 Campus Rd., Box 447, Honolulu, HI 96822, 808/956-5666 or 800/862-6628, www.outreach.hawaii.edu/summer).

Make the **Campus Center** your first stop. As you mount the steps, notice the idealized mural of old Hawaii: smiling faces of contented natives all doing interesting things. Inside is the **Information Center,** which dispenses information not only about the campus, but also about what's happening socially and culturally around town. Stop here for a campus map and self-guided tour brochure, and, if you're into it, pick up brochures on public artwork and significant plants on campus. The food in the cafeteria is institutional but cheap and has a Hawaiian twist. The best places to eat are the Manoa Garden Restaurant on the ground floor of the Hemenway Center or at the Paradise Palms Cafe next to Hamilton Library, although there are other smaller cafés and food kiosks around campus.

The **University Bookstore** (open Mon.–Fri. 8:15 A.M.–4:45 P.M., Sat. 8:15–11:45 A.M.) on the lower level of the Campus Center is excellent. The bookstore is worth coming to for its excellent specialty items, like language tapes and a whole range of Hawaiiana. The **Commons Gallery,** an adjunct of the University Art Gallery open only during regular school sessions, is on the third floor and is worth a look. The exhibits change regularly; admission is free. Next to the gallery is a lounge with overstuffed chairs and big pillows, where you can kick back and even take a quick snooze. This is not a very social campus. By 4:30 or 5 P.M. the place is shut up and no one is around. Don't expect students gathered in a common reading room or the activity of social and cultural events. When school lets out at the end of the day, people simply go home.

East-West Center

Follow Dole Avenue to East-West Road and make a left. The center's 21 acres were dedicated in 1960 by the U.S. Congress to promote better relations between the nations of Asia and the Pacific with the United States. In 1975, the center was incorporated and officially separated from the university. Many nations, as well as private companies and individuals, fund this institution of cooperative study and research. The center's staff, with help from University of Hawai'i students and scholars and professionals from throughout the region, focus on four broad but interconnected issues: regional security, social and cultural changes, the changing domestic political scene in nations of the region, and regional economic growth and its consequences. John Burns Hall's main lobby dispenses information on what's happening, along with maps. The murals inside are excellent, and the lobby also contains a large reading room with relaxing couches. While you're here, check out the bookstore, which carries an impressive selection of Hawaiiana and books on Asia, or have a peek at the East-West Center Gallery (open Mon.–Fri. 8 A.M.–5 P.M., Sun. noon–4 P.M.) Imin Center-Jefferson Hall, fronted by Chinese lions, has a serene and relaxing Japanese garden behind it, complete with a little rivulet and a teahouse named Jakuan (Cottage of Tranquility).

The impressive solid teak Thai Pavilion was a gift from the king of Thailand in 1967, where it was built and sent to Hawaii to be reconstructed. Due to deterioration, the original was replaced by another in 2006, also as a gift of the Thai king. The Center for Korean Studies (not part of the East-West Center, but just up the road) is also outstanding. A joint venture of Korean and Hawaiian architects, its inspiration was taken from the classic lines of Kyongbok Palace in Seoul. Most of the buildings are adorned with fine artworks: tapa hangings, murals, calligraphy, paintings, and sculpture. The entire center is tranquil, and along with the John F. Kennedy Theater of Performing Arts just across the road, is indeed fulfilling its dedication as a place of sharing and learning, culture and art.

MANOA VALLEY

Manoa Valley, a tropical palette of green ablaze with daubs of iridescent color, has a unique designation most aptly described as urban rainforest. Although not technically true, the valley, receiving more than 100 inches of rainfall per year, is exceptionally verdant even by Hawaiian standards, but it wasn't always so. In the late 1800s, the overpopulated valley was almost denuded of trees, only to be reforested by Dr. Harold Lyon, the founder of Lyon Arboretum, who planted trees gathered from around the world. The runoff from Manoa would flood the relatively dry Waikiki until the Ala Wai Canal was built in the 1920s as a catchment for its torrential flash floods. Only a short drive from arid Waikiki, Manoa was the first place in Hawaii where coffee was grown and pineapple was cultivated.

The great Queen Ka'ahumanu, who died here in 1832, favored the cool hills of the valley as a vacation spot to escape the summer heat. Manoa, favored by royalty ever since, has maintained itself as one of the most fashionable residential areas in Hawaii, even boasting its own country club at the turn of the 20th century, which is yet memorialized by the Manoa Cup, an amateur match-play golf championship, held yearly at the O'ahu Country Club. In 1893, just before annexation, a bewildered and beaten group of royalists came to Manoa to hide out. They were subsequently captured by a contingent of pursuing U.S. Marines and imprisoned in an area called The Pen, on the grounds of the now-defunct Paradise Park, at the upper end of the valley.

Taking Manoa Road, you pass **Punahou School,** one of the oldest and most prestigious schools in Hawaii. Built in 1841 from lava rock, children of the missionary families of wealthy San Franciscans attended, getting the best possible education west of the Rockies. Manoa Road eventually crosses O'ahu Avenue—an extension of University Avenue. There at the intersection is the **Wai'oli Tea Room,** set within a small parklike property. Owned and operated by the Salvation Army, this unique restaurant features fresh-baked pastries and serves breakfast, lunch, and high tea. Also featured here is the Little Grass Shack, supposedly lived in by Robert Louis Stevenson when he was a resident of Waikiki. Visit the chapel with its distinctive stained-glass windows. Above Punahou School, East Manoa Road splits off

Manoa Road. After crossing O'ahu Avenue, it leads to **Manoa Marketplace,** where you find plenty of shops and eateries, and the Manoa Valley Theater.

Lyon Arboretum

The Lyon Arboretum (3860 Manoa Rd., 808/988-0464, www.hawaii.edu/lyonarboretum, open Mon.–Fri. 9 A.M.–4 P.M.) is situated on 194 acres at the upper end of Manoa Road. Open to the public, it's principally a research facility and academic institution of the University of Hawai'i, a quiet shaded retreat from the noise of the city. While well cared for and orderly, this is not a highly manicured garden, just a natural beauty and profusion of greens. It not only has sections set aside for research and horticultural plants, but there is also an herb garden, ethnobotanical garden, and hundreds of tropical plants that include ginger, *ti,* heliconia, hibiscus, palms, and bromeliads. While guided tours are occasionally offered, you can look around on your own. Walking-tour maps are available; sign in at the main office and leave a donation.

The arboretum book and gift shop is a great place to pick up a memento or one of numerous books on the flora of Hawaii and other Hawaiian subjects. In addition, various horticultural and related classes are held at the arboretum, usually on Thursday and Saturday mornings. Classes are open to anyone but require a fee and reservation.

Free parking for arboretum visitors is near the visitors center gift shop. Do not park in the arboretum parking lot if you're planning to walk up the Manoa Valley Trail to Manoa Falls. If hiking to Manoa Falls, park inside the trailhead gate, down the road at the pay ($5) parking lot next to the Tree Tops Restaurant, or farther down in the residential neighborhood.

Wa'ahila Ridge State Recreation Area

On the ridge east of Manoa Valley—follow St. Louis Drive up to its end through St. Louis Heights—you will discover tall coniferous trees in the coolness of the mountains. This recreation area (open 7 A.M.–7:45 P.M.) has picnic tables, covered pavilions, plenty of parking spots, views out over Manoa Valley, and the trailhead for a trail that heads some distance up Waʻahila Ridge.

◖ BISHOP MUSEUM

Otherwise known as the Museum of Natural and Cultural History, this group of stalwart stone buildings holds the greatest collection of historical relics and scholarly works on Hawaii and the Pacific in the world. It refers to itself as a "museum to instruct and delight," and in one afternoon walking through its halls you can educate yourself about Hawaii's history and people and enrich your trip to the islands tenfold.

Officially named Bernice Pauahi Bishop Museum, the museum came about through the bequests of the last three royal women of the Kamehameha dynasty. Princess Bernice married Charles Reed Bishop, a New Englander who became a citizen of the then-independent monarchy in the 1840s. The princess was a wealthy woman in her own right, with lands and an extensive collection of things Hawaiian. Her cousin, Princess Ruth Keʻelikolani, died in 1883 and bequeathed Princess Bernice all of her lands and Hawaiian artifacts. Princess Bernice then owned about 12 percent of all Hawaii! Princess Bernice died less than two years later and left all of her landholdings to the **Bernice Pauahi Bishop Estate,** which founded and supported the Kamehameha School, dedicated to the education of Hawaiian children. (Although this organization is often confused with the Bishop Museum, they are totally separate. The school once shared the same grounds with the museum, but no school funds were, or are, used for the museum.) Bernice left her personal property, with all of its priceless Hawaiian artifacts, to her husband, Charles. Then, when Queen Emma, her other cousin, died the following year, she wished Charles Bishop to add her Hawaiian artifacts to the already formidable collection and establish a Hawaiian museum.

Bishop began construction of the museum's

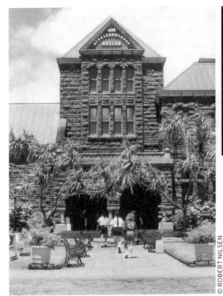

The stately Bishop Museum is the most respected museum of Polynesian culture in the world.

© ROBERT NILSEN

main building on December 18, 1889, and within a few years the museum was opened. In 1894, after 50 years in Hawaii, Bishop moved to San Francisco, where he died in 1915. He is still regarded as one of Hawaii's most generous philanthropists. In 1961, a science wing and planetarium were added, and in late 2005 the new Science Adventure Center was opened.

The museum (1525 Bernice St., 808/847-3511, www.bishopmuseum.org) is open daily 9 A.M.–5 P.M., except Christmas Day. Admission is $14.95 adults, $11.95 ages 4–12 and seniors; kids under four and museum members are free, but some exhibits and the planetarium are closed to children under six. *Kamaʻaina,* military, and other discounts are available upon request. It's sometimes best to visit on weekends because many weekdays bring teachers and young students who have more enthusiasm for running around than for checking out the exhibits. Food, beverages, and smoking are all strictly prohibited in the museum. The natural light in the museum is dim, so if you're into photography you'll need super-fast film (400 ASA performs only marginally) or a flash.

To get there, take exit 20A off the H-1 freeway, which puts you on Route 63, the Likelike Highway. Immediately get into the far right lane. In only a few hundred yards, turn onto Bernice Street, where you'll find the entrance to the museum. Or, use exit 20B West off H-1 to access Houghtailing Street. Keep your eyes peeled immediately for a clearly marked but small sign directing you to the museum. The-Bus no. 2 (School-Middle Street) runs from Waikiki to Kapalama Street, from which you walk two blocks, and the Waikiki Trolley (Red line) also makes this the farthest stop before its return to Waikiki.

Exhibits

It's easy to become overwhelmed at this museum, so just take it slowly. The number of exhibits is staggering: more than 1 million artifacts; about 22 million specimens of insects, shells, fish, birds, and mammals; an extensive research library; a photograph collection; and a fine series of maps. Only a small portion of the total can be shown. Get a map at the front desk that lists all of the halls, along with descriptions. Throughout the week, demonstrations in various Hawaiian crafts like lei-making, featherwork, and quilting are offered at 10 A.M. The following is just a small sample of the highlights.

The **main gallery** is highlighted by the rich tones of koa, the showpiece being a magnificent staircase. The floors of the main hall are perhaps the most interesting because they deal with old Hawaii. Here are magnificent examples of *kahili,* feathered capes, plumed helmets—all the insignia and regalia of the *ali'i.* To the right of the main entranceway is a fascinating exhibit of the old Hawaiian gods. Most are just called "wooden image" and date from the early 19th century. Among them are Kamehameha's war-god, Ku; the tallest Hawaiian sculpture ever found, from Kaua'i; an image of a god from a temple of human sacrifice; and lesser gods, personal *'aumakua* that controlled the lives of Hawaiians from birth until death. You wouldn't want to meet any of them in a dark alley!

In the main hall is a grass shack, a replica of what Captain Cook might have seen. Over your head a 55-foot sperm whale hangs from the ceiling. It weighed more than 44,000 pounds alive. You'll learn about the ukulele, and how vaudevillians spread its music around the world. Don't miss the koa wood collection of medicine bowls, handsome calabashes, some simple home bowls, and one reputed to be the earthly home of the wind goddess, which had to be refitted for display in Christianized 'Iolani Palace. A model *heiau* tells of the old religion and the many strange *kapu* that governed every aspect of life. Clubs used to bash in the brains of *kapu*-breakers sit next to benevolent little stone gods, the size and shape of footballs, that protected humble fishermen from the sea. As you ascend to the upper floors, the time period represented becomes increasingly closer to the present. The missionaries, whalers, merchants, laborers, and Westernized monarchs have arrived. Yankee whalers from New Bedford, New London, Nantucket, and Sag Harbor appear determined and grim-faced as they scour the seas, harpoons at the ready. Great blubber pots, harpoons, and figureheads are preserved from this perilous and unglamorous life. Bibles, thrones, and the regalia of power and of the new god are all here. In adjacent rooms are artifacts from the rest of the Pacific island cultures.

Outside, in the **Hawaiian Courtyard,** are implements used by the Hawaiians in everyday life, as well as a collection of labeled plants. The Courtyard Gallery features shells, and across the way is the Hawaii Sports Hall of Fame. Lying across the lawn from the main building, new **Science Adventure Center** houses an artificial volcano and numerous smaller exhibits where visitors can learn about Hawaii's natural environment. Special exhibits are shown in the Castle Memorial Building.

Before leaving the grounds, make sure to take in the hula performances at 11 A.M. and 2 P.M. The **planetarium** opens up its skies weekdays at 11:30 A.M., 1:30 P.M., and 3:30 P.M., and the first Friday of each month at 7 P.M. by reservation (808/848-4168) and $4 fee. Both the library (808/848-4148) and archives (808/848-4182) are open to the public Tues.–Fri. noon–4 P.M. and Sat. 9 A.M.–noon. The snack shop has reasonable prices, and **Shop Pacifica,** the museum bookstore and boutique, has a fine selection of materials on Hawaii and the Pacific, plus some authentic and inexpensive souvenirs.

OTHER MUSEUMS AND GALLERIES
Law Enforcement Museum
The Honolulu Police Department's Law Enforcement Museum (801 Beretania St., 808/529-3351, open weekdays 9 A.M.–3 P.M.) is housed at the police department headquarters, located between city hall and the Honolulu Academy of Arts. Thoroughly engaging, this free museum presents in broad strokes the history of law enforcement in the state, from its humble origins in 1834 to the modern and efficient force of today. Many weapons, badges, uniforms, and other police paraphernalia, as well as documents and photographs, are on display. Special attention is given to Detective Chang Apana, the real-life Charlie Chan, and other police officers of note. You'll need to go through a security check and sign in to enter the building.

◖ Hawaii State Art Museum
In 2002, the State Foundation of Culture and Arts finally got its wish—a location to house and display part of its large collection of Hawaiian art by Hawaiians. This collection is open to the public on the second floor of the No. 1 Capitol District Building (250 South Hotel St.), a Spanish Mission–style stucco building kitty-corner from 'Iolani Palace, which sits on the site of the original Royal Hawaiian Hotel, the finest of Honolulu's early hotels. The museum's two galleries and lobby house several hundred works of art by Hawaiian artists, mostly paintings, ceramics, and sculpture. These pieces are part of the foundation's Art in Public Places collection and together offer a glimpse of the diverse cultural

mix of people who make Hawaii their home and their expression of the islands. The museum (808/586-0304 or 808/586-0900 for recorded exhibit information, www.state.hi.us/sfca, open Tues.–Sat. 10 A.M.–4 P.M.) offers guided tours of the galleries at 11 A.M. and 2 P.M. Otherwise, you can walk through at your own pace. There is no entrance fee but donations are appreciated. The museum now sports a café on the first floor. Outdoor concerts of music and dance are showcased on the museum's front lawn 5–9 P.M. on the first Friday of each month to coordinate with Chinatown's First Fridays Gallery Walk events.

◖ Honolulu Academy of Arts
Enjoy the magnificent grounds of this perfectly designed building, a combination of East and West with a Hawaiian roof and thick white stucco walls reminiscent of the American Southwest, created by architect Bertram Goodhue and benefactor Anna Rice Cooke. The museum (900 S. Beretania St. 808/532-8700 or 808/532-8701 for recorded exhibition information, www.honoluluacademy.org, open Tues.–Sat. 10 A.M.–4:30 P.M., Sun. 1–5 P.M.) lies opposite Thomas Square. Admission fees are $7 adults, $4 seniors, students, and military personnel. Members and children under 12 get in free, as does everyone on the first Wednesday of the month and the third Sunday of the month. Guided docent tours, free with admission, are conducted daily at 10:15 A.M., 11:30 A.M., and 1:30 P.M., and Sun. at 1:15 P.M. Audio tours at $5 plus admission are also available. The academy houses a brilliant collection of classic and modern art, strongly emphasizing Asian artwork. It is Hawaii's premier general fine arts museum.

James Michener's outstanding collection of Japanese *ukiyo-e* is here. The story goes that an unfriendly New York cop hassled him on his way to donate it to a New York City museum, whereas a Honolulu officer was the epitome of *aloha* when Michener was passing through, so he decided that his collection should reside here. This collection is rotated frequently and displayed in a specially designed gallery to

Shangri La, a symphony of Islamic art and architecture, was once home to the heiress and art patron Doris Duke.

highlight and protect the prints. Magnificent Korean ceramics, Chinese furniture, and Japanese prints, along with Western masterworks from the Greeks to Picasso, make the academy one of the most well-rounded art museums in America. Some collections are permanent but others change, so the museum remains dynamic no matter how many times you visit. Discover delights like Paul Gauguin's *Two Nudes on a Tahitian Beach,* James Whistler's *Arrangement in Black No. 5,* and John Singer Sargent's *Portrait of Mrs. Thomas Lincoln Hansen Jr.* An entire wing is dedicated to religious art, while another holds furniture from medieval Europe. A small gallery displays Islamic art from the collection of Doris Duke, and other galleries hold works of Hawai'i and the Philippines. The courtyards are resplendent with statuary from the 6th century A.D. and a standing figure from Egypt, circa 2500 B.C. The Hawaiian climate is perfect for preserving artwork. In 2001, the new Luce Pavilion Complex opened, with a downstairs gallery focused on traveling exhibitions and an upstairs gallery

that displays engaging works on the history of art in Hawaii.

Educational programs, films, and concerts are also supported by the museum and held in the Academy's theater, known as the Doris Duke Theatre at the Academy, and the Robert Allerton Library is a fine reference library open to the public for research. For those looking for something extra, try the Art after Dark program (808/532-8734, www.artafterdark.org, $7) on the last Friday of the month 6–9 P.M., for art tours, discussions, musical concerts, films, food, and ideas. Stop at the Academy Shop, specializing in art books, museum reproductions, Hawaii out-of-print books, jewelry, notebooks, and postcards. The Pavilion Café (808/532-8734, open Tues.–Sat. 11:30 A.M.–2 P.M.) offers a light but terrific menu; a trip to the Academy demands a luncheon in the café.

The Waikiki Trolley and TheBus nos. 2 and 13 stop out front when going toward downtown (catch the return bus along S. King Street), but if you are driving, parking is in a lot to the rear of the Academy Art Center; $3 for four hours with validation, $2 per hour during the day, or $4 flat rate in the evening. A second lot one block east of the main building is open to the public only in the evening and on weekends at the same rate. On the far side of Thomas Square is the Blaisdell Center parking lot.

The Academy now offers tours of **Shangri La,** the former home of Doris Duke, a tobacco heiress and a wealthy patron of the arts in Hawaii and elsewhere. Shangri La sits on the ocean below Diamond Head and tours include transportation to and from the house. Over the years of her life, Doris Duke collected a vast quantity of Islamic Art and much of it is displayed at Shangri La, the interior of which was renovated to display the art to its best advantage. This house is simply full of treasures from the Middle East, and a tour through the house is a superb experience. Tours are run six times a day Wed.–Sat. only by advance reservation. Because these tours are so popular, they may be filled several months ahead. Call to reserve well in advance (808/532-3853 or 866/385-3849, www.shangrilahawaii.org, $25 per person, no children under age 12). The 2.5-hour tours leave from the Honolulu Academy of Art; van transportation is provided.

Academy Art Center at Linekona

Kitty-corner from the Honolulu Academy of Arts, and affiliated with it, is the Academy Art Center; admission is free. Built in 1908 as McKinley High School, and later used as Lincoln (Linekona) Elementary School, it is now on both the National and State Registers of Historic Places. The building was renovated and reopened in 1990 as a place where art students can create and display artwork, and where annual and changing special exhibitions are held. It's a functioning art center, so it's a good place to see what kinds of artwork young, contemporary Hawaiian artists are doing. Works are displayed in a large, wooden-floored room with a vaulted ceiling, perhaps the old school gymnasium, where banks of windows provide plenty of natural light.

The Contemporary Museum

The Contemporary Museum (2411 Makiki Heights Dr., 808/526-0232, www.tcmhi.org, open Tues.–Sat. 10 A.M.–4 P.M., Sun. noon–4 P.M., closed Monday and major holidays, $5 general admission, $3 students and seniors, free on the third Thursday of the month) welcomes you with two copper-green gates that are sculptures themselves. This open and elegant structure, the former Spalding House, yields seven galleries, a gift shop, an art library, and an excellent gourmet restaurant, the Contemporary Cafe. Acquired through the generosity of the *Honolulu Advertiser*'s stockholders, the building was donated to the museum as a permanent home in 1988. The focus is on exhibitions, not collections, although works by David Hockney are on permanent display, and there are others by such well-known artists as Andy Warhol and Jasper Johns. Always-changing exhibits reflect different themes in contemporary art—from 1940 onward. Guided tours of the exhibitions are given Tues.–Sat. at 1:30 P.M.; call 808/536-1322 for details at least a week in advance. Parking is free.

Surrounding the building are three magnificent acres sculpted into gardens perfect for strolling and gazing at the sprawl of Honolulu far below. You can follow the walking paths on your own (pick up a map on entry) to admire the outside sculptures, or take a 45-minute tour of the gardens led by museum volunteers and offered by appointment only.

This museum also displays works at The Contemporary Museum at First Hawaiian Center, a free gallery on the second floor of First Hawaiian Bank building in the center of town (999 Bishop St., open Mon.–Thurs. 8:30 A.M.–4 P.M. and Fri. until 6 P.M.).

Tennent Art Foundation Gallery

This private gallery (201-203 Prospect St., 808/531-1987, open Tues.–Sat. 10 A.M.–noon, Sun. 2–4 P.M., free) is located on the 'ewa slope of Punchbowl. With such limited hours, you have to plan a visit well to this gallery. The walls hold the paintings of Madge Tennent, one of Hawaii's foremost artists. According to her wishes, her remaining works are housed and displayed here, in what was her studio, rather than being sold or given for display elsewhere. Designed in 1953 by Vladimir Ossipoff, one of Hawaii's well-known architects, the two-level gallery with its undulating roof has been placed on the State Historical Record. The gallery is a quiet sanctuary in a residential neighborhood and worth a visit. Head up Ward Avenue until it meets Prospect Street. Turn left and proceed around to the west side of the hill. Look for the salmon-colored wall and gate.

University of Hawai'i Art Gallery

Housed in the Department of Art along The Mall on the Manoa campus, the art gallery (808/956-6888, www.hawaii.edu/artgallery) exhibits various art shows, both national and international, as well as student art works. Its yearly International Shoebox Sculpture Exhibition is well known. The Commons Gallery, a smaller gallery in the student center, also displays pieces by students and visiting artists. Both galleries are open to the public free during the school year, Mon.–Fri. 10:30 A.M.–4 P.M. and Sun. noon–4 P.M.

While on the university campus, you may want to have a look at the **East-West Center Gallery** (John A. Burns Hall, 1601 East West Rd., open weekdays 8 A.M.–5 P.M., Sun. noon–4 P.M.) or the **John Young Museum of Art** at Krauss Hall (2500 Dole St., 808/956-3634, open weekdays 11 A.M.–2 P.M., Sun. 1–4 P.M.).

GARDENS
Foster Botanical Garden

Many of these exotic trees have been growing in this 13.5-acre manicured garden (180 N. Vineyard Blvd., 808/522-7065, open daily 9 A.M.–4 P.M. except Christmas and New Year's Day, $5 nonresidents, $3 residents, $1 children 6–12) for more than 100 years. In the mid-1800s it was the private estate of Dr. William Hillebrand, physician to the royal court; he brought many of the seedlings from Asia. Now that the garden is on the National Register of Historic Places, two dozen of these trees enjoy lifetime protection by the state, and oth-

ers are examples of rare and endangered species. A few of the huge and exceptional trees are kapok, bo, banyan, and Mindanao gum, several from the 1850s, and other sections of the garden show orchids, palms, poisonous plants, herbs, and "primitive" plants. While guided tours are given Mon.–Sat. at 1 P.M. (808/522-7066 for reservations), free self-guided tour brochures are available on entry. Give yourself at least an hour for a leisurely stroll; bring insect repellent. Along with four others on the island, these gardens are administered by the Honolulu Botanical Gardens. Before leaving, stop in for a look at the Foster Garden Gallery and Bookstore for books, postcards, tapa cloth, T-shirts, and other gift items. Use TheBus no. 4 from Waikiki.

Lili'uokalani Botanical Garden

A stone's throw to the north over the freeway and set along the Nu'uanu Stream are the 7.5 acres of this garden. Once the secluded private garden of the last Hawaiian monarch, it is now hemmed in by private homes and apartment buildings and part of the Honolulu Botanical Garden system. Unlike the imported magnificence of the Foster Botanical Garden, this garden features mostly native Hawaiian plants in a natural setting. The bottom end near the freeway is more pleasant than the upper end near the parking lot, although there is more noise, and it seems to be used mostly for picnics.

Moanalua Gardens

The private gardens of the Damon Estate were given to the original owner by Princess Bernice Bishop in 1884. On the mountain side of the Moanalua Freeway, these gardens (808/833-1944, open weekdays 7 A.M.–6 P.M., weekends from 7:30 A.M.) are open to the public but not heavily visited. More like a park with open grassy lawns and spaced monkeypod trees than a typical botanical garden, it is a welcome respite from the hustle and bustle of the city. Some magnificent old trees include a Buddha tree from Ceylon and a monkeypod called "the most beautifully shaped tree" in the world by *Ripley's Believe It or Not!* On the grounds are a Chinese Hall, once used to entertain guests, and a cottage built by King Kamehameha V in the 1850s. Take exit 3 (Tripler Hospital exit) off Highway 78 (Moanalua Road), a connector between H-1 and H-3. Slow down on the exit ramp, as the garden entrance is along this exit ramp. If this exit is closed, proceed up the exit ramp to the cross street, turn right and then take the first left turn. This road loops around and under the cross street, bringing you to a parking lot for the Moanalua Recreation Center and Moanalua Gardens.

The nonprofit cultural and educational Moanalua Garden Foundation (www.mgf-hawaii.com,), not affiliated with the Damon Estate, presents the noncompetitive Prince Lot Hula Festival in the Moanalua Gardens yearly on the third Saturday in July.

HONOLULU BEACHES AND PARKS

The beaches and parks listed here are found in and around Honolulu's city limits. (World-famous Waikiki has its own section.) The good thing about having Waikiki so close is that it lures most bathers away from other city beaches, which makes them less congested. The following list contains most of Honolulu's beaches, ending at Ala Moana Beach Park, just a few hundred yards from where the string of Waikiki's beaches begins.

Ke'ehi Lagoon Beach Park

At the eastern end of Honolulu International Airport, this park is at the inner curve of Ke'ehi Lagoon, just off Route 92 (the Nimitz Highway). The water at this park is not the cleanest, but people do swim here. Local canoe clubs use it, and outrigger canoes can be seen skimming the water of the lagoon in the afternoon. Mostly, local people use the water for pole fishing and crabbing, and the rest of the park for picnicking, ball games, and tennis. There are restrooms, pavilions, picnic tables, a pay phone, and lots of parking. One entrance to the Disabled American Veterans Memorial, adjacent to the east, is through this park.

Sand Island State Recreation Area

You enter this park by way of the Sand Island Access Road, clearly marked off the Nimitz Highway. On the way, you pass through some ugly real estate—scrapyards, petrochemical tanks, warehouses, and other such beauties. It's not bad once you get past this commercial/industrial strip. Don't get discouraged—keep going! After crossing the bridge, hurry past a wastewater treatment center (hold your nose!) and pass the entrance to the U.S. Coast Guard base before entering the park (open 7 A.M.–6:45 P.M.), a 14-acre reserve landscaped with picnic, playground, and sporting facilities. The park is not well maintained, but it has pavilions, cold-water showers, walkways, and restrooms. However, the camping area is usually empty (state permit required). The sites are out in the open, but a few trees provide some shade. Unfortunately, you're under one of the main glide paths for Honolulu International Airport. From the campground end of the park, you have a view of part of the inner Honolulu harbor and downtown Honolulu, with Diamond Head making a remarkable counterpoint. Many local people come to fish, and the surfing can be good, but the snorkeling and swimming are fair at best. The currents and wave action aren't dangerous, but remember that this is at the harbor entrance and it receives more than its share of pollutants.

Kaka'ako (Point Panic) Waterfront Park

This small state facility was carved out of a piece of land next to Kewalo Basin Harbor and donated by the University of Hawai'i's Biomedical Research Center; at one time it was used as a dump. Follow 'Ohe or Ko'ula streets seaward from Ala Moana Boulevard to the park. From the huge parking lot, walking paths lead over the rise (which blocks out the noise of the city) to a grand promenade and picnic tables set under stout trellises. This area is poor for swimming, but it's great for fishing and surfing. Others come to enter the water for scuba dives. If you're lucky, you may spot a manta ray, known to frequent these waters. Unfortunately, novices will quickly find out why it's called Point Panic. As at the Kewalo Basin Park across the opening to the adjacent harbor, a long seawall with a sharp drop-off runs the entire length of the area. The wave action is perfect for riding, but all wash against the wall. Beginners stay out! The best reason to come here is for the magnificent and unobstructed view of the Ala Moana Beach, the Waikiki skyline, and Diamond Head beyond.

To the side of the park is the **Hawaii Children's Discovery Center** (111 'Ohe St., 808/524-5437, www.discoverycenterhawaii.org, open Tues.–Fri. 9 A.M.–1 P.M., weekends 10 A.M.–3 P.M., $8 adults, $5 seniors, $6.75 ages 2–17), an interactive educational institution where kids can learn about themselves, the community in which they live, the special things about Hawaii, and the different peoples of the world.

Kewalo Basin State Park

Kewalo Basin Marina, developed in the 1920s to hold Honolulu's tuna fleet, is home to many charter boats for water activities, including fishing, parasailing, sunset tours, and underwater excursions. Pay parking is to the side. On the ocean side of the marina, stretching along the breakwater, is this state park (free parking) with its promenade and covered picnic tables. Surfers congregate here for the good waves that develop because of the offshore reef, which continues all the way along the front of Ala Moana Beach Park.

Ala Moana Beach Park

Ala Moana (Path to the Sea) Beach County Park is by far Honolulu's best. Most visitors congregate just around the bend at Waikiki, but residents head for Ala Moana, the place to soak up the local color. During the week, this beautifully curving white-sand beach has plenty of elbowroom. Weekends bring families that come for every water sport O'ahu offers. The swimming is great, with manageable wave action, plenty of lifeguards, and even good snorkeling along the reef. Board riders have their favorite spots, and bodysurfing is excellent. The huge area has several restrooms, food concessions, tennis courts, softball fields, a bowling green, and parking for 500 cars. Many O'ahu outrigger canoe clubs practice in this area, especially in the evening; it's great to come and watch them glide along. A huge banyan grove provides shade and strolling if you don't fancy the beach, or you can bring a kite to fly aloft with the trade winds. Ala Moana Park stretches along Ala Moana Boulevard between the Ala Wai and Kewalo Basin boat harbors. It's across from the Ala Moana Shopping Center on the east end and Ward Centre on the west end, so you can rush right over if your credit cards start melting from the sun.

'Aina Moana (Land from the Sea) Recreation Area used to be called Magic Island because it was reclaimed land. It is actually the point of land stretching out from the eastern edge of Ala Moana Beach Park, contiguous with it. The beach here is a fine crescent strand that's protected by a breakwater and backed by broad lawns, trees, and picnic tables.

Entertainment

Music and Dancing

Anna Bananas (2440 S. Beretania St., 808/946-5190, open 11:30 A.M.–2 A.M.) is the "top banana" for letting your hair down and boogying the night away. It's just west of the S. King Street and University Avenue intersection, across from Star Market. Bananas has a laid-back atmosphere, reasonable beer prices, usually a small cover of about $5 that goes to the band, no dress code, and a friendly student crowd. The bar downstairs is dark and upstairs there's usually live music on the weekends. You get the whole spectrum of music styles coming through here. Pub food is served downstairs and there's a backyard to cool off in between sets. Great place, great fun!

Located at Restaurant Row, the **Ocean Club** (808/526-9888, open Tues.–Fri. 4:30 P.M.–4 A.M., Sat. 7 P.M.–4 A.M.) is one of Honolulu's consistent hot spots for the young crowd. With its DJ and a large dance floor, it can get active. The cocktail hour, with reduced-price *pu pu* and light meals, runs 4:30–8 P.M., while happy hour on Friday starts at 8 P.M. The age limit for entrance is 23 and over (21 and over on Thursday only), and there is a dress code. Apparently, the owners want a more sophisticated crowd, not a bunch of rowdy first-timers.

Rumours Nightclub (808/955-4811) in the Ala Moana Hotel is an established DJ disco that cranks up around 9 P.M. Thurs.–Sat. and seems to attract a crowd over 35, perhaps wanting to relive disco days. A dress code is enforced, and a $10 cover is charged. Closing time is usually 2–2:30 A.M.

Evening music is almost always on tap at one of the fine restaurants at Aloha Tower Marketplace. **Don Ho's Island Grill** (808/528-0807) and **Gordon Biersch Brewery and Restaurant** (808/599-4877) schedule live bands to accompany their menus. Also at Aloha Tower Marketplace, **Chai's Island Bistro** (808/585-0011) has some of the best island musicians performing weekly, including the Brothers Cazimero, Sistah Robi, Melveen

Leed, Jerry Santos, Hapa, and Makaha Sons. Each is a class act, and together they make the best lineup of local musicians on the island. Music runs 7–9 P.M. Reservations are suggested. Free valet parking is provided.

For a complete listing of what's happening in town on the music and dance scene for the weekend and coming week, have a look at the Calendar of Events section of the Friday edition of the newspaper.

Note: Also see the *Waikiki* chapter for more entertainment options.

Polynesian Revue

Kalo's South Seas Revue (808/941-5205), a nightly Polynesian revue and buffet dinner show, happens at the Ala Moana Hotel's South Seas Village. Dinner starts at 5:30 P.M. and the show gets going about 6:30 P.M. Dinner includes prime rib and dozens of other treats, and the show is a mixture of music, hula, and a fire dance. This is a fun, tourist-oriented affair that caters largely to Japanese. Tickets run $61 for adults and $36 for children.

Performance Arts

Like any big city, Honolulu has a whole host of musical and performance art venues and high-quality productions. Some of the best known are as follows:

The **Honolulu Symphony** (808/792-2000, www.honolulusymphony.com) performs indoors at the Neil S. Blaisdell Center Concert Hall and outdoors at the Waikiki Shell. Various programs take place throughout the year, with most tickets ranging $20–65, with students and seniors half price.

Hawaii Opera Theater (808/596-7858, www.hawaiiopera.org) also puts on shows at the Neil S. Blaisdell Center Concert Hall. The six-week season for this professional company runs late January through early March. Tickets run $29–120.

Ballet Hawaii (www.ballethawaii.org) also uses the Neil S. Blaisdell Center Concert Hall

FREE ENTERTAINMENT IN HONOLULU

At **Centerstage,** Ala Moana Shopping Center, various shows are presented – mostly music (rock, gospel, jazz, Hawaiian) and hula. Performances usually start at noon, sometimes at 2 P.M., and include local as well as national musical groups. The **Keiki Hula Show,** every Sunday at 10 A.M., is fast becoming an institution. Here, hula is being kept alive, with many first-time performers interpreting the ancient movements they study in their *halau.*

The stage at the west end of Ward Warehouse also offers free hula performances Thursday 6-8 P.M. and live music Sunday at 1 P.M.

The **Royal Hawaiian Band,** founded more than 170 years ago, performs Friday at noon at the 'Iolani Palace Bandstand and on Sunday 2-3 P.M. at the Kapi'olani Park Bandstand. Call (808/527-5666) for other band performance locations, or visit the band website (www.royalhawaiian band.com).

Honolulu Hale (City Hall) presents periodic free musical concerts in the central courtyard and art exhibitions in the central courtyard, Lane Gallery, or Third Floor Gallery. All are welcome Mon.-Fri. 8 A.M.-5 P.M.

with its variety of shows over the years at 1130 Bethel Street at the edge of Chinatown. This theater hosts local and off-island music and theater shows and is a venue of the annual Hawaii International Film Festival. For information on what's happening or to buy tickets, stop by the box office Tues.–Sat. 9 A.M.–5 P.M. and half an hour before shows. There's ample pay parking nearby.

The **Honolulu Theatre For Youth** (808/839-9885, www.htyweb.org) is a nonprofit organization that puts on professional shows with youth and families in mind at the Tenney Theatre, St. Andrew's Cathedral in Honolulu. Tickets run a reasonable $8–16.

The **Kumu Kahua Theater** (808/536-4441, www.kumukahua.org) is a small theater that produces half a dozen plays annually about life in Hawaii by Hawaiian playwrights. Set on the corner of Bethel and Merchant Streets, this 100-seat theater opens its doors Thurs.–Sat. at 8 P.M. and Sunday at 2 P.M. Admission is a reasonable $16 general, $13 seniors, and $10 students, with discounts on Thursday.

On the University of Hawai'i, Manoa campus, the **Kennedy Theatre** (808/956-7655, www .hawaii.edu/kennedy) hosts university stage productions. The building, designed by the noted architect I. M. Pei, is of interest in itself but is of greater interest for theater buffs because it is made to easily stage both Western- and Asian-style productions. Shows generally run Fri.–Sat. at 8 P.M. and Sunday at 2 P.M., with tickets at $16 regular, $14 seniors, $112 students. Box office hours are weekdays 10 A.M.–3 P.M.

The smaller and more intimate **Manoa Valley Theatre** (2833 East Manoa Valley Rd., 808/988-6131, www.manoavalleytheatre.com), Hawaii's own "off-Broadway" theater, produces half a dozen experimental stage shows throughout the year. The theater is adjacent to the Manoa Marketplace shopping center and has limited parking. Shows run Wed.–Thurs. at 7:30 P.M., Fri.–Sat. 8 P.M., and Sunday 4 P.M., with tickets in the $25–30 range.

The **Doris Duke Theatre** (808/532-8768) at the Honolulu Academy of Arts hosts a full schedule of film, music, and theatrical

for its few performances during the year but rehearses and runs a school at its studio at Dole Cannery Square.

Diamond Head Theatre (520 Makapu'u Ave., 808/733-0274, www.diamondhead theatre.com) performs at its own location just below Diamond Head. This company has been presenting live theatrical shows since 1915 and never fails to impress. Performances are Thurs.–Sat. at 8 P.M. and Sunday at 4 P.M., and tickets range $12–42.

Built in 1922 and renovated inside in 1996, the **Hawaii Theatre** (808/528-0506, www.hawaiitheatre.com) has thrilled crowds performances throughout the year, along with lectures and other educational functions. Tickets for film showings run $7 general or $5 members; other events vary in price.

Movies

For second-run Hollywood movies, try **Restaurant Row 9 Theatres** at Restaurant Row (808/526-4171) for the cheapest shows in town at $0.50 before 3:30 P.M. and $1 after 3:30 P.M., with validated parking in the complex parking structure.

First-run moviehouses are the **Kahala 8 Theater** at the Kahala Mall (593-3000, $8 adults, $5.75 children), the **Ward 16 Theatres,** 2nd floor at the Ward Entertainment Center (808/594-7000 or 593-3000, $8.75 adults, $6.25 children), or the 18-screen Signature **Regal Cinemas** at the Dole Cannery (808/526-3456, $8.50 adult, $6.50 children).

About the only place in town to see art films at a commercial theater is the two-screen **Varsity Twin Theater** (1106 University Ave., 808/593-3000, $8.25 adults, $6 children), near the university. The **Doris Duke Theatre** (808/532-8768) at the Honolulu Academy of Arts shows films many nights of the week, often with an international flavor. Occasionally, films are shown at various university auditoriums; look for fliers and promotional literature on campus.

The **Movie Museum** (3566 Harding Ave., 808/735-8771) in Kaimuki also shows art, international, and short-run films at its tiny theater located one block south of Wai'alae Avenue between 11th and 12th Avenues, across from the city parking lot. Here, film fanatics have the pleasure of sitting in cushy recliner chairs as they enjoy the flick. Entrance is $5 general. Call for movies and show times.

Shopping

If you don't watch the time, you'll spend half your vacation moving from one fascinating store to the next. Luckily, in greater Honolulu most shopping is clustered in malls, with specialty shops scattered around the city, especially in the nooks and crannies of Chinatown. Below is just a quick snapshot of some of the unique shops the town has to offer.

Ala Moana Shopping Center

This is the largest shopping center in the state, and if you want to get all of your souvenir hunting and special shopping done in one shot, this is the place. Because it serves as the main terminal for TheBus, you could make a strong case that this mall is the heart of shopping on O'ahu. It's on Ala Moana Boulevard just across from the Ala Moana Beach Park and is open Mon.–Sat. 9:30 A.M.–9 P.M., Sunday 10 A.M.–7 P.M. The center has large free parking lots but can also be reached by the Waikiki Trolley pink line, otherwise known as the Ala Moana Shopping Shuttle, which runs every eight minutes daily during

business hours from more than half a dozen locations in Waikiki for $2 each way. TheBus nos. 8, 19, 20, 42, and 58 also connect Ala Moana Shopping Center to Waikiki. Recently, the Ala Moana Shopping Center has taken off its comfortable Hawaiian shirt and shorts and donned designer fashions by Christian Dior and Gianni Versace. Local people have been irritated by this move, and they have a point, to a point. The center has plenty of down-home shopping left, but it now caters as much to the penthouse as it does to the one-room efficiency. It used to be where the *people* shopped, but now portions are being aimed at the affluent tourist, especially affluent Japanese tourists who flaunt designer labels. If anything, the shopping has gotten better, but you'll have to look around a bit more for bargains.

Plenty of competition keeps prices down, with enough of an array to suit any taste and budget. There are about 250 stores, including the major department stores **Sears, Macy's,** and **Neiman Marcus.** Utilitarian shops and boutiques feature everything from wedding rings to swim fins, while the food court and freestanding restaurants feed hungry shoppers with a multitude of ethnic foods. It's also a great place to see a cross-section of Hawaiian society. Another pleasant feature is the free Keiki Hula Show every Sunday at 10 A.M. on the Centerstage, but there are literally hundreds of other performances throughout the year. The center maintains an information kiosk near Centerstage to answer questions and point you in the right direction. Aside from all the shops, services include a Honolulu satellite city hall, post office, several banks, and a Continental Airlines office.

For books, try **Barnes and Nobles Booksellers** (808/949-7307), which has a large selection of books and an inclusive Hawaiiana section, or **Borders Express** (808/942-1605) for a smaller but sufficient stock. Books make inexpensive, easy-to-transport, and long-lasting mementos of your trip to Hawaii. **Longs Drugs** (808/941-4433) has good prices for film, but you might also check at **Ritz Camera** (808/943-6391). The **Crack Seed Center** (808/949-7200) offers the best array of crackseed (spiced nuts, seeds, and fruits), which has been a treat for island children for years. Prices are somewhat inflated here, but the selection can't be beat, and you can educate yourself about these same products in smaller stores around the island. Crackseed is not to everyone's liking, but it does make a unique souvenir. **Shirokiya** (808/973-9111) is a Japanese-owned department store near Macy's on the mountain side of the complex. It has a fascinating assortment of gadgetry, knickknacks, handy items, and nifty stuff that Nippon is so famous for. It's fun just to look around, and the prices are reasonable. Japanese products are also available at **S.M. Iida Limited** (808/973-0320), a local store dating back to the early 1900s, featuring garden ornaments and flower-arrangement sets. Specialty shops in the center include **Products of Hawai'i, Too** (808/949-6866), **Hawaiian Quilt Collection** (808/946-2233), and a **Hilo Hattie** (808/973-3266) shop.

Ward Centers

This cluster of more than 120 shops and nearly two dozen eateries occupies four clusters of buildings spread over a four city block area, west of Ala Moana Shopping Center and across from Kewalo Basin and the west end of Ala Moana Beach Park. Shopping hours vary somewhat by store, but generally run Mon.–Sat. 10 A.M.–9 P.M. and Sunday 10 A.M.–5 P.M. The centers can be reached by Waikiki Trolley red line, near the end of its loop through town, and by TheBus nos. 19, 20, and 42 from Waikiki, but there is also plenty of free parking. For the entertainment of shoppers, a free hula show on Thursday 6–8 P.M. and a Sunday concert at 2 P.M. are held at the stage near the parking structure of the Ward Warehouse section of shops.

The modern two-story **Ward Warehouse** complex lives up to its name, with a motif from bygone days when stout wooden beams were used instead of steel. The wide array of shops includes inexpensive restaurants and clothing stores, but the emphasis is on arts, crafts, and clothing. Among the many shops here, be sure to stop at **Native Books/Na Mea Hawaii** (808/596-8885, www.nativebookshawaii.com) for unique and authentic high-quality gifts, crafts, artwork, clothing, food items, books, and music CDs made in Hawaii. This store is an excellent place to start looking for an authentic gift to take home from the islands. One of the premier shops in the Ward Warehouse—there is another at Ward Centre—is **Nohea Gallery** (808/596-0074). *Nohea* means beautiful or handsome in Hawaiian, and this typifies the work displayed in these two galleries by more than 500 local artists and craftspeople. Nohea Gallery is where you can see the heart of Hawaii through the eyes of its artists. Have a look! Other notable shops are **Island Soap and Candle Works** (808/591-0533), which produces handmade products with scents of the islands; **My Little Secret** (808/596-2990), for quilt items; and the **Liquor Collection** (808/542-8808), for a great supply of wine, beer, liqueur, and other alcoholic beverages.

Down Ala Moana Boulevard from Ward Warehouse is **Ward Centre,** a string of exclusive shops and upscale eateries. It also has one of the few microbreweries on the island.

The Ward Centre is appointed in light wood and accentuated by brick floors that give the feeling of an intimate inside mall, although much is outside. Plenty of clothing and accessory stores fill these shops, as do a number of art retailers. The **Honolulu Chocolate Co.** (808/591-2997), a smug little devil, tempts with chocolate truffles, mocha clusters, and fancy nut rolls, and the **Black Pearl Gallery** (808/597-1477) tempts you with pretty things to wear. **Borders Books and Music** (808/591-8995) anchors the end of this center and is a full-selection outlet with books, music, newspapers, and magazines from around the world, a very good Hawaiiana section, ongoing events, and a gallery and coffee shop upstairs.

Across Auahi Street are the **Ward Gateway Center, Ward Farmers Market,** and the **Ward Village Shops,** each with several freestanding specialty stores and restaurants. The **Ward Entertainment Center** boasts additional restaurants, a huge movie theater complex, and the three-story **Dave and Buster's** (808/ 589-2215) restaurant and entertainment arcade for adults.

Aloha Tower Marketplace

Constructed in 1994, the Aloha Tower Marketplace is a unique shopping plaza, one frequented by tourists and locals alike. Set to the side of the Aloha Tower and fronting the working harbor of Honolulu, where ships from all over the world load and unload their goods, this marketplace is an old warehouse that's been tastefully converted into an upscale group of more than 100 shops offering food and beverages, apparel, art, gifts, jewelry, and specialty items. Shops are open Mon.–Sat. 9 A.M.–9 P.M., Sunday 9 A.M.–6 P.M. The vintage-looking, open-air red line Waikiki Trolley makes the connection from Waikiki to Aloha Tower many times a day and stops right at the front. Alternately, TheBus no. 19 and 20 from Waikiki get you close. If driving, use the pay parking lots in front of Aloha Tower or near Piers 5 and 6.

Aloha Tower Marketplace is an indoor-outdoor affair, where the sea breezes blow right through. The central courtyard atrium, in the shadow of the tower, is the spot for free musical entertainment performed throughout the week. Stop at **Hawaiian Pacific Crafts** (808/528-2388) and **Island Art Galleries** (808/528-5880) for a take-home souvenir, or **Wyland Galleries** (808/536-8973) for a classic piece of island art. The **World of Hats** (808/548-0717) carries everything from baseball caps to woven Panama hats to keep the sun at bay, and you can find island musical instruments and hula instruments at **Hawaiian Ukulele Company** (808/536-3228). The outside area in front of the tower is called the Boat Days Bazaar, and it's filled with cabana-type booths selling mostly apparel, gifts, and souvenirs. Most of the shops in this complex are locally owned, independent outfits. Have a walk through and support the local economy. After having a look at the shops, sit down for a snack or a meal at one of the many food vendors or have a drink at the watering holes. At several of these fine establishments you'll find evening entertainment virtually every night of the week.

Downtown Financial District

Fort Street in the center of town has many fine old buildings along its length. Most of Fort Street has been set aside as a pedestrian walkway, or mall, that's closed to vehicular traffic and makes a fine unencumbered way through downtown. Sections of Front Street are set aside on Tuesday, Wednesday, and Friday 8 A.M.–2 P.M. for vendors to set up movable carts and sell their wares in an open-air market setting. If you're downtown during these times, stop by and see what bargains you can find.

Chinatown

For shopping in Chinatown, head to the **Chinatown Cultural Plaza Shopping Center** on the corner of Maunakea and Beretania Streets, where you'll find such stores as Dragon Gate Book Store, Bin Ching Jade Center, Excellent Gems and Diamonds, and a slew of restaurants. In some ways it's more fun to look at than to shop in. Here also you'll find the Cultural Plaza Moongate Stage, where you can periodically catch a performance of Chinese dances and plays, and where you can herald the Chinese New Year. If a presentation is happening, attend.

At the corner of Hotel and Maunakea Streets is the compact **Maunakea Marketplace,** a tight little jumble of shops with souvenirs, gifts, and an indoor food court with mostly Asian vendors that seems more vibrant than the Cultural Plaza. A half block away along Kekaulike Street is the **Kekaulike Market,** with similar diversity and many shops selling ethnic foods and ingredients.

Nearby and close to the river is an open market of cooperative stalls that's been operating for over a century. Follow your nose to the pungent odors of fresh fish at **O'ahu Market** on King Street, where ocean delectables can be had for reasonable prices. Numerous other fish markets line the streets nearby.

Cindy's Lei & Flower Shoppe, on the corner of Hotel and Maunakea Streets, has fresh lei at cheap prices. At Beretania and Smith Streets is **Lita's Lei,** famous for good products and prices. Several others in the nearby streets are **Maunakea Street Florist, Lin's Lei Shop,** and **Violet Lei Stand,** which form a garland of flower shops.

Chinatown has been growing its art galleries as well as its flower stalls. The following are longstanding places that have created a niche for themselves and are worth a look. The **Pegge Hopper Gallery** (1164 Nu'uanu St., 808/524-1160, open Tues.–Fri. 11 A.M.–4 P.M. and Sat. 11 A.M.–3 P.M., www .peggehopper.com) displays only works by Pegge Hopper. Hopper is one of the three most famous working artists in all of Hawaii. Her original works grace the walls of the most elegant hotels and homes in the islands. If you would like to purchase one of her bold and amazing serigraphs, lithographs, or giclées, this shop has the best and widest selection. Only a few steps down the street is the **Studio of Roy Venter** (1160 Nu'uanu Ave., 808/381-3445), open by appointment and during the First Friday art Walk event. One block away on Smith Street is **Ramsay Galleries** (1128 Smith St., 808/537-2787, www.ramsaymuseum.org, open weekdays 10 A.M.–5 P.M., Sat. 10 A.M.–4 P.M.), and on Bethel Street is the cooperative and more experimental **Bethel Street Gallery** (1140 Bethel St., 808/524-3552, www.bethelstreetgallery.com, open Tues.–Fri. 11 A.M.–6:30 P.M., Sat. 10 A.M.–3 P.M.). **The ARTS at Marks Garage** (1159 Nu'uanu Ave., 808/521-2903, www.artsatmarks.com, open Tues.–Sat. 11 A.M.–6 P.M.) is an exhibit and performance space that usually does non-mainstream arts. This space was started as an art incubator and has been a resounding success.

Hilo Hattie and Dole Cannery

West of downtown is the well-known **Hilo Hattie** shop (700 Nimitz Hwy., 808/535-6500, open daily 8 A.M.–6 P.M.). At this store you can find an incredible variety of island fashions, gifts, crafts, and food items at reasonable prices. Shopping here is a good introduction to what the islands have to offer, and to make it a sweeter deal, the store offers free trolley transportation every 20 minutes (8:20 A.M.–4:50 P.M.) to its store from numerous hotel locations in Waikiki on its own shuttle buses. Hilo Hattie is one of the largest manufacturers of alohawear in the state. It's hard to resist spending: Prices and craftsmanship are good, and designs are contemporary.

For decades, the Dole Cannery produced the bulk of the world's pineapples. At the height of the harvest, this factory could process more than three million cans of fruit per day. Now the cannery and its attendant buildings have been silenced and turned to other uses. A part of the old cannery was transformed in 1988 to a minimall located at 650 Iwilei Road, only a short distance from Hilo Hattie. On the two levels you'll find a cluster of shops laid out as traditional storefronts, but many are taken by professional businesses or empty. There is a small minimart here, though, and across the street are the Regal Signature 18-screen movie theaters. On the larger Dole Cannery property are huge box stores **Best Buy, Costco,** and **Home Depot.**

Kahala Mall

The Kahala Mall is the major shopping mall on the eastern side of Honolulu, lying just east of Diamond Head at the edge of the upscale Kahala area and catering to the eastern suburbs of

Honolulu. **Macy's, Longs Drug, Star Market,** and the eight-screen **Kahala Theaters** anchor this mall, surrounded by dozens of mall-standard apparel outlets, gift shops, novelty stores, electronics chains, jewelry stores, and specialty shops. As with most malls, there are about a dozen fast-food outlets, from pizza to plate lunch and sushi, to refresh yourself for more shopping. If you're on the east end of the city, this is the shopping center of choice. General store hours are Mon.–Sat. 10 A.M.–9 P.M., Sunday 10 A.M.–5 P.M. The Kahala Mall is serviced by the Waikiki Trolley blue line and TheBus nos. 22 and 58 from Waikiki.

Bookstores

Honolulu has the bulk of the bookshops on the island. Right downtown at Bishops Square, on the bottom floor of the Pauahi Tower, is **Bestsellers Books** (808/528-2378, open Mon.–Fri. 7:30–5:30 P.M., Sat. 9 A.M.–3 P.M.), which not only has a large collection of books, including Hawaiiana, but also magazines, music, and videos. Bestsellers also has smaller shops at the Hilton Hawaiian Village in Waikiki, at the Honolulu International Airport, and at Koko Marina Shopping Center.

In Honolulu, **Barnes & Noble Booksellers** has one store at the Kahala Mall (808/737-3323, open Mon.–Sat. 9 A.M.–10 P.M., Sun. 9 A.M.–9 P.M.) and another at the Ala Moana Shopping Center (808/949-7307, open Mon.–Fri. 9:30 A.M.–9 P.M., Sun. 10 A.M.–7 P.M.). The **Borders Books and Music** in Honolulu is at the Ward Centre (808/591-8995, open Mon.–Thurs. 9 A.M.–11 P.M., Fri.–Sat. 9 A.M.–midnight, Sun. 9 A.M.–10 P.M.).

For a fine selection of Hawaiiana, try the **Shop Pacifica** (808/848-4158, open daily 9 A.M.–5 P.M.) at the Bishop Museum, the **Mission Houses Museum** gift shop (553 S. King St., 808/531-0481, open Tues.–Sat. 10 A.M.–4 P.M.) in downtown Honolulu, and **Native Books/Na Mea Hawaii** (808/596-8885, open Mon.–Thurs. 9:30 A.M.–9 P.M., Fri.–Sat. 9:30 A.M.–9:30 P.M., Sun. 9:30 A.M.–5:30 P.M.) in the Ala Moana Shopping Center. The **Palace Shop** (808/532-1050, open Tues.–Sat. 8:30 A.M.–4 P.M.) at 'Iolani Palace has a selection of books on the monarchy era, and the **Queen Emma Summer Palace Gift Shop** (808/595-3603, open daily 9 A.M.–4 P.M.) has additional volumes on Hawaiian royalty.

Both the **Honolulu Academy of Arts** (808/532-8703) and the **Contemporary Museum** (808/523-3447) have fine bookshops that focus on the arts, with many titles on various aspects of Hawaiian art. The **East-West Center** bookstore also carries a substantial collection of Hawaiiana as well as books on Asia, many of them published by the center. Aside from its academic books for classes, the **University of Hawai'i Bookstore** (808/956-4338, open Mon.–Fri. 8:15 A.M.–4:45 P.M., Sat. 8:15–11:45 A.M.) carries many trade books on all aspects of Hawaii.

For books on the natural environment and flora of Hawaii, try the gift shops at **Lyon Arboretum** or the **Foster Botanical Garden.**

Film and Camera

Although film is available at most gift shops and convenience stores around town, the cheapest place to buy film might be at **Sears** or **Longs Drugs.** Both have good selections and numerous stores on the island. **Ritz Camera** (808/943-6391) at the Ala Moana Center is also good and convenient.

Although camera repair shops are woefully absent on the outer islands, O'ahu does have at least one service center, but even this repair shop may not want or be able to repair certain brands of equipment. Try **Photo Tech** (1413 S. King St., Ste. 201, 808/952-6161, open Mon.–Fri. 9 A.M.–5 P.M., Sat. 9 A.M.–3 P.M.).

Consignment

Ladies looking for appropriate islandwear and designer fashions that won't break the budget should head for the **Pzazz** consignment boutique (3057 Wai'alae Ave., 808/732-5900, open Mon.–Sat. 10 A.M.–5 P.M.) at the lower end of Kaimuki, which sells used designer clothing. Pzazz has won accolades for being the best designer resale shop in town for moderately priced quality women's clothing.

Recreation

SAIL AND DINNER CRUISES

If you're taking a tour at all, a good choice is a dinner cruise. They're touristy, but a lot of fun and actually a good value. Money-saving coupons for these cruises can often be found in the free tourist magazines. Most cruises depart around 5:30 P.M. from the Kewalo Basin Marina or one of the piers near the Aloha Tower and cruise Waikiki toward Diamond Head before returning about two hours later. On board is a buffet, an open bar, live entertainment, and dancing.

High-tech hits the high seas on the **Navatek I** (808/973-1311 or 800/548-6262, www.atlantis adventures.com), a unique bi-hulled ship operated by Atlantis Adventures that guarantees the "most stable ride in the islands." Sailing from Pier 6, various cruises are available, including a whale-watching cruise in season for $58 and $29 children; a sunset buffet cruise, $75 adults and $50 children; and a sunset dinner cruise, $105 adults and $67 children, featuring gourmet food and some of the best island entertainers.

Paradise Cruises (808/983-7827 or 800/ 334-6191, www.paradisecruises.com) also does dinner cruise and show combinations on the *Star of Honolulu* and *Starlet* ships, both leaving from Pier 8 next to Aloha Tower Marketplace. The 340-passenger *Starlet* goes at 5:15 P.M. for a two-hour cruise and prices range $44–66 for adults. During morning hours, this ship offers a water fun tour for $63 adults and $38 children, as well as a whale-watching tour in season. The larger, 1,500-passenger *Star of Honolulu* offers four options from $68 to the $165 five-star, seven-course French dinner cruise. It also departs from Pier 8 near Aloha Tower at 5:30 P.M. and returns at 7:30 P.M. During the day, this ship does whale-watching in season and Hawaiian cultural cruises for $29 adults and $18 children, or $45 and $27, respectively, with the meal package.

The *Ali'i Kai* catamaran (808/539-9400 or 866/898-2519, www.robertshawaii.com) packs them in (1,000-passenger capacity) for a sunset dinner cruise and dancing to a live band nightly at 5:30 P.M. from Pier 5 near the Hawaii Maritime Center. The buffet dinner runs $59 adults and $34 children. The ride includes dinner, a Polynesian show, one free cocktail, and dancing. For $80 adults, $53 children, you have the sunset dinner cruise with buffet plus a seat at the Magic of Polynesia illusion show in Waikiki.

The big luxury catamaran *Makani* (808/591-9000 or 888/462-5264, www.sailmakani.com) leaves from the Kewalo Basin for two-hour morning, afternoon, and sunset sails that range in price $35–55 per person. Private charters are also available.

SCUBA

Diamond Head Divers (808/224-2770, www .diamondheaddivers.com) runs out of Kewalo Basin marina for tours of wrecks and natural features in the Honolulu/Waikiki area. Their 2-tank dive runs $99, an introductory dive is $125, and several certification and other specialty courses are also taught.

PARASAILING

For a once-in-a-lifetime treat, try parasailing where you're strapped into a harness complete with lifejacket and towed aloft to glide effortlessly over the waters off Waikiki and Ala Moana. Boats leave out of Kewalo Basin. Take-off and landing is done from the back end of the boat and you get about 600 feet of loft. Boats usually have up to 12 riders, singles and tandems, so you might be on the water for about an hour. The basic ride lasts 9–10 minutes and runs $40, or $35 for kids 12 and under. For a parasail adventure, try **Aloha Parasail/Jet Ski** (808/521-2446) and **Hawaiian Parasail** (808/591-1280). **Extreme Parasail** (808/737-3559, www.x-tremeparasail .com) offers a similar ride, as well as a 12–13 minute ride for $70 and a long 14–15 minute ride for $82.

Aloha Parasail and Xtreme Parasail also rent jet skis if you want to stay closer to the water. Expect jet ski prices to be about $40 for 30 minutes on the water.

SPORTFISHING
Numerous private sportfishing boats operating out of Kewalo Basin. They include the 44-foot *Sea Verse* (808/591-8840), **Kamome Sport Fishing** (808/593-8931) with its 53-foot boat, the long-established *Maggie Joe* (808/591-8888 or 877/806-3474, www.fish-hawaii.com), **Magic Sportfishing** (808/596-2998, www.magicsportfishing.com), **Kuu Huapala Fishing Co.** (808/596-0918), **The Wild Bunch** (808/596-4709) with their 41-foot Hatteras, *Kono* (808/593-8472) a 61-foot Sampan, and **Blue Nun Sports Fishing** (808/596-2443 or 866/596-2445, www.bluenunsportfishing.com). Although rates vary by boat, expect a half-day trip to cost $675–750, a three-quarters-day trip $775–850, and a full-day for $825–975.

HIKING
Manoa Valley Trail
Less than one mile long and not too steep, the Manoa Valley Trail is one of the easiest in town to negotiate and easy to get to. Follow Oʻahu Avenue past the university, then turn onto Manoa Road. Follow this until it turns sharply to the left and up the hill to Lyon Arboretum. At this sharp turn is the trailhead. If the gate at the trailhead is open, park inside the gate in the small parking lot. Otherwise, go back down the road to the Tree Tops Restaurant pay parking lot or farther into the neighborhood. The trail roughly follows the Manoa Stream up this tight valley. It's a fairly easy trail that goes through mostly introduced trees and bamboo, but it is rocky in places and may be muddy if it's rained recently. The hike takes a bit more than 30 minutes up and ends at a small pool into which the tall and narrow falls drop.

From near the end of this trail, the **Aihualama Trail** heads up the west side of the valley, zigzagging up the steepest parts, eventually connecting with the **Pauoa Flats Trail** that can lead you down to the various Tantalus and Makiki Valley trails or over that ridge and down the **Nuʻuanu Trail** to meet the **Judd Trail** and Nuʻuanu Pali Drive.

Judd Trail
This is an excellent trail to take to experience Oʻahu's "jungle" while visiting the historic and picturesque Nuʻuanu Pali nearby. From the Pali Highway, Route 61, turn right onto Nuʻuanu Pali Drive. Follow it for just under a mile to a water company building, near a reservoir spillway, shortly after a sharp S curve. The trail begins on the right side of the road near the bridge and leads through fragrant eucalyptus and a dense stand of picture-perfect Norfolk pines. It continues through the forest reserve and makes a loop back to the starting point. En route you pass Jackass Ginger Pool. Continue down the trail to observe wild ginger, guava, and *kukui*, but don't take any confusing side trails. If you get lost, head back to the stream and follow it until it intersects the main trail. From this trail, the **Nuʻuanu Trail** heads uphill to connect with the trails on Tantalus.

Tantalus and Makiki Valley Trails
Great sightseeing and hiking can be combined when you climb the road atop Tantalus, which has the greatest concentration of easy-access hiking trails on the island. Trails in this area offer magnificent views. To get there, head past Punchbowl along Puowaina Drive; just keep going until it turns into Tantalus Drive. The road switchbacks past some incredible homes and views until it reaches the 2,000-foot level, where its name changes to Round Top Drive, then heads down the other side. To approach from the other side, take Keʻeaumoku Street across H-1. Turn right on Nehoa, then left in one block to Makiki Street. Follow this a short distance to Round Top Drive and you're on your way. Trailhead signs are along the road.

One place to start is at the mile-long **Moleka Trail,** which offers some excellent views and an opportunity to experience the trails in this area without an all-day commitment. The trails are expertly maintained by the State Division of

Forestry and Wildlife. Your greatest hazard here is mud, but in a moment you're in a handsome stand of bamboo, and in 10 minutes the foliage parts onto a lovely panorama of Makiki Valley and Honolulu in the background. These views are captivating, but remember to have "small eyes"—check out the variety of colored mosses and fungi, and don't forget the flowers and fruit growing around you. A branch trail to the left leads to Round Top Drive, and if you continue the trail splits into three: the right one is the **Makiki Valley Trail,** which cuts across the valley for about one mile, ending up at Tantalus Drive; **'Ualaka'a Trail** branches left and goes for another half mile, connecting the Makiki Valley Trail with Pu'u 'Ualaka'a State Wayside; straight ahead is the **Maunalaha Trail,** which descends for just over one mile to the bottom of the valley at the Hawaii Nature Center and Forestry Baseyard.

On the mountain side of the road across from the Moleka Trailhead, the **Manoa Cliff Trail** heads inland and swings in a 5.5-mile arch back around to meet Tantalus Drive. Intersecting this trail at approximately the halfway point is the **Pu'u 'Ohi'a Trail,** which leads to the highest point on Tantalus and the expected magnificent view. It continues inland via the **Pauoa Flats Trail,** which ends at a lookout over Nu'uanu Valley and its reservoir. Partway along this trail, the **Nu'uanu Trail** heads west down to connect with the Judd Trail. A short way farther, the **'Aihualama Trail** heads east to Manoa Falls and down the **Manoa Valley Trail** to the end of Manoa Valley Road, exiting near Lyon Arboretum.

Environmental Outings

The **Hawaii Nature Center** (2131 Makiki Heights Dr., 808/955-0100, www.hawaii naturecenter.org) is a nonprofit organization dedicated to environmental education through a hands-on approach. Primarily geared toward school-age children but welcoming the young at heart, the Hawaii Nature Center offers weekend community programs for families and the public to share in the wealth of Hawaii's magnificent natural environment through interpretive hikes, earth care projects, and nature crafts. This is a wonderful opportunity for visitors to explore Hawaii through direct interaction with the environment. Outings are usually run on Saturdays or Sundays. Contact the center for its current calendar of events.

BIKING
Bike Rental and Bike Shops

For bicycle rentals, try **The Bike Shop** (1149 S. King St., 808/596-0588, www.bikeshop hawaii.com, open weekdays 9 A.M.–7 P.M., Sat. 9 A.M.–5 P.M., Sun. 10 A.M.–5 P.M.), where road bikes run $40 a day or $200 a week, and cruisers go for $20 a day or $100 a week. Periodically, the Bike Shop sponsors road and off-road rides and races.

While they come and go, there are always many small, sidewalk bike rental stalls in Waikiki, often at a place that also rents other modes of transportation. Not all shops carry all types, so inquire first, but many of the dealers in the Waikiki area have mountain or hybrid bikes. Expect to pay about $20–30 per day, depending on the type.

For sales and repairs, try The Bike Shop, the **Bikefactory** (740 Ala Moana Blvd., 808/596-8844, www.bikefactoryhawaii.com, open daily 9 A.M.–7 P.M.), **Island Triathlon and Bike** (569 Kapahulu Ave., 808/732-7227, www.islandtriathlonandbike.com, open Mon.–Sat. 10 A.M.–6 P.M., Sun. 11 A.M.–4 P.M.), or the more family oriented **McCully Bicycle** (2124 S. King St., 808/955-6329, www.mccullybike.com, weekdays 9 A.M.–8 P.M., Sat. 9 A.M.–6 P.M., Sun. 10 A.M.–5 P.M.) and **Eki Cyclery** (1603 Dillingham Blvd., 808/847-2005, www.ekicyclery.com, open Mon.–Fri. 10 A.M.–6:30 P.M., Sat. 10 A.M.–5 P.M., Sun. 11 A.M.–3 P.M.).

Bike Tours

For a downhill ride above Honolulu or off-road adventure in Ka'a'awa Valley on the windward side, the organized bike tour company to try is **Bike Hawaii** (808/734-4214 or 877/682-7433, www.bikehawaii.com). Tours run $96; bikes, helmets, water, and snacks are provided. Full-day bike, hike, and snorkel tours are also available. John Alford, the owner of this company, is also the author of *Mountain Biking the Hawaiian Islands,* the only book on biking the islands of Hawaii.

AIR TOURS
Fixed Wing Tours

A throwback to the days when tourists arrived in the islands by clipper planes is a seaplane tour by **Island Seaplane Service** (808/836-6273, www.islandseaplane.com) located on a floating dock at 85 Lagoon Dr., on the back side of the Honolulu International Airport. These four to six-passenger planes take off and land in Keʻehi Lagoon, just like the Pan Am China Clippers did in the 1930s. Two runs are offered: a half-hour circle of southeastern Oʻahu to get a look at Honolulu, Waikiki, Diamond Head, and the lower Windward *pali,* and a one-hour ride that gives you all of that plus takes you all the way up the Windward Coast, circling back over the Leilehua Plateau and Pearl Harbor before landing. Six flights per day fly 9:15 A.M.–4:45 P.M. and run $109 per person for the shorter flight, $199 for the longer. Reservations are required, and you can be shuttled from/to Waikiki if needed.

All Island Aviation (99 Mokuea Pl., 808/839-1499 or 888/773-0303) flies out of Honolulu in a nine-passenger twin-engine Piper Chieftain. It runs a six-island, three-hour scheduled excursion for $389 per person leaving Honolulu at 9 A.M. on various days of the week. A minimum of six passengers is needed to fly, so flights may not go every day. All flights include narration on ecology, culture, and history of the islands. Private charters can also be scheduled with this plane. Reservations are necessary at least two days in advance.

Helicopters

Helicopter companies rev up their choppers to flightsee you around the island, starting at about $89 per person for a short 15-minute trip over Honolulu/Waikiki. Prices rise from there up to about $225 for a one-hour Honolulu, Windward, North Shore narrated tour. Thirty- and 45-minute flights are options, plus night flights over Honolulu and Waikiki may also be offered. Transport to and from the heliport is usually included in the cost. Helicopter offices are located off Lagoon Drive, ocean side of the airport. **Makani Kai Helicopters** (110 Kapalulu Pl., 808/834-5813 or 877/255-8532, www.makanikai.com) offers standard options at a fair price using Astar six-passenger aircraft. This is a respected company with a great track record. **Offshore Helicopters** (100 Iolana Pl., 808/838-0007) also offers about the same flights at the same pricing.

Accommodations

The vast majority of O'ahu's hotels are strung along the boulevards of Waikiki. The remainder of greater Honolulu has relatively few accommodations, but they are fairly economical in relation to other similar accommodations on the island.

DOWNTOWN

YMCA Nu'uanu (men only) (1441 Pali Hwy., 808/536-3556), at the intersection of S. Vineyard Blvd., is a few minutes' walk from downtown Honolulu. You'll find a modern, sterile facility with a swimming pool, exercise room, and public telephones, but no parking on the premises. This is a clean, well-kept place that has set rules of conduct for its guests. The 70 single rooms do not have televisions. This is a first-come, first-served facility; call in the morning for a room, which run $32 per night for a single or $175 per week, and $39 for a room with a private bath. All rooms require a refundable $5 key deposit.

The only upscale hotel right in downtown Honolulu is the **ResortQuest at the Executive Centre Hotel** (1088 Bishop St., 808/539-3000 or 866/7742924, fax 808/523-1088, www.rqexecutivecentre.com). This triangular glass and steel building puts both businesspeople and travelers in the heart of Honolulu's financial and capitol districts. Rooms look out over city streets and harbor and provide fine views of the city lights at night. Each spacious air-conditioned suite is outfitted with an entertainment center, telephones, data ports, and in-room safe. A continental breakfast and local newspaper are available complimentary for all guests, and an on-site restaurant, daily maid service, 24-hour business center, coin laundry, 24-hour swimming pool, fitness center, and sauna are all amenities. Business suites with a refrigerator run $220–240, while the one-bedroom suites with kitchen are $280–295. Substantial discounts are offered for corporate and government guests. If you need to be in the city for business, the Executive Centre is a perfect location.

NEAR WAIKIKI

The **YMCA Central Branch** (401 Atkinson Dr., 808/941-3344, fax 808/941-8821, www .centralymcahonolulu.org) is the most centrally located and closest to Waikiki, and it's open to both men and women. Call ahead and make reservations at least two weeks in advance. A definite checkout date is a must. There is no curfew, but no visitors are allowed in the rooms, no loud noise is permitted after 10 P.M., no smoking or drinking, no cooking in rooms, and a $10 key deposit is required. Amenities include an outside swimming pool, sauna, weight room, gym, and racquetball court open to all guests, as well as a courtyard cafe that's open all day except for Sunday. Parking is limited to two stalls and the fee for each is $5 per day. There are 114 single and double rooms, with shared or private baths. Rooms are spartan but clean with a bed, desk, and telephone. Rates for rooms with shared baths (men only) are $35 per night single; weekly and monthly rates are available. For rooms with a private bath (open to men and women), rates are $43 per day single and $53 double; rates go down after eight consecutive days. This Y is just up from the eastern end of Ala Moana Park across from the tall Ala Moana Hotel, only a 10-minute walk to Waikiki.

The **Pagoda Hotel** (1525 Rycroft St., 808/941-6611 or 800/367-6060, fax 808/955-5067, www.pagodahotel.com) is behind Ala Moana Shopping Center between Kapi'olani Boulevard and S. King Street. Because this hotel is away from the action, you get good value for your money. Rooms are located in one low-rise building and one high-rise tower. All rooms in the Terrace Tower come with kitchenettes and run $120–215 for studio, one-, and two-bedroom suites. The Hotel Tower has mostly standard rooms at $120, but a few deluxe rooms cost $141; numerous packages are available. Substantial discounts are given to residents. Rooms come in a mixture of twin, double, and/or queen-size beds, so inquire. All rooms have a TV, air-conditioning, an in-room safe, and a small refrigerator. There's free parking, laundry facilities, a sundries shop, two swimming pools, and access to the well-known Pagoda Restaurant, a favorite of locals for its Asian ambience, theme lunch and dinner buffets, koi pond, and manicured garden. The Pagoda Hotel is locally owned and operated and, although not luxurious, is sufficient for a fine stay on the island.

The 36-story, 1,152-room **Ala Moana Hotel** (410 Atkinson Dr., 808/955-4811 or 800/367-6025, fax 808/944-6839, www.ala moanahotel.com) is just off the Waikiki strip, which means that its rates are slightly better than comparable rooms a few blocks away. Located between Ala Moana and Kapi'olani Boulevards, it's only steps from the Hawaii Convention Center and has a walking ramp connecting it directly with the Ala Moana Shopping Center for easy access. City-view and partial oceanview rooms in the back Kona Tower run $195–215, while those in the main Waikiki Tower run $235–295, and suites are $395–2,500; corporate and government rates are available. Each room has a/c, a TV, a mini refrigerator, direct-dial telephones, data ports, and all the comforts you would expect from a quality hotel. The hotel contains a third-level swimming pool, sundries shop, laundry facilities, the Rumours nightclub, a cocktail lounge, Japanese and Chinese restaurants, a Polynesian Revue with buffet dinner, and the first-rate Aaron's restaurant on the top floor for elegant Continental dining.

NEAR THE UNIVERSITY

The (**Hostelling International Honolulu** hostel (2323-A Seaview Ave., 808/946-0591, fax 808/946-5904, www.hostelsaloha.com) is near the main entrance to the university. It's an official Hostelling International hostel, so members with identity cards are given priority, but nonmembers are accepted on a space-available day-by-day basis. This hostel has 43 beds in male and female dorms and two private rooms. A bed in a dormitory runs $16 per night for members and $19 for nonmembers; the studio rooms run $42 for members or $48 for nonmembers. The office is open 8 A.M.–

noon and 4 P.M.–midnight. It has travel and sightseeing information, can offer suggestions for what to see and do, and hosts periodic barbecues. This hostel is always busy, but it takes reservations by phone with a credit card. There is no curfew, but the expectation is that everyone keeps appropriate quiet hours. A full kitchen is open for use, and there is a grill on the back patio for daytime barbecuing. A washer and dryer are available, storage lockers are available for use with your own lock, and there's limited off-street parking. Kick back in the communal room for TV, free movies, or to meet other travelers. From the hostel to the airport, take TheBus no. 6 to Ala Moana Shopping Center and transfer there to bus no. 19 or 20 on the ocean side of the mall; to Waikiki, take bus no. 4 direct.

YWCA Fernhurst (women only) (1566 Wilder Ave., 808/941-2231, fax 808/945-9478, fernhurst@ywcaoahu.org, www.ywcaoahu.org) just off Manoa Road, across from Punahou School, offers single and double rooms with shared baths, 24-hour security, a laundry facility, and television lounge. Women from around the world have found this a safe and convenient home while on the island. The Fernhurst YWCA recently went through major renovation and now offers rooms at $38 for a shared room, $48 single room. Membership is required.

The (**Manoa Valley Inn** (2001 Vancouver Dr., 808/947-6019, fax 808/946-6168, manoavalleyinn@aloha.net, www.manoa valleyinn.com) offers a magnificent opportunity to lodge in early-1900s elegance. Formerly the John Guild Inn, this country inn is listed on the National and State Registers of Historic Places. Built in 1915 by Milton Moore, an Iowa lumberman, the original structure was a modest, two-story, boxlike home. It was situated on seven acres, but the demand for land by growing Honolulu has whittled it down to the present half acre or so. Moore sold the house to John Guild in 1919. A secretary to Alexander and Baldwin, Guild added the third floor and back porch, basically creating the structure you see today. The home went through

© ROBERT NILSEN

Manoa Valley Inn

several owners and even survived a stint as a fraternity house. It ended up as low-priced apartment units until it was rescued and renovated in 1982 by the former owner of Crazy Shirts and one of Hawaii's patrons of arts and antiques. He outfitted the house from his warehouse of antiques with furnishings not original to the house but true to the period. Since then it has been sold several times and undergone additional refurbishing and landscaping. The eight lavishly furnished rooms run $105–145 in the low season and $125–165 during the high season. Most rooms have queen- or king-size beds, and about half the rooms share a bathroom. A continental breakfast and local phone calls are included in the room charge. The exemplary continental breakfasts are prepared on the premises. In the morning, the aroma of fresh-brewed coffee wafts up the stairs. Daily and Sunday newspapers are available. Pick one and sink into the billowy cushions of a wicker chair on the lava-rock-colonnaded back porch. Free off-street parking is provided. Check-in is at 3 P.M., checkout at 11 A.M.

NEAR THE AIRPORT

Nimitz Shower Tree (3085 N. Nimitz Hwy., 808/833-1411) is a converted warehouse building with cubicle-type rooms, run somewhat like a hostel with a number of house rules for the comfort and safety of guests. Single rooms are $25; a double goes for $43. If all you need is a shower and a rest during a layover, you can arrange that too. Weekly rates are available. Only cash is accepted. Rooms are given on a first-come, first-served basis. The Shower Tree has a bathroom, TV lounge, pay phone, and laundry for guests only, and you must use your own lock and key on your room. Located only five minutes from the airport, directly to the side of the double-decker Nimitz highway, this is one you should consider only if price is your main concern and you need to stay in this area.

A bit farther from the airport is the **Pacific Marina Inn** (2628 Waiwai Loop, 808/836-1131). This three-story, cement block affair backs up against Ke'ehi Beach park and is a basic, utilitarian accommodation with a small pool in its courtyard. It is nothing fancy but neat and tidy, and rates run $89 during the week and $99 on weekend nights.

One of the closest hotels to the airport is Best Western's **The Plaza Hotel** (3253 N. Nimitz Hwy., 808/836-3636 or 800/800-4683, fax 808/834-7406, www.best westernhonolulu.com). This 12-story tower has 274 small a/c rooms, each with king- or queen-size bed, a full bath, entertainment center, and a small refrigerator. Amenities include an on-site restaurant and bar, coin laundry, sundries shop, small swimming pool, and courtesy van service for the few blocks to and from the airport. Rates run $179–199 and $349 for a suite, with discounts for AAA members, seniors, government employees, and military personnel. Al-

though not in the center of the city or along the sands of Waikiki, it is convenient for air travel and close to the military facilities and tourist attractions that surround Pearl Harbor.

With nearly the same amenities as the Best Western, the **Honolulu Airport Hotel** (3401 N. Nimitz Hwy., 808/836-0661 or 800/800-3477, fax 808/833-1738, www.honolulu airporthotel.com) is even a bit closer to the airport terminal. Here you have more than 300 rooms on four floors, with a standard room from about $185, a suite substantially higher, and discounts for seniors, AAA members, airline, military, and government personnel. There is an on-site restaurant, free hotel parking, and complimentary shuttle service to and from the airport.

Food

The restaurants mentioned in this section are outside of the Waikiki area, although some are close, and located in the less touristy areas of greater Honolulu. Some are first-class restaurants; others are just local eateries where you can get a satisfying plate lunch. The restaurants are listed according to location. Besides the sun and surf, the amazing array of food found on O'ahu makes the island extraordinary.

SHOPPING CENTER DINING
Ala Moana Shopping Center

The majority of restaurants at the Ala Moana Shopping Center are located in the Makai Food Court, a huge central area on the first floor where you can inexpensively dine on dishes from San Francisco to Tokyo—most for under $10. Counter-style restaurants serve island favorites, reflecting the multiethnic culinary traditions from around the Pacific. You take your dish to a nearby communal dining area, great for people-watching. For more class and a finer environment, head for **Assaggio** (808/942-3446, open daily 11 A.M.–3 P.M., Sun.–Thurs. 4:30–9:30 P.M., and Fri.–Sat. 4:30–10 P.M.), on

the ground level next to Macy's. This award-winning Italian restaurant serves tasty dishes your mama would be proud to put on the table. Just as reputable are the second-floor **Longhi's** (808/947-9899, open Mon.–Sat. 9:30 A.M.–9 P.M., Sun. 10 A.M.–7 P.M.), a branch of a well-known Maui eatery which serves Mediterranean food, and **Morton's The Steakhouse** (808/949-1300, open weekdays 5:30–11 P.M., Sat. 5–11 P.M., Sun. 5–10 P.M.). You might not expect to find a fine restaurant in a department store, but Alan Wong operates the **Pineapple Room** restaurant and Patisserie Bar (808/945-6573, open weekdays 11 A.M.–9 P.M., Sat. 8 A.M.–9 P.M., Sun. 9 A.M.–3 P.M.) on the third floor of Macy's department store. This is great food for great shopping. The fourth floor Ho'okipa Terrace also has several fun restaurants including **Romano's Macaroni Grill** (808/356-8300, open Sun.–Thurs. 11 A.M.–10 P.M., Fri.–Sat. 11 A.M.–11 P.M.) and the **Mai Tai** bar (808/947-2900, open Mon.–Sat. 9:30 A.M.–9 P.M., Sun. 10 A.M.–7 P.M.), where you can mellow out after pounding the walkways to a drink and soft island music.

Ward Centre

This multi-building shopping center along Ala Moana Boulevard has a range of restaurants, from practical to semi-chic, all reasonably priced. On the ground floor of the Ward Warehouse is the **Chowder House** (808/596-7944, open Mon.–Thurs. 11 A.M.–9 P.M.), principally a seafood place with such items as fresh-grilled ahi, snow crab salad, Manhattan clam chowder, bay shrimp cocktail, and deep-fried shrimp. Upstairs is the **The Old Spaghetti Factory** (808/591-2513, open Mon.–Thurs. 11:30 A.M.–2 P.M. and 5–10 P.M., Fri. 11:30 A.M.–2 P.M. and 5–10:30 P.M., Sat. 11:30 A.M.–10:30 P.M., Sun. 4–9:30 P.M.), a huge chain restaurant that feels a bit like you might imagine a San Francisco eatery at the turn of the 20th century—almost Victorian. It serves a wide variety of pasta not quite like Mama makes, but passable, and a variety of other traditional Italian dishes at a reasonable price, with many around $10. More modern and expensive is **Kincaid's Fish, Chop & Steak House** (808/591-2005, open Mon.–Sat. 11 A.M.–10 P.M., Sun. 11:30 A.M.–5 P.M.), also on the second floor with views out over Kewalo Basin Marina. The lunch menu includes many sandwiches in the under-$12 range, while the dinner menu includes sirloin steak, pasta and roasted chicken Dijon, and grilled mixed seafood. Many entrées run about $20. Kincaid's serves generous portions of honest food at decent prices.

The Ward Centre restaurants lie directly across the street from Ala Moana Park and next door to the Ward Warehouse. Most seem to be a step up in quality and price. For a quick lunch, try **Mocha Java Cafe** (808/591-9023, open Mon.–Thurs. 9 A.M.–3 P.M., Fri.–Sat. 7 A.M.–10 P.M., Sun. 8 A.M.–5 P.M.), a yuppie, upscale, counter-service-type place with a few tables. It has a selection of sandwiches with an emphasis on vegetarian. If you want a designer lunch, that's the place to go. Along the interior walkway, **Sushi Masa** (808/593-2007, open Mon.–Sat. 10 A.M.–9 P.M., Sun. 10 A.M.–5 P.M.) serves reasonably priced Japanese food such as tempura, chicken teriyaki, and *tanuki* udon, as well as more expensive sashimi plates and sushi. Created by the owner of the upscale Alan Wong's Restaurant, **Kaka'ako Kitchen** (808/596-7488, open Mon.–Sat. 9 A.M.–9 P.M., Sun. 7 A.M.–5 P.M.) puts out more inexpensive plate lunches and sandwiches, as well as breakfasts and pastries, for shoppers on the go. Although most items, such as roast turkey sandwich, yaki tofu stir-fry, and chicken katsu curry, are familiar, others, like shichimi-dusted ahi steak with avocado poke and crispy fried sweet chili chicken, are a bit more exotic. Always tasty and easy on the pocketbook, meals here run mostly in the $7–10 range. This is a bargain. Across the way is **Kua 'Aina** (808/591-9133, open Sun.–Thurs. 10:30 A.M.–9:30 P.M., Fri.–Sat. 10:30 A.M.–11 P.M.), one of the island's favorite burger and sandwich shops. Offered here are hearty eats for an easygoing price. Some say Kua 'Aina burgers are the best on the island. Upstairs, **Compadres Bar and Grill** (808/591-8307, open daily 11 A.M.–1 A.M.) offers made-to-order health-conscious Mexican cuisine. The menu is huge, and no lard is used in any of the dishes except carnitas, which are pork anyway. Try the big, two-hands-required burritos, Baja-style tacos, or gulf prawns. Besides these, the menu comprises standard enchiladas, chiles rellenos, chimichangas, and a few vegetarian selections, and almost no dish more than $25. The bar complements the meal with a full selection of domestic and imported beers, tequila drinks, margaritas by the glass or pitcher, and island exotic drinks. Although part of a small chain, Compadres is an excellent choice for a meal in a hospitable atmosphere where the price is right and the service excellent. You can't go wrong! Next door is **Ryan's Grill** (808/591-9132, open Mon.–Sat. 11:15 A.M.–2 A.M., Sun. 10:30 A.M.–2 A.M.), a modern yet comfortable establishment dominated by a huge bar and open kitchen. The menu offers standards along with nouveau cuisine. Sandwiches are everything from hot Dungeness crab to a grilled chicken club. More substantial meals from the grill include coffee-crusted chicken with lychee relish and pasta dishes. Most menu items, along with plenty of munchies and *pu pu,* are served until the early morning hours, so Ryan's Grill makes a perfect late-night stop. Also upstairs you'll find **Brew Moon Restaurant and Micro Brewery** (808/593-0088, open Sun.–Thurs. 11 A.M.–1 A.M., Fri.–Sat. 11 A.M.–2 A.M.), where the food is casual American with a blend of the islands and a hint of Asian, but the real reason for stopping by is the beer. On tap are half a dozen beers brewed on-site, with others offered seasonally. The standards include Pacific Pale Ale; Moonlight, a light-bodied lager; and Hawaii 5 Ale, a heartier amber ale. Happy hour is 3–6 P.M., and there's music most nights from about 8 P.M.

Kitty-corner across the street, on the ground level below the multiplex theater in the Ward Entertainment Center, is **Wolfgang Puck Express** (808/593-8528, open Sun.–Thurs. 11 A.M.–10 P.M., Fri.–Sat. 11 A.M.–midnight), which offers quick and nutritious salads, sandwiches, pizza, and a few hot entrées for reasonable prices, mostly $7–10. Some of the meat is done in a rotisserie for that special flavor, and the pizza is baked in a wood-fired oven. Order at the counter and grab one of the few tables inside or head outside for bistro seating. Next door is **Big City Diner** (808/591-8891, open Sun.–Mon.7 A.M.–11 P.M., Tues.–Thurs. 7 A.M.–midnight, Fri.–Sat. 7 A.M.–1 A.M.). The old neighborhood restaurant from Kaimuki has opened a branch here and offers the same good food, good service, and good value here.

Aloha Tower Marketplace

Some years ago, a law was passed in Hawaii allowing beer to be sold at the place at which it was made. This allowed breweries to open pubs on premises. **Gordon Biersch Brewery & Restaurant** (808/599-4877, open Sun.–Thurs. 10 A.M.–midnight, Fri.–Sat. 10 A.M.–1 A.M.) has taken advantage of this opportunity and opened a fine establishment at the Aloha Tower Marketplace. Five beers are brewed here, with the addition of seasonal favorites: Golden Export, a smooth, medium hop, full-bodied beer similar to a pilsner but less bitter; Marzen, an Oktoberfest beer with a little extra oomph from a combination of malts; Dunkles, a dark beer served unfiltered in the old Bavarian tradition; Hefeweisen, a light crisp beer; and Blonde Bock, a sweet light golden drink. The lunch and dinner menus are similar, aside from the sandwiches offered at lunch and more hearty main dishes in the evening. Appetizers include fried calamari and crispy artichoke hearts, and there are small pizzas, pasta, and stir-fry dishes. These and the various salads are just preparation for the main courses, like barbecue salmon with sweet ginger rice, gorgonzola bone-in rib eye steak, or chicken marsala over linguine, most under $20. Dine inside or out—inside, with its leather booths, is more elegant and quieter for conversation. In the more casual alfresco portico, sit at stout wooden tables under canvas umbrellas and watch the tugboats shuttle ships through the harbor as the city lights sparkle across the water. The inside bar is good for a quiet drink, while you can boogie at the outside bar, where different bands come to play Wed.–Sat. evenings.

Across the walkway, **Don Ho's Island Grill** (808/528-0807, open daily 10 A.M.–9 P.M.) serves lunch and dinner daily and offers live evening music most nights of the week. Cashing in on one of the best-known names in island music, this is a casual, easygoing place with good food. Try surfboard-shaped pizzas, fresh fish, pasta, and Hawaiian desserts. Entrés run mostly $14–20.

At the entrance to the Marketplace is **[Chai's Island Bistro** (808/585-0011, open Tues.–Fri. 11 A.M.–4 P.M., daily from 4 P.M.), a great stop for Hawaiian regional cuisine but also the most happening place in town for the sweet sounds of island music, provided by famous island artists 7–9 P.M. For lunch, try such delicacies as the Japanese eggplant and zucchini soufflé, roasted fresh corn chowder, or a marinated and grilled chicken breast pita bread sandwich. The dinner menu is partially the same, with additional intriguing items like Long Island duck bistro style

MIXED CUISINE OF HAWAII

Hawaii is a gastronome's Shangri-la, a sumptuous smorgasbord in every sense of the word. The varied ethnic groups that have come to Hawaii in the last 200 years have each brought their own special enthusiasm and culture. Luckily for all, they didn't forget the cook pots, hearty appetites, and exotic taste buds.

The Polynesians who first arrived found a fertile but uncultivated land. Immediately they set about growing taro, coconuts, and bananas, and raising chickens, pigs, fish, and dogs, although the latter were reserved for the nobility. Harvests were bountiful, and the islanders thanked the gods with the traditional feast called the lu'au. Most foods were baked in the underground oven, the *imu*. Participants were encouraged to feast while relaxing on straw mats and enjoying the hula and various entertainments. The lu'au is as popular as ever and a treat guaranteed to delight anyone with a sense of eating adventure.

The missionaries and sailors came next, and their ships' holds carried barrels of ingredients for puddings, pies, dumplings, gravies, and roasts – the sustaining "American foods" of New England farms. The mid-1800s saw the arrival of boatloads of Chinese and Japanese peasants, who wasted no time making rice instead of bread the staple of the islands. The Chinese added their exotic spices, creating complex Szechuan dishes as well as worker's basics like chop suey. The Japanese introduced *shoyu* (soy sauce), sashimi, boxed lunches *(bento),* delicate tempura, and rich, filling noodle soups. The Portuguese brought their luscious Mediterranean dishes of tomatoes, peppers, and plump, spicy sausages, nutritious bean soups, and mouthwatering sweet treats like *malasadas* (holeless donuts) and *pao dolce* (sweet bread). Koreans carried crocks of zesty kimchi and quickly fired up grills for *pulgogi,* a thinly sliced marinated beef cooked over a fire. Filipinos served up their delicious *adobo* stews – fish, meat, or chicken in a rich sauce of vinegar and garlic.

Recently, Thai and Vietnamese restaurants have been offering their irresistible dishes next door to restaurants serving fiery burritos from Mexico or elegant marsala sauces from France. The ocean breezes of Hawaii not only cool the skin but also waft with them some of the most delectable aromas on earth, to make the taste buds tingle and the spirit soar.

and braised boneless short ribs with kabocha pumpkin. Chai's has established a great reputation and works hard at keeping the accolades coming. Lunch entrée prices run $12–25, dinner prices $26–43.

Restaurant Row

This new-age complex at 500 Ala Moana Boulevard points the way to people-friendly development in Honolulu's future. It houses shops and businesses, adequate public parking, and a nine-theater cineplex, but mostly restaurants on its ground level, all set along its central courtyard and strolling area. Some restaurants are elegant and excellent, whereas others are passable and plain. But they are all in a congenial setting, and you can pick your palate and style preference as easily as you'd pick offerings at a buffet. Three of the best are real treats.

The owner of the inspirational Sansei Seafood Restaurant and Sushi Bar has changed its format and opened two restaurants in its place. **Hiroshi** (808/533-4476, open daily 5:30–9:30 P.M.) serves "small plate" tapas that are a mix of Old Europe, modern Asia, and seafood from Hawaii. **Vino** (808/524-8466, open Wed.–Thurs. 5:30–9:30 P.M., Fri.–Sat. 5:30–10:30 P.M.) attempts to create the atmosphere of an Italian wine bar, and it also serves tapas to complement the wide variety of wines available each night by the glass.

Head to **Yanni's** (808/585-8142, open Mon.–Wed. and Sat. 5 P.M.–1 A.M., Thurs.–Fri. 11 A.M.–1 A.M.) for authentic Greek and Mediterranean cuisine. Perhaps the best is the lamb cutlet, but you can't go wrong with calamari or the pizza done in the *keawe* oven. Most entrées are under $25. A semi-formal place, it

Why then was "tourist food" in Hawaii so woeful for so long? Of course, there had always been a handful of fine restaurants, but for the most part the food lacked soul, with even the fine hotels opting to offer second-rate renditions of food more appropriate to large Mainland cities. Surrounded by some of the most fertile and pristine waters in the Pacific, you could hardly find a restaurant offering fresh fish, and it was an ill-conceived boast that even the fruits and vegetables lying limply on your table were imported. Beginning with a handful of extremely creative and visionary chefs in the early 1980s who took the chance of perhaps offending the perceived simple palates of visitors, a delightfully delicious new cuisine was born. Starting with the finest traditions of Continental cuisine − including, to a high degree, its sauces, pastas, and presentations − these chefs boldly added the pungent spices of Asia, the fantastic fresh vegetables, fruits, and fish of Hawaii, and, at times, the earthy cooking methods of the American Southwest. The result was and still remains a cuisine of fantastic tastes, subtle yet robust, and satiating but health-conscious −

the perfect marriage of fresh foods prepared in a fresh way. Now restaurants on every island proudly display menus labeled "Hawaiian Regional," "Pacific Rim," "fusion," or some other such name as a proud sign of this trend. As always, some are better than others, but the general result is that the "tourist food" has been vastly improved and everyone benefits. Many of these exemplary chefs left lucrative and prestigious positions at Hawaii's five-diamond hotels and opened signature restaurants of their own, making this fine food much more available and affordable.

In 1998, a new and younger group called Hawaiian Island Chefs came together to further enhance the variety and availability of innovative foods made with island-grown produce and the bounty of the sea. In addition, this group strives to influence culinary programs in the state to help carry on this fine tradition. With the incredible mix of peoples and cultures in Hawaii, the possibilities are endless, and this new group of chefs intends to shepherd the experience along, while promoting local farming enterprises and more nutritious food for everyone in the process.

instills the feeling of a fine seaside eatery. To add to the ambience, there is live Greek music and dance on Friday evenings.

AT THE ART GALLERIES

The **Pavilion Cafe** (900 S. Beretania St., 808/532-8734, open Tues.−Sat. 11:30 A.M.−1:30 P.M.) at the Honolulu Academy of Arts is a classy place for lunch. Dine inside or out. Menu items include soups, salads, and sandwiches, perhaps a goat cheese salad and tenderloin steak sandwich, and other entrées like pasta, mostly for under $10. An assortment of desserts and beverages can also be ordered. The food is delicious, but be aware that the portions are not for the hungry, being designed primarily for patrons of the arts, who seem to be wealthy matrons from the fashionable sections of Honolulu who are all watching their waistlines.

Don't let the Porsches, Mercedes, and BMWs parked vanity plate to vanity plate in the parking lot discourage you from enjoying the **Contemporary Cafe** (2411 Makiki Heights Dr., 808/523-3362, open Tues.−Sat. 11:30 A.M.−2:30 P.M., Sun. noon−2:30 P.M.) at the Contemporary Museum. The small but superb menu is as inspired as the art in the museum, and the prices are astonishingly inexpensive. Dine inside or out. Appetizers might be chicken satay or crostini, and salads include garden salad, soba noodle salad, or a miso Caesar. Sandwiches include hummus and pita, salmon patty burger, and blackened chicken wrap for $10 or less. An array of desserts includes cheesecake or flourless chocolate roulade, and beverages include homemade lemonade and cappuccino. For a wonderful cultural outing combined with a memorable lunch, come to the Contemporary

Cafe. It's just so . . . contemporary. Reservations are recommended.

CHINATOWN

You can eat delicious ethnic food throughout Chinatown. If not Honolulu's best, the entire district is definitely one of Honolulu's best culinary deals. On almost every corner you've got basic and cheap eateries whose ambience is Formica-topped tables and linoleum floors. Excellent Vietnamese and Thai restaurants have also sprung up like bamboo sprouts along Chinatown's streets, along with a smattering of Filipino, Korean, Japanese, and Indian places. A few bars with pub food round out the selection. Most are meticulously clean, and the moderately priced food is "family-pride gourmet." The decor ranges from oil-cloth table coverings topped by a bouquet of plastic flowers and a lazy Susan filled with exotic spices and condiments, to down-to-earth chic with some mood lighting, candles, and even linen place settings.

One place you shouldn't miss is **Shung Chong Yuein** (1027 Maunakea St., 808/531-1983, Mon.–Sat. 6 A.M.–4:30 P.M., Sun. 6 A.M.–2 P.M.), a Chinese cake shop. Look in to see yellow sugar cakes, black sugar cakes, shredded coconut with eggs, salted mincemeat, Chinese ham with egg, lotus seeds, and steamed buns.

The ◖ **Little Village** noodle house (1113 Smith St., 808/545-3008, open Sun.–Thurs. 10:30 A.M.–10:30 P.M., Fri.–Sat. 10:30 A.M.–midnight) is a pleasure. It's a gaily decorated place with large windows that look out onto the street, the service is efficient, and the menu has plenty of choices that are sure to please. While there are many noodle dishes, the restaurant also carries a great assortment of meat, poultry, seafood, and vegetarian dishes. Signature dishes include seafood with mixed vegetables, dried beef chow fun, sizzling scallops, and Szechuan spicy chicken, and most fall into the $7–13 range. As portions are large, you won't go away hungry. The Little Village has a diverse clientele and always seems to be buzzing. Besides that, it stays open late

into the evening for those enjoying the nightlife of Chinatown.

My Lan (1160 Maunakea St., 808/528-3663, open daily 9 A.M.–10 P.M.) is one of the best of the many Vietnamese restaurants in Chinatown. Aside from the usual spring rolls, green papaya salad, the *pho* beef noodle soups, the large and varied menu has plenty of porridge bowls, as well as rice, vermicelli, and egg noodle dishes, with many options for the vegetarian. The interior decoration and Vietnamese music help put you in the mood, so if you haven't tried this cuisine yet, My Lan is a good choice for your first Vietnamese meal.

Next door is **Sweet Basil Thai Restaurant** (1152 Maunakea St., 808/545-5800, open Mon.–Sat. 10:30 A.M.–2 P.M., Fri.–Sat. 5–9 P.M.), which does buffets of Thai food at a reasonable $10–15 per person.

Rosarina Pizza (1111 Maunakea St., 808/533-6634, open daily except Sunday 11 A.M.–2:30 P.M. and 5–9 P.M.) is an alternative to Asian cuisine. You can buy a slice of pizza here, or a whole pie for under $18. You can also order 12-inch sub sandwiches or an à la carte dinner like spaghetti with meat sauce or sausage, cannelloni, or manicotti, all for under $10.

Also for an alternative, try **Zaffron** (69 N. King St., 808/533-6635, open Mon.–Sat. 11 A.M.–2 P.M., Wed.–Sat. 5–9 P.M. for Indian tandoori, curry, biryani, and other spicy selections. Most à la carte items are under $11, while the buffet runs about $10 for lunch or $20 for dinner.

Grand Cafe and Bakery (31 North Pauahi St., 808/531-0001, open weekdays 7 A.M.–1:30 P.M., Sat. 8 A.M.–1 P.M.) presents good old American food with a down-home, made-from-scratch attitude. Try Bananas Foster French toast or old-fashioned oatmeal for breakfast or smoked turkey breast sandwich or meat loaf for lunch. Most items are priced less than $10. Not everyone stops by for a full meal—some come for the sweet treats: cakes, pies, puddings, tortes, and other delicacies line the deli case at the entry for you to choose from.

Chinatown Cultural Plaza

As with the shops at the Chinatown Cultural Plaza, the restaurants there also come and go. One to check out is the **Buddhist Vegetarian Restaurant** (808/532-8218, 10:30 A.M.–2 P.M. except Wednesday), which is basic and about as antiseptic as a monk's cell, but the food is healthy. Serving only lunch, the varied menu includes inexpensive dim sum dishes, stir-fry vegetables, spicy hot and sour soup, and many braised or fried vegetable or tofu dishes. Most are in the under-$10 category.

Royal Kitchen (808/524-4461, Mon.–Fri. 5:30 A.M.–5 P.M., Sat. 6:30 A.M.–2:30 P.M., Sun. 6:30 A.M.–2 P.M.) is a popular place with local families and businesspeople. It's especially known for its takeout baked manapua, soft dough buns stuffed with pork, char siu, or vegetables, and for its Chinese sausage, lup-cheung, char siu, roast pork, and roast duck.

Won Kee Sea Food Restaurant (808/524-6877, daily 11 A.M.–2:30 P.M., 5–9:30 P.M.) is an eatery where you get delicious seafood in tasteful surroundings. A place for Honolulu's in-the-know crowd.

Two doors down from the Won Kee, the **Legend Seafood Restaurant** (808/532-1868, open weekdays 1:30 A.M.–2 P.M., weekends 8 A.M.–2 P.M., and daily 5:30–9 P.M.) emphasizes fish and seafood but also serves inexpensive Hong Kong–style dim sum in small, medium, large, and super-size plate sizes. The especially long menu indicates the variety of foods available, and the numbers of people waiting to be seated at this sizable establishment lets you know of its popularity, especially on weekends. The prices too are an indication why Legend Seafood is so popular, as even the seafood dishes are mostly under $15.

Local pubs

A local bar with an easygoing atmosphere and a *pu pu* and pita-deli sandwich menu is **Hanks Cafe Honolulu** (1038 Nu'uanu Ave., 808/526-1410, open 1 P.M.–2 A.M. Mon.–Sat., Sun. opens at 3 P.M.). Though a small place, Hanks occasionally host musicians and comics. While you're there, have a look at the paintings on the walls—all Hank's.

At the bottom end of Nu'uanu Avenue are **O'Toole's Irish Pub** (902 Nu'uanu Ave., 808/536-4612), open for drinks, casual pub grub 11 A.M.–9 P.M., and live music each evening; and **Murphy's Bar and Grill** (2 Merchant St., 808/531-0422, open daily until 2 A.M. except Sunday, when it closes at midnight). At Murphy's, you can not only order such items as fish and chips and Gaelic steak that you might expect from an Irish bar, but you can also get fresh grilled island fish, a chicken breast sandwich, or a Cajun burger, all at fairly reasonable prices.

MO'ILI'ILI

Within one block or so of the University Avenue and S. King Street intersection, just below the University of Hawaii in an area known as Mo'ili'ili, a number of local eateries and food outlets, plus a collection of many other shops, cater to students and nonstudents alike.

The minute you walk into **Imanas Tei** (2626 S. King St., 808/941-2626, open Mon.–Sat. 5–11:30 P.M.) you know you're in for a special treat. The ambience is traditional and the smells are authentic. It's like being in a neighborhood restaurant in small-city Japan. Selections off the long menu include deep-fried and grilled tofu, meat, and fish. Sushi rolls and plates, sashimi, and stews and noodle dishes round out the list. It's just what you'd expect from a traditional Japanese restaurant. Most items run $4–10—you'll want more than one—but the stews and other full meals are $20 and more. Some claim that Imanas Tei has the best Japanese food in town; because it always seems to be busy, regulars would probably agree. Limited parking.

Across the street is **India House** (2633 S. King St., 808/955-7552, open Mon.–Fri. 11 A.M.–2 P.M., Mon.–Sat. 5–9:30 P.M., Sun. 5–9 P.M.). Extraordinary Indian dishes include a wide selection of curries, tandoori specials, vegetarian dishes, special naan bread, kabobs, and fish tikka. Specialty desserts include halawas, gulab jamun, and kheer. On the other side of the intersection is **Maharani** (2509 S.

King St., 808/951-7447, open daily 5–9 P.M.), a somewhat cramped restaurant that also produces wonderful spiced dishes of the subcontinent. Both are a treat with entrées in the $12–$16 range.

Closer to the corner of King Street and University Avenue are the very reasonable **Magoo's Pizza** (1015 University Ave., 808/949-5381), a lively local hangout for cheap beer and pizza that's boisterous and busy most days but especially on the weekends; and the **Greek Corner** (1025 University Ave., 808/942-5503), which weighs in with the hearty dishes of the Mediterranean, like hummus, gyro sandwiches, falafel plate, and souvlaki chicken kabob, most under $12.

Half hidden in the residential neighborhood south of this intersection is **The Willows** (901 Hauston St., 808/952-9200). This restaurant specializes in buffets and has been open for years. Weekday buffets run 11 A.M.–2 P.M., weekends 10 A.M.–2:30 P.M. Dinner buffets are 5:30 P.M.–9 P.M., from 5 P.M. on weekends. While the offerings are somewhat different at all the buffets, nothing seems to be missing from the serving table as the spread is a mixture of good old American, Hawaiian, and Asian. Prices run $17–28 adults and $8.50–14 kids.

Directly across from the University, inside the Atherton YMCA building at the corner of Metcalf Avenue is **Volcano Joe's** island bistro (1810 University Ave., 808/941-8449, open 11 A.M.–10 P.M.) and coffeehouse (weekdays 6 A.M.–8 P.M., weekends 7 A.M.–8 P.M.), where coffees and teas, many other drinks, as well as pizza, pita wraps, toasted sandwiches, salads, and pastries are available. Perfect for students on a budget or others looking for inexpensive eats and something healthy to fill your belly.

Market/Deli

Down to Earth Natural Foods and Lifestyle (2525 S. King St., 808/947-7678, open daily 7:30 A.M.–10 P.M.) is a kind of museum of health food stores serving filling, nutritious health food dishes for reasonable prices. Get sandwiches (like a whopping avocado, tofu, and cheese) and other items such as veggie stroganoff, eggplant parmigiana, and lasagna at the deli counter, or try the salad and hot entrée bars for other prepared foods. Healthwise, you can't go wrong, and the price is right! The selection of produce, fruits, and bulk foods is tops.

MANOA VALLEY

In the Manoa Marketplace are a good number of small ethnic restaurants and coffeehouses. Among these are **Paesano** (808/988-5923), a small Italian eatery open for lunch and dinner that has garnered a good reputation because of its authentic Italian preparations. Here as well are **Ramen** (open daily 11 A.M.–9 P.M.) for inexpensive Japanese noodle dishes, and **Pearl's Korean BBQ** (808/988-1088, open Mon.–Sat. 10:30 A.M.–9 P.M., Sun. 11 A.M.–9 P.M.) for easy-on-the-pocketbook, zesty Korean barbecue meals. If you care to just sit for a while, read the paper, or have a light bite to eat, stop at **Coffee Bean & Tea Leaf** (open Mon.–Thurs. 5:30 A.M.–10:30 P.M., Fri. 5:30 A.M.–11 P.M., Sat. 6 A.M.–11 P.M., Sun. 6 A.M.–10 P.M.) for an assortment of coffee, tea, chai, and pastries.

A short distance away is the **Wai'oli Tea Room** (2950 Manoa Rd., 808/988-5800, open weekdays 10:30 A.M.–3:30 P.M., weekends 8 A.M.–3 P.M.) owned and operated by the Salvation Army. Set within a small parklike property, the restaurant features fresh-baked pastries and serves a breakfast of quiche, frittatas, omelettes, and waffles; lunch brings salads and sandwiches, and a formal high tea (24-hour reservation requested) is offered daily with desserts, finger sandwiches, and scones.

If you are heading up to Lyon Arboretum or to Manoa Falls around midday, you might stop at the **Tree Tops Restaurant at Paradise Park** (808/988-6838, open 11 A.M.–2 P.M.), literally at treetop level and offering very good food and superlative views overlooking the old Paradise Park garden in upper Manoa Valley. It serves a daily lunch buffet only and is a bargain at $13.50.

KAIMUKI

Kaimuki was one of the first suburban areas of Honolulu to be developed. It lies on both sides of Waiʻalae Avenue, inland of Waikiki and east of the University. Many of the Kaimuki restaurants lie between 11th and 12th Avenues, although some are a bit farther afield. Literally within a few steps of each other are Italian, Japanese, Chinese, Korean, Mexican, Vietnamese, and Thai restaurants, as well as a coffee shop and bakery or two.

The **C Big City Diner** (3565 Waiʻalae Ave., 808/738-8855) is a well-known establishment in Kaimuki. Open for breakfast, lunch, and dinner, it serves huge portions and is so much a local favorite that you'll have to wait in line to get a seat on Saturday morning. It's great for families. Your breakfast might be Our Famous Big Breakfast of three eggs and choice of meat, Loco Moco, or Murphy's Famous Fresh Apple Pancakes. The lunch and dinner menu are pretty much the same, and from them you can order chow mein noodles, hamburger steak with grilled onions and mushrooms, baby back ribs with guava barbecue sauce, kimchi fried rice, burgers, or sandwiches. Most come for the food, but there's also satellite TV and live Monday night sports. Park in the city parking lot behind.

12th Avenue Grill (1145C 12th Ave., 808/732-9469, open Mon.–Thurs. 5:30–9 P.M., Fri.–Sat. 5:30–10 P.M.), one block off the main drag, is a cozy bistro with subdued lighting and an open kitchen that serves wholesome yet creative foods with plenty of wine choices to complement any meal. While the menu changes by the season, some appetizer selections might be crispy fried ravioli and crab and Kahuku corn cakes, while entrées could be cinnamon braised short ribs, pan-seared rib eye, or kim chee steak. Every night there are specials.

Hale Vietnam (1140 12th Ave., 808/735-7581, open daily 11 A.M.–10 P.M.) has built an excellent and award-winning reputation for authentic and savory dishes at moderate prices. It gets the highest praise from local people, who choose it again and again for an inexpensive evening of delicious dining. Try such items as deep-fried Imperial roll appetizers, catfish soup, chicken curry, braised shrimp in black pepper sauce, one of the numerous vegetarian dishes, or the Vietnamese fondue.

Another eatery close by that draws a local crowd is the somewhat sterile **Green Papaya**

THE LEGENDS OF MANOA VALLEY

Kahala-o-puna, known for her exceptional beauty, was betrothed to Kauhi, a young chief who was driven mad by unfounded jealousy. He falsely accused his lovely wife of faithlessness and killed her five times, only to have her resurrected each time by her sympathetic guardian *aumakua*. Finally, left for dead, Kahala-o-puna was found by a young prince who fell in love with her. Beseeching his animal spirits, he brought her to life one last time, and through them turned the jealous Kauhi into a shark. Kahala-o-puna, warned never to go into the ocean, disobeyed, and was seized in the massive jaws of Kauhi, who crushed the life from her, never to be rekindled. The warm misty rains of Manoa are the tears of the mother of Kahala-o-puna, and the gentle winds are the soft sobs of her bereaved father, who together forever lament the loss of their beloved daughter.

Another legend sings of the spring, Wai-a-ke-akua, created spontaneously by the great gods Kane and Kaneloa, who came to visit this valley. While overindulging in 'awa they became intoxicated and decided that they would dawdle in the lovely valley. Lying down, the gods could hear water running underground, so Kane took his great staff and struck the earth, causing Wai-a-ke-akua to appear. Because of the spring's divine origin, it became known as "water of the gods," making it *kapu* to all but the highest *aliʻi*. When Kamehameha conquered Oʻahu, only he could drink from the spring, which flows with cool sweet water to this day.

(3579 Wai'alae Ave., 808/737-8820), serving Vietnamese *pho* soups, noodle soups, and a healthy mix of vegetarian and meat and rice and noodle dishes, all for easy-on-the-budget prices.

Café Laufer (3565 Wai'alae Ave., 808/735-7717, open Sun.–Thurs. 10 A.M.–9 P.M., Fri.–Sat. 10 A.M.–10 P.M.) puts out fine pastries, coffee, and light foods; while **JJ Bistro and French Pastry** (3447 Wai'alae Ave., 808/739-0993, open weekdays 9 A.M.–9 P.M., Sat. 9 A.M.–7 P.M., Sun. noon–6 P.M.) is a tiny place that does a mix of pasta, pizza, and fish dishes, but its specialties are the sweet treats from the oven.

Coffee Talk (3601 Wai'alae Ave., 808/737-7444) is a coffee shop that also serves light breakfasts and sandwiches, as well as providing Internet service.

ALONG KAPAHULU AVENUE

Once Kapahulu Avenue crosses Ala Wai Boulevard going away from Waikiki, it passes excellent inexpensive to moderately priced restaurants, one after the other. Kapahulu was the area in which the displaced Chinese community resettled after the great Chinatown fire at the turn of the 20th century. Kapahulu translates as poor soil, and unlike most areas of Hawaii it could barely support vegetables and plants. Undaunted, the Chinese brought in soil with wagons and wheelbarrows, turning the area productive and verdant. The restaurants along Kapahulu Avenue are only a short drive away for those staying in Waikiki.

A large establishment with decor that shouts China, **Hee Hing** (449 Kapahulu, 808/735-5544, open 10:30 A.M.–9:30 P.M.) has a menu so big you might take longer deciding what you want than actually eating your meal. Along with the usual soups and noodle and rice dishes, you'll find other specialties like earthen pot casseroles, sizzling plates, traditional Szechuan and Northern Chinese dishes, and plenty of selections from the sea. All this comes at a reasonable price, with most dishes under $13, except for a few lobster and crab entrées.

The sit-down **Irifune Japanese Restaurant** (563 Kapahulu Ave., 808/737-1141, open Tues.–Sat. 11:30 A.M.–1:30 P.M. and 5:30–9:30 P.M.) is directly across from Zippy's, a fast-food joint. Irifune serves authentic, well-prepared Japanese standards in its small dining room, including stir-fry plates, rice bowls, tempura, and katsu dishes. Most dinner meals begin at around $10, while lunch dishes are somewhat less. One item that Irifune has become especially known for is its garlic ahi. Irifune is a great deal for Japanese food, much cheaper and easily as good as most other Japanese restaurants on the Waikiki strip. The decor is not special, but it's a popular neighborhood place so get there early. Having been around for more than 30 years, it's a winner!

Up a ways and on the other side of the road is **Ono Hawaiian Foods** (726 Kapahulu Ave., 808/737-2275, open Mon.–Sat. 11 A.M.–7:45 P.M.), an institution in down-home Hawaiian cooking. This is the kind of place a taxi driver takes you when you ask for "the real thing." It's clean and basic, and the decor is photos of local performers—all satisfied customers—hung on the wall. If you want to try *lomi lomi* salmon, poi, or *kalua* pig, this is *da' kine place, brah!* Chicken long rice, butterfish luau, chop steak, poke fish, and *opihi* are others worth a try. Prices are cheap, with plates at $10–13 and à la carte dishes mostly $5–7.

The Pyramids (758 Kapahulu Ave., 808/737-2900, open daily 11 A.M.–2 P.M. and 5:30–10 P.M., until 9 P.M. on Sunday) is the place to head for Egyptian and Mediterranean cuisine. It's a small place, so reservations are recommended. You might imagine yourself to be inside King Tut's tomb with hieroglyphics and painted stone blocks on the walls. Live music and belly dancing accompany the meal every evening. All the usual favorites are on the menu: tabbouleh and shawarma salads; hummus, baba ghanouj, falafel, and stuffed grape leaves appetizers; and entrées like shish kabob, moussaka, and kebbeh. Dinner prices, most below $20 for entrées, are a few dollars more than those at lunch, although the lunch buffet is a bargain at $9.95. The lunch menu also has a few sandwiches, while the dinner menu has some vegetarian options.

If you have a sweet tooth, try **Leonard's**

Bakery (933 Kapahulu Ave., 808/737-5591, open Sun.–Thurs. 6 A.M.–9 P.M., until 10 P.M. on Fri. and Sat. nights). Specializing in hot *malasadas* (original, custard, *haupia*, and guava) and pao dolce, Leonard's has garnered an islandwide reputation since 1952.

OTHERS AROUND TOWN
Local Style
At the corner of Pali Highway and Vineyard Boulevard is **People's Cafe** (808/536-5789, open Mon.–Sat. 10 A.M.–8 P.M.). A family affair, this down-home restaurant has seen several generations serving excellent and inexpensive Hawaiian food for years. Plate lunches are the least expensive, and combination lunches like the Laulau plate, which is *lomi* salmon, pipikaula, chicken lu'au or chicken long rice, and poi or rice, are only about $10 and served on sectioned trays. Although there's no decor to speak of, the place is clean and the people are friendly. If you want a real Hawaiian meal at a reasonable price, this is the place to come!

On Jin's Cafe (401 Kamake'e St., 808/589-1666, open Sun.–Thurs. 7 A.M.–9 P.M., Fri.–Sat. until 10 P.M.) behind Pier 1 Imports at the Ward Centers, is a pleasant surprise. Chef On Jin Kim, who used to run the kitchen at the Hanatei Bistro before it closed, has a much smaller and more intimate restaurant here. The food is eclectic with definite Pacific and European overtones. The clean, modern style, marble tables decorated with orchids, tile floor, and semi-open kitchen set the mood. Lunch is inexpensive, with plate lunches and sandwiches that run mostly $7–8.50, but even these show class. Dinners are the best—more sophisticated and more expensive but not outrageous. Appetizers such as charred ahi and lobster ravioli, lead to entrées like crispy snapper, bouillabaisse, duck à l'Orange, and kalbi ribs are mostly $12–24. Savor the sauces.

Waterfront
Fisherman's Wharf (1009 Ala Moana Blvd., 808/538-3808, open weekdays 11 A.M.–9 P.M., weekends 4–9 P.M.) on the Kewalo Basin is a Honolulu institution and has been here since

LA MARIANA SAILING CLUB

This small marina at 50 Sand Island Access Road is a love song in the middle of an industrialized area. The marina is Annette La Mariana Nahinu's labor of love that has remained true since 1955. You can read her fantastic story on the menu of the marina's Hideaway Restaurant. In 1955 this area was forgotten, forsaken, and unkempt. Ms. Nahinu, against the forces of nature and the even more unpredictable and devastating forces of bureaucracy, took this land and turned it into a yacht harbor. The main tools were indefatigable determination, God listening to her prayers, and a shovel and rake. It's one of the last enclaves of old Hawaii, a place to come for dinner or drink, or just to look at the boats. Annette, the founder, is now a little gray-haired woman (92 years old in 2007 and still going strong), a motherly type in Birkenstocks, who still spreads her magic while talking to old salts, new arrivals, and guests at the restaurant. La Mariana is a unique statement in a city where unique statements are not necessarily encouraged.

1952. The restaurant's theme is nautical, and the place exudes the feel of decades past as you watch fishing boats and pleasure craft arrive and depart as they have done for decades. For lunch, start with oysters on the half shell or fresh steamed clams. Follow this with Boston-style clam chowder and a Caesar salad. Lunch sandwiches, fish, and other entrées run mostly under $10. The dinner menu is similar, except pricier, but without the sandwiches and with the addition of pastas and other special entrées.

La Mariana Restaurant (50 Sand Island Access Rd., 808/848-2800, open daily 11 A.M.–9 P.M.) at La Mariana Sailing Club is the only real restaurant in this neck of the woods. This hideaway serves appetizers like sashimi, lumpia, and sautéed mushroom buttons. From the broiler come steaks, pork chops, and burgers with all the fixings. From the sea, seafood brochette, shrimp scampi served over linguini, or Cajun-style ahi will fill your plate. Most entrées cost less than $18. The lunch menu is simpler, with soups, salads, hot and cold sandwiches, and a handful of fish and stir-fry selections. The chef is also known for his onion rings. They're not on the menu; you have to know about them. Now you know! La Mariana is an out-of-the-way place—local, with a real Polynesian feel. Located at a working marina, this is where all the yachties come. Half hidden behind a stand of trees and a fence, only one small sign at the entrance points the way. Most evenings there's piano music from about 6 P.M., so stop by for a drink at the bar and enjoy.

Italian

Auntie Pasto's Restaurant (1099 S. Beretania St., 808/523-8855, open Mon.–Thurs. 11 A.M.–10:30 P.M., Fri. 11 A.M.–11 P.M., Sat. 4–11 P.M., Sun. 4–10:30 P.M.), at the corner of Pensacola, has a comfortable vibe. This casual and friendly neighborhood Italian eatery has a menu like Mama used to provide. Most entrées run $13–20, and these include eggplant parmesan, manicotti, calamari steak piccata, and veal marsala, and then there are the antipasti plates, pasta selections, and wonderful pizzas. Soups come by the cup or bowl, and salads range from a garden green salad to a chicken Caesar. No reservations necessary.

Korean

The Korean restaurant **Sorabol** (805 Ke'eaumoku St., 808/947-3113, open 24 hours a day) is located just down the road from the Pagoda Hotel. Unlike the majority of Korean food outlets in the state, this one has not Americanized most of its menu—what you get is pretty much what you might expect to get if you were in Korea. Many people know of the Korean Kalbi (marinated ribs) and Bulgogi (marinated beef), both braised on a griddle, but the menu also contains such typical dishes as tofu stew, ginseng chicken, mixed rice bowl, and dumplings in beef broth soup. The menu is long and traditional, reasonably priced with most dishes under $15, and also offers plate lunch, sushi, and sashimi choices. For a true taste of Korean cooking, try Sorabol.

Hawaiian Regional

As large a city as Honolulu is, it's able to support many innovative restaurants where locally grown foods are combined with preparation techniques from around the world to produce new and intriguing flavors. The following are restaurants where something new is always on the menu and the combination of ingredients, textures, and tastes is sure to please. Reservations are recommended.

In the semi-industrial area of Iwilei, **Sam Choy's Breakfast, Lunch, and Crab** (580 N. Nimitz Hwy., 808/545-7979, breakfast Mon.–Fri. 6:30–10:30 A.M. and Sat. and Sun. 7–11 A.M. , lunch until 3 P.M. or 4 P.M., and dinner Sun.–Thurs. 5–9:30 P.M. and until 10 P.M. Fri.–Sat.) is as popular as any. Some stop for the hearty breakfasts of omelettes, loco moco, and griddle items, while others make it during the day for a sandwich lunch or fish dinner. Many island favorites are on the menu, and there are always generous portions. Sam brews beer at this site, and the brewpub is open nightly until 10 P.M. Here you get *pu pu* specials and live music periodically. Valet parking only.

Indigo (1121 Nu'uanu Ave., 808/521-2900, open Tues.–Fri. 11:30 A.M.–2 P.M., Tues.–Sat. 6–9:30 P.M.), in Chinatown across from the Hawaii Theatre, serves what some classify as Eurasian cuisine. Chef Glenn Chu offers such savory items as Chinese steamed buns filled with eggplant and sun-dried tomatoes, crispy goat cheese wonton filled with fruit sauce, roasted tomato garlic crab soup, lilikoi-glazed sweet and sour baby back ribs, or Mogul lamb shanks vindaloo. Some vegetarian items are available, and there are many desserts to ponder. There's live music, dancing, and drinks at the adjacent Green Room Bar and Lounge until midnight. Valet parking is provided.

On the third floor of the Harbor Court building, set on the edge of Chinatown and overlooking Honolulu harbor, is the chic and contemporary **Palomino** (66 Queen

St., 808/528-2400, open weekdays 11 A.M.–2:30 P.M. and 5–10 P.M., Sat. 4–11 P.M., Sun. 4–10 P.M.), an innovative restaurant that combines fresh island ingredients with an old-world Italian twist. Specialties here are the wood-fired oven and rotisserie, which produce some exquisite flavors. The menu changes periodically but retains such favorites as chop chop salad, huli-huli lemon sage chicken, paella, and braised lamb shank. Always great are the diverse pizza and pasta dishes, the assortment of intriguing appetizers, and the delicious desserts. Expect lunch entrées, which also include sandwiches, to be in the $8–15 range, while dinner entrées run mostly under $35 with many less than $20. Only two blocks from the Hawaii Theatre, Palomino caters to the late-night theater crowd with late hours and a bar that stays open even later.

Alan Wong's (1857 S. King St., 808/949-2526, open at 5 P.M. nightly), just north of Waikiki is a Best Restaurant of the Year award-winner. Try nori-wrapped tempura ahi or manapua quesadillas as appetizers. Although the menu changes periodically, entrées might be mochi-crusted opakapaka, beef roulade, slow-poached lamb rib eye, or sautéed shrimp and clams penne pasta. Yum! Most selections run $26–36. The contemporary style of the restaurant matches the contemporary style of the food and its presentation. Valet parking is offered.

Near where the road crests the hill in Kaimuki is **3660 On the Rise** (3660 Wai'alae Ave., 808/737-1177, open Tues.–Sun. 5:30–9 P.M.), a casually elegant place where you can watch the cooks create behind the glass wall of the kitchen. The menu changes somewhat every night, but Chef Russell Siu's "first flavors" include ahi katsu and potato-crusted crab cakes, while "second flavors" are soups and salads. "Feature presentations" might be grilled ginger breast of duckling, Burgundy braised short ribs of beef, or Chinese steamed fillet of snapper lightly seared and simmered in a Chinese black bean broth. Round out your meal with one of the "sweet endings": harlequin crème brûlée or mile-high Wai'alae pie, perhaps, or indulge in a cup of coffee or glass of cognac or port. Delightful presentation and attentive service. Reservations are necessary.

One of the city's fine restaurants that has made a superb name for itself is █ **Chef Mavro** restaurant (1969 S. King St., 808/944-4714, Tues.–Sun. 6–9:30 P.M.) at the corner of McCully. Formerly the executive chef of the Four Seasons Resort on Maui and before that the executive chef at the Halekulani in Waikiki, Chef Mavro is now king of his own domain, and he reigns with distinction. The restaurant is not large but comfortable and personal, tastefully elegant yet not extravagant. Booths line the perimeter of the room, tables are set in the middle, paintings of tropical flowers and raku pottery with flowers line the walls, and low lighting, linen, and crystal set the mood. Basically, there is one seating a night. The intent is for guests to slowly savor their meals and leisurely enjoy their company. Chef Mavro offers a mix of à la carte and prix fixe menus with four or six options, with or without wine. The food is exceptional in its own right, but an important factor of dining here is the pairing of wine and food, a complementary union where neither overpowers the other. Each item is introduced and explained as it's set on the table, and wines are chosen for each individual dish. Nearly the entire menu changes by season, but no matter what the choices, the freshest of Hawaiian produce and seafood are always infused with subtle yet intense flavors and prepared with a French flair, resulting in tropical cuisine with French soul. This is an exceptional restaurant with masterful food. For a special night out, this is a great choice. Dining here can be expensive, but it's worth every penny. Entrées generally run $36–44, while the prix fixe dinners are $71 and $102, or $111 or 150 with wine pairings.

On the top floor of the Ala Moana Hotel, a short hop west of Waikiki, is **Aaron's** (808/955-4466, open daily 5–11 P.M.). This location affords an unsurpassed view out over the Waikiki strip as well as over downtown Honolulu. It is as much for its fabulous location that people come to dine, yet the food is first-class as well. And to add to the mix, there is live R&B music Wed.–Sat. evenings. Start your dinner with tiger eye sushi tempura, Manila clams, or *kalua* pork potsticker appetizer, and follow this with a daily selection of soup or a nutritious baby spinach salad. Entrées include steamed island onaga with baby Shanghai cabbage, soy-nori vinaigrette, and hot peanut oil; blackened "double" pork chop with pineapple marmalade, curry sauce, and toasted macadamia nuts; and veal scalloppine. Appetizers run $9–18 and entrées fall mostly in the $26–35 range. Couple the food and location with a select wine and you have the makings for a romantic evening. Call for reservations.

■ L'Uraku (1341 Kapi'olani Blvd., 808/955-0552, open daily 11 A.M.–2 P.M. and 5:30–10 P.M.) is on the ground floor of a building of the same name, not far from the Ala Moana Shopping Center. Complimentary parking is in the basement garage. Here, plate glass windows look out onto the lawn, while inside, brightly painted and upturned umbrellas adorn the ceiling and splashy, imaginative, modernistic paintings fill the walls. White linens and playfully colored napkins cover each table, and soft music sets the mood for a memorable meal. L'Uraku presents Euro-Japanese food and artfully combines the flavors, spices, and ingredients of Asia, the Continent, and the Pacific. Starting off with an appetizer like seared foie gras sushi, beef carpaccio, or takana crab cakes sets the table for the remainder of the meal. One of the salads refreshes the palate for the coming entrée, which might be misoyaki butterfish, steamed New Zealand tai snapper, garlic rosemary lamb chops, or vegetable saffron risotto with asparagus and mushrooms. Selecting from the extensive menu is a rewarding chore, but choosing the four-course "tasting" menu is also an excellent alternative. Entrées run mostly $20–30, while the tasting menu is $39, or $53 with wine pairings. If you still have room, try one of the many desserts like flourless chocolate cake or Hawaiian vanilla bean panna cotta to round out your fine dining experience and leave with a smile on your face.

WINE SHOPS

Wine is available at many markets and shops in Honolulu and Waikiki, yet several shops in town carry a good selection of bottles that would make a great complement to an everyday meal as well as to that special night where the wine should set the tone. If you are interested in selecting your own bottle of domestic or international wine, head to **The Wine Stop** (1809 S. King St., 808/946-3707, open Mon.–Thurs. 10 A.M.–9 P.M., Fri.–Sat. 10 A.M.–10 P.M., Sun. 11 A.M.–7 P.M.). This shop does wine-tastings, offers suggestions for food and wine parings, and also offers a section of microbrews and spirits.

In Chinatown, stop at **HASR Wine Co.** (31 N. Pauahi St., 808/535-9463, open weekdays 10 A.M.–8 P.M., weekends 10 A.M.–9 P.M.) to peruse the excellent wine collection. Tastings are given on Tuesday and Thursday 5–7 P.M. and during the First Friday art walk event.

R. Field Wine Co. (1460 S. Beretania St., 808/596-9463) in the Foodland supermarket is a purveyor of fine wines, exquisite foods, crackers, cookies, cheeses, imported pastas, caviar, and some organic produce and Hawaiian food products. Most of the wines are top-shelf Californian, with a nice variety of reserve wines going back years. International wines are also available, and while you're there check the humidor for a fine cigar. Look here for something special for that important evening.

FARMERS MARKETS

The island of O'ahu sports many large- and small-scale farmers markets throughout the week. The city and county sponsor what's known as the People's Open Markets in many of the neighborhoods. Too many to list, places and times can be found on the Internet (www.co.honolulu.hi.us/parks/programs/pom), but the most convenient to downtown is the Monday market 11:45 A.M.–12:30 P.M. at the city hall parking lot desk.

Perhaps the best true farmers market is the **Kapi'olani Community College Farmers Market** (www.hfbf.org/FarmersMarket.html), located at parking lot C at the college on Saturdays 7:30–11:30 A.M. A great place to get farm fresh vegetables and fruits, chef-prepared delicacies, and special treats. Local farmers come from all over the island to sell their crops here, and some of the best local chefs come here to buy for their restaurants.

FISH AUCTION

After 25 years and a move from its former site at Kewalo Basin, the **Honolulu Fish Auction** is doing business Mon.–Sat. at about 5:30 A.M. on Pier 38 at the United Fishing Agency, harborside of Nimitz Highway. You have to be there early to catch the action. This is one of the few live fish auctions in the state, and a joy for those with an interest in how fish catches are sold. Besides, your dinner might be coming off one of these boats.

ISLAND FISH AND SEAFOOD

Anyone who loves fresh fish and seafood has come to the right place. Island restaurants specialize in seafood, and it's available everywhere. You'll find it served in every kind of restaurant, and most often it is the fresh catch of the day. The following is a sampling of the best.

Mahimahi is an excellent eating fish, one of the most common, most popular, and least expensive in Hawaii. It's referred to as Dorado or "dolphin fish" but is definitely a fish, not a mammal. The flesh of Mahimahi is moderately firm, light, flaky, and moist. While different preparations are available, this mild-flavored fish is perhaps best seared, sautéed, baked, or broiled. You will find it served as a main course and as a patty in a fish sandwich. This fish is broadest at the head. When caught, it has iridescent shades of blue, green, and yellow, but after a while the skin turns a dark olive color.

The **a'u**, a broadbill swordfish or marlin, is a true island delicacy. It's expensive even in Hawaii because the darn thing's so hard to catch. The meat is moist and white – truly superb – and the flavor is definitely pronounced. If it's offered on the menu, order it. It'll cost a bit more, but you won't be disappointed.

Ono means delicious in Hawaiian, so that should tip you off to the taste of this wahoo, or king mackerel. An open-ocean fish, ono is regarded as one of the finest eating fishes, and its mild, sweet meat lives up to its name. Its white, delicate, and lean flesh can be done in almost any preparation.

Ulua, a bottomfish and member of the crevalle jack family, has white flesh with a steak-like texture. Delicious when baked, sautéed, or broiled.

Opakapaka is a pink snapper, the most preferred of the bottomfish. It has light pink, clear, and firm flesh that has a delightfully delicate flavor. Whole fish with the head on are often baked or steamed; larger fillets can be baked, poached, or sautéed.

Cousin to the *Opakapaka*, **Uku** is a gray snapper that is a favorite with local people for its moderately firm and slightly flaky flesh. It can be prepared like its relative but is often steamed.

Ahi, a yellowfin tuna with distinctive firm, pinkish meat, is a great favorite cooked or served raw in sushi bars, but can be prepared in almost any way.

Two moderately firm, open-ocean fish that sometimes appear on menus are **Opah**, or moonfish (as its shape is nearly that round when seen from the side), and **Monchong.** *Opah* is more moist and tender, while *Monchong* is denser, but both have full flavor.

Moi is the Hawaiian word for king, and this fish was traditionally the privilege of royalty. This fish has large eyes and a sharklike head. Considered one of the finest eating fishes in Hawaii, it's best during the autumn months. It doesn't often show up at restaurants, but try it when it does.

For the uninitiated, **sushi** is a finger-size block of sticky rice topped with a slice of (usually) raw fish or other sea creature. A delicacy in Japan, it has become very popular and much appreciated in Hawaii (and on the Mainland) as a fine food. In addition to the traditional offerings, cutting-edge chefs now create a mind-boggling variety of innovative sushi morsels.

WAIKIKI

Waikiki (Spouting Water) is a classic study of contradictions. Above all, it is an example of basic American entrepreneurialism taken to the nth degree. Along the main strip, high-powered businesspeople cut multimillion-dollar deals, but on the sidewalks it's a carnival midway with hucksters, handbillers, and street people selling everything decent and indecent under the tropical sun. To get a true feeling for Waikiki, you must put this amazing strip of land into perspective. The area covers only seven-tenths of a square mile, which, at a good pace, you can walk the length of in half an hour. On any given day, about 110,000 people crowd its beaches and boulevards, making it one of the most densely populated areas on earth. Sixty thousand of these people are tourists; 30,000 are workers who commute from various towns of O'ahu and cater to the tourists, and the remaining 20,000 actually call Waikiki home. The turnover is about 80,000 new tourists per week, and the pace rarely slackens. To the head shakers, these facts condemn Waikiki as a mega-growth area gone wild. To others, these same figures make Waikiki an energized, fun-filled place to be, where if you don't have a good time, it's your own fault.

For the naive or the out-of-touch looking for grass-shack paradise, the closest they'll come to it in Waikiki is painted on a souvenir ashtray. Those drawn to a smorgasbord of activities, who are adept at choosing the best and ignoring the rest, can't go wrong! People and the action are as constant in Waikiki as the ever-rolling surf.

© ROBERT NILSEN

HIGHLIGHTS

◖ Diamond Head: This is the quintessential symbol of Waikiki. From the rim of this ancient tuff cone, the world-renowned beach and tightly packed streets of Waikiki spread before you (page 98).

◖ Honolulu Zoo: This wonderful menagerie of (mostly) tropical animals is worth a visit (page 102).

◖ Waikiki Aquarium: Monk seals, jellyfish, sharks, live coral, and a host of other marine creatures are the stars here (page 102).

◖ U.S. Army Museum of Hawaii: This museum succinctly captures the role of the military in Hawaii from the days of Hawaiian royalty to the present (page 103).

◖ Waikiki Beach: Whether in the bright sunshine or pale moonlight, the romance begins immediately when visitors first see it (page 105).

◖ International Market Place: Visitors come to Waikiki for the fun and sun, but they also come to shop. The most unique shopping venue in town is this open-air market (page 115).

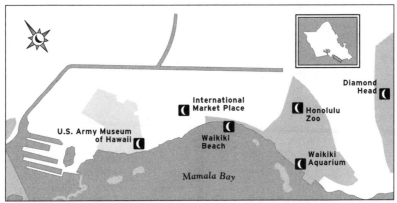

LOOK FOR **◖** TO FIND RECOMMENDED SIGHTS, ACTIVITIES, DINING, AND LODGING.

PLANNING YOUR TIME

In truth, little planning is required for your time in Waikiki. Waikiki is tiny, with accommodations, restaurants, and activities close at hand—and it's easy to get around. All of what you need for a good vacation is here. What you *do* need to decide, however, is how long you'll want to stay. Of course, spend some time on the beach. What's a Waikiki vacation without getting into the water? Shopping is a big draw, so you'll inevitably give your credit cards a good workout. There are so many fine restaurants that you'd be at it a month of Sundays to try only a small portion of the great foods offered here. And don't forget to

see the sights: Diamond Head, Honolulu Zoo, or the Waikiki Aquarium are all activities that could easily take a full morning or afternoon. At least one evening of your stay should be spent listening to the sweet sounds of Hawaiian music or enjoying one of the many dinner shows Waikiki is so well known for. While Waikiki is a grand place, it's good to get out and about to see the rest of the city of Honolulu, as well as the rest of the island, as Waikiki isn't all that O'ahu has to offer.

HISTORY

The written record of this former swampy area began in the late 1790s. The white man,

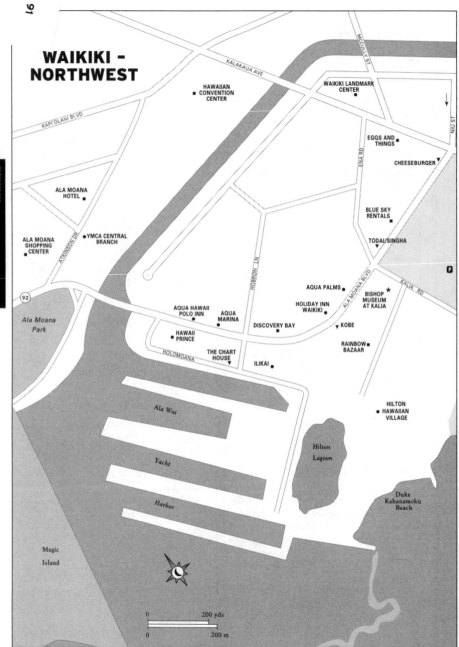

WAIKIKI - NORTHWEST

HAWAIIAN CONVENTION CENTER

WAIKIKI LANDMARK CENTER

KALAKAUA AVE

MCCULLY ST

KAPI'OLANI BLVD

EGGS AND THINGS

CHEESEBURGER

NIU ST

ALA MOANA HOTEL

BLUE SKY RENTALS

TODAI/SINGHA

ENA RD

ALA MOANA SHOPPING CENTER

YMCA CENTRAL BRANCH

HOBRON LN

KALIA RD

AQUA PALMS

BISHOP MUSEUM AT KALIA

92

ATKINSON DR

HOLIDAY INN WAIKIKI

ALA MOANA BLVD

Ala Moana Park

AQUA HAWAII POLO INN

AQUA MARINA

DISCOVERY BAY

KOBE

HAWAII PRINCE

RAINBOW BAZAAR

HOLOMOANA

THE CHART HOUSE

ILIKAI

HILTON HAWAIIAN VILLAGE

Ala Wai

Hilton Lagoon

Yacht

Duke Kahanamoku Beach

Harbor

Magic Island

0   200 yds

0   200 m

WAIKIKI

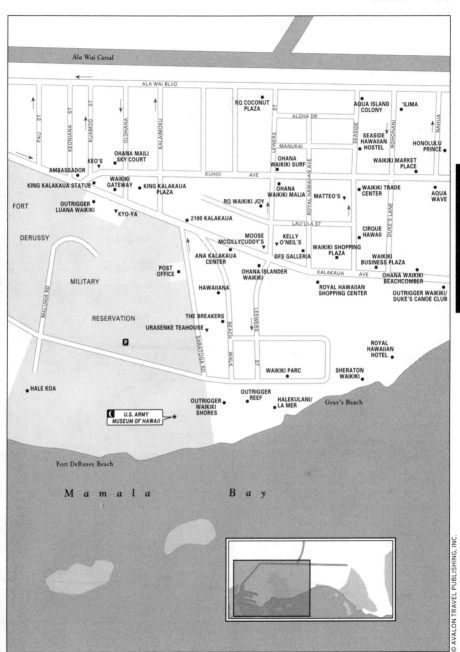

Ala Wai Canal

ALA WAI BLVD

PAU ST
KEONIANA ST
KUAMOO ST
OLOHANA
KALAIMOKU

RQ COCONUT PLAZA
AQUA ISLAND COLONY
'ILIMA

ALOHA DR

SEASIDE
NOHONANI
NAHUA

SEASIDE HAWAIIAN HOSTEL
HONOLULU PRINCE

MANUKAI

OHANA MAILI SKY COURT
KEO'S

WAIKIKI MARKET PLACE

OHANA WAIKIKI SURF

KUHIO AVE

AMBASSADOR

WAIKIKI GATEWAY
KING KALAKAUA STATUE
KING KALAKAUA PLAZA

OHANA WAIKIKI MALIA
MATTEO'S
WAIKIKI TRADE CENTER
AQUA WAVE

FORT

RQ WAIKIKI JOY

OUTRIGGER LUANA WAIKIKI
KYO-YA
2100 KALAKAUA

LAU'ULA ST
CIRQUE HAWAII

DERUSSY

MOOSE MCGILLYCUDDY'S
KELLY O'NEIL'S
WAIKIKI SHOPPING PLAZA
WAIKIKI BUSINESS PLAZA

MILITARY

POST OFFICE
ANA KALAKAUA CENTER
DFS GALLERIA

KALAKAUA AVE
OHANA WAIKIKI BEACHCOMBER

OHANA ISLANDER WAIKIKI
ROYAL HAWAIIAN SHOPPING CENTER
OUTRIGGER WAIKIKI/ DUKE'S CANOE CLUB

RESERVATION

HAWAIIANA

THE BREAKERS
URASENKE TEAHOUSE

MALUHIA RD

BEACH WALK
SARATOGA RD
LEEWERS ST

ROYAL HAWAIIAN HOTEL

WAIKIKI PARC
SHERATON WAIKIKI

HALE KOA

OUTRIGGER REEF
OUTRIGGER WAIKIKI SHORES
HALEKULANI/ LA MER
Gray's Beach

U.S. ARMY MUSEUM OF HAWAII

Fort DeRussy Beach

M a m a l a   B a y

WAIKIKI

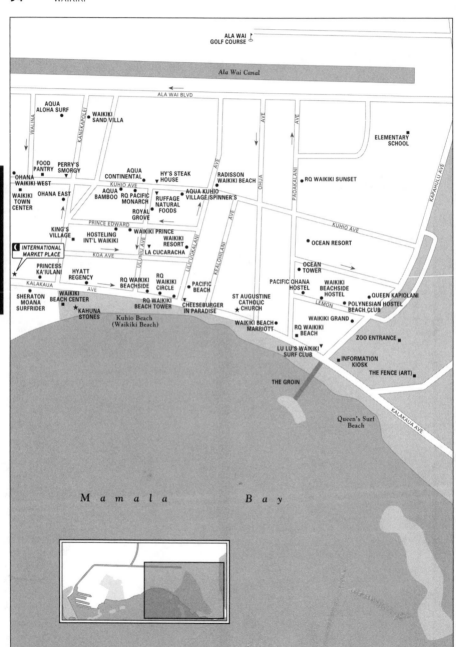

WAIKIKI

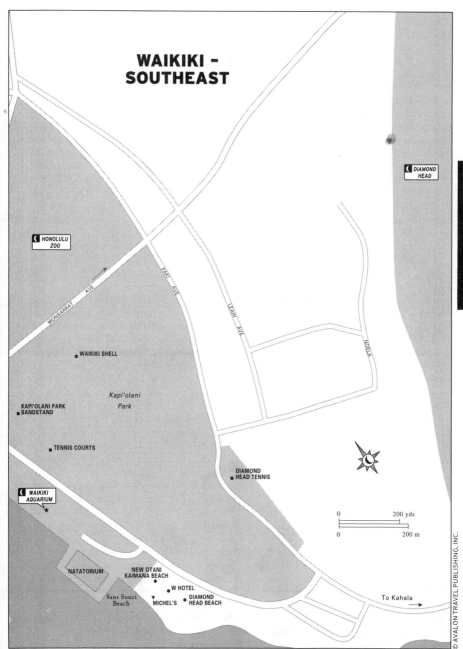

WAIKIKI - SOUTHEAST

DIAMOND HEAD

HONOLULU ZOO

PAKI AVE

MONSARRAT AVE

LEAHI AVE

NOELA

WAIKIKI SHELL

Kapiʻolani Park

KAPIʻOLANI PARK BANDSTAND

TENNIS COURTS

DIAMOND HEAD TENNIS

WAIKIKI AQUARIUM

| 0 | 200 yds |
| 0 | 200 m |

NATATORIUM

NEW OTANI KAIMANA BEACH

W HOTEL

Sans Souci Beach

MICHEL'S

DIAMOND HEAD BEACH

To Kahala

© AVALON TRAVEL PUBLISHING, INC.

WAIKIKI

along with his historians, cartographers, artists, and gunpowder, was already an undeniable presence in the islands. Kalanikupule, ranking chief of O'ahu, hijacked the *Jackall*, a small ship commanded by Captain Brown, with which he intended to spearhead an attack against Kamehameha I. The chief held the *Jackall* for a while, but the sailors regained control just off Diamond Head and sent the Hawaiians swimming for land. The ship then hastened to Kamehameha to report the treachery and returned with his armada of double-hulled canoes, which beached along Waikiki. The great king then defeated Kalanikupule at the famous battle of Nu'uanu Pali and secured control of the island. Thereafter Waikiki, pinpointed by Diamond Head, became a well-known landmark.

Waikiki's interior was low-lying swampland, long known to be good for fishponds, taro, rice, and bananas, but hardly for living. The beach, however, was always blessed with sunshine and perfect waves, especially for surfing, a sport heartily loved by the Hawaiians. The royalty of Hawaii, following Kamehameha, made Honolulu their capital and kept beach houses at Waikiki. They invited many visiting luminaries to visit them at their private beach. All were impressed. In the 1880s, King Kalakaua was famous for his beach house hospitality. One of his favorite guests was Robert Louis Stevenson, who spent many months here writing one of his novels. By the turn of the 20th century, Waikiki, which had been little more than a handful of grass-shack cottages, had become a highly exclusive vacation spot and home to some of the island's wealthiest families.

In 1901 the Moana Hotel was built, but immediately a protest was heard because it interfered with the view of Diamond Head. In 1906, Lucius Pinkham, then director of Hawaii's Board of Health, called the mosquito-infested area "dangerous and unsanitary," and proposed to drain the swamp with a canal so that "the whole place can be transformed into a place of unique beauty." By the early 1920s, the Ala Wai Canal was built, its dredgings used to reclaim land, and Waikiki was demarcated.

By the end of the 1920s, the Royal Hawaiian Hotel, built on the site previously occupied by the royal beach house, was receiving very wealthy guests who arrived by ocean liner, loaded down with steamer trunks. They ensconced themselves at Waikiki, often staying for the duration of the season.

For about 40 years, Waikiki remained the enchanted domain of Hollywood stars, dignitaries, and millionaires. But for the brief and extraordinary days of World War II, which saw Waikiki barricaded and barbed-wired, GIs—regular guys from the Mainland—were given a taste of this paradise while on R&R. They brought home tantalizing tales of wonderful Waikiki, whetting the appetite of Middle America.

Beginning just before statehood and continuing through the 1960s to the mid-1970s, hotels and condos popped up like fertilized weeds, and tourism exploded with the advent of the jumbo jet. Discounted package tours began to haul in droves of economy-class tourists. Businesses catering to the tastes of penny-pinchers and first-timers elbowed their way into every nook and cranny. For the first time, Waikiki began to be described as tacky and vulgar. For the old-timers, Waikiki was in decline. The upscale and repeat visitors started to snub Waikiki, heading for hidden resorts on the Neighbor Islands. But Waikiki had spirit and soul and never gave in. Its declining hotels started a campaign to regain their illustrious images. Millions upon millions of dollars have been poured into renovations and remodeling. Luxury hotels renting exclusive and expensive rooms have reappeared and are doing a booming business. To give you some perspective of just what's here, Waikiki has roughly 100 hotels, condominiums, and hostels with 29,000 guest rooms, 300 bars and lounges, and 250 restaurants, not to mention the hundreds of shops, sundry stores, and entertainment spots.

Waikiki Today

The Neighbor Islands are pulling more and more tourists away, and depending on your

WAIKIKI SEWAGE SPILL

With all of the fine improvements the city has made in Waikiki, there have been some mishaps along the way. Perhaps the most damaging of these was in the spring of 2006 when 48 million gallons of raw sewage spewed into the Ala Wai Canal and onto Waikiki beaches, due to a broken sewer line. This episode was a symptom of a deteriorating infrastructure that the city is constantly dealing with and for which a permanent solution has yet to be found. The spill closed beaches for days, and in Waikiki, that had a profound effect on tourism and the visitors who had come for beach time. Local health officials eventually reopened the beaches, deeming them safe, but there have been incidents following the spill where visitors and residents developed skin ailments that could easily be traced to their exposure to tainted water. City and tourism officials were quick to downplay the debacle. While this incident did tarnish the state's shining tourism image, luckily the hit seems to have been temporary and tourism has recovered – as, we are told, have the beaches.

point of view, this is either a boon or a bust for Waikiki. Direct flights to Maui, the Big Island, and Kaua'i allow more tourists than ever to bypass O'ahu, but still a whopping 80 percent of the people visiting the islands spend at least one night in Waikiki hotels, which offer, on average, the lowest room rates in Hawaii. The sublime and the gaudy are neighbors in Waikiki. But it somehow works, and works well. You may not find paradise on Waikiki's streets, but you will find a willing dancing partner, and if you pay the fiddler, she'll keep the beat.

For years, the city of Honolulu has been spending a great deal of money in Waikiki upgrading its infrastructure so that it works and looks better. By and large, the city has succeeded admirably with its improvements, and Waikiki has a new shine that brightens everyone's smile. Private industry has also gotten into the act. Not only have individual hotels improved their properties, but the big corporations also have made big changes. The most significant of these is the Waikiki Beach Walk renovation, about eight acres between Kalakaua Avenue and the beach, encompassing Kalia, Beach Walk, and Lewers Streets. Spearheaded by the Outrigger hotel corporation, this project is set to revitalize this tired, aging, and somewhat substandard section of town into a bright, pedestrian-friendly, and completely modern area by reconfiguring roads and walkways, putting in new landscaping, tearing down old structures, renovating some existing accommodations, building a new hotel, and creating a new shopping and entertainment complex. The goal is to bring new life into this significant but woefully inadequate section of town. The Waikiki Beach Walk project has ballooned into a $525 million development project, said to be the most ambitious redevelopment in Waikiki's history.

Sights

To see Waikiki's attractions, you can simply perch on a bench or loll on a beach towel. Its boulevards and beaches are world-class for people-watching. Some of its strollers and sunbathers are visions, whereas others are real sights. And if you keep your ears open, it's not hard to hear every American accent and a dozen foreign languages being spoken. Some actual sights are intermingled with the hotels, boutiques, bars, and restaurants. Sometimes, too, these buildings are the sights. Unbelievably, you can even find plenty of quiet spots—in Kapi'olani Park, Fort DeRussy, and at churches, temples, and ancient Hawaiian special places—sitting unnoticed amid the grand structures of the 20th century. Also, both the Honolulu Zoo and Waikiki Aquarium are well worth a visit.

Waikiki Historical Trail Markers

Some 20 surfboard-shaped historical markers have been set up at various points around Waikiki that give a brief description of important places, persons, and happenings in Waikiki's history. These markers are a quick introduction to the area and, if you follow them all, provide a good walk over a two-mile route. To follow along on your own, pick up a copy of the *Waikiki Historic Trail* brochure (www.waikikihistorictrail.com).

Run by the Native Hawaiian Hospitality Association (808/441-1404), guided and fee-based **walking tours** of these historical sites are offered by appointment only and last about two hours. Wear a hat and comfortable walking shoes. Call for exact details and reservations.

◖ DIAMOND HEAD

If you're not sandwiched in a manmade canyon of skyscrapers, you can look eastward from anywhere in Waikiki and see Diamond Head, which *says* Waikiki. Western sailors have used it as a landmark since the earliest days of contact, and the Hawaiians undoubtedly before that. Ships' artists etched and sketched its motif long before the names of the newfound lands of

Hawaii, Waikiki, and O'ahu were standardized and appeared on charts as Owyhee, Whytete, and Woohoo. The Hawaiian name was Le'ahi (Brow of the Ahi); legend says it was named by Hi'iaka, Madame Pele's younger sister, because she saw a resemblance in its silhouette to the yellowfin tuna. The name Diamond Head comes from a band of wild-eyed English sailors who found calcite crystals on its slopes and thought they'd discovered diamonds. Hawaii had fulfilled so many other dreams—why not a mountain of diamonds? Kamehameha I immediately made the mountain *kapu* until his advisor, John Young, informed him that what the seamen had found, later known as "Pele's tears," were worthless, except as souvenirs. No fortune was made, but the name stuck. The Hawaiians considered Diamond Head a power spot. Previously, Kamehameha had worshipped at a *heiau* on the western slopes, offering human sacrifice to his bloodthirsty war god, Ku.

Geologically, the 761-foot monolith is about 350,000 years old, said to have formed from one gigantic eruption when seawater came into contact with lava bubbling out of a fissure. This tuff cone is now a Hawaii state monument and a national natural landmark since its designation in 1968. Its 350-acre crater serves as a Hawaii National Guard depot; a hiking trail to the summit leads through an installation left over from World War II. The site of music festivals during the heady days of the 1960s and 1970s, Diamond Head held music festivals inside the crater once again starting in 2005. The southeast *(makai)* face has some of the most exclusive and expensive real estate in the islands. The Kahala Hotel is regarded by many to be one of the premier hotels in the world, and nearby is the super-snobbish Wai'alae Country Club. Many private estates—homes of multimillionaires, Hawaii's well-known, and high-powered multinational executives—cling to the cliffside, fronting ribbons of beach open to the public by narrow rights-of-way often hemmed in by the walls of the estates.

WAIKIKI

© ROBERT NILSEN

The volcanic tuff cone Diamond Head punctuates the eastern end of Waikiki, overlooking Kapi'olani Park.

The Hike

The most recognized symbol of Hawaii, Diamond Head is the first place you should head to for a strikingly beautiful panorama of Waikiki and greater Honolulu.

Getting there takes only 15 minutes from Waikiki, either by TheBus nos. 22 or 58 or by car following Kalakaua Avenue south from Waikiki and turning onto Monsarrat Avenue just beyond the Honolulu Zoo. Monsarrat turns into Diamond Head Road, then quickly a sign points you to the Diamond Head Crater entrance. Pass through a tunnel and into the militarized section in the center of the crater; the trail starts at the end of the parking lot. Although the hike is moderate, you should bring along water, and binoculars if you have them. Run by the Division of State Parks, the park is open daily 6 A.M.–6 P.M., and the entrance fee is $1 per person, but there is a $5 fee for parking. The trail is seven-tenths of a mile long and was built to the 761-foot summit of Le'ahi

Point in 1908 to serve as a U.S. Coast Artillery Observation Station. It was heavily fortified during World War II, and part of the fun is exploring the old gun emplacements and tunnels built to link and service them.

Wildflowers and chirping birds create a peaceful setting, although the inside of the crater is mostly an arid environment. When you come to a series of cement and stone steps, walk to a flat area to the left to find an old winch that hauled the heavy building materials to the top. Here's a wide panorama of the sea and Koko Head. Notice too that atop several little hillocks along the rim are old gun emplacements. Next comes a short but dark tunnel (a flashlight used to be needed, but now lights have been installed) and immediately a series of 99 steps. Following the steps is a spiral staircase that leads up into the four-level command post/ gun emplacement and out to the ridge. Once on top, another stairway and ladder take you to the very summit, where Waikiki lies below.

WAIKIKI FREE SIGHTS AND CURIOSITIES

On the beach near the Sheraton Moana Surfrider hotel are the **kahuna stones,** a lasting remnant of old Hawaii. The Hawaiians believed these stones were imbued with *mana* by four hermaphroditic priests from Tahiti: Kinohimahu, Kahaloamahu, Kapunimahu, and Kapaemahu (*mahu* in Hawaiian signifies homosexuality). They came to visit this Polynesian outpost in ancient times and left these stones for the people, who have held them in reverence for more than 600 years. About 40 years ago, a group of local historians went looking for the stones but couldn't find them. Around that time, there was a bowling alley along the beach, and when it was finally torn down, it was discovered that the stones had been incorporated into the foundation. Most visitors and islanders alike no longer revered the stones and often used them as a handy spot to scrape sand off their feet. That was the case until the recent renovation of Kalakaua Avenue, when the stones were fenced off and once again given prominence as a tangible element of ancient Hawaiian belief. *Kupuna* versed in the old ways say that the *mana,* once put in and strengthened by reverence, is dissipating.

Even if you're not a guest at the following hotels, you should at least drop by their lobbies for a quick look. Dramatically different, they serve almost as a visual record of Waikiki's changing history. Those who have a fondness for the elegance of days gone by should tour the **Sheraton Moana Surfrider** and steep in the history of the hotel, admiring its early-1900s artifacts and memorabilia. The Moana, Waikiki's oldest hotel, dating from 1901, is a permanent reminder of simpler times when its illustrious clientele would dance the night away at an open-air nightclub suspended over the sea. The Moana houses the Banyan Court, named for the enormous banyan tree just outside. From here, *Hawaii Calls* beamed Hawaiian music to the Mainland by shortwave radio for 40 years beginning in 1935. In its heyday, the show was carried by more than 700 stations. The hotel's architecture is a classic example

of the now quaint colonial style. Free one-hour tours are offered Monday, Wednesday, and Friday at 11 A.M. and 5 P.M. starting at the second-floor historical room.

The **Royal Hawaiian Hotel,** built in 1927 on the site of the old royal beach house, once had fresh pineapple juice running in its fountains. Now surrounded by towering hotels, it's like a guppy in a sea of whales. However, it does stand out with its Spanish-Moorish style, painted in distinctive pink, and is surrounded by huge old tropical trees and huge coconut palms. In the old days, only celebrities and luminaries came to stay – who else could afford $3 per day? Although it's younger than the Moana, many consider it the grande dame of Hawaiian hotels. The entranceway is elegantly old-fashioned, with rounded archways, overstuffed couches, and lowboys. At the end of the main hallway, Diamond Head is framed in the arches. Historical guided tours of the building and grounds are offered free every Monday, Wednesday, and Friday at 2 P.M. Meet in the registration lobby.

Across the street from the Sheraton Moana are the giant, modernistic, twin towers of the **Hyatt Regency Waikiki.** The lobby, like those of most Hyatts, is wonderful, with a large waterfall and a jungle of plants, all stepped down the series of floors, making an effect like the Hanging Gardens of Babylon.

The **Pacific Beach Hotel** is a first-rate hotel and a great place to stay in its own right. But if you don't, definitely visit the Oceanarium Restaurant just off the lobby, which has an immense three-story aquarium dedicated to holding 280,000 gallons of seawater and scores of colorful tropical fish. It is said that the old Mafia Dons used to send their rivals to "sleep with the fishes"; here, you have an opportunity to dine with the fishes. Usually you go snorkeling to watch the fish eat, but in this particular instance the fish watch you eat.

At the corner of the DFS Galleria Waikiki building is a two-story aquarium called **The Tube.** Running up through it from the first to the second floor is a spiral staircase, so as you

Sheraton Moana Surfrider

walk up you can see the tropical fish, small sharks, and rays from all angles – a nice touch.

In a nondescript building along Kuhio Ave. is the **Lucoral Museum** (2414 Kuhio Ave., 808/922-5381, open weekdays 9 A.M.-5:30 P.M.), a showcase, gift shop, and factory of gemstones, minerals, pearls, and coral. Not your typical museum, this compact, almost claustrophobic, collection has an amazing display of large and small items. Some jewelry is for sale in the gift shop.

Delineating Waikiki from the rest of the city is the nearly two-mile-long **Ala Wai Canal.** Created in the 1920s to drain the swamps that filled this flat oceanfront land, it now channels runoff from the mountains to the sea. The banks of the canal are used extensively by walkers, joggers, and runners, particularly shortly after sunrise and again before sunset; many come here to sit, relax, and watch the parade of paddlers practice for outrigger canoe races. It's cheap entertainment for one of Hawaii's favorite sports. Anglers also use the canal, trying their luck near its mouth near the Ala Moana bridge.

Just across the canal from Waikiki proper is the new and impressive **Hawaii Convention Center.** Built to attract more convention business to the state, it's a combination of large and small meeting halls, exhibition rooms, and banquet facilities, with high-tech sound and light capabilities and instantaneous translation services. Appealing to the aesthetic side of anyone who takes the time to look inside are several waterfalls and pools, tall palm trees, numerous artworks, and a glass ceiling that brings the outside in. This building also has several million dollars worth of artwork on display, like the *Gift of Water* statue in the entrance and Jean Charlot frescos depicting scenes of ancient Hawaiian life.

WAIKIKI

◖ HONOLULU ZOO

The trumpeting of elephants and chatter of monkeys emanates from the jungle at the 42-acre Honolulu Zoo (151 Kapahulu Ave., 808/971-7171, www.honoluluzoo.org, open daily except Christmas and New Year's Day, 9 A.M.–4:30 P.M., $8 adults, $4 locals, $1 children 6–12 with an adult, children under five free, and $25 for an annual family pass). Other special programs at an additional cost include a tour with a zookeeper, a campout with breakfast and tour, a moonlight stroll through the zoo, and stargazing at the zoo with an astronomer. Special evening concerts featuring local artists happen every Wednesday 6–7 P.M. June–August. The gates reopen at 4:35 P.M. for the fre e evening show.

The zoo holds the expected animals from around the world: monkeys, giraffes, lions, big cats, a hippo, elephants, even a sun bear (what else in Hawaii?). The Honolulu Zoo had the only large snake in Hawaii—a male Burmese python named Monty—until his demise in 2005. (Only the zoo can legally import snakes, geckos, iguanas, and similar reptiles.) Many islanders love this exhibit because reptiles in Hawaii are so exotic! Just as exotic is the Komodo dragon exhibit. From Indonesia, Komodo dragons are the world's largest lizards, often measuring three meters long. But the zoo is much more than just a collection of animals. It is an up-close escapade through the "jungle" of Hawaii. Moreover, the zoo houses Hawaii's indigenous birdlife, which is fast disappearing from the wild: Hawaiian gallinules, coots, hawks, owls, and the *nene,* the state bird, which is doing well in captivity, with breeding pairs being sent to other zoos around the world. The zoo is also famous for its Manchurian cranes, extremely rare birds from East Asia, and for successfully mating the Galapagos turtle. The **Keiki Zoo,** much enlarged over the previous children's petting zoo area, has barnyard animals, small reptiles, and other kid-safe animals. Its tropical bird and African savanna sections are also sure to please. Before leaving, have a look at the Zootique shop, where you can pick up T-shirts, postcards, posters, stuffed animals, books, and other gift items. The parking lot ($0.25 an hour) on the Kapahulu Avenue side is for zoo-goers only.

◖ WAIKIKI AQUARIUM

The first Waikiki Aquarium (then called the Honolulu Aquarium) was built in 1904, its entranceway framed by a torii gate. Rebuilt and restocked in 1954, it took on its current focus as an outreach and educational facility in the 1970s. Located in Kapi'olani Park, the aquarium (2777 Kalakaua Ave., 808/923-9741, www.waquarium.org, open daily except Christmas Day, 9 A.M.–5 P.M., with entrance until 4:30 P.M., $9 adults, $6 seniors, $4 youths 13–17, $2 juniors 5–12) has undergone a facelift with a new entranceway, touch tanks, and an opening directly to the sea. An audio wand tour in English and Japanese, included in the price of admission, explains the exhibits. Walk from points in Waikiki, take TheBus no. 2, or use the Waikiki Trolley blue line.

Although more than 400 species of Hawaiian and South Pacific fish, flora, and mammals live in its sparkling waters, the aquarium is much more than just a big fish tank. The floor plan contains four galleries of differing themes, all related to marine communities of the Pacific. One exhibit shows fish found in waters from Polynesia to Australia. Tanks hold sharks, turtles, eels, rays, clams, a seahorse, and colorful coral displays. Another exhibit, perhaps the most amazing of all, contains live coral that seem more like extraterrestrial flowers than specimens from our own seas. Some are long strands of spaghetti with bulbous ends like lima beans, others are mutated roses, or tortured camellias, all moving, floating, and waving their iridescent purples, golds, and greens in a watery bouquet. An Edge of the Reef exhibit shows how the low coastal waters and immediate shoreline relate to sustain the very busy reef environment.

Watch the antics of the monk seals—shameless hams—from the side of their 85,000-gallon tank, which now has a "variegated coastline" of natural nooks and crannies patterned after sections of O'ahu's coast. Hawaiian monk seals are one of only two species of tropical seals on earth.

Endangered, only about 1,400 individuals still survive, and the performances are more of a detailed description of the seals' day-to-day life in their dwindling environment. The seals inhabiting the tank are all males because placing a breeding couple would almost certainly result in the birth of a pup. Marine biologists anguished over the decision and ultimately decided that seals raised in captivity and then released back into the natural environment might introduce a devastating disease to the native population. This was considered too great a danger to risk.

The aquarium contains a bookshop with a tremendous assortment of titles on sealife and the flora and fauna of Hawaii, plus great gifts and mementos. The University of Hawai'i, which has run the aquarium since 1919, offers seminars and field trips through the aquarium, everything from guided reef walks to mini-courses in marine biology; information is available at the aquarium. The Waikiki Aquarium is a special opportunity for fun and education that will be enjoyed by the entire family. Don't miss it!

MUSEUMS
◖ U.S. Army Museum of Hawaii
This museum, with the hulks of tanks standing guard, is one long corridor where you feel the strength of the super-thick reinforced walls of this once-active gun emplacement. U.S. Army Museum of Hawaii (808/955-9552, www.hiarmymuseumsoc.org, open Tues.–Sun. 10 A.M.–4:15 P.M., except Christmas and New Year's Day, free) is at Battery Randolph in Fort DeRussy, on the corner of Kalia and Saratoga Roads. Battery Randolph once housed two 14-inch coast artillery rifles meant to defend Honolulu and Pearl harbors. The architecture is typical of the Taft Period forts constructed 1907–1920. The battery is listed in the National Register of Historic Places. At the entrance is the Museum Store, dedicated to things military, from flying jackets to wall posters. Walk the halls to learn the military history of Hawaii traced as far back as Kamehameha I. Here are rifles, swords, and vintage photos of Camp McKinley, an early 1900s (1898–1907) military station in the shadow of Diamond Head.

A side room holds models of artillery used to defend Waikiki when Battery Randolph was an active installation. One room shows how the guns worked in a method called "disappearing guns." The gun would raise up and fire. The recoil of the gun would swing it back down and lock it in position. After it was reloaded, a 50-ton counterweight would pop it up ready to fire. The explosive sound would rattle the entire neighborhood, so they were seldom test-fired.

Exhibits show the fledgling days of Army aviation in Hawaii, when on July 13, 1913, 14 officers began a military flying school. There are beautiful models of military equipment, especially one of an old truck unit. Then comes the ominous exhibit of Rising Japan, with its headlong thrust into World War II. Hawaii, grossly overconfident, felt immune to attack because of the strong military presence. Photos from the 1930s and 1940s depict the carefree lifestyle of visiting celebrities like Babe Ruth and Shirley Temple, which ended abruptly on December 7, 1941, in the bombing of Pearl Harbor.

An entire room is dedicated to the Pearl Harbor attack and is filled with models of Japanese planes, aircraft carriers, and real helmets and goggles worn by the Zero pilots. Most interesting are the slice-of-life photos of Hawaii mobilized for war: defense workers, both men and women, sailors, soldiers, entertainers, and street scenes. Pamphlets from the time read, "Know Your Enemies," and there's a macabre photo of people gathered at a stadium to see a demonstration of the devastating effect of flamethrowers that would be employed upon the Japanese enemy. Bob Hope is here entertaining the troops, while a 442nd Regimental Battle Flag bears testament to the most decorated unit in American history, composed mostly of *nisei* Japanese from Hawaii. Then come photos and exhibits from the soul-wrenching conflicts in Korea and Vietnam.

A new exhibit is dedicated to General Eric Shinseki, an Asian-American and Hawaii's own four-star general and former chief of staff 1999–2003. Some of Gen. Shinseki's personal possessions are on display, and the story of his life may serve to promote others to achieve.

WAIKIKI

A gallery on the upper level tells of the heroics of Hawaiian soldiers who have been awarded the Congressional Medal of Honor and Distinguished Service Cross for combat valor, almost all posthumously. Go outside to the upper-level exhibit to see one of the old guns still pointing out to sea, which seems incongruous with sunbathers just below on the quiet and beautiful stretch of beach. On the upper deck are depth charges, torpedoes, and shells, along with a multimedia slide show. Your eyes will take a few minutes to refocus to the glorious sunshine of Waikiki after the cold gloom of the bunker. Perhaps our hearts and souls could refocus as well.

Bishop Museum at Kalia

An offshoot of the main Bishop Museum in Honolulu, the Waikiki branch of the Bishop Museum (open daily 10 A.M.–5 P.M., $7 general, $5 military, *kama'aina,* and Hilton Hawaiian Village guests, free for kids age 12 and under) is housed in the Kalia Tower of the Hilton Hawaiian Village Resort. Much smaller in size and more focused in concept, this museum still offers galleries dedicated to the music, craftsmanship, and beliefs of Hawaiians, navigation, the monarchy period, and historical Waikiki. As at the main museum, the items shown here are excellent examples and the displays are well done. In addition, various activities, such as *lau hala* weaving, *kapa* making, navigation techniques, games, and music and musical instruments, are scheduled throughout the day for the enjoyment of guests, and a stars and skies mini-planetarium program relates to the wisdom and beliefs of the ancient Hawaiians. In this location, the Bishop Museum is able to bring a glimpse of ancient Hawaii to the traveling public who do not have the time or the desire to have a look at the extensive collection of the main museum. Give it at least an hour.

King's Guard Museum

The free King's Guard Museum (131 Kai'ulani Ave., 808/944-6855, open daily 5:30–10 P.M.) at

Blue sky, sunshine, and gentle surf: a typical Waikiki scene set in front of the Royal Hawaiian Hotel, looking toward Diamond Head.

© ROBERT NILSEN

the King's Village shops displays artifacts of the King's Guard Drill Team, an organization that honors the original king's guards from the days of King Kalakaua. Displays include uniforms, flays, rifles, photographs, posters, and other items. Catch the 6:15 P.M. guard ceremony and lowering of the Hawaiian flag each evening.

Damien Museum

As you walk along Kalakaua Avenue, directly across from the Kuhio Beach section is St. Augustine Catholic Church. This modernistic building squashed between high-rises is worth a quick look. The interior, serene with the diffused light of stained glass, looks like a series of A-frames. The Damien Museum (130 Ohua Ave., 808/923-2690, open Mon.–Fri. 9 A.M.–3 P.M.) is housed in a separate building to the rear, displaying photos and other artifacts of Father Damien, the Belgian priest who humanely cared for the lepers of Kalaupapa, Moloka'i, until his own death from complications of leprosy. Although museum entrance is free, donations are gratefully accepted because they are the museum's only source of revenue.

◖ WAIKIKI BEACH

In the six miles of shoreline from Kahanamoku Beach fronting the Hilton Hawaiian Village at the west end of Waikiki to the section of Kahala Beach fronting the Kahala Hotel, there are at least a dozen choice spots for enjoying swimming or surf activities. The central Waikiki beaches are so close to each other that you can hardly tell where one ends and another begins. They are basically just names for different sections of one long strand of sand. All are generally gentle, but as you head toward Diamond Head the beaches get farther apart and have their own personalities. Sometimes they're rough customers, particularly during winter. As always, never take *moana* for granted, especially during periods of high surf. There are seven lifeguard stations in Waikiki, staffed daily 9 A.M.–5:30 P.M. year-round. Now that you've finally arrived at a Waikiki beach, the one thing left to do is kick back and R-E-L-A-X.

Waikiki Beach stretches for two miles, broken into separate areas. It's not news that this beach is crowded. Sometimes when looking at the rows of glistening bodies, it appears that if one person wants to tan her other side, everybody else has to roll over with her. Anyone looking for seclusion here is just being silly. Take heart—a big part of the fun is the other people.

Stands set up along Waikiki Beach fronting Kalakaua rent boogie boards, surfboards, aqua cycles, and snorkel gear. The prices are sometimes more than many shops offering the same—but think of the convenience. However, all offer decent prices for surfing lessons and rides in outrigger canoes, which get you two waves and about 20 minutes of fun. Find other outrigger canoe rides—you help paddle—in front of the big hotels. Try the Outrigger Waikiki. They're great fun and a bargain at $15 per person.

Kahanamoku Beach

This stretch of sand fronting the lagoon at the Hilton Hawaiian Village is named after Hawaii's most famous waterman, Duke Kahanamoku. Duke's extended family lived here, and the Kahanamoku boys learned to play in the water. The man-made beach and lagoon were completed in 1956, and the beach here is the widest of any section in Waikiki. The swimming is great inside the reef, and a concession stand offers surfboards, beach equipment, and catamaran cruises.

Fort DeRussy Beach

You pass through the right-of-way of Fort DeRussy military area, where you'll find restrooms, picnic facilities, volleyball courts, and food and beverage concessions. Lifeguard service is provided by military personnel—no duty is too rough for our fighting men and women! A controversy raged for years between the military and developers who coveted this valuable piece of land. The government has owned it since the early 20th century and has developed what once was wasteland into the last non-cement, non-high-rise piece of real estate left along Waikiki. And it's a beauty. Because the public has access to the beach and its landscaped lawns, and because Congress has voted that the lands cannot be sold, it'll remain under military jurisdiction.

Gray's Beach

This section's name comes from Gray's-by-the-Sea, a small inn once located here. The narrow white-sand beach lies in front of the House Without a Key restaurant at the Halekulani Hotel, which replaced Gray's. Approach this section via rights-of-way on either side of the hotel, or get to the beach from behind the U.S Army Museum. The sea is generally mild here and the swimming is always good, with shallow waters and a sandy bottom. Offshore is a good break called Threes, a favorite with surfers.

The next section is referred to as **Royal Moana Beach** because it lies between Waikiki's oldest man-made landmarks, the Royal Hawaiian and Moana Surfrider hotels. Access is unlimited off Kalakaua Avenue. The inshore waters here are also gentle, and the bottom is sandy and generally free from coral. Offshore are three popular surfing areas: Paradise, Populars, and Canoes. Many novices have learned to surf here because of the predictability of the waves, but with so many rookies in the water and beach activities going on all around, you have to remain alert for runaway boards and speeding outrigger canoes.

Prince Kuhio Beach and Beach Park

When people say Waikiki Beach, this is the section to which they're usually referring. Named for Prince Kuhio—a tireless worker for Hawaiian rights and the Hawaiian representative to the U.S. Congress in the years following the demise of the Hawaiian Kingdom—this county-maintained park fronts Kalakaua Avenue as far as Kapahulu Avenue and "the groin," a cement pierlike protuberance running out into the water. Here, you'll find surfing, canoeing, and generally safe year-round swimming along the gently sloping, sandy-bottomed shoreline. The Waikiki Beach Center is at the in-town end of this beach, where you'll find comfort stations, concession stands, lifeguards, and a police

substation. Be careful of the rough coral bottom at the Diamond Head end of Kuhio Beach. A long retaining wall called Slippery Wall fronts the beach and runs parallel to it, creating a semi-enclosed saltwater pool. Coated with slick seaweed, Slippery Wall definitely lives up to its name. Although local youngsters play on the wall, the footing is poor and many knees have been scraped and heads cracked after spills from this ill-advised play. The surf on the seaward side of the wall churns up the bottom and creates deep holes that come up unexpectedly, along with an occasional rip current. A statue of Duke Kahanamoku, Hawaii's most famous native son, stands prominently in this park. At the beach stage near the statue, a free presentation of torch-lighting, hula, and music is presented nightly just before sundown.

KAPI'OLANI REGIONAL PARK

In the shadow of Diamond Head is Kapi'olani Park, a quiet 140-acre oasis of greenery, just a coconut's roll away from the gray cement and flashing lights of central Waikiki. It has proved to be one of the best gifts ever received by the people of Honolulu. King Kalakaua donated this section of crown lands to them in 1877, requesting that it be named after his wife, Queen Kapi'olani. A statue of her now stands near the bandstand in the park. In times past, it was the site of horse and car races, polo matches, and Hawaii's unique *pa'u* riders, fashionable ladies in long, flowing skirts riding horses decked out with lei. The park was even the site of Camp McKinley, the U.S. Army headquarters in the islands 1898–1907.

The park remains a wonderful place for people to relax and exercise away from the hustle of Waikiki. The park is a mecca for jogging and exercise, with many groups and classes meeting here throughout the day. It also serves as the finish line for the yearly Honolulu Marathon, one of the most prestigious races in the world. Its **Waikiki Shell,** an open-air amphitheater, hosts many visiting musical groups, especially during Aloha Week. The Honolulu Symphony is a regular here, providing free concerts, especially on summer evenings. Nearby, the rebuilt **Kapi'olani Bandstand** hosts the Royal Hawaiian Band on Sunday afternoons at 2 P.M. and other concerts on Friday evenings at 5:30 P.M. The area around the bandstand has been landscaped, and a small lagoon once again graces its side, harkening back to the early days of the park when it had several such lagoons.

Also, under the shade of the trees toward Waikiki Beach, plenty of street entertainers, including clowns, acrobats, and jugglers, congregate daily to work out their routines to the beat of conga drums and other improvised music supplied by wandering musicians. Families and large groups come here to picnic, barbecue, and play softball. The park grounds are also home to the Honolulu Zoo, Waikiki Aquarium, and Natatorium War Memorial. Just in front of the zoo, by the big banyan, are hundreds and hundreds of pigeons, the "white phantoms of Waikiki." In the morning they are especially beautiful darting through the sunshine like white spirits. Also in front of the zoo is a statue of Mohandas Gandhi and a raised octagonal monument surrounded by a wrought iron fence that's dedicated to Hawaiian royalty once buried in the sands of Waikiki.

Although Kapi'olani Beach Park is only a short stroll down the beach from Waikiki central, it gets much less use. This is where local families and those in the know come to get away from the crowds, just a few beach-blanket lengths away. In the park and along the beach are restrooms, volleyball courts, picnic tables, lifeguard towers, and a concession stand. At water's edge near the aquarium is the **Waikiki Natatorium,** a saltwater swimming pool built in 1927 as a World War I memorial. This pool was allowed to decay over the years until it was closed in 1980. The main gate and outer walls have been refurbished, but work to do the same to the pool enclosure has not materialized. Be careful of the rocky areas to the front of its stone enclosure. The section of the beach between Kuhio Beach Park and the Natatorium is called **Queen's Surf Beach.** The swimming is generally good here, with the best part at the Waikiki end, where it's at its widest and the bottom is gently sloping sand. Within this section, an area called The Wall has been designated as

a special bodysurfing and boogie boarding area. Supposedly, board riders are restricted from this area, but if the surf is good they're guaranteed to break the rules. Experts can handle it, but novices, especially with runaway boards, are a hazard. Beyond the Natatorium is **Sans Souci Beach,** the quiet southern end. Many families with small children come to Sans Souci because it is so gentle, yet for another crowd it's called "dig me beach" by locals because of the bronzed bodies who come to strut.

The **Waikiki Marine Life Conservation District** occupies an area that stretches from the "groin" (a seawall at the end of Kapahulu Avenue) to the Natatorium, basically the Queen's Surf Beach area, and out 500 yards into the water. It's a fish management area, so fishing is not allowed, but other water sports can be enjoyed.

The Kapi'olani Park **Visitor Information Kiosk** is on the corner of Kapahulu and Kalakaua Avenues. The kiosk uses vintage photos to give a concise history of Kapi'olani Park. An overview map shows all the features of the park. Information is available here concerning events at the aquarium, zoo, Waikiki Shell, Kapi'olani Bandstand, and the Art at the Zoo Fence (a collection of island artists selling their creations along the fence at the Zoo). Across the street on the sand, at the end of Queen's Surf Beach near the Groin, free movies and music happen every Friday and Saturday evenings.

AROUND DIAMOND HEAD

There are a number of small and narrow, mostly secluded beaches around the perimeter of Diamond Head. Generally, these beaches are not easy to access and have limited or no parking. Most back against a seawall or steep cliff and are fringed by rock and coral, so not really good for sunbathing or swimming. The exception is **Kahala Beach,** which parallels Kahala Avenue from Black Point to the Kahala Hotel and can be reached by marked rights-of-way between the high fences of estates in the area. The protrusion of land known as Black Point is the western end of ritzy residential Kahala. This section is the Beverly Hills of Honolulu, where many

WAIKIKI

celebrities have homes. The swimming at Kahala Beach is not particularly good, but there are plenty of pockets of sand and protected areas. Local people come to fish, and the surfing can be good beyond the reef. The Kahala Hotel is at the eastern end of this beach. The swimming there is always safe and good because the hotel has dredged the area to make it deeper. Just before the Kahala Hotel, where Kapakahi Stream enters the sea, the county has constructed **Wai'alae Beach County Park.** This park is generally empty during the week but may be crowded on weekends. Split by the stream with a footbridge crossing, it's a small beach park with basic amenities in a beautiful location. Looking to the east, Koko Head gives the impression that there is an island off in the distance, but it's just the way O'ahu bends at this point.

For visitors, the best reason for coming this way is for the sights along Diamond Head Road. There are three parking areas along the road. At one of these is a memorial plaque dedicated to the famous American aviator Amelia Earhart. Lining these parking areas are unofficial gardens of grass and flowers, envisioned, planted, and maintained by a couple of surfing oldsters who wanted to replace the hardpan dirt that flanked the top of the cliff with something more visually pleasing that would also cut down on the dust. Below you is **Kuilei Cliffs Beach Park.** Diamond Head Lighthouse sits prominently along the shore here and a Coast Guard reservation is set just beyond. Kuilei Cliffs Beach Park lies below Diamond Head Road and you can walk down the cliff trails to the beaches below. Here are plenty of secluded pockets of sand for sunbathing but poor swimming. The surf is generally rough, and the area is frequented by surfers. Surfing breaks offshore are known as Diamond Head, Lighthouse, and Cliffs. When the winds are right, sailboarders also come. Offshore is hazardous with submerged rocks, and currents can be fierce. Whales can sometimes be spotted passing this point, and to add to the mystique, the area is considered a breeding ground for sharks. Most visitors just peer down at the surfers from Diamond Head Road.

Entertainment

Waikiki swings, beats, bumps, grinds, sways, laughs, and gets down. If Waikiki has to bear being called a carnival town, it might as well strut its stuff. Dancing, happy hours, cocktail shows, lounge acts, Polynesian extravaganzas, and the street scene provide an endless choice of entertainment. Small-name Hawaiian groups, soloists, pianists, and sultry singers featured in innumerable bars and restaurants woo you and keep you coming back. Big-name island entertainers and visiting international stars play the big rooms. Free entertainment includes hula shows, ukulele music, street musicians, and artists. For a good time, nowhere in Hawaii matches Waikiki. The Friday edition of both city newspapers contains a Calendar of Events section that lists events and activities throughout the area for the weekend and coming week. The free *Honolulu Weekly* also sports such a listing. Also see the *Honolulu* chapter above for other happenings around town.

Bars and Lounges

While there are many more venues than those listed below, this coverage will get you started for evening entertainment along the Waikiki strip.

Spinner's (2463 Kuhio Ave., 808/923-5538, open 11 A.M.–4 A.M.) is a relaxed, easygoing, good-time, neighborhood-type bar with an outside patio that advertises the coldest beer in town, sports televisions, darts, billiards, and karaoke.

In the center of the International Market Place, the open-air **Coconut Willy's Bar and Grill** (808/923-9454) offers live music nightly from about 5 P.M., with no minimum or cover, while it serves mostly burgers and sandwiches for under $9.

In business for nearly 30 years, the gay-friendly and alternative-lifestyle nightclub **Hula's Bar and Lei Stand** (134 Kapahulu Ave., 808/923-0669) operates on the second floor of the Waikiki Grand Hotel building. There's music and dance that everyone can get down to until early morning.

The kitchen at **Kelly O'Neil's** Irish pub and grill (311 Lewers St., 808/926-1777) produces large portions of dishes like fish and chips, corned beef and cabbage, cottage pies, as well as sandwiches and burgers. The kitchen is open until 10 P.M. and the bar stays open until 4 A.M. Happy hour runs 11 A.M.–8 P.M., and music of the unplugged variety starts at 9 P.M., so if the noise of the Moose McGillycuddy's across the street is too overwhelming, head to the shamrock for something more mellow. Kelly O'Neil's is a smokers' place, so a layer of haze may hang in the room. Cigars are sold to smoke in-house.

For contemporary jazz or hip-hop in a happening place, visit the **Wonder Lounge** (808/922-3734, open Wed.–Thurs. 8 P.M.–midnight, Fri.–Sat. 10 P.M.–2 A.M.) of the Diamond Head Grill at the exclusive W Honolulu Hotel, at the far end of Kapiʻolani Park below Diamond Head. This has become one of the city's hot spots, particularly on Fridays and Saturdays for the younger and more affluent crowd.

Lu Lu's Waikiki Surf Club (2589 Kalakaua Ave., 808/926-5222, open 24 hours) has great views out over the Queen's Surf section of Waikiki Beach. The restaurant serves breakfast (starting at 2 A.M.), lunch, and dinner (until 11 P.M.) each day and *pu pu* for those desiring a lighter snack with their drinks. Call and request a seat along the outside open railing for the best scenery. Friday and Saturday brings DJ music until 4 A.M.

Many hotel cocktail bars and restaurants offer evening entertainment. One is the **Shore Bird Beach Bar** (808/922-2887) at the Outrigger Reef Hotel, where you can catch live local music 4:30 P.M.–1 A.M.

Duke's Canoe Club (808/922-2268) on the beach at the Outrigger Waikiki Hotel has a great lineup of well-known local talent playing every night of the week 4–6 P.M. and then 10 P.M.–midnight.

The **Paradise Lounge** at the Hilton Hawaiian Village presents the harmonies of Olomana, a well-appreciated old-time trio, Friday and Saturday evenings 8 P.M.–midnight. Also at the Hilton, the **Tapa Bar** and **Shell Bar** offer nightly entertainment 8–11 P.M., sometimes with hula accompaniment; no cover. On Friday night, the **Tropics Bar** becomes entertainment central, when you not only get Hawaiian entertainment at poolside, but also a ringside seat for fireworks over the water.

The **Banyan Court** at the Sheraton Moana Surfrider Hotel was the home of the famous *Hawaii Calls* radio show of years gone by. Now you don't have to dial in. Just walk down and sit under the banyan tree for the sweet sounds of contemporary Hawaiian music and hula every evening 5:30–10:30 P.M.

The Halekulani offers superb nightly entertainment. There is no lovelier location for a sunset cocktail than **House Without a Key,** where Aloha Serenaders, Hiram Olsen Trio, Poʻokela, or Paʻahana perform contemporary tunes nightly 5–8:30 P.M. Gracing the stage are two former Miss Hawaii beauty queens, Kanoe Miller and Debbie Nakanelua, who perform their inspired hula. Sunday brunch at the hotel's **Orchids Dining Room** is made even more genteel with the musical strains of harpist Carol Miyamoto, accompanied by flutist Aileen Kawakami, who perform the hit songs of Broadway musicals. Nightly 8:30 P.M.–midnight (or after) from the wood-paneled **Lewers Lounge** flows contemporary jazz selections with Noly Paʻa on piano, the duo of Jim Howard on keyboard and Bruce Hamada on bass and vocals, and Lenny Keyes on piano accompanied by Rocky Holmes on woodwinds.

Poolside at the Sheraton Waikiki you can find several Hawaiian music and dance groups performing on a rotating schedule. Visit the Hanohano Room's Cobalt Lounge on the 30th floor of the Sheraton for dancing to jazz and top 40 music 8:30–11:30 P.M. nightly.

FREE OR LOW-COST ENTERTAINMENT IN WAIKIKI

Although other types of entertainment come and go, the listing below gives you a fairly good idea of many of the longstanding free entertainment opportunities in Waikiki.

Every evening at King's Village behind the Hyatt Regency, a **Changing-of-the-Guard** show (www.kings-village.com/kingsguard .html) is performed at 6:15 P.M. The King's Guards wear uniforms from the period of the monarchy to give you a peek into one of the rituals of royal ceremony.

The **Royal Hawaiian Band** (www.royal hawaiianband.com) plays free concerts on Sunday afternoons at 2 P.M. at the bandstand in Kapi'olani Park, often with singers and hula dancers, and again on Friday at noon at the 'Iolani Palace in downtown Honolulu. Formed in 1836, the band plays mostly classical music and Hawaiian traditional tunes.

The Royal Hawaiian Shopping Center (808/922-2299) provides free **craft demonstrations and lessons** at various times throughout the week, including quilting, hula, lei-making, and ukulele instruction. Free hula shows and musical entertainment are sched-uled daily at the new Royal Court in the center of the complex.

A free **hula show and fireworks** are performed every Friday around sundown at the super pool at the Hilton Hawaiian Village. Other music and dance performances follow a torch-lighting ceremony on other days of the week. Anyone can come and stand for the show, but if you occupy a seat you must purchase at least one drink. On Saturday, performers from the Polynesian Cultural Center put on a free show 6–6:45 P.M.

Also staging a free hula show, albeit in a more mundane setting, is the Waikiki Town Center at the International Market Place. Come to the second floor of the shopping mall Monday, Wednesday, and Thursday 8:30–9:15 P.M. for the fun. Most other days of the week, musical groups perform in the market 7–9 P.M.

A slice of old Hawaii comes to life every evening for an hour starting at 6 P.M. (6:30 P.M. during winter months) at the Kuhio Beach Park. **Kuhio Beach Torchlighting and Hula Show,** complete with Hawaiian music

Across the road at the **Sheraton Princess Kaiulani Hotel,** there is poolside musical entertainment nightly 6:15–11:30 P.M. The stage location is such that music wafts across the pool and into the hotel lobby.

Every evening at the outdoor **Moana Terrace** bar and grill on the third floor of the Waikiki Beach Marriott there are great Hawaiian entertainers like Auntie Genoa Keawe, George Kua, and Martin Pahinui. Music usually starts at 6 P.M. and runs to about 9 P.M.

For light live jazz, head for the gentle ambience of the **Veranda Lounge** at the Kahala Hotel, where vocalists hold court nightly 7:30–10 or 11 P.M.

Dancing and Nightclubs

Waikiki has a number of discos, dance clubs, and live music nightclubs. Most have videos, a theme, a dress code of alohawear and shoes (no sandals), and start hopping around 10 P.M. with the energy cut off around 4 A.M.

Nick's Fishmarket restaurant (2070 Kalakaua Ave., 808/955-6333), ground floor oceanside at the Waikiki Gateway Hotel, swings with contemporary dance music every Saturday 10 P.M.–2 A.M. Expect a mixed but mostly mature crowd who have stayed on to dance after a magnificent meal, which Nick's is known for.

Everyone trumpets the mating call at **Moose McGillycuddy's Pub and Cafe** (310 Lewers St., 808/923-0751), especially every Wednesday, which is Ladies' Night, and Sunday, when there's a bikini contest, but really every night there's a party. The Moose serves breakfast, lunch, and dinner (until 10 P.M.) in the downstairs restaurant; head upstairs for the music and dancing. The nightclub rocks 7:30 P.M.–4 A.M. every night, with live music until about and authentic hula performed by various *halau*, is offered free to the public. Head for the beach stage near the Duke Kahanamoku statue and you'll be in the right spot. You might want to bring your beach mats for this casual show.

Sunset on the Beach is an event of sunset, music, and movies, Friday and Saturday at the Queen's Surf Beach section of Waikiki near the Groin. Starting around 4 P.M. music is performed free by some of the island's known bands while food stalls dispense quick, easy, and inexpensive eats for dinner. Once the sun goes down, a free family-oriented movie is shown on a 30-foot screen. Bring your appetite and something to sit on.

The **Urasenke Teahouse** (245 Saratoga Rd., 808/923-3059) is an authentic teahouse donated to Hawaii by the Urasenke Foundation of Kyoto, Japan, which lies along the Waikiki side of Fort DeRussy. Every Wednesday and Friday at 10 A.M. and 11 A.M., volunteer students and teachers perform the ancient aesthetic art of *chanoyu* (tea ceremony); make reservations a few days prior. A minimum donation of $3 is asked of those who want to watch the ceremony and partake of the frothy *matcha*, a grass-green tea made from the delicate tips of 400-year-old bushes, and the accompanying sweets. Comfortable long pants and socks are requested. To find delight and sanctuary in this centuries-old ritual among the clatter and noise of Waikiki offers a tiny glimpse into the often-puzzling duality of the Japanese soul.

A potpourri of contemporary **street entertainment** is also found in Kapi'olani Park on weekends. You might find musicians, jugglers, clowns, unicyclists, and acrobats putting on a free, impromptu circus just across from the zoo. Likewise, street musicians perform along Kalakaua and Kuhio Avenues at appropriate spots where large groups of people can stop, listen, drop bills into an open instrument case, or buy a CD.

Just for the thrill of it, ride the outside **glass elevators** of the Sheraton Waikiki, Ilikai, or Hawaii Prince hotels to see great sights. Daytime sights are good but the nighttime lights are even more spectacular.

1 A.M. To help get the evening started, half-price happy hour runs 4–8 P.M., and various specials on *pu pu* in the pub are always posted. This is a wild and zany place: good food, good fun, cheap drinks, and a young, energetic crowd. Try here to answer the call of the wild.

The **Esprit Nightclub** (808/922-4422) at the Sheraton Waikiki presents dance music by local bands Sunday, Wednesday, and Thursday 8:30 P.M.–midnight and Fri.–Sat. 9:30 P.M.–1:30 A.M. Come casual or dressed to the hilt. Good dance floor, $5 cover or $2 for hotel guests, one-drink minimum. It's the only nightclub in Waikiki that's right on the beach. Cocktails are served from 4 P.M.

Scruples Beach Club (2310 Kuhio Ave., 808/923-9530, open nightly 8 P.M.–4 A.M.), in the Waikiki Marketplace across from the end of Duke's Lane, is a disco that attracts dancers to its mostly Top 40 and live DJ music, with an older crowd usually before 11 P.M. and a younger crowd after 11 P.M. The cover charge is $5.

Near the corner of Kuhio and Walina, in the basement of the Ohana Waikiki West Hotel, is **Nashville Waikiki** (2330 Kuhio Ave., 808/926-7911, open 4 P.M.–4 A.M.), a country bar with inexpensive drinks, pool tables, and line dancing with instruction. It also plays classic rock and roll some nights. No cover.

The **Zanzabar** nightclub (2255 Kuhio Ave., 808/924-3939) in the Waikiki Trade Center is supposedly the largest nightclub in Waikiki. It may also be the fanciest. Dance to live music or DJ tunes of all types, from Latin to rock to hip-hop Tuesday 8 P.M.–4 A.M., Wed.–Sun. 9 P.M.–4 A.M.; $10 cover, 21 and older with 18 and older admission on some nights; there is a dress code.

Fashion 45 Nightclub (808/922-4599,

www.fashion45hawaii.com, open nightly 9 P.M.–4 A.M.) is on the 2nd floor of the Waikiki Trade Center. With three bars, two DJ stands, occasional live music, and ample dance floor, this contemporary-style nightclub is for the 21 and over crowd. Dress code required.

Dinner Shows

Although hotel concierge staff and various ticket agents around town can sell or arrange tickets to the following shows, each show has its own dedicated ticket booth at the establishment where it performs. It's best to check in the morning for ticket availability or several days in advance during summer and winter peak seasons.

The multimillion-dollar, 700-seat showroom at the Ohana Waikiki Beachcomber Hotel fills with magical vibrations when headliner John Hirokawa suddenly appears out of nowhere. The **Magic of Polynesia** (808/971-4321, www .magic-of-polynesia.com) is a journey into the realm of enchantment and beauty that the entire family can enjoy. Sleight of hand, disappearing maidens, decapitated heads, swaying hula dancers, fantastic costumes, and audience participation are all part of the magical extravaganza. A nightly show starts at 8 P.M., with an additional show at 5 P.M. during summer. Dinner seating runs $77–135 adults, $67–125 kids 4–11; cocktail seating runs $51 adults or $45 children.

Also playing at the Ohana Waikiki Beachcomber is **Blue Hawaii: The Show** (808/923-1245), a tribute to Elvis by impersonator Jonathon Von Brana. This show of music and dance is held nightly except Wednesday 6:15–7:40 P.M. Dinner and show runs $62–82, with seating at 4:45 P.M. If you want to come just for a cocktail and the show, it will set you back $36. Children's prices are about 30 percent less.

Society of Seven (808/922-6408), a well-established local cabaret ensemble, appears nightly except Monday at the Outrigger Waikiki's Main Showroom, performing musical tunes from the last 50 years, with plenty of humor and antics thrown in for good measure. In various permutations, this band has been performing locally since the late 1960s.

Show time is 8:30 P.M., and tickets run $39 adults or $33 kids if you only want drinks with your show, or $56 adult or $50 kids for the show with buffet dinner. Dinner starts at 7 P.M.

The 'Ainahau Showroom at the Sheraton Princess Ka'iulani Hotel presents **Creation: A Polynesian Odyssey** (808/931-4660), a story of the origins of man and the movement of the Polynesian peoples across the Pacific islands to Hawaii. Overall, this is a quick glimpse of the people who have made Hawaii home. Dramatically produced, with plenty of flash and flair, this show is an eyeful. One show nightly except Monday and Wednesday at 6 P.M. with dinner or cocktails (7 P.M. seating). Cocktail prices are $39 and the dinner fare runs $68–105, depending on your choice of food.

Cirque Hawaii (808/922-0017) performs its extravaganza of dance, comedy, contortion, and heart-stopping aerobatics in the former IMAX theater on Seaside across from the Waikiki Shopping Plaza. Two shows nightly except Wednesday at 6:30 P.M. and 8:30 P.M. run for $55–75 adults and $42–57 for kids ages 3–11.

Lu'au

The **Royal Lu'au** (808/931-7194), held every Monday 6–8:30 P.M. on the Ocean Lawn of the Royal Hawaiian Hotel, *is* the classic Hawaiian feast, complete with authentic foods, entertainment, and richly spiced with *aloha*. Authenticity is added by lawn seating on traditional *lau hala* mats (table seating is available, too) while the sun sets on Waikiki Beach and the stars dance over Diamond Head. Entertainment is an hour-long Polynesian extravaganza featuring Tahitian and traditional hula, a Samoan fire dance, and bold rhythmic drumming, and the buffet is a lavish feast of traditional favorites. You are presented with a fresh flower lei and welcomed at the open bar for mai tais and other tropical drinks. This lu'au is not cheap, priced at $97 adults and $53.50 for children ages 5–12.

The **South Pacific Cultural Center** (808/922-3705, www.southpacificcultural centerwaikiki.com) puts on a Polynesian

Show each evening at the Waikiki Shell Amphitheater in Kapiʻolani Park. This dinner show runs 6–8:30 P.M. and includes entertainment from the islands of Samoa, Tonga, Tahiti, Fiji, New Zealand, and Hawaii. The show and meal run $64–130 adults or $50–80 for children 3–12 years old, or the show and a cocktail drink (for adults) runs $48 and $35, respectively. In addition to the evening show, three-hour daytime craft fairs with brunch give you a glimpse of Hawaiian arts and crafts. The daytime events start at 8:30 A.M. and 11:30 A.M. and run $57 adults and $42 children.

Shopping

The biggest problem concerning shopping in Waikiki is to keep yourself from burning out over the endless array of shops and boutiques. Everywhere you look someone has something for sale, and with the preponderance of street stalls lining the boulevards, much of the merchandise comes out to greet you. The same rule applies to shopping as it does to everything in Waikiki—class next door to junk. Those traveling to the Neighbor Islands should seriously consider a shopping spree in Waikiki, which has the largest selection and most competitive prices in the islands. A great feature about shopping in Waikiki is that most shops are only a minute or two from the beach. This enables your sale-hound companion to hunt while you relax. There's no telling how much money your partner can save you! "Ingrate! This bathing suit could have cost $50, but I got it for $25. See, you saved $25 while you were lying here like a beached whale." Everyone concerned should easily be mollified. Charge!

Art in the Park

The best place to find an authentic Hawaii painting or photograph at a reasonable price is at The Fence, along the fence of the Honolulu Zoo fronting Kapiʻolani Park. Also referred to as Art at the Zoo Fence (www.artat thezoofence.com), the Fence gathers some of the island's best artists to display and sell their works on weekends 9 A.M.–4 P.M., as they have for decades. Established in 1953, the Fence was the good idea of Honolulu's former mayor, Frank Fasi, who decided that Oʻahu's rich resource of artists shouldn't go untapped. There are plenty of excellent artists whose works are sure to catch your fancy.

A newer event also happening on Saturdays and Sundays, 9 A.M.–4 P.M. across from the zoo in Kapiʻolani Park, is the **Waikiki Artfest.** This weekend gathering of local artists displays other types of artwork for sale, among them, jewelry, ceramics, clothing, stained glass, quilts, and woodcarvings, plus there is live local entertainment to enjoy as you shop.

Gifts, Souvenirs, and Sundries

ABC Stores scattered throughout Waikiki were founded by a local man, Sid Kosasa, who learned the retail business from his father. Jokingly referred to as the "**A**ll **B**locks **C**overed" store, this "everything store" sells groceries, sundries, and souvenirs. Prices are good, especially on specials like lotions and beach mats. The stores are very conveniently located just about everywhere in Waikiki. Although they are fewer and farther in between, **E-Z Discount Stores** offer the same basic selection.

Most people just can't leave the island without buying an aloha shirt or a muʻumuʻu. And why not? They *say* Hawaii. Dozens of shops in Waikiki handle these trademark items, but to get an idea of what's out there at a decent price, try **Touch of Aloha** (205 Lewers St., 808/922-1492). Alternately, search the numerous shops at the International Market Place. For something more classy (and more expensive), look to the upscale shops in the larger shopping malls or the boutiques at the luxury hotels along this strip.

For classic Hawaiian shirts, head for **Bailey's Antique and Aloha Shirts** (517 Kapahulu, 808/734-7628, open daily 10 A.M.–6 P.M.), where you will find thousands of the vintage "collectible garments" on display. The best are made from rayon manufactured before 1950. Prices range $100–2,000. Reproductions of these old wearable artworks are also available, as are clothing, jewelry, lamps, figurines, and the like. Although not technically in Waikiki, it's close enough to count.

For photo finishing and photo supplies, try **Ritz Camera** (808/922-4340) at the Sheraton Moana Surfrider or **Outrigger Kuhio Photo** (2330 Kuhio Ave., 808/923-5505).

Duty-free goods are always of interest to international visitors. You can find a duty-free store at **DFS Galleria Waikiki** (330 Royal Hawaiian Ave.), opposite the Bank of Hawaii—how convenient! If you want to see a swarm of Japanese visitors jostling for position in a buying frenzy, that's the spot.

Waikiki Shopping Centers

The largest credit card oasis in Waikiki is the **Royal Hawaiian Shopping Center** (808/922-0588, open daily 10 A.M.–10 P.M., www.shopwaikiki.com). This massive complex is four stories of nonstop shopping, running for three blocks in front of the Sheraton and Royal Hawaiian hotels. Reopened in 2007 after an extensive and costly redevelopment and reconstruction, this complex now provides an excellent mixture of intimate shops, large chain stores, international luxury boutiques, with an abundance of clothing and jewelry stores. A number of specialty shops include the Little Hawaiian Craft Shop, which carries an amazing array of high-quality, handmade gift items, most made by local craftspeople; Hilo Hattie, the quintessential store of Hawaii; and Hawaiian Heirloom Jewelry. Restaurants are located mostly on the ground and third levels. There is an information desk on the first level, about in the middle of the complex, and the Polynesian Cultural Center has a kiosk also on the ground level. Palm trees will once again be a

centerpiece at the new Royal Court, as they historically were on this site, and it is there that entertainment of all sorts will take place. A pay parking structure is attached to the center; turn on Royal Hawaiian Avenue and then turn immediately right into the garage.

Across Royal Hawaiian Avenue is the three-story **DFS Galleria Waikiki** (330 Royal Hawaiian Ave., 808/931-2655. www.dfsgalleria.com). This chic shopping plaza has little but luxury fashion shops and the third-floor duty-free shops. The ground floor is designed to give the impression of early-1900s plantation storefronts, all gathered around a banyan tree. A two-story aquarium sits at the corner of this building, and a staircase spirals up to the second floor through it.

West of the DFS Galleria has become a high-end shopping ghetto with Louis Vuitton and Prada a few steps away, Burberry across the street, and the **2100 Kalakaua** center with Tiffany, Coach, Yves St. Laurent, Chanel, Gucci, Tods, Bottege Venetto shops just up the road. If you've got plenty of dough to drop, you can feel comfortable heading this way; otherwise you may have trouble getting past the front door security guards. Down Kalakaua Avenue a bit farther, in the **King Kalakaua Plaza** are the more middle-of-the-road Nike and Banana Republic stores.

The **Hyatt Regency Shopping Center** (open daily 9 A.M.–11 P.M.) also called the Atrium Shops, is on the first three floors of the Hyatt Regency Hotel. The 60 or so shops are mighty classy: If you're after exclusive fashions or a quality memento, this is the place. There's a continental-style sidewalk café, backed by a cascading indoor waterfall. Various shops often put on free entertainment and fashion shows.

King's Village (www.kings-village.com, open 9 A.M.–11 P.M.) directly behind the Hyatt Regency, takes its theme from the late 1800s, with boardwalks passing 19th-century look-alike shops on two levels, complete with a changing-of-the-guard ceremony nightly at 6:15 P.M. Apparel and jewelry shops make up the bulk of the stores here, but there are gift shops and several restaurants, too. Around the walkways historical plaques briefly relate the reign of the Hawaiian kings and queens, and the King's Guard Museum is located in the back. Enter at Ka'iulani Street and Koa Avenue.

The **Rainbow Bazaar** (9 A.M.–10 P.M.) is a unique mall at the Hilton Hawaiian Village on the far western end of Waikiki. Fun just to walk around, the bazaar feature three main themes: Imperial Japan, Hong Kong Alley, and South Pacific Court. The shops here sell fashions, gifts, fine arts, jewelry, and sundries.

◀ International Market Place

The International Market Place (www .internationalmarketplacewaikiki.com, open daily 10 A.M.–10:30 P.M.) is an open-air shopping bazaar that feels a bit like a slice of Asia. Its natural canopy is a huge banyan, and the entire complex is tucked between the Beachcomber and Princess Ka'iulani hotels. This warren of shops has some fine merchandise, a treasure or two, and lots of great junk! If you're

after souvenirs like bamboo products, shellwork, hats, mats, lotions, alohawear, jewelry, and carvings, you can't do better than the International Market Place. When you get hungry from all the looking around, head to the food court in the back on the Duke's Lane side. The worst thing is that everything starts to look the same; the best is that the vendors will bargain. Make offers and try hard to work your way through the gauntlet of shops without getting scalped. In 2006, there was some controversy over the future of this marketplace, as the owners wanted to tear it down and build a modern new structure for shops. There was a great outcry from vendors, residents, and Waikiki businesspeople alike who were keen on retaining the feeling of the place. Only time will tell what changes might finally be in store for this prime location.

In **Duke's Lane,** a shortcut between Kuhio and Kalakaua Avenues, you'll find a row of open-air stalls selling mostly jewelry and knickknacks.

Recreation

At Waikiki, it's mostly about water activities. For other types of recreation, you must venture to other parts of the island.

Surfing

Several enterprises in Waikiki offer beach services. These concessions are often affiliated with hotels, and almost all hotel activities desks can arrange surfing lessons for you. A lesson and board will run about $45 per hour, half that for the board alone. Most guarantee that they will get you standing, and as in skiing, a good lesson to start you off is well worth the time and money. Some reputable surfing lessons along Waikiki are provided by Outrigger Hotel and Hilton Hawaiian Village. Also check near the huge rack of surfboards along Kalakaua Avenue, just near Kuhio Beach at the Waikiki Beach Center, where you'll find beach boy enterprises at more competitive rates.

Surfing schools usually charge a bit more for their services, but you get great instruction and a wide range of options. In Waikiki, try **Hans Hedemann Surf School** (808/924-7778, www.hhsurf.com) for instructions and lessons; it costs $75 per person for a group lesson of up to four people, $125 for a semiprivate lesson for two individuals, or $150 for a private lesson. Hedemann has shops at the Outrigger Reef Hotel, Sheraton Waikiki, New Otani Kaimana Beach Hotel, and Park Shore Hotel in Waikiki, at the Kahala Hotel, and also gives lessons at the Turtle Bay Resort on the North Shore.

Hawaiian Fire Surf School (808/737-3473 or 888/955-7873, www.hawaiianfire.com), run by off-duty city firefighters, offers two lessons each day, using a beach along the southwest coast of the island. Two-hour lessons are $97 for up to three persons and $139 for an adult private lesson. Transportation to and from Waikiki is included.

Loco Boyz (744 Kapahulu Ave., 808/739-5588, www.locoboyzsurf.com) also offers surf instruction, lunch, and transportation for $79 group, $100 semi-private, or $140 private lessons at a location close to Waikiki.

Kayak

Go Bananas Kayaks (799 Kapahulu Ave., 808/737-9514, www.gobananaskayaks.com, open 9 A.M.–7 P.M.) is way into kayaks. Single-person kayaks run $30 per day, $42 for two-person kayaks, and $50 for a three-person kayak. All rentals include car racks, paddles, and all needed gear. Lessons are available upon request. In addition to renting kayaks, the store sells kayak and canoe gear and equipment. Although not in Waikiki, it's close—only a few minutes up Kapahulu Avenue from the zoo.

Sailing

For the pure thrill of running under the wind in the waters off Waikiki, have a sail with *Maitai* catamaran (808/922-5665 or 800/462-7975, www.leahi.com). Ninety-minute sail and snorkel trips leave several times per day for $45 per adult and $27 for kids, while the sunset cocktail cruise goes for $34 adults and $17 for kids. These cruises leave from the beach between the Sheraton Waikiki and Halekulani hotels and cruise the waters off Waikiki.

The **Outrigger Catamaran** (808/922-2210) sets sail right from Waikiki Beach in front of the Outrigger Reef on numerous daily sailings. The early morning snorkel-sail runs on Tuesday, Thursday, and Saturday, 8–10:30 A.M. for $42 per person. When the wind picks up a bit, the cat goes for as fast a sail as it can several times from late morning to mid-afternoon for $30 per person. Come sunset, the catamaran heads out again for a sunset sail at 5 P.M. for $35 per person. The sights are great off Waikiki and this experience couldn't be more convenient.

Leaving from in front of the Outrigger

Waikiki, the *Kepoikai II* makes four daily, one-hour catamaran rides for $15, plus a sunset trip. These are basic rides, but they get you out on the water for some breeze in your hair. Contact **Waikiki Beach Services,** which has a booth in front of the hotel.

Underwater Cruises

As beautiful as O'ahu is topside, it can be more exquisite below the waves. **Atlantis Submarines** (808/973-9811 or 800/548-6262, www.atlantisadventures.com, $84 adults, $42 children 12 and under and at least 36 inches high) trips depart daily every hour on the hour 9 A.M.–3 P.M. from the Hilton Hawaiian Village pier, where you board the Hilton Rainbow Catamaran, which ferries you to the waiting sub. Once aboard, you're given a few instructions and then it's "run silent, run deep, run excited" for about 45 minutes. The sub is amazingly comfortable. Seats are arranged so that everyone gets a prime view through the large windows, and the air is amazingly fresh. The larger futuristic sub measures 96 feet and carries 64 passengers; the smaller is 65 feet long and carries 48 passengers. Outfitted with video cameras, it allows passengers to view the undersea world in every direction and glide slowly by artificial reefs and wrecks of a ship and an airplane, while listening to explanations of the varied sealife through a multilanguage audio system. This one is the thrill of a lifetime.

Scuba

In Waikiki, try the following for scuba tours and instruction. **Waikiki Diving Center** (424 Nahua St., 808/922-2121, www.waikikidiving.com) does PADI and NAUI certification and beach and boat dives. Boat dives go mostly to the Koko Head area. Some of the prices are $99 for a two-tank boat or introductory dive, $115 for a wreck dive, and $350 for an open-water certification course. **South Seas Aquatics** (2155 Kalakaua Ave., Ste. 112, 808/922-0852, www.ssahawaii.com) calls itself a "discount dive shop." It provides competitive pricing for certification, tours, and rentals, with two-tank dives that run $90–100, including hotel pick-up; certification courses run $400. **Reef Trekkers** (808/943-0588 or 877/359-7333, www.reeftrekkers.com) has established a good reputation for scuba tours. Introductory dives run $120, two-tank dives for certified divers are $95, and night dives go for $105. Dive sites are picked according to ocean conditions and divers experience. An open water certification course runs $455. Hotel pick-up is included. **Aqua Zone** (808/923-3483 or 866/3483, www.aquazone.net) offers tours and instruction for both beginners and advanced divers. Find them at the Outrigger Waikiki on the Beach Hotel and at the Waikiki Beach Marriott Hotel. Both beach and boat dives are given and prices are competitive.

Gear Rentals

Of the beachside sport rental shops, **Prime Time Sports (PTS)** (808/949-8952) is a good bet. At Fort DeRussy Beach in front of the Hale Koa Hotel, it rents all sorts of water equipment, beach chairs, and umbrellas, and gives surf and sailboarding lessons, all at reasonable prices. Sample fees are: surfboard, $10 per hour; surf lesson, $45 per hour; $20 per hour for a two-person kayak rental; snorkel gear, $12 all day; and aqua cycles, $20 per hour.

Waikiki Beach Services, located in front of the Outrigger Waikiki hotel, also rents some beach equipment. Some are surf boards at $15 for the first hour and $5 each hour after that, boogie boards at $7 for the first hour and $3 each hour after that, as well as beach chairs, umbrellas, and backrests.

Snorkel Bob's (700 Kapahulu Ave., 808/735-7944, open daily 8 A.M.–5 P.M., www.snorkelbob.com) operates on O'ahu, as it does on all the outer islands. Always a good deal, Snorkel Bob's may be a bit higher priced here than on the Neighbor Islands, but it has the same great gear. Depending on the quality, snorkel sets run from $3.50 per day to $29 per week. And if you're traveling to one of the other islands, you can drop your gear off at one of the shops there free. Find Snorkel Bob's at the corner of Kapahulu and Date Street, across

from the corner of the Ala Wai Golf Course, just outside of Waikiki proper.

Not all activities and sports rentals in Waikiki are done at the umbrella stands set up along Waikiki Beach. For a reputable shop, try **Blue Sky Rentals** (1920 Ala Moana Blvd., 808/947-0101, open daily 8 A.M.–5 P.M.), street level at the Inn on the Park Hotel. Here staff provide rental equipment and can arrange ground, air, and sea activities; cash only. Snorkeling gear or boogie boards are $12 per day. Introductory scuba dives can be arranged, as can deep-sea fishing trips, paragliding, and skydiving. Mountain bikes rent for $15 for four hours, $20 for eight hours, or $25 for a full day; mopeds run $30, $40, and $50 for the same time increments. See also **Coconut Cruisers** (305 Royal Hawaiian, 808/924-1644 or 800/536-4434) for bike rentals, $15 a day for a mountain bike or $30 a day for a road bike.

Other bike rental shops in Waikiki, including the motorcycle shops that also rent bikes, will set you on a mountain bike, cruiser, or a hybrid for about $10 for four hours for $20 for a day, sometimes with a $50 security deposit besides.

Walking and Wheeling Tours

The volunteer organization **Clean Air Team** (808/948-3299) hosts two hikes on Diamond Head on the first Saturday of each month, regardless of weather, leaving from near the Mohandas Gandhi statue at the front entrance of the Honolulu Zoo. The Diamond Head Story hike runs 9 A.M.–noon, and the Diamond Head Lighthouse Walk runs 1–4 P.M. There is no cost for these hikes, but donations are accepted to further programs of this nonsmoker's rights advocacy group.

Segway of Hawaii (808/941-3151, www.segwayofhawaii.com) runs tours on their two-wheel electric vehicles. Riders must be over 16 years old and weigh 100–280 pounds. Rides include a 2.5-hour Waikiki/Diamond Head tour for $125, and sightseeing glide rides to Ala Moana Park for $99–110. It's best to reserve a few days ahead. Find them at the Hilton Hawaiian Village.

WAIKIKI

Accommodations

Waikiki is loaded with places to stay. These come in all categories from deluxe to dingy, and there are many crossover accommodations that have amenities and services typical to both hotels and condos. Your problem won't be finding a place to stay, but choosing from the enormous selection. During peak season (Christmas to Easter and in summer) you'd better have reservations, or you could easily be left out in the *warm*. The good news is that, room for room, Waikiki is the cheapest place to stay in the state. Hotels along the beach are more expensive than their counterparts away from the water. The beachfront hotels have the surf at the doorstep, but those a block away have a little more peace and quiet. The following listings are not exhaustive—they couldn't be! Here are just some from all categories, which you can use as a barometer to measure what's available.

Military

If you are in the military, you can check out **Hale Koa Hotel** (2055 Kalia Rd., 808/955-0555 or 800/367-6027, fax 808/955-9670, information@halekoa.com, www.halekoa.com), the Fort DeRussy Armed Forces Recreational Center. On the beach at Fort DeRussy, this hotel is solely operated for active-duty U.S. military personnel, Department of Defense civilians, and a few other categories of former military and defense-related personnel. But anyone can walk in and have a look around. This well-run and well-maintained hotel has all the dining facilities, entertainment options, activity programs, and amenities of other large hotels in Waikiki. Depending on military rank or government status, there is an array of prices for the seven categories of rooms, all at rates ($77–198) well below the going rate for similar hotels in Waikiki—especially as it's right on the beach, and a wonderful section at that.

UNDER $50

Hosteling International Waikiki (2417 Prince Edward St., 808/926-8313, fax 808/ 922-3798, www.hostelsaloha.com) is located two streets behind the Hyatt Regency. A dorm room bunk here is $20 for members and $23 for nonmembers. Dorm rooms are sexually integrated, and you must be at least age 18 to stay unaccompanied by an adult. Couples can rent a studio for $48 members and $54 nonmembers. It's recommended that reservations be made at least two weeks in advance, particularly during peak season. There is a seven-day maximum stay. Credit cards can be used for reservations. The business office is open 7 A.M.–3 A.M., but there is no curfew as the hostel is open 24 hours. Baggage may be stored for $5 for the day after checkout if you have a late flight. There is limited parking for a minimal fee, and Internet access is for guests only. Key deposits will not be refunded if keys are not returned by 11 A.M., checkout time. Visitors are not allowed at any time, and neither alcohol nor smoking is permitted. Lockers—small, gym locker-types not big enough for a backpack but adequate for valuables—are available, but you must provide your own lock. The hostel gets visitors from around the world. It's clean and safe. The common area/TV lounge, kitchen, and bathrooms are shared by all. This is a very good choice for an economical place to stay in Waikiki.

The **Waikiki Beachside Hostel** (2556 Lemon Rd., 808/923-9566 or 866/478-3888, fax 808/923-7525, contact@waikikibeachside-hostel.com, www.waikikibeachsidehostel.com) is the largest hostel in town, so there is plenty going on here. It has eight-person, coed or female dorm rooms for $25 per person, with four-person dorms at $35–38, and $75–83 for a semiprivate room. There is a 30-day stay limit and you must have an out-of-state ID to check in. All rooms have full baths and kitchens with refrigerator, air-conditioning, TV, and daily maid service. On property there's a large outdoor lounge, pool table, laundry facilities, large storage lockers, and some parking. On the first floor is an Internet café. The Waikiki Beachside Hostel is a clean, well-furnished, and well-kept place.

Just down the road is the **Polynesian Hostel Beach Club** (2584 Lemon Rd., 808/922-1340, fax 808/262-2817, polynesian@hostelhawaii.com, www.hostelhawaii.com). Only one block from the beach, the Polynesian is in a converted condo-apartment building. A space in a shared room with shared bath runs $20–25, single/double rooms with in-room baths are $45–54, and a private studio with kitchen goes for $67–77. The hostel has a common room for reading and watching TV, free movies, a communal kitchen, laundry facilities, free use of some water equipment, and some hostel-sponsored activities. Internet connection is available. There are storage lockers for luggage if you want to go interisland, and small valuable lockers area also available. Somewhat rough around the edges, this conveniently located hostel is a good place to meet people from other countries.

The **Pacific Ohana Hostel** (2552 Lemon Rd., 808/921-8111 or 877/467-8350) was once a small apartment building, much like the other hostels along this road. Reasonably clean dorm rooms for up to four people, either coed or women-only, run $21 per person with a $25 key deposit, shared private rooms for one or two are $30–40, and private studios with kitchenettes run $50 per night. Weekly and monthly rates are an option. All rooms have air-conditioning. Other amenities include a community kitchen, coin laundry, vending machines, Internet access, and a big-screen TV in the lounge; there is staff on duty 24 hours a day, and a small parking area.

Seaside Hawaiian Hostel (419 Seaside Ave., 808/924-3303 or 866/924-3303, fax 808/923-2111, resinfo@seasidehawaiianhostel.com, www.seasidehawaiianhostel.com) is the most centrally located of the hostels in Waikiki, but farther from the beach. Relatively quiet and nestled under a banyan tree, this low-rise hostel is a home away from home for short-term foreign and domestic guests. There is a two-night minimum and seven-night maximum stay; identification and departure information are required. Women-only and coed bunk rooms run $27 per person May–Dec. or $23

through the winter, while semi-private rooms with a TV, mini-fridge, and shared bath go for around $40 per room. Some of the amenities include Internet access, in-room storage lockers, clean linens, a communal kitchen, continental breakfast, lounge, outdoor courtyard, coin laundry, and low-cost outings and activities. For check-in and check-out, the office is open 8 A.M.–noon and 4 P.M.–midnight, but there is no curfew and the clean, safe hostel is open 24 hours a day.

For additional listings of inexpensive hostels, YMCAs, and YWCAs, see *Accommodations* in the *Honolulu* chapter.

$50-100

When the hostels are full, try the **Waikiki Prince Hotel** (2431 Prince Edward St., 808/922-1544, fax 808/924-3712, info@waikikiprince.com, www.waikikiprince.com), next door to Hosteling International Waikiki. This little hotel of 30 units is about the cheapest in Waikiki at $50–65 per night for a standard room or $65–100 for a room with a kitchenette during low season—April–November. Weekly rates get you a seventh night free. While the rooms are quite small, everything is as neat as a pin. All rooms have air-conditioning and cable television, and there's a coin laundry and limited fee parking on premises. One of the best bargains in town, this is a quiet alternative to the noisier and busier hostels in the area.

The **Royal Grove Hotel** (151 Uluniu Ave., 808/923-7691, fax 808/922-7508, www.royalgrovehotel.com), built in 1951 and run by the Fong family since 1970, gives you a lot for your money. You can't miss its "paint-sale pink" exterior, but inside it's much more tasteful. Rooms with kitchenettes in the older wing run $46.50 for two guests; the newer upgraded wing of studios and one-bedroom apartments with kitchenettes and a/c run $64–80; $10 for an extra person. A tiny pool in the central courtyard offers some peace and quiet away from the street. The Royal Grove passes the basic tests of friendliness and cleanliness. It's used but not abused, and the price is right.

WAIKIKI

During low season, April 1–November 30, the Royal Grove offers reduced rates; weekly and monthly rates are possible except in January and February.

$100-150

◖ **The Breakers** (250 Beach Walk, 808/ 923-3181 or 800/426-0494, fax 808/923- 7174, breakers@aloha.net, www.breakers- hawaii.com) is a friendly, family-style, two- story hotel, where if you're a repeat visitor, the staff may remember your name—and they get plenty of repeat guests. Only minutes from the beach, this little gem of a hotel somehow keeps the hustle and bustle far away. Certainly, this is what staying at Waikiki was like before the high-rises blocked the sight of the beach from street level. Having done a superb job since 1954, The Breakers is tastefully decorated and well kept. Each of the 65 units has a complete kitchenette and overlooks the shaded courtyard of coconut and banana trees. In the garden is an ample swimming pool, and off to the side you can relax with a snack or light meal and tropical drink at the Cafe Terrace pool bar and lounge. Complimentary coffee is offered near the front desk all day. The rates for studios are $96–103 single or $99–105 double; garden suites run $130–171. For additional persons in any room, there is an additional $10 per- person fee. Studios hold up to three, suites five. All units have a/c, color TV, telephone, and a safe. There's limited parking at the back. The Breakers claims to be "Waikiki's most distinc- tive resort hotel" and it's right. It's a winner.

Next door is the **Hawaiiana Hotel** (260 Beach Walk, 808/923-3811 or 800/367-5122, fax 808/926-5728, www.hawaiianahotel.com), a low-rise cinderblock hotel with a distinctly local flavor. The Hawaiiana is a bit boxier than the Breakers but is painted in pleasing whites and light blues and presents a homey feeling. Two pools set off the nicely landscaped garden, onto which each of the fewer than 100 rooms in the six buildings has a view. All clean and comfy rooms have air-conditioning, a kitch- enette, and electronic safe; most have showers, but a few have baths. Complimentary morn- ing coffee and juice are served at poolside, and barbecue grills are set up for guest use. In addi- tion, the hotel offers limited parking and laun- dry facilities. Rates for rooms, single or double, run $105–215, with the one-bedroom units at $235. There's no glitz here, just good honest value and close proximity to the beach.

The minute you walk into the **ResortQuest Coconut Plaza Hotel** (450 Lewers St., 808/923-8828 or 877/997-6667, fax 808/923- 3473, www.rqcoconutplaza.com) with planta- tion decor in its lobby, you feel at home and comfortable. With the Ala Wai Canal to its side, the hotel is not in the midst of the ac- tion, but it's only a few blocks to dining and entertainment. Rates are $115–145 for hotel rooms and studios and up to $195 for suites. Bright and cheery, all rooms are air-condi- tioned and the studios and suites have kitch- enettes. There is a small pool off the lobby, where a complimentary continental breakfast is offered daily.

Aqua Hotels (866/406-2782, www.aqua resorts.com) is a relatively new accommoda- tion brand in Waikiki that specializes in small, chic, boutique hotels and economy class ho- tels. Its properties are renovated older hotels that have been brought up-to-date and given a spit-polish shine. Generally, the rooms are moderate to small, but all are well kept and seem to be of good value. Reservation for all can be made through the toll-free number or website. Aqua's economy hotels, called Aqua Lite Hotels, have rooms that generally run in the $100–180 range, but you can often find specials and discounts. The Aqua Lite hotels include **Aqua Continental** (2426 Kuhio Ave., 808/922-2232) and **Aqua Kuhio Village** (2463 Kuhio Ave., 808/791-7171), both located near the Aqua Bamboo hotel; **Aqua Hawaii Polo Inn** (1696 Al Moana Blvd., 808/949-0061) and **Aqua Marina** (1700 Ala Moana Blvd., 808/942-7722), neighbors across from the Hawaii Prince Waikiki hotel; **Aqua Island Colony** (445 Seaside Ave., 808/923-2345), overlooking the Ala Wai Canal; and **Ocean Tower Hotel** (129 Paoakalani Ave., 808/687- 7700), on the west end of Waikiki.

WAIKIKI

$150-200

Ohana Hotels (800/462-6262, www.ohana hotels.com) is a branch of the Outrigger Hotels and Resorts family of accommodations. Ohana has six properties in Waikiki offering more than 2,600 rooms. All fall into the economy to moderate categories. Although not luxurious, they do offer comfortable, family-friendly accommodations, and all have full baths, air-conditioning, TV, and entertainment centers. Four have kitchenettes, and some properties have recently been renovated. Several of the Ohana Hotels have restaurants, lounges with entertainment, shops, and swimming pools on property, and similar services. Except for the Ohana Beachcomber (see the *$200–250* section), rates start at $159–219, with all rooms no more expensive than $479. Additional adults in a room are $20 per night. These Ohana hotels are the well-situated **Ohana East** (150 Ka'iulani Ave., 808/922-5353, fax 808/926-4334); **Ohana Islander Waikiki** (270 Lewers, 808/923-7711, fax 808/924-5755), located at the entrance to the Waikiki Beach Walk redevelopment area; the largest with over 600 rooms is the **Ohana Waikiki West** (2330 Kuhio Ave., 808/922-5022, fax 808/924-6414); the **Ohana Waikiki Malia** (2211 Kuhio Ave., 808/923-7621, fax 808/921-4804); and the high-rise **Ohana Maile Sky Court** (2058 Kuhio Ave., 808/947-2828, fax 808/943-0504).

Of contemporary design is the **Waikiki Sand Villa Hotel** (2375 Ala Wai Blvd., 808/922-4744 or 800/247-1903, fax 808/923-2541, www.waikikisandvillahotel.com). Reasonably small, with just over 200 rooms, it has all the amenities of a big hotel, including a large pool, sundries shop, and on-site restaurant and bar. A complimentary breakfast is served daily. Housed in one tower and a three-story Mediterranean-style building to the rear, rooms run $140–185; the larger and more spacious rooms that overlook the pool are $245; and the upper-floor suites are $365. Prices run $10–15 less during spring and autumn.

A sister hotel, the **Waikiki Gateway Hotel** (2070 Kalakaua Ave., 808/955-3741 or 800/247-1903, fax 808/955-1313, www.waikikigateway.com) is across from the King Kalakaua statue near where Kalakaua and Kuhio Avenues meet. Somewhat trapezoidal in shape, this hotel is the home of Nick's Fishmarket (one of the town's best seafood dinner choices), a sundries shop, and small pool, and it serves a daily complimentary breakfast with a view up on one of the top floors. Generally, the bed arrangement is one double and one single in a room, but two doubles and three singles are also available. Room rates run $135–170, $180 for one of the few rooms with a kitchenette, and $80 for a single room; subtract about 10 percent during spring and autumn. The guest rooms and upper floor public spaces were renovated during 2006–2007.

Of newer design is the **Holiday Inn Waikiki** (1830 Ala Moana Blvd., 808/955-1111 or 888/992-4545, fax 808/947-1799, www.waikikihi.holiday-inn.com). The approximately 200 rooms here are clean, decent, and only steps away from the beach, restaurants, and shopping. They are reasonably priced at $140–180, with suites for $350, plus there are reduced rates at various times of the year according to availability. Although it's not chic, the Holiday Inn is comfortable, convenient, and predictable. It has its own swimming pool and small fitness center, and you always get good service.

With its off-the-strip location and magnificent views of Diamond Head, the **Queen Kapiolani Hotel** (150 Kapahulu Ave., 808/922-1941 or 800/367-2317, fax 808/922-2694, www.queenkapiolani.com) is one of the best and quietest hotels for the money in Waikiki. The spacious lobby is open and airy with the living mural of Diamond Head in the background. You're only seconds from the beach, but there is an outside swimming pool on the third floor, off which is the reasonably priced Garden Lanai restaurant. There's ample parking, coin laundry, an activities desk, and a sundries shop. Rates begin at $140 standard to $220 for an ocean view and run $235–250 for studios with kitchenettes. One-bedroom suites with kitchenettes run $325–500 per night and must be one of the best deals in town. Several packages with great discounts are available. Although it's not luxurious, the Queen Kapiolani has all you need for a comfortable and convenient vacation and is a good value.

One block behind the Queen Kapiolani is her sister property, the **Ocean Resort Hotel Waikiki** (175 Paoakalani Ave., 808/922-3861 or 800/367-2317, fax 808/922-3773, www.oceanresort.com). The Ocean Resort is as good a deal as the Queen, but it does not have as nice a location. Perhaps a bit more refined than the Queen, the Ocean Resort's two towers offer everything from standard rooms at $147–173, studios with kitchenettes for $193–230, and suites for $225–500, and there is an on-site restaurant and lounge, a gift shop, two swimming pools, and limited parking.

The **'Ilima Hotel** (445 Nohonani St., 808/923-1877 or 800/801-9366, fax 808/924-2617, www.ilima.com) overlooks the Ala Wai Canal and golf course, so it is away from the beach. This high-rise condo-style hotel has the friendly *aloha* spirit and maintains a quiet and safe environment. A small native Hawaiian garden welcomes all guests at the entry to the hotel. As soon as you enter you are greeted by bold paintings that depict scenes from Hawaiian mythology. From Christmas to Easter, studio units begin at a reasonable $167, one-bedroom suites at $243, two-bedroom suites at $344, with $10 each for extra persons. For families of up to eight, the three-bedroom, two-bath penthouse suite at $527 per night is an option. These rates are $30–80 less during low season, April–mid-December, and discounts are given for corporate, military, and government travelers, AARP seniors, and AAA members. All units are spacious, have full kitchens, a/c, TV, and maid service. For amenities, you'll find a small pool, exercise room, sauna, laundry facilities, a travel desk, and limited free parking. The staff even serenades guests in the lobby on Fridays at 11:30 A.M. At the 'Ilima you get all the necessities and plenty of space at a reasonable rate. A great choice and a favorite.

Directly across from the beach, the **ResortQuest Waikiki Circle Hotel** (2464 Ka-lakaua Ave., 808/923-1571 or 877/977-6667, fax 808/926-8024, www.rqwaikikicircle.com) has one of the best locations in Waikiki at a reasonable rate. An older landmark hotel that has been totally refurbished in a clean and cheery, whimsically modern mode, the building is built in the round so that many have at least a partial view of the ocean. With 14 guest floors, this hotel is dwarfed by its neighbors, but it makes it all the more intimate for its guests. Guest rooms run $175–205. Rooms and amenities include a/c, private lanai, cable TV, laundry facilities, on-premise restaurant, parking, and a tour desk. For its location, this moderate establishment is a bargain.

Upon arrival, step onto a path of white tile leading through a tiny but robust garden to a translucent dome sheltering the outdoor reception area of the **ResortQuest Waikiki Joy Hotel** (320 Lewers St., 808/923-2300 or 877/997-6667, fax 808/924-4010, www.rqwaikikijoy.com), a lotus flower that blooms in the heart of Waikiki. Immediately, marble steps rise to a veranda, where every morning a complimentary continental breakfast is served accompanied by the soft sounds of a tiny fountain. The hotel, with only 94 rooms, is divided into two towers: the Hibiscus and the Gardenia. It's intimate enough to make everyone feel like an honored guest. Typical hotel rooms, $170–190, and suites, $210–250, are amazingly spacious, and bigger yet are the executive one-bedroom suites with kitchen, $295. The hotel rooms all feature a refrigerator and writing desk. The suites in the Gardenia Tower feature a bedroom and attendant sitting area complete with couch and a large private lanai. Here, bathrooms feature a wonderful hot tub. The hotel restaurant is Cappuccino's, a European-style bistro. The Waikiki Joy, aptly named, is the epitome of the adage that "wonderful things come in small packages."

Renovated in 2001, the **Aqua Bamboo** (2425 Kuhio Ave., 808/922-7777 or 866/406-2782, fax 808/922-9473, www.aquabamboo.com) is a smart boutique hotel near the action. Thai-inspired, with decorative touches of bamboo, this older 12-story building has been transformed into a pleasing and intimate accommodation—and one easy on the budget. All rooms are air-conditioned, come with daily maid service, and have a lanai, color TV, and all comforts of a fine establishment; studios and suites have kitchens or kitchenettes. One thing you don't have, however, is a beach view, yet the pool area with its spa and surrounding tropical greenery make for a secluded spot to lounge. A continental breakfast is served daily, coffee is going all day in the lobby, you can enjoy a weekly hosted cocktail get-together, laundry facilities are on property, and daily newspapers are available. Parking is available but limited—reserve ahead. Room rates run $180–191 for a hotel room, $196–200 for a studio, $216–287 for one of the suites, and $627 for the penthouse if you're so inclined. Children under 18 stay free with parents using existing beds. For a small, charming, comfortable hotel, the Bamboo is hard to beat.

Aside from the Aqua Bamboo, others in the Aqua boutique listing, with nearly the same amenities, are the **Aqua Palms** (1850 Ala Moana Blvd., 808/946-7256), located near the Hilton Hawaiian Village; **Aqua Wave** (2299 Kuhio Ave., 808/922-1262), near the International Market Place; and **Aqua Aloha Surf** (444 Kanekapolei St., 808/923-0222), near the Ala Wai Canal. These hotels have chic contemporary or retro decor and so set the mood for a relaxing vacation. Room rates for these Aqua boutique hotels (866/406-2782, www.aquaresorts.com) generally fall into the $160–310 range.

$200-250

At the far eastern end of the bay next to Kapi'olani Park and just below Diamond Head is a small group of hotels and condos, amid a handful of apartments and single-family homes. One landmark of this area is the refurbished, small and intimate **The New Otani Kaimana Beach Hotel** (2863 Kalakaua Ave., 808/923-1555 or 800/356-8264, fax 808/922-9404, www.kaimana.com). Built in 1964, it has the look of that era but has been totally brought up to date. The New Otani has all the amenities and niceties that you'd expect from

such a hotel, but a big plus is that it sits on the quiet Sans Souci Beach with no building between it and the view of central Waikiki down the shore. On property are two fine restaurants, Hau Tree Lanai and Miyako, plus the Sunset Lanai bar, a travel desk, sundries shop, laundry facilities, fitness center, and off-street parking. Depending on direction of view, rooms run $150–345 and suites are $220–1,095, slightly more from Christmas through mid-March; $30 per additional person. If you're looking for a quiet hotel on a superb spot, yet want to be near the heart of Waikiki for easy access, the New Otani Kaimana Hotel is a great choice.

A few steps away is the **Diamond Head Beach Hotel** (2947 Kalakaua Ave., 808/922-1928 or 800/535-0085, fax 808/924-8980, www.marcresorts.com). Small and slender in stature, this Marc Resort property rises up at a slight angle, making the top floors narrower than the bottom floors. Tucked between tall apartments, most rooms offer little horizon view, except for those at the ocean end of the building. This hotel is a great find on the quiet end of Waikiki and good value for your outlay. Each room is privately owned, but all have full and modern conveniences and amenities. Studio rooms have kitchenettes and suites have full kitchens. Rates run $220–240 for rooms and $360–480 for one-bedroom suites. For those with vehicles, there is limited secure parking.

Sometimes you just hit it lucky and get much more for your money than you expected, and delightfully so. The **Ohana Waikiki Beachcomber** (2300 Kalakaua Ave., 808/922-4646 or 800/462-6262, fax 808/923-4889, www.ohanawaikikibeachcomber.com) is definitely one of those values. The Beachcomber is right in the heart of town—you couldn't be more central. The Beachcomber, living up to its name, is just a minute from the beach, and the professional and amiable staff know exactly what you want and how to deliver it. The 500 guest rooms all feature a private lanai, a/c, TV, phone, room safe, and convenient refrigerator. The Hibiscus Cafe, a casual restaurant on the second floor, serves meals all day, from a light breakfast starter to an international evening

WAIKIKI

entrée. On the property are a swimming pool, boutique shops, covered parking, and laundry facilities. Offered throughout summer, the Beachcomber Kids program can entertain and feed children over five years old while their parents are off doing other activities. To add to its image as an entertainment center, the Beachcomber also presents both the "Magic of Polynesia Show," a nightly illusionist spectacular, in its 700-seat showroom, and "Blue Hawaii: The Show," an Elvis impersonation and musical revue. The rates for guest rooms range $269–329, while the sumptuous suites run $459 and $700. There is a $30 charge for an additional adult, and children 17 and under stay free in their parents' room. Various bargain rates help keep down the costs. To stay within budget while having a quality experience, the Beachcomber is a sure bet!

Just off Lewers Street is the modern but casual **Waikiki Parc Hotel** (2233 Helumoa Rd., 808/921-7272 or 800/422-0450, fax 808/923-1336, www.waikikiparc.com), where the beach is just a stroll away. The entranceway is done in marble, carpet, and soft lighting, and coolness seems to permeate the entire property. Subdued elegance is the mode here—the building and surroundings speak for themselves, particularly after the 2006 property refurbishment. Rooms are not spacious, yet eminently efficient, comfortable, and pleasing, some with lanai and others with balconies. On the oceanview side, you look down on the distinctive orchid pool at its sister property, the Halekulani, across the street. Depending on location in the building, rooms run $235–345 per night. Several special room packages are available to reduce costs. The hotel pool is on the eighth floor. While all of Waikiki offers a variety of food, on property is the new Nobu Waikiki restaurant, serving imaginative Japanese cuisine. A business center, fitness room, and hospitality room for early check-ins or late checkouts are additional amenities. Validated valet parking is standard. As a small property close to the beach, with elegant, contemporary touches, this is a fine choice.

Across the road from her sister hotel, the Sheraton Moana Surfrider, is the **Sheraton**

Princess Ka'iulani Hotel (120 Ka'iulani Ave, 808/922-5811 or 800/782-9488, fax 808/931-4577, www.princess-kaiulani.com). With grace and grandeur, the Princess takes her place as one of the royalty of this strip, and this is immediately apparent as you enter the hotel lobby. Princess Ka'iulani was the last generation of Hawaiian royalty, but unfortunately she died in 1899 at the young age of 23, six years after the end of the monarchy. Portraits of her hang in the lobby of the hotel, and a statue has been placed in 'Ainahau Park, the small triangular park around the side and one block back from the hotel. Now over 50 years old but well kept, this hotel is built on what was her estate, 'Ainahau, and it's a big place with 1,150 rooms in three towers. Rooms run from $185 for a cityside room and $225 for a standard to $380 for a deluxe ocean view, with suites running upward from $625. Guest service helps with arranging activities and dining, older kids can be taken care of through the hotel's *keiki* program, and you can safely deposit your car in the hotel parking lot. When looking for food, you need not look far. The Princess Ka'iulani has the Momoyama Japanese restaurant, the open-air Pikake Terrace, known for its evening buffets and nightly Hawaiian entertainment—music wafts across the torchlight pool for the enjoyment of all—and the open-all-day Princess Food Court along Kalakaua Avenue. In addition, the Princess presents theatrical performances in its 'Ainahau showroom.

The small but sumptuous **ResortQuest Waikiki Beachside Hotel** (2452 Kalakaua Ave., 808/931-2100 or 877/997-6667, fax 808/931-2129, www.rqwaikikibeachside.com) is a boutique hotel with style and class, from the Italian Travertine marble floor covered with pink floral carpet to the hand-painted silk artwork hanging on the walls. Every little touch says classical elegance. Outside, a tiny courtyard is serenaded by a bubbling Italian fountain, perfect for complimentary breakfast of coffee and croissants, or the special weekend tea service. In the 12 floors above, 78 luxurious rooms await, ranging in price $200–405. Each tastefully decorated room comes with daily maid service, a mini-fridge, entertainment center, room safe, and free morning newspaper. To make your visit even more carefree, the concierge service will help with all your activities and travel plans. While not cheap, this is a gem.

Near the eastern end of the strip is the **ResortQuest Waikiki Beach Hotel** (2570 Kalakaua Ave., 808/922-2511 or 877/997-6667, fax 808/923-3656, www.rqwaikiki beachhotel.com). Remodeled in 2002 to the tune of $30 million, this 644-room, 25-floor property has been totally reconditioned and brought up to date with retro architectural features and hip Hawaiian decor. Each room has a contemporary island feel with bold, bright colors and furnishings, and while they're small, the bathrooms are finely done. Check-in is on the second floor, and across the pool deck is Tiki's Grill and Bar, a lively, casual place with indoor and outdoor seating that looks out over Kalakaua Avenue to the beach. More than just a casual eatery, as its name and decor seem to imply, Tiki's serves contemporary island favorites, offers a bar menu until midnight, and is the venue of soothing music every evening. Rising over the bar is a tapered hood with a flood of red light shining up the wall, mimicking a volcano. One of the special features of this hotel is its breakfast on the beach concept, where a continental breakfast is served each morning on the pool deck. This breakfast is a wide assortment of pastries, cereal, yogurt, fruit, and drinks, which you can have on one of the poolside chaise lounges, in your room, or load into the soft-sided cooler from your room and carry across the street to enjoy while you sit under a palm tree with your feet in the sand. This hotel has valet parking only and a string of street-level shops. Room rates are standard $260, partial ocean view $300, ocean view $350, oceanfront $410, and suites $450. An older establishment brought back to life as a fashionable, chic spot, the ResortQuest Waikiki Beach Hotel is a great choice for comfort and convenience.

Standing as one of the pillars of the eastern end of the strip is **Pacific Beach Hotel** (2490 Kalakaua Ave., 808/922-1233 or 800/367-6060, fax 808/922-0129, www.pacificbeachhotel.com). This two-tower, 837-room hotel has a perfect spot along the shore and is only on the edge of most of the busy shopping bustle. Rooms have full baths, lanai, a/c, complete entertainment centers, refrigerators, and coffeemakers. On property are a swimming pool, two tennis courts, a fitness center, a bevy of shops, laundry services, and valet or self parking. The concierge or tour desk will arrange activities for the family, and the kids' program is set up to take care of the younger set. For the convenience of guests, the Pacific Beach has three restaurants: the unique Oceanarium, which has a three-story aquarium wall; Neptune's Garden, where the focus is on seafood; and Shogun, for Japanese dining fine enough to win local acclaim. Room rates run $260–290 for standard and partial oceanview rooms, $340–390 for oceanview and oceanfront rooms; slightly higher from just before Christmas to the end of February. In addition, a handful of suites on the top floors of each tower run $700–2,200 per night and provide you the best of the best. For location, amenities, and ease of use, this fine hotel is hard to beat.

$250 AND UP
Outrigger Hotels
Outrigger Hotels and Resorts (www.outrigger .com) manages the most hotel and condo rooms in the state for any single owner-operator. Outrigger is an island-owned chain that has five high-end properties in Waikiki, six economy Ohana Hotel properties also in Waikiki (see the *$150–200* section), hotels and condos on the other three major islands, and properties throughout the South Pacific. Its flagship property and fanciest Waikiki hotel is the ⟨C⟩ **Outrigger Waikiki** (2335 Kalakaua Ave., 808/923-0711 or 800/688-7444, fax 808/921-9749, www.outriggerwaikiki.com, $359–639), which sits right on the beach next to the Royal Hawaiian Shopping Center, between the classic Royal Hawaiian Hotel and Sheraton Moana Surfrider. A few properties to the west and also on the beach is the **Outrigger Reef** (2169

WAIKIKI

© RI

WAIKIKI

Rainbow Tower at the Hilton Hawaiian Village

Kalia Rd., 808/923-3111 or 800/688-7444, fax 808/924-4957, www.outriggerreef.com, $269–599 for rooms, $529–2,100 for one-bedroom units), the company's number-two property in Waikiki, which received a complete renovation 2006–2007. Both Outrigger hotels have multiple restaurants on property, lounges, and in-house entertainment on a daily basis. In addition, the Outrigger Waikiki presents a popular entertainment show at its Main Showroom. Both properties have a pool, laundry facilities, shops, a travel desk, a/c, in-room refrigerators and safes, a kids' program, and all the amenities you'd expect from a quality establishment. Outrigger operates its own catamaran from the beach for snorkel tours and sunset sails. Outrigger can help you reduce your expenses with one of its many discount programs, like a free night with a minimum stay; room and car package; bed-and-breakfast package; and over 50, AAA, AARP, military, and corporate rates. Having been around for decades, the Outrigger gives good value and plenty of service and knows how to treat its guests right.

Hilton Hawaiian Village

This mammoth first-rate resort, a 22-acre oasis of tranquility, sits in its own quiet corner of Waikiki. You are greeted at the entrance by a larger-than-life sculpture of three Hawaiian hula dancers and a reflecting pond. The Hilton Hawaiian Village (2005 Kalia Rd., 808/949-4321 or 800/445-8667, fax 808/947-7898, www.hiltonhawaiianvillage.com) is at the far western end of Waikiki, lying between Fort DeRussy and Ala Wai Yacht Harbor. Enter along 200 yards of private hotel driveway, passing the Rainbow Bazaar mall with its exclusive shopping and dining. Facing you are the Hilton's six towers: the Tapa, Diamond Head, Lagoon, and Rainbow, the prestigious Ali'i Tower, and the newest, the Kalia. With more than 3,400 rooms, this resort complex is by far the largest in the state, having nearly twice as many rooms as its nearest rival. The huge multistoried rainbows on both sides of the Rainbow Tower are, according to the *Guinness Book of World Records,* the tallest ceramic-tile mosaics in the world. Created in 1968, these two murals have recently gone through a refurbishment to correct missing and defaced tiles. All rooms are deluxe and most have magnificent views. Amenities include color TV, a/c, self-service bar, refrigerator, 24-hour room service, voicemail, and a safe for personal belongings. The beachside Ali'i Tower pampers you even more with a private pool, turndown service, and concierge service. The Lagoon Tower overlooks the huge lagoon, while the others lie back from the water. The Kalia, newest of the bunch, has the business traveler in mind. It has several dedicated executive floors, a bridge connection to the Mid-Pacific Conference Center, its own set of shops, a restaurant, a branch of the Bishop Museum, the Mandara Spa and fitness center, and the Holistica Hawaii Health Center, a preventive health clinic. Room rates are $209–569 throughout the village, with suites up to $4,700. One- and two-bedroom condo units are available in the Lagoon Tower for $289–1,200.

The towers form a semicircle fronting the beach, creating about as private a public beach as you can get. Few come here unless they're staying at the Hilton. It's dotted with palms—tall royal palms for elegance, shorter palms for shade. The property has five pools. The main pool, surrounded by luxuriant tropical growth and called the super pool, is the largest in Waikiki. Torches of fire, and ginger, banana trees, palms, ferns, and rock gardens fill the grounds, where several dozen birds, including half a dozen penguins, make their home.

The action of Waikiki is out there, of course, just down the shore, but you don't feel it unless you want to. Relax and enjoy the sunset accompanied by contemporary Hawaiian music at any of the five bars and lounges. Exotic and gourmet dining from throughout the Pacific rim is available at the village's eight restaurants, especially the hotel's signature Bali by the Sea and Golden Dragon restaurants. Additional restaurants, like Benihana of Tokyo and Sergio's, are just across the driveway at the Rainbow Bazaar shopping mall, while more boutique shops can be found in each of the towers. Exclusively for kids 5–12, the Rainbow Express Keiki Club offers fun things to do each day of the week year-round. Reflecting the large-scale nature of this resort, a long list of free activities and entertainment is scheduled throughout the week. Of special note are the evening torch-lighting ceremony and the Friday sunset King's Jubilee entertainment of Polynesian music and dance that's accompanied by fireworks over the water. The hotel has everything to keep its villagers contented and happy. As a complete destination resort where you can play, relax, shop, dine, dance, and retreat, the Hilton Hawaiian Village knows what it's about and has found its center.

Hyatt Regency Waikiki
The Hyatt (2424 Kalakaua Ave., 808/923-1234 or 800/233-1234, fax 808/923-7839, www.waikiki.hyatt.com) is a hotel resort of grand proportions. Standing directly across from the beach, two geometrical towers rise up in symmetry to the warm tropical sun. Anchoring these modernistic pillars are three floors of shops and restaurants, a day spa, and meeting

and convention space. Imitating a jungle forest, the entrance atrium sports copious tropical greenery and a broad waterfall that spills into a refreshing pool. Up the stairs on the second level is the front desk. More than 1,200 rooms occupy this mini-city, and each is large and plush with the latest in adornments and amenities. Nothing is skimped on when it comes to guest comforts, and luxury is assured. Hotel room rates run roughly $300–600 per night. Special deals and packages are always available, but these may change throughout the year. As with many other Hyatt hotels, this one provides professional spa service. At Na Ho'ola, you can maintain your workout regimen at the fitness center or be pampered with massage, sauna, body work, or Hawaiian healing treatments of herbal preparations. Don't want to walk across the street to the beach? Then have a dip in the hotel pool or the hot tub. Four restaurants, serving everything from award-winning Chinese cuisine to standard American steaks, grace this hotel, and there is the customary lounge and bar for relaxation. Soft sounds of Hawaiian music waft through the hotel every evening from the lobby bar. With practiced efficiency, the Hyatt will provide a memorable stay.

Hawaii Prince Hotel Waikiki
The dynamic seascape of the tall masted ships anchored in the Ala Wai Yacht Harbor reflects in the shimmering pink-tinted glass towers of the Hawaii Prince Hotel Waikiki (100 Holomoana St., 808/956-1111 or 866/7746236, fax 808/946-0811, www.princeresortshawaii.com). The twin towers, Diamond Head and Ala Moana, are scaled by a glass elevator affording wide-angled vistas of the Honolulu skyline. Decorated in green and tan with light burnished maple, the rooms, all oceanview, feature a marble-topped desk with full mirror, a/c, functional windows, and a full entertainment center. Each room has its own refrigerator, walk-in closet with complimentary safe, and a king-size bed. The marble bathrooms have separate shower stalls, tubs, and commodes with a full set of toiletries. Room rates are from

$340 for an Oceanfront Marina to $485 for an Oceanfront Top (floors 30–33), while suites range $575–2,500; $60 per extra person. Special business rates are offered (ask when booking), and golf and other packages are available. Ride the elevator to the fifth floor, where you will find a keyhole-shaped pool and canvas shade umbrellas overlooking the harbor below. The business center gives you access to a secretary, computers, fax machines, modems, and a conference room. Other amenities include two excellent restaurants—the Prince Court and Hakone—a lobby lounge with evening music, a full fitness center, spa and massage service, valet parking, and a courtesy shuttle. The Hawaii Prince boasts its own golf course, an Arnold Palmer–designed 27-hole championship course, and two tennis courts, at the Hawaii Prince Golf Club, at 'Ewa Beach, 40 minutes away, the only one of its kind belonging to a Waikiki hotel. The Hawaii Prince, at the gateway to Waikiki, is away from the action of the frenetic Waikiki strip, but close enough to make it easily accessible.

Sheraton Waikiki

Dominating the center of Waikiki are the 30 floors and 1,823 rooms and suites of the Sheraton Waikiki (2255 Kalakaua Ave., 808/922-4422 or 888/488-3535, fax 808/923-8785, www.sheraton-waikiki.com). Built in 1971 as one of the area's first convention centers, it has a perfect location on the beach—and a long stretch of the beach. Recent refurbishment brings the spirit of the sea into the hotel; the *honu* (green sea turtle), which has come back from the brink of extinction and feeds in the evening in the waters of Waikiki, has been incorporated into the hotel logo. Rooms are basically either ocean view or city view, and all have full amenities, including air-conditioning, TV and movies, mini-refrigerators, and in-room safes. Rooms with views away from the water run $320–455. For an oceanview or oceanfront room, rates are $500–650. Suites start at $950. The hotel has two dozen shops for apparel, jewelry, gifts, and sundries; two freshwater swimming pools; a fitness center;

business center; and plenty of parking. On the dining and entertainment side, the Sheraton has the only Waikiki beachfront nightclub, two cocktail lounges, nightly poolside Hawaiian music entertainment, and three fine restaurants, including the Hanohano Room (its signature restaurant on the 30th floor), Yoshiya for Japanese specialties and sushi, and the more casual Ocean Terrace Restaurant, known for its buffets. Guests have signing privileges at the other Sheraton properties in Waikiki, all three of which are only minutes away. Water activities like sailing, surfing, snorkeling, and outrigger canoe and catamaran rides can all be arranged at the hotel beach center. Outside activities can be arranged through the activities desk, and guests who have early arrivals or late-night departures can use the lockers, showers, restrooms, and lounge in the Hospitality Center. The Keiki Aloha Club can keep your kids busy with age-appropriate, supervised activities, and baby-sitting services are also available. As the second largest resort complex in Hawaii, the Sheraton Waikiki offers something for everyone.

Sheraton Moana Surfrider

The **C Sheraton Moana Surfrider** (2365 Kalakaua Ave., 808/922-3111 or 888/488-3535, fax 808/923-0308, www.moana-surfrider.com) is the oldest and most venerable hotel in Waikiki. More than just recapturing early-1900s grandeur, the Moana has surpassed itself by integrating all of the modern conveniences. The original Italian Renaissance style is the main architectural theme, but like a fine opera, it joins a variety of themes that blend into a soul-satisfying finale. Later construction and restoration has connected the three main buildings—the Banyan, Tower, and Diamond wings—to form an elegant complex of luxury accommodations, gourmet dining, and distinctive shopping. The renovated Moana, filled with memories of times past, is magical. It's as if you stood spellbound before the portrait of a beautiful princess of long ago, when suddenly her radiant granddaughter, an exact image, dazzling in jewels and grace, walked into the room.

You arrive under the grand columns of a porte cochere, where you are greeted by doormen in crisp white uniforms and hostesses bearing lei and chilled pineapple juice. The lobby is a series of genteel parlor arrangements conducive to civilized relaxation. Art, urns, chandeliers, sofas, koa tables, flowers, vases, and glass-topped pedestal tables wait in attendance. An elevator takes you to the second floor, where a room filled with 100 years of memorabilia whispers names and dates of the Moana's grand past.

Upstairs, the rooms are simple elegance. Queen-size beds, rattan chairs, and fluffy pillows and bedspreads extend their waiting arms. All rooms have a/c, and the Banyan Wing features a remote-control master keyboard for TV, lights, and music. But this is the Moana! Bathrooms are tile and marble, appointed with huge towels and stocked with fine soaps, shampoos, creams, makeup mirrors, and a bathroom scale, which you can hide under the bed.

Being the first hotel built in Waikiki, it sits right on the beach with one of the best views of Diamond Head along the strip. A swimming pool with sundeck is staffed with attentive personnel, and the activities center can book you on a host of activities, including a classic outrigger canoe ride or a sunset sail on a catamaran. Two casual restaurants and a lounge take care of all your dining needs; the Banyan Veranda is known for its sumptuous Sunday Brunch, and you can take afternoon tea on the veranda. Many rooms overlook the central Banyan Court, scene of nightly entertainment that can be chamber music or soft Hawaiian tunes. Open the windows, allowing the breezes to billow the curtains while the waves of Waikiki join with the music below in a heavenly serenade. Rooms are $350–660, with suites priced from $1,100. The Sheraton Moana Surfrider is a superb hotel offering exemplary old-fashioned service. Whether you're a guest here or not, join one of the free guided tours of the hotel's restored and refurbished original section, offered Monday, Wednesday, and Friday at 11 A.M. and 5 P.M.

Royal Hawaiian Hotel

(**The Royal Hawaiian** (2259 Kalakaua Ave., 808/923-7311 or 888/488-3535, fax 808/931-7098, www.royal-hawaiian.com), the second oldest hotel along Waikiki, provides an ongoing contemporary experience in early-1900s charm. Affectionately known as the Pink Palace, this Spanish-Moorish–style hotel has been through a restoration, which has recaptured the grand elegance of the historic boat days. Its doors first opened in 1927, at a cost of $4 million, an unprecedented amount of money in those days for a hotel. The Depression brought a crushing reduction in Hawaiian tourism, bringing the yearly total down from 22,000 to less than 10,000 (today more visitors arrive in one day), and the Royal Hawaiian became a financial loss. During World War II, with Waikiki barbed-wired, the hotel was leased to the Navy as an R&R hotel for sailors from the Pacific Fleet. After the war, the hotel reverted to Matson Lines, the original owner, and reopened in 1947 after a $2 million renovation. Sheraton Hotels purchased the Royal in 1959, built the tall, curved Royal Tower Wing in 1969, sold the hotel in 1975, but continued to remain as operating manager.

When you visit the Royal Hawaiian, the most elegant lobby is not where you check in. Rather, follow the long hallway toward the sea. This becomes an open breezeway, with arches and columns in grand style. Here is the heart of the hotel, with Diamond Head framed in the distance. Although hemmed in by taller and larger buildings and its property shrunk in size to a mere 12 acres, the Royal Hawaiian still maintains a fabulous garden. Feel free to walk around and see what the grounds offer, but to make the best of it, pick up a copy of the hotel's *Self-guided Garden Walking Tour* brochure.

Original double doors featured one solid door backed by a louvered door so you could catch the ocean breezes and still have privacy. Today, the hotel is air-conditioned, so the old doors have been removed and new solid rosewood doors carved in the Philippines have replaced them. Rooms might have four-poster beds, canopies, twins, or kings. All rooms have

Royal Hawaiian Hotel

remote-control TV, refrigerators, electronic safes, and computer hookups on telephones for laptop computers. Furniture is French provincial, with bathrooms fully tiled. Completely renovated rooms in the original section have kept the famous pink motif but are slightly more pastel. They have a marble tile bathroom, a brass butler, and louvered drawers. The tall ceilings are even more elegant with molded plaster cornices. Guests are treated to banana bread on arrival, a daily newspaper on request, and turndown service. A Hospitality Suite is provided for early morning check-ins or late checkouts and offers complimentary shower facilities. The Royal Tower is preferred by many guests because every room has an ocean view and the bathrooms are generally larger. From the balcony of most, you look down onto the swimming pool, the beach, palm trees, and Diamond Head in the distance. Not as large as its neighbors, the Royal Hawaiian has 528 rooms, 35 of which are suites. A basic guest room is $420–725, with suites ranging upward from $900.

The main dining room at the Royal is the beachfront Surf Room, open all day every day, and perhaps best known for its Friday evening seafood buffet. Lighter food is also available at the Beach Club next to the pool. If you stay at the Royal Hawaiian, you can dine and sign at the Moana Surfrider, Sheraton Waikiki, or Princess Ka'iulani, all operated by Sheraton Hotels. One of the best features of the Royal, open to guests and nonguests, is the remarkable lu'au every Monday night. Drinks and entertainment are provided daily at the hotel's famous Mai Tai bar.

Halekulani

The Halekulani (2199 Kalia Rd., 808/923-2311 or 800/367-2343, fax 808/926-8004, www.halekulani.com) was an experiment of impeccable taste that paid off. Some years ago the hotel was completely rebuilt and refurnished with the belief that Waikiki could attract the luxury-class visitor, and that belief has proven accurate. Since opening, the hotel has gained international recognition and has been named as a member of the prestigious Leading Hotels of the World and Preferred Hotels and Resorts Worldwide. It is one of few AAA four-diamond award hotels in Hawaii. In addition, its signature restaurant, La Mer, has been given a five-diamond award rating, and the Orchids Dining Room has received a four-diamond award, making the Halekulani one of the best.

The soothing serenade of the Halekulani begins from the moment you enter the porte cochere, where an impressive floral display welcomes you. The property was first developed in 1907 by Robert Lewers as a residential grouping of bungalows, none of which survive. However, still preserved is the Main Building, dating from the 1930s when the hotel became a fashionable resort owned by Juliet and Clifford Kimball. The Main Building, a plantation-style mansion, houses the hotel's second-floor La Mer restaurant, along with the ground-floor Orchids Dining Room; Lewer's Lounge for an intimate cocktail and nightly entertainment; the genteel Living Room, where you can enjoy refreshments; and the Veranda, where afternoon tea is held. Notice the Main Building's distinctive "Dickey Roof," patterned after a Polynesian longhouse, perfectly sloped to catch island breezes while repelling a sudden rain squall. Wander the grounds to be pleasantly surprised that so much is given to open space, accented with trimmed lawn, reflecting pools, and bubbling fountains. The heated Orchid Pool, with its signature mosaic orchid, is always inviting and within earshot of the surf. Close by is House Without a Key, an indoor/outdoor buffet restaurant also serving light snacks and perhaps one of the best locales in all of Waikiki for a sunset cocktail.

Enter the guest room through a solid teak door into an antechamber that opens into the room, done in shades of white. Awaiting is a platter of fine china bearing a display of fresh fruit and complimentary "Bakeshop" chocolates. King-size beds require only a small portion of the rich Berber carpet–covered floors. For ultimate relaxation and added convenience, all rooms feature a writing desk, small couch,

reclining chair, and Oriental-style lamps, while bathrooms have separate soaking tubs and showers. Additional amenities include a remote-controlled entertainment center with DVD player, mini-fridge, three cordless telephones, and in-room safe. Sliding louvered doors lead to a private tiled lanai. Prices are $385–670 for guest rooms, $860–2,115 for suites, with the Vera Wang and Royal suites at prices available on request. A third-person charge is $125 for anyone over 18 years of age or $40 for a child if a rollaway bed is needed. Additional amenities include daily newspapers, free local telephone calls, a full-service fitness center, and the totally healthy SpaHalekulani. The Halekulani awaits to show you its version of classic island charm. You won't be disappointed.

Waikiki Beach Marriott Resort & Spa

The Waikiki Beach Marriott (2552 Kalakaua Ave., 808/922-6611 or 800/367-5370, fax 808/921-5255, www.marriottwaikiki.com) has a long history of treating guests like royalty. The hotel now stands on the original site of Queen Lili'uokalani's summer cottage. The grand tradition of the hotel is reflected in the open sweeping style, and after more than three decades, it appears extremely modern because its design was so visionary when it was built. The more than 1,300 rooms fall into many categories, but most range $289–459, with suites up from there. All rooms are oversize and include cable TV, a/c, nightly turndown service, and in-room safes. You can step across the street to mingle with the fun-seekers on Waikiki Beach, relax at one of the hotel's two pools, or work up a sweat at the fitness center. The hotel offers a host of exclusive shops in an off-lobby mall, and an on-site beauty shop and health spa can revitalize you after a hard day of having fun in the sun. For food and entertainment, try the family-style Kuhio Beach Grill, the Moana Terrace bar, the Japanese noodle shop Restaurant Run, or the Italian restaurant Arancino di Mare. The finest eateries on property, however, are the Sansei Seafood Restaurant and Sushi Bar and d.k Steak House. If you're after peace and quiet, head for the Garden Courtyard in the center of the hotel, where you can sit among flowers and full-grown coconut and bamboo trees. Periodically throughout the week, you can attend activities here to learn lei-making, hula, or even Hawaiian checkers from *kupuna* who come just to share their *aloha*. The Marriott is a first-class hotel that really knows how to make you feel like a visiting monarch. Rule with joy!

The Kahala Hotel & Resort

Long considered a standard-setter for Hawaiian deluxe hotels, the Kahala Hotel & Resort (5000 Kahala Ave., 808/739-8888 or 800/367-2525, www.kahalaresort.com) is not actually in Waikiki, but in Kahala, an exclusive residential area just east of Diamond Head. The hotel, built more than 30 years ago and refurbished in 1996–1997 to the tune of $80 million, is proud that many of its key employees have been there from the first days and that they have formed lasting friendships with guests who happily return year after year. Surrounded by the exclusive Wai'alae Country Club (not even hotel guests are welcome unless they are members), the hotel gives a true sense of peace and seclusion and rightly boasts a "Neighbor Island Experience" only minutes from bustling Waikiki.

Adjacent to the lobby is the indoor-outdoor Verandah lounge; lunch, tea and light foods are served here in the afternoon, and entertainment is scheduled every evening. Beyond the lounge and overlooking the garden and bay is the hotel's signature restaurant, Hoku's. One of many imaginative restaurants in town, Hoku's serves a grand combination of ethnic dishes encompassing the Pacific, East, and West from its open kitchen, and is open for dinner daily and Sunday brunch. Guests really into cooking should consider the Kahala Culinary Academy held at Hoku's every Saturday; reservations are required. The more informal and open-air Plumeria Beach Cafe offers à la carte and buffet choices every day from morning until evening. If that's not enough, Tokyo-Tokyo offers superb Japanese food each

evening, and the poolside Seaside Grill is a perfect spot for a light lunch and quiet afternoon or evening drink.

The Kahala Hotel has 345 rooms in two towers and low-rise bungalows set around a lagoon. Average rooms are extra large and have full entertainment centers with 27-inch televisions, bathrooms with his and hers sections, a wet bar, small refrigerators, and in-room safes. Rates are $395 for a courtyard-view room, $450 for a garden-view room, $515–575 for a mountain-view room, up to $685 for a lagoon or oceanview room, and $820 for a room on the water; add $140 for a third adult in any room. Suites run $1,400–4,600. Numerous promotions and packages are available.

The hotel, fronting the sheltered Maunalua Bay, features a perfect crescent beach, the most secluded of hotel beaches in the city. Also on property are a swimming pool and beach cabana with all water-sports gear available. Behind, a waterfall cascading from a free-form stone wall forms a rivulet that leads to a dolphin lagoon and a series of saltwater ponds teeming with reef fish. Various dolphin experiences are offered in and out of the water by an independent company, Dolphin Quest (www.dolphinquest.org). A Hawaiian cultural program offers classes free to guests, including lei-making, hula dance, or ukulele instruction. Other offerings are its arcade shops, scheduled shuttle service to Waikiki and major shopping malls, fitness and executive business centers, and the Kahala Kids club for those 5–12 years old. The Kahala Hotel is an AAA five-diamond award winner and pays excellent attention to detail and service. While not for everyone, there's no doubt you get all you pay for.

W Honolulu Hotel

The W Honolulu Hotel (2885 Kalakaua Ave., 808/922-1700 or 877/946-8357, fax 808/923-2249, www.whotels.com) lies below Diamond Head. Small and intimate, at the quiet end of Waikiki on Sans Souci Beach, this is a chic modern affair at the forefront of contemporary design and features, with a touch of Asia, yet the elegance is understated. Each spacious room has a superb view of Diamond Head or the ocean, and only the best of amenities and finest of service are allowed. The W Honolulu Hotel does cater to business travelers, although not exclusively. To satisfy your most discriminating tastes, the Diamond Head Grill, one of the city's most chic food purveyors and entertainment spots, is in the building. This hotel comprises only four dozen rooms, so each guest is treated with a familiarity that is not possible at a larger resort. Rooms are $465–570, with the two-bedroom penthouse suite at $3,700; $65 extra guest charge, no charge for kids under 18 using existing beds.

CONDOMINIUMS
$100-150

One company that manages many condominium and hotel properties around the state is **ResortQuest** (www.resortquesthawaii.com). Several of its Waikiki condominiums, from economy to luxury, are listed in the following sections.

You can capitalize on the off-beach location of the **Aston Honolulu Prince** (415 Nahua St., 808/922-1616 or 877/997-6667, fax 808/922-6223, www.honoluluprince.com), a ResortQuest property, where you'll find a modest hotel/condo offering remarkably good value for your money. This 10-floor, 119-room property invites you into its newly refurbished hotel rooms and one- and two-bedroom suites. All offer a/c, color cable TV, and daily maid service, while the suites have fully equipped kitchens. Prices begin at $110–130 for a standard room, $170 for a one-bedroom, and $200 for a two-bedroom unit. The apartments are oversized, with a huge sitting area that includes a sofa bed for extra guests. The Honolulu Prince is not fancy, but it is clean, decent, and family-oriented, and its location up from behind the International Market Place puts you in the center of Waikiki. A fine choice for an affordable price.

$150-200

You can't beat the value at the **ResortQuest**

Pacific Monarch (2427 Kuhio Ave., 808/923-9805 or 877/997-6667, fax 808/924-3220, www.rqpacificmonarch.com) condo resort directly behind the Hyatt Regency,. It offers some great features for a moderately priced property. Fully furnished studios are $180–200; one-bedroom condo apartments cost $230–260, all a/c, with on-site parking for a fee. The rooms are bright and cheery with full baths, living/dining areas, kitchens or kitchenettes, and cable TV. End units of each floor are larger, so request one for a large party. The swimming pool, with a relaxing hot tub, perches high over Waikiki on the 34th floor of the hotel, offering one of the best cityscapes in Honolulu. The lobby is sufficient but small. Save money and have a great family experience by setting up temporary housekeeping at the Pacific Monarch.

$200-250

Twinkling lights descending the residential valleys of the Ko'olau Range with Diamond Head framed in perfect symmetry are an integral part of the natural room decor of the **ResortQuest Waikiki Sunset** (229 Paoakalani St., 808/922-0511 or 877/997-6667, fax 808/923-8580, www.rqwaikikisunset.com). Although a condominium, the Waikiki Sunset offers all of the comfort and convenience of a hotel, including 24-hour front desk service, daily maid service, and amenities like a swimming pool, sauna, lighted tennis court, travel desk, and sundries shop. The entrance, cooled by Casablanca fans whirring over marble floors, sets the mood for this charming accommodation tucked away only one block from the Kuhio Avenue strip. One-bedroom units range $210–295, and two-bedroom units run $380–690, making this an appropriate size for families. All feature full kitchens for in-room cooking and dining. All suites feature a private lanai, an entertainment center with remote-control color TV, and a tiled bath with a soaking tub perfect for the start of a cozy evening.

Snuggled into a corner of Fort DeRussy is the **Outrigger Luana Waikiki** (2045 Kalakaua Ave.,

808/955-6000 or 800/348-8181, fax 808/943-8555, www.outriggerluanawaikiki.com) condominium hotel. This hotel looks out over the green space, with a nearly unobstructed view to the beach. While not on the water, it's just a short stroll away. There is a swimming pool at the hotel, a fitness center, and a sundries shop, but no restaurant, although the well-liked Kyo-Ya Japanese restaurant is next door. Each room is air-conditioned and has a lanai, color TV, and daily maid service. Studio suites (no kitchens) run $210–235, studios with kitchenettes are $240–265, while the one-bedroom suites with full kitchens are $325–375. You'll love the comfort and convenience of the Outrigger Luana Waikiki.

$250 and Up

A tunnel of white thunbergia tumbling from a welcoming arbor leads to the entrance of the **ResortQuest Waikiki Beach Tower** (2470 Kalakaua Ave., 808/926-6400 or 877/997-6667, fax 808/926-7380, www.rqwaikikibeachtower.com) one of Waikiki's newest luxury condos and the poshest of the ResortQuest properties. A lustrous patina shines from brown on tan marble floors; glass-topped tables of black and gold lacquer hold magnificent displays of exotic blooms; and fancy French mirrors and cut-glass chandeliers brighten the small but intimate reception area. Enter your suite through a vestibule onto a white carpet leading to a combination dining/living room, accented with contemporary paintings and koa trim. The modern kitchen has all amenities, the master bedroom has its own entertainment center and huge private lanai from which you can overlook Waikiki, and the full bathroom has a huge walk-in closet. Rates range $525–585 for one-bedroom suites, $610–775 for two-bedroom suites, with the addition of more opulent units up to $1,300. Special amenities include twice-daily maid service, concierge desk, valet parking, a swimming pool, jet spa, and sauna. For a condo, this one is right at the top, and you get all the extra amenities that make your stay a pleasure, plus you have the beach at your doorstep.

The only condominium right on the beach is the **Outrigger Waikiki Shore** (2161 Kalia Rd., 808/923-3111 or 800/688-7444, fax 808/924-4957, www.outriggerwaikikishore.com, $275–480), Outrigger's premier resort condominium in Waikiki. Newest to the Outrigger condo list is the **Outrigger Regency on Beach Walk** (255 Beach Walk, 808/923-9000 or 800/688-7444, $250–405), which opened in early 2007 as an upscale, chic accommodation in the heart of the redevelopment area.

Food

The streets of Waikiki are an international banquet, with more than a dozen cuisines spreading their tables for your enjoyment. Because of the culinary competition, you can choose restaurants in the same way that you peruse a smorgasbord, for both quantity and quality. Within a few hundred yards are all-you-can-gorge buffets, fast-food snack bars, gourmet restaurants, casual open-air eateries, ice cream shops, dinner shows, and a lu'au or two. The free tourist literature runs coupons, and placards advertise specials for breakfast, lunch, and dinner. Bars and lounges sometimes give free pu pu and finger foods that can easily make a light supper. As with everything in Waikiki, its restaurants are a close-quartered combination of the best and the worst, but with only a little effort it's easy to find great food, great atmosphere, and mouthwatering satisfaction.

Note: At many of the moderately priced restaurants listed and at all of the expensive restaurants *reservations are highly recommended.* Also, many of the restaurants along the congested Waikiki strip provide valet parking (usually at no charge) or will offer validated parking at a nearby lot. So check when you call to reserve. If you're staying in Waikiki, it's best to walk. Attire at most Hawaiian restaurants is casual, but at the better restaurants it's dressy casual, which means closed-toe shoes, trousers, and a collared shirt for men, and a simple but stylish dress for women. At some of the very best restaurants you won't feel out of place with a jacket, but ties are not usually worn.

Local Style

Eggs and Things (1911 Kalakaua Ave., 808/949-0820, open 11 P.M.–2 P.M. the following afternoon) is a late-night institution located just where Kalakaua Avenue meets McCully. The clientele in the wee hours is a mix of revelers, hotel workers, and boat captains; by breakfast time, it's mostly tourists. The decor is tile floors and Formica tables. The waitresses are top-notch and friendly, but they get slammed as it's such a popular place. The food is absolutely excellent, the portions are huge, and it's hard to spend more than $10. Daily specials are offered 1–2 A.M., while the morning special runs 5–9 A.M. Waffles and pancakes are scrumptious with fresh fruit or homemade coconut syrup. Besides the eggs, omelettes, and crepes, the most popular item is fresh fish, usually caught by the owner, who goes out almost every day on his own boat. Casual attire is the norm.

Natural Foods

Ruffage Natural Foods (2443 Kuhio Ave., 808/922-2042, open Mon.–Sat. 9 A.M.–6 P.M.) is one of a very few natural food restaurants in Waikiki. It serves a wide assortment of tofu sandwiches, burritos, natural salads, tofu burgers, fresh island fruits, and smoothies. Everything is homemade, and the restaurant tries to avoid processed foods as much as possible. Just about everything on the menu is less than $7. Food supplements, minerals, vitamins, and things of that nature are also available. It's a small hole-in-the-wall-type eatery around the corner from the Royal Grove Hotel that's easy to miss. A few wooden tables are available for eating outside under a portico.

Marie's Health Foods Organic Café (2155 Kalakaua Ave., 808/926-3900, open Mon.–Sat. 11 A.M.–8 P.M.) is an eat-in/takeout place along Beach Walk on the ground level in the ANA Kalakaua Center. An alternative to the big restaurants with full, heavy meals, here you can get health-conscious, organic salads, wraps, sandwiches, and lasagna for less than $11, as well as smoothies, coffee, and other drinks, while supplements and other health products are also for sale.

American

Perry's Smorgy (2380 Kuhio Ave., 808/926-0184) is the epitome of the budget traveler's "line 'em up, fill 'em up, and head 'em out" kind of restaurant. What you'll find is good ol' American food. There is no question that you'll waddle away stuffed, but forget about any kind of memorable dining experience. When you arrive, don't be put off by the long lines. They move! First, you run a gauntlet of salads, breads, and potatoes, in the hopes that you'll fill your plate. Try to restrain yourself, because then comes the meat, fish, and chicken. The breakfast buffet, 7–11 A.M., is actually very good at $6.95, with all the standard eggs, meats, juices, and rolls, and the food in general, considering the price, is more than acceptable. The lunch buffet, 11:30 A.M.–2:30 P.M., is priced equally well at $7.95, and the all-you-can-eat dinner, 5–9 P.M., is a bargain at $9.95, as is Sunday brunch, 11:30 A.M.–2:30 P.M.

Building on its success in Lahaina, Maui, as a fun-loving place with good eats and affordable prices, all in a location that gives great sunsets, with the added benefit of lively music in the evening, **Cheeseburger in Paradise** (2500 Kalakaua Ave., 808/923-3731) opened shop in Waikiki right across from the beach. A second restaurant is located across from Fort DeRussy (1945 Kalakaua Ave., 808/941-2400). Try an omelette, pancakes, or French toast to get you going in the morning. For the rest of the day, burgers (meat or meatless), sandwiches, salads, and fries will do. Lots of options, and lots of logo items, too. You won't have to try too hard to get out the door for under $10, while a few menu items range up to $15. Cheeseburger is a casual, open-air place that fits the breezy tropical setting perfectly, but everyone seems to like the ambience, so it can get busy. Expect a wait.

Chuck's Steak House began operation in 1959 and, while the original place has now closed due to the huge Waikiki Beach Walk renovation, Chuck's is still going strong in two other locations, so they're doing something right! **Chuck's Steak House** (808/923-1228, open 4:45–10 P.M.), which has a prime location on the second floor overlooking the water at the Outrigger Waikiki Hotel and **Chuck's Cellar** (808/923-4488, open 5:30–10 P.M.), on the basement level at the Ohana East Hotel, have the same basic menu and reputation. Chuck's has a fairly simple menu—steak, with the addition of some seafood items. There is nothing extraordinary here, just plain good food prepared in a straightforward manner. All meals come with potatoes or rice, salad bar or soup, and bread. Most entrées run $22–32, with the Cellar's prices a few bucks less, and each place has early-bird and nightly specials. You can't go wrong at Chuck's for a decent meal, and Chuck's Cellar has live music nightly to entertain diners.

The **Shore Bird Beach Broiler** (2169 Kalia Rd., 808/922-2887, open 7 A.M.–10 P.M.), open for breakfast buffet, a lunch lanai menu, and dinner, is on the beach at the Outrigger Reef Hotel, giving this restaurant one of the best gourmet locations in all of Waikiki. A walk through the lobby to the beach for a remarkable sunset takes you right past the restaurant, where you'll find a limited but adequate menu of "cook-your-own" selections for under $23. Included is a fresh salad bar of vegetables and fruits. Beverages are included, the setting is wonderful, and the value is excellent. Across the lobby, the Shore Bird Beach Bar serves a grill menu 11 A.M.–1 A.M. plus offers evening entertainment nightly until 1 A.M.

The **Oceanarium** (808/921-6111, open 6 A.M.–10 P.M.) at the Pacific Beach Hotel offers a full breakfast, lunch, and dinner menu. While limited à la carte menus are always available, buffets, like the daily breakfast buffet for

$15.50 and nightly prime rib and seafood buffet at $31.95, are what it does best. The Oceanarium is done in elegant muted colors as if you were under water, and, in fact, a three-story aquarium lines one wall. A unique treat.

The Chart House (1765 Ala Moana Blvd., 808/941-6669), on the ground floor of the Ilikai Marina Building across from Ala Wai Yacht Harbor, is open daily 4 P.M.–12 A.M. (from 5 P.M. on the weekends), with food served Mon.–Thurs. 5:30–9:30 P.M. (until 10 P.M. Fri.–Sat.). Seafood and beef are its specialties, with most entrées in the $25–40 range. Selections off the menu include rib eye steak, grilled lamb chops, Kahuku prawns, and bouillabaisse. It offers a happy hour until 7 P.M., *pu pu* off the lounge menu until midnight, and nightly entertainment. The Chart House has a great reputation with locals and visitors alike, and because it's one of the oldest restaurants in Waikiki, it definitely is doing something right. You can't go wrong here.

Hy's Steak House (2440 Kuhio Ave., 808/922-5555, open at 6 P.M. on weekdays, from 5:30 P.M. on weekends) is one of those rare restaurants that not only is absolutely beautiful (decorated in dark wood and low light like a Victorian sitting room) but serves great food as well. Its award-winning menu offers entrées other than steak and chops, but these are the specialties and worth the stiff-upper-lip price. Great care is taken in the preparation and presentation of all dishes. Expect most entrée prices in the $25–43 range. Dress is resort casual; reservations are necessary.

Japanese

Ezogiku is a small chain of Japanese restaurants that has three locations in Waikiki (2146 Kalakaua Ave., 2420 Koa Ave., and 2546 Lemon Rd.). Open until the wee hours, these no-atmosphere restaurants serve inexpensive hearty bowls of Sapporo ramen (renowned as the best), curry rice, and gyoza. Ezogiku is a no-frills kind of place: small, smoky, counter seating, and totally authentic. It's so authentic that on the dishes they spell ramen as larmen. You not only eat inexpensively, but you also get an authentic example of what it's like to eat in Japan...cheaply. Eat heartily for around $8.

Like its sister restaurant in Lahaina, the Waikiki **Kobe Japanese Steak House and Sushi bar** (1841 Ala Moana Blvd., 808/941-4444, open from 5 P.M. nightly) is a fun eatery with plenty of slicing, dicing, and chopping at the teppanyaki table. The flash of the chef's knives and the flame of the grill will keep you occupied as you sample your freshly prepared sushi and sip sake, beer, or an exotic mixed drink as you wait for your meal. Most entrées fall in the $22–33 range, but it's well worth the entertainment value. Kobe's Japanese country inn ambience will set the mood and the chef will perform with skill. All that's left is for you to enjoy.

Todai Restaurant (1910 Kalakaua Ave., 808/947-1000, open 11 A.M.–2 P.M. and 5–9:30 P.M.) does Japanese sushi and seafood buffets, so you can choose what appeals to you from the food table without having to learn your way through a menu. Prices are $14.95 for lunch on weekdays and $17.95 on weekends and $27.95 for dinners.

An exceptional restaurant worth visiting for authentic Japanese food is 🄲 **Kyo-Ya** (2057 Kalakaua Ave., 808/947-3911, open Mon.–Sat. 11 A.M.–1:30 P.M., daily 5:30–9:15 P.M.). This contemporary restaurant has western seating downstairs and tatami rooms with foot wells on its second floor. For dinner, complete *teishoku* (set menu) meals are available, as are nabemono, sukiyaki, and shabu shabu dishes for several people, as well as à la carte plates and sushi and sashimi; *teishoku* prices run $23–38. Lunch prices are substantially less, and the meal offerings also include donburi, udon, and soba. Kyo-Ya has an excellent reputation for outstanding food.

The **Shogun Restaurant** (808/921-6113, open 6–10 A.M., 11 A.M.–2 P.M., and 5–10 P.M.) at the Pacific Beach Hotel is an award-winner and a favorite spot for residents to take their visiting guests. This is a high-class place and a definite cultural experience. Shogun offers breakfast, lunch, and dinner buffets, some à la carte selections, and a *teppan* and sushi bar. The dinner buffet runs $26.95, except on Monday and Thursday when it's $31.95 and crab is the feature. Definitely make reservations.

Hakone (808/944-4494, open Wed.–Thurs. 6–9:30 P.M., Fri.–Sun. 5:30–9:30 P.M.), the Hawaii Prince Hotel's fine Japanese restaurant, is appointed with shoji screens and wooden tables with high-backed chairs in front of a glass wall that frames the still life of the Ala Wai Yacht Harbor. Dishes are typical, with *teishoku* like lobster onigarayaki and wafu sirloin steak at $45, nabemono $55, and a sushi buffet at $42.

Chinese

The **Golden Dragon** (808/946-5336, open nightly except Monday 6–9:30 P.M.) would tempt any knight errant to drop his sword and pick up chopsticks. One of the two fine restaurants at Hilton Hawaiian Village, the Golden Dragon has walls decorated with portraits of emperors, and the plates carry the Golden Dragon motif. The interior color scheme is a striking vermilion and black, with the chairs and tables shining with a lacquerware patina. The Golden Dragon isn't your average chop suey house, but the menu has all of the standard Cantonese fare (with some Szechuan dishes) from crispy lemon chicken to firecracker crispy noodles, but it doesn't end there. The food is expertly prepared, and two fine choices are the exotic Imperial Beggar's Chicken, feeding two for $48.50, which is a chicken wrapped in lotus leaves, encased in clay, and baked (requires 24 hours' notice to prepare); and Chef Chiang's Signature Selection (for two), which includes chicken egg rolls, crispy wontons, island pork char siu, hot and sour soup, stir-fry chicken, scallops with lychee and asparagus, beef with snow peas, tastes of lobster and shrimp, and duck fried rice, with green tea ice cream for $39 per person. For a first-class restaurant with impeccable food and service, the prices at the Golden Dragon are reasonable.

Korean

Located in the Waikiki Resort Hotel, **Seoul Jung** (130 Lili'uokalani, 808/921-8620, open 6 A.M.–2 P.M. and 5–10 P.M.) has a fine Korean menu with plenty of traditional side dishes to accompany each main entrée. The soup, rice, hot pot, and meat dishes run mostly $12–20, with a few stews for several people up to $45. For a taste of Korea, this is the place to come.

Thai

Singha Thai Cuisine (808/941-2898, open daily 4–10 P.M.), owned and operated by the owner of renowned Chai's Bistro at Aloha Tower Marketplace, presents some of the best-tasting Thai food in the city. A selection of wok stir fries, curries, and seafood dishes run mostly $16–28. Specialties of the house include braised duck legs, BBQ honey hoisin baby back ribs, seared jumbo black tiger prawns, and spicy Siamese fighting fish. To add to the joy of dinning here, Thai dancers perform for guests nightly 7–9 P.M. Find this fine restaurant at the corner of Ala Moana Boulevard and Ena Street, kitty-corner from the Hilton Hawaiian Village.

Whether you've tried Thai food or not, **Keo's in Waikiki** (2028 Kuhio Ave., 808/951-9355, open 7 A.M.–2 P.M. and 5–10 P.M., Fri.–Sat. until 11 P.M.), at the Ambassador Hotel near where Kalakaua and Kuhio Avenues merge, is a very good choice. Keo's has the full range of Thai entrées, from meat selections through noodles, seafood, and vegetarian dishes, and all can be adjusted from mild to fiery hot to suit your taste. Try a spicy lemongrass soup or green papaya salad to start your meal. These and appetizers are priced mostly under $12, while entrées, like Thai garlic beef with mushrooms, Thai crispy fish with red chili, pad Thai noodles with vegetables, or yellow curry with chicken, generally run a reasonable $12–16. The lunch and dinner menus are basically the same, but breakfast combines both Asian and American choices. Reservations would be a good idea because this is a popular place.

At the Ohana East Hotel, **Keoni's** (2375 Kuhio Ave., 808/922-9888, open daily 7 A.M.–11 P.M.), a sister restaurant of Keo's, also serves Thai cuisine alongside many Western dishes at similar prices. On the Thai side, you find Thai crispy calamari appetizers, hot basil chicken, panang curry with shrimp, and spicy scallops with lemongrass. From the Western side comes onion soup au gratin, spaghetti Bolognese, and roasted chicken.

Mexican

La Cucaracha (2446 Koa Ave., 808/924-9889, open daily noon–10:30 P.M.) Mexican Bar and Grill advertises great margaritas and attracts crowds with its lively music and bright and appealing decorations. The menu offers the usual list of tacos, burritos, quesadillas, chimichangas, as well as chiles rellenos, flautas, chicken mole, fajitas, and seafood dishes that you might expect at a fine Mexican restaurant. Portions are sizeable, and most dishes are under $16. For those coming for *bebidas,* the bar has a broad selection of Mexican and domestic beer. A sister restaurant (2310 Kuhio Ave., 808/922-2288) is located close by, so you have a choice.

Island Fresh

Duke's Canoe Club, Waikiki at the Outrigger Waikiki Hotel (808/922-2268, open 7 A.M.–10 P.M.) has an unbeatable location fronting Waikiki Beach. Basically a steak and seafood restaurant, it's a happening place, with plenty of Duke Kahanamoku and surfing memorabilia on the wall, with cocktails and lively local music every evening. Aside from the steak, fish, and seafood items there are such selections as Hawaiian *huli huli* chicken and baby back pork ribs, all $18–29. The food is tasty, but you generally come here as much for the atmosphere, music, and chance to see the sun sink into the sea. Just another part of the restaurant, the **Barefoot Bar** has a lighter and cheaper menu of sandwiches, burgers, pizza, and *pu pu* until midnight.

Following in the footsteps of its sister restaurant on Maui's Ka'anapali Beach, the **Hula Grill, Waikiki** (808/923-4852, open 6:30–10:30 A.M. and 5–10 P.M.) has opened on the 2nd floor of the Outrigger Waikiki Hotel overlooking the beach. Featuring foods of the islands, breakfast might be buttermilk pancakes with bananas and macadamia nuts or a *paniolo* omelette. Dinner selections include any number of local fish or the grill traditions of lemon-ginger roasted chicken, shrimp scampi, shrimp kung pao stir fry, or prime bone-in New York steak. Dinner entrée prices range $16–32, but you get the view thrown in free. Operating 4–6 P.M., the **Plantation Bar** at Hula Grill has *pu pu* and a limited light menu for those wanting less of a meal with the same fine view.

House Without a Key (808/923-2311), a casual outdoor-indoor restaurant in a magnificent oceanside setting at the Halekulani Hotel, is open for breakfast, lunch, and dinner. Named after the first novel written about Charlie Chan, Honolulu's famous fictional detective, the restaurant offers unsurpassed views in every direction and is one of the best spots on the island to enjoy a sunset cocktail and evening entertainment. Although casual, the seating is comfortable with padded chairs at simple wood-trimmed tables. Like the environment, the menu is casual, with prices fairly easy on the budget. Breakfast is buffet only at $24. Lunch and dinner are à la carte, with such entrées as grilled mahi fillet sandwich, garlic shrimp pasta, and catch of the day, most for $12–16.

At the eastern end of Waikiki, in the boutique W Honolulu Hotel, is the **Diamond Head Grill** (808/922-3734, open 7–10:30 A.M. and 6–11 P.M.). This chic eatery serves three meals a day (lunch only as room service to W Honolulu Hotel guests), and the menu items are as light and modern as the decor. The breakfast menu has everything from a vegetable frittata to Belgian waffles. While not overly complex, dinner entrées are well seasoned and freshly creative. Roasted center cut of Chilean sea bass, Colorado rack of lamb, and filet mignon of bison are three specialties. Expect most entrées in the $25–39 range. After dinner, the Wonder Lounge comes alive with live guitar or DJ dancing music.

Neptune's Garden Restaurant (808/921-6112, open Tues.–Sat. 5:30–9:30 P.M.) is the Pacific Beach Hotel's fine-dining restaurant; as its name implies, its focus is fish and seafood. Entrées run mostly $23–40 and include such delicacies as seafood paella, wild Alaskan salmon, garlic prawns, and steamed Maine lob-

ster. Soft, soothing music accompanies dinner. Reservations recommended.

One of the most unusual restaurants in Waikiki is the **Top of Waikiki** (808/923-3877, open nightly 5–9:30 P.M.), the revolving round top of the Waikiki Business Plaza. The food and drink are good here, but many come for the great view over the town as the restaurant makes a slow revolution. Seating is tiered so that everyone has a good view. Come before sunset and watch the lights of the city come on and the sun sink into the sea. Start with an appetizer like seared scallops with braised pancetta before moving on to an entrée like beef Wellington, seafood paella, risotto, steak and shrimp Napoleon, or island-style mango chicken, with most in the $24–33 range.

French

Michel's (2895 Kalakaua Ave., 808/923-6552, open daily from 5:30 P.M., plus Sunday brunch) at the Colony Surf is literally on the beach, so your appetite is piqued not only by sumptuous morsels, but also by magnificent views of the Waikiki skyline boldly facing the Pacific. The interior is neo-French elegant, with the dining rooms appointed in soft pastels, white tablecloths, crystal chandeliers, heavy silver service, and tasteful paintings. The bar, serpentine and made of polished koa, features Bloody Marys. Food is traditional French continental, and dinner is *magnifique* with such entrées as fresh Maine lobster, potato-crusted opakapaka, duckling à l'Orange, steak Diane flamed at tableside, and chateaubriand for two; $28–42. The dining experience at Michel's, which has serviced guests for over 40 years, is completely satisfying with outstanding food and outstanding service, all in an outstanding setting.

Italian

Matteo's (364 Seaside, 808/922-5551, open daily 5:30–11 P.M.), in the Marine Surf Hotel, is a wonderfully dark and romantic Italian restaurant that sets the mood even outside by welcoming you with a red canopy and brass rail that leads to a carved door of koa and crystal.

WAIKIKI

WAIKIKI

Inside is stylish, with high-backed booths, white tablecloths, and marble-top tables. On each is a rose, Matteo's signature. Dinners begin with hot or cold antipasti, such as portobello crostini, artichokes alla Matteo's, or seafood medley vinaigrette. Light fare of *insalata e zuppe* (salad and soup) matched with garlic bread or bruschetta make an inexpensive but tasty meal. Entrée suggestions are chicken Florentino, veal osso bucco Milanese, Grenadine of beef tenderloin, or cioppino alla Livornese. Complete dinners come with Matteo's special salad, soup, and coffee or tea and include seafood lasagna and veal parmigiana and are priced under $36. Pastas are reasonable and traditional. An extensive wine list complements the food; after dinner, coffee, a cordial, or cognac might suit the mood. This restaurant gets the thumbs up from local critics and has garnered awards of excellence. If you are out for a special evening of fine dining and romance, Matteo's will set the mood, and the rest is up to you.

Sarento's, Top of the "I" (808/955-5559, open 5:30–9 P.M., until 9:30 Fri.–Sat.) occupies the top floor of the Ilikai Hotel and, like its sister restaurant, Aaron's, on the top floor of the Ala Moana Hotel, it has a fabulous location that looks out over the Ala Wai Yacht Club, down along the Waikiki strip, and over downtown Honolulu. The quality of the fine Italian food at Sarento's matches its setting. Start with appetizers like bruschetta rustica or steamed clams in wine broth. Soups and salads follow but are only a preview to the many fine entrées that might include pan-roasted opakapaka, veal scaloppine, filet mignon Marchand, kiawe-smoked pork chops, and penne pasta with pancetta, Maui onions, and tomato sauce. Most entrées run $28–34, with the pastas about $10 less.

Fine Dining

A few restaurants in Waikiki are a cut above the many fine restaurants in town. In essence, these are the best of the best, and a meal at any one would be a perfect spot for that special one night out with your sweetheart. They are expensive, and all expect guests to dress in neat resort-wear or better. Reservations recommended. A short list of these fine restaurants follows.

Softly the soprano sea sings, while the baritone breeze whispers in melodious melancholy, as you float ephemerally above the waves at **La Mer** (808/923-2311, open 6–10 P.M.), the open-air signature dinner restaurant at the Halekulani. Splendid in their appointment, the walls, filigreed panels of teak covered in Chinese silk screen, are predominantly browns and whites, the traditional colors of Hawaiian tapa. The superb French continental menu, with its numerous selections of seafood, is bolstered by a huge wine list and a platter of select cheeses to end the meal. Entrées like roasted Chilean sea bass, bouillabaisse in a puff pastry, breast of Barbary duck à l'Orange, and rack of lamb with dijon mustard crust are generally in the $39–46 range, with two set dinner menus at $89 and $128 (for two). La Mer sets the standard, and if you were to choose one restaurant for a night of culinary bliss, this is a perfect choice. Long sleeve shirts and coats are required for men.

White, purple, and yellow orchids tumble from trellises, cascade from clay planters, and always grace your table at **Orchids Dining Room** (808/923-2311, open 7:30–11 A.M., 11:30 A.M.–2 P.M., and 6–10 P.M.), another seaside, indoor-outdoor restaurant at the Halekulani. Specializing in contemporary American cuisine, Orchids is also famous for its fabulous and legendary Sunday buffet brunch. Beautifully appointed with teak wood and Hawaiian eucalyptus flooring, the setting is casual-elegant with white starched linen tablecloths and of course heavy silver and crystal. La Mer is arranged with a trilevel central dining area that spreads out to a covered veranda, so all tables enjoy a panoramic view of the sea with Diamond Head in the distance. Start the day with a continental or American breakfast, or try it Japanese-style with grilled fish, steamed rice, pickles, miso soup, seaweed, and green tea. Lunch is also casual, with the Sunday brunch drawing visitors and residents alike. The dinner specialty is seafood, although meat and poultry are available. Entrées might be luscious Oriental-style onaga, Madras seafood curry, charbroiled ahi steak, and roasted lamb chops. Most entrées run $27–36.

The Hilton Hawaiian Village is one of the finest destination resorts in Hawaii. Its signature restaurant complements the resort perfectly. **Bali by the Sea** (808/941-2254, open Mon.–Sat. 6–9:30 P.M.), on the first floor of the Rainbow Tower, may sound like Indonesian cuisine, but it's more continental and Pacific Rim cuisine than anything else, and it's a consistent AAA four-diamond award winner. The setting couldn't be more brilliant. Sit by the open windows so the sea breezes fan you as you overlook the gorgeous beach with Diamond Head off in the distance. Choose appetizers like sugarcane-crusted scallops or duck confit with wild mushroom risotto. Ranging mostly $28–44, entrées include a magnificent selection of fish from Hawaiian waters, each prepared to bring out its essential flavor and many covered with a delightfully complementary sauce. Meat entrées are grilled breast of chicken, filet mignon, or oven-roasted rack of lamb. Bali by the Sea is a superb choice for an elegant evening of fine dining.

The signature restaurant at the Sheraton Waikiki is the **Hanohano Room** (808/922-4422, open daily 5:30–9 P.M.) atop the building on its 30th floor. From here, the vista before you sweeps from Pearl Harbor to Diamond Head, and behind you, the city of Honolulu runs up into the hills. The view at night is stunning with the twinkle of city lights below. This formal, fine dining restaurant features Pacific Island cuisine. Select your entrée from such items as sautéed onaga, crispy skin *moi* (threadfish), filet mignon, and prime rib, ranging $27–39. A wonderful meal may be even more romantic here to the sounds of light piano music or later in the evening when a local trio called Stardust plays contemporary jazz and top 40 tunes in the Cobalt Lounge. The dance floor is always open.

One of the most laudable achievements in the restaurant business is to create an excellent reputation and then to keep it. **Nick's Fishmarket** (2070 Kalakaua Ave., 808/955-6333, open nightly 5:30–10 P.M., until 11 P.M. Fri.–Sat.) at the Waikiki Gateway Hotel has done just that. Many gourmets consider Nick's *the* best dining in Waikiki, and it's great fun to find out if they know what they're talking about. Adventurous and highly skilled, the chefs here, like the master of an old sailing ship, will take you to culinary ports of call rarely visited. Highly professional waiters, knowledgeable about every dish, are friendly and efficient and always at hand to suggest just the right wine from the extensive list to perfectly complement your choice of dish. Start with fresh-baked oysters Rockefeller or blackened sashimi. The New England clam chowder is unbeatable, while the Caesar salad prepared at your table has long won honors as the best available west of California! Although Nick's is primarily renowned for its fish and lobster, don't overlook the veal, steaks, and chicken with sides of pasta. Most entrées run $32–42, while the lobster dishes run $50–78. The sinless—along with those expecting salvation "tomorrow"—will enjoy the dessert menu.

For other fine-dining options around town, several of which are close to Waikiki, refer to *Food* in the *Honolulu* chapter.

Markets

The only real grocery store in Waikiki is **Food Pantry** (2370 Kuhio Ave., 808/923-9831, open 6 A.M.–1 A.M.), which carries groceries, bakery goods, and deli items at the corner of Kuhio Avenue and Walina Street. Otherwise, you must find snacks and select grocery items at the corner convenience stores and sundries shops around town.

Information and Services

Tourist Information

Numerous activity booths are strewn throughout the Waikiki area, most touting one or several particular attractions. They're set up to sell, so expect their pitch. Hotel concierge and activity desks also have plenty of information.

Your best source of general tourist information in Waikiki for brochures, booklets, and questions is the **Hawaiian Visitors Bureau** office (2270 Kalakaua Ave., Ste. 801, 808/923-1811, open Mon.–Fri. 8 A.M.–4:30 P.M.) in the Waikiki Business Plaza at the corner of Kalakaua and Seaside Avenues.

While on the street, stop by the **visitor information kiosk** at the corner of Kalakaua and Kapahulu Avenues near the Honolulu Zoo entrance to pick up brochures about town, TheBus, and events happening in the area.

Post Office

In Waikiki, the post office is at 330 Saratoga Rd., 800/275-8777. Window service is offered Mon.–Fri. 8 A.M.–4:30 P.M., Sat. 9 A.M.–1 P.M.

Medical Services

For immediate care medical services in Waikiki, see one of the following: **Straub Doctors on Call** (808/971-6000 or 808/923-9966 for Japanese-speaking doctors) for emergencies and "house calls" to your hotel, 24 hours a day; **Kuhio Walk-in Medical Clinic** (2310 Kuhio Ave., Ste. 223, 808/924-6688, open Mon.–Fri. 9 A.M.–4:30 P.M., Sat. until 1 P.M.) at the corner of Nahua in Waikiki; **Urgent Care Clinic of Waikiki** (2155 Kalakaua Ave., Ste. 308, 808/924-3399, open daily 8:30 A.M.–7 P.M.) in the ANA Kalakaua Building, with lab and x-ray capabilities; **The Medical Corner** (1860 Ala Moana Blvd. #101, 808/943-1111, open daily 8 A.M.–8 P.M.) for minor emergencies; and **Waikiki Health Center** (277 'Ohua Ave., 808/922-4787, open Mon.–Thurs. 9 A.M.–8 P.M., Fri. until 4:30 P.M., Sat. until 2 P.M.), for low-cost care including pregnancy and confidential STD testing.

Pharmacies

Kuhio Pharmacy (2330 Kuhio Ave., 808/923-4466, open weekdays 9 A.M.–5 P.M. for prescriptions), ground level in the Ohana Waikiki West Hotel, is the only full-service pharmacy in Waikiki.

Getting Around

Far and away the best way to get around Waikiki is on foot. For one, it's easily walked from one end to the other, and walking saves you hassling with parking and traffic jams. Also, TheBus and taxis are abundant. Those who have opted for a rental car should note that many of the agencies operate Waikiki lots, which for some can be more convenient than dropping your car at the airport on the day of departure. Check to see if this suits you.

Waikiki does an excellent job of conveying **traffic,** both auto and pedestrian, along Kalakaua Avenue, the main drag fronting Waikiki Beach. To give the feeling of an outdoor strolling mall, sidewalks along Kalakaua have been widened and surfaced with red brick, and the section right along the sand has been updated with flagstone walkways, old-fashioned lampposts, tiki torches, benches, trellises, landscaping, and water fountains. If you're driving, pay attention to one-way street signs. Kalakaua Avenue, for example, is one-way going south, Ala Wai Boulevard is one-way running north, and Kuhio Avenue runs both ways—for most of its length. Many of the short cross streets also have one-way traffic only. What appears to be inconvenient at first actually helps the traffic flow and reduces congestion.

Public parking in Waikiki can be a hassle, although there are plenty of parking garages, most attached to hotels and shopping centers. A good place to park not far from the beach is the strip running parallel to Kapi'olani Park at one end and along Saratoga Street at the other. There are plenty of two-hour parking meters available, especially if you arrive before 9 A.M. Also, inexpensive (for Waikiki) parking is available at the Waikiki Parking Garage (333 Seaside Ave.), the Royal Hawaiian Shopping Center garage (2201 Kalakaua Ave.), and at the Waikiki Trade Center garage (2255 Kuhio Ave.), but most don't allow overnight parking. Parking at the Fort De-Russy parking lot runs $3 for the first hour, $2 for additional hours, and $24 for a maximum of 24 hours. Parking at hotel or private parking lots can also be expensive. Hotels usually charge $15–18 for their daily rate; some have valet parking, whereas at others you self-park. Parking lot fees often run $10–15 overnight.

Trolleys

The **Waikiki Trolley** (808/593-2822, www .waikikitrolley.com), an open-air bus, will take you on a tour of Waikiki and surrounding areas for $25 adults, $12 children ages 4–11. This all-day pass lets you board, exit, and reboard at any stop along three specific routes. Multiday passes for four consecutive days on these same routes are available for $45 and $18, respectively. A one-way fare for the pink line within Waikiki is $2 per ride. Starting from the rear of the DFS Galleria in Waikiki, trolleys run every 45 minutes on the red and blue lines and every eight minutes on the pink line. The **red line** (Honolulu City route) operates 10:15 A.M.–6:30 P.M., leaving its last starting point at 4:15 P.M. This line basically connects Waikiki with historical and cultural sights in downtown Honolulu, going as far as the Bishop Museum. The **blue line** (Ocean Coast route) starts at 9 A.M. and runs until 6:50 P.M., leaving its last starting point at 4:30 P.M. It heads east to the coastal sights of southeast O'ahu and as far as Sea Life Park. The **pink line** (the Ala Moana Shopping Shuttle) operates 9:30 A.M.–9:40 P.M., leaving its last starting point at 9 P.M. This line connects Waikiki to the Ala Moana Shopping

© ROBERT NILSEN

One of the easiest means of transportation in the city, the Waikiki Trolley can shuttle you around town in its open-air carriages.

Center and the Ward Centre shops. In addition, a free **DFS Galleria trolley** operates roughly 11 A.M.–11 P.M., connecting the DFS Galleria to several major hotels in Waikiki. The **Waikele Trolley** (808/591-2561 or 800/824-8804) runs round-trips between various hotels in Waikiki and the Waikele premium outlets in Waipahu twice in the morning, returning twice in the afternoon for $24 adult and $8.75 children. Pick up a map/brochure from any activity desk or call the information number for times and stops. Tickets can be purchased from booths at the DFS Galleria, the Ala Moana trolley depot, and at the Hilton Hawaiian Village Tapa Tower stop.

A few other independent trolleys operate in Waikiki, such as the Maui Divers Jewelry, which takes guests to its factory, and a Hilo Hattie trolley, which runs to its flagship store in Iwilei. In addition to these, many activity vendors provide shuttle pickup and returns for paying guests of their activities.

For express shuttle service to various points beyond Waikiki, such as Diamond Head, Lanikai Beach in Kailua, the Aloha Stadium Swap Meet, and the Arizona Memorial, try **Ohana Express Shuttle** (808/753-5593) or **Hawaii Super Shuttle** (808/841-2928).

TheBus

Many popular island destinations and attractions are reachable by the Honolulu public bus system, called TheBus, directly from Waikiki, or from the Ala Moana Shopping Center bus depot after a short ride from Waikiki. Refer to the short list below for some popular destinations.

From Kuhio Avenue going west:

- Airport (1 hour 15 minutes): nos. 19, 20
- Ala Moana Shopping Center: nos. 8, 19, 20, 42, 58
- Aloha Tower, Arizona Memorial, Aloha Stadium flea market: nos. 20, 42
- Downtown Honolulu, Chinatown, Honolulu Academy of Arts: nos. 2, 13, 20

- University of Hawaii, Manoa campus: no. 4
- Bishop Museum: no. 2

From Kuhio Avenue going east:

- Diamond Head, Kahala Mall, Hanauma Bay, Sandy Beach, and Sea Life Park: no. 22 (Beach Bus)
- Diamond Head, Kahala Mall, and Sea Life Park: no. 58

From the Ala Moana Shopping Center:

- North shore (circle-island clockwise, 4–5 hours): no. 52
- Windward shore (circle-island, counter-clockwise, 4–5 hours): no. 55
- Kailua and Waimanalo (1.5 hours): no. 57
- Manoa Falls, Lyon Arboretum: no. 5
- Leeward Coast: no. C (express)

Rental Cars

Aside from the national chains, which all have booths and baseyards at or near the Honolulu International Airport and offices somewhere in Waikiki, there are several smaller independent car rental companies that rent vehicles, including sedans, four-wheel drives, SUVs, and convertibles at lots in Waikiki. Among these are **Paradise Rent A Car** (1879 Kalakaua Ave., 808/946-7777; 151 Uluniu Ave., 808/926-7777; and 355 Royal Hawaiian Ave., 808/924-7777 or 888/882-2277, open 8 A.M.–5 P.M.) and **VIP (Very Inexpensive Prices) Car Rentals** (234 Beach Walk, 808/922-4605; 1944 Kalakaua Ave., 808/946-7733).

Vanity Rentals

The most distinctive and fun-filled cars in Waikiki are the sports cars and luxury imports available from **Exotic Car Rentals** (2025 Kalakaua Ave., 808/942-8725, open 8 A.M.–6 P.M.). This company has a fleet of American and European classic cars, like the

Viper, Corvette, Ferrari, Porsche, Maserati, Mercedes, and BMW. The finest of these vehicles may rent for $900 a day, the lowly Corvette for the mere pittance of around $250 per day.

Paradise Rent A Car (1879 Kalakaua Ave., 808/946-7777; 151 Uluniu Ave., 808/926-7777; and 355 Royal Hawaiian Ave., 808/924-7777 or 888/882-2277, open 8 A.M.–5 P.M.) also rents luxury cars like the Prowler, Viper, Mercedes, Porsche, Jaguar, and Corvette convertible at comparable rates.

Motorcycle and Moped Rentals

For rentals, try **Big Kahuna Motorcycle Tours and Rentals** (407 Seaside Ave., 808/924-2736 or 888/451-5544, www.bigkahunarentals.com, open 8 A.M.–6 P.M.), where rentals run $100–180 for four hours, with full day and weekly rentals available. **Cruzin Hawaii Motorcycles** (1980 Kalakaua Ave., 808/945-9595 or 877/945-9595, www.cruzinhawaii.com,

open 8:30 A.M.–5:30 P.M.) rents only Harley-Davidsons at its shop near the Ambassador Hotel. Fat Boy, Road King, and Heritage Softails run $99 for three hours or $149 all day, and Sportsters go for $79 for three hours or $99 all day; 24-hour, three-day, and weekly rates can also be arranged. **Hawaiian Peddler** (2139 Kuhio Ave., 808/926-5099) carries Rebels, Nighthawks, and Fat Boys ranging $115–189 a day.

Aside from a variety of motorcycles, you can pick up mopeds and electric cars at the two locations of **Paradise Cruisers** (2446 Koa Ave. and 1994 Kalakaua Ave., 808/368-4223 or 808/926-2847, open 7 A.M.–9 P.M.). Mopeds and scooters can also be rented from **Adventure on 2 Wheels** (1946 Ala Moana Ave., 808/944-3131; 2552 Lemon Rd., 808/921-8111). **Coconut Cruisers** (305 Royal Hawaiian, 808/924-1644 or 800/536-4434) rents motor scooters at $100, mopeds at $35, and bicycles at $15–30 per day.

WAIKIKI

CENTRAL O'AHU AND 'EWA

For most uninformed visitors, central O'ahu is a colorful blur as they speed past in their rental cars en route to the North Shore. Slow down—there are things to see! For island residents, the suburban towns of 'Aiea, Pearl City, Waipahu, Mililani, and Wahiawa are considered home. The three routes heading north from the coast meet in Wahiawa, the island's most central town. The roads cross just near the entrance to Schofield Barracks, which served as a warm-up target for Japanese Zeros as they flew on their devastating bombing run over Pearl Harbor.

As with central O'ahu, 'Ewa, the southwestern corner of the island, holds few attractions for the average visitor; most tourists simply buzz right through. Once a broad expanse of sugarcane fields and a huge naval air station, this land now provides room for some of the fastest-growing suburban areas on the island, 'Ewa, 'Ewa Beach, and Kapolei, as well as for expansive golf courses, a huge industrial estate, plenty of commercial development, and a new tourist resort with hotels, condominiums, a marina, and…another golf course. Still, great expanses of 'Ewa have either been left fallow or are as yet as undeveloped.

PLANNING YOUR TIME

It's fair to say that most visitors to Central O'ahu are just passing through so will spend little time there. However, those who have an interest in symbols of World War II should spend the better part of a day visiting and paying respects at the USS *Arizona* Memorial, the USS *Bowfin* submarine, and the USS *Missouri* battleship. These should be everyone's first

© ROBERT NILSEN

HIGHLIGHTS

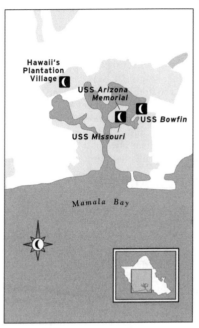

◖ USS *Arizona* Memorial: This is one of the nation's most solemn and hallowed sites. It's a symbol of tragedy and honor, and now a memorial to those who were baptized by the flames of war (page 148).

◖ USS *Bowfin* Submarine: To help avenge the fiery start of World War II, the *Bowfin* and others like it prowled the sea to inflict damage on enemy ships. This workhorse of the deep now lies snug at its final harbor (page 150).

◖ USS *Missouri:* The end of World War II came on the deck of the USS *Missouri*, where the surrender of the Japanese was finalized. It and the USS *Arizona* now stand as bookends, representing the start and end of that war (page 151).

◖ Hawaii's Plantation Village: This living museum offers a glimpse into the life and times of Hawaii sugar plantations and the people from around the world who came to labor in the fields and, in the process, build a better life for themselves and their families (page 154).

LOOK FOR ◖ TO FIND RECOMMENDED SIGHTS, ACTIVITIES, DINING, AND LODGING.

stops on a tour of the area. In addition, several hours might be well spent at Hawaii's Plantation Village in Waipahu for an introduction to plantation life and the lives of the people who helped build the sugar economy of the islands. There is at least one good hiking trail to get away from the suburban sprawl for a few hours. Wahiawa, with its cultural, botanical, and military sites, could also easily take the better part of a day. Because the Central O'ahu and 'Ewa areas are relatively spread out, plan on spending plenty of time in your vehicle between destinations, particularly if you're staying in Waikiki.

CENTRAL O'AHU AND 'EWA

'Aiea, Pearl City, and Waipahu

These towns ring the northern edge of Pearl Harbor. The twin cities of 'Aiea and Pearl City, except for the World War II military memorials and perhaps a football game at Aloha Stadium, have little to attract the average tourist. They are mainly residential areas for greater Honolulu and the large numbers of military families throughout this area. Likewise, Waipahu doesn't hold much attraction to the tourist because of its largely agricultural base, but Hawaii's Plantation Village is an attempt to interpret the importance of plantation culture for visitors.

PEARL HARBOR HISTORICAL SITES
◖ USS *Arizona* Memorial Visitor Center

The USS *Arizona* Memorial (www.nps.gov/usar) is a joint venture of the U.S. Park Service and the navy. It's free, but donations are accepted. The Park Service runs the visitors center (808/442-0561, open 7:30 A.M.–5 P.M.) and

the navy operates the shuttle boats that take you out to the memorial shrine. The displays, museum, and gift shop at the complex are open daily except Thanksgiving, Christmas, and New Year's Day, with programs at the theater and the actual shuttle ride to the memorial operating only 8 A.M.–3 P.M. If the weather is stormy, or waves rough, they won't sail. As many as 5,000 people visit per day in winter and twice that many go in summer. Your best time to avoid delays is before 9:30 A.M., but a line often starts to form by 7 A.M. With 1.5 million visitors yearly, this is one of the most heavily visited sites in the state.

As you enter the visitors center, you're handed a numbered ticket. Until it's called, you can visit the bookstore/gift shop and museum or, if the wait is long, the USS *Bowfin*, moored within walking distance. The bookstore specializes in volumes on World War II and Hawaiiana. The museum is primarily a pictorial history, with a strong emphasis on the

THE COMING OF WAR

Even as you approach the pier to board a launch to take you to the USS *Arizona*, you know that you're at a shrine. Very few spots in America carry such undeniable emotion, so easily passed from one generation to another: here, Valley Forge, Gettysburg, not many more. On that beautiful, cloudless morning of December 7, 1941, at one minute before 8 o'clock, the United States not only entered the war but lost its innocence forever.

The first battle of World War II for the United States actually took place about 90 minutes before Pearl Harbor's bombing, when the USS *Ward* sank an unidentified submarine sliding into Honolulu. In Pearl Harbor, dredged about 40 years earlier to allow superships to enter, the heavyweight champions of America's Pacific Fleet were lined up, many flanking the near side of Ford Island. The naive deployment of this

"Battleship Row" prompted a Japanese admiral to remark that never, even in times of world peace, could he dream that the military might of a nation would have its unprotected chin stuck so far out, just begging for a right cross to the jaw. When it came, it was a roundhouse right, whistling through the air, and what a doozy!

Well before the smoke could clear and the last explosion stopped rumbling through the mountains, 3,566 Americans were dead or wounded, six mighty ships had sunk into the ooze, 12 other ships stumbled around battered and punch-drunk, and 323 warplanes were useless heaps of scrap. The Japanese fighters had hardly broken a sweat, and when their fleet, located 200 miles north of O'ahu, steamed away, the "east wind" had indeed "rained." But this downpour was only the first squall; the American hurricane followed.

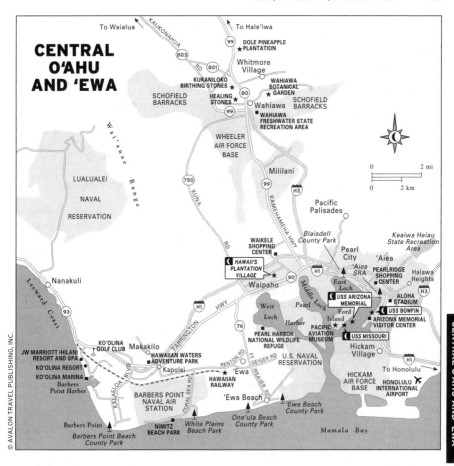

CENTRAL O'AHU AND 'EWA

To Waialua

To Hale'iwa

DOLE PINEAPPLE PLANTATION

Whitmore Village

KUKANILOKO BIRTHING STONES

WAHIAWA BOTANICAL GARDEN

SCHOFIELD BARRACKS

HEALING STONES

Wahiawa

SCHOFIELD BARRACKS

WAHIAWA FRESHWATER STATE RECREATION AREA

WHEELER AIR FORCE BASE

Mililani

Waianae Range

LUALUALEI

NAVAL

RESERVATION

Pacific Palisades

Keaiwa Heiau State Recreation Area

Blaisdell County Park

Pearl City

'Aiea

Halawa Heights

0   2 mi

0   2 km

WAIKELE SHOPPING CENTER

HAWAII'S PLANTATION VILLAGE

'Aiea SRA

PEARLRIDGE SHOPPING CENTER

Leeward Coast

Nanakuli

Waipahu

East Loch

USS ARIZONA MEMORIAL

ALOHA STADIUM

USS BOWFIN

West Loch

Pearl Loch

Middle Loch

Ford Island

ARIZONA MEMORIAL VISITOR CENTER

PACIFIC AVIATION MUSEUM

USS MISSOURI

Harbor

PEARL HARBOR NATIONAL WILDLIFE REFUGE

U.S. NAVAL RESERVATION

Hickam Village

KO'OLINA GOLF CLUB

Makakilo

HAWAIIAN WATERS ADVENTURE PARK

JW MARRIOTT IHILANI RESORT AND SPA

KO'OLINA RESORT

Kapolei

'Ewa

HICKAM AIR FORCE BASE

HONOLULU INTERNATIONAL AIRPORT

To Honolulu

KO'OLINA MARINA

Barbers Point Harbor

HAWAIIAN RAILWAY

BARBERS POINT NAVAL AIR STATION

'Ewa Beach

'Ewa Beach County Park

One'ula Beach County Park

Barbers Point

NIMITZ BEACH PARK

White Plains Beach Park

Mamala Bay

Barbers Point Beach County Park

© AVALON TRAVEL PUBLISHING, INC.

CENTRAL O'AHU AND 'EWA

involvement of Hawaii's Japanese citizens during the war. There are instructions of behavior to "all persons of Japanese ancestry," from the time when bigotry and fear prevailed early in the war, as well as documentation of the 442nd Battalion, made up of Japanese-American soldiers, and their heroic exploits in Europe, especially their rescue of Texas's "lost battalion." Preserved newspapers of the day proclaim the "Day of Infamy" in bold headlines.

When your number is called, you proceed to the comfortable theater where a 20-minute film includes actual footage of the attack. The film is historically factual, devoid of an over-

abundance of flag waving and Mom's apple pie. After the film, you board the launch: no bare feet, no bikinis or bathing suits, but shorts and T-shirts are fine. Thirty years ago visitors wore suits and dresses as if going to church! The film, boat ride there, tour of the memorial, and boat ride back lasts about 80 minutes.

After several decades of steady use, the visitors center is showing signs of deterioration. Plans call for a new structure (www.pearl harbormemorial.com) to house the museum, gift shop, and theater to better handle the visitor load, but its construction will be at an undetermined future date.

Security measures in place following the September 11, 2001, terrorist attacks on the Mainland include not allowing any backpacks, strollers, purses, bags, camera bags, and other such items of potential concealment to be brought into this memorial, the Bowfin Museum, or the USS *Missouri*. A storage place that charges $2 per bag has been set up in the parking lot between the Arizona Memorial and the Bowfin Museum so you can safely leave larger items that you don't want left in your car. This parking lot has been a notoriously unsafe spot often hit by thieves looking to rifle through the parked cars but is now patrolled by security personnel on bicycles so it's much, much better protected than in the past. Adjacent to this storage place are a row of gift shops and snack bars.

The Memorial

The launch, a large, mostly open-air vessel deftly handled and piloted by naval personnel, heads for the 184-foot-long alabaster memorial straddling the remains of the ship that still lies on the bottom. Some view the memorial as a tombstone; others see it as a symbolic ship, bent by struggle in the middle, but raised at the ends pointing to glory. The USS *Arizona* became the focus of the memorial because its casualties were so severe. When it exploded, the blast was so violent that it lifted entire ships moored nearby clear out of the water. Less than nine minutes later, with infernos raging and huge hunks of steel whizzing through the air, the *Arizona* was gone. Its crew went with it; more than 1,100 men were sucked down to the bottom, and only 289 managed to struggle to the surface. To the left and right are a series of black-and-white moorings bearing the names of the ships that were tied to them on the day of the attack.

The deck of the memorial can hold about 200 people. The ship's bell is on display, and a chapel-like area at the far end displays a marble tablet with the names of the dead. Into a hole in the center of the memorial, flowers and wreaths are dropped on special occasions. Part of the superstructure of the ship still rises above the water, but it is slowly being corroded away

by wind and saltwater. The flag, waving overhead, is attached to a pole anchored to the deck of the sunken ship. Many visitors are Japanese nationals, who often stop and offer their apologies to these Pearl Harbor survivors, distinguished by special military-style hats. The navy ordered that any survivor wishing to be buried with his crew members had that right. Several veterans have been laid to rest with their buddies. In 1989, the USS *Arizona* was made a National Historical Landmark.

◖ USS *Bowfin* Submarine and Museum

The USS *Bowfin* (SS-287), a World War II submarine, is moored a few short steps from the Arizona Memorial Visitor Center. Access to the submarine is the highlight, but don't miss a look at the museum. In the museum building, a short pictorial history depicts progress in undersea warfare from Revolutionary times to the present. Battle flags, recruiting posters, photographs, uniforms, military medals, and weapons and hardware are displayed, while a cutaway model of the *Bowfin* depicts life aboard ship. Unique to the museum, and the only one displayed for public viewing, is a daunting Poseidon C-3 submarine missile. An ongoing film in the mini-theater describes life below the surface for the modern submarine force. For the real aficionado, the museum archives and library of submarine-related literature is open by appointment only. Here and there across the four-acre grounds lie artillery pieces, torpedoes, missiles, and the conning tower and periscope of the USS *Parche*. Next to the museum is a gift shop and snack bar.

The private, nonprofit organization Pacific Fleet Submarine Memorial Association (808/423-1341, www.bowfin.org) maintains the *Bowfin* and museum as a memorial and educational exhibit. Both are open daily 8 A.M.–5 P.M., except Thanksgiving, Christmas, and New Year's Day. Audio tours take you through the sub; last entry is at 4:30 P.M. Admission to the sub and museum is $10 adults or $4 for the museum only; $7 for military, seniors, and *kama'aina* or $4 for the museum only; and

ONBOARD THE *BOWFIN*

Launched one year to the day after the Pearl Harbor attack, the USS *Bowfin* completed nine patrol tours during World War II. Nicknamed the "Pearl Harbor Avenger," it was responsible for sinking an incredible 44 enemy ships before the end of the war. Retired in 1979, restored and opened to the public in 1981, it was put on the National Historical Landmark list in 1986. It's a 312-foot-long sausage of steel with a living area only 16 feet in diameter. As you enter the sub, you're handed an audiotape machine, which explains different areas on the sub and life onboard. The deck is made from teak wood, and the deck guns could be moved fore or aft, depending on the skipper's preference. You'll also notice two anchors. As you descend, you feel as if you are integrated with a machine, a part of its gears and workings. In these cramped quarters of brass and stainless steel lived 90 to 100 men, all volunteers. Freshwater was in short supply, and the only man allowed to shower was the cook. Officers were given a dipper of water to shave with, but all the other men grew beards. With absolutely no place to be alone, the men slept on tiny stacked shelves, and only the officers could control the light switches. The only man to have a minuscule private room was the captain.

Topside, twin 16-cylinder diesels created unbelievable noise and heat. A vent in the passageway to the engine room sucked air with such strength that if you passed under it, you'd be pulled to your knees. When the sub ran on batteries under water, the quiet became maddening. The main bunkroom, not much bigger than an average bedroom, slept 36 men. Another 30 or so ran the ship, while another 30 lounged. There was no night or day aboard ship, just shifts. Coffee was constantly available, as well as fresh fruit, and the best mess in all the services. Subs of the day had the best radar and electronics available. Aboard were 24 high-powered torpedoes and ammunition for the topside gun. Submariners, chosen for their intelligence and psychological ability to take it, knew that a hit from the enemy meant certain death. The USS *Bowfin* is fascinating and definitely worth a visit.

$4 children ages 4–12 or $2 for the museum only. Children three and under are free for the museum tour but not admitted into the submarine. Rates to visit both the USS *Bowfin* and take an unguided tour of the USS *Missouri* run $20 adult and $10 for a child.

◖ USS *Missouri*

On June 22, 1998, the USS *Missouri* came home. Whereas the destruction of the USS *Arizona* and other ships in the harbor brought the United States into war with Japan, it was on the deck of the USS *Missouri* that Japan, bruised and bloodied, surrendered to the United States, ending this most costly of world conflicts. Docked on Ford Island just a rifle shot from the USS *Arizona,* it proudly takes its place on "Battleship Row." At 887 feet long and 108 feet wide, this battleship is a behemoth, one of the largest ever built and the last taken off active service. Like a floating city, it had a crew of around 2,500. Commissioned in June 1944, this ship participated in many battles during World War II and later during the Korean War and the Persian Gulf War. Money collected by the private, nonprofit USS *Missouri* Memorial Association is used to refurbish and maintain the "Mighty Mo." Since January 1999, visitors have been allowed onto the deck, where the signing of the surrender took place, and to view the bridge, climb the stairs from level to level, peer into officers' and enlisted men's quarters, enter the galley and dining rooms, and see the armaments for which the ship was well known and feared. Although later retrofitted with more sophisticated weapons, the original huge 16-inch guns could fire a 2,700-pound shell more than 23 miles, and even the smaller five-inch guns could send their projectiles a respectable nine miles. This was no light-duty ship. For protection, some of its armor plating was 17 inches

© ROBERT NILSEN

Still an imposing ship, the USS *Missouri* is now open to visitors.

thick! Several videos and other displays along the way explain the ship's history and function. A plaque on the surrender deck indicates the spot where the table used by representatives of the Japanese, U.S., and Allied governments and armed forces signed the surrender document. In future years, other areas of the ship may also be opened to tourists.

The USS *Missouri* is open daily 9 A.M.– 5 P.M. Entrance runs $16 adults and $8 children for an unguided tour, with reduced rates for *kama'aina* and military personnel. Add $6 per person for the one-hour guided tours or for an audio phone tour. The special Explorers guided tour, which takes you to various parts of the ship that are not open to the general public, is offered at $45 adult and $20 children. Combined tour tickets for the USS *Missouri* and the USS *Bowfin* run $12 self-guided and $26 guided for adults, and $10 unguided and $16 guided for children. Shuttle trolleys depart every 10 minutes starting at 9 A.M. from a stand in front of the USS *Bowfin* Museum and run over the new Ford Bridge to the ticket

office for the ship. The ticket window closes at 4 P.M. and everyone must by off the ship by 5 P.M. For nonmilitary personnel, the shuttle is the only way to get to the ship. It's worth a couple of hours, and the emotional impact will remain much longer. For more information, contact the USS Missouri Memorial Association (808/423-2263, or 877/644-4866, www.ussmissouri.org).

Pacific Aviation Museum

With its first phase opened in December 2006, the **Pacific Aviation Museum** (808/690-0169, www.pacificaviationmuseum.org, open daily 9:30 A.M.–4:30 P.M.) brings another World War II–related exhibit to Pearl Harbor. This exhibit has as its focus aviation history and will, when completed in 2009, occupy three military airplane hangers and the control tower on Ford Island. Displays will include events about and following World War II, numerous airplanes, and a partial aircraft carrier deck. Other sections of the museum will open through 2009.

Getting to Pearl Harbor

There are a few options for how to visit Pearl Harbor and its historical military sites. If you're driving, the entrance is along Route 99, Kamehameha Highway, about one-half mile south of Aloha Stadium; well-marked signs direct you to the ample parking area. If you're on H-1 west, take exit 15A and follow the signs. You can also take TheBus, nos. 20 or 42 from Kuhio Avenue in Waikiki or nos. 20, 42, or 52 from Ala Moana Center or downtown and be dropped off within a minute's walk of the entrance. Depending on stops and traffic, this trip could take over an hour.

The Arizona Memorial Bus Shuttle (808/839-0911), a private operation from Waikiki run by VIP Transportation, takes about half an hour and will pick you up at any Waikiki hotel. It charges $11 round-trip; reservations are necessary, so call a day in advance. It runs every 30 minutes to the memorial 7 A.M.–1 P.M. For your return trip, just find the bus in the parking lot and board. Return trips run until 5:15 P.M.

To see all three of these memorials—a definite recommendation—plan to be at Pearl Harbor by midmorning and make a half day of your visit. Start with the USS *Arizona* and then proceed to the other two.

PARKS AND CULTURAL SITES

Blaisdell County Park

The park's waters, part of Pearl Harbor's East Lock, are too polluted for swimming. It's sad to think that in the late 19th century it was clear and clean enough to support oysters. Pearl Harbor took its name from Waimomi, Water of Pearls, which were indeed harvested from the oysters and a certain species of clam growing here. Today, however, we see firsthand the devastation caused by sewage and uncountable oil spills. Oysters from the Mainland's East Coast have been introduced, but signs still warn of polluted fish and shellfish. Open until 10 P.M., the park has broad grass lawns and young monkeypod and other trees. Facilities include a picnic tables and restrooms. From here you can see the back side of Ford

Island and a few naval ships parked on its periphery. From this point, the water looks like a lake. Local people gather here on weekends and in the cool of the evening. It's a quiet spot to watch the evening turn to night. Access is off Route 99 at the junction of Ka'ahumanu Avenue, about 1.5 miles past Aloha Stadium and just before you enter Pearl City.

The **Pearl Harbor Bike Path,** a biking/jogging right-of-way, skirts the water through this park. It runs for several miles from near the Arizona Memorial, around the top of the bay, and out to Waipahu Depot Road in Waipahu. This path is part of the Pearl Harbor Historic Trail system, an effort by the city and community action groups to expand the recreational opportunities of city residents; it consists of this trail, future biking/jogging trails through golf courses, wildlife refuges, the 'Ewa Plain, additional parkland, the Hawaiian Railway line in 'Ewa, and a future extension of that line into Waipahu.

A short way east of Blaisdell County Park is the much smaller **'Aiea State Recreation Area.** Also set on the water, this diminutive green area has grass lawns, picnic benches, restrooms, and a parking lot, but it seems much less used. As with its neighbor up the road, the Pearl Harbor Bike Path runs along the edge of this park.

Keaiwa Heiau State Recreation Area

As you travel up 'Aiea Heights Road, you get a world-class view of Pearl Harbor below. It's not glorious because it is industrialized, but you do ride through suburban sprawl Hawaiian-style until you come to the end of the road at Keaiwa Heiau State Recreation Area. In the cool heights above 'Aiea, these ancient grounds have a soothing effect the minute you enter. Overnight tent camping, at exceptionally large sites, is allowed here with a permit; for other visitors, the gates open at 7 A.M. and close at 7:45 P.M. (6:45 P.M. in winter). As you enter the well-maintained park (a caretaker lives on the premises), tall pines to the left give a feeling of alpine coolness—great for a picnic.

Below, Pearl Harbor lies open, like the shell of a great oyster.

Keaiwa Heiau was a healing temple, surrounded by gardens of medicinal herbs tended by Hawaii's excellent healers, the *kahuna lapa'au*. Roots, twigs, leaves, and bark from the garden were ground into potions and mixed liberally with prayers and love. These potions were amazingly successful at healing Hawaiians before the white explorers brought diseases. Inside the *heiau* compound, it's somehow warmer and the winds seem quieter. Toward the center are numerous offerings, simple stones wrapped with *ti* leaves. Some are old, while others are quite fresh. Follow the park road to the top and the entrance to the **'Aiea Loop Trail,** which makes a 4.8-mile round-trip loop along the ridges that create the boundary of this park. You'll pass through a forest of tall eucalyptus trees and view canyons to the left and right. Partway up is a bench in a small clearing with a grand view over the mountains and valleys. Notice, too, the softness of the "spongy bark" trees growing where the path begins. Allow three hours for the loop.

Hawaii's Plantation Village

Hawaii's Plantation Village, an open-air museum set below the now-abandoned O'ahu Sugar Mill and smokestack, in Waipahu Cultural Garden Park (94-695 Waipahu St., 808/677-0110, www.hawaiiplantationvillage.org, open Mon.–Sat. 9 A.M.–3 P.M., $13 adults, $7 military and *kama'aina,* $10 seniors, and $5 students 4–11) offers a stroll down memory lane. Plantation buildings have been moved from other locations to create this museumlike village. Among the restored structures are homes and dormitories, a store, camp office, Buddhist shrine, cookhouse, and community bathhouse. The 30 original structures and the photos, artifacts, and memorabilia they contain testify to the hard work performed by Hawaii's sugar plantation communities and provide insight into the eight ethnic groups represented. From 1852 to 1946, nearly 400,000 immigrants were brought to the islands to work in the field industries. Although the Chinese were first and their numbers amounted to 46,000, the Japanese were the largest group at 180,000. These were followed by Portuguese, Puerto Ricans, Okinawans, Koreans, and a smaller number of northern Europeans. The last major influx was by the Filipinos, whose numbers swelled to about 125,000. Each group contributed greatly to the economic health of the islands and over the following decades became part of the cultural mix the state is known for today. In the museum building are homey displays illuminating everyday plantation life of the workers and the industry as a whole. The main museum building functions as an education center and is the start of all tours. It is a fine but brief introduction to the reality of the sugar economy in the islands. Out in the yard stands a train engine, once used to pull cane from the fields to the mill. The displays in the museum building you can see on your own, but the plantation village is open for guided tours only. Tours run about 90 minutes and start every hour 10 A.M.–2 P.M. On Saturdays, the village has hands-on demonstrations and participatory activities that make the entire tour a great learning experience. This is a worthy stop. From Farrington Highway, turn inland onto Waipahu Depot Street and then follow Waipahu Street around to the left to the entrance.

PRACTICALITIES
Shopping

The main shopping center in 'Aiea is the **Pearlridge Shopping Center** (open Mon.–Sat. 10 A.M.–9 P.M., Sun. 10 A.M.–6 P.M.). This is a typical "Anywhere, USA" indoor mall with prices geared toward island residents, not tourists. Some of the larger stores include Macy's, Sears, Longs, and Borders Books and Music. More than 150 smaller boutiques and specialty shops are also here, along with two food courts, more than 25 restaurants, and a 16-screen movie theater. Consisting of two main buildings—the "Uptown" and "Downtown" centers—and several smaller annexes, the entire complex is air-conditioned, and the two major sections are connected by a monorail for your shopping convenience. The Skycab monorail costs $0.50 each way and runs during shopping hours. For your enjoyment, music is performed throughout the week in the Uptown section, second level, and at the Downtown section center court. Plenty of parking is available.

Across the street to the west is the smaller **Westridge Shopping Center,** and across the highway to the south, the **Pearl Kai Shopping Center,** both clusters of shops and eateries. At intervals along Route 99 to the west are additional suburban shopping malls for everything from groceries to fashions.

Along H-1 in Waipahu, the shopping that attracts the most attention is the large **Waikele Shopping Center,** with its typical mall selection of shops like Old Navy, Sports Authority, Big K, and Borders Books and Music. North across Lumiaina Street at **Waikele Premium Outlets** (open Mon.–Sat. 9 A.M.–9 P.M., Sun. 10 A.M.–6 P.M.), you can save money on fashions, furnishings, and specialty items. You'll only find big-name stores at the outlets—think Levi's, Polo Ralph Lauren, Calvin Klein, Banana Republic, and the like—with hardly an island shop in sight. If you need to travel thousands of miles to spend money at logowear shops, this is the place. A favorite of locals, it's also well used by visiting Japanese tourists. For the convenience of shoppers, the Waikele Trolley connects the outlet mall with the shopping center. It also connects the mall with hotels in Waikiki, leaving various locations in Waikiki twice in the morning and returning three times every afternoon and evening; $22 round-trip adults, $8 kids. Reservations preferred (808/591-2561), or have your hotel concierge make the arrangements. A free intra-mall shuttle runs between these two Waikele shopping centers.

Swap Meets

Next to the Westridge complex is the **Kam Swap Meet** site; the **Aloha Stadium Swap Meet** operates in the Aloha Stadium parking lot. Both swap meets run Wednesday, Saturday, and Sunday from early morning until mid-afternoon. More typical outdoor markets than antique or junk markets, these swap meets offer clothing, accessories, bags, jewelry, snack foods, and a great assortment of other goods sold at reasonably low prices.

Accommodations

Except for a handful of long-term apartment hotels, accommodations are virtually nonexistent in this area. One of the available places is the **Harbor Shores Apartment Hotel** (98-145 Lipoa Place, 808/488-5742 or 800/227-8796, fax 808/486-8537, hshores@aloha.net, www.harbor-shores.com). This older but well-cared-for three-story building has 42 two-bedroom apartments that go for around $125 per night, with reduced TLA (temporary lodging allowance) rates for military families. Each furnished unit has linoleum floors and air-conditioning, a complete kitchen, a living room with color cable television, free local phone calls, and a full bath. As a family-oriented hotel, the Harbor Shores has a small swimming pool, fenced children's play area, barbecue grills for outdoor cooking, a laundry facility, parking, and complimentary transportation to nearby military bases and the airport. Only the Pearl Harbor Bike Path lies between it and the water. Located just off Kamehameha Highway and close to H-1, the Harbor Shores is not bothered by traffic noise yet is close to transportation routes and military bases.

Just down the road, the **Harbor Arms Apartment Hotel** (98-130 Lipoa Pl., 808/488-5556 or 800/360-5556, fax 808/488-8385, information@harborarms.com, www.harborarms.com) offers fully furnished air-conditioned studios and apartments, all with kitchens and baths, TV, and phone. Expect rates from about $100 a night, but rates vary according to occupancy and season, so be sure to contact the hotel for a current quote. A coin laundry and swimming pool are also available on property, and there's plenty of parking. The Harbor Arms is a three-story cement block affair, not fancy by any means but clean and well maintained with all the necessary comforts. Because it's TLA-approved, many military personnel use this facility as temporary housing. Airport transportation is provided.

Food
Buzz's Steak House (98-751 Kuahao Pl., 808/487-6465, open weekdays 11 A.M.–2 P.M.,

daily 5–10 P.M.) is at the corner of Ka'ahumanu Avenue, just off H-1. It's futuristic, like something a kid would build with an erector set. It'd be perfect if it were down by the sea, but from where it's located you can peer at Pearl Harbor in the distance or have a world-class view of the freeway. The steakhouse is owned and operated by an old island family whose business grew into a small chain of restaurants from the original location in Kailua. This is one of the remaining two. Buzz's is an institution where islanders go when they want a sure-fire good meal with large portions and a salad bar. Generally, you can get lunch sandwiches and salads for under $12, while the dinner menu has finer meat and fish dishes mostly under $24.

Just down Ka'ahumanu Avenue toward the sea, try **Stuart Anderson's Cattle Co. Restaurant** (808/487-0054, open Mon.–Thurs. 11 A.M.–10 P.M., Fri.–Sat. 11 A.M.–10:30 P.M., Sun. noon–9:30 P.M.). Stuart Anderson's focus is red meat, and they cut their own daily so it's fresh and tasty, but chicken and seafood are also available. Whatever the meal, it'll "come with all the fixin's."

For something Asian, try the Japanese **Gyotaku Restaurant** (98-1226 Ka'ahumanu Ave., 808/487-0091, open 11 A.M.–9 P.M., until 10 P.M. Fri.–Sat.), a few steps away. Stop here for sushi, salad, miso soup, udon or soba noodle dishes, and various full meal or combination plates. Most meals are under $20; luncheon and dinner specials and senior and *keiki* meals all help keep the price down even further.

Wahiawa and Vicinity

Wahiawa is like a military Jeep: basic, but indispensable. This is a real military town, with personnel from Schofield Barracks or nearby Wheeler Air Force Base shuffling along the streets. Most are young, short-haired, and dressed in fatigues. Everywhere you look are cheap bars, liquor stores, burger joints, rundown adult video stores, pawn shops, used car dealers, tattoo parlors, used-furniture stores, and a few Christian fellowship chapels thrown in to save the fallen. Just south of town, Route 99 turns into Route 80, which goes through Wahiawa, crosses the Wahiawa reservoir (fishing is available here), then crosses California Avenue, the main drag, before rejoining Route 99 north of town. Wahiawa has seemingly little to recommend it, and maybe because of its ugliness, when you do find beauty it shines even brighter. As you gain the heights of the Leilehua Plateau, spread between the Waianae and Ko'olau mountain ranges, a wide expanse of green is planted in pineapple. As a traveler's way station, central O'ahu blends services and just enough historical sites to warrant stretching your legs, but not enough to bog you down for the day.

SIGHTS
Schofield Barracks

Stay on Route 99 (here called Wilikina Drive), skirt Wahiawa to the west, and go past the main entrance to Schofield Barracks. Notice the Kemoo Farms building about 50 yards past the entrance. This former outlet for farm produce is now a café/bakery and bar that caters largely to off-duty military personnel who live and work across the road. Stop here and look behind the shops at a wonderful still life created by the Wahiawa Reservoir.

Schofield Barracks dates from the early 1900s, named after General John Schofield, an early proponent of the strategic importance of Pearl Harbor. A sign proclaims it is still Home of the Infantry, Tropic Lightning. Open to the public, the base remains one of the prettiest military installations in the world, and one of the largest, as home to more than 20,000 military personnel and dependents.

You can visit the small **Tropic Lightning Museum** (808/655-0438, open Tues.–Sat. 10 A.M.–4 P.M. except federal holidays, free), with its memorabilia going back to the War of 1812. There are tanks from World War II, Chinese

© ROBERT NILSEN

This tank sits in the front yard of the Tropic Lightning Museum at Schofield Barracks. The museum has a good collection of material relating to the militarization of O'ahu.

rifles from the Korean War, and deadly *pungi* traps from Vietnam. Mostly, it's a portrayal of the history of Schofield Barracks and the 25th Infantry Tropic Lightning Division. The museum is on Waianae Avenue, straight up from Macomb Gate, but entrance to the base is via the Lyman Gate on Kunia Avenue (Route 750). Follow the signs for parking. Since the September 11, 2001, terrorist attacks on the Mainland, nonmilitary visitors need to sign in at Lyman Gate before entering the base. While at the museum, pick up a copy of the Schofield Barracks *Historic Guide,* and spend some time seeing the other sites on the compound or drive up to the Kolekole Pass, where you get a sweeping view of inland and coastal Wai'anae.

Wahiawa Botanical Garden

In the midst of town is an oasis of beauty, 27 acres of developed woodlands and ravine featuring exotic trees, ferns, and flowers gathered from around the world. Part of the Honolulu botanical park system, Wahiawa Botanical

Garden (1396 California Ave., 808/621-7321, open daily 9 A.M.–4 P.M. except Christmas and New Year's Day, free) is just beyond the district park and recreational center. The parking lot is marked by an HVB Warrior; walk through the main entranceway and take a pamphlet from the box (when available) for a self-guided tour. When it rains, the cement walkways are treacherously slippery, especially if you're wearing flip-flops. The nicer paths have been left natural, but they can be muddy. Inside the grounds are trees from the Philippines, Australia, and Africa, and a magnificent multihued Mindanao gum from New Guinea. Fragrant camphor trees from China and Japan and the rich aroma of cinnamon bombard your senses. Everywhere are natural bouquets of flowering trees, entangled by vines and highlighted by rich green ferns. Most specimens have been growing for a minimum of 40 years, so they're well established, and some have been around since the 1920s when this area was an experimental tree farm. This well-kept garden is a delightful little surprise in the midst of this heavily agricultural and military area.

The Healing Stones

Belief in the healing powers of these stones has been attracting visitors since ancient times. When traveling through town on Kamehameha Highway (Route 80), take a left on California Avenue and follow it to Ka'alalo Place. To glimpse the religion of Hawaii in microcosm, in a few blocks you pass the Ryusenji Soto Buddhist Mission, followed by the healing stones, next door to Olive United Methodist Church. If you've never experienced a Buddhist temple, make sure to visit the grounds of this one. Usually no one is around, and even if the front doors are locked you can peer in at an extremely ornate altar graced by a statue of the Buddha, highlighted in black lacquer and gold. On the grounds look for a stone *jizo*, patron of travelers and children. In Japan he often wears a red woven hat and bib, but here he may have on a straw hat and mu'umu'u.

Just past the Ka'ala Elementary School and right at the edge of the street, a small, white, humble cinder-block building built in 1947 houses the healing stones. Although normally locked, the iron gate strikes a deep mournful note when swung open, as if it were an instrument designed to announce your presence and departure. Inside the building, three stones sit atop rudimentary pedestals. It is said that the mystic vibrations of these three stones cured the maladies of sufferers. Little scratches mark the stones, and an offertory box is filled with items like oranges, bread, a gin bottle, coins, and chocolates. A few votive candles flicker before a statue of the Blessed Virgin.

Kukaniloko Birthing Stones

Follow Route 80 through town for about a mile. At the corner of Whitmore Avenue is a stoplight. Right takes you to Whitmore Village; left puts you on a short dirt track that leads to a eucalyptus grove in the midst of fallow pineapple fields marking the birthing stones. About 40 large boulders are in the middle of a field with a mountain backdrop. One stone looks like the next, but on closer inspection you see that each has a personality. Kukaniloko was of extreme cultural and spiritual importance to pre-contact Hawaiians. It is said this site has been used for at least 800 years; the royal wives would come here, assisted by both men and

A BRIEF MILITARY HISTORY

A few military strategists realized the importance of Hawaii early in the 19th century, but most didn't recognize the advantages until the Spanish-American War. It was clearly an unsinkable ship in the middle of the Pacific from which the United States could launch military operations. Pearl Harbor was first surveyed in 1872 by General Schofield, and this world-class anchorage was given to the United States Navy for its use in 1887 as part of the Sugar Reciprocity Treaty. In August 1898, four days after the United States annexed Hawaii, United States Army troops created Camp McKinley at the foot of Diamond Head, and American troops were stationed there until it became obsolete in 1907. Named in General Schofield's honor, Schofield Barracks in central O'ahu became (and remains) the largest military installation in the state. It first housed the U.S. 5th Cavalry in 1909 and was heavily bombed by the Japanese at the outset of World War II. Pearl Harbor, first dredged in 1908, was officially opened on December 11, 1911. The first warship to enter was the cruiser *California*. The Japanese navy attacked Pearl Harbor and other military installations on December 7, 1941. The flames of Pearl Harbor ignited World War II's Pacific theater operations, and there has been no looking back. Ever since that war, the military has been a mainstay of island economy. Following the war, the number of men and installations decreased; today it maintains a force of roughly 35,000, with all branches of the military represented.

© ROBERT NILSEN

Of major cultural significance, the Kukaniloko Birthing Stones lie in a surprisingly mundane setting on the Leilehua Plateau.

women of the ruling *ali'i* class, to give birth to their exalted offspring and future nobles of the islands. On the edge of this group of stones is a special stone that appears to be fluted all the way around, with a dip in the middle. It, along with other stones nearby, seems perfectly fitted to accept the torso of a reclining woman. Nearby was the *heiau* Ho'olono-pahu, where the newborns were consecrated and the baby's umbilical cord, a sacred talisman, was cut. This was followed by the pounding of a drum to announce the birth of a chief.

Dole Pineapple Plantation

North of Wahiawa you begin to pass row upon row of pineapples. Hawaiian pineapple production started in this area at the turn of the 20th century, and it has remained a strong, but now diminishing, force in the economy of O'ahu since then. A few minutes up Route 99 you come to Dole Pineapple Plantation (64-1550 Kamehameha Hwy., 808/621-8408, www.dole-plantation.com), where there's a small demonstration garden of pineapple varieties. Look for

all the tour buses lined up outside. The Dole stop is a monument to retailing with its huge gift shop (open 9 A.M.–5:30 P.M.), where packaged and ready-to-eat pineapples and other food items, logowear, and souvenirs made in Hawaii are yours to purchase. While at the Dole Plantation, visit the "World's Largest Maze." Certified by the *Guinness Book of World Records,* the maze is nearly two acres in area and formed by more than 11,000 native Hawaiian bushes and flowering plants. The maze (open 9 A.M.–5 P.M., $5 adults and $3 children 4–12) will take 20–30 minutes to find your way through—it's a chore and a blast. Here too is the Pineapple Express Train (9 A.M.–5 P.M., $7.50 adults and $5.50 kids), a miniature train that rides a two-mile narrow-gauge rail line for a 20-minute tour through plantation fields. While not a great attraction, this narrated tour is a pleasant ride for the kids. The newest activity is the Garden Tour (9 A.M.–5 P.M., $3.75 adults and $3 for kids), a narrated walk through eight small gardens with commentary on life in the communities that served this plantation.

PINEAPPLE

Ananas comosus of the family Bromeliaceae is a tropical fruit that originated in southern South America. During the 1500s and 1600s, ships' captains took this unusual and intriguingly sweet fruit around the world on their journeys. Pineapples seem to have been brought to Hawaii from somewhere in the Caribbean in the early 1800s, but it wasn't until the mid-1880s that any experimentation was done with them, using the "smooth Cayenne," which is still the dominant commercial fruit variety. The first commercial plots of pineapple production were planted on the Leilehua Plateau at Wahiawa by James Dole just after the turn of the 20th century. To preserve the fruit, he built a cannery there in 1903 and later a second in Iwilei in Honolulu. Expanding his operation, Dole bought the island of Lana'i in 1922 and proceeded to turn the Palawai Basin into one huge pineapple plantation – some 18,000 acres at its greatest extent, producing a million pineapples a day during peak harvest. Relying heavily on canning, Dole made the "king of fruits" a well-known and ordinary food to the American public.

© ROBERT NILSEN

Production of pineapples is a lengthy process. First the ground must be tilled and harrowed to ready the soil for planting. The crowns of the pineapple fruit (which themselves look like miniature pineapple plants) or slips from the stem are planted by hand into long rows – some 30,000 plants per acre. A drip-irrigation system is then installed and the soil covered with ground cloth to help control pests and weeds. Fertilizers and pesticides are sprayed as needed, and the plants grow in the warm tropical sun. After 11–13 months these plants fruit, and some seven months later the first crop is harvested. Generally each plant yields one fruit, which grows on a center stalk surrounded by sharp and spiky curved leaves. The fruit sprouts again and, about 13 months later, a second crop is taken. Sometimes a third crop is also harvested from these same plants, before the remainders are tilled into the soil and the process begins again. Pineapples are picked by hand – a hot, dusty, and prickly job – and then placed on a boom conveyor that dumps them into trucks, which then take them to the cannery. There, all are pressure-washed and sorted by size and quality before being canned or fresh-packed into boxes and shipped to market. Generally about two-thirds are sold as fresh fruit; the remainder is canned. All aspects of production are rotated to keep pineapples available for market throughout the year.

PRACTICALITIES

The streets of Wahiawa are lined with stores that cater to residents, not tourists. This means that the prices are right, and if you need supplies or necessities, this would be a good place to stock up. Up California Avenue toward the botanical garden is **Wahiawa Town Center,** with eateries, a Longs Drugs for sundries, a bank, video store, and laundry; and the smaller **Wahiawa Shopping Center** directly adjacent with a Foodland grocery store and a variety of small ethnic eateries.

Dot's Restaurant (130 Mango St., 808/622-4115, open weekdays 7 A.M.–2:30 P.M. and 5–9 P.M., weekends 7 A.M.–9 P.M.) is a homey, family-style restaurant specializing in standard American and Japanese dishes. The interior is a mixture of Hawaiian and Asian in dark tones. Most selections are under $11, but the nightly prime rib special runs $12–18, depending upon size. At Dot's, you get a good square meal for your money. It's nothing to write home about, but you definitely won't go away hungry.

'Ewa

As far as the average tourist is concerned, the road to 'Ewa is not a road to anywhere of interest. Located just west of Pearl Harbor and not long ago a great expanse of sugarcane fields, 'Ewa now sprouts little more than residential subdivisions and golf courses. It has also been a military stronghold for decades. Military bases edge the western shore of Pearl Harbor, and a huge expanse was taken by the former Naval Air Station Barbers Point, now slowly being turned to other uses. A few isolated and little-used beaches line the 'Ewa south shore, and while not the best for swimming, they are great for seclusion. West of 'Ewa is Kapolei, a new high-tech town with much development that does attract tourists to its luxury hotel, marina, man-made swimming lagoons, water park, and lu'au grounds.

Although it's still in the early stages of development, the 640-acre Ko Olina Resort is set up like other high-class resorts around the islands. Away from the hustle and bustle of the big city, it's a huge, manicured property of well-tended and landscaped lawns, tree-lined boulevards, the respected championship Ko Olina Golf Club, one luxury hotel (for now), several townhouse properties, and a time-share accommodation. Here as well are the Paradise Cove Lu'au park, a marina and public boat launch, four perfectly shaped man-made lagoons for sunbathing and swimming, a seaside pathway, and public access parks—all with plenty of space for growth. Set between the Barbers Point Harbor and the bottom end of the Wai'anae Mountain Range, this resort has a very agreeable location—it gets the most sun and the least rain of any section of the island. The only drawback, which may be less obvious as the resort becomes more built up, is the specter of Campbell Industrial Park down the coast toward Barbers Point.

SIGHTS
Hawaiian Railway Line
No commercial passenger train lines operate in the islands today, but two trains do run for tourists: the Sugar Cane Train on Maui and the Hawaiian Railway train on O'ahu. In 'Ewa, the Hawaiian Railway Society (91-1001 Renton Rd., 808/681-5461, www.hawaiianrailway.com) gives rides, restores and shows engines and train cars, and maintains an open-air train exhibit and gift shop. This organization does more than give tourist rides; it provides an educational adventure. The 90-minute round-trip, fully narrated rides start at 1 P.M. and 3 P.M. on Sunday only; $10 adults and $7 for seniors and children 2–12. No reservations are accepted; it's first-come, first-served. On the third Sunday of every month, the Dillingham parlor car with its luxury appointments is added to the train on both runs. Fares for the parlor car seats are $20. Group charter rides can be arranged weekday mornings. The train runs about seven miles along narrow-gauge track from the 'Ewa station at the end of Renton Road west to the Leeward Coast at Kahe Point, just past the Ko Olina Resort. Don't expect a rail burner—this baby moves at a mild 15 miles an hour. All aboard!

At one time, the O'ahu Railway and Land Company (OR&L) railroad totaled 72 miles of track that ran from Honolulu around Pearl Harbor, up the Leeward Coast, and across the north coast all the way to Kahuku, with another line up from Honolulu to the inland town of Wahiawa. It was a workhorse of a system, hauling people and goods (mostly sugar and molasses), servicing farms and commercial establishments, and, later, transferring troops and bulk items during World War II. After the war, the railroad couldn't compete with the burgeoning bus and trucking firms and the growing importance of the automobile, so the line was shut down at the end of 1947 after 58 years of service, and most of the track taken up. After much labor was expended restoring a section of the remaining track and some rolling stock, the Hawaiian Railway Society began to offer rides to the public in 1989.

'Ewa Beaches
Unlike the small plantation-era town of 'Ewa with its renovated structures, skeleton mill, and

orientation to the farm, 'Ewa Beach is a beach community and working-class town. Near the end of Fort Weaver Road and located across from the NOAA Pacific Tsunami Warning Center is the small **'Ewa Beach County Park.** A broad, grassy area with a few coconut trees and restrooms fronts its narrow sand beach; you can see Honolulu and Diamond Head way off in the distance to the east. Although better swimming beaches are found elsewhere on the island, this is a good place to come if you want to have the beach to yourself.

At the west end of Papipi Road is **One'ula Beach Park,** larger than 'Ewa Beach Park but farther off the main drag. There are some athletic fields and picnic tables here, and many young guys come to surf the mostly gentle waves or shore fish.

Farther west and reached by driving down Coral Sea Road through the old Barbers Point air base is the small and well-maintained **Nimitz Beach Park,** with picnic tables, a covered pavilion, and a lawn. On the way is **White Plains Beach Park,** a surfers' hangout with covered picnic areas, restrooms, and the Shore Break bar and grill (open 11 A.M.–9 P.M.), which serves inexpensive sandwiches, burgers, and beverages. White Plains is a family park with periodic lifeguard coverage. If you are out that way, White Plains is a decent place, but, like all other beaches along this coast, it's a bit far removed just for a spot on the sand. Follow the signs along Coral Sea Road before Nimitz Beach.

Barbers Point Beach County Park

This county park is at the end of Olai Road off Kalaeloa Boulevard. The point was named after Captain Henry Barber, who was shipwrecked near here in 1795. Few people, even island residents, visit this beach park because the shoreline is a limestone shelf, it still hasn't fleshed out to become very pretty, and you have to get to it by driving through the Campbell Industrial Park. One pocket of white-sand beach is open to the public, although it fronts the adjacent Germaine's Lu'au grounds, and you will find picnic tables and restrooms. The

swimming is safe only in summer, but most come for shore fishing.

ENTERTAINMENT
Lu'au

Germaine's Lu'au (808/949-6626 or 800/367-5655, www.germainesluau.com, open Tues.–Sun. 6–8:45 P.M.), often claimed by local people to be *the* best, is held at a private beach at Barbers Point. Of all the lu'au on the island, Germaine's is the most down-home Hawaii of the bunch. The cost for dinner, cocktails, and the Polynesian show runs $65 adults, $55 ages 14–20, and $45 kids 6–13. A free shuttle (reservations required) from Waikiki-area hotels can be booked when calling for tickets.

Paradise Cove Lu'au (808/842-5911 or 800/775-2683, www.paradisecove.com, open daily 5–8:30 P.M.) at the Ko Olina Resort boasts a wonderful dinner with arts-and-crafts displays, games, and other activities on a private beach along the Leeward Coast. Tickets run $73 adults, $63 youth 13–18, and $53 kids 4–12, with enhanced packages at greater cost. Paradise Cove is in a well-landscaped 12-acre parklike setting, and the production is definitely tourist-oriented. Transportation by shuttle bus from Waikiki is included in the admission. The shuttle bus departs from various hotels starting at 3:45 P.M. and returns by about 9:30 P.M.

SHOPPING

In Kapolei, you will find the **Kapolei Shopping Center,** the **Marketplace at Kapolei,** and other nearby shopping areas, perfect for those staying on this coast. Among the numerous shops are a Longs Drugs, Blockbuster Video, UPS Store, plenty of boutiques, a Safeway for food shopping, three banks with ATMs, three gas stations, and plenty of fast-food eateries for inexpensive dining. A movie theater, post office, and several big box stores are a short distance to the west on Kamokila Boulevard.

RECREATION
Hawaiian Waters Adventure Park

Whether it's barreling down the four-story slide, bodysurfing at the wave pool, floating leisurely

HAWAIIAN LU'AU

The lu'au is an island institution. For a fixed price, you get to gorge yourself on a tremendous variety of island foods, sample a few island drinks, and have an evening of entertainment as well. Generally, lu'au run from about 5 P.M. to 8:30 P.M. On your lu'au day, eat a light breakfast, skip lunch, and do belly-stretching exercises! This tourist variety lu'au is a lot of fun, but definitely a show. The least expensive, most authentic, and best lu'au are often put on by local churches or community groups. If you ask locals which is the best, you won't get two to agree. It's literally a matter of taste.

All commercial lu'au have pretty much the same format, though the type of food and entertainment differ somewhat. To have fun at a lu'au you have to get into the swing of things. Entertainment is provided by local performers in what is usually called a Polynesian Revue. This includes the tourist's hula – the fast version with swaying hips and dramatic lighting – a few wandering troubadours singing Hawaiian standards, and someone swinging flaming torches. Although individual lu'au vary, some offer an *imu* ceremony where the pig is taken from the covered oven, as well as traditional games, arts, and crafts. Food is usually served buffet-style, although a few do it family-style. All of the Hawaiian standards are usually served, but if those don't suit your appetite, various Asian dishes, plus chicken, fish, and roast beef are most often also on the table. If you leave a lu'au hungry, it's your own fault!

The lu'au master starts the *imu* on the morning of the gathering; stop by and watch if it's permitted. He lays the hot stones and banana stalks so well that the underground oven maintains a perfect 400°F. In one glance, the lu'au master can gauge the weight and fat content of a succulent porker and decide just how long it should be cooked. The water in the leaves covering the pig steams and roasts the meat so that it falls off the bone. Local wisdom has it that "All you can't eat in the *imu* are the hot stones."

down the curvaceous and continuous "river" in an inner tube, or playing with the kids in the *keiki* pool, a day at Hawaiian Waters is good, clean fun in a safe environment, with appropriate activities for all ages. Opened in 1999 in Kapolei, this 25-acre water-theme park is the only one of its kind in Hawaii. Other amenities include a picnic area, bathrooms and changing rooms, lockers, a first-aid station, food concessions, gift shops, a musical performance stage, and plenty of free parking. Don't forget your hat and sunscreen. This is the sunniest side of the island! Hawaiian Waters (400 Farrington Hwy., 808/674-9283, www.hawaiianwaters.com) is open 10:30 A.M.–5 P.M. through the summer, until 3:30 P.M. on weekdays, and until 4 P.M. on weekends the rest of the year, with periodic days off for maintenance. All-day admission runs $35 adults, $25 kids 3–11, with *kama'aina,* senior, and group rates for savings.

Ocean Activities

Ocean activities for this section of O'ahu focus on boats that operate out of the private Ko Olina Marina, the newest and most modern facility on the island. There is pay parking at the marina for all marina users. Aside from slip space, you will find the **Ko Olina Marina Store and Deli** (808/676-3348, open 6:30 A.M.–6 P.M.) for sundries, clothing, and a limited deli menu of pastries, soups, salads, plate lunches, and sandwiches, with most items $6.50 or less.

Offering water activities along the leeward shore is **Ko Olina Ocean Adventures** (808/396-2068, www.koolinaoceanadventures.net). Running its boat from the Ko Olina Marina, this company offers four-hour excursion including snorkeling and a passive swim with the dolphins daily at 7 A.M. and 11:30 A.M. at $95 for adults and $68 for kids. During the months of winter and spring when the whales come to spend time in the warm Hawaiian waters, guests on these tours have the extra treat of a whale-watching experience. Ask about the snuba option, which costs extra. Transportation to or from Waikiki can be arranged for an extra fee.

Hawaii Nautical (808/234-7245, www.hawaiinautical.com) runs its *Ko Olina Cat* catamaran on morning and afternoon snorkel trips up the coast as well as a sunset sail. Snorkel trips run $99.50 for adults and $83.50 for kids, while the sunset sail is $45 and $35, respectively. The *Lied Back* does private half-day sails for $700 and dinner cruises at $190 per person. Late morning scuba trips can also be arranged on the monohull *Sea Dreams II* at $125 per person with equipment. Depending on water conditions and divers' experience, operators choose any of about a dozen coral, cave, or wreck sites to visit.

For competitive rates, the large and sleek *Ka ʻOli ʻOli* catamaran also cruises up the coast to Kaʻena Point on snorkel/sail and sunset sail excursions, where you'll almost always see dolphins. Contact **Ocean Joy Cruises** (808/677-1277 or 888/677-1277, www.oceanjoycruises.com).

For sportfishing, inquire with **Boom Boom Sportfishing** (808/306-4162, www.boomboomsportfishing.com), where boats run from either the Ko Olina Marina or from the Waianae Harbor up the coast. From Ko Olina, rates run $500 for a four-hour charter or $175 shared, or $700 for an eight-hour charter or $125 shared.

Golf and Tennis

The green velvet of the **Ko Olina Championship Golf Course,** designed by Ted Robinson and named one of the finest courses in America by *Golf Digest,* fronts the hotel. Open since 1990, the course is fully matured and has already hosted prestigious tournaments. If you'd rather play tennis, day or evening (sunrise–8:30 P.M.), the JW Marriott Ihilani has three hard plexipave and three artificial grass Kramer surface tennis courts on top of the hotel's parking structure. Court time can be arranged for $22 per hour, and instruction, round robins, and clinics are offered for extra fees.

ACCOMMODATIONS
JW Marriott Ihilani Resort and Spa

The 🄲 **JW Marriott Ihilani Resort and Spa** (92-1001 Olani St., 808/679-0079 or 800/626-4446, fax 808/679-0080, www.ihilani.com),

an alabaster specter floating amid the emerald-green acres of the Ko Olina Resort, rises above a white-sand beach at the southern end of the Waiʻanae coast. It's about one-half hour west of the Honolulu airport—simply follow the H-1 expressway to the clearly marked Ko Olina exit. You approach the resort by way of a cobblestone drive that winds its way up to a porte cochere. The open breezeway leads to a towering glass-domed atrium brightened by cascading trellised flowers and ringed by living green ferns. Below, rivulets trickle through a series of free-form ponds, some like glass-reflecting sculptures, others alive and tinkling a natural refrain. The guest rooms, huge at almost 700 square feet, are pleasantly appointed in pastels and white, and all feature air-conditioning, ceiling fans, louvered doors, remote-control entertainment centers, in-room safes, mini-bars, and private lanai. Bathrooms, an intricate play of marble and tile, feature double sinks, separate commode and shower stalls, and deep oversize tubs. Evening brings turndown service. Mountain- and garden-view rooms run $425–465, while oceanview rooms go for $545–585 per night; suites run $850–4,500. Many spa, golf, tennis, and honeymoon packages are available, and these save a good deal on room rates. With time and maturity, the Ihilani Resort and Spa, tucked away from the madding crowd, has become one of Oʻahu's premier destinations and has received the prestigious AAA four-diamond award for excellence in service and accommodations.

Other amenities are 24-hour room service, concierge service, a small clutch of boutiques, a *keiki* beachcomber club, tennis courts, and a full-service spa. Free cultural activities are scheduled throughout the week, and there's evening entertainment at poolside. For the more adventurous, interactive explorations of the saltwater pools and the sharks, rays, fish, and other sea creatures that inhabit them are offered daily for a fee. The terrace is a perfect place to relax after a dip in the circular freshwater pool, but for a more athletic swim, try the gentle lagoon down below.

In a separate facility just a short walk across

from the main entrance is the **Ihilani Spa** (808/679-3321), a magnificently soothing, re-vitalizing, and uniquely Hawaiian spa experience. This facility is centered on Thalasso water therapy, a computer-controlled water-jet massage utilizing fresh seawater and seaweed. After being immersed in this state-of-the-art tub, you move on to the Vichy Shower, Grand Jet, or Needle Pavilion, where 12 shower heads poke stimulating sprays into every nook and cranny. Next, the superbly trained staff offers therapeutic massage, including Swedish, *lomi lomi,* or shiatsu. You can also opt for a mani-cure, pedicure, or skin-rejuvenating facial. To keep trim and supple, head for the fitness fa-cility on the third level, where you will find a lap pool, hot tub, aerobics room, and strength-training equipment.

FOOD
At the Resort
Dining at the Ihilani is a fantastic blending of East and West, relying heavily on locally grown herbs, vegetables, meats, and most im-portant, island seafood. It is a blissful marriage of Mediterranean, Oriental, and Hawaiian cuisine that can easily be influenced by ingre-dients from around the world. The Ihilani's signature restaurant, a AAA four-diamond award winner, is **Azul** (808/679-0079, open for dinner only Tues.–Sat. 6–9 P.M., Sunday brunch 10 A.M.–2 P.M.), complemented by a magnificent wine cellar. Here the flavors of fish and seafood, mixed with the cuisines of the Mediterranean, are cooked to their finest over the wood-fired oven and grill. Select en-trées might include poached Maine lobster and tiger shrimp, seared tenderloin of beef, slow braised lamb shank, or peppercorn ahi, most in the $30–40 range. Breakfast, lunch, and din-ner of more contemporary Hawaiian cuisine and buffets three nights a week are served at the open-air (**Naupaka Terrace** (808/679-0097, open 6:30 A.M.–10 P.M.), with views of the pool and lagoon, with most entrées in the

$21–34 range. Traditional Japanese fare, which includes Monday, Friday, and Saturday night buffets, is offered for dinner only at **Ushio Tei** (808/679-0097, open Thurs.–Mon. 5:30–9 P.M.). For snacks and drinks during the day, try the **Poolside Grill**; for cocktails and small plates in the evening, head to the **Hokule'a Lounge.** In additional to these options, health-conscious breakfasts and lunch spa cuisine are also offered at the Ihilani Spa.

Golfers and others who are into the casual setting overlooking the golf course's 18th hole and perimeter pond will enjoy clubhouse din-ing at the Ko Olina Golf Club's **Roy's Ko Olina** (808/676-7697, open noon–2 P.M. and 5:30–9 P.M.). During the day, your order might be a sandwich or seafood pasta medley. In the evening, the options are more filling, with plenty of favorites from the land and sea, with most entrées in the $25–34 range.

In Town
Located across the road from the Kapolei Theater, **Buono Pasto Assaggio Ristorante Italiano** (open Thurs.–Tues. 11 A.M.–3 P.M., daily 4:30–9:30, Fri.–Sat. until 10 P.M.) is more upscale than most nonresort restaurants in the area—and perhaps the best restaurant in Kapolei. It has a traditional Italian menu with the usual pasta and house specials, but also a good number of seafood items, with most din-ner entrées in the $18–22 range.

Also worth a try is the nearby and less expen-sive **Kapolei Chinese Restaurant** (808/674-8888, open daily 10 A.M.–9 P.M.), where most dishes run $6.25–8.25.

In the Marketplace at Kapolei (590 Far-rington Hwy.), you will find a number of ethnic eateries generally open 9 A.M.–9 P.M. Among the many are **En Fuego** (808/674-8805), which does a variety of home-style dishes and *poke;* **Kapolei Korean B.B.Q.** (808/674-8822); **Tokyo Noodle House** (808/692-9888); and **Julie'z Restaurant** (808/693-8778), for down-home Filipino cooking.

THE LEEWARD COAST

The Wai'anae (Mullet Waters) coast, the leeward face of O'ahu, is separated physically from the rest of the island by the Wai'anae Range. Spiritually, culturally, and economically, the separation is even more profound. This area is O'ahu's last stand for ethnic Hawaiians, and for that phenomenal cultural blending of people called *locals*. Some warn tourists against going to Wai'anae because the idea of "us against them" permeates the consciousness of the area. If you follow this poor advice, you miss not only the last of undeveloped coastal O'ahu, but also the absolute pleasure of meeting people who will treat you with genuine *aloha*. Along the coast are magnificent beaches long known for their surf and one small humble community after another. Wai'anae is the home to families that hold *lu'au*

on festive occasions, where the food and entertainment are the real article. Anyone lucky enough to be invited into this quickly disappearing world will be blessed with one of the last authentic cultural experiences in Hawaii.

The possibility of hassles shouldn't be minimized because they do happen. The biggest problem is thievery, of the sneak-thief variety. The toughness of Wai'anae is self-perpetuating, and frankly some of the locals *like* the hard reputation. In years past, *pakalolo* (marijuana) has had a tremendous effect on the area. The *pakalolo* trade brought some money back into the depressed region, and it changed the outlook of some of the residents. They felt camaraderie with other counterculture people, many of whom happened to be *haole*. They could relax and not feel so threatened with pursuing an

HIGHLIGHTS

◖ **Poka'i Bay Beach County Park:** A near-idyllic bay for playing in the sand and warm water, this beach park makes a great stop for your time on the Leeward coast (page 169).

◖ **Makaha Beach County Park:** This is the best spot on the Leeward Coast to see local surfers riding the waves and a good place, most of the year, for you to give it a go as well (page 169).

◖ **Ka'ena Point State Park:** One of the few places on the island of O'ahu – and in the state as a whole – that still preserves a coastal dune ecosystem. It is a nature reserve for several threatened and endangered plants and birds (page 170).

◖ **Kane'aki Heiau:** O'ahu's long and dry Leeward Coast had a large and sustained population in pre-contact times. This rebuilt *heiau* is the best physical representation of an ancient Hawaiian cultural site on this coast (page 171).

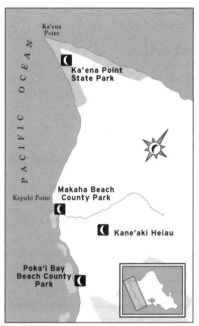

LOOK FOR ◖ TO FIND RECOMMENDED SIGHTS, ACTIVITIES, DINING, AND LODGING.

often elusive materialistic path. Many became more content with their laid-back lifestyle and genuinely less interested in the materialistic trip all the way around.

Years ago, it was thought that this northwest coast would be the next large region of development, and indeed some was done. However, with the downturn in the Hawaiian economy throughout the 1990s and into the 2000s, less was accomplished than some had envisioned.

PLANNING YOUR TIME

A trip up the Wai'anae Coast should take just one day, unless you intend to stay and let the slow pace of life become your pace of life. Except for Kane'aki Heiau, all sights of interest along

this coast are along the ocean; more specifically, they are the beaches. It's perhaps best as a first-time visitor to make the drive to the end of the road and then stop on the way back down to swim or surf. If you intend to hike to Ka'ena Point, beyond the end of the road, plan on several hours there and back from the state park parking lot. Remember that Kane'aki Heiau is open only for a few hours during the middle of the day, so plan a stop there accordingly.

SIGHTS

Many of the sights along this coast are beach parks. Four of the beach parks offer camping. Some campers are local people in semipermanent structures. Remember that this is the Leeward Coast, which gets plenty of sunshine. Many of the beach parks do not have shade trees, so be prepared. June is the prettiest month because all the flowers are in bloom, but it's one of the worst times for sunburn. The entire coast is great for snorkeling, with plenty of reef fish. However, keep your eyes on the swells, and always stay out of the water during rough seas, when waves can batter you against the rocks. The parks listed in this section run from south to north.

Kahe Point Beach County Park and Tracks Beach Park

These parks are just where the Farrington Highway curves north along the coast. They're the first two *real* Wai'anae beaches, and they're symbolic of the divide between "local" O'ahu and the rest of the island. You come around the bend to be treated to an absolutely pristine view of the coast with the rolling sea, a white-sand beach, a cove, and the most hideous power plant you've ever seen. Facilities at Kahe Point Beach County Park are restrooms, a phone, a pavilion, and picnic tables. The beach is poor except for a section just north of the improved park, and this is known as Electric Beach because it sits just opposite the power plant. Swimming is dangerous except on calm summer days. More often, you'll find people surfing and bodysurfing here, and some scuba companies bring guests here to enter the water.

A short way along is a mostly undeveloped area known as Tracks to island surfers because of the railroad tracks that run along the shore here. The white-sand beach is wide, and the swimming generally safe. The mild waves are perfect for learning how to surf. If you keep your eyes trained out to sea, the area is beautiful.

Nanakuli Beach County Park

This park is on the southern outskirts of Nanakuli (Pretend to be Deaf) town, the first real town of the Wai'anae coast. The beach park is community-oriented, with recreational buildings, basketball courts, a baseball diamond, and children's play area. Camping is permitted with a county permit. Lifeguards

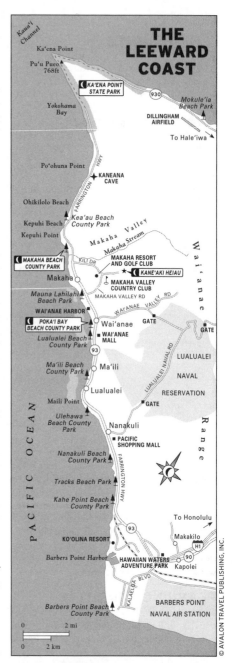

work on a daily basis, and the swimming is generally safe except during periods of high winter surf. The southern section, called Piliokahe, is fronted by a cliff with a small cove below, and you'll often see fishermen casting off the cliff edge here. This cliff is lithified sandstone overlaying lava. During periods of calm surf, the waters are crystal clear and perfect for snorkeling. The northern section, called Kalaniana'ole, is generally calmer than the southern end. A pathway runs between these sections.

Ulehawa Beach County Park

Just north of Nanakuli and running for a good long way along the coast, this park offers restrooms, picnic facilities, lifeguards, and sometimes camping. The best swimming is in a sandy pocket near the lifeguard tower at the south end. Surf conditions make for good bodysurfing. Most of the park, along a rocky cliff, is undeveloped, although the parking areas have been improved. Here you'll find unlimited fishing spots. A shallow lagoon is generally safe for swimming year-round. As always, it's best to check with the local people on the beach.

Ma'ili Beach County Park

This park stretches along the length of Ma'ili (Pebbly) town. It lies between two streams coming down from the mountains. Amenities include restrooms, picnic facilities, and lifeguard towers, and the site is one of the best beaches along the coast. Camping is permitted with a county permit on weekends only. The best swimming is in front of the lifeguard towers at the northern end. In wintertime the beach disappears, but it returns wide and sandy for the summer. Plenty of coral pockets offer good snorkeling. Don't just jump in—ask the locals or swing by the lifeguard tower to make sure it's safe.

Lualualei Beach County Park

This beach lies in the town of Wai'anae across from the Wai'anae Mall and is generally decent for swimming in summer. Directly south of

there and along the highway is a narrow strip of sand between the road and the water lying directly below Pu'u Ma'ili'ili, a fist of a hill that pushes nearly to the water. This park has restrooms, picnic facilities, and camping during summer. The entire park is largely undeveloped and lies along low cliffs and raised coral reef. Swimming is almost impossible. It's primarily good for fishing and looking.

((Poka'i Bay Beach County Park

This park is one of the nicest along the Wai'anae coast, just off the main drag in Wai'anae town. It provides restrooms, picnic facilities, lifeguards, and a boat ramp, which brings plenty of small craft into the area. Set on Kane'ilio Point is Kuiluiloa Heiau. Don't be surprised to see a replica of a double-hulled canoe. It's been used for publicity purposes and has appeared in a beer commercial. The park is reasonably well maintained and family-oriented. There's surfing, sailboarding, snorkeling, and safe swimming year-round. If you're heading for one beach along Wai'anae, this is a top choice.

Mauna Lahilahi Beach Park

As you proceed north, you pass the Wai'anae intermediate and high schools, as well as Wai'anae Small Boat Harbor. As you approach the town of Makaha, you can't help spotting the dominant headland called Mauna Lahilahi, a onetime island. Called Black Rock by the local fishermen, it still marks Makaha. Below it, at the Makaha Valley Road turn, is the small Mauna Lahilahi Beach Park, without amenities.

((Makaha Beach County Park

This beach is famous for surfing. Surfing competitions have been held here since the Makaha International Surfing Competition began in 1952. Years later, a local lifeguard named Richard "Buffalo" Keaulana, known to all who've come here, began the Annual Buffalo Big Board Riding Championship. Paul Strauch Jr., a local surfing legend and inventor of the "cheater five," came to Makaha whenever he had a chance, along with Buffalo's sons and other pro surfers, many of whom live in the area. In 1995, Buffalo retired after 36 years as a lifeguard.

The swimming can be dangerous during high surf but excellent on calm days of summer. Winter brings some of the biggest surf in Hawaii. Always pay heed to the warnings of the lifeguards. Extra parking, bathrooms, and a canoe shed have been created across the road.

Kea'au Beach County Park

This park has restrooms, picnic facilities, and the greatest number of camping spots on the coast. The improved part of the park has a small sandy beach, but most is fronted by coral and lava and is frequented mostly by fishermen and campers. The unimproved section is not good for swimming, but it does attract a few surfers; it's good for snorkeling and scuba only during calm periods. The improved section is a flat, grassy area with picnic tables, a few shade trees, and pavilions. Farther on is Ohikilolo Ranch, a couple of homeless camps along the water, a few private homes, and more strands of solitary beach.

K Ka'ena Point State Park

Once past Makaha, there are plenty of private places to pull off. This crab claw of land, which ends at Ka'ena Point, forms a lightly indented bay. The seascape demands attention, but look into the interior. The mountains seem naturally terraced as they form dry, deep valleys. All are micro-habitats, each different from the other.

Keawa'ula Bay, also called Yokohama Bay, is the end of the line; the pavement ends here at a long stretch of sandy beach. If you're headed for Ka'ena Point or beyond to the north coast, you'll have to walk through this windswept coastal park. The park is mostly unimproved except for a lava-rock bathhouse on the right just after the entrance. The area was named because of the multitude of Japanese fishermen who came to this lonely site to fish. It's still great for fishing! The swimming can be hazardous because of the strong wave action and rough bottom, but sunbathing is tops. Lifeguards are on duty during summer. Mostly the area is used by surfers and local people, including youngsters who dive off the large lava rocks. This is inadvisable for people who are unfamiliar with the area. Yokohama is a great place to come if you're after a secluded beach. Weekdays, you'll have it to yourself, with a slightly greater number of people on the weekends. Definitely bring cold drinks, and remember that there are no shade trees whatsoever, so a hat or beach umbrella is a necessity. You can still see cement railroad track abutments and embedded railroad ties, remnants of the rail line that once ran around the point to the North Shore. A gigantic golf ball—really a U.S. satellite tracking station—caps the ridge above this park.

The hike out to the point or around to the end of the road on the North Shore is hot and dry. There is no shade and no amenities. Bring plenty of water and a hat. The trail is level and easy to follow because it was the old rail bed, but parts are rocky and may be muddy. In at least one spot the trail has been washed away, so you will have to scramble down into and out of a low gully. When the trade winds are blowing, this south side is protected from the wind, but once at the point you feel the trades. The point has been set aside as the **Ka'ena Point Natural Area Reserve** and the low sand dune environment here harbors hardy and mostly ground-hugging plant species like the beach naupaka, 'ilima, pa'u o Hi'iaka, and pohinahina. This point is also home to various shore nesting and breeding seabirds like the Laysan albatross; others, such as the wedgetail shearwater, red-footed booby, and brown noddy are also seen. On occasion, Hawaiian monk seals and *honu* (green sea turtles) may also be seen on the beach. Leave them alone and give them plenty of space. During winter, you'll undoubtedly spy humpback whales frolicking off the point.

A few minutes south of Yokohama Bay on the inland side as you head down the coast is **Kaneana Cave.** You probably wouldn't notice it on your way north because of the land formation that conceals the mouth in that direction, but it is obvious as you drive south. Legend has it that this cave was the home of Nanue the shark man. Look for three yellow cement blocks, like road dividers, right in front of the cave's yawing mouth. It's at the foot of a 200-foot outcropping of stone.

◖ Kane'aki Heiau

Makaha can translate as Water Breaking Out to Sea because of the area's propensity for damming runoff waters from the mountains behind the beach until enough pressure forces it to "break out." However, there is another meaning for Makaha that doesn't help its image. The second translation, Fierce, aptly describes a gang of bandits who long ago lived in the surrounding hills and terrorized the region. They would wait for small bands of people walking the road, then swoop down and relieve them of their earthly goods.

If you follow Kili Drive inland, you pass condos and high-rises clinging to the arid walls of this leeward valley. Turning right onto Huipu Drive, or alternately, driving up Makaha Valley Road from the highway, you reach an artificial oasis of green that is the Makaha Resort and Golf Club and Makaha Valley Country Club. Continue inland on Maunaolu Street to visit the Kane'aki Heiau, a 16th- or 17th-century temple restored under the direction of the Bishop Museum in 1970. This temple was dedicated to Lono, the benevolent god of harvest and fertility, but later may have been converted to a *luakini heiau* for human sacrifice. The thatched huts used as prayer and meditation chambers, along with a spirit tower and carved images, have all been replicated. Because the *heiau* is within a private gated community, access is limited to Tues.–Sun. 10 A.M.–2 P.M. It may be closed even during those times when it's too rainy or muddy. Stop at the guard house and let them know where you're heading. They will ask to see your identification and car registration or car rental agreement before they sign you in.

SHOPPING AND SERVICES

The **Wai'anae Mall** is the largest and most complete shopping facility on the coast. The

Oracle towers and carved wooden figure at Kane'aki Heiau

mall holds all you need, including a few clothing and gift shops, Blockbuster Video, Longs Drugs, and a coin laundry in the back. Banking needs can be taken care of at the Bank of Hawaii or American Savings Bank branch offices. Just a short way up the highway on the seaward side is a post office.

For Internet access, head for **Michelle Lee's** (85-794 Farrington Hwy., #A1, 808/696-8809, open Mon.–Fri. 8 A.M.–5 P.M., Sat. 10 A.M.–2 P.M.) in Wai'anae, where you can get online for $0.10/minute, $2 minimum.

There are a number of small markets and convenience stores up and down this coast. At the Makaha Valley Road intersection in Makaha is a 7-Eleven convenience store with an attached **gas station,** your last chance to fill your tank as you head up the coast. Across the street is the **Makaha Wash Spot** (808/695-8307, open 6:30 A.M.–9 P.M.), a self-serve laundry that also has drop-off service for those who are too busy to do their own.

RECREATION
At Wai'anae Small Boat Harbor

To get a look at a small working harbor or for ocean activities, visit the Wai'anae Small Boat Harbor, located next to Wai'anae High School. Huge installed stones form an impressive man-made harbor, with everything from luxury yachts to aluminum fishing boats.

Ocean Concepts (808/696-7200, www.ocean concepts.com) runs scuba tours from its office at the harbor. Half-day, one-tank boat dives run $125; shore dives at Electric Beach and certification courses are also offered.

Wild Side Specialty Tours (808/306-7273, www.sailhawaii.com) runs a catamaran up the Leeward Coast on morning wildlife sails at $95, afternoon reef snorkel trips at $75, and sunset sails for $95, narrated by the knowledgeable crew.

Boom Boom Sportfishing (808/306-4162, www.boomboomsportfishing.com) runs half- and full-day deep-sea fishing trips off the Leeward Coast for $400–600 or $100–150 for a shared ride. The smaller 30-foot *kaimalolo* of

Kaimalolo Sportfishing (808/695-3474) runs half-day charters for $275, $400 for 8 hours, and $550 for 12 hours.

For sports rental gear while on the Wai'anae Coast, head to **Hale Nalu Surf & Bike** (85-876 Farrington Hwy., 808/696-5897, open daily 10 a.m.–7 p.m., www.halenalu.com), just up from the Wai'anae Mall in the center of Wai'anae town. Hale Nalu rents mountain and hybrid bikes at $24/day, snorkel gear at $8/day, body boards at $11/day, and surf boards at $19–22/day. Three-day and weekly rates are also available, as are beach chairs, umbrellas, life vests, and other beach gear.

Golf

Wai'anae sports two fine but not luxury golf courses, both located up Makaha Valley Road. The Makaha Resort Golf Club is located at the Makaha Resort, and the Makaha Valley Country Club is a short distance away at a turn in the road just before the resort. Both courses are well kept with plenty of good views over the coast and up onto the

SEASICKNESS

Many people are affected by motion sickness, particularly on sailing vessels. If you tend to get queasy, try one of the following to prevent symptoms. Although there are others, oral medications widely available in pharmacies are Dramamine, Bonine, and Triptone. Dramamine and Bonine may cause drowsiness in some people; Triptone seems not to. Although these medications are usually taken just before boarding a ship, they might work better if a half dose is taken the night before and the second half dose is taken the morning of your ride. In all cases, however, take medication as prescribed by the manufacturer.

Other people swear by ginger capsules; take as directed. Look for these at health food stores, nutrition centers, or alternative medicine dealers.

An alternative to medication is Sea-Bands, elastic bands worn around the wrists that put gentle pressure on the inside of the wrist by way of a small plastic button. Sea-Bands are available at pharmacies and at most scuba shops and can be reused until the elastic wears out. Follow directions for best results.

Without medication or pressure bands, you can still work to counter the effects of motion sickness. The night before, try not to eat too much, particularly greasy food, and don't drink alcohol to excess. If your stomach begins to feel upset, try eating a few soda crackers. If you begin to feel dizzy, focus on the horizon or a mountaintop – something stationary – and try to direct your thoughts to something other than your dizziness or queasiness. With children (and perhaps adults as well), talking about what animal figures they can see in the clouds or how many houses they can spot along the shoreline may be enough to distract them until they begin feeling better.

mountainside. Rates for both are around a moderate $80 for 18 holes.

ACCOMMODATIONS
◖ Makaha Resort and Golf Club

After several years of closure, then a major renovation and refurbishment, the old Sheraton Makaha Resort was reopened under new ownership as the Makaha Resort and Golf Club (84-626 Makaha Valley Rd., 808/695-9544 or 866/576-6447, fax 808/695-7558, www.makaharesort.net). This property has a wonderful location set back in the Makaha Valley, surrounded by the *pali,* and is accompanied by a great golf course. Its western orientation allows for perfect sunsets, which are common because this is the sunniest and driest part of the island. The location gives this resort seclusion, yet it is close enough to reach the water by a short drive. From the reception building, which houses the registration desk, the hotel's one restaurant and lounge, and golf pro shop, detached buildings step down the gentle slope of the property. Somewhat dated by their design and style and sweeping Polynesian-style wood-shingle roofs—it was built in the 1960s—each of these buildings contains several rooms, and all of the buildings are connected by walkways. Because of the layout, you and your bags will be driven to your room by golf cart, but it's only a short walk to any point on the property. The entire property has gone through a thorough renovation, and all rooms and public areas have been brought up to date. Rooms, with their pleasing island colors and decor, contain king-size or double beds, a full bath and private lanai, writing desk and chairs, coffeemaker, television, and small refrigerator, and all are air-conditioned. The large, inviting swimming pool provides sweeping views of the mountains and coast. Standard rooms start at around $129 per night, suites from about $219, with several discounted rates offered. For its location and amenities, the Makaha Resort and Golf Club offers a great deal for a reasonable price.

Condominiums

Except for camping, most inexpensive places to stay along the Wai'anae Coast are in condos. Depending on the season, number of rooms, and property, rates generally fall into the $400–500 per week range for studios, $500–700 for one-bedroom units, and up to $1,000 for two bedrooms. Monthly rates are also available, and you usually get substantial savings for longer rentals. Most require a minimum stay of four to seven days, while some can only be rented by the month.

The three-story **Maili Cove** (87-561 Farrington Hwy.) in Ma'ili is a beachfront complex with one-bedroom apartments, a swimming pool, and parking. The least expensive accommodations are at the four-story **Makaha Surfside** (85-175 Farrington Hwy.), just up the coast north of the high school. The beach may be rocky in front of this condo, but it makes up for this with two pools. All units are individually owned and fully furnished. Next up the way, at Lahilahi Point, are the **Makaha Beach Cabanas** (84-965 Farrington Hwy.). This nine-story complex is not fancy, but it's clean and serviceable. Next door and a step up in quality and price is the taller **Hawaiian Princess** (84-1021 Farrington Hwy.). Farthest up the coast, the **Makaha Shores** (84-265 Farrington Hwy.) overlook the beautiful white-sand Makaha Beach and provide great viewing of the surfers challenging the waves below.

Two other complexes are inland and away from the water. **Makaha Valley Towers** (84-749 Kili Dr.) rise dramatically from Makaha Valley, but they don't fit in. They're either a testament to man's achievement or ignorance, depending on your point of view. The condo provides fully furnished studio, one-, and two-bedroom units. If you're staying in this tall high-rise, try to get an upper floor, where you can take advantage of the remarkable view. Just below the Towers is the **Makaha Valley Plantation** (84-786 Ala Mahiku), an aesthetic low-rise community with generally larger units that better fits the land.

For condominium rentals along this coast, contact Inga's Realty (808/695-9055, fax 808/695-8060, www.ingasrealty.com), Sugar Kane Realty (808/696-5833, fax 808/696-7573, www.sugarkanerealty.com), or Hawaii

MEAL MONEYSAVERS

Only one thing is better than a great meal: a great meal at a reasonable price. The following are island institutions and favorites that will help you eat well yet keep prices down.

KAUKAU WAGONS

These are lunch wagons, but instead of slick, stainless-steel jobs, most are old delivery trucks converted into portable kitchens. Some say they're a remnant of World War II, when workers had to be fed on the job; others say the meals they serve were inspired by the Japanese *bento*, a boxed lunch. You'll see the wagons parked along beaches, in city parking lots, or on busy streets. Usually a line of local people will be placing their orders, especially at lunchtime – a tip-off that the wagon serves delicious, nutritious island dishes for reasonable prices. They might have a few tables, but basically they serve food to go. Kaukau wagons specialize in the plate lunch.

PLATE LUNCH

One of the best island standards, these lunches give you a sampling of authentic island food that can include teriyaki chicken, mahimahi, *laulau*, and *lomi* salmon, among others. They're served on paper or Styrofoam plates, are packed to go, and usually cost less than $7. Standard with a plate lunch is "two-scoop rice," and a generous dollop of macaroni or other salad. These full meals are great for keeping down food costs and for instant picnics. They are available everywhere from *kaukau* wagons to restaurants.

An innovation on the regular plate lunch is starting to pop up here and there in finer restaurants and even at a few *kaukau* wagons. This is a better-quality plate lunch with the freshest ingredients, more health-conscious preparation, and a greater inventiveness in the foods chosen, and they're often served in a classier manner. As would be expected, these meals are not available everywhere yet and cost up to twice as much as the ordinary plate lunch, but they're still a good deal for this variation on a standard Hawaiian tradition.

BENTO

Bento are the Japanese rendition of the box lunch. Aesthetically arranged, they are full meals often sold in supermarkets and in some local eateries with takeout counters.

Hatfield Realty (808/696-4499, fax 808/696-1805, www.hawaiiwest.com).

In addition, many individuals rent condos along this coast. Don and Pat Maxwell (808/395-5960 or 808/554-8282, maxwellcondos@hawaii.rr.com, www.hawaiibeachcondos.com) have several moderately priced studio and one-bedroom units in three beachfront condos in Makaha. All have full kitchens, tropical furnishings and decor, and most have cool tile floors. Queen-size beds predominate, and some units have a queen sofa bed for up to two additional guests. Most units are in properties with swimming pools, outdoor barbecue areas, and coin laundry facilities. Nightly, weekly, and monthly rates are available; some units have a five-night minimum stay (seven nights during high season), while others are

rented by the month. Email to see what might fit your needs best. Email is much preferred over a phone call. They promise a speedy reply.

Inquire also with Noreen Conlin (808/372-0855, www.beachlovershawaii.com), who, along with friends, rents a number of studio, one-bedroom, and two-bedroom condos in the Makaha Surfside and Makaha Beach Cabanas. Only some of these units can be rented short term. All have the amenities and comforts to make a fine vacation and all are reasonably priced.

FOOD
At Makaha Resort

The **◖ Kaiona Restaurant** (808/695-7515) offers sit-down service for three meals a day. Its short but adequate menu features a com-

SAIMIN

Special saimin shops, as well as restaurants, serve this hearty, Japanese-inspired noodle soup. Saimin is a word unique to Hawaii. In Japan, these soups would be called *ramen* or *soba*, and it's as if the two were combined into saimin. A large bowl of noodles in broth, stirred with meat, chicken, fish, shrimp, or vegetables, costs only a few dollars and is big enough for an evening meal. The best place to eat saimin is at a local hole-in-the-wall shop run by a family.

OKAZU-YA

A Hawaiian adaptation of the Japanese restaurant that sells side dishes and inexpensive food, *okazu-ya* usually have a full menu of savory entrées as well as side dishes that take their inspiration, like much in the islands, from all the peoples who have made Hawaii their home. Sometimes, they specialize in one type of dish or another. Usually small family-run shops that cater to the local community, they have loyal clients who demand top quality and cheap prices. Although not usually on the list of dieters' delights, the food at these fine places is filling and will sustain you through the day; some places are beginning to adapt to a leaner menu selection. Some but not all have *okazu-ya* as part of the restaurant name.

EARLY-BIRD SPECIALS

Even some of the island's best restaurants in the fanciest hotels offer early-bird specials – the regular-menu dinners offered to diners who come in before the usual dinner hour, which is approximately 6 P.M. You pay as little as half the normal price and can dine in luxury on some of the best foods. The specials are often advertised in free tourist brochures, which might also include coupons for two-for-one meals or limited dinners at much lower prices.

BUFFETS

Buffets are also quite common in Hawaii, and like lu'au are all-you-can-eat affairs. Offered at a variety of restaurants and hotels, they usually cost $12 and up, but will run $25-35 in the better hotels. The food ranges considerably from passable to quite good. At lunchtime, they're lower priced than dinner, and breakfast buffets are cheaper yet. Buffets are often advertised in free tourist literature, which often includes discount coupons.

bination of reasonably priced appetizers and entrées that, at dinner, run $15–23. Breakfast has mostly standard American eggs and griddle choices, but there is a buffet on the weekends. The lunch menu is easy-on-the-pocketbook salads, sandwiches, and lighter meals. Dinner offers heartier, contemporary Hawaiian meals that may include choices like chicken piccata, rib eye steak, pasta primavera, or fish and seafood selections. On Friday and Saturday there are special dinner buffets. Although not gourmet, these meals are filling and nutritious. Whether dining inside or out on the balcony, try to time your dinner meal for sunset. After dinner or a round of golf, stop for a cool drink at the **Puamana Lounge** (open 11 A.M.–9:30 P.M.), where there's live music on weekends, or drop by the **19th Hole** near the pro shop, where snacks are available throughout the day.

Other Restaurants

There are no fine dining restaurants along the coast, but there are plenty of local eateries. Finding a plate lunch is no problem. Little drive-in lunch counters are found in every Wai'anae community. Each serves hearty island food such as teriyaki chicken, pork, or mahimahi with "two-scoop" rice. Favorites of plate lunch lovers are the **L&L Drive-In** (808/696-7989) and **Barbecue Kai** (808/696-7122), both in Wai'anae. In Makaha, try **Lahi Lahi Drive-In** (7 A.M.–3 P.M.) at the intersection of Farrington Highway and Makaha Valley Road. Order at the walk-up window and eat at one of the tables under the canopy or take your food across the road to the beach. This restaurant offers quick breakfasts like omelettes, eggs, and waffles for under $4.50 and lunch of loco moco, chicken cutlets, hamburger steaks, teriyaki beef, and various sandwiches and burgers for less than $7.

In the Pacific Shopping Mall complex is **Nanakuli Chop Suey Restaurant** (808/668-8006, open 10 A.M.–8:30 P.M.), serving standard Chinese fare at local down-home prices. Just behind McDonald's at the mall, the **Nanakuli Korean Bar-B-Que** (808/668-2722, open 9 A.M.–9 P.M.) offers sit-down and take-out Korean food at moderate prices.

Beaches (87-070 Farrington Hw., 808/697-8999, open 11 A.M.–2 P.M.), a local bar and restaurant located right across from Ma'ili Beach park, is the place to go for sunset dinner views and periodic live evening music.

Markets

In Nanakuli, try the **Sack 'N Save Foods** (808/668-1277) in the Pacific Shopping Mall, where you'll find the largest supermarket in the area for groceries, bakery, and a deli.

For ethnic flavor, try the full-service **Tamura Super Market** (86-032 Farrington Hwy., 808/696-3321, open weekdays 7 A.M.–8:30 P.M., weekends 7 A.M.–8 P.M.), which stocks plenty of ingredients used in ethnic foods, along with its usual line of groceries. You'll find the Tamura market a short way north of the Wai'anae Mall.

GETTING THERE

The Wai'anae coast is very accessible. One road takes you there. Simply follow the H-1 freeway from Honolulu until it joins the Farrington Highway (Route 93), which runs north, opening up the entire coast. A handful of side roads lead into residential areas, and that's about it! A strange recommendation, but sensible on this heavily trafficked road, is to drive north to the end of the line and then stop at the scenic sights on your way back south. This puts you on the ocean side of the highway, where you won't have to worry about cutting across a steady stream of traffic. If at all possible, avoid early morning rush hour traffic going down the coast and into Honolulu and late afternoon and evening traffic going up the coast. The worst of it may mean a bumper-to-bumper ride for half the distance of the coast.

TheBus no. 40 and express bus C run at intervals all day long from Ala Moana Shopping Center bus depot up the Wai'anae coast to Makaha Beach Park and stop at all the beaches on the way.

SOUTHEAST O'AHU

It's amazing how quickly you can leave the frenzy of Waikiki behind. Once you round the bend past Diamond Head and continue traveling east toward Koko Head, the pace slackens measurably . . . almost by the yard. A minute ago you were in traffic, now you're cruising. It's not that this area is undeveloped; other parts of the island are much more laid-back, but none so close to the action of the city. In the 12 miles you travel from Honolulu to Makapu'u Head, you pass the natural phenomenon of Koko Crater, an arid-zone botanical garden, a reliable blowhole, the most aquatically active marine preserve in the islands, and a string of beaches, each with a different personality.

Humanity has made its presence felt here, too. The area has some of the most exclusive homes on the island, as well as Hawaii Kai, a less exclusive project developed by the visionary businessman Henry Kaiser, who years ago created this harbinger of things to come. There's Sea Life Park, offering a day's outing of fun for the family, plus suburban shopping centers. The lack of development past Hawaii Kai preserves the area as scenic and recreational, prized attributes that should definitely be taken advantage of.

PLANNING YOUR TIME

A trip through Southeast O'ahu could easily take a full day, especially if you spend part of it snorkeling at Hanauma Bay—and Hanauma Bay should not be missed. Plan on at least a morning or afternoon there and then the rest of the day sightseeing along the coast. Water activities in Maunalua Bay, a hike to Mariner's

© ROBERT NILSEN

SOUTHEAST O'AHU

HIGHLIGHTS

◖ **Hanauma Bay Nature Preserve:**
This is truly one of the most wonderful natural and best protected snorkeling spots in all the islands (page 180).

◖ **Sandy Beach Park:** This is the island's premier site for boogie boarding. It has, seemingly, the perfect bottom to create the right waves, but it can be treacherous. Unless you're an expert, it's best to watch and enjoy, and not risk being pummeled like a rag doll (page 182).

◖ **Makapu'u Point:** The views from here – up the Windward coast, back along the south shore, down onto the surf, and out across the channel to Moloka'i – are some of the prettiest O'ahu has to offer (page 183).

◖ **Sea Life Park Hawaii:** This marine animal park is an attraction that can introduce you to the wonders of the deep, entertain you with its shows, and educate you with a variety of interactive training programs (page 184).

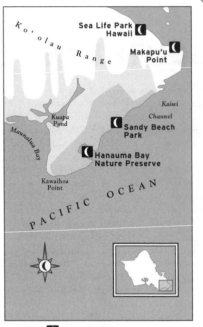

LOOK FOR ◖ TO FIND RECOMMENDED SIGHTS, ACTIVITIES, DINING, AND LODGING.

Ridge, a stroll through Koko Crater Botanical Garden, and a hike to Makapu'u Point all will require an hour and a half or more, so plan your time accordingly. If you are coming back into Honolulu along the coast road, plan to have dinner along the way before returning to your hotel in Waikiki. Otherwise, complete the circle of this southeastern corner of the island and enter Honolulu through the Nu'uanu Valley. The night lights of the Windward side as seen from the Nu'uanu Pali Lookout are as fine as the daytime scene from that same spot.

The Coastal Drive

The drive out this way accounts for about one-third of what is called **The Circle Route.** Start by heading out along coastal Route 72, hitting the sights on the way, travel up through Waimanalo, and loop back into the city via Kailua and the Pali Highway—or do the reverse. Really, the only consideration is what time of day you'd rather stop at the southeast beaches for a dip in the ocean. For the most part, the beaches of this area *are* the sights, although the road abounds with scenic points and overlooks. It's hard to find a road on any of the Hawaiian Islands that's more scenic than this one. The countryside is dry because this is the leeward side. The road is a serpentine ribbon with one coastal vista after another, a great choice for a joyride just to soak in the sights.

SIGHTS
Maunalua Bay

Maunalua (Two Mountain) Bay is a four-mile stretch of sun and surf between Diamond Head and Koko Head, with a small beach park about every half mile. **Wailupe Beach County Park** lies on the Waikiki side of the residential Wailupe Peninsula, once a shoreline pond. This pocket-size beach park comes up first along Kalaniana'ole Highway, providing restrooms and picnic facilities. Swimming is officially not recommended. Be careful of the boat channel surrounding the area because the deep drop-off is abrupt.

After another fancy neighborhood and beyond the 'Aina Haina Shopping Center is **Kawaiku'i Beach County Park.** No lifeguard is present, but the conditions are safe year-round, and the bottom is shallow and overgrown with seaweed. In times past, islanders came to the confluence of a nearby spring to harvest special *limu* that grow only where freshwater meets the ocean. You'll find parking stalls, picnic facilities, and restrooms. Few people use the park, and it's ideal for sunning, but for frolicking in the water, give it a miss.

In quick succession come **Niu and Paiko Beaches,** lying along residential areas. Although there is public access, few people take advantage of them because the swimming, with a coral and sand bottom, is less than ideal. It's shallow and best at high tide, when

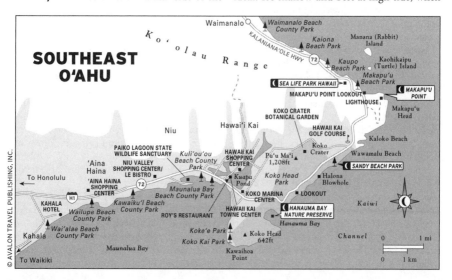

a kayak works well to scoot across the water. Some residents have built a pier at Niu Beach past the mudflats, but it's restricted to their private use. **Paiko Lagoon** is a state wildlife sanctuary; binoculars will help with sightings of a variety of coastal birds.

On the east side of the Paiko Lagoon is **Kuli'ou'ou Beach Park.** Even with its broad lawns, picnic tables, children's play area, and shallow beach, this "everyman's" park at the end of a string of exclusive neighborhoods is not a very enticing place for swimming.

The residential area in the hills behind **Maunalua Bay Beach Park** is Hawaii Kai, built by Henry Kaiser, the aluminum magnate. The controversial development was often denigrated as suburban blight. Many felt it was the beginning of O'ahu's ruination. On the ocean side of Kuapa Pond, the park fronts Maunalua Bay. At one time the pond was a huge fishpond, later dredged by Kaiser, who used the dredged material to build the park, which he donated to the city in 1960. The boat launch constitutes the primary attraction of the park, and except for this boat launch (the only one on this side of the island), the area is of little recreational use because of the coral bottom. Outrigger canoe clubs come here to push off for morning canoe practice, and some scuba companies use the boat ramp for their excursions to the outer reef.

Koke'e and Koko Kai Beach Parks, two undeveloped parks, are along Po'ipu Drive in the wealthy Portlock area below Koko Head. Basically just house lots with access to the water, Koke'e has a small sand beach, while Koko Kai is just a rock ledge. The currents make both largely unsuitable for swimming, but they're popular with surfers. Few others come here, but the views of the bay are lovely.

◖ Hanauma Bay Nature Preserve

One of the premier seaside spots in Hawaii is in the sea-eroded crater of an extinct volcano just below Koko Head. People flock here to snorkel, scuba, picnic, and swim. Hanauma Bay, meaning Curved Bay and pronounced as three syllables—"ha-nau-ma," gets on average about 3,000 people a day. That's over one million visitors a year! During the day, the parking lot at the top of the hill overlooking the crescent bay below looks like a used-car lot, jammed with Japanese imports, vans, and tour buses. Parking ($1 per vehicle) is severely restricted, so use TheBus no. 22 ($2), which has a stop at the entrance. If you want to avoid the crowds, go in the early morning or after 4 P.M. when the sun dips behind the crater and most tourists leave on cue. There's still plenty of daylight, so plan your trip accordingly.

After years of overuse, this recreation area has gone through several improvements, including new facilities and an educational program. Hanauma Bay Nature Preserve (808/396-4229, www.hanaumabayhawaii.org) is open 6 A.M.–7 P.M. (6 P.M. in winter), except for Tuesday when the bay is closed, and is open until 10 P.M. on the second and fourth Saturdays of each month in summer and on the second Saturday of each month in winter. A $5 entrance fee is charged for nonresidents older than age 12 going down to the water, but it is free after 4:30 P.M. Before you actually head down the road to the beach, you are obliged to view a seven-minute video about the bay, its marinelife, and how to best protect this fragile environment. A look at the Marine Education Center environmental display next door adds to your understanding of how the whole ecosystem works. A small food concession, gift shop, and restrooms are located near the ticket windows up top; snorkel rental booth, an information booth, showers, and additional restrooms are down at the beach. Lifeguards are on duty all day. Neither smoking nor alcohol consumption are allowed beyond the entrance center. From the top, you can walk down or take the trolley ($0.50 down, $1 up, or $2 for all-day use); scuba tanks and other large items require an extra fee.

The reef protects the bay and sends a maze of coral fingers right up to the shoreline. A large sandy break in the reef, **Keyhole,** is a choice spot for entering the water and for swimming. The entire bay is alive with tropical fish. Many fish have become so accustomed to snorkelers

CORAL

Whether you're an avid scuba diver or novice snorkeler, you'll become aware of O'ahu's underwater coral gardens and grottoes whenever you peer at the fantastic seascapes below the waves. Coral in Hawaii grows in many shapes, sizes, and colors, like it does elsewhere in the world. Although there is plenty of it, the coral in Hawaii doesn't do as well as in other more equatorial areas because the water is too wild and it's not quite as warm. Hawaii has some 400,000 acres of coral, and each island is surrounded by unconnected stretches of coral reef. Most is of the hard coral type, as opposed to the soft coral or sponge varieties. Coral looks like a plant fashioned from colorful stone, but it's actually the skeleton of tiny animals, zoo-phytes, which need algae in order to live. Coral grows best in water that is quite still, where the days are sunny and the algae can thrive. Coral can be fragile. Please do your part to protect these underwater gardens by not stepping on coral, breaking off pieces, or dragging anything across it. Look, but do not touch. Many of Hawaii's reefs have been dying in the last 20 years, and no one seems to know why. Pesticides and fertilizers used in agriculture have been pointed to as a possible cause, but other major concerns for coral health are algae bloom and the resultant smothering of coral, sedimentation and erosional runoff of silt from the land, global warming, abuse by humans engaging in recreational activities, and even oil from skin and sunblock.

that they've lost their fear entirely and come nibbling at your fingers for food. Please do not feed the fish. It's illegal to do so and carries a stiff fine. Let the fish feed naturally to maintain a better balance and prevent them from becoming food beggars. Most important, the reef is being destroyed by people walking on it. Please do everything you can to avoid this harm. Also, leave the sea turtles alone, and all rocks, shells, and coral as you find them. With care, Hanauma Bay will remain beautiful for all future generations.

Before you enter the water, do yourself a favor and visit the information booth that describes conditions. It divides the bay into three areas, ranging from beginner to expert, and warns of sections to avoid. Be especially careful of **Witches Brew,** a turbulent area on the right at the mouth of the bay that can wash you into the Moloka'i Express, a notoriously dangerous rip current. Follow a path along the left-hand seacliff to **Toilet Bowl,** a natural pool that rises and falls with the tides. If the conditions are right, you can sit in it to float up and down in a phenomenon very similar to a flushing toilet. However, conditions are often too dangerous for this stunt.

Koko Head

For a sweeping view, you used to be able to hike to the summit of **Koko Head,** not to be confused with Koko Crater farther east, but it's now off limits. The 642-foot summit of Koko (Blood) Head was the last place that young, wandering Madame Pele attempted to dig herself a fiery nest on O'ahu; as usual, she was flooded out by her jealous sister. The bowl of Hanauma Bay lies at the feet of Koko Head; below are two small extinct craters, Nono'ula and 'Ihi'ihilauakea.

Halona Cove

As you round a bend on Route 72 past Hanauma Bay, you come to two scenic lookouts and the natural lookout of Halona Cove (The Peering Place), an excellent vantage point from which to see whales in season. Just before Halona stands a monument and stone wall erected by the **Honolulu Japanese Casting Club.** Below on the rocks, men come to cast into the surf. The monument at one time was of O Jisan, the Japanese god of protection, but it was destroyed by overzealous patriots during World War II. The current monument was erected after the war, and O Jisan was carved into it. Below is a secluded little beach perfect for sunbathing. The only way to reach it is to scramble down the cliff. Swim only on calm days, or the waves can pull you out to sea and then suck you into the chamber of the famous **Halona Blowhole** just around the bend. There's a turnout at the blowhole for parking. The blowhole is a lava tube at the perfect height for the waves to be driven into it. The water compresses, and the pressure sends a spume into the air through a hole in its ceiling. For safety's sake, stay up by the lookout and don't venture down to the blowhole itself.

Sandy Beach Park

The fine sand of Sandy Beach forms one of the best boogie-boarding beaches on O'ahu, and the most rugged of them all. It's also a great surfing beach—for experts. It is said that more necks and backs are broken or injured on this beach than on all the other O'ahu beaches combined. But because of the east-breaking waves, and bottom, the swells are absolutely perfect for boogie-boarding. The lifeguards at the two towers use a flag system to inform you about conditions. The red flag means "stay out." When checking out Sandy Beach, don't be fooled by boogie-boarders who make it appear easy. These are experts who are intimately familiar with the area, and even they are injured at times.

Local people refer to the beach as "Scene Beach" because this is where young people come to strut their stuff. This is where the boys are because this is where the girls are. There are restrooms, a large parking area, and two lifeguard towers. Rip-offs have happened, so don't leave valuables in your car. A *kaukau* wagon often parks in the area, selling refreshments. When wind conditions are right, you may see a whole parade of colorful exotic-shaped kites flying across the sky here. Some even come to practice flying kites to work on skills for kiteboarding.

As the road skirts the coastline, it passes a string of beaches that look inviting but are extremely dangerous because there is no protecting reef. The best known is **Wawamalu,**

© ROBERT NILSEN

When the winds are right, the skies above Sandy Beach may be filled with a great variety of kites.

where people come to sunbathe only. Across the road is **Hawaii Kai Golf Course,** an excellent public course.

Koko Crater Botanical Garden

The rim of the Koko Crater tuff cone rises to 1,208 feet. On the floor is the 60-acre **Koko Crater Botanical Garden** (open daily sunrise to sunset, except Christmas and New Year's Day, free), which, because of the unique conditions, specializes in succulents, cacti, and other dry land plants from Hawaii, the Americas, Africa, and Madagascar. Opened in 1958, this garden is little developed and has but one circular trail and no other amenities. Expect to spend 90 minutes on the two-mile circle path. To reach the gardens, follow Route 72 east to just past Sandy Beach Park and then take a left on Kealahou Street. Turn left again at a sign that points to a riding stable and the botanical garden, and follow the road to its end, where a walking path leads into the crater. If you come in spring or early summer, the entrance to the

© ROBERT NILSEN

Unlike most botanical gardens on the island, Koko Crater Botanical Garden is the preserve of dryland plants, so cacti and succulents predominate.

garden will be ablaze with plumeria blossoms of various colors.

🄲 Makapu'u Point

The southeasternmost point of land on O'ahu is Makapu'u (Bulging Eye) Point. This headland overlooks Makapu'u Beach Park and supports an important lighthouse. This lighthouse uses prism glass in its lamp and has been functioning for more than 100 years. Bunkers near the top were constructed during World War II and referred to by James Jones in his novel *From Here to Eternity*. They were manned during the war to protect the deep-water Makapu'u Bay from possible Japanese attack. A moderate one-mile hike over an asphalt road leads to the top. Park in the daytime only parking lot along the highway and give yourself at least 90 minutes for the round-trip hike. It's dry and windy, so bring plenty of water and a hat to shade your eyes. During winter this is an excellent spot to watch for whales. Some energetic people bring a picnic lunch and hike down the sheer outer

face of this promontory to a rocky tidepool area along the water to sunbathe and fish.

A second parking lot (open day and night) is a bit farther up the road at **Makapu'u Lookout,** from where you have a good view down on Makapu'u Beach and up the Windward Coast. Here too is an excellent spot for whale-watching in season.

Makapu'u Beach Park

This beach park below Makapu'u Point is a favorite launching pad for hang gliding. Makapu'u is *the* most famous boogie-boarding beach in the entire state and also used for surfing. It can be extremely rugged, however, and many people have been rescued here. In winter the conditions are hazardous, with much of the beach eroded away, leaving exposed rocks. With no interfering reef, the surf can reach 12 feet—perfect for boogie-boarding, if you're an expert. In summer, the sandy beach reappears, and the wave action is much gentler, allowing recreational swimming. There are restrooms, lifeguard towers with a flag warning system, and picnic facilities.

Offshore is **Manana (Rabbit) Island.** Curiously, it does resemble a rabbit, but it's so named because rabbits actually live on it. They were released there in the 1880s by a local rancher who wanted to raise them but who was aware that if they ever got loose on Oʻahu they could ruin much of the croplands. During the impotent counterrevolution of 1894, designed to reinstate the Hawaiian monarchy, Manana Island was a cache for arms and ammunition buried on its Windward side. Nearby, and closer into shore, is tiny Kaohikaipu Island, which, along with Manana and several other islands along this coast, is reserved as a seabird sanctuary. Efforts were made to attract albatross to this island, but they just never took to it. This tiny island is great for ground-nesting seabirds, as there are no natural predators like mongooses, cats, and dogs.

◖ Sea Life Park Hawaii

Nestled below the lush Koʻolau Mountains inland of Makapuʻu Point is Sea Life Park Hawaii (808/259-7933 or 866/365-7446, www .sealifeparkhawaii.com, open daily 9 A.M.–5 P.M., $31.20 adult and $24.95 children 4–12). The Waikiki Trolley's Ocean Coast Blue Line shuttle runs round-trip from Waikiki to Sea Life Park Hawaii every 45 minutes throughout the day for $25 adult, $12 child 4–11, and $18 seniors. Alternately, take TheBus nos. 58 or 22 ($2) from Kuhio Avenue in Waikiki. For self-drivers, Kalanianaʻole Highway takes you past Makapuʻu Point to the park's front entrance; parking costs $3 per vehicle.

Within the park, a cluster of tanks hold an amazing display of marine animals that live freely in the ocean just a few hundred yards away. The park hosts a variety of shows throughout the day by trained sea lions, dolphins, and penguins and other activities with turtles, seals, and rays in the various pools and at the informative Hawaii Ocean Theater. The park's most impressive feature is the Hawaiian Reef Tank, a massive 300,000-gallon fish bowl where guests come face to face through walls of glass with more than 2,000 specimens of the island's rich marinelife as they descend three fathoms down an exterior ramp. For a more in-depth and intense exposure to the training and care of dolphins, sea lions, and stingrays, several interactive programs are offered that mostly run $114–199 and require about 45 minutes, although the two-hour Sea Life Interactive is $335 adult and $299 for children. The Sea Trek program lets guests actually enter the big tank in wet suits and a diver's helmet to meet the fish mask to mouth for $108. The shorter Hawaiian Ray Encounter, where you enter the stingray tank to float among those graceful creatures runs $45 adults or $40 children. All of the special program prices include regular admission to the park. These popular sessions are held several times a day, and reservations must be made well in advance. Sea Life Park Hawaii is a great learning and entertaining experience for the entire family or for anyone interested in exploring Hawaii's fascinating marinelife.

RECREATION
Water Activities

The Japanese-owned Koko Marina Center has several water sport and thrill-ride booking agencies. They will take any tourists out, but these outfits are used largely by Japanese tourists who come here by the busload and immediately head out on one of these thrill rides. They've already booked from Japan, so it's all set up and off they go.

Keep in mind that personal watercraft rentals are not allowed on weekends and holidays, so make your plans for some other day. Generally, self-powered watercraft rides, parasailing, and scuba diving happens from a floating dock out in Maunalua Bay, while activities pulled by a boat take place inside the marina.

Hawaii Sports (808/395-3773) offers nearly a dozen water sports to choose from, like a 20-minute banana boat ride for $29 per person, 30-minute personal watercraft use for $49, parasail ride for $59 (10 minutes in the air), wakeboarding or water-skiing for $69 for a 30-minute pull, and an introductory scuba dive for $59.

Several other water sports companies offer

the same activities at roughly the same prices, while a few also have speed and sailboat rides or transportation to Hanauma Bay for a day of snorkeling. Other companies at the Koko Marina Center to check with are **Sea Breeze Watersports** (808/396-0100) and **Aloha Ocean Sports** (808/395-7474), which also offer a combination of powered watercraft activities and introductory scuba diving.

For those intending to head to Hanauma Bay to snorkel but not wanting to deal with the traffic or parking should contact **Hawaii Ocean Promotions** (808/395-0001) in the Koko Marina Center which, for $20 adult or $15 children 3–11, picks you up in Waikiki, arranges transportation to/from Hanauma Bay, and gives you snorkel gear for the day. The $5 entrance fee into Hanauma Bay is your responsibility.

Scuba

The **Aloha Dive Shop** (808/395-5922, www .alohadiveshop.com) is a full-service dive shop located at the Hawaii Kai Shopping Center. You can rent or buy snorkeling and scuba gear. Two-tank, two-location dives run $100 for beginners and feature all-boat diving at Maunalua Bay, Koko Head, and/or Diamond Head. Pickup in Waikiki is about 8:30 A.M. and return is 1:30–2 P.M. Three-day, open-water certification courses are given for about $400; advanced and search-and-rescue courses are also taught. This is the shop of Jackie James, first lady of Hawaiian diving. She's been diving here for more than 30 years.

Surfing Lessons

Hawaiian Surf Adventures (808/396-2324, www.hawaiiansurfadventure.com) takes you by boat to beginning surfing locations near Koko Head. Two-hour small group lessons run $79 with private lessons at $125. If you don't want to drive yourself, transportation to/from Waikiki will run you $10.

Mariner's Ridge Trail

Up above Hawaii Kai is a ridgetop subdivision called Mariner's Ridge. Turn onto Kaluanui Road just past the post office on the north side of Hawaii Kai Marina to get there. Follow the road all the way as it snakes up to the top. At the end of the road, park your car and head up the ridge trail. A steady uphill climb most of the way, this trail should take about 45 minutes and is the shortest route to the Ko'olau Ridge. The bottom half is fairly open, with views over the entire residential area surrounding Maunalua Bay, but the upper portion is partly through trees and somewhat cooler. At the ridge, you're rewarded with spectacular views down onto Waimanalo and north toward Kailua and Kane'ohe. From here, it's easy to see just how agricultural Waimanalo is—and how close to Waikiki—and what wonderful beaches the Windward side has. This area is the tail end of the rugged and jagged Ko'olau Range, which can be seen running up to the northwest.

SHOPPING

One of the first places to pick up supplies as you head east on Route 72 is at the **Niu Valley Shopping Center**, about halfway between Diamond Head and Koko Head. Aside from foodstuffs, you can also get your prescription filled here, pick out flowers for your sweetie, or grab a sandwich for your trip down the highway. A little less ideal for location and a bit closer to Diamond Head, the **'Aina Haina Shopping Center** still has restaurants, a grocery store, two banks, a branch post office, and a gas station. Enter from West Hind Drive.

On the west side of Kuapa Pond in Hawaii Kai are two shopping malls. Try **Hawaii Kai Towne Center** for General Nutrition Center, Costco, or more than a dozen other shops. Safeway, Longs Drugs, Aloha Dive Shop, and numerous other stores and restaurants are in the neighboring **Hawaii Kai Shopping Center** just up the road.

Along the highway in Hawaii Kai, on the east side of Kuapa Pond is **Koko Marina Center**. This is the largest and easiest-access shopping center you'll find on the way to Hanauma Bay. There are three banks, several gift shops, a number of shops for beachwear, a Bestsellers book and music shop, and Koko Marina 8 Theaters. Foodland provides most supplies for picnics and camping, and the eateries serve everything from fast food to fine dining meals.

FOOD

In the Niu Valley Shopping Center is 🄲 **Le Bistro** (808/373-7990, open nightly 5:30–9 P.M. except Tuesday) a small neighborhood restaurant owned by a local boy that's getting rave reviews from patrons. A mixture of Continental cuisine with a dash of the East, Le Bistro serves such items as an ahi and salmon sashimi appetizer, short ribs, scallops, and steak. It's small and intimate with midrange to expensive prices.

🄲 **Roy's Restaurant** (6600 Kalaniana'ole Hwy., 808/396-7697, open Mon.–Thurs. 5:30–9:30 P.M., until 10 P.M. on Friday, Sat. 5–10 P.M., and Sun. 5–9:30 P.M.), in the Hawaii Kai Corporate Plaza, presents Pacific Rim cuisine at its very best. Even if you're staying in Waikiki—only about 20 minutes away—it's definitely worth the trip. Through experimentation and an unfailing sense of taste, Roy Yamaguchi has created dishes using the diverse and distinctive flavors of French, Italian, Chinese, Japanese, Thai, and Hawaiian cuisine and blended them into a heady array of culinary delights that destroy the adage "East is East and West is West." The twain have definitely met, and with resounding success. Roy's dining rooms—one up and one down—are elegant and casual, much like the food, featuring an open kitchen, and although pleasant enough, it is not designed for a lengthy romantic evening. Roy's dining philosophy seems to be the serving of truly superb dishes posthaste with the focus on the food as the dining experience, not the surroundings. The menu changes somewhat every evening, but you might find blackened ahi and *opakapaka* potstickers and wild mushroom and escargot cassoulet for appetizers, various salads, or an individual *imu*-oven pizza. Entrées like grilled loin of lamb with rosemary, crab meat, and risotto sauce; slow braised and charbroiled

---

ISLAND TREATS

Certain finger foods, fast foods, and island treats are unique to Hawaii. These are some of the best and most popular.

Pronounced as in "Winnie the Pooh Pooh," and originally the name of a small shellfish, *pu pu* now is a general term that has come to mean hors d'oeuvres, or any finger food. *Pu pu* can be anything from crackers to cracked crab. Often, they're given free at lounges and bars and can even include chicken drumettes, fish kabobs, and tempura. At a good display you can have a free meal.

A sweet of Chinese origin, **crackseed** can be any number of preserved and seasoned fruits and seeds. Favorites include coconut, watermelon, pumpkin seeds, mango, plum, and papaya. Distinctive in taste, they take some getting used to but make great trail snacks. They are available in most island markets. **Li Hing Mui,** one version of crackseed, has become very popular over the past few years. While it comes in a variety of "flavors," it's basically dried plums with a coating of salt and sugar, sometimes with other ingredients or coloring added.

Also look for dried fish (cuttlefish) on racks, usually near the crackseed. Nutritious and delicious, it makes a great snack.

Shave ice, a real island institution, makes the Mainland "snow cone" melt into insignificance. Special machines literally shave ice to a fluffy consistency. It's mounded into a paper cone, and your choice of dozens of exotic island syrups is generously poured over it. Given a straw and a spoon, you just slurp away.

Taro chips are like potato chips but are made from the taro root. If you can find them fresh, buy a bunch because they are mostly available packaged.

Two sweets from the Portuguese are *malasadas,* holeless donuts, and *pao dolce,* a sweet bread. Sold in island bakeries, they're great for breakfast or as treats.

short ribs; or Hawaiian-style misoyaki butterfish are mostly under $32. Desserts are superb and include individually prepared (order at the beginning of dinner) fresh fruit cobbler in sauce Anglaise, or a richer-than-rich chocolate soufflé. Roy's is a dining experience that is universally appreciated. This was Roy's first restaurant and is still his flagship. From here the empire spread—now nearly three dozen strong.

At the Koko Marina Center

The Coffee Bean & Tea Leaf (open Sun.–Thurs. 5:30 A.M.–10 P.M., Fri.–Sat. 5:30 A.M.–9 P.M.) is a stylish coffee shop that also does teas, pastry, and inexpensive and healthy light lunches.

Loco Moco Drive Inn (808/396-7878, open Mon.–Sat. 9:30 A.M.–9 P.M., Sun. 9 A.M.–8 P.M.) serves quick plate lunches and sandwiches for under $6.

The finest food here is available at **Assaggio Hawaii Kai** (808/396-0756, open daily 11:30 A.M.–2:30 P.M., Sun.–Thurs. 5–9:30 P.M., Fri.–Sat. 5–10 P.M.), which overlooks the marina. Although a shopping center restaurant, Assaggio's does wonderful, traditional Italian food that will have you smiling when you leave. A long list of antipasti, soups, and salads start your dinner, but the real treat comes when you pick from the lengthy menu of pasta, chicken, fish, and meat dishes. You will be rewarded with a tasty meal, reasonably priced at $18–22. Have a glass of wine with your meal and leave room, if you can, for one of the fine desserts. Assaggio's is a good choice for a special night out.

The **Kona Brewing Company, Koko Marina Pub** (808/394-5662, open Mon.–Sat. 11 A.M.–11 P.M., Sun. 9 A.M.–11 P.M.) sits right over the water, a good location with views of the marina and the low Ko'olau ridgeline beyond. The pub doesn't brew beer here but serves beer it brews in Kona, which includes Longboard Lager, Fire Rock Pale Ale, Big Wave Golden Ale, and Pipeline Porter. This pub specializes in pizza, salads, and sandwiches, but you can also get an assortment of *pu pu* and more hearty meat and fish plates. Pizzas run $13–23, while other choices range mostly $8–18. Happy hour runs 3–6 P.M. weekdays, and there is live music during the early evenings from midweek on through the weekend. The Koko Marina Pub has better than average pub grub and is a friendly, pleasing, and fun place for food and entertainment.

The **Greek Marina** restaurant (808/396-8441, open Mon.–Sat. 11 A.M.–3 P.M., Sun.–Thurs. 5–9 P.M., Fri.–Sat. 3–10 P.M.) is a utilitarian place that does tasty food worthy of its name. Appetizers include spanikopita, dolmadas, and tzatziki, while entrées might be gyros, calamari steak, moussaka, or souvlaki. Nothing is too fancy here, and all dishes are at affordable prices, with many in the $10–15 range.

Lu'au

Sea Life Park Hawaii presents **Sea Life Lu'au** daily 6–9 P.M. This entertainment includes a dolphin show, buffet dinner, and a Polynesian Revue show by Tihati Productions. Tickets run $84 adults and $50 children under 13.

WINDWARD O'AHU

O'ahu's Windward Coast never has to turn a shoulder into a harsh and biting wind. The trades do blow, mightily at times, but always tropical warm, perfumed with flowers, balmy and bright. Honolulu is just 12 miles over the hump of the *pali,* but a world apart. When *kama'aina* families talk of going to "the cottage in the country," they're most likely referring to the Windward Coast. In the southern parts, traditionally known as Ko'olaupoko, the suburban towns of Kailua and Kane'ohe are modern in every way, with the lion's share of the services on this side. With populations of more than 35,000 each, these two towns together make the second most densely populated area on the island. Kailua has O'ahu's best sailboarding beach and a nearby *heiau,* preserved and unvisited, while Kane'ohe sits

on a huge bay dotted with islands and fringed by a reef. To add to the mix, the much smaller, slower, and very Hawaiian town of Waimanalo contributes hugely to the island's fresh produce bins with its extensive farmlands.

North, in the stretch of Windward O'ahu called Ko'olauloa, are a string of beaches that offer the full range of O'ahu's coastal outdoor experience. You can meander side roads into the mountains near the Hawaiian villages of Waiahole and Waikane, where the normal way of life is ramshackle cottages on small subsistence farms. The coast bulges at Ka'a'awa, where the Crouching Lion, a natural stone formation, seems ready to pounce on the ever-present tour buses that disturb its repose. Inland lies a valley that is Ahupua'a 'O Kahana State Park, where O'ahu's beautiful and natu-

HIGHLIGHTS

◖ **Waimanalo Bay State Recreation Area:** This is one of the best beaches and parks along this coast. Many people who live on the island consider it the best. If you are unable to visit this beach, others that are equally nice, perhaps better in some ways, are Kailua Beach, Lanikai Beach, and the beach at Malaekahana State Recreation Area (page 192).

◖ **Ulupo Heiau:** One of the last remaining large, precontact cultural sites on the Windward Coast. This restored religious center overlooks Kawainui Marsh in Kailua (page 195).

◖ **Valley of the Temples:** Built in commemoration of Japanese immigrants to Hawaii, Byodo-In Temple occupies a jaw-droppingly beautiful spot below the rippled and verdant paliin Kaneʻohe (page 206).

◖ **Laʻie Mormon Temple:** This striking building set in a tidy town is the center for the Mormon congregation in Hawaii (page 219).

◖ **Polynesian Cultural Center:** One of the most frequented tourist attractions in the state, the Polynesian Cultural Center is a showcase of Polynesian culture and arts, a testament to the enduring legacy of Pacific Island peoples (page 219).

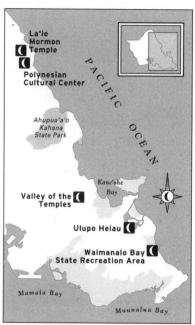

LOOK FOR ◖ TO FIND RECOMMENDED SIGHTS, ACTIVITIES, DINING, AND LODGING.

ral heart flashes in greenery. Suddenly, you're in manicured Laʻie, where Hawaii's Mormon community has built a university, a temple perfect in its symmetry, and the Polynesian Cultural Center, a sanitized replica of life in the South Seas. The northern tip at Kahuku is the site of one of Oʻahu's oldest sugar mills. Just outside of town is the James Campbell National Wildlife Refuge, and beyond that Kahuku Point, where the North Shore begins.

More than a dozen beaches line the 35 miles of the Windward Coast from Waimanalo to Kahuku. Most offer a wide range of water sports and a few have camping. A handful of offshore islands, one or two close enough to

wade to, can be visited and explored. Others are refuges for Hawaiian water birds and off limits to visitors.

It makes little difference in which direction you travel the Windward Coast, but the following is listed from south to north. The slight advantage in traveling this direction is that your car is in the right-hand lane, which is better for coastal views. But, as odd as it may seem, this dynamic stretch totally changes its vistas depending on the direction you travel. You can come one way and then retrace your steps, easily convincing yourself you've never seen it before. The road, Kalanianaʻole Highway (Route 72) through Waimanalo and Kamehameha

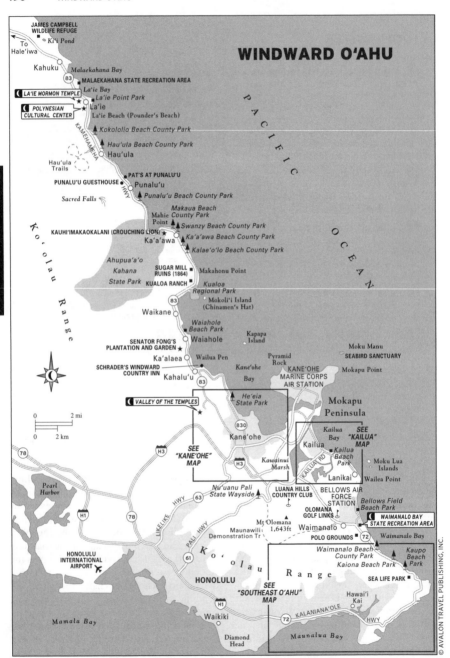

WINDWARD O'AHU

JAMES CAMPBELL
WILDLIFE REFUGE
To
Hale'iwa • Ki'i Pond

Kahuku   Malaekahana Bay
83   MALAEKAHANA STATE RECREATION AREA
☾ LA'IE MORMON TEMPLE   La'ie Bay
★   La'ie Point Park
☾ POLYNESIAN   ★ La'ie
CULTURAL CENTER   La'ie Beach (Pounder's Beach)
▲ Kokololio Beach County Park

▲ Hau'ula Beach County Park
Hau'ula
Hau'ula
Trails

★ PAT'S AT PUNALU'U
PUNALU'U GUESTHOUSE ● Punalu'u
▲ Punalu'u Beach County Park
Sacred Falls
Makaua Beach
Mahie County Park
Point ▲▲ Swanzy Beach County Park
KAUHI'IMAKAOKALANI (CROUCHING LION) ★ ▲ Ka'a'awa Beach County Park
Ka'a'awa   ▲ Kalae'o'lo Beach County Park

Ahupua'a o
Kahana   SUGAR MILL   Makahonu Point
State Park   RUINS (1864) ■
KUALOA RANCH ■   Kualoa
Regional Park
83   ● Mokoli'i Island
(Chinamen's Hat)
Waikane
Waiahole
Beach Park   Kapapa
SENATOR FONG'S   Waiahole   Island
PLANTATION AND GARDEN ★   Moku Manu
Ka'alaea   Wailua Pen   Pyramid   SEABIRD SANCTUARY
SCHRADER'S WINDWARD   Rock   Mokapu Point
COUNTRY INN   Kane'ohe   KANE'OHE
Kahalu'u   83   Bay   MARINE CORPS
AIR STATION
He'eia   Mokapu
☾ VALLEY OF THE TEMPLES   State Park   Peninsula
★   830   Kailua
Kane'ohe   Bay   SEE
"KAILUA"
SEE   Kailua   MAP
"KANE'OHE"   ● Kailua
MAP   H3   Beach   ● Moku Lua
Kawainui   Park   Islands
H3   Marsh   Lanikai   Wailea Point
Pearl   Nu'uanu Pali   BELLOWS AIR
Harbor   63   State Wayside   LUANA HILLS   FORCE
COUNTRY CLUB   STATION   Bellows Field
OLOMANA   Beach Park
GOLF LINKS   ☾ WAIMANALO BAY
78   78   Mt Olomana   Waimanalo   STATE RECREATION AREA
Maunawili   1,643ft   POLO GROUNDS ■   72   Waimanalo Bay
H1   Demonstration Tr   Waimanalo Beach
61   County Park   Kaupo
Waimanalo   Beach
Kaiona Beach Park   Park
HONOLULU   SEA LIFE PARK ■
INTERNATIONAL   K o 'o l a u   Hawai'i
AIRPORT   Kai
HONOLULU   R a n g e
SEE
"SOUTHEAST O'AHU"
MAP
Mamala Bay   H1
72   KALANIANA'OLE
Waikiki   HWY
Diamond   Maunalua Bay
Head

PACIFIC OCEAN

K o 'o l a u R a n g e

KAMEHAMEHA HWY

PALI HWY

LIKELIKE HWY

0   2 mi
0   2 km

© AVALON TRAVEL PUBLISHING, INC.

Highway (Route 83) north from Kailua, is clearly marked.

PLANNING YOUR TIME

It would be a shame not to spend at least a full day along the long and lovely Windward Coast. Rather than zipping through on the way to the North Shore or making a quick day trip from the big city, take this coast slowly—there is truly much fine scenery to appreciate and plenty of activities to pursue. If possible, plan on staying a couple of days, one for Kailua and south, the other for Kane'ohe and north. There are plenty of accommodations and sufficient amenities. Playing at any one of the many fine beaches will certainly be a good morning or afternoon's activity. A day trip by boat to the Kane'ohe Bay sandbar or activities at the Kualoa Ranch could take much of the day; if you plan on kayaking, surfboarding, or participating in any of the many other water- or land-based activities this coast has to offer, count more time in. The Windward Coast also has a good number of cultural sites each worth a short visit. Give them some time and plan your stops between other activities. Don't skimp, don't rush, don't just drive blindly through. Slow down to explore and let the slower pace of life on this coast become your pace for a couple of days.

Waimanalo

This small rural town at the bottom end of the Ko'olau Range is a largely Hawaiian community. It was at one time the center of a thriving sugar plantation owned by the *hapa* Hawaiian nobleman, John Cummins, who was responsible for introducing rabbits to Manana Island, just offshore. The area has fallen on hard times ever since the plantation closed in the late 1940s, but now it produces much of Honolulu's bananas, papayas, and anthuriums from small plots and farms, and a great deal of organic greens that end up on the plates of many fine restaurants on the island. The town sits in the center of Waimanalo Bay, which has the longest stretch of sand beach (three miles) on O'ahu, and to many people, especially those who live on O'ahu, it is also the best. The backdrop for this rather ordinary town is a finely sculpted *pali* that rises precipitously into a variegated curtain of green—and it's close. This part of O'ahu is absolutely beautiful in its undevelopment, yet adequate travelers' services are in town. Coming up from the arid southeastern coast, you think you're in Waimanalo when you pass the first built-up beach area, but that isn't it. Keep going about a mile or two and then you'll come to the older section of town, which is Waimanalo proper.

BEACHES AND PARKS
Kaupo Beach Park

Between Sea Life Park and Waimanalo, this is the first park along the coast that's safe for swimming. The park is undeveloped and has no lifeguards, so you are advised to exercise caution. The shore is lined with a protective reef and rocks, and the swimming is best beyond the reef. Close to shore, the jutting rocks discourage most swimmers. Surfers frequent Kaupo, especially beginners, lured by the ideal yet gentle waves. At the southern end of this park is Makai Research Pier. Part of this pier is open to the public, but the rest is closed for use by government ocean research organizations. Many locals come to fish off the pier or spearfish along the coast. Some companies run scuba tours to the reef offshore.

Kaiona Beach Park

Just before you enter Waimanalo from the south, you pass Kaiona Beach Park. Local people are fond of the area and use it extensively. Look inland to view some remarkable cliffs and mountains that tumble to the sea. The area was once called Pahonu, "Turtle Enclosure," because a local chief who loved turtle meat erected a large enclosure in the sea into

© ROBERT NILSEN

From the ridge of the Ko'olau Range, it's easy to see how agricultural Waimanalo is and what great beaches it has.

which any turtle caught by local fishermen had to be deposited. Parts of the pond perimeter wall can still be seen at low tide. Facilities include restrooms, showers, and a picnic area. Swimming is safe year-round.

Waimanalo Beach County Park

The fine powder sand of Waimanalo beaches stretches virtually uninterrupted from Sea Life Park, past the town of Waimanalo, and through Bellows Air Force Base to Wailea Point. At the south end of town, Waimanalo Beach County Park provides camping with a county permit. The beach is well protected, and the swimming is safe year-round. Snorkeling is good, and there are picnic tables, restrooms, and recreational facilities, including a ballpark, basketball courts, and children's play equipment. The park is right in the built-up beach area and not secluded from the road. Although the facilities are good, the setting could be better.

◖ Waimanalo Bay State Recreation Area

Just up the road is Waimanalo Bay State Recreation Area. This park is good for picnicking and swimming, which can sometimes be rough. The area, surrounded by a dense ironwood grove, is called "Sherwood Forest" or "Sherwoods," because of many rip-offs by thieves who fancy themselves as Robin Hood, plundering the rich and keeping the loot for themselves. Fortunately, this problem of breaking into cars is diminishing, but take necessary precautions. This is the best beach on this section of the island.

Bellows Field Beach Park

Part of this onetime active air force base, now used only as a rest and recreational facility, is one of O'ahu's finest beach parks, and there's camping too! The water is safe for swimming year-round, and lifeguards are on duty on the weekends. Bodysurfing and board surfing are also excellent in the park, but snorkeling is mediocre. After entering the main gates, follow the road for about two miles to the beach area. You'll find picnic tables, restrooms, and cold-water showers. The combination of shade trees and adjacent beach make a perfect camping area that's often full. The park is marked by two freshwater streams, Waimanalo and Puha, at either end. Because the military has security issues, this park is only open Friday afternoon to Sunday evenings for non-military persons.

RECREATION

The **Olomana Golf Links** (808/259-7926), a relatively easy public course, is close to town. It's also a good place to go for breakfast.

For those who enjoy the sport of kings, **polo matches** are held at about 2:30 P.M. on Sunday from May (or June) to October at the polo field in Waimanalo across from Waimanalo Bay State Recreation Area. Sponsored by the Honolulu Polo Club (www.honolulupolo.com), matches usually last 90 minutes and entrance is $3 adults, with kids 12 and under free.

FOOD AND SHOPPING

As you enter the beach section of Waimanalo, look on the ocean side for **Ⓒ Keneke's** (41-855 Kalaniana'ole Hwy., 808/259-5266, open daily 9:30 A.M.–5:30 P.M.). A local eatery next to the post office, Keneke's offers plate lunches with a long list of options for $4.50–7, as well as burgers, sandwiches, shave ice, smoothies, and drinks. It's a great place to fill up for an afternoon on the beach, and the crowd tells you what a good reputation it has. Order at the window and sit at a picnic table under the canopy to the side.

Nearby in what looks like an old gas station building is a small "no-name" market for sundries and snacks. A short mile north of Keneke's is **Mel's Market** (41-1029 Kalaniana'ole Hwy., 808/259-7550), where you can pick up almost all supplies, and you definitely have a better selection. The **Naturally Hawaiian** (41-1025 Kalaniana'ole Hwy., 808/259-5354, open daily 10 A.M.–6 P.M.) gift gallery is next door for a good selection of artwork.

Keep going along the Kalaniana'ole Highway for a mile or so to find **Waimanalo Shopping Center** in the middle of town. In this shopping center are **New Hawaii's Treasures** (808/259-9799) for inexpensive jewelry, gifts, and souvenirs; **Sumo Connection Hawaii** (808/259-8646), where sumo wrestler Yokozuna Akebono's mother presides over sumo memorabilia and aloha shirts; the well-managed **Waimanalo Laundry** (808/259-5091); **Dave's Ice Cream** (808/259-0356, open daily 9 A.M.–9:30 P.M.); and a gas station.

Across the road and down a bit is **Shima's Market** (41-1606 Kalaniana'ole Hwy., 808/259-9921, open Mon.–Sat. 8 A.M.–8 P.M., Sun. 9 A.M.–6 P.M.), a small but full-service food and sundries outlet that's the best in town.

Kailua

Kailua (Two Seas) is developed with shopping centers, all modern services, and one of the *best* sailboarding beaches in the state. The easiest way into town is over the Ko'olau Range on Route 61, most widely known on the island as the Pali Highway. As soon as you pass through a long tunnel just after the Nu'uanu Pali Lookout and your eyes adjust to the shocking brilliance of sunshine, look to your right to see **Mt. Olomana.** Its 1,643-foot peak is believed to be a remnant of the volcanic caldera which was the origin of Windward O'ahu. Below lies Kailua and the Kawainui (Big Water) Marsh, perhaps the oldest inhabited area on this side of the island. Kamehameha I, after conquering O'ahu in 1795, gave all this land to the chiefs who had fought for him. The area became a favorite of the ruling *ali'i* until the fall of the monarchy at the turn of the 20th century.

SIGHTS

A good touring loop is to continue straight on Route 61 until it comes to the coast. Route 61, the Pali Hwy., changes its name to Kailua Rd. when it passes Castle Medical Center and then becomes Ku'ulei Rd. oceanside of the main intersection in town. Turn right onto Kalaheo

Avenue, which takes you along the coast to Kailua Beach Park. In the waters offshore will be a spectacle of sailboarders, with their sails puffed out like the proud chests of multicolored birds. Follow the road around the shoulder of the headland as it gains the heights from the beach; a pull-off here affords an expansive panorama of the bay below. By daytime it's enjoyable, but in the evening local kids come here to hang out and drink beer. Continuing, the road takes you through an area of beautiful homes strung along Lanikai Beach. At one time trees came down to the shoreline, but it has steadily eroded away. The Navy attempted to start a retaining reef by dumping barge loads of white bath tile just offshore. Their efforts were not successful, but many homes in town now have sparkling new, white-tiled bathrooms! As this road, 'A'alapapa Drive, loops back toward town, it changes name to Mokulua.

At the north end of Kailua Beach is **Mokapu (Sacred District) Peninsula,** home of the Marine Corps Base Hawaii (MCBH) in Kan'eohe—closed to civilians except on the fourth of July for its typically American Bay Fest holiday celebration. Most of the little islands in the bay are bird sanctuaries. The

FIRST HAWAIIANS

The Mokapu Peninsula, now occupied by the Marine Corps Air Station, is a sacred site for Hawaiians. Mololani is the small crater on this stub of land and its morning-sun facing eastern side has red soil with some black mixed in. Legend says that it is here that the first Hawaiians were created. The gods Kane, Kanaloa, Ku, and Lono had gathered by the sea. Kane drew an image of a man in the sand in the likeness of the gods. Boasting that he had the power to bring life to such a form, Kanaloa also drew a human likeness in the sand, commanded it to come to life – but nothing happened. Then Kane asked for help from his two other companions, who after chanting the proper words, brought life to the image drawn by Kane. They called this man Kanehulihonua, and they took him to live in Hale-kou, a house made by the gods. When the man went out, he could see that his shadow was always at his side. One morning, Kanehulihonua woke to see a woman at his side, and he believed that the gods had created her from his shadow. He named her Keakahulilani, or Shadow Changed by Heaven. From these two individuals have sprung the people of Hawaii and, according to legend, all the people who populate the islands of the Pacific Ocean.

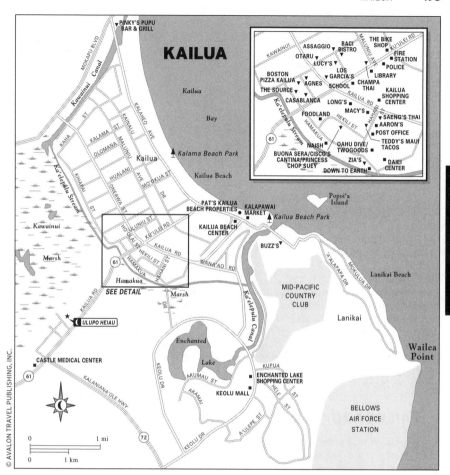

WINDWARD O'AHU

farthest, **Moku Manu,** is home to terns and man-o'-wars, birds famous for leading fishermen to schools of fish. Between the base and the rest of town are several delicate fishponds; the hill that rises from the center of the base is an old traditional Hawaiian sacred site.

☾ Ulupo Heiau

Ulupo (Night Inspiration) is dedicated to the Ulu line of *ali'i*, who were responsible for setting up *heiau* involving the sacred births of chiefs. The umbilical cord was often cut as a drum was sounded, and then the cord *(piko)*

was placed in a shallow rock depression at a *heiau*. This temple, supposedly built by the legendary *menehune,* who usually accomplished their task within the span of one night, shows remarkable stone craftsmanship, measuring 140 feet wide by 180 feet long by 30 feet high at its tallest edge, although the stepped front wall has partially collapsed by rock fall. Although the *heiau* is not officially used today, you can still sometimes see *ti* leaf–wrapped offerings on the top platform. The *heiau* overlooks Kawainui Marsh. Below the *heiau*, traditional-style Hawaiian *lo'i* (flooded paddy fields) are still raising taro. Ulupo Heiau was one of three *heiau* that once overlooked the former fishpond. The other two, located on the west side of the marsh, are Pahukini and Holomakani *heiau*. Some restoration has been done to Pahukini Heiau, but both remain largely untouched and inaccessible.

To get to Ulupo Heiau as you approach Kailua on the Pali Hwy., turn left at the Castle Medical Center onto Uluoa Street, following it one block to Manu Aloha Street, where you turn right. Turn right again onto Manu O'o and park in the Windward YMCA parking lot. The *heiau* is directly behind the YMCA building. Alternately, follow a short paved access road from a pull off along Kailua Road (Route 61), that is located across the highway from a Tesoro gas station.

Beaches

Along the shoreline of an exclusive residential area, just south of Kailua, sits the gentle **Lanikai Beach**. For access, more than half a dozen marked rights-of-way run off Mokulua Drive, the main thoroughfare, but there is not good parking. No facilities are provided, but good snorkeling, kayaking, and swimming is possible year-round, with generally mild surf and a long, gently sloping, sandy beach. The beach runs south for almost a mile, broken by seawalls designed (unsuccessfully in most cases) to hold back erosion. Many outrigger canoes use the sandy-bottomed shore to launch and land. Popular with local people but not visited much by tourists, this beach is consistently rated one of the best in the state.

Kailua Beach is the main beach in the area and is often regarded as the best overall beach on the island. Of wide, soft, powdery sand, it runs for nearly two miles along the front of town, with the Kailua Beach Park at its southern end. Great for family outings, with safe conditions and fine facilities, this beach has become a hot sailboarding spot, and more recently kiteboarders have found it a great place for this new sport. The wind conditions attract a daily flotilla of sailboarders and kiteboarders, but they must stay beyond marked buoys that delineate the swimming area at the center of the park. Sailboarders and kiteboarders must launch their gear only from the left side of the swimming area. The park boasts a pavilion, picnic facilities, restrooms, cold-water showers, lifeguards, a boat ramp at its south end,

---

SAILBOARDING AND KITEBOARDING

The sport of sailboarding is commonly known as windsurfing, after the name of one of the most famous sailboard manufacturers. A combination of surfing and sailing, the equipment is a rather large and stable surfboard mounted with a highly maneuverable sail. It sounds difficult, but most people find it slightly easier than surfing because you're mobilized by the wind and not at the mercy of the waves. You don't have to read the waves as well as a surfer, and, like riding a bicycle, as long as you keep moving you can hold your balance. Kailua Bay has perfect conditions for this sport, and you can go there any day to see sailboarders skimming the waves with their multihued sails displayed like proud peacocks.

A cross between wakeboarding and flying a kite, kiteboarding (also known as kitesurfing) is one of the newest water sports to hit the island. With kiteboarding, a large foil-sail kite is attached by long ropes to a grab bar clipped to a harness worn around the waist. Steering is done by pulling one end of the bar or the other to raise or lower the kite, catching more or less wind. A wide ski is used, similar to a wakeboard ski, except that this one has a short rudder. Booties – a neoprene version of snowboard boots – keep you attached to the board. Proficient kitesurfers skim the water as fast and as freely as sailboarders. Those who really know how to use the wind to their advantage can get 20-30 feet of loft. Those who know the sport say that it's not for the timid, nor as easy as it might appear. Definitely begin with lessons.

and sometimes a food concession (they come and go); the gates are closed at night, roughly sunset to sunrise. The surf is gentle year-round, and the swimming safe. Children should be careful of the sudden drop-offs in the channels formed by the Ka'elepulu Canal as it enters the sea in the middle of the beach park. Good surfing and diving are found around Popoi'a Island, another bird sanctuary, just offshore.

Kalama Beach Park is reached by driving *makai* (toward the sea) on Route 61, which turns into Kailua Road and then Kuulei Road, and making a left at the T intersection onto North Kalaheo. Wedged between large beachfront lots and stylish houses, this small park has only parking and restroom facilities but allows access to the central stretch of Kailua Beach and is less frequented than Kailua Beach Park. At the far north end of Kailua Beach, a reef break makes better wave action for body boarders than any other place in the bay.

SHOPPING

The two towns of Kailua and Kane'ohe have the lion's share of shopping on the Windward Coast. You can pick up basics in the small towns as you head up the coast, but for any unique or hard-to-find items, Kailua/Kane'ohe is your only bet. In Kailua, there are some shops near the main intersection of Kailua Road (The Pali Highway/Route 61) and Oneawa Street, but you'll find more in the small shopping centers around town. The **Kailua Shopping Center** has limited shopping that includes **Under A Hula Moon** (808/261-4252) for gifts and souvenirs, and the well-stocked and great independent bookshop **Bookends** (808/261-1996, open Mon.–Sat. 9 A.M.–8 P.M., Sun. 9 A.M.–5 P.M.), for a full range of reading material, including a large Hawaiiana section. Across the street in the **Kailua Town Center** are **Macy's** (808/262-5395) and **Longs Drugs** (808/261-8537), for pharmacy items, film and film developing, and sundries. A few steps down Hahani Street is the large **Don Quijote** (formerly Daiei) store (808/266-4400), where you can find just about anything.

For antiques and collectibles of all sorts stop at **The Hunter Collectibles** (764 Kailua Rd., 808/262-4868, open 10 A.M.–4 P.M.). If you're really into old finds and one shop isn't enough, head to **Old Pali Road Antiques** (320 Ku'ulei Rd., 808/261-7946), only a few blocks away across from the elementary school, or around the corner to **Ali'i Antiques of Kailua** (21 Maluniu Ave., 808/261-1705), both old fixtures in town.

For new collectibles and other artwork, try **Island Treasures** (629 Kailua Rd., 808/261-8131, open daily 10 A.M.–6 P.M., Sun. until 4 P.M.) gallery next to Longs Drugs. This shop represents Hawaiian artists only and then only if the work has an island flavor. Its fine collection, perhaps the best in town, includes paintings, pottery, woodwork, greeting cards, handmade gifts, some jewelry, etched glass, and trinkets.

Closer to the water is the small **Kailua Beach Center,** with its **Kailua First Stop Convenience Store** (808/262-0480), clothing shops, and water gear store.

Other small malls with retail stores, food outlets, and sundry other shops are the **Enchanted Lake Shopping Center** and neighboring **Keolu Mall** on the south side of Enchanted Lake, and **Aikahi Park Shopping Center** near the Kane'ohe Marine Corps Base.

RECREATION
Sailboarding and Kiteboarding

Far and away the most famous sailboarding and kiteboarding beach on O'ahu is Kailua Beach Park on the Windward Coast. Daily, a flotilla of boarders glide over its smooth waters, propelled by the constant breezes. In town, several enterprises build, rent, and sell sailboards, kiteboards, and other water equipment. Commercial ventures are allowed to operate along Kailua Beach on weekdays and weekend mornings, but weekend afternoons and holidays are *kapu!*

Kailua Sailboards and Kayaks (130 Kailua Rd., 808/262-2555, www.kailuasailboards .com, open 8:30 A.M.–5 P.M. daily), with a perfect location only a minute from Kailua Beach, is a full-service sailboard and kayak store. Sailboard rentals run $59 per day or $49 for a half

Both sailboarders and kiteboarders find Kailua Beach to be the most consistent place to ride on the island.

day; weekly rates are also available. Beginning group lessons are $69 for a three-hour session. Surfing lessons run $69 and kiteboarding lessons are $119. In addition, boogie boards, snorkel gear, and bicycles are rented.

Naish Hawaii (155 Hamakua Dr., 808/262-6068 or 800/767-6068, www.naish.com, open daily 9 A.M.–5:30 P.M.) is a very famous maker of custom boards, production boards, sails, hardware, accessories, and repairs. T-shirts, bathing suits, beach accessories, hats, and slippers are also for sale. Naish is the largest and oldest sailboarding company in Hawaii. The famous Naish Windsurfing School gives 90 minutes of personal instruction at Kailua Beach including all equipment for $75 for one person or $100 for two people. Private instruction goes for $65 an hour and group lessons run $45 per person. Kiteboarding lessons, 1.5 hours, will set you back $125, with additional lessons for $100 each. Naish rents boards and rigs for beginners, intermediate, and advanced riders from $25 for two hours to $250 for one week.

Hawaiian Watersports (354 Hahani St., 808/262-5483, www.hawaiianwatersports.com, open daily 9 A.M.–5 P.M.) also offers sales, lessons, and rentals for sailboarding, kiteboarding, and surfing, as well as kayak and snorkel gear rentals.

Kayaking

Near the beach in Kailua, **Kailua Sailboards and Kayaks** (130 Kailua Rd., 808/262-2555, www.kailuasailboards.com, open daily 8:30 A.M.–5 P.M.) also rents kayaks and other water gear as well as offers guided tours. Half-day rentals for single and tandem kayaks are $39 and $49, with full-day rentals at $49 and $59. A guided tour of the coast and islands off Kailua Beach, with an emphasis on education, runs $119 adults or $95 for kids 3–12. Good service, good prices, and free pickup in Waikiki are offered. Its prices are about the same as **Twogood Kayaks Hawaii** (345 Hahani St. 808/262-5656, www.twogoodkayaks.com, open Mon.–Fri. 9 A.M.–6 P.M., Sat.–Sun.

and holidays 8 A.M.–6 P.M.), which also offers kayak rentals, sales, lessons, and group tours, as well as snorkeling gear, boogie boards, dry bags, and more. Half-day kayak rentals are $39 single and $49 tandem, full-day rental is $49 single and $59 tandem, and the kayak will be dropped off free at the Kailua Beach Park (other drop-off locations in Kailua will run you an additional $15 delivery fee). Multi-day rates are also an option, as are various lessons and self-guided trips. A full-day, fun-filled, guided, and educational tour to Kailua Bay and offshore islands, which includes all gear, a bag lunch, and transportation to/from Waikiki, is available for $109 per person.

See also **Hawaiian Watersports** (354 Hahani St., 808/262-5483, www.hawaiianwatersports.com, daily 9 A.M.–5 P.M.) for its similar guided kayak tours.

Scuba

In Kailua, try these full-service dive shops: **Aaron's Dive Shop** (307 Hahani St., 808/262-2333, www.hawaii-scuba.com); or **Oahu Dive Center** (345 Hahani St., 808/263-7333 or 866/933-3483, www.oahudivecenter.com) at the Don Quijote Shopping Center. Aaron's offers a discover scuba trip that gives you two dives for $125, and a three-day certification course for $389. Oahu Dive Center runs similar dives for $150 and $350, respectively, plus it offers specialty dives and instruction. Both are reputable companies with many years of service.

Hiking

The **Maunawili Demonstration Trail** is one of O'ahu's newest trails. The trailhead is just above St. Stephen's Seminary along the Pali Highway, but you can't turn left into the trailhead parking lot when going uphill. Approach it from the Honolulu side or head uphill through the Pali tunnel and turn off onto Nu'uanu Pali Drive. Follow this up past the Nu'uanu Pali Lookout and get back onto the highway going toward Kailua. After passing through the tunnel again, a sign points to a scenic overlook a short ways down at a large curve in the road. Pull off into the parking area and look for the trail sign and entrance through the highway guardrail near the overlook turnout entrance. This trail can also be accessed by walking down the Old Pali Road from the Nu'uanu Lookout. The beauty of this trail is that it is reasonably flat with little elevation gain or loss as it winds its way along the Windward side of the Ko'olau Range. The whine of the Pali Highway abates almost immediately and you are suddenly in a brilliant highland tropical forest. You can continue to the end (upper Waimanalo, about three hours one-way) for a full day's hike, or just find a secluded spot after a mile or so for a picnic. The views are spectacular, and vantage points display the coast all the way from Rabbit Island to Chinaman's Hat. Remember, however, that as with all Hawaiian trails, recent rainfall makes for treacherous footing.

Biking

Across the road from the library is **The Bike Shop** (270 Ku'ulei Rd., 808/261-1553, www.bikeshophawaii.com, open Mon.–Fri. 10 A.M.–7 P.M., Sat. 9 A.M.–5 P.M., Sun. 10 A.M.–5 P.M.), which does bike sales and repair and also rents mountain bikes at $20–40 per day or $100–200 per week, depending upon the quality.

ACCOMMODATIONS
Vacation Rentals

If looking for a rental house in Kailua, start by contacting **Pat's Kailua Beach Properties** (204 South Kalaheo Ave., Kailua, HI 96734, 808/261-1653 or 808/262-4128, fax 808/261-0893, info@patskailua.com, www.patskailua.com). Pat's has more than 30 separate units in Kailua and Lanikai, ranging in price $100–500 per night; monthly rates are also available, and some properties can only be rented by the month. Stays of a week or longer are appreciated, although shorter stays are accepted when they fit between other reservations. All units are fully furnished, and most are within two blocks of the water. The options are many, and Pat's has something for everyone from a young couple out for a week of water activities looking for an inexpensive vacation, all the way to a large family needing a four-bedroom luxury beachside home for a family reunion. This first-rate company can find the right place to meet your needs.

Located one block from the beach, **Savannah's Cabana** (808/292-1348) is a one-bedroom detached cottage that's great for a vacationing couple. Cool and comfortable, this newly built hideaway has all modern amenities and comes with a king-size bed, cable color TV, an efficiency cooking area, and some beach gear to borrow. Rent is $125 per night with a cleaning fee for less than four nights; no credit cards please. Stays of seven nights or more are encouraged with a discount.

Kailua Beach Vacation Accommodations (808/262-5409 or 800/484-1036, book@ hawaiibestrentals.com, www.hawaiibestrentals .com) has rentals on or near Kailua and Lanikai beaches. These clean and modern studio, one-bedroom, and two-bedroom units have all you need for a comfortable vacation. The three Kailua units rent for $155–185 a night with a minimum of seven nights, while the two studios in Lanikai run $115 a night with a five night minimum.

Lanikai Beach Rentals (1277 Mokulua Dr., 808/261-7895 or 800/258-7895, fax 808/262-2181, www.lanikaibeachrentals@hawaii.rr.com, www.lanikaibeachrentals.com) can also put you in a fine beach house either in Lanikai or Kailua. Rates run $125–625 a day, but the majority are under $185. In addition, there a couple rentals that go only by the month.

Pacific Hawaii Reservations (571 Pauku St., Kailua, HI 96734, 808/262-8133, fax 808/262-5030, pir@aloha.net, www.oahu-hawaii-vacation.com) and **Affordable Paradise Bed and Breakfast** (332 Ku'ukama St., Kailua, HI 96734, 808/261-1693, info@affordable-paradise.com, www.affordable-paradise.com), both reputable agencies with offices in Kailua, list private vacation rental homes in and around town, up and down the coast, throughout the island, and around the state. Rates and homes differ dramatically, but all are guaranteed to be comfortable and accommodating.

Bed-and-Breakfast

One of the finest guest homes in Kailua, a beautiful property that sits on a quiet side street, is ◖ **Sharon's Serenity B&B** (127 Kahahiaka St., 808/262-5621 or 800/914-2271, sharon@sharonsserenity.com, www.sharons serenity.com). Sharon goes out of her way to make you feel comfortable and welcome, and the coffee is always fresh-perked. Sharon also takes the time to sit with you, giving advice on where to dine, what to see, and a candid description of activities that are worthwhile. The meticulously clean, beautifully appointed home of open contemporary design features guest rooms with color TV and refrigerator, Mexican tile throughout, a spacious family room, backyard swimming pool and lanai, and views of the Ka'elepulu Canal, golf course, and hills beyond. The Blue Room has a queen-size bed and its own attached private bath. The Poolside Room, also with an in-room bath, has both a king-size bed and a twin bed. The suite could easily accommodate a small family, with its queen-size bed and twin bed; a twin bed set up like a daybed can be put in for a fourth person. The suite features an in-room sliding partition for privacy and its own bath just across the hall. Rates are $80–130, depending upon the room and number of guests, with no additional cleaning fee, and the price includes a continental breakfast, which Sharon will have waiting in the morning. This B&B is a short walk to the beach and close to the center of town if you want to walk. Sharon's Serenity is an excellent choice for the Windward Coast, perfect for getting away from it all.

FOOD

Kailua is rich in foods of the world, and the following list gives you a sampling. Most of these restaurants are in the moderate range, several are classier fine-dining places, and a few are downright inexpensive. Enjoy!

Natural Foods

Head to **Down to Earth Natural Food and Lifestyle** for wholesome, nutritious, and inexpensive wraps, sandwiches, and other quick foods at a reasonable price from the deli counter, or pick up a salad or hot entrée to go from the salad and hot food bar at $7 a pound.

Bakery

For a little pick-me-up or a sweet treat, try **Agnes' Portuguese Bake Shop** (46 Ho'ola'i St., 808/262-5367, open Mon.–Sat. 6 A.M.–6 P.M., Sun. 6 A.M.–2 P.M.) for Portuguese-style *malasadas* and *pao dolce,* other breads, pies, and cakes, or soup, salad, cappuccino, or espresso. This cool, clean, and inviting place is a popular stop in town and has a loyal following. For those interested, there is Internet access.

Pizza

For a lot of something more common, try **Boston's Pizza Kailua** (29 Ho'ola'i St., 808/263-7757, open Sun.–Thurs. 11 A.M.–8 P.M., Fri.–Sat. 11 A.M.–9 P.M.), which serves one size—a huge three-pound, 19-inch pizza. Prices vary $17–24 depending on the number of toppings or $4.25–6 by the slice (a quarter of a pizza), while smaller calzones run $5 each. A few tables inside and out accommodate guests, but most people stop here for takeout.

Burgers

Teddy's Bigger Burger (539 Kailua Rd., 808/262-0820, open 10:30 A.M.–9 P.M.) is a retro place with a 1950s look: bright lights, bright colors, Formica, and rock and roll music. Stop here for large "hand-pattied" charbroiled burgers, crispy fries, extra thick shakes, and fountain drinks. Most everything on the menu is under $9. Teddy says that here bigger really *is* better.

Island Style

For down-home island cooking, stop at **Boots and Kimo's Homestyle Kitchen** (131 Hekili St., 808/263-7929, open weekdays 7 A.M.–2 P.M., weekends 6:30 A.M.–2:30 P.M.) for island favorite plate lunches.

If that's not enough, across the street in the Kailua Foodland Marketplace is **Big City Diner** (808/263-8880, open Sun.–Thurs. 7 A.M.–10 P.M., Fri.–Sat. 7 A.M.–midnight), a

sister restaurant to the original in the Kaimuki area of Honolulu. The Big City Diner serves ordinary American egg and griddle breakfasts, and sandwiches, burgers, fish, and a variety of other comfort foods for lunch and dinner. Portions are large.

At the north end of town overlooking Kawainui Canal is **Pinky's Pupu Bar and Grill** (970 N. Kalaheo Ave., 808/254-6255, open Mon.–Fri. 3–10 P.M., Sat. 4–10 P.M., Sun. 8 A.M.–2 P.M. and 4–10 P.M.). Pinky's is a good-time, cheery place, open and breezy, with lots of stuff hanging from the ceiling and a set of shelves that shouts vintage Hawaii. This is the place to come for familiar, feel-good food and large portions. The lunch menu has soup and salads and plenty of sandwiches for under $10. Dinner is heartier, with baby back ribs, fish tacos, beer can chicken, steak, grill items, and all those meals you know and love for less than $19. It's also family-friendly with a good kids' menu. Full bar is available.

Lucy's Grill N' Bar (33 Aulike St., 808/230-8188, 5–10 P.M. daily) is a fun, fine-dining place with an eclectic menu, open kitchen, and full bar. On the menu are such items as ahi and crab cakes and coconut-crusted shrimp sticks for appetizers, Italian sausage and shiitake mushroom pizza, and hibachi salmon, braised lamb shanks, and Mongolian-style pork ribs for entrées. When locals want a special night out on the town, Lucy's is often the choice. Most main dishes run $16–28.

Steakhouse

Buzz's Original Steakhouse (413 Kawailoa Rd., 808/261-4661, open daily 11 A.M.–10 P.M.) is really *the* original steakhouse of this small island chain owned by the Schneider family. Buzz's is just across the road from Kailua Beach Park, situated along the canal. This restaurant is an institution with local families. It's the kind of place that if you can't think of where to go, you head for Buzz's. The food is always good, if not extraordinary, and charbroiling is the theme. Lunch is served until 3 P.M. and consists of salads and burgers, mostly $9–14. For dinner, from 5 P.M., some menu items are top sirloin, chicken teriyaki, rack of lamb, and fresh fish, with entrées in the $15–28 range except for the lobster and crab legs. Salad bar is included with all entrées, or you can order it or the soup and salad bar as your meal. No credit cards are accepted.

Italian

Let the pungent aroma of garlic frying in olive oil lead you to **Assaggio Italian Restaurant** (354 Uluniu St., 808/261-2772, open Mon.–Fri. 11:30 A.M.–2:30 P.M., Sun.–Thurs. 5–9:30 P.M., until 10 P.M. Fri.–Sat.). You are welcomed into an open contemporary dining room done in the striking colors of black, red, teal, and magenta, where tables covered in white linen and black upholstered chairs line the long window area. The typical and traditional Italian menu, served with crusty Italian bread, begins with a full line of antipasti, soups like pasta e fagioli and vichyssoise. Pastas range in price $12–16 and include linguine, fettuccine, and ziti, covered in your choice of marinara, clam, carbonara, pesto, or other sauce. Entrées are chicken cacciatore, baked ziti with eggplant and mozzarella, and grilled dishes such as New York strip steaks, pork chops, and osso bucco all make up this long menu; all are priced below $22. From the sea comes fresh fish sautéed in garlic, scallops and shrimp in wine, or calamari alla parmigiana. Desserts are homemade and the full bar serves imported and domestic beers, liquors, coffee, espresso, and plenty of wine varietals.

A few steps down Aulike Street, the smaller, more intimate, and more informal **Baci Bistro** (30 Aulike St., 808/262-7555, open weekdays 11:30 A.M.–2 P.M., daily 5:30–10 P.M.) has both indoor and outdoor café seating. Soup, salad, and hot or cold appetizers prepare you for the tasty entrées to come. Try one of the traditional pastas, like rigatoni with sausage and basil or spinach tagliatelle and porcini mushrooms in cream sauce; choose a meat or fish dish, like veal scallopine or fresh fish of the day; or select one of the fine risotto dishes, all $13–20. Baci Bistro serves a memorable meal with class.

An easygoing place with linens, **Buona Sera** (131 Hekili St., 808/263-7696, open daily 5:30–9 P.M.) does reasonably priced Italian food with main entrées under $15. Expect all your traditional favorites. This is a tiny place with row upon row of empty Chianti bottles along the walls.

Located next to the Down To Earth Natural Foods grocery store is the casual **Zia's Caffé Kailua** (201 Hamakua Dr., 808/262-7168, open daily 11 A.M.–10 P.M.). Come for pasta, sandwiches, fresh fish and seafood, soups, or special salads, where a nutritious lunch will run $8–12 and a more filling dinner $13–22.

Moroccan

C Casablanca (19 Ho'ola'i St., 808/262-8196, open Tues.–Sat. 6–8:30 P.M.) serves Moroccan cuisine, one of the unusual tasty treats of town. Meals are served prix fixe at $32.75 with your choice of entrée, while the house specials run $38.50. Appetizers, a soup, dessert, and mint tea come with each meal, as does B'stilla, baked phyllo dough with saffron chicken, almonds, and egg. Couscous is a mainstay and comes with vegetables, chicken, or lamb. Other herbed delicacies are fish charmoula, pan-fried calamari with garlic and capers, spiced Cornish hen, and lamb *tagine* with eggplant. Diners sit on cushions or on the floor, and as these meals are usually eaten with the fingers, you'll have to ask for eating utensils if you need them. Dining at Casablanca will be a cultural experience.

Japanese

If Japanese food is what you're after, try **Otaru** (442 Uluniu St., 808/261-7802, open Mon.– Fri. 11 A.M.–2 P.M., nightly 5–9:30 P.M.). Otaru can fill your every wish for sushi, sashimi, and full sukiyaki, tempura, and *teishoku* meals for both lunch and dinner. Sushi runs $3.50–12 and you won't run out of choices, while most dinners are $13–19.

Chinese

Princess Chop Suey (131 Hekili St., 808/262-7166, open Mon.–Sat. 10 A.M.–9 P.M., Sun. 11 A.M.–9 P.M.) is your basic chop suey joint. Its theme is Naugahyde and Formica, and everything on the menu is under $8.

Thai

A few steps down Kuʻulei Road is **Champa Thai** (306 Kuʻulei Rd., 808/263-8281, open Mon.–Fri. 11 A.M.–2:30 P.M., nightly 5–9:30 P.M.). A comfortable place with linens and white tablecloths and a mixture of Thai and beach decoration, Champa Thai gets praise from locals for its extensive menu of well-prepared dishes that can be made to your desired spiciness level. All of the usual offerings from spring roll appetizers to green papaya salad, hot and sour lemongrass soup, curries, vegetarian dishes, rice, noodles, meat, and seafood dishes are available. Most entrées are under $8. BYOB is OK (small corkage fee).

Saeng's Thai Cuisine (315 Hahani St., 808/263-9727, open Mon.–Fri. 10 A.M.–2 P.M., daily 5–9:30 P.M.) has been around the longest. Saeng's offers spicy Thai food with an emphasis on vegetarian meals, all at an agreeable price. Starters are Thai crisp noodles, fish patties, green papaya salad, yum koong shrimp salad, and chicken coconut soup. Specialties include spicy stuffed calamari, Thai red curry, and à la carte beef, pork, and chicken dishes.

Mexican

Near the main intersection of town is **Los Garcia's** (14 Oneawa St., 808/261-0306, Sun.–Thurs. 11 A.M.–9 P.M., Fri.–Sat. 11 A.M.–10 P.M.), a better than average Mexican restaurant owned by a family from Guadalajara. Simple yet tasteful, the south-of-the-border decor is achieved with adobe-like arches, wooden tables, Mexican ceramics placed here and there, and plenty of cacti and hanging plants. The menu features combination dinners of burritos, chiles rellenos, enchiladas, tacos, or tamales all priced under $14. Shrimp and seafood dishes and the special meat plates cost about the same. Less expensive dishes are asada burritos, tacos de ceviche, carnitas, plus the more traditional Mexican plate dishes, like alegrias, gordita Jalisco, and quesadilla Michoacana. There are even a half dozen dishes for the vegetarian. Los Garcia's is definitely worth the money!

Cisco's Cantina (131 Hekili St., 808/262-7337, open Sun.–Thurs. 11 A.M.–10 P.M., Fri.–Sat. 11 A.M.–11 P.M.) features complete Mexican cuisine. Tostadas, tacos, burritos, enchiladas, and chiles rellenos are mostly under $13; fajitas are more expensive at $21.75 for one or $26.75 for two. All come with Mexican corn, sautéed Tex-Mex mushrooms, and beans and rice. Inside, the south-of-the-border atmosphere is created with hanging piñatas, stucco walls, and blue-tile tables.

Maui Tacos (539 Kailua Rd., 808/261-4155, open daily 9 A.M.–9 P.M.) serves quick Mexican food with an attitude and Hawaiian twist—always good. Expect meals in the $4–8 range.

Farmers Market

If you're looking for fresh vegetables, fruits, flowers, and other locally grown and produced food items, try the **Kailua Thursday Night Farmers Market,** held downtown at the Kailua Town Center parking garage behind the Longs Drug store every Thursday 5–7:30 P.M. Stop by and support local farmers.

Supermarkets

There are several large, full-service grocery stores in town that also have meat and deli departments. **Times Supermarket** (open daily 7 A.M.–10 P.M.) is centrally located in the Kailua Shopping Center. **Safeway** has supermarkets on Hamakua Street, in the Enchanted Lake Shopping Center, and at the Aikahi Park Shopping Center near the Kaneʻohe Marine Corps Base. On the corner of Hamakua and Hekili streets sits a new **Foodland.** Incorporated into this supermarket is **R. Field,** a wine company that carries a gourmet selection of cheeses, crackers, jams, jellies, and all sorts of other prepared foods, both local and international.

Kalapawai Market (306 S. Kalaheo Ave., 808/262-4359, open daily 6 A.M.–9 P.M.) is the closest shop to the beach at the corner of Kailua Rd. and Kalaheo Avenue. Stop for sundries and beach supplies, basic food and drink supplies, wine and beer, and an adjacent deli that carries tasty hot and cold sandwiches and salads for under $7.

For a full line of fresh, organic, and whole foods, plus an assortment of supplements and health products, try the large **Down to Earth Foods and Lifestyle** (201 Hamakua Dr., 808/262-3838, open daily 8 A.M.–10 P.M., www.downtoearth.org). This store also has a salad and hot food bar, deli counter, and an Internet corner.

The smaller but well-established health food store **The Source Natural Foods** (32 Kainehe St., 808/262-5604, open weekdays 9 A.M.–9 P.M., Sat. 9 A.M.–6 P.M., Sun. 9 A.M.–5 P.M.) has a good selection of bulk foods, some organic fresh fruit and produce, vitamins and minerals, cosmetics and hygiene products, as well as lots of essences, oils, and natural healing products to help with whatever ails you and to keep you on the straight and narrow.

INFORMATION AND SERVICES

The **Kailua Information Center** (808/261-2727, open weekdays 10 A.M.–4 P.M., Sat. 10 A.M.–2 P.M.), staffed by the Chamber of Commerce, is located in the Kailua Shopping Center. Pick up brochures for businesses on the Windward Coast, free maps to both the Kailua and Kane'ohe areas, and the answers to your questions about the immediate area.

Campers can get information and **camping permits** at the satellite city hall (1090 Keolu Dr.) in the Keolu Mall near Enchanted Lake.

The Keolu Mall has a post office, and there is another in town at the corner of Kailua Road and Hahani Street, just across from a First Hawaiian National Bank.

Medical aid is available from **Castle Medical Center** (808/263-5500), a hospital at the intersection of the Pali Highway (Route 61) and Kalaniana'ole Highway (Route 72).

Find the Kailua Washerette next to Lucy's on Aulike Street. The U-Wash-N-Dry (open 24 hours) is located next to the Casablanca restaurant on Ho'ola'i Street.

There are **gas stations** at the Kailua Shopping Center in the center of town and at the Aikahi Park Shopping Center.

Kane'ohe

The bedroom community of Kane'ohe (Kane's Bamboo) lies along Kane'ohe Bay, protected by Hawaii's only large barrier reef, easily seen from the Nu'uanu Pali Lookout high above to the west. Around the edge of the bay lie six of the original 30 fishponds that once graced this fine shore. A lush, fertile land of bountiful farms, historically one of the most productive areas of O'ahu, Kane'ohe was, in centuries past, the second most populous area on the island, and (combined with neighboring Kailua) remains so today. Through the years, the major crops of this coastal town have shifted from taro to rice, sugarcane, pineapples, and bananas, and today a variety is still grown.

Where Route 83 intersects the Likelike Highway on the southern outskirts of Kane'ohe, it branches north and changes its name from the Kamehameha Highway to the Kahekili Highway until it hits the coast at Kahalu'u. This four-mile traverse passes two exceptionally beautiful valleys: Ha'iku Valley and the Valley of the Temples. Neither should be missed. The Hawaii State Veterans Cemetery lies along Kamehameha Highway, and three golf courses grace these green hills, one near the water and two tucked into the folds of the encircling *pali*.

Offshore is Moku O Lo'e, commonly called **Coconut Island.** It became famous as the opening shot in the TV show *Gilligan's Island*, although the series was shot in California. Now home to the University of Hawai'i Marine Lab, it was *kapu* in ancient times and during World War II served as an R&R camp for B-29 crews. Many of the crews felt the island had bad vibes and reported having a streak of bad luck. In recent times, Frank Fasi, Honolulu's former mayor, suggested that Hawaii's gate-crashing guests, Ferdinand and Imelda Marcos, should lease Coconut Island. It never happened.

A **sandbar** known as Ahu O Laka (Altar of Laka), approximately one mile wide and three

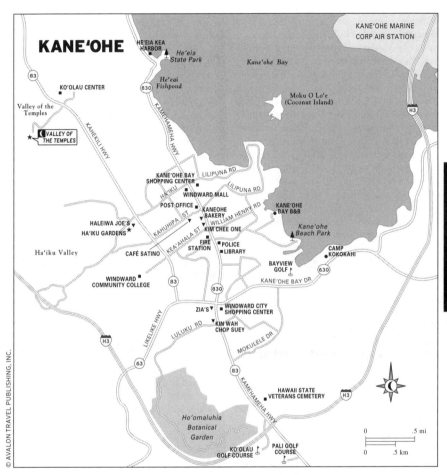

KANE'OHE

miles long, occupies the center of Kane'ohe Bay, making a perfect anchorage for catamarans, pontoon boats, and powerboats. These boat people drop anchor, jump off, and wade to the bar through knee-deep, clear waters. It has become an unofficial playground where you can fling a Frisbee, play volleyball, drink beer, or just float around. Part of the sandbar may rise above the water if tides are right, and some barbecue chefs even bring their hibachis and have a bite to eat. Surrounding you is Kane'ohe Bay, with Chinaman's Hat floating off to the north and a perfect view of the *pali* straight ahead. This

place is the epitome of la dolce vita, Hawaiian style. Fortunately, in recent years, the once crystal-clear bay, which was becoming murky with silt because of development, is clearing again as a result of conservation efforts.

SIGHTS
Ho'omaluhia Botanical Garden

Lying below the encircling H-3 freeway at the south edge of town is this 400-acre tract (808/233-7323, open daily 9 A.M.–4 P.M. except Christmas and New Year's Day), one component of the Honolulu Botanical Gardens system that previously was agricultural land. Find it at the end of Luluku Road. Although it includes a 32-acre lake, no swimming is permitted. This dammed reservoir, part of the flood control plan for Kaneʻohe, was created following several devastating floods in the 1960s. The focus of this garden is on trees and plants from various areas of the world, including Hawaii, the Philippines, India, Africa, and tropical America. Day-use and weekend overnight camping are permitted, walking is encouraged along its many trails, and jogging and bicycling can be done on its paved road. Do yourself a favor and walk down to the lake to see the ducks, geese, and moorhens, but don't forget to turn around and look up at the *pali* that rises up precipitously right behind you. Free guided nature walks are given at 10 A.M. on Saturday and 1 P.M. on Sunday. Bring mosquito repellent and an umbrella. Before you leave, have a look at the visitors center art gallery for the fine art exhibits staged there.

Haʻiku Gardens

Haʻiku (Abrupt Break) Gardens (46-336 Haʻiku Rd.) is a lovely section of a residential area that includes a restaurant and some quiet condominiums. After you pass Kaneʻohe District Park and Windward Community College, turn left onto Haʻiku Road and proceed for .5 mile uphill. The gardens date from the mid-1800s, when Hawaiian *aliʻi* deeded 16 acres to an English engineer named Baskerville. He developed the area, creating spring-fed lily ponds, building estate homes, and planting flowers, fruits, and ornamental trees. Later a restaurant was built, and the grounds became famous for their beauty, often used for special gatherings. You're welcome to walk through the gardens, but they are closed at sunset. Proceed from the restaurant down a walkway to the grassy lawn and pond, where perhaps you'll attract an impromptu entourage of ducks, chickens, and guinea fowl that squawk along looking for handouts. Amid the lush foliage is a gazebo used for weddings. A path leads around the pond, whose benches and small pavilions are perfect for contemplation, and continues under a huge banyan, while a nearby bamboo grove serenades with sonorous music if the wind is blowing.

◖ Valley of the Temples

The concept of this universal faith cemetery, Valley of the Temples Memorial Park (47-200 Kahekili Hwy.), is as beautiful as the sculpted *pali* that serves as its backdrop. A rainy day makes it better. The *pali* explodes with rainbowed waterfalls, and the greens turn a richer emerald, sparkling with dewdrops. High on a hill sits a Christian chapel, an A-frame topped by a cross. The views can be lovely from up there, but unfortunately the large windows of the chapel perfectly frame some nondescript tract housing and a shopping center below. Great planning! Different areas are set aside for Catholics, Chinese, and other groups.

The crown jewel of the valley is **Byodo-In Temple** (Temple of Equality), a superbly appointed replica of the 900-year-old Byodo-In of Uji, Japan (depicted on the 10-yen coin). This temple dates from June 7, 1968, 100 years to the day after Japanese immigrants first arrived in Hawaii. It was erected through the combined efforts of an American engineering firm headed by Ronald Kawahara and a plan designed by Kiichi Sano, a famed Kyoto landscape artist. Byodo-In Temple is open daily 8 A.M.–4:30 P.M. Admission, for the Byodo Temple only and payable at the cemetery front entrance, is $2 adults, $1 seniors and children 2–12, or *kamaʻaina* rates of $5 per carload, but you have to prove you're from Hawaii.

Across the low arched bridge and to the left as you approach the temple hall is a three-ton brass bell. This bell, which you're invited to strike after making an offering, creates the right vibrations for meditation and symbolically spreads the word of Amida Buddha. Follow the path behind the bell to a small gazebo. Here a rock, perfectly and artistically placed, separates a stream in two, sending the water to the left and right. The pagoda at the top of the path is called the Meditation House. Go to this superbly manicured area to get a sweeping view of the grounds. In front of the Meditation House is a curious tree; pick up one of the

Byodo-In Temple

fallen leaves and feel the natural velvet on the back. Once down below again, remove your shoes before entering the temple hall proper. The walls hold distinctive emblems of different Buddhist sects. The 18-foot-tall Buddha figure was hand-carved, finished in lacquer, and then covered in gold leaf. Upstairs wings are roped off, with no entry permitted. Stand on the gravel path opposite the main temple. You'll see a grating with a circle cut in the middle. Stick your face in to see the perfectly framed contemplative visage of Amida Buddha. A small gift shop selling souvenirs, cards, film, and some refreshments is to the right of the temple. If you wish to photograph the complex, it's best to come before noon, when the sun is at your back as you frame the red and white temple against the deep green of the *pali*.

Senator Fong's Plantation and Gardens

Just north of Kahalu'u is Senator Fong's Plantation and Gardens (47-285 Pulama Rd., 808/239-6775, www.fonggarden.com, open daily 10 A.M.–4 P.M. except Christmas and New Year's Day, $14.50 adults and $9 children). Follow Pulama Road inland about .5 mile to the garden entrance. Guided and narrated walking tours occur at 10:30 A.M. and 1 P.M., taking visitors through about 200 acres of the garden. The plantation is a labor of love created by Hiram Fong, who served as state senator 1959–1977. Upon retirement he returned to his home and beautified the gardens he started in the 1950s. The result is 725 acres of natural beauty that rise to 2,600 feet at the ridge of the Ko'olau Range above. The five major valleys and ridges of this garden—each named for a president Senator Fong served under—preserve the native flora and fauna of the land, along with planted flower and fruit gardens and groves of trees, palms, bushes, and ferns. Senator Fong died in 2004 at the age of 97, but his work and the gardens are being carried on by his family members. The large open-air entrance pavilion houses a snack window and a small but well-appointed souvenir shop, where you can get everything from aloha shirts to postcards. Tables are set with baskets of flowers inside the pavilion, where you can make your own keepsake lei for $6.50.

Along the Shore

The shoreline from Mokapu Peninsula past the downtown area is chockablock with homes and condos and a handful of private yacht clubs and marinas. Beyond, it's much more open and rural, more like it was in decades past. The shoreline drive out of Kane'ohe offers some of the most spectacular views of a decidedly spectacular coast, with few tourists venturing along this side road.

The tiny **Kane'ohe Beach Park** is accessible off Route 830 as it heads northward through town; turn onto Waikalua Road at the corner that has both the police and fire stations. This park is better for the views of Kane'ohe Bay than for any beach activities, although there are restrooms and a few picnic tables. The water is safe year-round, but it's murky and lined with mudflats and coral heads.

He'eia State Park is designated as an interpretive park. It sits low on Kealohi Point overlooking He'eia Fishpond and Kane'ohe Bay below. Kealohi translates as The Brightness, because it was a visible landmark to passing voyagers, but there is a much deeper interpretation. To the Hawaiians this area was a jumping-off point into the spirit world. It was believed that the souls of the recently departed came to this point and leapt into eternity. The right side, He'eia-kei, was the side of light, while the left side, He'eia-uli, was the domain of darkness. The wise *kahuna* taught that you could actually see the face of God in the brilliant sun as it rises over the point. This point is also the site of an ancient *heiau* called Kalae'ulu'ula, but it was removed when sugar was planted in the 19th century. On the grounds are a pavilion and restrooms. The park contains some indigenous plants and mature trees. Because it's an interpretive park, periodic programs are offered for the community and visitors alike by the Friends of He'eia State Park.

Below is **He'eia Fishpond,** the finest remaining example of the many fishponds that once lined this bay. Now privately owned, it is still used to raise mullet *('ama),* the traditional fish raised by the ancient Hawaiians and *kapu* to all except the *ali'i.*

Just north of this park is the state-operated **He'eia Kea Harbor.** Generally, small fishing boats and pleasure craft use the boat launch and other facilities, and several water activity companies start their tours here. The Deli gift shop/snack bar at the end of the pier is a good place to pick up last-minute supplies, get a bite to eat, and ask about what's operating from the harbor.

The Waihe'e Stream, meandering from the *pali,* empties into the bay and deposits freshwater near the ancient **Kahalu'u Fishpond,** a picture-perfect tropical setting; it is private property—no admittance. So picture-perfect is the place that it has provided the background scenery to TV and Hollywood productions such as an episode of *Jake and the Fat Man,* a setting for *Parent Trap II,* and the famous village scene from *The Karate Kid II.* On the west side of the fishpond, a spit of land holds a wedding chapel, regularly used by Japanese visitors for a memorable wedding spot.

At the mouth of Waihe'e Stream is **Kahalu'u Park,** little more than a dirt parking lot. A public boat launch well used by fishermen and a canoe club, this undeveloped land has recently been cleared of its brush and invasive trees so you can once again see the water.

SHOPPING

With a series of shopping malls, independent stores, restaurants, banks, government offices, the police and fire stations, a post office, and library, the major business route through town is Kamehameha Highway (Rte. 830). Toward the north end of this strip is the **Windward Mall** (46-056 Kamehameha Hwy., open Mon.–Sat. 10 A.M.–9 P.M., Sun. 10 A.M.–5 P.M.), the premier full-service mall on the Windward Coast. Besides department stores like Macy's and Sears, typical mall shops sell everything from shoes to jewelry. There is Borders Express bookshop, small and unique shops like Seeds and Things, which sells crackseed and other snacks, the requisite food court, a multiplex movie theater, and a satellite city hall office.

The **Kane'ohe Bay Shopping Center** across from the Windward Mall is a little more down-home, featuring a Longs Drugs, Blockbuster Video, FedEx Kinko's copy center, and several restaurants.

At the corner of Kamehameha Highway and Kane'ohe Bay Drive is the smaller **Windward City Shopping Center.** Here you'll find a few clothing stores, Longs Drugs, two banks, and plenty of ethnic eateries.

Across from the Valley of the Temples Memorial Park is the **Ko'olau Center,** which provides a gas station, several local eateries, and the Koolau 10 Cinema.

The community of Kahalu'u is near the convergence of Kahekili Highway, Route 83, and Route 830, an extension of the Kamehameha Highway that cuts through Kane'ohe and hugs the coastline heading north from town. This wide spot in the road is not much more than a gas station and the **Hygienic Store** (808/239-8381), which sells liquor, groceries, soda, ice, and all you'll need for an afternoon lunch.

A short way beyond is **Sunshine Arts Hawaii** (47-653 Kamehameha Hwy., 808/239-2992, open Mon.–Sat. 9 A.M.–5:30 P.M., Sun. 10 A.M.–5 P.M.). This art gallery (look for the big yellow building with a beach scene painted on its side) has a better than average collection of paintings and prints, photographs, and turned wooden bowls. Well-known island artists featured include Kathy Long, Avi Kiriaty, and Harry Wishard, plus many others who are not as well known. This shop also frames artwork and can ship purchased pieces.

RECREATION

Most organized water activities in Kane'ohe use the He'eia Kea Harbor as their home base.

Generally catering to Western tourists, **Captain Bob's** (808/942-5077) tours Kane'ohe Bay aboard the *Barefoot I* catamaran daily except Sunday and features a picnic lunch and all the water activities you can handle on its four-hour sail 10:30 A.M.–2:30 P.M. Prices run $72 adults, $61 ages 13–17, and $51 ages 4–12.

You can work off lunch snorkeling or playing volleyball on the sandbar. The food is passable, but the setting offshore with the *pali* in the background is world-class. Transportation from Waikiki is included.

For a fun-filled day on the water, far from the crowds of Waikiki, try **Schrader's Windward Country Inn** (47-039 Lihikai Dr., 808/239-5711). Its two-hour pontoon boat cruise runs from the resort property to the sandbar on Wednesday and Saturday (weather permitting), where you can swim, snorkel, or kayak to your heart's content. Departure time is usually around 10 A.M. but may depend on the tides, so call a day in advance. The trip is complimentary for those staying at the resort and only $20 for others.

ACCOMMODATIONS

Kane'ohe has far fewer places to stay than Kailua just over the hill to the south, but a few accommodations are hidden here and there around town.

Hotels $100-150

(Schrader's Windward Country Inn (47-039 Lihikai Dr., 808/239-5711 or 800/735-5711, fax 808/239-6658, info@schradersinn.com, www.schradersinn.com) has been accommodating guests for over three decades at its lovely spot overlooking Kahalu'u Fishpond at the end of Wailau Peninsula. At first it may look like a hodgepodge of a place, but it's really a nice little community of about two dozen units in several separate buildings. Some of these units sit along the water, while others step up the steep embankment. Studios and one- to five-bedroom units are available, some fully furnished and others with kitchenettes. Surprisingly large, all are neat and clean, with a/c, telephone, television, and daily maid service. A complimentary breakfast is available each morning (7–10 A.M.) on the lanai outside the office on the top level of the main building, and a local-style dinner is served free to all guests on Wednesday evening (7–9 P.M.), accompanied by a local musician. Also complimentary is the twice-weekly pontoon boat trip to snorkel sites and the sandbar in the bay. On property are a swimming pool, laundry, and barbecue pit. Room rates run $98–165 for studios and one-bedroom rooms, $220–265 for two-bedroom units, $275 for a three-bedroom suite, and $385–535 for the four- and five-bedroom deluxe suites. Ask about off-season rates, weekly and monthly discounts, and the room and car package. This rural motel on the water is a fine alternative for those looking for peace and quiet.

Bed-and-Breakfast

Right over the water opposite the private Makani Kai Marina is **Kane'ohe Bay B&B** (45-302 Pu'uloko Pl., 808/235-4214, kaneohebaybnb@aol.com). The downstairs rental room in this contemporary-style house not only faces east toward the bay and morning sun but is also set next to the courtyard saltwater swimming pool and hot tub. The tile floor and tradewind breezes help keep the room cool during the day, and while not overly large, this room has an attached full kitchen. A somewhat larger upstairs room with its own lanai is also rented, and like the one downstairs is only appropriate for one or two people. A fully prepared breakfast is served each morning at the poolside lounge or on the back patio. The rooms runs $150 per night ($175 over the Christmas season) with a three-night minimum. Located in a quiet residential neighborhood, Kane'ohe Bay B&B is a convenient home-away-from-home, and the gracious hosts will welcome you like old friends, offer advice for sightseeing and meals, but give you space if you desire.

Camping

Camping, allowed Friday 9 A.M.–Monday 4 P.M. only, at the designated spots in **Ho'omaluhia Botanical Garden** is allowed with a permit from the garden office. Make your application Mon.–Sat. 9 A.M.–4 P.M. Be aware that the gates to the garden are locked throughout the night, except for entrance 5:30–6:30 P.M. and exit only 9–9:15 P.M.

Camp Kokokahi (45-035 Kane'ohe Bay Dr., 808/247-2124, fax 808/247-6124) has semiprivate cabins that are open to visitors on weekends. Cabins are for sleeping only; restrooms, a kitchen, and a laundry facility are separate. Rates in a shared cabin are $19 per person, and you must bring your own bedding or sleeping bag. Tent camping is also an option for $10 per night per person, also only available on weekends. Located at the water's edge under tall monkeypod trees, Camp Kokokahi is a restful and attractive place. Call for information and reservations at least one week in advance.

FOOD

Kane'ohe is a bit of a wasteland as far as tourist services, nightlife, and eating out are concerned. Most people who live here head for the action in Honolulu. Kane'ohe has mostly ordinary midrange restaurants, many located in the shopping malls, and all with respectable menus, while more upscale eateries are located in Kailua.

Bakery

The **Kaneohe Bakery** (45-1026 Kamehameha Hwy., 808/247-0474, open 4 A.M.–midnight) will tempt you with all sorts of fresh delights to satisfy your sweet tooth.

Korean

One of the best cheap deals in town is at **Kim Chee One** (46-010 Kamehameha Hwy., 808/235-5560, open weekdays 9 A.M.–9 P.M., weekends 7 A.M.–9 P.M.), which has a few sister restaurants scattered around O'ahu. The setting is plain, but you'll have no trouble finding an excellent Korean mixed barbecue plate for $7.25 or a selection of other Korean and Americanized Korean dishes.

Chinese

Highly recommended is **Kin Wah Chop Suey** (808/247-4812, open Sat.–Sun. 10 A.M.–2 P.M., daily 5–9 P.M.), for the best Chinese food in the area. Find Kin Wah Chop Suey in a small strip mall at the corner of Luluku Place across from the Windward City Shopping Center. The menu contains the full litany of meat and vegetarian dishes, plus rice, noodles, and daily specials. Most items are under $10, except for the multiple-person meals.

Contemporary Hawaiian

True to its name, **Haleiwa Joe's Seafood Grill at Ha'iku Gardens** (46-336 Ha'iku Rd., 808/247-6671, open daily 4:30–9:30 P.M., Sat. until 10 P.M., Sun 10 A.M.–2 P.M.) is an open-air restaurant that sits surrounded by a fragrant garden in the lovely and secluded Ha'iku Valley. This valley is considered one of the most beautiful places on O'ahu, and people have long come here to be married. Haleiwa Joe's specializes in fresh fish, steak, and prime rib, although the menu is much longer than that, and food is prepared with the flavors and spices of the Pacific and Asia. Appetizers can be Thai fried calamari or crunchy coconut shrimp, and entrées include half a dozen kinds of fish in various preparations, chicken satay, sticky ribs, and prime rib, mostly in the $15–27 range. The bar opens at 4:30 P.M. and there are bar specials and *pu pu* until 6:30 P.M. This restaurant is first-come, first-served; no reservations are accepted.

Italian

Cafe Satino (46-138 Kahuhipa St., 808/236-0062, open daily from 5 P.M.) creates Italian food that's like homemade. In a no-nonsense, no-atmosphere, cinderblock building, set between an upholstery shop and an auto parts store, Satino creates wonderfully tasty food.

Ordinary lasagna and ravioli are on the menu, but other selections of greater interest are chicken Sorrentino, veal Venezia, and calamari Capri, most at a reasonable $12–15.

Zia's Caffé Kane'ohe (45-620 Kamehameha Hwy., 808/235-9427, open Mon.–Fri. 10 A.M.–9:30 P.M., Sat.–Sun. 11 A.M.–10 P.M.) is a sister restaurant to Zia's in Kailua. This is a place of European ambience, soft lighting, sweet music, attentive waitstaff, and good wine. While the lunch menu is simpler, dinner might be Tuscan-style rib eye steak, fresh fish picatta, seafood florentine, saltimbocca, or eggplant parmesan, with most dinner entrées in the $13–22 range. Zia's is a friendly, family place that also makes the romantic couple feel at home. This is a good choice for a fine meal.

Farmers Market

The parking lot of He'eia State Park turns into a farmers market on Sunday 9 A.M.–2 P.M., with plenty of produce from nearby towns.

Supermarkets

For those staying in the area, there are a number of easy-access grocery stores in Kane'ohe, including a **Safeway** at the Kaneohe Bay Shopping Center, **Foodland Supermarket** at the Windward City Shopping Center, and a **Times Supermarket** at the Koolau Center. All are open from early morning until late in the evening.

WINDWARD O'AHU

North Windward Towns

WAIAHOLE AND WAIKANE

If you want to fall in love with rural, old-time O'ahu, go to the northern reaches of Kane'ohe Bay around Waiahole and Waikane, a Hawaiian grassroots area that has so far eluded development. Alongside the road sit some of the best fruit stands on O'ahu, plus several flower stands and nurseries. Do yourself a favor and have one of the cold coconuts. Sip the juice, and when it's gone, eat the custardlike contents. This is a real island treat, nutritious and delicious. For a glimpse of what's happening, turn inland and drive up Waiahole Valley Road. The road twists its way into the valley, becoming narrower. Left and right in homey, ramshackle houses lives down-home Hawaii, complete with taro patches in the backyards and fruit and nut trees to the sides. Waikane Valley Road, another road of the same type about a half mile up Route 83, lays out a simi-

lar rural scene. If you're staying in Waikiki, compare this area with Kuhio Avenue only 45 minutes away!

At the Waiahole Valley Road turn, stop for a bite to eat at the **Ono Loa Hawaiian Foods** restaurant (808/239-2863, usually open Mon.–Wed. and Sat. 10 A.M.–2 P.M., Sun. noon–3 P.M.), a local place at the Waiahole Poi Factory building. This is the real thing, with real Hawaiian food like poi, haupia, and taro pudding, along with other local favorites like *kalua* pig and chicken long rice. Plate lunches go for about $7 (cash only), or just sample one of the traditional treats. Sit outside on a picnic table or take your food to one of the nearby beach parks.

Up the highway is the old-style **Waikane Store** (808/239-8522), a short distance before the much newer **Coral Kingdom** gift shop (808/239-4899). The Coral Kingdom is a large

Mokoli'i Island, also known as Chinaman's Hat, lies off Kualoa Regional Park and is only a short kayak ride across the water.

© ROBERT NILSEN

commercial establishment set up to cater to busloads of Japanese tourists. It's fun to have a look inside at the cases of coral and diamond jewelry, other gifts, trinkets, clothing, crafts, and island memorabilia.

KUALOA

Continuing on, the road passes through what was once sugarcane country. Most of the businesses failed in the 1800s, but you will see the ruins of the Kualoa Sugar Mill along the road. Although it closed well over a century ago, the dilapidated mill still stands, its stone chimney the most obvious remnant. Kualoa is one of the most sacred areas on Oʻahu, and the *aliʻi* brought their children here to be reared and educated. Indeed, it was once owned by high Oʻahu chiefs and then taken by the Kamehameha family when they conquered the island. In 1850, following the Great Mahele, Kualoa was sold to Dr. Jerritt Judd, an early missionary and later advisory to King Kamehameha III, who turned it into a ranch, which has remained in the family ever since. While sugarcane is gone, the working ranch still has about 500 head of cattle and has diversified into flowers, aquaculture, and ecotourism.

Offshore stands a recognizable island. Mokoliʻi (Small Lizard) Island is commonly called **Chinaman's Hat** for its obvious resemblance to an Asian chapeau. Legend says that Mokoliʻi Island is the tail of a lizard that was killed by the goddess Hiʻiaka. Where's the body? The flat land near the old overgrown mill ruins.

Along the highway before the open ranchland is **Tropical Farm at Kualoa Nursery and Garden** (open daily 9:30 A.M.–5 P.M.), a macadamia nut outlet that also sells local coffee and plenty of other goodies. This farm has about 1,700 macadamia nut trees that produce all the nuts sold in the shop, both plain and flavored varieties. Like the Coral Kingdom, this shop receives plenty of tour buses, so stop when the parking lot is not so full.

Kualoa Regional Park

With the *pali* in the background, Chinaman's Hat offshore, and a glistening white strand shaded by swaying palms, Kualoa is one of the finest beach parks on Windward Oʻahu, with one of its longest, if very narrow, beaches. It has full facilities and services, including lifeguards on weekends and summers, restrooms, picnic tables, and an expansive parking area. Because of its exposure to winds, Kualoa is sometimes chilly. The park is popular and often used by athletic groups for games and competitions. The park is open daily 7 A.M.–7 P.M., and overnight camping is allowed with a county permit. The swimming is safe year-round along a shoreline dotted with pockets of sand and coral, but you still have to be careful of the sometimes-strong currents. The snorkeling and fishing are good, but the real treat is walking the 500 yards to Chinaman's Hat at low tide. You need appropriate footgear (old sneakers are fine) because of the sharp coral heads. The island is one of the few around offshore Oʻahu that are not official bird sanctuaries, although many shorebirds do use the island and should not be disturbed. At the end of the park road is the small, inland Apua Fishpond and bordering its side is the Moliʻi Fishpond, one of the largest on the coast.

Kualoa Ranch

The 4,000-acre Kualoa Ranch (49-560 Kamehameha Hwy., 808/237-8515 or 800/231-7321, www.kualoa.com, open daily 9 A.M.–3 P.M., except Christmas and Thanksgiving), just past Kualoa Regional Park, offers organized, prepackaged outdoor activity tours on its working cattle ranch. Your choice of activities includes horseback riding, all-terrain vehicle (ATV) and 6WD rides into the valley, gun range firing, kayaking, a movie set ride, and more. Numerous Hollywood movies and television shows have filmed parts of their action on the ranch. A Hawaiian exhibit is available free, and there is a restaurant for lunch. The Half-day Package Tour runs $94 adults, $59 children 3–11 and includes three activities or tours, transportation to and from Waikiki, as well as a barbecue lunch. The Full-Day Package Tour at $139 and $79, respectively, is much the same with four activity choices. Individual activities are one- and two-hour horseback rides that run $69 and $99; you must be at least age 10 and not weigh more than 230 pounds. For the same price guests 16 and older can take a guided one- or two-hour ATV ride into one of the valleys. Both the 6WD Pinzgauer truck trip and the movie set tour run $20 per adult. For some activities, there are stipulations for the age of participant and adult accompaniment. The Kualoa Ranch is not a cultural experience. It's an outing for activities, adventure, and fun. Periodically the list of activities and tours changes, so call for current information. It's best to reserve a few days in advance, as these activities are popular.

KA'A'AWA

When you first zip along the highway through town you get the impression that there isn't much here, but there's more than you think. The town stretches back toward the *pali* for a couple of streets. On the ocean side is Swanzy Beach Park, primarily a local hangout. Across the road is the tiny post office and a plate lunch place. Behind the post office is **Pyramid Rock,** obviously named because of its shape.

O'ahu's Windward *pali* are unsurpassed anywhere in the islands, and they're particularly beautiful here. Take a walk around. Stroll the dirt roads through the residential areas and keep your eyes peeled for a small white cross on the *pali* just near Pyramid Rock. It marks the spot where a serviceman was killed during the Pearl Harbor invasion. His spirit is still honored by the perpetually maintained bright white cross. While walking you'll be treated to Ka'a'awa's natural choir—wild roosters crowing any time they feel like it and the din of cheeky parrots high in the trees. A pair of parrots escaped from a nearby home years ago, and their progeny continue to relish life in the balmy tropics.

As you approach the bend of Mahie Point, staring down at you is a popular stone formation, the **Crouching Lion.** Undoubtedly a tour bus or two will be sitting in the lot of the Crouching Lion Inn. As with all anthro-pomorphic rock formations, it helps to have an imagination. Anyway, the inn is much more interesting than the lion. George Larsen built the inn in 1928 from rough-hewn lumber from the Pacific Northwest; the huge stones were excavated from the site. The inn went public as a restaurant in 1957 and has been serving tourists ever since.

While at the Crouching Lion Inn, stop next door at the **Crouching Lion Art Gallery** (808/237-8545, open daily 11 A.M.–6 P.M.). This gallery displays an excellent representation of original paintings, sculptures, some jewelry and gifts, and edition prints of both internationally acclaimed and local island artists.

Beach Parks

Four beach parks in as many miles lie between Ka'a'awa Point and Kahana Bay. **Kalae'o'io Beach County Park,** the first, is a shaded short strip that has roadside parking only. There are a few picnic tables but no restrooms, and the beach is good but the bottom is a bit rocky. The second park, a short distance beyond, is **Ka'a'awa Beach County Park,** a popular beach with restrooms, lifeguards, picnic facilities, and limited parking at its northern end. An offshore reef running the entire length of the park makes swimming and snorkeling safe year-round, except during strong storms. Lots of people come to shorefish this coastal strip.

Swanzy Beach County Park, two minutes north, offers a broad, grassy expanse and basketball courts and has camping with a county permit on weekends only. The sand and rubble beach lies below a long retaining wall, often underwater during high tide. The swimming is safe year-round but is not favorable because of the poor quality of the beach. Swanzy is one of the best squidding and snorkeling beaches on the Windward Coast. A break in the offshore reef creates a dangerous rip that should be avoided. Just beyond is the smaller and narrower **Makaua County Beach Park.**

Ahupua'a 'O Kahana State Park

This state park (formerly called Kahana Valley State Park) is a full-service park with picnic facilities, restrooms, camping, a boat launch on the beach, and hiking trails inland. Camping is allowed with state permit at the beach; restrooms and information are on the mountain side of the road. It's perfectly situated for a quiet picnic under the coconut trees. Swimming is good year-round, although the waters can be cloudy at times. A gentle shorebreak makes the area ideal for bodysurfing and beginner board riders. This entire beach area is traditionally excellent for *akule* fishing, with large schools visiting the offshore waters at certain times of year. The bay and valley once supported a large Hawaiian community, and many cultural remains dot the area, including *heiau,* housing sites, terraced fields, and irrigation ditches. Remnants of the seven-acre **Huilua Fishpond** lie just outside the park boundary on the south shore of the bay. Running up the valley, past a small in-park residential neighborhood, is the rest of the park. Few people visit there, as it's overgrown and access is limited to a few hiking trails. This park encompasses the Kahana Valley, historically an *ahupua'a,* and runs from water's edge to over 2,600 feet.

You can follow two trails within the park, one that loops about three miles back into the valley and the other a one-mile round-trip along the bayfront mountainside past a fishing shrine to a lookout once used to watch for fish in the bay. For the **Kapa'ele'ele Ko'a and Keaniani Kilo Trail** to the shrine and lookout, the hike starts to the side of the park information center. This trail begins on what was a train track bed but shortly begins to climb up the hillside to a height of about 150 feet to the lookout, passing the small fishing shrine on the way. Return the same way or head down the hill and follow the roadside trail back. To reach the **Nakoa Trail,** which runs into the valley, head up the road through the residential neighborhood—park your car at the entrance to the village. From the check-in station beyond the far end of the village you can follow the loop trail either right or left. Much of this trail winds around the hillsides through stands of *hala* trees. It's wet back in the val-

ley and often rains, so be prepared to get wet. It's also a great environment for mosquitoes. Once at the back end of the loop and again a couple hundred yards from the trailhead at a swimming hole, this trail crosses the Kahana Stream. Because there are no bridges, you must wade through.

Food

There was a time when *everyone* passing through Ka'a'awa stopped at the **Crouching Lion Inn.** Built in 1928, it was the only place *to* stop for many, many years. The inn (808/237-8511, open daily 11 A.M.–3 P.M., 5–9 P.M.) has seen its ups and downs over the years, and now, fortunately, seems to be in a strong stable pattern. It's beautiful enough to stop at just to have a look, but if you want a reasonably quiet meal, avoid lunchtime and come in the evening when all of the tour buses have long since departed. Sitting high on a verdant green hill, the inn's architectural style is a mixture of English Tudor and country Hawaiian. The view from the veranda is especially grand, but inside it's cozy with a fireplace and open-beamed ceilings—even with the dart machines, pool tables, and sports television. Lunch can be a simple order of Portuguese bean soup, or a heartier seafood plate, mahimahi melt sandwich, *kalua* pork plate, or deep-fried shrimp, all priced $8–11. Dinner entrées, accompanied by fresh-baked rolls, soup or salad, vegetables, and choice of rice or potatoes, include Slavonic steak, sautéed seafood, Hawaiian chopped steak, or shrimp kebabs and run $15–20. The limited-menu early-bird specials are a real bargain at $11. The inn's famous mile-high coconut pie, macadamia nut cream pie, and double-crusted banana cream pie are absolutely delicious. To complement your menu selection, a full bar serves cocktails, beer, wine, and liquors.

PUNALU'U

Punalu'u (Coral Diving) is a long, narrow ribbon of land between the sea and the *pali,* a favorite place to come for a drive in the country. Its built-up area is about a mile or so long but only a hundred yards wide. It has gas, supplies, and camping. In town is **St. Joachim Church.** There's nothing outstanding about it, merely a one-room church sitting meekly on a plot of ground overlooking the sea. But it's real and home-grown, where the people of this district come to worship. Just look and you might understand the simple and basic lifestyle that persists in this area.

In town is **Ching Punalu'u Store** (808/237-7017, open Mon.–Sat. 8 A.M.–7 P.M., Sun. 8 A.M.–6 P.M.), a mini-mart in an old building for basic food supplies. **Kaya's Store** (808/293-9095), across the road from St. Joachim Church, is another mini-mart with similar hours that carries sundries, snacks, liquor, and fishing gear.

On the northern outskirts of town is **Sacred Falls State Park;** it is closed indefinitely because of a landslide that killed eight hikers in 1999. There is a barricade across the entrance. The area's Hawaiian name was Kaliuwa'a (Canoe Leak), and although the original name isn't as romantic as the anglicized version, the entire area was considered sacred. It's a narrow valley where the gods would show disfavor by dropping rocks onto your head. Hawaiians used to wrap stones with *ti* leaves and leave them along the trail as an appeasement to the gods, so they weren't tempted to brain them. The walls of this deep valley are 1,600 feet high, but the falls drop only 90 feet or so. Although you can't hike there now, you can get a glimpse of the falls way back in the valley from over the roof of the Church of Latter-Day Saints along the highway just north of the park or from the end of the road to the side of the church.

Beach

Right along the highway is **Punalu'u Beach County Park,** with restrooms, picnic tables, lots of shade, and decent snorkeling, but no lifeguards. The swimming is safe year-round inside the protected reef. Local fishermen, usually older Filipino men who are surfcasting, use this area frequently. They're friendly and a great source of information for anyone trying to land a fish or two. They know the best baits and spots to dunk a line.

Art Galleries

Three small galleries here make this a mini-center for viewing artwork. The **Lance Fairly Gallery** (53-839 Kamehameha Hwy., 808/293-9009 or 888/293-1188, www.lancefairly.com), displays colorful landscapes and seascapes by fine artist Lance Fairly. Both his plein air and studio paintings seem to have a luminescence or inner light, and there's an enhancement of color for a pleasing yet somewhat magical or mystical tone. Lithographs and giclée (prints created by a computer-based method that reproduces the original almost perfectly) are available for purchase. Fairly also does some unique paintings on metal, and his techniques render a three-dimensional quality to his subjects. The gallery is open pretty much every day, but because this is Fairly's studio, you may have to ring the front bell to have the door opened.

A few steps up on the mountain side of the road is the **Kim Taylor Reece Gallery** (53-866 Kamehameha Hwy., 808/808/293-2000 or 800/657-7966, www.kimtaylorreece.com, open Thurs.–Sat. only noon–5 P.M.). Reece is a fine photographer of renown, and many of his large-size prints are of nudes or hula dancers in traditional Hawaiian dress. The bulk of the work is black and white, but some prints are hand-tinted.

Between these two galleries is the more down-home and local **Kahaunani Woods & Krafts,** displaying wooden bowls, boxes, and other such objects made of native woods by the owner in his shop in the back.

Accommodations

Pat's at Punalu'u is one of the few condos along this coast, and one of the few buildings that approaches the height of coconut trees. Even though it's rather out of place along this coast, the building is painted light green to blend into the background color. Pat's is right on the water, and every unit has a lanai that overlooks the sea. On property are a swimming pool, sauna, patio next to the beach, and parking. Units are fully furnished with kitchens, televisions, and washers and dryers, and run $100 for a studio, $125 for one bedroom, and $235 for a two-bedroom deluxe or three-bedroom penthouse, with the addition of a $75–150 cleaning charge. There is a three-day minimum; weekly and monthly rates can be arranged. A $150–200 damage deposit is required within 10 days of booking, and full payment is to be made one month before arrival. Punalu'u and vicinity is an easygoing area, a throwback to Hawaii as it used to be years ago, yet it's so close to the big city and all it offers. If you're looking for quiet and relaxation at a decent price, this could be the spot. Room arrangements are made through Paul Comeau Condo Rentals (P.O. Box 589, Ka'a'awa, HI 96730, 808/293-2624 or 800/467-6215, fax 808/293-0618, comeaup001@hawaii.rr.com, www.patsinpunaluu.com).

The **Punalu'u Guesthouse** (53-504 Kamehameha Hwy., 808/293-8539) provides simple, basic accommodations. This house in a residential area across the street from the ocean provides three rooms with two single beds each and an ample clean bathroom. It's like a bed-and-breakfast, but no breakfast is provided. However, guests may use the kitchen to do their own cooking. There is also a living room that guests share, small lockers available for use, and a coin laundry. Rates run $25 adults, with a $10 key deposit. Check in is 3–5 P.M. or by arrangement. Reservations are made through the Hostelling International Honolulu hostel (808/946-0591, fax 808/946-5904), located near the University of Hawai'i, Manoa.

Food
Keep a sharp eye out for a truck and a sign featuring shrimp just along the road. Turn in to **Maliko O Punalu'u Bar and Grill** (53-146 Kamehameha Hwy., 808/237-8474, open daily except Tuesday 11 A.M.–9 P.M.). This is the first place of note after passing the Ahupua'a 'O Kahana State Park. The shrimp couldn't be fresher—it comes from local fishermen. In this no-frills, friendly restaurant, you can have a half pound of shrimp cooked to order as scampi, tempura, spicy, or in a cocktail for $14.25! Shrimp is the pièce de résistance, but basic sandwiches and burgers for under $11.50

are also on the menu, as well as other inexpensive entrées like spaghetti, breaded chicken cutlet with gravy, and steak and mahimahi combo. Complete meals come with cooked vegetables, bread, and rice or potatoes. There are plenty of appetizers and side dishes on the menu and a good selection of beer and wine. Screened, yet open to the breezes, the restaurant offers inside and outside seating. Maliko O Punalu'u is the kind of place locals frequent because they know the food is good and the prices fair.

HAU'ULA
This speck of a town is just past Punalu'u between mile markers 21 and 22. The old town center is not much more than two soda machines, the **Hau'ula Gift Shop and Art Gallery** (54-042 Kamehameha Hwy., 808/293-5145) in the pink Ching Tong Leong store, and **Wu's Sundries** (open weekdays 9:30 A.M.–8 P.M., weekends 9:30 A.M.–10 P.M.). A small restaurant and a little church up on the hill with the *pali* as a backdrop add the finishing touches. Up the road in the new section of Hau'ula, look for the **Hau'ula Kai Center,** a small shopping center with a post office, Tamura's Market, and a couple of eateries.

Beaches
At the estuary of a little stream across from the fire station in the middle of town is **'Aukai Beach Park,** a small flat beach. There are better choices nearby.

Hau'ula Beach County Park is an improved beach park with picnic facilities, restrooms, pavilion, volleyball court, and camping. There's safe swimming year-round inside the coral reef, with good snorkeling; surfing is usually best in winter. Rip currents are present at both ends of the beach at reef breaks, and deep holes in the floor of a brackish pond are formed where Ma'akua Stream enters the sea. Across the road are the ruins of the historic **Lanakila Church** (1853), partially dismantled at the turn of the 20th century to build a smaller church near Punalu'u. The newer Hau'ula Congregational Church stands next to it.

Kokololio Beach County Park is next—a fine spot with lots of parking. A little dune protects the beach from road noise. There is good swimming, but many locals come to boogie board, mostly at the northern end where the beach makes a slight curve. With lots of shade trees and picnic tables, it's good for a day trip or to camp with a county permit. This beach is also known as Kekela.

Hiking

Outdoor enthusiasts will love the little-used **Hau'ula Trails.** These ridge and valley trails offer just about everything you can expect from a Hawaiian trail: the mountains, the valleys, and vistas of the sea, but they don't run high in elevation. Built by the Civilian Conservation Corps during the Depression, these manicured trails are wide, and the footing is great most of the way, even in rainy periods. They run up and down several ridges and into interior valleys through the extraordinary jungle canopy. The hard-packed loop trail, covered in a soft carpet of ironwood needles, offers magnificent coastal views once you reach the heights and sights of inland verdant gulches and valleys. The area flora consists of ironwoods, passion fruit, thimbleberries, *'ohi'a,* and wild orchids, among other native and introduced species. The ridge trail has a completely different character as it passes through sections of *hau* trees and some hardwoods. It starts with a steep zigzag up the hillside to a covered picnic table and overlook and from there heads up the ridge only to circle back around. All three trails start beyond the end of Ma'akua Road, which is off Hau'ula Homestead Road, only a minute or so from the highway. Pass a hunters' check-in station and continue on the paved trail. On your right is the start of the **Hau'ula Loop Trail,** otherwise known as the Papali Trail; a short way farther, the **Ma'akua Ridge Trail** heads off to the left. Both are 2.5 miles long. The **Ma'akua Gulch Trail** goes straight ahead up the valley. Each trail round-trip should take less than two hours. The Gulch Trail may be closed periodically because of hazardous conditions.

along the Hau'ula Loop Trail

© ROBERT NILSEN

Food

You'll find the **Hawaiian Seafood Grill and Bar** (open daily 11 A.M.–8 P.M.) near the Hau'ula Kai Center at the north end of Hau'ula. It's a basic eatery that does shrimp in several different ways, fish and chips, clam strips, and chicken, mostly in the $10–14 range, with less-expensive sandwiches.

If you'd rather have a more ethnic meal, try **Korean BBQ** (808/293-8404) across the street.

LA'IE

The "Saints" came marching into La'ie (Leaf of the 'Ie Vine) in 1864 and set about making a perfect Mormon village in paradise. What's more, they succeeded! The town is squeaky clean, with well-kept homes and manicured lawns that hint of suburban Midwest America. Dedicated to education, they founded a branch of **Brigham Young University** (BYU, www.byuh.edu) in 1955, which now attracts students from all over Polynesia, many of whom work in the nearby Polynesian Cultural Center. The students vow to live a clean life, free of drugs and alcohol, and to not grow beards. In the foyer of the main entrance, look for a huge mural depicting Laʻie's flag-raising ceremony in 1921, which symbolically established the colony. To reach the university from the highway, turn onto Hale Laʻa Boulevard and at the traffic circle follow Kulaniu Street directly to the campus. Alternately, take Naniloa Loop off the highway. Free campus tours are offered by appointment (808/293-3660, weekdays 9 A.M.–4 P.M.).

◖ Laʻie Mormon Temple

The first view of the Mormon Temple, built in 1919 as the church's fifth temple, is impressive. Square and somewhat blocky, with simple architectural lines, yet reverential in its aesthetic, this house of worship sits pure white against the *pali* and is further dramatized by a reflecting pool and fountains spewing fine mists. The visitors center of this tranquil, shrine-like church is open daily 9 A.M.–8 P.M. Displays show aspects of the church's mission and a video relates the history of the Laʻie colony. Greeters, while not pushy, definitely want to engage you in a discussion about your religious beliefs. They are missionaries after all, so it's not surprising, but they'll leave you alone if you desire. Smoking is prohibited, and modest shirts (no halter tops) must be worn to enter. It is said that this temple attracts more visitors than any other Mormon site outside of the main temple in Salt Lake City.

◖ Polynesian Cultural Center

The real showcase in Laʻie is the Polynesian Cultural Center (808/293-3333 or 800/367-7060, www.polynesia.com). The PCC, as it's called by islanders, began as an experiment in 1963. Smart businessmen said it would never thrive way out in Laʻie, and tourists didn't come to Hawaii for *culture* anyway. Well, they were wrong, and the PCC now rates as one of Oʻahu's top tourist attractions, luring about one million visitors annually. Miracles do happen! The PCC is a nonprofit organization, with proceeds going to the Laʻie

---

LANILOA LEGEND

Laniloa Peninsula is a spit of land that pushes out to Laʻie Point. It's a residential area that ends in an undeveloped country park, from where you can get scenic views up and down the coast and of the small islands offshore. While the peninsula is a low, rocky promontory, beaches line the coast in both directions. Of the offshore islands, there are several legends. One states that Laniloa was a legendary *moʻo* (lizard) that terrorized the inhabitants of this area and anyone who happened to pass this way. The lizard was finally dispatched by the heroic warrior and demi-god named Kana, who had it out for all lizards after one had terrorized his mother. Kana cut this lizard's head into five pieces and threw them into the ocean, and these pieces are now seen as the five small islands off the end of the Laniloa Peninsula.

BYU students' educational funds and to maintaining the center.

Covering 42 acres, the PCC's primary attractions are eight model villages including examples from Hawaii, Samoa, the Marquesas, Fiji, Aotearoa (New Zealand), Tonga, Tahiti, and Rapa Nui (Easter Island). The villages are primarily staffed with people from the representative island homelands. Remember that most are Mormons, whose dogma colors the attitudes and selected presentations of the staffers. Still, all are genuinely interested in dispensing cultural knowledge about their traditional island ways and beliefs, and almost all are characters who engage in lighthearted bantering with their willing audience. Walk through the villages on your own or take a canoe ride over the artesian-fed waterways. Other attractions include a Migrations Museum, art and handicraft shops, and an IMAX theater that presents a colorful movie about the sea. In addition, a shuttle tram runs outside the center and will take you on a guided tour to the BYU campus, the temple, and the community.

The Pageant of Canoes is one of the highlights for visitors to the Polynesian Cultural Center.

© ROBERT NILSEN

The undeniable family spirit and pride at the PCC makes you feel welcome, while providing a clean and wholesome experience, with plenty of attention to detail. It's this quality approach and good value that has sustained the "miracle."

Throughout the day, there are various cultural presentations at each village. The Pageant of Canoes sails at 2:30 P.M. and is a waterborne show of music and dance. All day, the Keiki Activities program offers children the opportunity to tune into these cultures with kid-oriented experiences. **Horizons,** the center's largest extravaganza, runs 7:30–9 P.M. at the indoor/outdoor amphitheater. This theater hosts a show of music, dance, and historical drama, put on by nearly 100 performers. The costumes and lighting are dramatic and inspired and the performance is spirited and genuine; it's hard to believe that the performers are not professionals.

Food is available from the Banyan Tree snack bar (11 A.M.–7 P.M.), and the Island BBQ (11 A.M.–1:30 P.M.) for an all-you-can-eat spread. For buffet dinners, you can dine at the Gateway restaurant (5–7 P.M.) or at the Ambassador restaurant (5–7 P.M.). Another option is the Hale Aloha Lu'au, which introduces you to the Hawaiian feast, the ceremony of removing the roasted pig from the *imu* pit, and a reenactment of a royal court procession.

The PCC is open daily except Sunday 12:30–9 P.M., general admission and the show costs $39 adults, $24 children, under five free, but dinner is on your own. Packages are also available; they include general admission to the villages, daytime activities, and preferred seating at the evening show, while some add dinner. The Admission/Show Package, $50 adults and $35 children or $45 and $26, respectively, with twilight admission 4–6:30 P.M. The Ali'i Lu'au Package, $80 adults and $56 children, lets you partake in the *lu'au* dinner show; this is $65 and $50 with twilight entry. The Ambassador Package, $110 adults and $76 children, provides a sit-down dinner at the Ambassador restaurant or at the Ali'i Lu'au, a guided tour, and special souvenirs, gifts, and other perks; this package is $95 and $66 with twilight entrance.

TheBus no. 52 ($2) runs to the PCC from Ala Moana Shopping Center but takes about 2.5 hours. The PCC runs its own bus transportation to the center from certain hotels in Waikiki for $16 per person round-trip and offers door-to-door mini-coach transportation for $25 round-trip from any point in Waikiki. A taxi ride one-way might set you back $80 from Waikiki. Most island hotels and tour companies can arrange a package tour to PCC.

Beaches

At the southern end of La'ie is **La'ie Beach County Park,** a mostly unimproved beach park with no facilities. The beach here is called **Pounders Beach,** so named by students of BYU because of the pounding surf. This beach experiences heavy surf and dangerous conditions in the winter, but its excellent shoreline break is perfect for bodysurfing for those with some skill. The remains of an old pier at which interisland steamers once stopped is still in evidence. The shoreline waters farther into town are safe for swimming inside the reef, but winter produces heavy and potentially dangerous surf. Good snorkeling, fishing, and net-throwing are possible here.

At the north end of town, just south of Malaekahana, is the tiny **Hukilau Beach**. This is the site of real neighborhood *hukilau* (pulling into shore a seine fishnet by a group of people) of decades past and the inspiration of the *hapa-haole* song "Hukilau." Penned in 1948 by Jack Owens, it refers to fishing with *hukilau* nets at La'ie Bay and is now part of the repertoire of most Hawaiian entertainers. It's a fine beach in summer, while winter winds bring kiteboarders.

Malaekahana State Recreation Area

This state recreation area is the premier camping beach and park along the north section of the Windward Coast. Separated from the highway by a large stand of ironwood shade trees, this 37-acre park offers showers, restrooms, picnic facilities, local-style beach cabins, and camping.

Malaekahana was Pu'uhonua of La'ie, a place of refuge and, according to legend, the only spot on O'ahu not conquered by King Kamehameha. The recent restructuring of the recreation area and administration by native Hawaiians was intended to bring back its traditional role as a healing and gathering place. An alternative learning center erected here is connected to Kahuku High School, where students come to reconnect culturally and spiritually.

Offshore is Moku'auia, better known as **Goat Island.** The island is only a stone's throw from shore, and you can reach this seabird sanctuary by wading across the reef during low tide from Kalanai Point. Reef walkers or tennis shoes are advised, but go only when the water is calm! You'll find a beautiful crescent white-sand beach and absolute peace and quiet. Relax and look for wedge-tailed shearwaters, a ground-nesting bird that burrows into the sand to nest, or try to spot hawksbill or green sea turtles. The swimming inside the reef is good, and it's amazing how little this area is used for such a beautiful spot. Farther offshore, about 200–300 yards, are two other small islands, to which *you cannot wade.* It's too far, and the currents are strong. Some kiteboarders now come to use this beach. There are two entrances to the park. The south entrance, closest to La'ie, puts you in the day-use area of the park, where there are restrooms and showers. The entrance to the camping section is north a minute or two (around mile marker 17) and is marked by a steel gate and a sign welcoming you to Malaekahana State Recreation Area. Be aware that the gate opens at 7 A.M. and is locked at 6:45 P.M.

Accommodations

The ◖ **Laie Inn** (55-109 Laniloa St., 808/293-9282 or 800/526-4562, fax 808/293-8115, laieinn@hawaii.rr.com, www.laieinn.com) is just outside the PCC on the mountain side of the highway. It's a humble cinderblock motel, and like the rest of town, basic, as neat as a pin, and secure. Although you won't find luxury, you won't go wrong here. Five two-story buildings with four dozen units surround a quiet and relaxing central courtyard and swimming pool. All rooms have a/c, TV, mini-fridges, microwaves, and island-inspired decorations and amenities; bathrooms have been renovated with new fixtures and accessories. Rooms run $99 king, $89 queen, $94 two doubles, a good value. The room fee includes a daily continental breakfast served 6–9:30 A.M. in the lobby, free local telephone calls, and parking. Not only is this inn close to BYU, the PCC, and the Mormon temple, but it's also near Windward and North Shore beaches. Hotel guests have access to a private beach area across the road near a barbecue grill. The Laie Inn is a good choice at reasonable rates.

Pounders Beach Rentals (55-161 Kamehameha Hwy., 808/293-1000, info@poundersbeachrentals.com, www.poundersbeachrentals.com) is between mile markers 19 and 20, ocean side, just south of Pounders Beach. Two upstairs suites are rented. The Plumeria Suite has a full kitchen and two queen-size beds, good for a small family. It runs $110 per night or $125 during the year-end holidays. The Honu Suite has a kitchenette and king-size bed and is best for a couple. It is $125 a night or $150 during the holidays. There is a three-day minimum (five nights during the holidays), a deposit of $100 is required to hold a reservation ($200 during the holidays), a 30-day cancellation period is in effect, and most credit cards are accepted. All guests have use of the washer and dryer, and there is good off-street parking. From the house, there's a short path to Pounders Beach, and an outdoor shower can be used to wash off beach sand when returning. This is good value in a quiet, if not spectacular, setting.

A stone's throw from the Polynesian Cultural Center is the one-unit vacation rental **Ala Mahina Beach Cottage** (55-455 Kamehameha Hwy., 808/293-2275). A tropical hideaway set among thick vegetation and right on the narrow but sandy beach, it has a good-size sitting room, small but fully furnished kitchen, and one bedroom with a queen-size bed and air-conditioning. It's just right for two guests, but the queen sleeper in the sitting room would make it comfortable for four.

All of the art hanging on the walls is by Michael, the owner. The rate is $150 per night plus a $75 cleaning fee, and weekly rates can be negotiated.

Camping at **Malaekahana State Recreation Area** is handled by the Friends of Malaekahana (P.O. Box 305, La'ie, HI 96762, 808/293-1736, fax 808/293-2066, malaekahana@hawaii.rr.com, www.alternative-hawaii.com/fom). Reservations are taken up to 12 months in advance and at least 14 days before planned arrival, although walk-in camping reservations are accepted if space is available. Check-in is handled 3–5 P.M.; checkout time is noon. The office is open Mon.–Fri. 10 A.M.–4 P.M. Write or call for information and reservation applications. Firearms, fireworks, pets, and drinking of alcoholic beverages are prohibited in the park, and a quiet time is enforced 10 P.M.–8 A.M. Tent campers pay $5 per person per night, and five camping yurts run $40–60. Outside hot showers and bathroom facilities are shared. Bring mosquito repellent. Parking is limited. Make sure to call and make arrangements with the staff if you will be arriving later than office hours. The park gate is locked—for your security—7 P.M.–7 A.M.

Food and Shopping

When you enter La'ie you will be greeted by the Stars and Stripes flying over the entrance of the PCC. Next door is a whopper of a McDonald's; in keeping with the spirit of Polynesian culture, it looks like a Polynesian longhouse. Just up the road at the **La'ie Village Shopping Center** you'll find a large and modern Foodland grocery store, along with a Bank of Hawaii, a post office, La'ie Cinemas, and a handful of restaurants—all that you'll need for a successful vacation.

Along a side street in La'ie is the **Hukilau Cafe** (55-662 Wahinepe'e, 808/293-8616, open Tues.–Fri. 7 A.M.–2 P.M., Sat. 7–11:30 A.M.), an inexpensive, no-nonsense, Hawaiian-style eatery that does eggs and griddle items for breakfast and plate lunches for lunch. This is as down-home local as you can get.

KAHUKU

This village—and it is a village—is where the workers of the North Shore live. Kahuku is "fo' real," and a lingering slice of what *was* not so long ago. Do yourself a favor, and turn off the highway for a two-minute tour of the dirt roads lined by proudly maintained homes that somehow exude the feeling of Asia. The older part of town is to the sea side of the mill; newer homes line well-paved streets up by the school, library, and hospital. When the sugar mill closed, this community, like many throughout the state, took a nosedive and lost its economic balance. Still looking for equilibrium, some locals have turned to raising freshwater shrimp in several shrimp farms just north of town, and others grow sweet corn. Along the beach is the local, nine-hole Kahuku Golf Course. It was built for plantation workers early in the 1900s, an unusual move by owners for their workers. It is now a municipal course.

Sights

On the north end of town is the Mill Shopping Center, which is part of the town's old sugar mill—recycled. The mill operated 1893–1971 and its large central building, with its huge gears and machinery, is gone. A couple small buildings have been turned into a little bazaar of shops and a restaurant, but it seems be difficult to keep the shops filled. Here as well are two condo offices for Turtle Bay Resort condos up the road, a post office, and a gas station out front.

On the northern outskirts of town are the two sections of the 164-acre **James Campbell National Wildlife Refuge.** Established in 1976, this refuge consists of marshland and man-made ponds harboring many varieties of waterfowl and shorebirds, including the endemic and endangered Hawaiian stilt, coot, duck, and moorhen. The refuge is open to the public from the third Saturday in October through the third Saturday in February. Free and educational guided tours are offered during these months on Saturday at 9–10:30 A.M. or 3:30–5 P.M. and Thursday 4–5:30 P.M. for up to 25 people. Call the refuge management office (808/637-6330) to make arrangements.

Shopping

Just a mile past Kahuku, beyond the shrimp farms, is the old Tanaka Plantation Store, a refurbished early-1900s company store that now houses the antique shop **The Only Show In Town** (56-901 Kamehameha Hwy., 808/293-1295, open daily 10:30 A.M.–5:30 P.M.). Blown to O'ahu's North Shore from Kaua'i by Hurricane 'Iniki, Paul Wroblewski reopened his antiques and collectibles shop, jamming it with Hawaiian artifacts, old bottles, costume jewelry, license plates, Japanese glass fishing floats, netsuke, scrimshaw, a collection of Marilyn Monroe memorabilia, and a full line of antique jewelry. Paul's an amiable fellow and is open to any reasonable offer. Remember, he may price according to your attitude. Also, if you have a collectible that you want to sell or get an estimate on, ask Paul to take a look.

Food

You can pick up supplies at the **Kahuku Superette** (808/293-9878), open from early morning until late evening and clearly marked along Route 83 across from the school.

For short-order food, stop across the road at **Amy's by the Green** (808/293-8896), a small plate lunch place that also serves grilled items and breakfast generally for under $7. Her hamburger steak and deep-fried teriyaki chicken are perhaps best known.

For another uniquely local experience, try **❰ Giovanni's** white *kaukau* wagon (808/293-1839, open 10:30 A.M.–6:30 P.M.), which sits across the roadway from the school. Giovanni's sells shrimp scampi, a demonically spicy shrimp, and shrimp in lemon juice that run $12 for a dozen in-the-shell pieces. Rice comes with all plates. Picnic tables sit under an awning attached to the wagon, and to the side is another *kaukau* wagon selling smoothies. You're guaranteed to get messy eating this meal, and you'll use a pile of napkins, but your sticky fingers and sated stomach are your reward.

Because of the popularity of these farm-raised

shrimp, Giovanni's has fielded stiff competition. Similar *kaukau* trucks selling shrimp can also be seen along the highway in the vicinity. One of these is **Romy's Kahuku Shrimp** (808/232-2202), a wayside restaurant with outdoor covered seating. Here, half a dozen pieces in four seasonings, plus two scoop rice, runs $11. This is also a tour bus favorite.

The **Kahuku Grill** (808/293-2110, open daily 8 A.M.–5 P.M.), an indoor-outdoor restaurant with a walk-up window, serves mostly Korean and American plate lunches; because of the area, it has several shrimp dishes as well. Most meal choices are under $9, with shrimp at $11.

On the second and fourth Saturdays of the month 8 A.M.–noon, the Kahuku Community Hospital sponsors a **farmers market** for produce, flowers, fish, and crafts, as well as a health screening.

THE NORTH SHORE

This shallow bowl of coastline stretches from Ka'ena Point in the west to Turtle Bay in the east. Mount Ka'ala, the verdant backdrop to the area, rises 4,020 feet from the Wai'anae Range, making it the highest peak on O'ahu. The entire stretch is a day-tripper's paradise, with plenty of sights to keep you entertained. But the North Shore is synonymous with one word: surfing.

Thunderous winter waves, often measuring 25 feet but sometimes up to 40 feet (from the rear!), rumble along the North Shore's world-famous surfing beaches lined up one after the other—Waimea Bay, Pipeline, 'Ehukai, Sunset. They attract highly accomplished athletes who come to compete in prestigious international surfing competitions. Other beaches, often less well known, like Mokule'ia Beach, also provide excellent waves without the crowds. Be aware that *all* North Shore beaches experience heavy surf conditions with dangerous currents throughout the winter months. The waters, at this time of year, are not for the average swimmer. Please heed all warnings. In summer *moana* loses her ferocity and lies down, becoming gentle and safe for nearly anyone—leap in!

The main attractions of the North Shore are its beaches, but interspersed among them are a few sights definitely worth your time and effort. The listings below run from east to west, as approached from Windward O'ahu. However, the most-traveled route to the North Shore is from Honolulu along the H-2 freeway to Wahiawa, and then directly to the coast from there along Route 99 or Route 803. At

THE NORTH SHORE

HIGHLIGHTS

◖ **The Great Surfing Beaches:** The North Shore of O'ahu is synonymous with surfing, and Sunset Beach,'Ehukai, Pipeline, and Waimea are the best of the best (page 231).

◖ **Waimea Valley Audubon Center:** This is a pearl of a botanical garden, with a diversity of tropical plants, Hawaiian cultural sites, and a very lovely waterfall (page 233).

◖ **Pu'u O Mahuka Heiau:** The largest of O'ahu's *heiau*, this was a place of human sacrifice, but now only its ruins testify to its significance (page 234).

◖ **Ka'ena Point State Park:** A lonely windswept spit of land that's great for a day hike, Ka'ena Point is a nature preserve for shorebirds, waterbirds, beach plants, and the occasional monk seal (page 247).

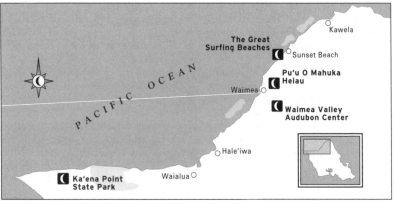

LOOK FOR ◖ TO FIND RECOMMENDED SIGHTS, ACTIVITIES, DINING, AND LODGING.

Weed Circle or Thompson Corner, where these routes reach the coastal highway, turn right along the Kamehameha Highway (Route 83), which heads around the coast all the way to Kane'ohe, or turn left along the Farrington Highway (Route 930), following it to road's end just before Ka'ena Point.

Hale'iwa has become the central town along the North Shore. Its main street is lined with restaurants, boutiques, art galleries, small shopping malls, and sports equipment stores. Waialua, just west, is a former sugar town with an old mill and farther west is Dillingham Airfield, where you can arrange to fly above it all in a small biplane, soar si-

lently in a glider, or give your heart a real jolt by jumping out of a plane for a free-fall parachute ride. The road ends for vehicles not far from there, and then your feet have to take you to Ka'ena Point, where large waves pound the coast and coastal sand dunes have been set aside as a nature reserve for native plants and birds. Heading east, you'll pass famous Pu'u O Mahuka Heiau, where human flesh once mollified the gods, and Waimea Valley Audubon Center, the premier botanical and cultural attraction of the North Shore. Then come the great surfing beaches and their incredible waves, followed by the wonderfully secluded Turtle Bay Resort.

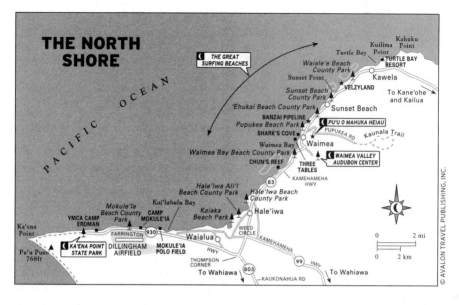

THE NORTH SHORE

THE GREAT SURFING BEACHES

PACIFIC OCEAN

Kahuku Point
Kuilima Point
Turtle Bay Point
TURTLE BAY RESORT
Waiale'e Beach County Park
Kawela
Sunset Point
VELZYLAND
Sunset Beach County Park
To Kane'ohe and Kailua
'Ehukai Beach County Park
Sunset Beach
BANZAI PIPELINE
Pupukea Beach Park
PU'U O MAHUKA HEIAU
SHARK'S COVE
PUPUKEA RD
Kaunala Trail
Waimea Bay
Waimea
Waimea Bay Beach County Park
CHUN'S REEF
WAIMEA VALLEY AUDUBON CENTER
THREE TABLES
KAMEHAMEHA HWY
83
Hale'iwa Ali'I Beach County Park
Hale'iwa Beach County Park
Kai'lahulu Bay
Mokule'ia Beach County Park
CAMP MOKULE'IA
Kaiaka Beach Park
Hale'iwa
YMCA CAMP ERDMAN
WEED CIRCLE
KAMEHAMEHA
Ka'ena Point
FARRINGTON 930
Waialua
KA'ENA POINT STATE PARK
DILLINGHAM AIRFIELD
MOKULE'IA POLO FIELD
Pu'u Pueo 768ft
THOMPSON CORNER
To Wahiawa
803
99 HWY
To Wahiawa
KAUKONAHUA RD

0   2 mi
0   2 km

© AVALON TRAVEL PUBLISHING, INC.

PLANNING YOUR TIME

If possible, come to the North Shore of O'ahu during the winter, for it's at that time of year that the great surfing beaches put on their best show. The winds are up, the surfers are showing their stuff, and the excitement of catching big waves is palpable. However, everyone else also wants to be there when the waves are thundering, so be sure to plan your trip well in advance and expect crowds. The beaches are, of course, what draws most people to the North Shore. During one day, you can easily see all the good surfing spots, but give each plenty of time as they change by the minute. Aside from the surf, this coast also offers a number of other sights worth a stop. Take an hour and stroll the lovely walkways of the Waimea Valley Audubon Center or peek at the ruins of Pu'u O Mahuka Heiau. If you feel like stretch-

ing your legs a bit more, take an afternoon to hike in the forested hills and valleys above the town of Waimea. The town of Hale'iwa cries out for you to stop and peruse its many shops. Take a few hours to look at its galleries and surf shops, or have a break for a meal at one of its many restaurants. Then there is the more remote west end of the coast, with untouched beaches for miles of beachcombing. While it's fastest and most convenient to get to the North Shore by going across the Leilehua Plateau of Central O'ahu, you can also get there in a more circuitous but vastly more scenic route via the Windward side. It can be "done" in one day, but it's wise to give it more, especially if you want to partake in activities. The North Shore is rural, quiet, scenic, and largely unspoiled, and no matter how long you stay, it will forever pull on your heart strings.

Turtle Bay

TURTLE BAY RESORT

The Turtle Bay Resort is a first-class resort of some 880 acres on Turtle Bay, the northern extremity of the North Shore. This resort was built in the 1960s as a self-contained destination and is surrounded by sea and surf on Kuilima Point, which offers protected swimming year-round at Kuilima Cove. The entrance road to the hotel is lined by blooming hibiscus outlining a formal manicured lawn. The Turtle Bay Resort hotel, with its associated cottages and villas, occupies Kuilima Point and the adjacent seashore. Condominiums flank the entrance road. Two 18-hole golf courses embrace the property, and there is a professional tennis facility on the grounds with plexi-pave courts. A helicopter company also runs its operation from here.

Recreation

Two very playable 18-hole **golf courses** grace the seashore at Turtle Bay. The premier course is the Arnold Palmer Course, home of the PGA Champions' Turtle Bay Championship. The front nine holes are links-style, cutting through the rolling sand dunes, while the back nine slice through stands of trees. Hosting the LPGA tour's Hawaiian Open is the George Fazio Course, the only Fazio-designed golf course in Hawaii. This course is broader and more open but still with challenges. Greens fees run $145 and $115 for resort guests and $175 and $155 for nonguests. Call the pro shop (808/293-8574) for reservations.

Managed by the well-known Peter Burwash International, the Turtle Bay **Tennis Center** (808/296-6024, open 8 A.M.–noon and 2–6 P.M.) has eight courts, two lit for night play. Sign up for court time or arrange for match play, clinics, or instruction. Rackets and ball machines are rented.

The stable at Turtle Bay Resort (808/293-8811) welcomes both resort guests and nonguests. Gentle guided **trail rides** through the ironwood forest and along the beach are offered several times daily. Regular rides cost

$50 adults and $30 children 7–12 for the 40-minute saunter. Advanced adult rides are $100, evening rides run $80 per person, and there's even a pony walk for kids under age seven for $25. On weekends, a wagon ride heads out to Kawela Bay, $20 for adults and $10 for kids 3–12 years old.

Paradise Helicopter (808/293-2570, www.paradisecopters.com) has its office and landing pad on the far side of the hotel parking lot, tucked behind a screen of vegetation. The company offers three different helicopter rides to meet everyone's needs for time and expense. For $120, the 20-minute North Shore and Waterfall Adventure will whisk you along the long line of north coast surf beaches and show you some of the island's most wonderful waterfalls. The 40-minute Best of O'ahu ride expands their flying territory and takes you over more picturesque O'ahu sites for $175. The ultimate 60-minute O'ahu Experience, which basically makes a circle of the entire eastern half of the island from Turtle Bay to Pearl Harbor, will set you back $220. Paradise Helicopter, which also operates on the Big Island of Hawai'i, uses four-passenger Hughes 500 helicopters for its O'ahu flights.

Accommodations

The █ **Turtle Bay Resort** hotel (57-091 Kamehameha Hwy., Kahuku, 808/293-6000 or 800/203-3650, fax 808/293-9147, www.turtlebayresort.com) is the main focus of this resort property. From 2001 to 2003, the hotel went through an extensive renovation that brought all exterior and interior public areas up to date. Along with a total room, restaurant, and meeting room renovation, the lobby was opened up to Kuilima Bay, letting in the light and making this enticing view part of the welcoming experience. The hotel offers a totally renovated and expanded swimming pool deck with hot tub and water slide; full water activities, including equipment rental and surfing and scuba lessons; horseback riding along the beach, through the oceanfront ironwood forest,

The Turtle Bay Resort hotel has a superb location on Turtle Bay.

the many massage, facial, or body treatment options. Several spa rooms on the floor above have direct access by dedicated elevator to the spa center. For a moderate additional fee, the summer Keiki Turtle Club program will keep kids ages 5–12 busy throughout the day with arts, crafts, and age-appropriate activities.

All 400 guest rooms and two dozen suites in the three-wing main hotel building are oceanview, but not all are oceanfront. No matter where you are, however, you have a great view, especially December through April, when humpback whales cavort in the waters off the point. Rooms are furnished with king-size or double beds, full baths, a mini refrigerator, ample closets, a/c, remote-control cable TV, in-room safe, and high-speed Internet access. The predominantly sand and light sea green colors are offset by bolder tropical fabrics; sparse ornamentation lets the beauty of the surroundings draw your attention. Suites come complete with a changing room, sitting area, and a large enclosed lanai. In addition, several dozen self-contained luxury cottages line Turtle Bay and offer more seclusion with direct access to lawn and shoreline. Rates are $440–520 for an oceanview or oceanfront room, $900 for a cottage, $1,200–2,400 for multi-bedroom villas, and $890–2,500 for suites; $50 for an extra adult. The family plan allows children under 18 to stay free in a room with their parents. Numerous room and car, golf, tennis, romance, and seasonal discount packages are available. The Turtle Bay Resort is a first-class destination resort, but because of its fabulous yet out-of-the-mainstream location, you get much more than you pay for. The Turtle Bay Resort is an excellent choice for a vacation with the feel of being on a Neighbor Island.

and across a wetland preserve; a small clutch of shops for jewelry, gifts, and sundries; and the fanciest dining on the North Shore. Because the hotel is an oasis unto itself, you should always call ahead to book any of the activities, even as a guest staying at the hotel, to avoid disappointment; the concierge desk in the lobby can help with any on-site or off-site arrangements. By all means, however, take a hike along part or all of the 12 miles of trails winding through the resort property. Ask for a copy of the resort's *Trail and Ocean Guide*. Although each has its own character, the trail to the banyan tree and Kawela Bay is superb. The resort's seaside Wedding Pavilion is splendid with open-beamed ceiling, stained glass, and eight-foot beveled windows that can be thrown open to allow the ocean breezes to waft through.

As part of the remodel, the hotel now sports Spa Luana, which has its own fitness center, half a dozen treatment rooms, including a wet room and outdoor massage cabanas, and a beauty salon. Pamper yourself with one of

Surrounded by golf links on the approach road to Turtle Bay Resort is a secure condominium complex of several hundred units that's split into two groups. Within this quiet and landscaped community at Kuilima are private tennis courts, swimming pools, and barbecue facilities, and you're only a short stroll away from the activity, shopping, and dining options at the resort. Vacation rentals in this

THE NORTH SHORE

tropical complex are studios to three-bedroom units, each with a full kitchen, one or more bathrooms, ceiling fans, washer and dryer, entertainment center with TV, telephone, and a lanai that opens onto the green lawn, palm trees, flowering bushes, and the fairway. Rates for these units generally run $90–105 studio, $115–155 one-bedroom, $160 two-bedroom, and $180 three-bedroom, although this could vary slightly depending on the condition of the unit. Fees may be slightly less during low season, April–May and September–November. There is a two-night minimum stay with a one-week minimum in place over the Christmas holiday. A down payment is required, as is a "guest service fee." These condos range from not so well taken care of to newly remodeled and fancy, so when you inquire about availability, be sure to be specific and ask just what sort of place is being offered to you. For information and reservations, contact either **The Estates at Turtle Bay** (56-565 Kamehameha Hwy., P.O. Box 366, Kahuku, HI 96731, 808/293-0600 or 888/200-4202, fax 808/293-0471, www.turtlebay-rentals.com), with about 150 units in its pool, or **Turtle Bay Condos** (56-565 Kamehameha Hwy., P.O. Box 248, Kahuku, HI 96731, 808/293-2800, fax 808/293-2169, www.turtlebay condos.com), with fewer units. Both have check-in offices at the Mill Shopping Center in Kahuku, just a few miles down the road on the Windward side.

Food

Because it is set in the country with little else around, the Turtle Bay Resort provides several options for meals. The **Palm Terrace** (808/293-6000) is the main hotel restaurant for all-day dining. Best known for its sumptuous buffets, menu service is also an option. The Palm Terrace serves hearty American favorites, from simple to fancy, supplemented by dishes from around the world. The breakfast buffet runs $19.95, lunch buffet is $22.95, and it's $27.95 for the prime rib buffet, except for Saturday when it become the prime rib and seafood fest for $31.95. The views overlooking the pool and beyond to Turtle Bay combined with excellent value for the money make the Palm Terrace the best *ordinary* restaurant on the North Shore.

For that extra-special dinner of contemporary island cuisine, make reservations at ◖ **21 Degrees North** (808/293-6000). This is the resort's redesigned fine-dining restaurant; resortwear is requested. Facing west and overlooking the charming Turtle Bay, it's a perfect place for sunset and a romantic retreat. Your start of soup or appetizer leads into the wonderfully prepared and presented entrée, which might be rosemary-crusted rack of lamb, nori-wrapped *moi* on jasmine rice, braised lobster, or broiled filet mignon, all priced at $28–44. A selection of wine would make a perfect match to the meal, while coffee, a cordial, or a luscious dessert would certainly finish it off in style. If you desire to just have it all up front, try the five-course tasting menu at $76 per person or $95 with wine.

The **Sunset Room** is synonymous with Sunday brunch at the Turtle Bay Resort. It enjoys a wonderful reputation, and if friends or family come visiting, islanders take them here to impress. Brunch (10 A.M.–2 P.M.) is buffet-style and features mounds of fresh fruits and pastries, fresh-squeezed fruit juices, imported cheeses, eggs in several styles, fresh fish, seafood, sashimi, and more. This feast costs $32.50 adults, $29.25 for seniors, and $16 for children 4–11. Reservations are recommended. Expect a wait, which goes quickly as you enjoy the magnificent scenery.

Located right on the Kuilima Cove beach, the open-air **Ola** restaurant (808/293-2801, open daily 11 A.M.–3 P.M., Sun.–Thurs. 5:30–9:30 P.M., Fri.–Sat. 5:30–10 P.M.) serves casual island fare using flavors and spices from Asia and Europe. Lunch is fresh salads and fish or chicken sandwiches. For a more filling dinner, start out with fresh Kahuku corn chowder and then move on to a lovely fish or meat dish, mostly $25–32.

Located at the golf clubhouse, **Lei Lei's** bar and grill (808/293-2662, open daily 7 A.M.–10 P.M.) offers large portions of tasty food in a relaxed and casual setting. During the day, sandwiches, burgers, and other quick foods are prepared mainly for golfers, but in the evening this restaurant shines with such items as crab-stuffed salmon, crunchy coconut shrimp, double-cut pork loin chop, and baby back ribs, all served with fresh vegetables and either garlic smashed potatoes or white rice. Expect most entrées in the $22–33 range.

Just off the lobby in a perfect spot overlooking Kuilima Bay, the **Bay Club** is a casual sports lounge and bar offering drinks and *pu pu* during the day. In the late evening, it offers music, dancing, and cocktails. When lounging by the pool, pick up a cool cocktail drink or *pu pu* from the **Hang Ten** bar, which also has live evening entertainment.

Lu'au

Legends of the North Shore Lu'au is a Friday-only dinner and Polynesian Revue at the Turtle Bay Resort. This entertaining evening starts at 6 P.M. with a full buffet dinner, followed by the show, which features music and dance from various islands around the Pacific. The full evening runs $75 adults and $45 children 4–11; for the show only, the prices are $50 and $30, respectively.

Waimea and the Great Surfing Beaches

The two-lane highway along the North Shore is pounded by traffic. Be especially careful around Waimea Bay, where the highway sweeps around below the steeple of **St. Peter and Paul Mission.** The steeple is actually the remnant of an old rock-crushing plant on the site. The town of Waimea sits on the east side of this bay and is a small one-horse town with little more than a fire station, beach park, supermarket, gas station, and a couple of shops.

The greatest surfing beaches of the North Shore stretch between the town of Waimea and Sunset Beach. Between these two points are several beach parks, a botanical garden, and an ancient Hawaiian *heiau*. The North Shore is an easygoing, laid-back section of the island. This is country O'ahu, far removed from the frenetic hustle of Honolulu.

SIGHTS
◀ The Great Surfing Beaches

East of Waimea Bay lies a series of great surfing beaches, most powerful and dramatic in winter when the big waves roll into shore. It is here, when the waves are at their best, that the big international surfing competitions are held and swarms of visitors drive up to watch. Unless you have experience in big waves, don't even think of going out. Generally, if the life-

guards here don't know you, you won't be allowed in the water during periods of dangerous surf. Just spend some time on shore admiring the power of the ocean and skill of those who know how to ride these monsters.

These beaches run end to end, and its hard to tell where one ends and the next begins. This is one of the longest white-sand beaches on O'ahu. While the entire stretch is sometimes referred to as Sunset Beach, each world-famous surfing spot warrants its own name, although they're not clearly marked and are tough to find . . . exactly. Winter surf erodes the beach, with coral and lava fingers exposed at the shoreline, but in summer you can expect an uninterrupted beach usually 200–300 feet wide. In years past, the beaches were not always well maintained, and the restrooms, even at Waimea Bay, were sometimes atrocious. The reason was politics and money. Efforts all went into Waikiki, where the tourists are. Who cared about a bunch of crazy surfers on the North Shore? Recently, however, some money has been put into this area to alleviate these problems, and a few new facilities have been constructed and others spiffed up.

Don't expect much when you come to **Sunset Beach County Park,** except for a grand beach that curves around to the east to Sunset Point.

Aside from a lifeguard tower, there's only a parking lot and bathrooms across the road. Almost as famous as the surfing break is the Sunset Rip, a notorious offshore current that grabs people every year. Summertime is generally safe, but never take *moana* for granted. Beyond Sunset to the east is the surf spot **Backyards** and farther is the locally well-known **Velzyland.** Just beyond, on the ocean side of the University Livestock Farm, is **Waiale'e Beach County Park.** Its rocky shoreline makes it not so good for swimmers except for a small sandy spot at the southern end, but many anglers come to try their luck. Across the street may be a stand selling fresh fruit and coconuts, and in the area you'll undoubtedly find others selling sweet corn, an unexpected treat on this tropical island.

For **'Ehukai Beach County Park,** look for Sunset Beach Elementary School on the inland side of the highway. There is a small parking lot on the ocean side, but you can park in the school's lot on days when school isn't in session. 'Ehukai has a lifeguard tower and restroom and provides one of the best vantage points from which to watch the surfing action on the **Pipeline,** as well as **Pupukea, Gas Chambers,** and **Kammie Land,** other breaks up the coast. Surfing competitions will often have their headquarters set up here, and broadcasting companies will televise from this beach.

Closest to Waimea is **Banzai Beach,** probably the best-known surfing beach in the world. Its notoriety dates from *Surf Safari,* an early surfer film made in the 1950s, when it was dubbed "Banzai" by Bruce Brown, maker of the film. The famous tubelike effect of the breaking waves comes from a shallow reef just offshore, which forces the waves to rise dramatically and quickly. This forces the crest forward to create "the Pipeline," hence the term **Banzai Pipeline** for this break. Other breaks at this beach are **Back Doors, Off the Wall,** and **Log Cabins.** A lifeguard tower near the south end of the beach at the stream entrance is all you'll find in the way of improvements. Parking is along the roadway.

Pupukea Beach Park

A perfect place to experience marinelife is the large tidepool next to Pupukea Beach Park, across the street from the Shell gas station in Waimea. The beach park has restrooms, picnic facilities, and fair swimming in sandy pockets

Shark's Cove is one of the best snorkel sites on the North Shore.

© ROBERT NILSEN

MAUI POHAKU LOA

Between Sunset and 'Ehukai beaches, on the inland side of the highway near mile marker 9, you can't help noticing a mammoth redwood log that has been carved into a giant statue called Maui Pohaku Loa. This carved log represents an ancient Hawaiian. Peter Wolfe, the sculptor, has done a symbolic sculpture for every state in the union, this being his 50th. This statue was extremely controversial. Some feel that it looks much more like an American Indian than a Hawaiian, and that the log used should have been a native koa instead of an imported redwood from the Pacific Northwest. Others say that its *intention* was to honor the living and the ancient Hawaiians, and that is what's important, not the exact design or type of wood.

between coral and rock, but only in summer. A long retaining wall out to sea forms a large and protected pool at low tide. Wear footgear and check out the pools with a mask. Don't be surprised to find large sea bass. Be careful not to step on sea urchins, and stay away from the pool during rough winter swells, when it can be treacherous. The western end of this park is called Three Tables. The eastern section of the park is called Shark's Cove, although no more sharks are here than anywhere else. The area is terrific for snorkeling, high visibility but not as many fish as Hanauma Bay, and a major destination for scuba tours in season. The Pupukea Marine Life Conservation District runs from Three Tables Cove past Shark's Cove to Kulalua Point and includes the tidal pools and shoreline. Most water activities are permitted, but spearfishing is not. If you had to pick a spot from which to view the North Shore sunset, Pupukea Beach Park is hard to beat. Convenient for those who are out for a bit of exercise, a jogging/bicycle path parallels the highway and links Pupukea Beach Park with Sunset Beach Park a couple of miles up the road.

Waimea Bay Beach County Park

Waimea Bay has some of the largest rideable waves in the world. This is the heart of surfers' paradise. The park, improved with a lifeguard tower, restrooms, and a picnic area, covers the bay where the river enters the ocean. The church steeple overlooks the beach's east end; kids dive off rocks at its western end. In summer, the bay can be as calm as a lake. During big winter swells, the bay is lined with spectators watching the surfers ride the monumental waves. People inexperienced with the sea should not even walk along the shorebreak in winter. Unexpected waves come up farther than you'd think, and a murderous rip lurks only a few feet from shore. The area is rife with tales of heroic rescue attempts, many ending in fatalities. A plaque commemorates Eddie Aikau, a local lifeguard credited with making thousands of rescues. In 1978, the *Hokule'a*, the Polynesian Sailing Society's double-hulled canoe, capsized in rough seas about 20 miles offshore. Eddie was aboard and launched his surfboard to swim for help. He never made it, but his selfless courage lives on. It's here at Waimea Bay, anytime between December 1 and February 28, when the surfing contest Quicksilver Big Wave Invitational in Memory of Eddie Aikau is held. While the North Shore produces big waves, the waves have to be consistently 20 feet or more to run the competition. It's happened only seven times in over 20 years.

◖ Waimea Valley Audubon Center

Look for the well-marked entrance to Waimea Valley Audubon Center (808/638-9199, open daily 9:30 A.M.–5 P.M., $8 adults, $5 seniors, children 4–12, and *kama'aina*.), directly mountain side of Waimea Bay on Highway 83, and then drive into the lush valley before coming to the actual park entrance. The park is the most culturally significant travel destination on the North Shore. Parenthetically, this valley was visited by the crew of Captain Cook's ships following his death in 1779, and in 1792 by Captain Vancouver, who stopped here to fill his water casks. Unfortunately, three of Captain

Vancouver's men were killed in a skirmish that erupted while fetching water.

This center provides a wonderful sanctuary for a plethora of tropical plants and has not lost sight of its ancient *aloha* soul. With 1,875 acres and 6,000 species of plants in about three dozen gardens, it is primarily a botanical garden, with a fascinating display of flowers and plants labeled for your edification, but it also collects, grows, and preserves extremely rare specimens of Hawaii's endangered flora. Guided historical walks on Tuesday and Saturday at 1 P.M. and a Hawaiian Plant Walk on Thursday and Sunday at 2 P.M. can make this a wonderful learning experience. Throughout the week, other botanical and cultural activities are scheduled.

At the upper end of the walkway is Waimea Falls. A graceful cascade for most of the year, it can turn into a frothing torrent of red erosional water when the rains in the hills above have been heavy and visitors are allowed to swim in the pool below the falls. Near the garden entrance is **Hale o Lono Heiau,** one of the island's largest and most ancient *heiau,* dedicated to the god Lono and used for agricultural purposes, and numerous other sites of ancient Hawaiian life and ethnology. A small restaurant near the ticket counter offers plate lunches and other quick food items that can be had throughout the day.

((Pu'u O Mahuka Heiau

Do yourself a favor and drive up the mountain road leading to this *heiau,* even if you don't want to visit it. The vast and sweeping views of the coast below to the west are incredible. Right in the center of Waimea is a Foodland supermarket. Turn here up Pupukea Road and follow the signs.

Pu'u O Mahuka Heiau, said to be the largest on O'ahu, covers a little more than five acres. Designated a National Historical Landmark, it has three sections that descend the hillside in huge steps. The *heiau* was the site of human sacrifice. People still come to pray, as is evidenced by offerings wrapped in *ti* leaves placed on the small altar at the upper end of the site. In the upper section is a raised mound sur-

© ROBERT NILSEN

Pu'u O Mahuka Heiau is O'ahu's largest ancient religious site.

rounded by stone in what appears to be a central altar area. The *heiau*'s stonework shows a high degree of craftsmanship throughout, but especially in the pathways. The lower section of the *heiau* appears to be much older and is not as well maintained, but in fact may be newer. Have a walk around the ruins, not through them, then walk through the grass to the west for a peek into the valley.

Drive past the *heiau* access road and in a minute or so make a left onto Alapio Road. This takes you through an expensive residential area called Sunset Hills and past a home locally called The Mansion which was purported to be Elvis Presley's island hideaway. The road straight up the hill leads to a Boy Scout Camp, beyond which a biking/hiking trail leads into the mountains.

RECREATION
Biking
Country Cycle (808/638-8866, open daily except Monday 10 A.M.–5 P.M.) offers bike rentals for biking the easy and convenient North Shore path or heading up into the forest.

Horseback Riding

In Pupukea, above the town of Waimea, **Happy Trails Hawaii** (59-231 Pupukea Rd., 808/638-7433, www.happytrailshawaii.com) can put you on horseback for an easy ride along the edge of the canyon looking into Waimea Valley. The two-hour and 1.5-hour rides run $78 and $57, respectively. The age requirement is six years old, and you cannot weigh more than 235 pounds to ride. Riding with Happy Trails Hawaii makes an easy, enjoyable experience for beginning riders.

Hiking

Above Waimea is one of the North Shore's most accessible hiking trails. Reasonably well marked, the **Kaunala Trail** should take 2–3 hours. This trail, which is open on weekends and holidays, can be extremely wet and slippery (and somewhat disorienting) during periods of heavy rain, so go only when it's dry. It's best to pick up a trail map and description from the Department of Forestry and Wildlife in Honolulu before you head out along this trail. Turn inland by the Waimea Foodland supermarket and head up Pupukea Road. Drive to the end of the road and park near the Boy Scout camp. There, head through the access gate and walk up the forest road. Less than one mile in, there is a trailhead marker on your left. Turn in there for the actual start of this 2.5-mile trail and follow it as it meanders in and out of numerous small valleys and crosses several small streams. The trail pops out onto an abandoned Jeep track. Turn right, and within a half mile or so, it connects with the main forest road. Turn right again, toward the sea, and shortly you'll pass a roadside picnic table, beyond which this downhill road takes you about two more miles back to your beginning.

ACCOMMODATIONS

The North Shore of O'ahu has long been famous for its world-class surfing. The area attracts enthusiasts from around the world who are much more concerned with the daily surfing report than they are with deluxe accommodations. The Kamehameha Highway is dotted with surfer rentals from Kawela Bay to Hale'iwa. Just outside their doors are famous surfing breaks. Some of these accommodations are terrific, whereas others are barely livable, and you'll find that most of both types are taken throughout the winter surfing season. The best deals are beach homes or rooms rented directly from the owners, but this is a hit-and-miss proposition. You have to check the local papers or the bulletin boards outside shops in Waimea and Hale'iwa; craigslist (honolulu.craigslist.org) may also provide some leads. Others are well-established, well-known accommodations that have been around for years. Many better homes are now handled by rental agents. The homes vary greatly in amenities. Some are palaces, whereas others are basic rooms perfect for surfers or those who consider lodging secondary.

Surfer Rentals

Shark's Cove Rentals (59-672 Kamehameha Hwy., 808/638-7980 or 888/883-0001, lanej003@hawaii.rr.com, www.sharkscoverentals.com) offers shared and private rooms in its houses directly across from Shark's Cove. Clean, safe, homey, and well maintained, Shark's Cove contains a living room, full kitchen, and shared bathroom in each of its three areas, and an outdoor covered patio, pay phone, and washer and dryer for use by all guests. Shark's Cove is small enough to get to know others easily yet large enough for some diversity. Three rooms in the back house, which has a full kitchen and shared bath, run $85. Downstairs bunk rooms in the middle house are $75; upstairs, the bunk rooms are $95 a night or $30 per person. There is even a deluxe tent in the side yard (electricity, bed, maid service) that goes for $60 a night. A new addition created two large studios above the main house and these run $165 and $185. Spacious, clean, and modern, one has an ocean view while the other looks out onto the mountain. As it's so close to the road, though, those sensitive to sound should consider a room in the back and not take the new rooms up front. Rates vary somewhat by season; weekly and monthly rates are an option. No breakfast is served, and there is a small key and linen deposit. These rentals are convenient for their location and definitely worth the price. Contact John or Wilma Lane for information or reservations.

Backpackers Vacation Inn and Plantation Village (59-788 Kamehameha Hwy., 808/638-7838, fax 808/638-7515, www.back packers-hawaii.com) specializes in budget accommodations for surfers, backpackers, and families. It has a perfect location fronting Three Tables Beach. Find it at mile marker 6, the fourth driveway past the church tower coming from Waimea Bay. On the mountain side of the road are two three-story, pole-style houses that offer hostel and private room accommodation, while on the ocean side is an additional building with studios. The basic rate is $25 for a bunk in the hostel-style rooms, which includes use of a kitchen, laundry facilities, and TV in the communal room. Each room has four bunks, a shower, and a bath. The feeling is definitely not deluxe, but it is adequate, and there can be a real communal vibe. The back house has several private rooms for two with shared kitchen and bath for $65–75. Studios in the building on the beach rent for $125–150 daily depending on the season, and each has a complete kitchen or kitchenette, two double beds, a foldout couch, a ceiling fan, and a world-class view of the beach from the lanai. Weekly rates with discounts are offered, and all payments are to be made in advance—no refunds. This inn and hostel is often full, so book ahead. In addition, guests have free use of boogie boards and snorkeling gear, Internet access, and bike rentals for $5–10 per day. Staff can arrange whale-watching or sunset sails, scuba lessons, kayak rental, and other activities and equipment, often at reduced rates. Small valuables can be locked away in an office safe, and larger items can also be stored. Van transportation to/from the airport and Waikiki is free for guests, and TheBus no. 52 ($2) stops directly in front. This friendly, laid-back place is a good choice.

About two hundred yards toward town is the **Plantation Village,** also operated by Backpackers. Nine private cottages, once the homes of real plantation workers, create a small community. These cottages are furnished with cable TV, linens, fans, and a full kitchen, and the lanai is a great place to catch the breezes. It's only a three-minute walk to the Foodland store for supplies. Everyone is free to use the washers and dryers and pay phone in the common area. One caveat, however: Some guests have complained that the cottages have, in some cases, been unkempt, in need of supplies, lacking in security, and generally not kept up to the best standards. Use your own judgment. Many of the fruit trees on the grounds provide guests with complimentary bananas, papayas, and mangos. A bunk in the dorm here goes for $25. The larger, multi-bedroom cottages run $180–280. An inexpensive and nutritious evening meal is served two or three nights a week in the garden area of the village for about $7. During surfing season, the Plantation Village is booked up, so reserve well in advance.

Vacation Rental Cottages

(Ke Iki Beach Bungalows (59-579 Ke Iki Rd., Waimea, 808/638-8829 or 866/638-8229, keikibeachbungalows@hawaii.rr.com, www .keikibeach.com) is a small beachfront cottage compound just past the Foodland supermarket heading east. The property has 200 feet of beach with a sandy bottom that goes out about 300 feet (half that in winter). The complex is quiet with a home-away-from-home atmosphere. Half the units are situated along the beach and half are in the garden. All have full kitchens, televisions, and a Weber barbecue. Three of the units are sized to be comfortable for a couple only, one has room for up to eight people, while most can sleep up to five easily. Rates are $165–210 for a two-bedroom unit, $135–195 for a one-bedroom unit, and $120 for the studio. In high season, December 1–January 6, rates are somewhat higher. A three-night minimum is required; weekly rates are available. A one-time cleaning fee is charged, which ranges $50–100 depending on the size of unit. This is a good choice for a stay on the North Shore.

Bed-and-Breakfast

Santa's By The Sea B&B (59-461 Ke Waena Rd., 808/638-7837, www.santasbythesea.com) is one studio apartment located between Banzai Pipeline and Log Cabins surfing spots. As this is the basement floor of a beachfront house, the view from the inside is not the best, so spend your time on the gazebo or beach. A full kitchen is stocked with all the goodies for you to make your own breakfast whenever you desire. There is a spacious bedroom and bath, washer and dryer, a telephone, and use of a computer. The small sitting room doubles as a sleeping area for the kids. There are plenty of water toys to borrow, and you will, as the water is literally steps away. A hot and cold outdoor shower is provided near the gazebo so you can wash off the sand before you head inside. The gazebo overlooks the beach, so you might find that you spend a good deal of time there. It's perfect for sunsets and for the gentle breezes. Despite its name, this studio is not decked out in Christmas decor; there are only a few decorative items that hint at the holiday season. The owner just loves Christmas. Santa's By The Sea is a very clean and well-kept establishment that runs $200 a night with a two-night minimum; one-night stays are possible for an extra charge if there is room between other bookings.

Rental Agencies

Various agencies handle rental homes and condos along the North Shore, mostly between Hale'iwa and Turtle Bay. The range is broad and prices vary greatly, even season to season, but generally you might expect to pay about $125 per night for a studio or condo on the beach, $150 for a one-bedroom rental, $200 for a two-bedroom unit, and $250–900 for a three- or more bedroom home. These homes are fully furnished with all you'll need for a relaxing vacation. Cleaning deposits are usually applied, and rental agreements are often for a minimum of one week, although sometimes less. By and large, full payment is expected in advance. For stays during holidays and the Vans Triple Crown surfing event, book 6–12 months in advance. At other times, a couple of months' advance reservation is usually enough.

To check on what is available, try the following agencies: **Sterman Realty** (66-250 Kamehameha Hwy., Ste. D100, Haleiwa, HI 96712, 808/637-6200, fax 808/637-6100, www.sterman.com), which has about 100 homes in its listing. With fewer but plentiful listings are **Team Real Estate** (66-250 Kamehameha Hwy., Ste. D103, Haleiwa, HI 96712, 808/637-3507 or 800/982-8602, fax 808/637-8881, www.teamrealestate.com), **Sunset Homes, LLC** (66-030 Kamehameha Hwy., Haleiwa, HI 96712, 808/637-2400 or 808/227-7092, fax 808/637-4200, www.sunsethomes.net), and **Hawaii Surf and Sand Vacations** (P.O. Box 961, Haleiwa, HI 96712, 808/638-7504 or 877/429-2448, fax 808/638-5336, www.hawaiivac.com).

FOOD

All food options in and near Waimea fall into the inexpensive to moderate range. For a full selection of food supplies, shop **Foodland** (59-720 Kamehameha Hwy., 808/638-8081, 6 A.M.–11 P.M.) along the highway in Waimea at the Pupukea Road intersection. In this town without a restaurant, the deli counter at Foodland could serve as a lunch stop, since you can get deli salads, cut meat, whole roasted chickens, chicken strips, and sandwiches until 9 P.M. Foodland also has a bakery counter, and there's a Starbucks (open 5 A.M.–9 P.M.) at the front.

Sharks Cove Grill (open daily 8:30 A.M.–5:30 P.M.), a *kaukau* wagon along the highway a few steps from Foodland and across from Shark's Cove, dispenses plate lunches for breakfast and lunch. Morning meals might be oatmeal, pancakes, and eggs for under $5. For lunch look for salads, fish and chicken sandwiches, and grilled meat skewers for $7–10.

Behind the Maui Pohaku Loa statue in a covered garden setting is **Island Shack** (59-254 Kamehameha Hwy., 808/638-9500, open daily 8:30 A.M.–10 P.M.). This covered outdoor eatery with its gravel floor produces better-than-average grinds, with live music on some evenings. Breakfasts are mostly eggs and griddle items. For lunch and dinner, you can have your choice of fish and meat items like fresh fish, grilled shrimp, beef stew, and chicken breast, or select one of the vegetarian items. Not inexpensive but not outrageous, most items run $10–14. Island Shack is a very casual and down-to-earth operation that aims to please.

Sunset Beach Store is the home of **Ted's Bakery** (59-024 Kamehameha Hwy., 808/638- 8207, open daily 7 A.M.–6 P.M.), where you can get a fine assortment of loaves, pies, cakes, sinfully rich pastries and sweet treats, drinks, and smoothies. Ted's also does breakfast omelettes and eggs for under $5, and burgers, plate lunches, and sandwiches for lunch for under $7. No seating; it's all takeout.

Hale'iwa

Hale'iwa (Home of the Frigate Birds) has become the premier town of the region, mainly because it straddles the main North Shore road where the highways over the Leilehua Plateau meet the coast, and it has most of the shopping, dining, and services along the North Shore. The coastal highway runs through town, but to ease traffic, Hale'iwa now has a bypass, the Joseph P. Leong Highway, around the back side of town. Unless you're really in a rush, follow the brown Welcome to Historic Hale'iwa Town sign into town because this is where it's all happening.

Many of the old buildings of town are of the single-story plantation-era variety from the early 1900s. Hale'iwa has managed to keep this old-style look fairly intact, and even the new North Shore Marketplace shopping mall has kept with the style and created mostly single-story false-front stores and covered wooden lanai.

Head through town going eastward and cross the graceful double-arch **Anahulu River Bridge.** Park for a moment and walk back over the bridge. Look upstream to see homes with tropical character perched on the bank of this lazy river. The scene is reminiscent of times gone by, and it is said that Queen Lili'uokalani

© ROBERT NILSEN

Hale'iwa Harbor lacks the hustle and bustle of Honolulu's harbors, and everyone on the North Shore likes it that way.

THE NORTH SHORE

TRADITIONAL HAWAIIAN FOODS

Hawaiian cuisine, the oldest in the islands, consists of wholesome, well-prepared, and delicious foods. An oft-heard island joke is that "local men don't eat until they're full; they eat until they're tired." Some Hawaiian dishes have become standard fare at a variety of restaurants, eaten at one time or another by anyone who spends time in the islands, but the best is still served at local-style restaurants. Hawaiian food in general is called *kaukau;* cooked food is *kapahaki,* and something broiled is called *ka'ola.* Any of these designations on a menu lets you know that Hawaiian food is served. Usually inexpensive, these dishes definitely fill you up and keep you going.

In old Hawaii, although the sea meant life, and indeed a great variety of fish and other seafood was eaten, many more people were involved in cultivating beautifully tended garden plots of taro, sugarcane, breadfruit, and various sweet potatoes *('uala)* than with fishing. They husbanded pigs—a favorite from the *imu* oven—and barkless dogs *('ilio),* and they prized *moa* (chicken) for their feathers and meat but found eating the eggs repulsive.

Their only farming implement was the *'o'o,* a sharpened hardwood digging stick. The Hawaiians were the best farmers of Polynesia, and the first thing they planted was taro, a tuberous root that was created by the gods at the same time as humans. This main staple of the old Hawaiians was made into poi. Every lu'au will have poi, a glutinous purple paste. It comes in liquid consistencies referred to as one-, two-, or three-finger poi. The fewer fingers you need to eat it, the thicker it is. Poi is one of the most nutritious carbohydrates known, but people unaccustomed to it find it bland and tasteless. Some of the best, fermented for a day or so, has an acidic bite. Poi is made to be eaten *with* something, but locals who love it pop it into their mouths and smack their lips. Those unaccustomed to it will suffer constipation if they eat too much.

Although poi fell out of favor during the middle of the 20th century, it is once again becoming more popular, and several sizable factories now produce poi for sale. You can find plastic containers of this food refrigerated in many supermarkets and local food stores. In addition, deep-fried slices of taro root, plain or spiced, are now packaged and sold like potato chips.

A favorite dessert is *haupia,* a custard made from coconut, found at most social gatherings. Like a tiny meal in a pouch, *laulau* is a package of meat, fish, and veggies wrapped in *ti* leaves and baked or steamed. *Poke* is a seafood salad made with a variety of seafood, seaweed, and onions that's frequently found on traditional island menus and more and more in fish markets or deli sections of supermarkets. One of the ingredients is *limu,* a generic term for edible seaweed that has been gathered as a garnish since precontact times. Many people still gather *limu* from the shoreline and eat it as a salad or mix with ground *kukui* nuts and salt as a relish. There's no other seaweed except *limu* in Hawaii. Because of this, the heavy, fishy-ocean smell that people associate with the sea but that is actually that of seaweed is absent in Hawaii.

A favorite Hawaiian snack is *'opihi,* small shellfish (limpets) that cling to rocks. *'Opihi* are cut from the shell and eaten raw by all peoples of Hawaii. Those who gather them always leave some on the rocks for the future. 'A'ama are the ubiquitous little black crabs that you'll spot on rocks and around pier areas. They're everywhere. For fun, local anglers will try to catch them with poles, but the more efficient way is to throw a fish head into a plastic bucket and wait for the crabs to crawl in and trap themselves. The *'a'ama* are about as big as two fingers and make delicious eating.

A traditional liquor made from *ti* root is *'okolehao.* It literally means "iron bottom," referencing the iron blubber pots used to ferment it.

THE NORTH SHORE

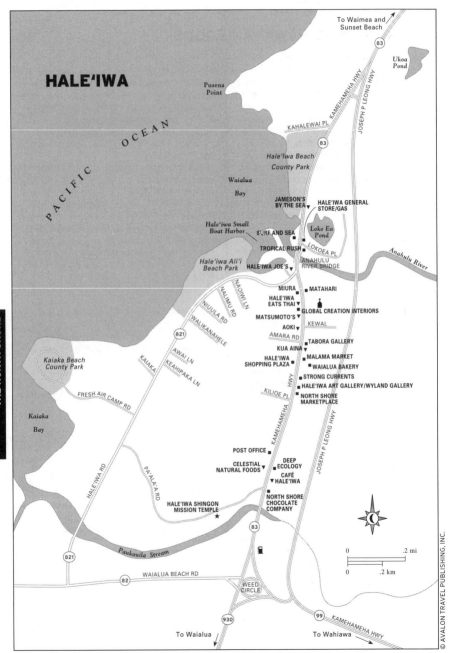

HALE'IWA

PACIFIC OCEAN

To Waimea and
Sunset Beach

83

Ukoa
Pond

Puaena
Point

KAHALEWAI PL

KAMEHAMEHA HWY

JOSEPH P LEONG HWY

83

Hale'iwa Beach
County Park

Waialua
Bay

JAMESON'S
BY THE SEA

HALE'IWA GENERAL
STORE/GAS

Hale'iwa Small
Boat Harbor

SURF AND SEA

Loko Ea
Pond

LOKOEA PL

Anahulu River

TROPICAL RUSH

ANAHULU
RIVER BRIDGE

Hale'iwa Ali'i
Beach Park

HALE'IWA JOE'S

MIURA

MATAHARI

HALE'IWA
EATS THAI

GLOBAL CREATION INTERIORS

MATSUMOTO'S

KEWAL

NAOWILN

NIULULA RD

NALIMU RD

WALIKANAHELE

821

AOKI

AMARA RD

AWAI LN

KEAHIPAKA LN

KUA AINA

TABORA GALLERY

Kaiaka Beach
County Park

KAIAKA

HALE'IWA
SHOPPING PLAZA

MALAMA MARKET

WAIALUA BAKERY

KAMEHAMEHA HWY

STRONG CURRENTS

HALE'IWA ART GALLERY/WYLAND GALLERY

FRESH AIR CAMP RD

KILIOE PL

NORTH SHORE
MARKETPLACE

JOSEPH P LEONG HWY

Kaiaka
Bay

HALE'IWA RD

PA'ALA'A RD

POST OFFICE

CELESTIAL
NATURAL FOODS

DEEP
ECOLOGY

CAFÉ
HALE'IWA

NORTH SHORE
CHOCOLATE
COMPANY

HALE'IWA SHINGON
MISSION TEMPLE

83

821

Paukauila Stream

82

WAIALUA BEACH RD

WEED
CIRCLE

0   .2 mi

0   .2 km

930

To Waialua

99

KAMEHAMEHA HWY

To Wahiawa

© AVALON TRAVEL PUBLISHING, INC.

once had a summer house on the riverbank here. The former Queen has left another mark on the town, the Lili'uokalani Protestant Church (founded in 1892) on the highway. Although the congregation is much older and the original church was from the late 1800s, the present church dates from 1961. Standing to the side in the cemetery are some headstones from the early days. Hale'iwa was an early focus for travelers and before 1900 sported a fashionable Victorian-style hotel near the river mouth for those able to get away from the hubbub of Honolulu. If you're heading to Waialua from Hale'iwa, take Hale'iwa Road, a back way through residential areas. Look for Pa'ala'a (Sacred Firmness) Road and take it past the Hale'iwa Shingon Mission temple, another vestige from Hale'iwa's past. This Buddhist mission hosts an Obon festival yearly, traditionally observed in July, a colorful cultural event that honors the dead. This quiet town with a sugar past and lazy days of surfers and hippies is still strong on cultural activities. If you're in town during the Hale'iwa Arts Festival and the taro festival, don't miss them. These days, major activities revolve around surfing; some of the biggest surfing events in the country are held at the beaches up the coast.

The best sources of current specific information pertaining to the North Shore are the bulletin boards outside many of the shops and restaurants. As you enter Hale'iwa from the west, you'll pass a gas station and a full-service post office; just east of the arched bridge is another gas station and the Hale'iwa General Store for basic supplies. Bank of Hawaii and First Hawaiian Banks are at the Hale'iwa Shopping Plaza. Hale'iwa Family Health Center (808/637-5087, open Mon.–Sat. 8 A.M.–5 P.M.) is a walk-in clinic at the rear of the Haleiwa Shopping Plaza.

SIGHTS
Beaches and Parks
Fronting town, **Hale'iwa Ali'i Beach Park** is on the western shore of Waialua Bay, set next to Hale'iwa Harbor. This beach park is improved with restrooms, a lifeguard tower, and a small boat launch. Lifeguards staff the tower throughout the summer, on weekends in winter. The shoreline is rocks and coral with pockets of sand, and although portions can be good for swimming, the park is primarily noted for surfing at a break simply called Hale'iwa. The park is popular with townspeople, and it became more widely known in the late 1990s because the then-popular TV program *Baywatch Hawaii* was based here, and some of the shows were filmed on the beach.

A little farther to the west, on Kaiaka Point, is **Kaiaka Beach County Park.** This is a good snorkeling beach, and you'll find restrooms and picnic areas here. Camping is allowed with a county permit.

Hale'iwa Beach County Park, clearly marked off the highway on the eastern side of Waialua Bay beyond the bridge, is right at the river mouth across from the marina. Here you'll find pavilions, picnic facilities, athletic grounds, restrooms, showers, and lots of parking, but no camping, except for the homeless who drift in periodically. The area is good for fishing, surfing, and, most important, for swimming year-round! It's about the only safe place for the average person to swim along the entire North Shore during winter. You can often see the canoe club practicing in the bay during late afternoon. This park is the site of the annual **Summer Artfest,** a confab of visual and performance artists that takes place in July.

Kawailoa Beach is the general name given to the waterfront stretching all the way from Hale'iwa Beach County Park to Waimea Bay. Cars park where the access is good. None of the shoreline is really suitable for the recreational swimmer. The surf sites, Laniakea, Jockos, Leftovers, and Alligators are all along this shoreline, but the most popular is Chun's Reef.

SHOPPING
In Town
In a little cluster at the north end of town, you'll find a few old and new shops, including the **H. Miura Store** (808/637-4845), in business since 1918, which has a few basic

dry goods but mostly cloth and brightly colored clothing. This is certainly the most well-known tailor shop in town. Across the street, **Matahari** (808/637-8515) carries women's fashions. A few steps away, **Global Creations Interiors** (808/637-1505, open Mon.–Sat. 10 A.M.–6 P.M., Sun. 11 A.M.–6 P.M.) handles furniture, artwork, home accessories, and some hand-painted silk clothing.

Along the highway near the center of town is **Hale'iwa Shopping Plaza,** which provides all the necessities in one-stop shopping: boutiques, **Haleiwa Pharmacy** (808/637-9393, open weekdays 9 A.M.–5:30 P.M., Sat. 9 A.M.–1:30 P.M.), photo store, a Bank of Hawaii and First Hawaiian Bank, and general food and merchandise.

North Shore Marketplace

The North Shore Marketplace is a newer complex with some unique shops. Most shops are open 9 A.M.–6 P.M., with restaurants serving until late. One of the most interesting shops is **Jungle Gem's** (808/637-6609), with a metaphysical assortment of crystals, crystal balls, African trading beads, and gems. The shop specializes in locally made jewelry that is reasonably priced and of excellent quality. The owners are knowledgeable gemologists and fine jewelers who do much of the work on display. **Silver Moon Emporium** (808/637-7710) has not only some jewelry but also a fine collection of boutique clothing. For something more gifty and island-oriented, have a look at **Polynesian and Global Handicrafts** (808/637-1288) and **Kama'ainas Hale'iwa** (808/637-1907).

To the left in the rear as you drive into the parking lot is **Twelve Tribes International Imports** (808/637-7634, open Mon.–Fri. 11 A.M.–6 P.M., Sat. 10 A.M.–6 P.M., Sun. noon–6 P.M.), a multicultural emporium with items from the global village. Although there are several racks of craft, jewelry, incense, and music items, much is clothing.

Across the way is **Oceans in Glass** (808/637-3366, daily 10 A.M.–6 P.M.), where hand-blown art glass is produced in the open-air studio. Most of what the artists make goes to the hotels, but they do have a good collection of retail items for sale in the studio. Pyrex is used for these delicate figures, many of them dolphins and other sea creatures. This is a fun little shop. Check it out to see how the work is done.

Next door is the **North Shore Surf and Cultural Museum** (808/637-8888). A walk through this compact showplace will teach you a bit about the history of surfing on the North Shore, and you'll have a chance to examine surfboards, clothing, photographs, and other artifacts of surfing life and the culture of the North Shore. Like the surging life on the North Shore, this museum is down-to-earth and very unpretentious, a seat-of-the-pants operation. The sign says Open Most Afternoons. Donations accepted.

Art Galleries and Shops

Wyland Gallery (808/637-8730, open daily 9 A.M.–6 P.M., www.wylandgalleries.com) at the North Shore Marketplace is the most well-known name in art galleries in Hawaii. Wyland is a famous environmental artist known for his huge whale and marinelife murals, in addition to watercolors and fine oil paintings. The gallery is large, spacious, and well lit, and is a relocation of the first galley he opened. Everything has a Hawaiian or sea theme. There are watercolors of Hawaiian maidens by Janet Stewart, the strong paintings of John Pitre and Scott Powers, and bronze sculptures of the sea by Scott Hanson. If the original artwork is too expensive, there are posters, mini-prints, and postcards.

Also at the North Shore Marketplace, **Hale'iwa Art Gallery** (808/637-3368, open daily 10 A.M.–6 P.M.) shows mostly original works by island artists, many from O'ahu, mostly up-and-comers who have not yet made it big but who show obvious talent. Lots of paintings are features, with a smaller selection of other forms and mediums. This is a good place to see the scope and quality of art being produced in the state.

The **Tabora Gallery** (66-160 Kamehameha Hwy., 808/637-5520) features the wonderfully evocative seascape paintings of Ray Tabora. It's easy to see how the subtle color, movement, and expression in his scenes has propelled him to become one of the most sought-after contemporary Hawaiian artists. Also displayed in this gallery are paintings by Rudolf and Rodel Gonzales, Tabora's cousins, who paint with a different feel. Landscape paintings of Daryl Millard and fantasy-scapes of James Coleman, who once was a Disney artist, also grace the gallery walls. Some evenings and weekends, there will be an artist in the shop working on a piece.

RECREATION
Sporting Goods Shops and Activities

The following shops are all along the main drag through Hale'iwa.

Barnfield's Raging Isle Surf and Cycle (808/637-7707, www.ragingisle.com, open daily 10 A.M.–6:30 P.M.) in the North Shore Marketplace is a full-service mountain bike and surf shop, and manufacturer of its own line of surfboards, the only major place on the North Shore doing so. Board repairs are also made. Aside from selling and repairing bikes, Barnfield's also rents mountain bikes at $40–60 for 24 hours and road bikes for $50 for 24 hours. Casual clothing and surfwear are stocked.

For surfboards, sailboards, boogie boards, snorkeling equipment, scuba gear, and other water toys, as well as beachwear of all sorts, try **Surf N Sea** (62-595 Kamehameha Hwy., 808/637-9887, www.surfnsea.com, open daily 9 A.M.–7 P.M.). The best-established place in town, Surf N Sea is a mustard yellow building near the bridge that offers great rentals and sales, boat trips, fishing charters, and daily scuba, surfing, and sailboarding lessons. Surf N Sea offers one- and two-tank scuba dives for $75–120 and an open water diver certification course at $375.

Another quality company offering scuba lessons is **Deep Ecology** (66-456 Kamehameha Hwy., 808/637-7946 or 800/578-3992, www.deepecologyhawaii.com). Deep Ecology also runs whale-watching tours on its Zodiac raft during winter.

Across the street next to the bridge, **Tropical**

Rush (808/637-8886) has a great selection of surfboards and beachwear for sale and boards for rent.

Along the highway in the center of town is **Strong Current** (808/637-3410), a surf shop that also has clothing and swimwear, but it's more than that. It's almost like a museum of surfing with all the collectibles on display.

North Shore Catamaran Charters (808/638-8279, www.sailingcat.com) does sailing throughout the year from Hale'iwa Harbor on its 40-foot *Ho'o Nanea*. Morning and afternoon picnic snorkels run May–September at $80–95 and $60–75 for kids, whale-watching rides December–May for $80 adults and $60 kids. Sunset cruises at $50 adults and $35 kids sail year-round.

The Watercraft Connection (808/637-8006) rents personal watercraft and kayaks from a small booth at the entrance to Hale'iwa marina. You can ride any day of the week—weather and water conditions permitting.

Leaving from Hale'iwa Harbor for part- or full-day charter fishing trips along the North Shore are **Chupu Charters Sportfishing** (808/637-3474) and **Kuuloa Kai Sportfishing** (808/637-5783).

Hawaii Shark Encounters (808/351-9373, www.hawaiisharkencounters.com) runs an exceptional tour out of Hale'iwa Harbor. They take you by boat to a site several miles out into the ocean, where you get into a metal and Plexiglas cage, around which sharks circle to have a look at you. Rates are $100 per person or $50 for boat riders. Three morning runs in summer, two throughout the rest of the year.

A number of companies and individuals offer surfing lessons on the North Shore. Try one of the following. **North Shore Surf Camp** (808/638-5914, www.northshoresurf camps.com) has $60 group lessons and $75 private lessons. **Surf N Sea** (808/637-9887, www.surfnsea.com) offers two-hour lessons at $75. **Surf Hawaii** (808/295-1241, www.surfhawaii4u.com) in the North Shore Marketplace runs three-hour group lesson at $100 and a private lesson for $130; multi-day lessons are also an option.

ACCOMMODATIONS

The Waimea area has numerous accommodations and few places to eat. Hale'iwa, on the other hand, has few accommodations and plenty of places for food. For vacation rentals in Hale'iwa, see the list of rental agents in the *Waimea* section.

FOOD
Sweet Treats

The **North Shore Chocolate Company** (open daily 11 A.M.–5 P.M.) will entice even the most ardent dieter with its hand-made chocolates and house-roasted coffee. Find it next door to the well-known **Cafe Hale'iwa.**

If the smells of fresh-baked bread and pastries don't bring you into the **Waialua Bakery** (66-200 Kamehameha Hwy., 808/637-9079, open daily except Sunday 9 A.M.–4 P.M.), nothing will. Aside from the breads, cookies, and muffins, the bakery makes filling and delicious sandwiches, smoothies, and juice, right for a "get-me-started" push in the morning or a "keep-me-going" nudge during the day. Here you can get out the door with something to eat for under $7.

Shave Ice

You can tell by the tour buses and cars parked outside that ◖ **Matsumoto's** (66-087 Kamehameha Hwy., 808/637-4827) is a famous store on the North Shore. What are all those people after? Shave ice. This is one of the best places on O'ahu to try this island treat. Not only do the tourists come here, but local families often take a Sunday drive just to get Matsumoto's shave ice. Try the Hawaiian Delight, a mound of ice smothered with banana, pineapple, and mango syrup, or any three of nearly two dozen flavors plus ice cream or sweet beans on the bottom. If lines are too long here or if you want to support the competition, try **Aoki's** shave ice or the **H. Miura Store**, both only a few steps away. Shave ice cones will run about $2.

Local Style

◖ **Cafe Hale'iwa** (66-460 Kamehameha Hwy., 808/637-5516, open daily 7 A.M.–2 P.M.), a casual hole-in-the-wall eatery on your right just as you enter town, serves one of the best breakfasts on O'ahu. Specials of the house are whole-wheat banana pancakes; the Dawn Patrol, which is two buttermilk pancakes with two eggs, off the wall omelettes; huevos rancheros; breakfast in a barrel, an egg and potato burrito with home fries and rice or beans; and steaming-hot Kona coffee. Lunch options include fish sandwiches, burritos with home fries, and grilled ham and cheese, with little on either the breakfast or lunch menus over $9. The café attracts many surfers, so it's a great place to find out about conditions.

If you missed the fresh shrimp trucks on your way up the Windward Coast or just haven't made it that far yet, stop at **Giovanni's** *kaukau* truck at the western end of town under a big tree by a dip in the road. Like at his original location in Kahuku, here you can get a dozen shrimp in various preparations for $11.

Sandwiches

Another place with great treats is **Kua 'Aina Sandwich** (66-160 Kamehameha Hwy., 808/637-6067, open daily 11 A.M.–8 P.M.) for a great assortment of sandwiches, salads, and—some claim—the best burgers on the island. Every item on the menu is under $7. Originally located in a small space down the road, this new spot has plenty of tables for the hungry mob. Kua 'Aina has gotten so popular that it now has a restaurant at the Ward Center in Honolulu.

If you're tired or just need a pick-me-up, head for the North Shore Marketplace, where you'll find the **Coffee Gallery** (66-250 Kamehameha Hwy., 808/637-5571, open daily 7 A.M.–8 P.M.), which has a large selection of fresh-roasted gourmet coffee, including Kona coffees and international selections of organically grown coffee. You can enjoy a steaming cup from its full-service espresso bar, along with fresh carrot juice and vegan pastries made without dairy products or eggs. Every day there is a homemade soup, fresh salad, and a fine selection of sandwiches that range from a vegetarian garden burger on a whole-wheat bun with lettuce and tomatoes, Maui onion, guacamole, and a side of tortilla chips to pita bread filled with eggplant, pesto, and veggies, all priced around $6. It's all vegetarian. Sit outside in the shaded and screened dining area and watch the character-laden "characters" of the North Shore come and go. Internet access is available.

Natural Foods

In the back of the Celestial Natural Foods market is **Paradise Found Cafe** (66-443 Kamehameha Hwy., 808/637-4540), a lunch counter that's open until 5 P.M. This little eatery serves vegetarian meals, healthful and nutritious, like plate lunches, tofu sauté wrap, garden burgers, and tempeh calzone. Smoothies, fresh juice drinks, teas, sodas, and sweets are also available. This food might take you to the stars, but portions are definitely not for the hungry.

Thai

Through the tall windows that front the cafe you see eccentric tile patterns on the floor and walls and an attempt at atmosphere with paper light shades and screens. But the focus at **(Hale'iwa Eats Thai** (66-079 Kamehameha Hwy., 808/637-4247, open Sun.–Thurs. noon–9 P.M., Fri.–Sat. noon–9:30 P.M.) is the food. Excellent by most estimates, you'll find the food creative yet traditional and the presentation bold. There are few surprises on the menu—all the usual Thai standards are there—but somehow the dishes just seem to be tastier. Most run $9–12, with the duck selections higher at $15. If you are into Thai food, this is one you should try.

Italian/Pizza

With a takeout window and a few seats under the canopy, **Spaghettini** (66-200 Kamehameha Hwy., 808/637-0104, open daily 11 A.M.–8 P.M.) dishes up full helpings of pasta, a few sandwich offerings, and New York–style pizza. It's quick and fun and draws those who want to fill up without spending too much. Get your plate of pasta for under $10, pizza for $10 and up, and sandwich for $6.

Pizza Bob's (66-145 Kamehameha Hwy., 808/637-5095, open daily 11 A.M.–9 P.M., Fri.–Sat. until 10 P.M.), in the Hale'iwa Shopping Plaza, has an excellent local reputation and serves not only delicious pizza, but also salads, pasta, burgers, and sandwiches. Dinner specials are offered nightly. Large pizzas run $19–23, while the other menu items are mostly $8–12. People are friendly, there's plenty of food, and the price is right. There may be live music on Friday evenings.

Mexican

Rosie's Cantina (66-165 Kamehameha Hwy., 808/637-3538, open daily 7 A.M.–9 P.M., Fri.–Sat. until 11 P.M.) in the Hale'iwa Shopping Plaza, prepares hearty Mexican dishes for a decent price. The inside is "yuppie Mex" with brass rails, painted overhead steam pipes, and elevated booths. Breakfast is mostly eggs and grill items, most with a south-of-the-border edge, but the full lunch and dinner menus are more typically Mexican, from burritos to quesadillas and fajitas. Expect to pay around $10 for most dishes. Full bar is available.

For south-of-the-border food, try **Cholo's Homestyle Mexican** (66-250 Kamehameha Hwy., 808/637-3059, open Sun.–Thurs. 11 A.M.–9 P.M., Fri.–Sat. 10:30 A.M.–9:30 P.M.). Plate items, which include rice and beans, run $6.50–15; dinners include rice, beans, salad, chips, salsa, and a choice of meat for $9–17.50. Many combinations and a variety of nacho plates are also available. Now more than twice the size of the original place, Cholo's always has lively activity; to help keep you interested while you wait for your food, the walls are festooned with masks, paintings, prints, crosses, figurines, and other works of art and crafts.

Hawaiian Contemporary Cuisine

(Jameson's by the Sea (62-540 Kamehameha Hwy., 808/637-4336, open daily 11 A.M.–9:30 P.M.) is the best that Hale'iwa has to offer. At the north end of town overlooking the sea, Jameson's has an outdoor deck perfect for a romantic sunset dinner, while inside the romantic mood is continued with shoji screens, cane chairs with stuffed pillows, candles with shades, and tables resplendent with fine linen. Lunch is lighter with sandwiches and salads, but for dinner the kitchen turns it up a notch or two. Appetizers include a salmon pâté, crab-stuffed mushrooms, and creamy clam chowder. Main dishes focus on seafood, like mahimahi, baked stuffed shrimp, ocean scallops, and seafood scampi, but also include filet mignon, chicken breast, and New York steak. Most entrées cost under $30. For dessert have the lemon macadamia nut chiffon pie. Brunch is served Sat.–Sun. 9 A.M.–noon. Reservations are highly recommended. Request a window seat for the sunset.

Hale'iwa Joe's Seafood Grill (66-011 Kamehameha Hwy., 808/637-8005, open daily 11:30 A.M.–9:30 P.M., Fri.–Sat. until 10:30 P.M.) is in a green cinder-block building on the left before you cross the Anahulu River bridge going east. Although purely utilitarian on the outside, the inside is modern and tasteful with a touch of North Shore surfing decor. This fine restaurant looks out over the Hale'iwa boat harbor, and some of what's on the menu comes directly from the fishing boats. Dine inside or out. Appetizers can be ahi spring roll, Thai fried calamari, and crunchy coconut shrimp. Main entrées here emphasize fish, but steak and ribs are also available. Fresh mahimahi is always a winner, grilled spicy shrimp starts the taste buds jumping, and the pork ribs marinated in soy-ginger and hoisin sauce tip the hat toward the Orient. Most entrées are under $24, but the range is $15–35. Hale'iwa Joe's is a good-time place with tasty food in a casual setting. Its full bar and live music (on some weekends) make this a lively hangout for the local crowd and visitors alike.

Markets
For food and picnic supplies, try the **Hale'iwa IGA** (66-197 Kamehameha Hwy., 808/637-5004, open Mon.–Sat. 8 A.M.–8 P.M., Sun. 8:30 A.M.–5:30 P.M.) in the center of town. Almost across the street is the smaller **Malama Market** (66-190 Kamehameha Hwy., 808/637-4520, open 7 A.M.–9 P.M.), a full-service grocery store with a deli and warm foods section.

Celestial Natural Foods (66-443 Kamehameha Hwy., 808/637-6729, open Mon.–Sat. 9 A.M.–6 P.M., Sun. 9 A.M.–5 P.M.), near the western end of town, is a complete natural and health food store.

Along the Farrington Highway

SIGHTS
Waialua
In the early 1900s, Waialua, a stop along the sugar-train railway, was a fashionable beach community complete with hotels and vacation homes. Today, it's hardly ever visited, and once in a while you can see horses tied up along the main street along with the parked cars in this real one-horse town.

The old sugar mill, an outrageously ugly mechanical monster, dominates the town. There is no sugar now, but the area does produce some coffee, corn, bananas, and other diversified crops on mostly small plots. Quiet Waialua, with its main street divided by trees running down the middle, *is* rural O'ahu. In town, there's a general store for supplies, a post office, a feed shop, a washerette, and two local eateries. On the highway near Thompson Corner is **The Bakery** (808/637-9795, open 5:30 A.M.–6 P.M.), a good stop for *malasadas* and pastries of all sorts. The Farmers Community Market operates Saturdays from 8:30 A.M. in the parking lot of the old sugar mill.

If **polo** is your game or if you're just curious, head west of town to the Mokule'ia Polo Field and catch a Hawaii Polo Club (www.hawaiipolo.com) match, Sunday at 2 P.M. from May to September, $7 general admission.

Beach Parks
Mokule'ia Beach County Park is the main

public access park along the highway. It provides rudimentary picnic facilities, restrooms, a playground area, and camping, but almost no shade. In summer, swimming is possible along a few sandy stretches protected by a broken offshore reef. Some come to kiteboard because of the steady trade winds.

Farther down, **Mokule'ia Army Beach** is a wider strand of sand that also has little shade. It's private, and the only noise interrupting your afternoon slumber might be planes taking off from the airfield. Local people have erected semipermanent tents in this area and guard it as if it were their own. A minute farther toward Ka'ena is an unofficial area with a wide sand beach. During the week you can expect no more than a half dozen people on this 300-yard beach. Remember that this is the North Shore and the water can be treacherous. Five minutes past the airfield, the road ends and the state park begins. This is a good place to check out giant waves in winter or have a good walk any time of year.

☾ Ka'ena Point State Park

Ka'ena Point lies about 2.5 miles down the dirt track after the pavement gives out. Count on three hours for a return hike and remember to bring water. The point can also be reached from road's end above Makaha on the Waianae (Leeward) side of the island. The sand dunes on the point are a nature reserve for nesting seabirds, so give them wide berth. Ka'ena often has *the* largest waves in Hawaii on any given day. In winter, these giants can reach above 40 feet, and their power, even when viewed safely from the high ground, is truly amazing. Surfers have actually plotted ways of riding these waves, which include being dropped by helicopter with scuba tanks. Reportedly, one surfer named Ace Cool has done it. For the rest of us mortals . . . who wants to have that much fun anyway? Ka'ena Point is the site of numerous *heiau*. Because of its exposed position, it, like similar sites around the islands, was a jumping-off point for the souls of the dead. The spirits were believed to wander here after death, and once all worldly commitments

were fulfilled, they made their leap from earth to the land beyond. Hopefully, the daredevil surfers will not revive this tradition! During winter, chances are good for seeing whales carousing off this point, and at other times of the year, you can see Laysan Albatross, shearwaters, other waterbirds, shorebirds, and an occasional monk seal. Fishermen also like to try their luck shore-fishing near the parking area at the end of the road.

RECREATION
Fixed-Wing Tours

Across the road from Mokule'ia Beach Park is Dillingham Airfield, small but modern, with restrooms near the hangars and a new parking area. Most days, especially weekends, a few local people sell refreshments from their cars or trucks. The main reason for stopping is to take a small biplane flight or glider ride or to try parachuting.

You can soar silently above the coast with **Honolulu Soaring** (808/677-3404, www.honolulusoaring.com), an outfit offering one- or two-passenger piloted rides that are infinitely more exciting than the company's name. A plane tows you aloft and you circle in a five-mile radius with a view that can encompass 40 miles on a clear day. The rides are available daily 10 A.M.–5:30 P.M. on a first-come, first-served basis. Rates for a 10-minute ride are $59 for a single person and $98 if there are two passengers, or $99 and $178, respectively, for 20 minutes. Add $20 single or $40 tandem for additional 10-minute segments if you want a longer ride. If you're really brave, a 15-minute aerobatic ride runs $149 for one passenger only. Lessons can also be arranged. Check in with "Mr. Bill."

Also at the Dillingham Airfield is **Soar Hawaii Sailplane** (808/637-3147, www.soarhawaii.com). This company offers 10- to 60-minute rides for $39–158 for one person, with the option of tandem rides available. Aerobatic rides for one passenger (with parachute!) are the same length as the standard rides but $70 more per ride. A reduction in rates is usually offered during summer. Open 10 A.M.–5:30 P.M.; reservations are recommended.

You can also take a **Stearman Biplane Ride** out of the Dillingham Airfield. A ride in this old-style bird brings back the days of barnstormers and pioneer aviation. Stearman runs a 45-minute historical flight for $205 and a one-hour flight for $295 in its open-cockpit biplane. There is space for one passenger only—aside from the pilot. If you're really a daredevil, you can ask for the aerobatic option, but it'll run you an extra $50.

Meant for extreme aerobatic flights, a **Pitts S-2B biplane** is a step up in adventure. Fifteen-minute single-passenger rollercoaster rides go for $180. Contact Skydive Hawaii (808/637-9700, www.hawaiiskydiving.com).

Parachuting

Two companies offer parachuting at the Dillingham Airfield. All drops are tandem with an instructor, unless you have certification for solo flights. After gaining 10,000–14,000 feet in elevation, you'll freefall for a minute and parachute for several more, landing lightly on the grass (God willing!) next to the airstrip. These companies usually operate 8 A.M.–3 P.M. daily. While their rates vary somewhat, expect a fee of about $225–250, but many discounts are available. Generally you must be 18 years old and less than 200 pounds to jump. For this thrill ride, contact **Pacific Skydiving** (808/637-7472, www.pacific-skydiving.com) or **Skydive Hawaii** (808/637-9700, www.hawaiiskydiving.com).

ACCOMMODATIONS

Mokuleia Beach Colony (68-615 Farrington Hwy.) is a private gated community of 26 duplexes along a wonderfully uncrowded beach just past the polo grounds. Some owners rent their condos out. For one, contact Marty (808/227-8416).

Just beyond the Colony is **Mokule'ia Sunset** (808/247-3637, fax 808/235-2644, hibeach@lava.net, www.hibeach.com), a cottage and studio set directly on the beach. Quiet, clean, but a little funky, these remodeled units would be a great place for a relaxing beach vacation. The two-bedroom, one-bath cottage that is good for up to three people has a full kitchen, queen-size and queen trundle beds, and a lanai. Rental rates are $115–135 a night with a three-night minimum or $785–985 a week. Just right for a couple, the studio also has a full kitchen and rents for $95–115 a week or $685–785 a week.

Camp Mokule'ia (68-729 Farrington Hwy., Waialua, 808/637-6241, fax 808/637-5505, www.campmokuleia.com) is owned and operated by the Episcopalian Church in Hawaii. This camp runs organized summer programs for kids and offers space for other group meetings and retreats throughout the year. In addition, rooms in its lodge building are open to individuals and families on a space-available basis. Reserve no more than 30 days in advance. Plain and simple, rooms run $65–75 per day. Tent camping is also an option at $10 per person per night. Large groups often take the summer camping space, so you will have better luck finding room the rest of the year. Meals can be purchased separately when the kitchen is open for groups or you can barbecue your own. As an added attraction, Camp Mokule'ia has protected swimming on an adjacent sand beach.

YMCA Camp H. R. Erdman (69-385 Farrington Hwy., Waialua, 808/637-4615, fax 808/637-8874, www.camperdman.net) is next, one of the best-known camps on O'ahu. This YMCA facility is named after a famous Hawaiian polo player killed in the 1930s. The full-service facility is used as a summer camp for children, throughout the year for special functions, and as a general retreat area by various organizations. Cabins are usually rented to groups of eight or more at $180 a cabin, and you must prepare your own meals. At least a 48-hour advance reservation is requested.

BACKGROUND

The Land

When Papa, the Hawaiian earth mother, returned from vacationing in Tahiti, she was less than pleased. She had learned through a gossiping messenger that her husband, Wakea, had been playing around. Besides simple philandering, he'd been foolish enough to impregnate Hina, a lovely young goddess who bore him island children. Papa, scorned and furious, showed Wakea that two could play the same game by taking a handsome young lover, Lua. Their brief interlude yielded the man-child Oʻahu, sixth of the great island children. Geologically, Oʻahu is the second oldest main island after Kauaʻi. It emerged from beneath the waves as hissing lava a few million years after Kauaʻi and cooled a little quicker than Papa's temper to form Hawaii's third largest island.

GEOGRAPHY

Oʻahu's most impressive natural features were formed after the heavy volcanic activity ceased and erosion began to sculpt the island. The most obvious are the wall-like *pali* cliffs—mountains eroded by winds from the east, valleys cut by streams from the west. Perfect examples of these *pali* are seen from Waimanalo to the north end of Kaneʻohe Bay, and examples of eroded valleys are **Nuʻuanu** and **Kalihi.**

© ROBERT NILSEN

windward side *pali* near Kane'ohe Bay

Other impressive features are **Diamond Head, Koko Head,** and **Punchbowl,** three tuff-cone volcanoes created after the heavy volcanic activity of early O'ahu. A tuff cone is volcanic ash cemented together to form solid rock. Diamond Head is the most dramatic, formed after a minor eruption about 100,000 years ago and rising 761 feet from its base.

O'ahu has the state's longest stream, **Kaukonahua,** which begins atop Pu'u Ka'aumakua at 2,681 feet in the central Ko'olau Range and runs westward 33 miles through the Leilehua Plateau, emptying at the North Shore. En route, it runs through the **Wahiawa Reservoir,** which, at 302 acres, forms the second largest body of freshwater in Hawaii. Three of O'ahu's taller, accessible waterfalls are 80-foot **Kaliuwa'a** (Sacred Falls), just west of Punalu'u; Manoa Falls, at the back of Manoa Valley above the University of Hawai'i; and **Waihe'e Falls,** in the Waimea Valley Audubon Center on the North Shore, which has a drop of more than 40 feet. O'ahu's main water concern is that usage may be outstripping supply.

East and west of O'ahu are two channels separating it from Moloka'i and Kaua'i. To the west, the 72-mile-wide **Kaua'i Channel,** the widest channel within the major Hawaiian Islands, runs more than 10,000 feet deep and is notoriously treacherous. The **Kaiwi Channel** to the east is only 26 miles wide and 2,200 feet deep. It too can be rough but is not generally as much of a problem for ships as the Kaua'i Channel. Yearly outrigger canoe races are held across this channel.

Island Builders

The Hawaiians worshiped Madame Pele, the fire goddess whose name translates equally well as Volcano, Fire Pit, or Eruption of Lava. When she was angry, she complained by spitting fire, which cooled and formed land. Vulcanologists say that the islands are huge mounds of cooled basaltic lava surrounded by billions of polyp skeletons that have formed coral reefs. O'ahu, like all the Hawaiian Islands, is in essence a shield volcano that erupted rather gently, creating an elongated dome much like a turtle shell.

© AVALON TRAVEL PUBLISHING, INC.

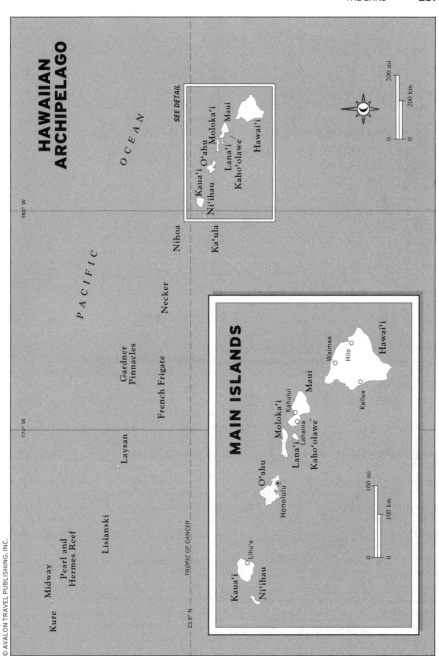

HAWAIIAN ARCHIPELAGO

PACIFIC

OCEAN

Kure

Midway

Pearl and
Hermes Reef

Lisianski

Laysan

Gardner
Pinnacles

French Frigate

Necker

Nihoa

Ka'ula

170° W

160° W

TROPIC OF CANCER

23.5° N

SEE DETAIL

Kaua'i O'ahu
Ni'ihau Moloka'i
Lana'i Maui
Kaho'olawe
Hawai'i

0   200 mi
0   200 km

MAIN ISLANDS

Kaua'i

Ni'ihau

Lihu'e

O'ahu

Honolulu

Moloka'i

Kahului

Lana'i

Lahaina

Kaho'olawe

Maui

Waimea

Hilo

Kailua

Hawai'i

0   100 mi
0   100 km

Once above sea level, its tremendous weight seals the fissure below. Eventually the giant tube that carried lava to the surface sunk in on itself and formed a caldera, as evidenced at Hanauma Bay, the famous snorkeling spot on O'ahu's southeast coast. Wind and water took over and relentlessly sculpted the raw lava into deep crevices and cuts that became valleys. The once-smooth windward O'ahu mountainside is now an undulating green monolith because of this process.

Lava

Lava flows in two distinct types, for which the Hawaiian names have become universal geological terms: **'a'a** and **pahoehoe.** They're easily distinguished in appearance, but chemically they're the same. 'A'a is extremely rough and spiny and will quickly tear up your shoes if you do much hiking over it. Also, if you have the misfortune to fall down, you'll immediately know why they call it 'a'a. Pahoehoe, a billowy, rope-like lava resembling burned pancake batter, can mold into fantastic shapes. While O'ahu has had no recent lava flows, examples of both are encountered on various hikes throughout the island.

Rivers and Lakes

O'ahu has no navigable rivers, but there are hundreds of streams. The two largest are Kaukonahua Stream, which runs through central O'ahu, and Waikele Stream, which drains the area around Schofield Barracks. A few reservoirs dot the island; Wahiawa Reservoir and Nu'uanu Pali Reservoir are both excellent freshwater fishing spots. The only sizeable and natural freshwater bodies of water on O'ahu, both altered by man, are Salt Lake in Honolulu and Enchanted Lake in Kailua. Hikers should be aware that the uncountable streams and rivulets can quickly turn from trickles to torrents, causing flash floods in valleys that were the height of hospitality only minutes before.

Tsunamis

Tsunami is the Japanese word for tidal wave. It ranks up there with the worst of them in sparking horror in human beings. But if you were to count up all the people in Hawaii who have been swept away by tidal waves in the last 50 years, the toll wouldn't come close to those killed on bicycles in only a few Mainland cities in just five years. A Hawaiian tsunami is actually a seismic sea wave that has been generated by an earthquake or landslide that could easily have originated thousands of miles away in South America or Alaska. Some waves have been clocked at speeds up to 500 mph. The safest place during a tsunami, besides high ground well away from beach areas, is out on the open ocean, where even an enormous wave is perceived only as a large swell. A tidal wave is only dangerous when it is opposed by land. The worst tsunami to strike the islands in modern times occurred on April 1, 1946. The Hana coast of Windward Maui bore the brunt with a tragic loss of many lives as entire villages were swept away; Hilo, on the Big Island, also suffered greatly.

Earthquakes

These rumblings can be a concern in Hawaii and offer a double threat because they can generate tsunamis. If you ever feel a tremor and are close to a beach, get as far away as fast as possible. O'ahu rarely experiences earthquakes, but like the other islands, it has an elaborate warning system against natural disasters. You will notice loudspeakers high atop poles along many beaches and coastal areas; these warn of tsunamis, hurricanes, and earthquakes. They are tested at 11 A.M. on the first working day of each month. All island telephone books contain a civil defense warning and procedures section with which you should acquaint yourself. Note the maps showing which areas traditionally have been inundated by tsunamis and what procedures to follow in case an emergency occurs.

CLIMATE

O'ahu, like all the Hawaiian Islands, has equitable weather year-round. The average daytime temperature in winter is about 72°F and the average summer day raises the thermometer only a few degrees to 78°F. Nighttime temperatures drop less than 10 degrees. Elevation, however, does drop temperatures about three degrees for every 1,000 feet you climb. The interior plateau of Oʻahu experiences about the same temperatures as the coastal areas because of the small difference in elevation. However, the *pali* are known for strong, cooling winds that rise up the mountainside from the coast. The coldest temperature recorded on the island was 43°F in Kaneʻohe on the Windward Coast, while the hottest was 96°F at Waiʻanae on the Leeward Coast.

Rainfall

Precipitation is the biggest differentiating factor in the climate of Oʻahu. Hardly a day goes by that it isn't raining somewhere on the island. Precipitation occurs mostly at and below the 3,000-foot level. Although rain can occur at any time of year, it's more plentiful in winter. Hawaiian rains generally aren't very nasty. Much of the time just a light drizzle, they hardly ever last all day. Mostly localized to a relatively small area, you can often spot rains by looking for the rainbows. An important rain factor is the mountains, which act like water magnets. Moist winds gather around them and eventually build rain clouds. The ancient Hawaiians used these clouds and the reflected green light on their underbellies to spot land from great distances.

Generally, the entire Leeward Coast, the "rain shadow," from Kaʻena to Koko Head, is dry. Waiʻanae, Honolulu International Airport, and Waikiki average only 20–25 inches of rain per year. The Leilehua Plateau in the center of the island does a little better at about 40 inches per year. Rain falls much more frequently and heavily in the Koʻolau Mountains and along the Windward Coast. The bay town of Kaneʻohe sees 75–90 inches per year, while the Nuʻuanu Reservoir in the mountains above Honolulu gets a whopping 120–130 inches yearly, with some years substantially greater than that. The maxim throughout the islands is "don't let rain spoil your day." If it's raining, simply move on to the next beach or around to the other side of the island where it'll probably be dry. You can

GREEN FLASH

Nearly everyone who has visited a tropical island has heard of the "green flash," but few have seen it. Some consider the green flash a fable, a made-up story by those more intent on fantasy than reality, but the green flash *is* real. This phenomenon doesn't just happen on tropical islands; it can happen anywhere around the midriff of the earth where an unobstructed view of the horizon is present, but the clear atmosphere of a tropical island environment does seem to add to its frequency. The green flash is a momentary burst of luminescent green color that happens on the horizon the instant the sun sets into the sea. If you've seen the green flash you definitely know; there is no mistaking it. If you think you saw something that might have been green but weren't sure, you probably didn't see it. Try again another day.

The green flash requires a day where the atmosphere is very clear and unobstructed by clouds, haze, or air pollutants. Follow the sun as it sinks into the sea. Be careful not to look directly at the sun until it's just about out of sight. If the conditions are right, a green color will linger at the spot where the sun sets for a fraction of a second before it too is gone. This flash is not like the flash of a camera, but more a change of color from yellow to an intense green that is instantaneous and momentary.

However romantic and magical, this phenomenon does have a scientific explanation. It seems that the green color is produced as a refraction of the sun's rays by the thick atmosphere at the extreme low angle of the horizon. This bending of the sun's light results in the green spectrum of light being the last seen before the light disappears.

Seeing the green flash is an experience. Keep looking, for no matter how many times you've seen it, each time is still full of wonder and joy.

usually depend on the beaches of Waikiki and Wai'anae to be sunny and bright. No matter where you go for that day on the beach, however, the temperature of the ocean water will run 75–80°F year-round.

As far as rainfall is concerned, some years surprise everyone—2006 was one of those years. From late February to early April, due to a low pressure system that kept the trade winds from blowing the moisture to the south, the island of O'ahu received more rain than anyone could remember. Statistics rank it as much or more than the record years of 1951 and 1925. This period saw almost continuous rain, with few breaks. Some locations on the island had 35–45 inches of rain each month! Even for Hawaii, this was unusual, and no one, visitors and locals alike, was very happy about it. April 1 brought downtown Honolulu a record-breaking amount of rain, causing widespread flooding. This was no April Fools joke!

"So Good" Weather

The ancient Hawaiians had words to describe climatic specifics such as rain, wind, fog, and even snow, but they didn't have a general word for weather. The reason is that the weather is just about the same throughout the year and depends more on where you

are on any given island than on what season it is. The Hawaiians did distinguish between *kau* (the drier and warmer summer months of May–October, with reliable trade winds from the northeast) and *ho'oilo* (the cooler and wetter winter months of November–April, with more erratic winds), but this distinction included social, religious, and even navigational factors, far beyond a mere distinction of weather variations.

The Trade Winds

Temperatures in the 50th state are both constant and moderate because of the trade winds, a breeze from the northeast that blows at about 5–15 miles per hour. These breezes are so prevailing that the northeast sides of the islands are always referred to as **Windward,** regardless of where the wind happens to blow on any given day. You can count on the trades to be blowing on an average of 300 days per year, hardly missing a day during summer and occurring half the time in winter. Although usually calm in the morning, they pick up during the heat of the afternoon, then weaken at night. Just when you need a cooling breeze, there they are, and when the temperature drops at night, it's as if someone turned down the giant fan.

O'AHU TEMPERATURE AND RAINFALL

TOWN		JAN.	MARCH	MAY	JUNE	SEPT.	NOV.
Honolulu	High	80	82	84	85	82	81
	Low	60	52	68	70	71	68
	Rain	4	2	0	0	0	4
Kane'ohe	High	80	80	80	80	82	80
	Low	67	62	68	70	70	68
	Rain	5	5	2	0	2	5
Waialua	High	79	79	81	82	82	80
	Low	60	60	61	63	62	61
	Rain	2	1	0	0	1	3

temperature in degrees Fahrenheit, rainfall in inches

HURRICANE FACTS

A **tropical depression** is a low-pressure system or cyclone with winds below 39 mph. A **tropical storm** is a cyclone with winds 39-73 mph. A **hurricane** is a cyclone with winds over 74 mph. These winds are often accompanied by torrential rains, destructive waves, high water, and storm surges.

The National Weather Service issues a **Hurricane Watch** if hurricane conditions are expected in the area within 36 hours. A **Hurricane Warning** is issued when a hurricane is expected to strike within 24 hours. The state of Hawaii has an elaborate warning system against natural disasters. You will notice loudspeakers high atop poles along many beaches and coastal areas; these warn of tsunami, hurricanes, and earthquakes. These sirens are tested briefly at the beginning of each month. As the figures below attest, property damage has been great but the loss of life has, thankfully, been minimal.

MAJOR HURRICANES SINCE 1950

NAME	DATE	ISLANDS AFFECTED	DAMAGES
Hiki	Aug. 1950	Kaua'i	1 death
Nina	Dec. 1957	Kaua'i	–
Dot	Aug. 1959	Kaua'i	$5.5 million
Fico	July 1978	Big Island	–
'Iwa	Nov. 1982	Kaua'i, O'ahu	1 death; $234 million
Estelle	July 1986	Maui, Big Island	$2 million
'Iniki	Sept. 1992	Kaua'i, O'ahu	8 deaths; $1.9 billion

The trade winds are also a factor in keeping down the humidity. They will suddenly disappear, however, usually in winter, and might not resume for a few weeks. The tropic of Cancer runs through the center of Hawaii, yet the latitude's famed oppressively hot and muggy weather is joyfully absent in the islands. Honolulu, on the same latitude as sweaty Hong Kong and Havana, has an acceptable 60–75 percent daily humidity factor.

Kona Winds

Kona means Leeward in Hawaiian, and when the trades stop blowing, these southerly winds often take over. To anyone from Hawaii, "kona wind" is a euphemism for bad weather because it brings in hot, sticky air. Luckily, kona winds are most common October–April, when they appear roughly half the time. The temperatures drop slightly during the winter, so these hot winds are tolerable, even useful for moderating the thermometer. In the summer they are awful, but luckily—again—they hardly ever blow during this season.

A kona storm is another matter. These subtropical low-pressure storms develop west of the Hawaiian Islands, and as they move east they draw winds up from the south. Common only in winter, they can cause considerable damage to crops and real estate. There is no real pattern to kona storms: Some years they come every few weeks, whereas in other years they don't appear at all.

Severe Weather

With all this talk of ideal weather, it might seem like there isn't any bad weather on O'ahu. Read on. When a storm does hit an island, conditions can be bleak and miserable. The worst storms occur in the fall and winter and often have the warped sense of humor to drop their heaviest rainfalls on areas that are normally quite dry. It's not unusual for a storm to dump more than three inches of rain per hour; this can go as high as 10 inches, making Hawaiian rainfalls some of the heaviest on earth.

Hawaii has also been hit with some walloping **hurricanes** in the last few decades. There haven't been many, but they have been destructive. Most hurricanes originate far to the southeast off the Pacific coast of Mexico and Latin America; some, particularly later in the season, start in the midst of the Pacific Ocean near the equator south of Hawaii. Hurricane season is generally considered June–November. Most hurricanes pass harmlessly south of Hawaii, but some, swept along by kona winds, strike the islands. The most recent and destructive was Hurricane 'Iniki, which battered the islands in 1992, killing eight people and causing an estimated $2 billion in damage. It had its greatest effect on Ni'ihau, the Po'ipu Beach area of Kaua'i, and the Leeward Coast of O'ahu.

Flora and Fauna

The Mystery of Migration

Anyone who loves a mystery will be intrigued by the speculation about how plants and animals first came to Hawaii. Most people's idea of an island paradise includes swaying palms, dense mysterious jungles ablaze with wildflowers, and luscious fruits just waiting to be plucked. In fact, for millions of years the Hawaiian chain consisted of raw and barren islands where no plants grew and no birds sang. Why? Because they are geological orphans that spontaneously popped up in the middle of the Pacific Ocean. The islands, more than 2,000 miles from any continental landfall, were therefore isolated from the normal ecological spread of plants and animals. Even the most tenacious travelers of the fauna and flora kingdoms would be sorely tried in crossing the mighty Pacific. Those that made it by pure chance found a totally foreign ecosystem. They had to adapt or perish. The survivors evolved quickly, and many plants and birds became so specialized that they were limited not only to specific islands in the chain but to habitats that frequently consisted of a single isolated valley. It was as if after traveling so far

and finding a niche, they never budged again. Luckily, the soil of Hawaii was virgin and rich, the competition from other plants or animals was small to nonexistent, and the climate was sufficiently varied and nearly perfect for most growing things.

The evolution of plants and animals on the isolated islands was astonishingly rapid. A tremendous change in environment, coupled with a limited gene pool, accelerated natural selection. For example, many plants lost their protective thorns and spines because there were no grazing animals or birds to destroy them. Before settlement, Hawaii had no fruits, vegetables, coconut palms, edible land animals, conifers, mangroves, or banyans. The early Polynesians brought 27 varieties of plants that they needed for food and other purposes. About 90 percent of plants on the Hawaiian Islands today were introduced after Captain Cook first set foot here. Tropical flowers, wild and vibrant as we know them today, were relatively few. In a land where thousands of orchids now brighten every corner, there were only four native varieties, the least in any of the 50 states. Today, the indigenous plants and animals have the highest rate of extinction anywhere on earth. By the beginning of the 20th century, native plants growing below 1,500 feet in elevation were almost completely extinct or totally replaced by introduced species. The land and its living things have been greatly transformed by humans and their agriculture. This inexorable process began when Hawaii was the domain of its original Polynesian settlers, then greatly accelerated when the land was inundated by Western peoples.

The indigenous plants and birds of O'ahu have suffered the same fate as those of the other Hawaiian Islands, and perhaps more so. These species are among the most endangered on earth and are disappearing at an alarming rate. Several sanctuaries on O'ahu harbor native species, but they must be vigorously protected. Do your bit to save them; enjoy but don't disturb.

FLORA
Introduced Plants

Hawaii's indigenous and endemic plants, flowers, and trees are both fascinating and beautiful, but, unfortunately, like everything else native, they are quickly disappearing. The majority of flora considered exotic by visitors was introduced either by the original Polynesians or by later white settlers. The Polynesians who colonized Hawaii brought foodstuffs, including coconuts, bananas, taro, breadfruit, sweet potatoes, yams, and sugarcane. They also carried along gourds to use as containers, 'awa to make a basic intoxicant, and the *ti* plant to use for offerings or to string into hula skirts. Non-Hawaiian settlers over the years have brought mangos, papayas, passion fruit, pineapples, and the other tropical fruits and vegetables associated with the islands. Also, most of the flowers, including protea, plumeria, anthuriums, orchids, heliconia, ginger, and most hibiscus, have come from every continent on earth. Tropical America, Asia, Java, India, and China have contributed their most beautiful and delicate blooms. Hawaii is blessed with national and state parks, gardens, undisturbed rainforests, private reserves, and commercial nurseries that offer an exhaustive botanical survey of the islands. The following is a sampling of common native and introduced flora that add the dazzling colors and exotic tastes to the landscape.

Native Trees

Koa and 'ohi'a are two indigenous trees still seen on O'ahu. Both have been greatly reduced by the foraging of introduced cattle and goats, and through logging and forest fires. The **koa,** a form of acacia, is Hawaii's finest native tree. It can grow to more than 70 feet high and has a strong, straight trunk, which can measure more than 10 feet in circumference. Koa is a quickly growing legume that fixes nitrogen in the soil. It is believed that the tree originated in Africa, where it was very damp. It then migrated to Australia, where it was very dry, which caused the elimination of leaves so that all that was left were bare stems that could survive in the desert climate. When koa came to the Pacific islands, instead of reverting to the true leaf, it just broadened its leaf stem into sickle-shaped, lifelike foliage that produces an inconspicuous, pale yellow flower. When the tree is young or damaged it will revert to the original feathery, fernlike leaf that evolved in Africa millions of years ago. The koa does best in well-drained soil in deep forest areas, but scruffy specimens will grow in poorer soil. The Hawaiians used koa as the main log for their dugout canoes, and elaborate ceremonies were performed when a log was cut and dragged to a canoe shed. Koa wood was also preferred for paddles, spears, and even surfboards. Today it is still considered an excellent furniture wood, and although fine specimens can be found in reserves, loggers are harvesting the last of the big trees.

The **'ohi'a** is a survivor and therefore the most abundant of all the native Hawaiian trees. Coming in a variety of shapes and sizes, it grows as miniature trees in wet bogs or as 100-foot giants on cool, dark slopes at higher elevations. This tree is often the first life in new lava flows. The 'ohi'a produces a tuftlike flower—usually red, but occasionally orange, yellow, or white, the latter being very rare and elusive—that resembles a natural pompon. The

PUBLIC AND PRIVATE BOTANICAL GARDENS

Honolulu Botanical Gardens comprises five separate gardens supported and maintained by the county. Three are open daily 9 A.M.-4 P.M.; two are open sunrise to sunset. No admission fee is charged, except for Foster Botanical Garden.

Foster Botanical Garden (50 N. Vineyard Blvd., Honolulu, 808/522-7066) is a 13-acre oasis of exotic trees and rare plants. Free guided tours are offered Mon.-Sat. at 1 P.M. Admission is $5 nonresidents, $1 children 6-12, and free children under 6.

Ho'omaluhia Botanical Garden (45-680 Luluku Rd., Kane'ohe, 808/233-7323) features free guided hiking tours Saturday at 10 A.M. and Sunday at 1 P.M.

Koko Crater Botanical Garden, inside Koko Crater, specializes in succulents, cacti, and other dry land plants. Open sunrise to sunset.

Lili'uokalani Botanical Garden on North Kuakini Street, Honolulu, features mostly native Hawaiian plants, Nu'uanu Stream, and Waikahalulu Waterfall. Open sunrise to sunset.

Wahiawa Botanical Garden (1396 California Ave., Wahiawa, 808/621-7321) has 27 acres of cultivated trees, flowers, and ferns from around the world.

Ha'iku Gardens (46-336 Ha'iku Rd., Kane'ohe) has many acres of flowers, ornamental trees, and a pond. There is also a restaurant on-site.

Lyon Arboretum (3860 Manoa Rd., Honolulu, 808/988-0464, open Mon.-Fri. 9 A.M.-4 P.M.) is a research facility of the University of Hawai'i. Dr. Harold Lyon planted 194 acres of trees, flowers, and bushes in the late 1800 s. Some guided tours are offered. Entrance is by donation.

Senator Fong's Plantation and Gardens (47-285 Pulama Rd., Kane'ohe, 808/239-6775, open daily 10 A.M.-4 P.M. except Christmas and New Year's Day, admission is $14.50 adults, $9 children 5-12) includes 725 acres of natural and cultivated flower, tree, palm, and fern gardens. Guided and narrated walks run several times per day.

Waimea Valley Audobon Center (808/638-9199, daily 9:30 a.m.-5 p.m., $8 adults, $5 seniors, children 4-12 and *kama'aina*) in Waimea Valley collects, grows, and preserves rare Hawaiian flora. Some flowers and plants are labeled. Afternoon guided walks are on Tuesday, Thursday, Saturday, and Sunday.

---

flower was considered sacred to Pele; it was said that she would cause a rainstorm if 'ohi'a blossoms were picked without the proper prayers. The flowers were fashioned into lei that resembled feather boas. The strong, hard wood was used to make canoes, poi bowls, and especially for temple images. 'Ohi'a logs were also used as railroad ties and shipped to the Mainland from the Big Island. It's believed that the "golden spike" linking rail lines between the U.S. East and West Coasts was driven into an 'ohi'a log from the Big Island when the two railroads came together in Ogden, Utah.

Tropical Rainforests

When it comes to pure and diverse natural beauty, the United States is one of the finest pieces of real estate on earth. As if purple mountains' majesty and fruited plains weren't enough, it even received a tiny, living emerald of tropical rainforest. A tropical rainforest is where the earth takes a breath and exhales pure sweet oxygen through its vibrant green canopy. Located in the territories of Puerto Rico and the Virgin Islands, and in the state of Hawaii, these forests comprise only one-half of one percent of the world's total, and they must be preserved. The U.S. Congress passed two bills in 1986 designed to protect the unique biological diversity of its tropical areas, but their destruction has continued unabated. The lowland rainforests of Hawaii, populated mostly of native 'ohi'a, are being razed. Landowners slash, burn, and bulldoze them to create more land for cattle and agriculture and, most distressingly, for wood chips to generate electricity! Introduced wild boar gouge the forest floor, exposing sensitive roots and leaving tiny, fetid ponds where mosquito larvae thrive. Feral goats that roam the forests are hoofed locusts that strip all vegetation within reach. Rainforests on the higher and steeper slopes of mountains have a better chance as they are harder for humans to reach. One unusual feature of Hawaii's rainforests is that they are "upside down." Most plant and animal species live on the forest floor, rather than in the canopy as in other forests.

Almost half of the birds classified in the United States as endangered live in Hawaii, and almost all of these make their home in the rainforests. We can only lament the passing of the rainforests that have already fallen to ignorance, but if this ill-fated destruction continues on the global level, we will soon be lamenting our own passing. We must nurture the rainforests that remain and, with simple enlightenment, let them be.

FAUNA

You would think that with O'ahu's dense human population, little room would be left for animals. In fact, they are environmentally stressed, but they do survive. The interior mountain slopes are home to **wild pigs,** and a small population of **feral goats** survives in the Wai'anae Range. Migrating whales pass by, especially along the Leeward Coast, where they can be observed from lookouts ranging from Waikiki to Koko Head. Half a dozen introduced game birds are found around the island, but O'ahu's real animal wealth is its indigenous birdlife.

Birds

One of the great tragedies of natural history is the continuing demise of Hawaiian bird life. Perhaps only 15 original species of birds remain of the more than 70 native families that thrived before the coming of humans. Since the arrival of Captain Cook in 1778, 23 species have become extinct, with 31 more in danger. And what's not known is how many species were wiped out before white explorers arrived.

Experts believe that the Hawaiians annihilated about 40 species, including seven species of geese, a rare one-legged owl, ibis, lovebirds, sea eagles, and honeycreepers—all gone before Captain Cook arrived. Hawaii's endangered birds account for 40 percent of the birds officially listed as endangered or threatened by the U.S. Fish and Wildlife Service. In the last 200 years, more than four times as many birds have become extinct in Hawaii as in all of North America. These figures unfortunately suggest that a full 40 percent of Hawaii's endemic birds no longer exist. Almost all of O'ahu's native birds are gone, and few indigenous Hawaiian birds can be found on any island below the 3,000-foot level.

Native birds have been reduced in number because of multiple factors. The original Polynesians helped wipe out many species. They altered large areas for farming and used fire to destroy patches of pristine forests. Also, bird feathers were highly prized for making lei, for featherwork in capes and helmets, and for the large *kahili* fans that indicated rank among the *ali'i*. Introduced exotic birds and the new diseases they carried are another major reason for reduction of native bird numbers, along with predation by the mongoose and rat—especially on ground-nesting birds. Bird malaria and bird pox were also devastating to the native species. Mosquitoes, unknown in Hawaii until a ship named the *Wellington* introduced them at Lahaina in 1826 through larvae carried in its water barrels, infected most native birds, causing a rapid reduction in birdlife. Feral pigs rooting deep in the rainforests knock over ferns and small trees, creating fetid pools in which mosquito larvae thrive. However, the most damaging factor by far is the assault on native forests by agriculture and land developers. Most Hawaiian birds evolved into specialists. They lived in only one small area and ate a very limited number of plants or insects, which once removed or altered, soon killed the birds.

The shores around O'ahu, including those off Koko Head and Sand Island but especially on the tiny islets of Moku Manu, Manana, and

O'AHU WILDLIFE REFUGES, BIRD SANCTUARIES, AND NATURE RESERVES

Two areas at opposite ends of the island and one high up in the Ko'olau Mountain Range have been set aside as national wildlife refuges (NWRs) and managed by the U.S. Fish and Wildlife Service. **James Campbell NWR,** above the town of Kahuku on the extreme northern tip, and **Pearl Harbor NWR,** in three separate units on the West Loch and Middle Loch of Pearl Harbor and at Kalaeloa near Barbers Point, were both established in the early to mid-1970s. They serve mainly as wetland habitats for the endangered **Hawaiian gallinule** ('alae'ula), **stilt** (ae'o), and **coot** ('alae ke'oke'o). Clinging to existence, these birds should have a future as long as their nesting grounds remain undisturbed. These refuges also attract a wide variety of other birds, mostly introduced species such as **cattle egrets, herons, doves, munia, cardinals,** and the **common finch,** as well as migratory birds like the **Pacific golden plover, bristle-thighed curlew,** and **wandering tattler.** In the midrange area above Pearl City and Wahiawa, the newer **O'ahu Forest NWR** has been established to protect upland native birds like the

'apapane, O'ahu 'elepaio, and pueo (Hawaiian owl), several varieties of rare tree snails, and the forest that sustains them.

Much of the area within the lowland refuges is natural marshland, but ponds, complete with water-regulating pumps and dikes, have been built. The mountain reserve is largely intact native forest. The general public is not admitted to these areas without permission from the refuge managers. For more information, and to arrange a visit to the James Campbell refuge October-February, contact Refuge Manager, O'ahu Natural Wildlife Refuge Complex (66-590 Kamehameha Hwy., Rm. 2C, Hale'iwa, HI 96712, 808/637-6330, www.fws.gov/oahurefuges).

The Nature Conservancy of Hawaii maintains two nature preserves in coordination with one public and one private owner. **Honouliuli,** a 3,582-acre tract on the southeast slope of the Wai'anae Range above Makakilo and Schofield Barracks, is home to more than 60 rare and endangered plants and animals, including a handful found nowhere else on earth. Two guided hikes into the preserve are

others on the Windward side, are home to thriving colonies of marine birds. On these diminutive islands it's quite easy to spot several birds from the **tern** family, including the white, gray, and sooty tern. All have distinctive screeching voices and wingspans of approximately 30 inches. Part of their problem is that they have little fear of humans. Along with the terns are **shearwaters.** These birds have normal wingspans of about 36 inches and make a series of moans and wails, often while in flight. For some reason shearwaters are drawn to the bright lights of the city, where they fall prey to house cats and automobiles. Sometimes Moku Manu even attracts an enormous **Laysan albatross** with its seven-foot wingspan. **Tropicbirds,** with their lovely streamerlike tails, are often seen along the Windward Coast.

To catch a glimpse of exotic birds on O'ahu you don't have to head for the sea or the hills. The city streets and beach parks are constantly aflutter with wings. Black **myna birds** with their sassy yellow eyes are common mimics around town. **Sparrows,** introduced to Hawaii through O'ahu in the 1870s, are everywhere, and **munia,** first introduced as caged birds from Southeast Asia, have escaped and can be found almost anywhere around the island. Another escaped caged bird from Asia is the **bulbul,** a natural clown that perches on any likely city roost and draws attention to itself with loud calls and generally ridiculous behavior.

If you're lucky, you can also catch a glimpse of the *pueo* (Hawaiian owl) in the mountainous areas of Wai'anae and the Ko'olau Range. Also, along trails and deep in the forest from offered once a month on Saturday or Sunday. Much smaller is the 30-acre **'Ihi'ihilauakea** preserve. In this shallow crater above Hanauma Bay at the southeastern tip of the island is a totally unique vernal pool and a rare *marsilea villosa* fern. Because of the nature of this extremely fragile ecosystem, visitation is limited. For more information on the infrequent hikes or volunteer activities, contact the Nature Conservancy (923 Nu'uanu Ave., Honolulu, HI 96817, 808/537-4508 or the hike line at 808/587-6220, www.nature .org/hawaii).

Dotting the Windward Coast from Makapu'u Point in the south to Kahuku in the north are more than a dozen small islands that compose the O'ahu section of the **Hawaii State Seabird Sanctuary.** None more than a half mile offshore, these islands are set aside to help seabirds nest, feed, and propagate, as well as to maintain native vegetation. Frequently seen on these islands are the **frigate bird, sooty tern, red-footed booby, wedge-tailed shearwater,** and **red-tailed tropicbird,** many of which lay their eggs and raise their chicks here. Others, like the wandering tattler and bristle-thighed curlew, migrate south from arctic regions to forage for food and spend the winter. Landing on Moku Manu and Manana islands is prohibited, but the rest can be visited if posted regulations are followed.

To help preserve specific land areas from greater degradation, three natural area reserves have been created on O'ahu. Lying on the coast at the western tip of the island is **Ka'ena Point Natural Area Reserve,** where natural sand dunes and low-lying shore plants predominate. It's also an area where the Laysan albatross mate and the Hawaiian monk seal is starting to return again after being driven nearly to the point of extinction. In the Wai'anae Range above Ka'ena is the lowland dry forest **Pahole Natural Area Reserve.** Here, isolated stands of native trees represent what some say is only about 10 percent of the dry-land forests that once swathed these islands. High above Pahole is **Mt. Ka'ala Natural Area Reserve.** Below the peak on this flattop mountain is a cloud forest and boggy plateau, while down its eastern slope cut deep gorges filled with drier forests. Native trees, ferns, flowers, and birds abound, and introduced plants and animals are being eradicated.

Tantalus to the Wai'anae Range you can sometimes see elusive native birds like the *'elepaio, 'amakihi,* and the fiery red *'i'iwi.*

The *'amakihi* and *'i'iwi* are endemic birds not endangered at the moment. The **'amakihi** is one of the most common native birds; yellowish green, it frequents the high branches of the 'ohi'a, koa, and sandalwood trees looking for insects, nectar, or fruit. It is less specialized than most other Hawaiian birds, the main reason for its continued existence. The *'i'iwi,* a bright red bird with a salmon-colored, hooked bill, is found in the forests above 2,000 feet. It too feeds on a variety of insects and flowers. The **'i'iwi** is known for a harsh voice that sounds like a squeaking hinge, but it's also capable of a melodious song. The feathers of the *'i'iwi* were highly prized by the *ali'i* for clothing decoration. The **'elepaio,** with its long tail (often held upright), is a fairly common five-inch brown bird (appearance can vary considerably) that can be coaxed to come within touching distance of the observer. Sometimes it will sit on lower branches above your head and scold you. This bird was the special *'aumakua* (personal spirit) of canoe builders in ancient lore. The **'apapane** is abundant in Hawaii, and being the most common native bird, is the easiest to see. It's a chubby, red-bodied bird about five inches long with a black bill, legs, wingtips, and tail feathers. It's quick and flitty and has a wide variety of calls and songs, from beautiful warbles to mechanical buzzes. Like the *'i'iwi,* its feathers were sought by Hawaiians to produce distinctive capes and helmets for the *ali'i.*

O'ahu is also home to several game birds found mostly in the dry upland forests. These include three varieties of **dove,** the **Japanese quail,** both the **green** and **ring-necked pheasant,** and **Erkel's francolin.**

MARINE LIFE
Hawaiian Whales and Dolphins

Perhaps it's their tremendous size and graceful power, coupled with a dancer's delicacy of movement, that render whales so aesthetically and emotionally captivating. In fact, many people claim that they even feel a spirit-bond to these obviously intelligent mammals that at one time shared dry land with us and then re-evolved into creatures of the great seas. Experts often remark that whales exhibit behavior akin to the highest social virtues. For example, whales rely much more on learned behavior than on instinct, one sign of a highly evolved intelligence. Gentle mothers and protective "escort" males join to teach the young to survive. They display loyalty and bravery in times of distress and innate gentleness and curiosity. Their "songs," especially those of the humpbacks, fascinate scientists and are considered a unique form of communication in the animal kingdom. Humpback whales migrate to Hawaii every year from November to May. Here, they winter, mate, give birth, and nurture their young until returning to food-rich northern waters in the spring. It's hoped that humankind can peacefully share the oceans with these magnificent giants forever. Then, perhaps, we will have taken the first step in saving ourselves.

The role of whales and dolphins in Hawaiian culture seems limited. Unlike fish, which were intimately known and individually named, only two generic names described whales: *kohola* (humpback whale) and *palaoa* (sperm whale). Dolphins were all lumped together under one name, *nai'a;* Hawaiians were known to harvest dolphins on occasion by herding them onto a beach. Whale jewelry was worn by the *ali'i.* The most coveted ornament came from a sperm whale's tooth, called a *lei niho palaoa,* which was carved into one large curved pendant. Sperm whales have more than 50 teeth, ranging in size from 4–12 inches and weighing up to two pounds. One whale could provide numerous pendants. The most famous whale in Hawaiian waters is the humpback, but others often sighted include the sperm, killer, false killer, pilot, Cuvier's, Blainsville, and pygmy killer. There are technically no porpoises, but dolphins include the common, bottlenose, spinner, white-sided, broad- and slender-beaked, and rough-toothed. The mahimahi, a favorite eating fish found on many menus, is commonly referred to as dolphin fish but is unrelated and is a true fish, not a cetacean.

Whale-Watching

If you're in Hawaii from late November to early May, you have an excellent chance of spotting a humpback. You can often see whales from a vantage point on land (good spots on O'ahu are in the southeast between Koko Head and Makapu'u Point and in the northwest off Ka'ena Point), but this is nowhere near as thrilling as seeing them close-up from a boat. Either way, binoculars are a must. Telephoto and zoom lenses are also useful, and you might even get a nifty photo in the bargain. But don't waste your film unless you have a fairly high-powered zoom: fixed-lens cameras give pictures with a lot of ocean and a tiny black speck. If you're lucky enough to see a whale breach (jump clear of the water), keep watching—they often repeat this stunt several times. If a whale dives and lifts its fluke high in the air, expect it to be down for at least 15 minutes and not come up in the same spot. Other times they'll dive shallowly, then bob up and down quite often.

History

THE ROAD FROM TAHITI
The Great Navigators

No one knows exactly when the first Polynesians arrived in Hawaii. The great "deliberate migrations" from the southern islands seem to have taken place A.D. 500–800, though anthropologists keep pushing the date backward in time as new evidence becomes available. Even before that, however, it's reasonable to assume that the first people to set foot on Hawaiian soil were probably fishermen, or perhaps defeated warriors whose canoes were blown hopelessly northward into unfamiliar waters. They arrived by a combination of extraordinary good luck and an uncanny ability to sail and navigate without instruments, using the sun by day and the moon and rising stars by night. They could feel the water and determine direction by swells, tides, and currents. The movements of fish and cloud formations were also utilized to give direction. Because their arrival was probably an accident, they were unprepared to settle on the fertile but uncultivated lands, having no stock animals, plant cuttings, or women. Forced to return southward, many undoubtedly lost their lives at sea, but a few wild-eyed stragglers must have made it home to tell tales of a paradise to the north where land was plentiful and the sea bounteous. This is affirmed by ancient navigational chants from Tahiti,

THE KUMULIPO

The great genealogies, finally compiled in the late 1800s by order of King Kalakaua, were collectively known as *The Kumulipo, A Hawaiian Creation Chant*, basically a Polynesian account of Genesis. Other chants related to the beginning of this world, but *The Kumulipo* sums it all up and is generally considered the best. The chant relates that after the beginning of time, there is a period of darkness. The darkness, however, mysteriously brims with spontaneous life; during this period plants and animals are born, as well as Kumulipo, the man, and Po'ele, the woman. In the eighth chant darkness gives way to light and the gods descend to earth. Wakea is "the sky father" and Papa is "the earth mother," whose union gives birth to the islands of Hawaii. First born is Hawai'i, followed by Maui, then Kaho'olawe. Apparently, Papa becomes bushed after three consecutive births and decides to vacation in Tahiti. While Papa is away recovering from postpartum depression and working on her tan, Wakea gets lonely and takes Ka'ula as his second wife, who bears him the island-child of Lana'i. Not fully cheered up, but getting the hang of it, Wakea takes a third wife, Hina, who promptly bears the island of Moloka'i. Meanwhile, Papa gets wind of these shenanigans, returns from Polynesia, and retaliates by taking up with Lua, a young and virile god, and soon gives birth to the island of O'ahu. Papa and Wakea finally decide that they really are meant for each other and reconcile to conceive Kaua'i, Ni'ihau, Ka'ula, and Nihoa. These two progenitors are the source from which all the *ali'i* ultimately traced their lineage, and from which they derived their god-ordained power to rule.

Basically, there are two major genealogical families: the Nanaulu, who became the royal *ali'i* of O'ahu and Kaua'i, and the Ulu, who provided the royalty of Maui and Hawai'i. The best sources of information on Hawaiian myth and legend are Martha Beckwith's *Hawaiian Mythology* and the monumental three-volume opus *An Account of the Polynesian Race*, compiled by Abraham Fornander 1878-1885. Fornander, after settling in Hawaii, married an *ali'i* from Moloka'i and had an illustrious career as a newspaperman, Maui circuit court judge, and finally Supreme Court justice. For years Fornander sent scribes to every corner of the kingdom to listen to the elder *kupuna*. They returned with the firsthand accounts, which he dutifully recorded.

Moorea, and Bora Bora, which passing from father to son revealed how to follow the stars to the "heavenly homeland in the north." Possibly a few migrations followed, but it's known that for centuries there was no real reason for a mass exodus, so the chants alone remained and eventually became shadowy legend.

From Where They Came

It's generally agreed that the first planned migrations were from the violent cannibal islands that Spanish explorers called the Marquesas, 11 islands in extreme eastern Polynesia. The islands themselves are harsh and inhospitable, breeding a toughness into these people that enabled them to withstand the hardships of long, unsure ocean voyages and years of resettlement. Marquesans were a fiercely independent people whose chiefs could rise from the ranks because of bravery or intelligence. They must also have been a fierce-looking lot. Both men and women tattooed themselves in complex blue patterns from head to foot. The warriors carried massive, intricately designed ironwood war clubs and wore carved whale teeth in slits in their earlobes that eventually stretched to the shoulders. They shaved the sides of their heads with sharks' teeth, tied their hair in two topknots that looked like horns, and rubbed their heavily muscled and tattooed bodies with scented coconut oils. Their cults worshiped mummified ancestors; the bodies of warriors of defeated neighboring tribes were consumed. They were masters at building great double-hulled canoes launched from huge canoe sheds. Two hulls were fastened together to form a catamaran, and a hut in the center provided shelter in bad weather. The average voyaging canoe was 60–80 feet long and could comfortably hold an extended family of about 30 people. These small family bands carried all the staples they would need in the new lands.

The New Lands

For five centuries the Marquesans settled and lived peacefully on the new land, as if Hawaii's *aloha* spirit overcame most of their fierceness. The tribes coexisted in relative harmony, es-

pecially because there was no competition for land. Cannibalism died out. There was much coming and going between Hawaii and Polynesia as new people came to settle for hundreds of years. Then, it appears that in the 12th century a deliberate exodus of warlike Tahitians arrived and subjugated the settled islanders. They came to conquer. This incursion had a terrific significance on the Hawaiian religious and social system. Oral tradition relates that a Tahitian priest, Pa'ao, found the *mana* of the Hawaiian chiefs to be low, signifying that their gods were weak. Pa'ao built a *heiau* at Waha'ula on the Big Island, then introduced the warlike god Ku and the rigid *kapu* system through which the new rulers became dominant. Voyages between Tahiti and Hawaii continued for about 100 years, and Tahitian customs, legends, and language became the Hawaiian way of life. Then suddenly, for no recorded or apparent reason, the voyages discontinued and Hawaii returned to total isolation.

The islands remained forgotten for almost 500 years until the indomitable English seaman, Captain James Cook, sighted O'ahu on January 18, 1778, and stepped ashore at Waimea on Kaua'i two days later. At that time Hawaii's isolation was so complete that even the Polynesians had forgotten about it. On an earlier voyage, Tupaia, a high priest from Raiatea, had accompanied Captain Cook as he sailed throughout Polynesia. Tupaia demonstrated his vast knowledge of existing archipelagoes throughout the South Pacific by naming more than 130 islands and drawing a map that included the Tonga group, the Cook Islands, the Marquesas, even tiny Pitcairn, a rock in far eastern Polynesia where the mutinous crew of the *Bounty* found solace. In mentioning the Marquesas, Tupaia said, *"He ma'a te ka'ata,"* which means "Food is man" or simply "Cannibals." But remarkably absent from Tupaia's vast knowledge was the existence of Easter Island, New Zealand, and Hawaii.

The next waves of people to Hawaii would be white, and the Hawaiian world would be changed quickly and forever.

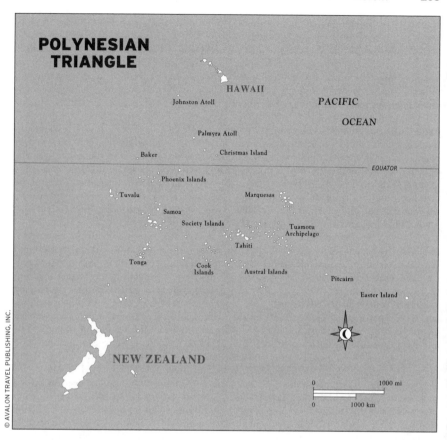

POLYNESIAN
TRIANGLE

HAWAII
Johnston Atoll

PACIFIC

OCEAN

Palmyra Atoll

Baker   Christmas Island

EQUATOR

Phoenix Islands

Tuvalu   Marquesas

Samoa
Society Islands   Tuamotu
Archipelago

Tahiti

Tonga   Cook
Islands   Austral Islands

Pitcairn

Easter Island

NEW ZEALAND

0   1000 mi

0   1000 km

© AVALON TRAVEL PUBLISHING, INC.

THE WORLD DISCOVERS HAWAII

The late 18th century was an extraordinary time in Hawaiian history. Monumental changes seemed to happen all at once. First, Captain James Cook, a Yorkshire farm boy, fulfilling his destiny as the all-time greatest Pacific explorer, found Hawaii for the rest of the world. For better or worse, it could no longer be an isolated Polynesian homeland. For the first time in Hawaiian history, a charismatic leader, Kamehameha, emerged, and after a long civil war he united all the islands into one centralized kingdom. The death of Captain Cook in Hawaii marked the beginning of a long series of tragic misunderstandings between whites and natives. When Kamehameha died, the old religious system of *kapu* came to an end, leaving the Hawaiians in a spiritual vortex. Many takers arrived to fill the void: missionaries after souls, whalers after their prey and a good time, traders and planters after profits and a home. The islands were opened and devoured like ripe fruit. Powerful nations, including Russia, Great Britain, France, and the United States, yearned to bring this strategic Pacific jewel under their own influence.

The 19th century brought the demise of the Hawaiian people as a dominant political force in their own land and with it the end of

Hawaii as a sovereign monarchy. An almost bloodless yet bitter military coup followed by a brief Hawaiian Republic ended in annexation by the United States. As the United States became completely entrenched politically and militarily, a new social and economic order was founded on the plantation system. Amazingly rapid population growth occurred with the importation of plantation workers from Asia and Europe, which yielded a unique cosmopolitan blend of races like nowhere else on earth.

By the dawning of the 20th century, the face of old Hawaii had been altered forever; the "sacred homeland in the north" was hurled into the modern age. The attack on Pearl Harbor saw a tremendous loss of life and brought Hawaii closer to the United States by a baptism of blood. Finally, on August 21, 1959, after 59 years as a "territory," Hawaii officially became the 50th state of the Union.

Captain Cook Sights Hawaii

In 1776, Captain James Cook set sail for the Pacific from Plymouth, England, on his third and final expedition into this still vastly unexplored region of the world. On a fruitless quest for the fabled Northwest Passage across the North American continent, he sailed down the coast of Africa, rounded the Cape of Good Hope, crossed the Indian Ocean, and traveled past New Zealand, Tasmania, and the Friendly Islands (where the "friendly" natives hatched an unsuccessful plot to murder him). On January 18, 1778, Captain Cook's 100-foot flagship HMS *Resolution* and its 90-foot companion HMS *Discovery* sighted O'ahu. Two days later, they sighted Kaua'i and went ashore at the village of Waimea. Although anxious to get on with his mission, Cook decided to make a quick sortie to investigate this new land and reprovision his ships. He did, however, take time to remark in his diary about the close resemblance of these newfound people to others he had encountered as far south as New Zealand and marveled at their widespread habitation across the Pacific.

The first trade was some brass medals for a mackerel. Cook also stated that he had never before met natives so astonished by a ship, and that they had an amazing fascination with iron, which they called *ko'i*, Hawaiian for adze. There is even some conjecture that a Spanish ship under one Captain Gaetano had landed in Hawaii as early as the 16th century, trading a few scraps of iron that the Hawaiians valued even more than the Europeans valued gold.

It was also noted that the Hawaiian women gave themselves freely to the sailors with the apparent good wishes of the island men. This was actually a ploy by the *kahuna* to test if the newcomers were gods or men—gods didn't need women. These sailors proved immediately mortal.

Cook was impressed with the Hawaiians' swimming ability and with their well-bred manners. They had happy dispositions and sticky fingers, stealing any object made of metal, especially nails. The first item stolen was a butcher's cleaver. An unidentified native grabbed it, plunged overboard, swam to shore, and waved his booty in triumph. The Hawaiians didn't seem to care for beads and were not at all impressed with a mirror. Cook provisioned his ships by trading chisels for hogs, while common sailors gleefully traded nails for sex. Landing parties were sent inland to fill casks with fresh water. On one such excursion a Mr. Williamson, who was eventually drummed out of the Royal Navy for cowardice, unnecessarily shot and killed a native. After a brief stop on Ni'ihau, the ships sailed away, but both groups were indelibly impressed with the memory of each other.

Cook Returns

Almost a year later, when winter weather forced Cook to return from the coast of Alaska, his discovery began to take on far-reaching significance. Cook had named Hawaii the Sandwich Islands in honor of one of his patrons, John Montague, the Earl of Sandwich. On this return voyage, he spotted Maui on November 26, 1778. After eight weeks of seeking a suitable harbor, the ships bypassed it, but not before the coastline was duly drawn by Lieutenant William Bligh, one of Cook's finest and most trusted officers. (Bligh would find his own drama almost 10 years later as commander of the infamous HMS *Bounty*.) The *Discovery* and *Resolution* finally found safe anchorage at Kealakekua Bay on the Kona coast of the Big Island. It is very lucky for history that on board was Mr. Anderson, ship's chronicler, who left a handwritten record of the strange and tragic events that followed. Even more important were the drawings of John Webber, ship's artist, who rendered invaluable impressions in superb drawings and etchings. Other noteworthy men aboard were George Vancouver, who would lead the first British return to Hawaii after Cook's death and introduce many fruits, vegetables, cattle, sheep, and goats, and James Burney, who would become a long-standing leading authority on the Pacific.

By all accounts Cook was a humane and just captain, greatly admired by his men. Unlike the many supremacists of that time, he was known to have a respectful attitude toward any people he encountered, treating them as equals and recognizing the significance of their cultures. Not known as a violent man, he would use his superior weapons against natives only in an absolute case of self-defense. His hardened crew had been at sea facing untold hardship for almost three years; returning to Hawaii was truly like reentering paradise.

A strange series of coincidences sailed with Cook into Kealakekua Bay on January 16, 1779. It was *makahiki* time, a period of rejoicing and festivity dedicated to the fertility god of the earth, Lono. Normal *kapu* days were suspended, and the Hawaiians enjoyed dancing, feasting, and the islands' version of Olympic games. It was long held in Hawaiian legend that the great god Lono would return to earth. Lono's image was a small wooden figure perched on a tall mastlike crossbeam; hanging from the crossbeam were long, white sheets of tapa. Who else could Cook be but Lono, and what else could his ships with their masts and white sails be but his sacred floating *heiau*? This explained the Hawaiians' previous fascination with his ships, but to add to the remarkable coincidence, Kealakekua Harbor happened to be considered Lono's private sacred harbor. Natives from throughout the land prostrated themselves and paid homage to the returning god. Cook was taken ashore and brought to Lono's sacred temple, where he was afforded the highest respect. The ships badly needed fresh supplies, and the Hawaiians readily gave all they had, stretching their own provisions to the limit.

The Fatal Misunderstandings

After an uproarious welcome and generous hospitality for over a month, it became obvious that the newcomers were beginning to overstay their welcome. During the interim a seaman named William Watman died, convincing the Hawaiians that the *haole* were indeed mortals, not gods. Watman was buried at Hikiau Heiau, where a plaque commemorates the event to this day. Incidents of petty theft began to increase dramatically. The lesser chiefs indicated it was time to leave by "rubbing the Englishmen's bellies." Inadvertently, many *kapu* were broken by the English, and once-friendly relations became strained. Finally, the ships sailed away on February 4, 1779.

After plying terrible seas for only a week, *Resolution*'s foremast was badly damaged. Cook sailed back into Kealakekua Bay, dragging the mast ashore on February 13. The natives, now totally hostile, hurled rocks at the sailors. Orders were given to load muskets with ball; firearms had previously only been loaded with shot and a light charge. Confrontations increased when some Hawaiians stole a small boat and Cook's men set after them, capturing the fleeing canoe, which held an *ali'i* named Palea. The Englishmen treated him roughly; to the Hawaiians' horror, they even smacked him on the head with a paddle. The Hawaiians then furiously attacked the mariners, who abandoned the small boat.

Cook Goes Down

Next the Hawaiians stole a small cutter from the *Discovery* that had been moored to a buoy and partially sunk to protect it from the sun. For the first time, Captain Cook became furious. He ordered Captain Clerk of the *Discovery* to sail to the southeast end of the bay and stop any canoe trying to leave Kealakekua. Cook then made a fatal error in judgment. He decided to take nine armed mariners ashore in an attempt to convince the venerable King Kalaniʻopuʻu to accompany him back aboard ship, where he would hold him for ransom in exchange for the cutter. The old king agreed, but his wife prevailed upon him not to trust the *haole*. Kalaniʻopuʻu sat down on the beach to think while the tension steadily grew.

Meanwhile, a group of mariners fired on a canoe trying to leave the bay, and a lesser chief, Noʻokemai, was killed. The crowd around Cook and his men reached an estimated 20,000, and warriors outraged by the killing of the chief armed themselves with clubs and protective straw-mat armor. One bold warrior advanced on Cook and struck him with his *pahoa* (dagger). In retaliation Cook drew a tiny pistol lightly loaded with shot and fired at the warrior. His bullets spent themselves on the straw armor and fell harmlessly to the ground. The Hawaiians went wild. Lieutenant Molesworth Phillips, in charge of the nine mariners, began a withering fire; Cook himself slew two natives.

Overpowered by sheer numbers, the sailors headed for boats standing offshore, while Lieutenant Phillips lay wounded. It is believed that Captain Cook, the greatest seaman ever to enter the Pacific, stood helplessly in knee-deep water instead of making for the boats because he could not swim! Hopelessly surrounded, he was knocked on the head, then countless warriors passed a knife around and hacked and mutilated his lifeless body. A sad Lieutenant King lamented in his diary, "Thus fell our great and excellent commander."

The Final Chapter

Captain Clerk, now in charge, settled his men and prevailed upon the Hawaiians to return Cook's body. On the morning of February 16 a grisly piece of charred meat was brought aboard: The Hawaiians, according to their custom, had afforded Cook the highest honor by baking his body in an underground oven to remove the flesh from the bones. On February 17, a group of Hawaiians in a canoe taunted the mariners by brandishing Cook's hat. The English, strained to the limit and thinking that Cook was being desecrated, finally broke. Foaming with blood-lust, they leveled their cannon and muskets on shore and shot anything that moved. It is believed that Kamehameha the Great was wounded in this flurry, along with four *aliʻi*, and 25 *makaʻainana* (commoners) were also killed. Finally, on February 21, 1779, the bones of Captain James Cook's hands, skull, arms, and legs were returned and tearfully buried at sea. A common seaman, one Mr. Zimmerman, summed up the feelings of all who sailed under Cook when he wrote, "… he was our leading star." The English sailed next morning after dropping off their Hawaiian girlfriends who were still aboard.

THE UNIFICATION OF OLD HAWAII

Hawaii was already in a state of political turmoil and civil war when Cook arrived. In the 1780s the islands were roughly divided into three kingdoms: venerable Kalaniʻopuʻu ruled Hawaiʻi and the Hana district of Maui; wily and ruthless warrior-king Kahekili ruled Maui, Kahoʻolawe, Lanaʻi, and later Oʻahu; and Kaeo, Kahekili's brother, ruled Kauaʻi. War ravaged the land until a remarkable chief, Kamehameha, rose and subjugated all the islands under one rule. Kamehameha initiated a dynasty that would last for about 100 years, until the independent monarchy of Hawaii forever ceased to be.

To add a zing to this brewing political stew, Westerners and their technology were beginning to come in ever-increasing numbers. In 1786, Captain Jean de François La Pérouse and his French exploration party landed in what's now La Perouse Bay, near Makena on Maui, foreshadowing European attention to the islands. In 1786 two American captains, Portlock and Dixon, made landfall in Hawaii. Also, it was known that a fortune could be made on the fur trade between the Pacific Northwest and Canton, China; stopping in Hawaii could make the trip feasible. After this was reported, the fate of Hawaii was sealed.

Hawaii under Kamehameha was ready to enter its "golden age." The social order was medieval, with the *ali'i* as knights, owing their military allegiance to the king, and the serf-like *maka'ainana* paying tribute and working the lands. The priesthood of *kahuna* filled the posts of advisors, sorcerers, navigators, doctors, and historians. This was Polynesian Hawaii at its apex. But like the uniquely Hawaiian silversword plant, the old culture blossomed, and as soon as it did, it began to wither. Ever since, all that was purely Hawaiian has been supplanted by the relentless foreign influences that began bearing down upon it.

Young Kamehameha

The greatest native son of Hawaii, Kamehameha was born under mysterious circumstances in the Kohala District of the Big Island, probably in 1753. He was royal born to Keoua Kupuapaikalaninui, the chief of Kohala, and Kekuiapoiwa, a chiefess from Kona. Accounts vary, but one claims that before his birth, a *kahuna* prophesied that this child would grow to be a "killer of chiefs." Because of this, the local chiefs conspired to murder the infant. When Kekuiapoiwa's time came, she secretly went to the royal birthing stones near Mo'okini Heiau and delivered Kamehameha. She entrusted her baby to a manservant and instructed him to hide the child. He headed for the rugged and remote coast around Kapa'au. Here Kamehameha was raised in the mountains, mostly by men. Always alone, he earned the nickname "The Lonely One."

Kamehameha was a man noticed by everyone; there was no doubt he was a force to be reckoned with. He had met Captain Cook when the *Discovery* unsuccessfully tried to land at Hana on Maui. While aboard, he made a lasting impression, distinguishing himself from the multitude of natives swarming the ships by his royal bearing. Lieutenant James King, in a diary entry, remarked that Kamehameha was a fierce-looking man, almost ugly, but that he was obviously intelligent, observant, and very good-natured. Kamehameha received his early military training from his uncle Kalani'opu'u, the great king of Hawai'i and Hana, who fought fierce battles against Alapa'i, the usurper who stole his hereditary lands. After regaining Hawai'i, Kalani'opu'u returned to his Hana district and turned his attention to conquering all of Maui. During this period, young Kamehameha distinguished himself as a ferocious warrior and earned the nickname of "the Hard-shelled Crab," even though old Kahekili, Maui's king, almost annihilated Kalani'opu'u's army at the sand hills of Wailuku.

When the old king neared death he passed on the kingdom to his son Kiwala'o. He also, however, empowered Kamehameha as the keeper of the family war god Kuka'ilimoku: Ku of the Bloody Red Mouth, Ku the Destroyer. Oddly enough, Kamehameha had been born not 500 yards from Ku's great *heiau* at Kohala and had heard the chanting and observed the ceremonies dedicated to this fierce god from his first breath. Soon after Kalani'opu'u died, Kamehameha found himself in a bitter war that he did not seek against his two cousins, Kiwala'o and his brother Keoua, with the island of Hawai'i at stake. The skirmishing lasted nine years, until Kamehameha's armies met the two brothers at Moku'ohai in an indecisive battle in which Kiwala'o was killed. The result was a shaky truce with Keoua, a much embittered enemy. During this fighting, Kahekili of Maui conquered O'ahu, where he built a house of the skulls and bones of his adversaries as a reminder of his omnipotence. He also extended his will to Kaua'i by marrying his half-brother to a high-ranking chiefess of that island. A new factor would resolve this stalemate of power—the coming of the *haole*.

The Olowalu Massacre

In 1790 the American merchant ship *Eleanora*, commanded by Yankee captain Simon Metcalfe, was looking for a harbor after its long voyage from the Pacific Northwest. Following a day behind was the *Fair American*, a tiny ship sailed by Metcalfe's son Thomas and a crew of five. Simon Metcalfe, perhaps by necessity, was a stern and humorless man who would allow no interference. While his ship was anchored at Olowalu, a beach area about five miles east of Lahaina, some natives slipped close in their canoes and stole a small boat, killing a seaman in the process. Metcalfe decided to trick the Hawaiians by first negotiating a truce and then unleashing full fury on them. Signaling he was willing to trade, he invited canoes of innocent natives to visit his ship. In the meantime, he ordered that all cannon and muskets be readied with scatter shot. When the canoes were within hailing distance, he ordered his crew to fire at will. Over 100 people were slain; the Hawaiians remembered this killing as "the Day of Spilled Brains." Metcalfe then sailed away to Kealakekua Bay and in an unrelated incident succeeded in insulting Kameiamoku, a ruling chief, who vowed to annihilate the next *haole* ship that he saw.

Fate sent him the *Fair American* and young Thomas Metcalfe. The little ship was entirely overrun by superior forces. In the ensuing battle, the mate, Isaac Davis, so distinguished himself by open acts of bravery that his life alone was spared. Kameiamoku later turned over both Davis and the ship to Kamehameha. Meanwhile, while harbored at Kealakekua, the senior Metcalfe sent John Young to reconnoiter. Kamehameha, having learned of the capture of the *Fair American,* detained Young so he could not report, and Metcalfe, losing patience, marooned his own man and sailed off to Canton. (Metcalfe never learned of the fate of his son Thomas and was later killed with another son while trading with Native Americans along the Pacific coast of the United States.) Kamehameha quickly realized the significance of his two captives and the *Fair American* with its brace of small cannons. He appropriated the ship and made Davis and Young trusted advisors, eventually raising them to the rank of chief. They would all play a significant role in the unification of Hawaii.

Kamehameha the Great

Later in 1790, supported by the savvy of Davis and Young and the cannon from the *Fair American,* which he mounted on carts, Kamehameha invaded Maui, using Hana as his power base. The island defenders under Kalanikupule, son of Kahekili who was lingering on O'ahu, were totally demoralized, then driven back into the deathtrap of 'Iao Valley. There, Kamehameha's forces annihilated them. No mercy was expected and none given, although mostly commoners were slain with no significant *ali'i* falling to the victors. So many were killed in this sheer-walled, inescapable valley that the battle was called *ka pani wai,* which means "the damming of the waters"—literally with dead bodies.

While Kamehameha was fighting on Maui, his old nemesis Keoua was busy running amok back on Hawai'i, again pillaging Kamehameha's lands. The great warrior returned home flushed with victory, but in two battles could not subdue Keoua. Finally, Kamehameha had a prophetic dream in which he was told that Ku would lead him to victory over all the lands of Hawaii if he would build a *heiau* to the war god at Kawaihae. Even before the temple was finished, old Kahekili attempted to invade Waipi'o, Kamehameha's stronghold. But Kamehameha summoned Davis and Young, and with the *Fair American* and an enormous fleet of war canoes defeated Kahekili at Waimanu. Kahekili had no choice but to accept the indomitable Kamehameha as the king of Maui, although Kahekili remained the administrative head until his death in 1794.

Now only Keoua remained in the way, and he would be defeated not by war, but by the great *mana* of Ku. While Keoua's armies were crossing the desert on the southern slopes of Kilauea, the fire goddess Pele trumpeted her disapproval and sent a huge cloud of poisonous gas and mud-ash into the air. It descended on and instantly killed the middle legions of Keoua's armies and their families. The footprints of this ill-fated army remain to this day outlined in the mud-ash as clearly as if they were deliberately encased in wet cement. Keoua's intuition told him that the victorious *mana* of the gods had swung to Kamehameha and that his own fate was sealed. Kamehameha sent word that he wanted Keoua to meet with him at Ku's newly dedicated temple in Kawaihae. Both knew that Keoua must die. Riding proudly in his canoe, the old nemesis came gloriously outfitted in the red and gold feathered cape and helmet signifying his exalted rank. When he stepped ashore he was felled by Kamehameha's warriors. His body was ceremoniously laid on the altar, along with 11 others who were slaughtered and dedicated to Ku, of the Maggot-dripping Mouth.

Increasing Contact

By the time Kamehameha had won the Big Island, Hawaii was becoming a regular stopover for numerous ships seeking the lucrative sandalwood trade with China. In February 1791, Captain George Vancouver, still seeking the Northwest Passage, returned to Kealakekua, where he was greeted by a throng of 30,000.

The captain at once recognized Kamehameha, who was wearing a Chinese dressing gown that he had received in tribute from another chief, who in turn had received it directly from the hands of Cook himself. The diary of a crew member, Thomas Manby, relates that Kamehameha, missing his front teeth, was more fierce-looking than ever as he approached the ship in an elegant double-hulled canoe sporting 46 rowers. The king invited all to a great feast prepared for them on the beach. Kamehameha's appetite matched his tremendous size. It was noted that he ate two sizable fish, a king-size bowl of poi, a small pig, and an entire baked dog. Kamehameha personally entertained the English by putting on a mock battle in which he deftly avoided spears by rolling, tumbling, and catching them in midair, all the while hurling his own spear a great distance. The English reciprocated by firing cannon bursts into the air, creating an impromptu fireworks display. Kamehameha requested from Vancouver a full table setting, with which he was provided, but his request for firearms was prudently denied.

Captain Vancouver became a trusted advisor of Kamehameha and told him about the white man's form of worship. He even interceded for Kamehameha with his headstrong queen, Ka'ahumanu, and coaxed her from her hiding place under a rock when she sought refuge at Pu'uhonua O Honaunau. The captain gave gifts of beef cattle, fowl, and breeding stock of sheep and goats. The ship's naturalist, Archibald Menzies, was the first *haole* to climb Mauna Kea; he also introduced a large assortment of fruits and vegetables. The Hawaiians were cheerful and outgoing, and they showed remorse when they indicated that the remainder of Cook's bones had been buried in a temple close to Kealakekua. John Young, by this time firmly entrenched in Hawaiian society, made no request to sail away with Vancouver. During the next two decades of Kamehameha's rule, the French, Russians, English, and Americans discovered the great whaling waters off Hawaii. Their increasing visits shook and finally tumbled the ancient religion and social order of *kapu*.

Finishing Touches

After Keoua was laid to rest, it was only a matter of time until Kamehameha consolidated his power over all of Hawaii. In 1794 the old warrior Kahekili of Maui died and gave O'ahu to his son Kalanikupule, while Kaua'i and Ni'ihau went to his brother Kaeo. In wars between the two, Kalanikupule was victorious, though he did not possess the grit of his father nor the great *mana* of Kamehameha. He had previously murdered a Captain Brown, who had anchored in Honolulu, and seized his ship, the *Jackall*. With the aid of this ship, Kalanikupule now determined to attack Kamehameha. However, while en route, the sailors regained control of their ship and cruised to the Big Island to inform and join with Kamehameha. An army of 16,000 was raised and sailed for Maui, where they met only token resistance, destroyed Lahaina, pillaged the countryside, and vanquished Moloka'i in one bloody battle.

The war canoes next sailed for O'ahu and the final showdown. The great army landed at Waikiki, and although defenders fought bravely, giving up Oʻahu by the inch, they were steadily driven into the surrounding mountains. The beleaguered army made its last stand at Nuʻuanu Pali, a great precipice in the mountains behind present-day Honolulu. Kamehameha's warriors mercilessly drove the enemy into the great abyss. Kalanikupule, who hid in the mountains, was captured after a few months and sacrificed to Ku, The Snatcher of Lands, thereby ending the struggle for power.

Kamehameha put down a revolt on Hawaiʻi in 1796. The king of Kauaʻi, Kaumualiʻi, accepted the inevitable and recognized Kamehameha as supreme ruler without suffering the ravages of a needless war. Kamehameha, for the first time in Hawaiian history, was the undisputed ruler of all the islands of "the heavenly homeland in the north."

Kamehameha's Rule

Kamehameha was as gentle in victory as he was ferocious in battle. Under his rule, which lasted until his death on May 8, 1819, Hawaii enjoyed a peace unlike any the warring islands had ever known. The king moved his royal court to Lahaina, where in 1803 he built the Brick Palace, the first permanent building of Hawaii. The benevolent tyrant also enacted the "Law of the Splintered Paddle." This law, which protected the weak from the exploitation of the strong, had its origins in an incident of many years before. A brave defender of a small overwhelmed village had broken a paddle over Kamehameha's head and taught the chief—literally in one stroke—about the nobility of the commoner.

Just as Old Hawaii reached its golden age, however, its demise was at hand. The relentless waves of *haole* both innocently and determinedly battered the old ways into the ground. With the foreign ships came prosperity and fanciful new goods after which the *aliʻi* lusted. The *makaʻainana* were worked mercilessly to provide sandalwood for the China trade. This was the first "boom" economy to hit the islands, but it set the standard of exploitation that would follow. Kamehameha built an ob-

servation tower in Lahaina to watch for ships, many of which were his own, returning laden with riches from the world at large.

In the last years of his life Kamehameha returned to his beloved Kona coast, where he enjoyed the excellent fishing that is renowned to this day. He had taken Hawaii from the darkness of warfare into the light of peace. He died true to the religious and moral *kapu* of his youth, the only ones he had ever known, and with him died a unique way of life. Two loyal retainers buried his bones after the baked flesh had been ceremoniously stripped away. A secret burial cave was chosen so that no one could desecrate the remains of the great chief, thereby absorbing his *mana*. The tomb's whereabouts remain unknown, and disturbing the dead remains one of the strictest *kapu* to this day. "The Lonely One's" kingdom would pass to his son, Liholiho, but true power would be in the hands of his beloved but feisty wife Kaʻahumanu. As Kamehameha's spirit drifted from this earth, two forces sailing around Cape Horn would forever change Hawaii: the missionaries and the whalers.

MISSIONARIES AND WHALERS

The year 1819 was of the utmost significance in Hawaiian history. It marked the death of Kamehameha, the overthrow of the ancient *kapu* system, the arrival of the first whaler in Lahaina, and the departure of Calvinist missionaries from New England determined to convert the heathen islands. Great changes began to rattle the old order to its foundations. With the *kapu* system and all of the ancient gods abandoned (except for the fire goddess Pele of Kilauea), a great void permeated the souls of the Hawaiians. In the coming decades Hawaii, also coveted by Russia, France, and England, was finally consumed by America. The islands had the first American school, printing press, and newspaper west of the Mississippi. Lahaina, in its heyday, became the world's greatest whaling port, accommodating more than 500 ships of all types during its peak years.

The Royal Family

Maui's Hana District provided Hawaii with one of its greatest queens, Ka'ahumanu, born in 1768 in a cave within walking distance of Hana Harbor. At the age of 17 she became the third of Kamehameha's 21 wives and eventually the love of his life. At first she proved totally independent and unmanageable and was known to openly defy her king by taking numerous lovers. Kamehameha placed a *kapu* on her body and even had her attended by horribly deformed hunchbacks in an effort to curb her carnal appetites, but she continued to flout his authority. Young Ka'ahumanu had no love for her great, lumbering, unattractive husband, but in time (even Captain Vancouver was pressed into service as a marriage counselor) she learned to love him dearly. She in turn became his favorite wife, although she remained childless throughout her life. Kamehameha's first wife was the supremely royal Keopuolani, who so outranked even him that the king had to approach her crawling on his belly. Keopuolani produced the royal children Liholiho and Kauikeaouli, who became King Kamehameha II and III, respectively. Just before Kamehameha I died in 1819 he appointed Liholiho his successor, but he also had the wisdom to make Ka'ahumanu the *kuhina nui* or queen regent. Initially, Liholiho was weak and became a drunkard. Later he became a good ruler, but he was always supported by his royal mother, Keopuolani, and by the ever-formidable Ka'ahumanu.

Kapu Is Pau

Ka'ahumanu was greatly loved and respected by the people. On public occasions, she donned Kamehameha's royal cloak and spear and, so attired and infused with the king's *mana,* she demonstrated that she was the real leader of Hawaii. For six months after Kamehameha's death, Ka'ahumanu counseled Liholiho on what he must do. The wise *kuhina nui* knew that the old ways were *pau* (finished) and that Hawaii could not hope to function in a rapidly changing world under the *kapu* system. In November 1819, Ka'ahumanu and Keopuolani prevailed on Liholiho to break two of the oldest and most sacred *kapu* by eating with women and by allowing women to eat previously forbidden foods, such as bananas and certain fish. Heavily fortified with strong drink and attended by other high-ranking chiefs and a handful of foreigners, Ka'ahumanu and Liholiho ate together in public. This feast became known as *'Ai Noa* (Free Eating). As the first morsels passed Ka'ahumanu's lips, the ancient gods of Hawaii tumbled. Throughout the land, revered *heiau* were burned and abandoned and the idols knocked to the ground. Now the people had nothing but their weakened inner selves to rely on. Nothing and no one could answer their prayers; their spiritual lives were empty and in shambles.

Missionaries

Into this spiritual vortex sailed the brig *Thaddeus* on April 4, 1820. It had set sail from Boston on October 23, 1819, lured to the Big Island by Henry Opukaha'ia, a local boy born at Napo'opo'o in 1792, who had earlier been taken to New England. Coming ashore in Kailua-Kona, where Liholiho had moved the royal court, the Reverends Bingham and Thurston were granted a one-year, trial missionary period by King Liholiho. They established themselves on Hawai'i and O'ahu and from there began the transformation of Hawaii. The missionaries were people of God, but also practical-minded Yankees. They brought education, enterprise, and most important a commitment to stay and build. By 1824, the new faith had such a foothold that Chieftess Keopuolani climbed to the firepit atop Kilauea and defied Pele. This was even more striking than the previous breaking of the food *kapu* because the strength of Pele could actually be seen. Keopuolani ate forbidden *'ohelo* berries and cried out, "Jehovah is my God." Over the next decades the governing of Hawaii slipped away from the Big Island and moved to the new port cities of Lahaina on Maui and, later, Honolulu.

Rapid Conversions

The year 1824 also marked the death of Keopuolani, who was given a Christian burial.

She had set the standard by accepting Christianity, and several of the *ali'i* had followed the queen's lead. Liholiho had sailed off to England, where he and his wife contracted measles and died. Their bodies were returned by the British in 1825, on the HMS *Blonde* captained by Lord Byron, cousin of *the* Lord Byron. During these years, Ka'ahumanu allied herself with Reverend Richards, pastor of the first mission in the islands, and together they wrote Hawaii's first code of laws based on the Ten Commandments. Foremost was the condemnation of murder, theft, brawling, and the desecration of the Sabbath by work or play. The early missionaries had the best of intentions, but like all zealots they were blinded by the single-mindedness that was also their greatest ally. They were not surgically selective in their destruction of native beliefs. *Anything* native was felt to be inferior, and they set about wiping out all traces of the old ways. In their rampage they reduced the Hawaiian culture to ashes, plucking self-will and determination from the hearts of a once-proud people. More so than the whalers, they terminated the Hawaiian way of life.

The Early Seamen

A good portion of the common seamen of the early 19th century came from the dregs of the Western world. Many a whoremongering drunkard had awoken from a stupor and found himself on the pitching deck of a ship, discovering to his dismay that he had been "pressed into naval service." For the most part, these sailors were a filthy, uneducated, lawless rabble. Their present situation was dim, their future hopeless, and they would live to be 30 if they were lucky and didn't die from scurvy or a thousand other miserable fates. They snatched brief pleasure in every port and jumped ship at any opportunity, especially in an easy berth like Lahaina. They displayed the worst elements of Western culture, which the Hawaiians naively mimicked. In exchange for *aloha* they gave drunkenness, sloth, and insidious death by disease. By the 1850s, the population of native Hawaiians tumbled from the estimated 300,000 reported by Captain Cook in 1778 to barely 60,000. Common conditions such as colds, flu, venereal disease, and sometimes smallpox and cholera devastated the Hawaiians, who had no natural immunities to these foreign ailments. By the time the missionaries arrived, *hapa haole* children were common in Lahaina streets.

The earliest merchant ships to the islands were owned or skippered by lawless opportunists who had come seeking sandalwood after first filling their holds with furs from the Pacific Northwest. Aided by *ali'i* hungry for manufactured goods and Western finery, they raped Hawaiian forests of this fragrant wood so coveted in China. Next, droves of sailors came in search of whales. The whalers, decent men at home, left their morals back in the Atlantic and lived by the slogan "no conscience east of the Cape." The delights of Hawaii were just too tempting for most.

Two Worlds Tragically Collide

The 1820s were a time of confusion and soul-searching for the Hawaiians. When Kamehameha II died, the kingdom passed to Kauikeaouli (Kamehameha III), who made his lifelong residence in Lahaina. The young king was only nine years old when the title passed to him, but his power was secure because Ka'ahumanu was still a vibrant *kuhina nui*. The young prince, more so than any other, was raised in the cultural confusion of the times. His childhood was spent during the very cusp of the change from old ways to new, and he was often pulled in two directions by vastly differing beliefs. Since he was royal born, he was bound by age-old Hawaiian tradition to mate and produce an heir with the highest-ranking *ali'i* in the kingdom. This mate happened to be his younger sister, Princess Nahi'ena'ena. To the old Hawaiian advisors, this arrangement was perfectly acceptable and encouraged. To the increasingly influential missionaries, incest was an unimaginable abomination in the eyes of God. The problem was compounded by the fact that Kamehameha III and Nahi'ena'ena were drawn to each other and were deeply in love. The young king could not stand the mental pressure imposed by conflicting worlds. He became a teenage alcoholic too royal to be restrained by anyone in the kingdom, and his bouts of drunkenness and womanizing were both legendary and scandalous.

Meanwhile, Nahiʻenaʻena was even more pressured because she was a favorite of the missionaries, baptized into the church at age 12. She too vacillated between the old and the new. At times she was a pious Christian, at others she drank all night and took numerous lovers. As the prince and princess grew into their late teens, they became even more attached to each other and hardly made an attempt to keep their relationship from the missionaries. Whenever possible, they lived together in a grass house built for the princess by her father.

In 1832, the great Kaʻahumanu died, leaving the king on his own. In 1833, at the age of 18, Kamehameha III announced that the "regency" was over and that all the lands in Hawaii were his, personally, and that he alone was the ultimate law. Almost immediately, however, he decreed that his half sister Kinaʻu would be "premier," signifying that he would leave the actual running of the kingdom in her hands. Kamehameha III fell into total drunken confusion, until one night he attempted suicide. After this episode he seemed to straighten up a bit and mostly kept a low profile. In 1836, Princess Nahiʻenaʻena was convinced by the missionaries to take a husband. She married Leleiohoku, a chief from the Big Island, but continued to sleep with her brother. It is uncertain who fathered the child, but Nahiʻenaʻena gave birth to a baby boy in September 1836. The young prince survived for only a few hours, and Nahiʻenaʻena never recovered from the complications. She died in December 1836 and was laid to rest in the mausoleum next to her mother, Keopuolani, on the royal island in Mokuhina Pond in Lahaina. After the death of his sister, Kamehameha III became a sober and righteous ruler. Often seen paying his respects at the royal mausoleum, he ruled longer than any other king until his death in 1854.

The Missionaries Prevail

In 1823, the first mission was established in Lahaina, Maui, under the pastorate of Reverend Richards and his wife. Within a few years, many of the notable *aliʻi* had been, at least in appearance, converted to Christianity. By 1828 the cornerstones for Waineʻe Church, the first stone church on the island, were laid just behind the palace of Kamehameha III. The struggle between missionaries and whalers centered on public drunkenness and the servicing of sailors by local native girls. The normally god-fearing whalers had signed on for perilous duty that lasted up to three years, and when they anchored in Lahaina they demanded their pleasure. The missionaries were instrumental in placing a curfew on sailors and prohibiting native women from boarding ships, which had become customary. These measures certainly did not stop the liaisons between sailor and *wahine*, but they did impose a modicum of social sanction and tolled the end of the wide-open days. The sailors were outraged; in 1825 the crew from the *Daniel* attacked the home of the meddler, Reverend Richards. A year later a similar incident occurred. In 1827, confined and lonely sailors from the whaler *John Palmer* fired their cannon at Reverend Richards' newly built home.

Slowly the tensions eased, and by 1836 many sailors were regulars at the Seamen's Chapel, adjacent to the Baldwin Home. Unfortunately, even the missionaries couldn't stop the pesky mosquito from entering the islands through the port of Lahaina. The mosquitoes arrived from Mexico in 1826 aboard the merchant ship *Wellington*. They were inadvertently carried as larvae in the water barrels and democratically pestered everyone in the islands from that day forward regardless of race, religion, or creed.

Foreign Influence

By the 1840s, Honolulu was becoming the center of commerce in the islands; when Kamehameha III moved the royal court there from Lahaina, the ascendant fate of the new capital was guaranteed. In 1843, Lord Paulet, commander of the warship *Carysfort*, forced Kamehameha III to sign a treaty ceding Hawaii to the British. London, however, repudiated this act, and Hawaii's independence was restored within a few months when Queen Victoria sent Admiral Thomas as her personal agent of good intentions. The king memorialized the turn of events by a speech in which he uttered the phrase, *"Ua mau ke e'a o ka'aina i ka pono,"* ("The life of the land is preserved in righteousness"), now Hawaii's motto. The French used similar bullying tactics to force an unfavorable treaty on the Hawaiians in 1839; as part of these heavy-handed negotiations they exacted a payment of $20,000 and the right of Catholics to enjoy religious freedom in the islands. In 1842 the United States recognized and guaranteed Hawaii's independence without a formal treaty, and by 1860 over 80 percent of the islands' trade was with the United States.

The Great Mahele

In 1840, Kamehameha III ended his autocratic rule and instituted a constitutional monarchy. This brought about the Hawaiian Bill of Rights, but the most far-reaching change was the transition to private ownership of land. Formerly, all land belonged to the ruling chief, who gave wedge-shaped parcels called *ahupua'a* to lesser chiefs to be worked for him. The commoners did all the real labor, their produce heavily taxed by the *ali'i*. The fortunes of war, the death of a chief, or the mere whim of a superior could force a commoner off the land. The Hawaiians, however, could not think in terms of owning land. No one could *possess* land, one could only *use* land, and its ownership was a foreign concept. As a result, naive Hawaiians gave up their lands for a song to unscrupulous traders, and land ownership issues remains a basic and unrectified problem to this day. In 1847 Kamehameha III and his advisors separated the lands of Hawaii into three groupings: crown land (belonging to the king), government land (belonging to the chiefs), and the people's land (the largest parcels). In 1848, 245 *ali'i* entered their land claims in the *Mahele Book,* assuring them ownership. In 1850 the commoners were given title in fee simple to the lands they cultivated and lived on as tenants, not including house lots in towns. Commoners without land could buy small *kuleana* (farms) from the government at 50 cents per acre. In 1850, foreigners were also allowed to purchase land in fee simple, and the ownership of Hawaii from that day forward slipped steadily from the hands of its indigenous people.

KING SUGAR

It's hard to say just where the sugar industry began in Hawaii. The Koloa Sugar Plantation on the southern coast of Kaua'i successfully refined sugar in 1835. Others tried, and one success was at Hana, Maui, in 1849. A whaler named George Wilfong hauled four blubber pots ashore and set them up on a rocky hill in the middle of 60 acres he had planted in sugar. A team of oxen turned "crushing rollers," and the cane juice flowed down an open trough into the pots, under which an attending native kept a roaring fire burning. Wilfong's methods of refining were crude, but the resultant high-quality sugar turned a neat profit in Lahaina. The main problem was labor. The Hawaiians hired for this work were basically indentured workers. They made excellent whalers but did not do well for such long and tiring hours on the soil. They became extremely disillusioned with their contracts, which could last up to 10 years. Most of their wages were eaten up by manufactured commodities sold at the company store, and it didn't take long for them to realize that they were little more than slaves. At every opportunity they either left the area or just refused to work.

Imported Labor

The **Masters and Servants Act of 1850,** which allowed importation of laborers under the contract system, ostensibly guaranteed an endless supply of cheap labor for the plantations. Chinese laborers were imported but were too enterprising to remain in the fields for a meager $3 per month. They left as soon as opportunity permitted and went into business as small merchants and retailers. In the meantime, Wilfong had sold out, releasing most of the Hawaiians previously held under contract, and his plantation fell into disuse. In 1860, two Danish brothers, August and Oscar Unna, bought land at Hana to raise sugar. They solved the labor problem by importing Japanese laborers, who were extremely hardworking and easily managed. The workday lasted 10 hours, six days a week, for a salary of $20 per month, with housing and medical care. Plantation life was very structured, with stringent rules governing even bedtimes and lights out. A worker could be fined for being late or for smoking on the job. The workers had great difficulty functioning under these circumstances, and improvements in benefits and housing were slowly gained.

Sugar Grows

The demand for "Sandwich Island Sugar" grew as California was populated during the gold rush and increased dramatically when the American Civil War required a constant supply. The only sugar plantations on the Mainland were small plots confined to the Confederate states, whose products could hardly be bought by the Union and whose fields were destroyed later in the war. By the 1870s it was clear to the planters, still mainly New Englanders, that the United States was their market; they tried often to gain closer ties and favorable tariffs. The Americans also planted rumors that the British were interested in annexing Hawaii; this put pressure on the U.S. Congress to pass the long-desired **Reciprocity Act,** which would exempt sugar from import duty. It finally passed in 1875, in exchange for U.S. long-term rights to use the strategic naval port of Pearl Harbor, among other concessions. These agreements gave increased political power to a small group of American planters, whose outlooks were similar to the post–Civil War South, where a few powerful whites were the virtual masters of a multitude of dark-skinned laborers. Sugar was now big business, and the Hana District alone exported almost 3,000 tons per year. All of Hawaii would have to reckon with the "sugar barons."

Changing Society

The sugar plantation system changed life in Hawaii physically, spiritually, politically, and economically. Now boatloads of workers came not only from Japan but also from Portugal, Germany, and even Russia. The white-skinned workers were most often the field foremen *(luna)*. With the immigrants came new religions, new animals and plants, unique cuisines, and a plantation language known as pidgin, or *da'kine*. Many Asians, and to a lesser extent the other groups—including the white plantation owners—intermarried with Hawaiians. A new class of people properly termed "cosmopolitan" but more familiarly and aptly known as "locals" was emerging. These were the people of multiple-race backgrounds who couldn't exactly say *what* they were, but it was clear to all just *who* they were. The plantation owners became the new "chiefs" of Hawaii who would carve up the land and dispense favors. The Hawaiian monarchy was soon eliminated.

A KINGDOM PASSES
The Beginning of the End

Like the Hawaiian people themselves, the Kamehameha dynasty in the mid-1800s was dying from within. King Kamehameha IV (Alexander Liholiho) ruled 1854–1863; his only child died in 1862. He was succeeded by his older brother Kamehameha V (Lot Kamehameha), who ruled until 1872. With his passing the Kamehameha line ended. William Lunalilo, elected king in 1873 by popular vote, was of royal, but not Kamehameha, lineage. He died after only a year in office, and being a bachelor left no heirs. He was succeeded by David Kalakaua, known far and wide as the "Merrie Monarch," who made a world tour and was well received wherever he went. He built 'Iolani Palace in Honolulu and was personally in favor of closer ties with the United States, helping push through the Reciprocity Act. Kalakaua died in 1891 and was replaced by his sister, Lydia Lili'uokalani, last of the Hawaiian monarchs.

The Revolution

When Lili'uokalani took office in 1891, the native population was at a low of 40,000, and she felt that the United States had too much

The King David Kalakaua statue stands along Kalakaua Avenue in Waikiki.

influence over her homeland. She was known to personally favor the English over the Americans. She attempted to replace the liberal constitution of 1887 (adopted by her pro-American brother) with an autocratic mandate in which she would have had much more political and economic control of the islands. When the McKinley Tariff of 1890 brought a decline in sugar profits, she made no attempt to improve the situation. Thus the planters saw her as a political obstacle to their economic growth; most of Hawaii's American planters and merchants were in favor of a rebellion. She would have to go! A central spokesperson and firebrand was Lorrin Thurston, a Honolulu publisher who, with a core of about 30 men, challenged the Hawaiian monarchy. Although Lili'uokalani rallied some support and had a small military potential in her personal guard, the coup was ridiculously easy—it took only one casualty. Captain John Good shot a Hawaiian policeman in the arm and that did it. Naturally, the conspirators could not have succeeded without some solid assurances from a secret contingent in the U.S. Congress as well as outgoing President Benjamin Harrison, who favored Hawaii's annexation. Marines from the *Boston* went ashore to "protect American lives," and on January 17, 1893, the Hawaiian monarchy came to an end.

The provisional government was headed by Sanford B. Dole, who became president of the Hawaiian Republic. Lili'uokalani surrendered not to the conspirators, but to U.S. Ambassador John Stevens. She believed that the U.S. government, which had assured her of Hawaiian independence, would be outraged by the overthrow and would come to her aid. Incoming President Grover Cleveland *was* outraged, and Hawaii wasn't immediately annexed as expected. When queried about what she would do with the conspirators if she were reinstated, Lili'uokalani said that they would be hung as traitors. The racist press of the times, which portrayed the Hawaiians as half-civilized, bloodthirsty heathens, publicized this widely. Because the conspirators were the leading citizens of the land, the queen's words proved untimely. In January 1895, a small, ill-fated counterrevolution headed by Lili'uokalani failed, and she was placed under house arrest in 'Iolani Palace. Officials of the Republic insisted that she use her married name (Mrs. John Dominis) to sign the documents forcing her to abdicate her throne. She was also forced to swear allegiance to the new Republic. Lili'uokalani went on to write *Hawaii's Story* and the lyric ballad "Aloha O'e." She never forgave the conspirators and remained queen to the Hawaiians until her death in 1917.

Annexation

An overwhelming majority of Hawaiians opposed annexation and desired to restore the monarchy, but they were prevented from voting by the new Republic because they couldn't meet the imposed property and income qualifications—a transparent ruse by the planters to control the majority. Most *haole* were racist and believed that the "common people" could not be entrusted with the vote because they were childish and incapable of ruling themselves. The fact that the Hawaiians had existed quite well for 1,000 years before white people even reached Hawaii was never considered. The Philippine theater of the Spanish-American War also prompted annexation. One of the strongest proponents was Alfred Mahon, a brilliant naval strategist who, with support from Theodore Roosevelt, argued that the U.S. military must have Hawaii in order to be a viable force in the Pacific. In addition, Japan, victorious in its recent war with China, protested the American intention to annex, and in so doing prompted even moderates to support annexation in fear that the Japanese themselves coveted the prize. On July 7, 1898, President McKinley signed the annexation agreement, and this "tropical fruit" was finally put into America's basket.

MODERN TIMES

Hawaii entered the 20th century totally transformed from what it had been. The old Hawaiian language, religion, culture, and leadership were all gone. Western dress, values, education, and recreation were the norm. Native Hawaiians were now unseen citizens who lived in dwindling numbers in remote areas. The plantations, new centers of social order, had a strong Asian flavor; more than 75 percent of the workforce was Asian. There was a small white middle class, an all-powerful white elite, and a single political party ruled by that elite. Education, however, was always highly prized, and by the late 1800s all racial groups were encouraged to attend school. By 1900, almost 90 percent of Hawaiians were literate (far above the national norm), and schooling was mandatory for all children ages 6–15. Intermarriage was accepted, and there was a mixing of the races like nowhere else on earth.

The military became increasingly important to Hawaii. It brought in money and jobs, dominating the islands' economy. The Japanese attack on Pearl Harbor, which began U.S. involvement in World War II, bound Hawaii to America forever. Once the islands had been baptized by blood, the average Mainlander felt that Hawaii was American soil. A movement among Hawaiians to become part of the United States began to grow. They wanted a real voice in Washington, not merely a voteless delegate as provided under their territory status. Hawaii became the 50th state in 1959, and the jumbo-jet revolution of the 1960s made it easily accessible to growing numbers of tourists from all over the world.

Pearl Harbor Attack

On the morning of December 7, 1941, the Japanese carrier *Akagi*, flying the battle flag of the famed Admiral Togo of the Russo-Japanese War, received and broadcast over its public address system island music from Honolulu station KGMB. Deep in the bowels of the ship a radioman listened for a much different message, coming thousands of miles from the Japanese mainland. When the ironically poetic message "east wind rain" was received, the attack was launched. At the end of the day, 2,325 U.S. servicemen and 57 civilians were dead; 188 planes were destroyed; 18 major warships were sunk or heavily damaged; and the United States was in the war. Japanese casualties were ludicrously light. The ignited conflict would rage for four years until Japan, through the atomic bombing of Nagasaki and Hiroshima, was vaporized into total submission. At the end of hostilities, Hawaii would never again be considered separate from America.

Statehood

Several economic and political reasons explain why the ruling elite of Hawaii desired statehood, but put simply, the vast majority of people who lived there, especially after World War II, considered themselves Americans. The first serious mention of making the Sandwich Islands a state was in the 1850s under President Franklin Pierce, but the idea wasn't taken seriously until the monarchy was overthrown in the 1890s. For the next 50 years statehood proposals were made repeatedly to Congress, but there was stiff opposition, especially from the southern states. With Hawaii a territory, an import quota system beneficial to Mainland producers could be enacted on produce, especially sugar. Also, there was prejudice against creating a state in a place where the majority of the populace was not white.

During World War II, Hawaii was placed under martial law, but no serious attempt to intern the Japanese population was made, as in California. There were simply too many Japanese, and many went on to gain the respect of the American people through their outstanding fighting record during the war. Hawaii's own 100th Battalion became the famous 442nd Regimental Combat Team, which gained notoriety by saving the Lost Texas Battalion during the Battle of the Bulge and went on to be *the* most decorated battalion in all of World War II. When these GIs returned home, *no one* was going to tell them that they were not loyal Americans. Many of these Americans of Japanese Ancestry (AJAs) took advantage of the GI Bill and received higher education. They were from the common people, not the elite, and they rallied grassroots support for statehood. When the vote finally occurred, approximately 132,900 voted in favor of statehood with only 7,800 votes against. Congress passed the Hawaii State Bill on March 12, 1959, and on August 21, 1959, President Eisenhower announced that Hawaii was officially the 50th state.

Government

The only difference between the government of the state of Hawaii and those of other states is that it's streamlined, and in theory more efficient. There are only two levels of government: the state and the county. With no town or city governments to deal with, considerable bureaucracy is eliminated. Hawaii, in anticipation of becoming a state, drafted a constitution in 1950 and was ready to go when statehood came. Politics and government are taken seriously in the Aloha State, which at one time consistently turned in the best national voting record per capita. For example, in the first state elections 173,000 of 180,000 registered voters voted—a whopping 94 percent of the electorate. These days, Hawaiians give greater importance to and show greater turnout for state elections. Because of Hawaii's location in the far west, when presidential elections are held, the results are often known before many in the state have time to cast their ballots. In the election to ratify statehood, hardly a ballot went uncast, with 95 percent of the voters opting for statehood. The bill carried every island of Hawaii except Ni'ihau, where most of the people (total population 250 or so) were of relatively pure Hawaiian blood. When Hawaii became a state, Honolulu became its capital. Since statehood, the legislative and executive branches of state government have been dominated by the Democratic party. Breaking a 40-year Democratic hold on power in the state and becoming the first woman to hold the position, former Maui mayor and Republican Linda Lingle was elected as governor in 2002 and reelected in 2006. Hawaii is represented in the U.S Congress by two senators, currently Daniel K. Inouye (D) and Daniel K. Akaka (D), and two representatives, currently Neil Abercrombie (D) and Mazie Hirono (D).

City and County of Honolulu

O'ahu has been the center of government for about 160 years, since King Kamehameha III permanently established the royal court there in the 1840s. In 1879–1882, King David Kalakaua built 'Iolani Palace as the central showpiece of the island kingdom. Lili'uokalani, the last Hawaiian monarch, lived after her dethronement in the nearby residence Washington Place. While Hawaii was a territory, and for a few years after it became a state, the palace was used as the capitol building, with the governor residing in Washington Place. Modern O'ahu, besides being the center of state government, governs itself as the City and

THE NORTHWESTERN ISLANDS

Like tiny gems of a broken necklace, the North-western Hawaiian Islands spill across the vast Pacific. Popularly called the Leewards, most were discovered in the 19th century.

The Leewards are the oldest islands of the Hawaiian chain, believed to have emerged from the sea 25–30 million years ago! Slowly they floated west-northwest past the suboceanic hot spot as the other islands were built. Measured from **Nihoa Island,** about 100 miles off the northwestern tip of Kaua'i, they stretch for just under 1,100 miles to **Kure Atoll.** There are islets, shoals, and half-submerged reefs in this chain: Kure, Midway, Pearl and Hermes Atolls, Lisianski, Maro Reef, Gardner Pinnacles, French Frigate Shoals, Necker, and Nihoa. Most have been eroded flat by the sea and wind, but a few tough volcanic cores endure. Together they make up a landmass of approximately 3,500 acres, the largest being the three Midway islands – taken together – at 1,580 acres, and the smallest the **Gardner Pinnacles** at six acres.

Politically, the Leewards are administered by the City and County of Honolulu, except for the Midway Islands, which are under federal jurisdiction. None, except Midway, are permanently inhabited, but there are some lonely wildlife field stations on Kure and the French Frigate Shoals. All, except for Midway Atoll, are part of the **Hawaiian Islands National Wildlife Refuge,** established at the turn of the 20th century by Theodore Roosevelt. In 1996, following the closure of the Naval Air Base on Midway Island, Midway Atoll was turned over to the Department of the Interior and is now administered as the **Midway Atoll National Wildlife Refuge.** In June 2006, this 140,000-square mile string of 10 islands and atolls and their surrounding waters, roughly 1,400 miles long and 100 mile wide, were officially designated a **Marine National Monument** (www .hawaiireef.noaa.gov), effectively creating the nation's largest wilderness preserve and world's largest marine preserve. This monument will be overseen jointly by the U.S. Fish and Wildlife Department and the National Oceanic and Atmospheric Administration.

MIDWAY ATOLL

Midway Atoll is about 1,250 miles northwest of and an hour behind Honolulu. It is only 150 miles or so east of the international date line. The atoll comprises three separate islands – Sand, Eastern, and Spit – within a 25-square-mile lagoon. Together, at about three square miles, the islands make up about half of the total land area of all the Northwestern Islands. These three islands and surrounding reef, only a dozen feet above the ocean level at their highest points, are coral growths that rise some 500 feet above the underlying volcanic peak.

First discovered in 1859 and named Brooks Islands, they were renamed Midway when annexed by the United States in 1867. In 1903, President Theodore Roosevelt put the islands under the control of the U.S. Navy. With the growing concern about Japanese aggression in Asia, a naval base was begun on Midway in 1940. This installation was bombed on December 7, 1941, after the attack on Pearl Harbor earlier in the day. In June of the following year, the Battle of Midway took place in the ocean off the atoll and was a turning point in the war of the Pacific. Until 1993, Midway continued to be used as a military base, housing up to 4,000 personnel during the 1960s. With the closure of the naval facility in 1993, Midway Atoll became the Midway Atoll National Wildlife Refuge (http://midway.fws.gov), administered starting in 1996 by the U.S. Fish and Wildlife Service for the Department of the Interior; it was folded into the new Marine National Monument in 2006. Today, Midway has only a small resident population that runs its facilities, maintains the refuge, and conducts scientific study. Limited tourism was allowed at Midway until 2002, when the concessionaire withdrew from its operations.

© ROBERT NILSEN

Hawaii State Capitol building in downtown Honolulu

County of Honolulu. The county covers not only the entire island of Oʻahu, but also all the far-flung Northwestern Islands except for Midway, which is under federal jurisdiction.

The island of Oʻahu has three times as many people as the other islands combined. Nowhere is this more evident than in the representation of Oʻahu in the state House and Senate. Oʻahu claims 18 of the 25 state senators and 35 of the 51 state representatives. These lopsided figures make it obvious that Oʻahu has plenty of clout, especially Honolulu urban districts, which elect more than 50 percent of Oʻahu's representatives. Frequent political battles ensue because what's good for the city and county of Honolulu isn't always good for the rest of the state. More often than not, the political moguls of Oʻahu, backed by huge business interests, prevail.

Like the rest of the state, the voters on the island of Oʻahu are principally Democratic in orientation, but not in as great a percentage as on the other islands. The current mayor is Mufi Hannemann, Democrat, the first Honolulu mayor of Samoan ancestry. He is assisted by an elected county council consisting of nine members, one from each council district around the island. The Oʻahu state senators are overwhelmingly Democratic, except for four Republicans. Democratic state representatives also outnumber Republicans, but not by quite as huge a margin. Most of the eight Republican districts are in urban Honolulu and the suburban communities of Kailua and Kaneʻohe. For Internet information about the city and county of Honolulu, see www.co.honolulu.hi.us.

Economy

Hawaii's mid-Pacific location makes it perfect for two primary sources of income: tourism and the military. Tourists come in anticipation of endless golden days on soothing beaches, while the military is provided with the strategic position of an unsinkable battleship. Each economic sector nets Hawaii billions annually, money that should keep flowing smoothly and even increase in the foreseeable future. Although money earned from tourism is more volatile, revenues from the military remain mostly removed from the normal ups and downs of the Mainland U.S. economy. Also contributing to the state revenue are, in descending proportions, manufacturing, construction, and agriculture (mainly sugar and pineapples). As long as the sun shines and the balance of global power requires a military presence, the economic stability of Hawaii is guaranteed.

Economically, O'ahu dwarfs the rest of the islands combined. A huge military presence, an international airport that receives the lion's share of visitors, and, unbelievably, half of the state's best arable lands keep O'ahu in the economic catbird seat. The famous "Big Five" and other major businesses all maintain their corporate offices in downtown Honolulu, from which they oversee vast holdings throughout Hawaii and the Mainland. The Big Five— C. Brewer and Co., Theo. H. Davies & Co., Amfac Inc., Castle and Cooke Inc. (Dole), and Alexander and Baldwin Inc., historically Hawaii's major economic powerhouses—controlled the economic lifeblood of the islands through their web of subsidiary corporations and holding companies and for all practical purposes controlled politics on the islands through their influence in government until World War II. Located in about the same spots as when their founders helped overthrow the monarchy, things are about the same as then, except that they're going strong, whereas the old royalty of Hawaii has vanished.

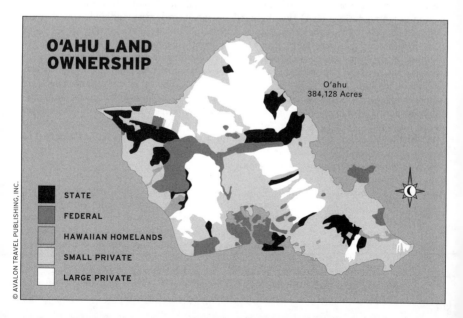

Tourism

The flow of visitors to O'ahu has remained unabated ever since tourism outstripped sugar and pineapples in the early 1960s, becoming Hawaii's top moneymaker. Of the more than seven million people who visit the state yearly, more than half stay on O'ahu. On any given day, O'ahu plays host to about 90,000 visitors, having rebounded from a major dip following the September 2001 terrorist attacks on the Mainland. Waikiki is still many people's idea of paradise. Most all the rest, en route to the Neighbor Islands, at least pass through O'ahu. The overwhelming number of these tourists are on package tours. Hotels directly employ more than 16,000 workers, nearly half the state's total, not including all the shop assistants, food servers, taxi drivers, and everyone else needed to ensure a carefree vacation. Of the state's 73,000 accommodation units, O'ahu claims 35,000; of those, about 29,000 are in Waikiki. The O'ahu hotels consistently have some of the highest occupancy rates in the state, hovering around 73 percent. In contrast, the average daily room rate is the lowest in the state, making accommodations on O'ahu slightly more of a bargain than on the other islands. The visitor industry generates more than $11 billion of yearly revenue, and this is only the amount that can be directly related to the hotel and restaurant trades. With the flow of visitors seemingly endless, O'ahu has a bright economic future.

The Military

Hawaii is the most militarized state in the United States: all five services are represented. Camp H. M. Smith, overlooking Pearl Harbor, is the headquarters of CINCPAC (Commander-in-Chief Pacific), which is responsible for 70 percent of the earth's surface, from California to the east coast of Africa and to both poles. The U.S. military presence dates back to 1887, when Pearl Harbor was given to the navy as part of the Sugar Reciprocity Treaty. The sugar planters were given favorable duty-free treatment for their sugar, while the U.S. Navy was allowed exclusive rights to one of the best harbors in the Pacific. In 1894, when the monarchy was being overthrown by the sugar planters, the USS *Boston* sent a contingency of U.S. Marines ashore to "keep order," which really amounted to a show of force, backing the revolution. The Spanish-American War saw U.S. troops billeted at Camp McKinley at the foot of Diamond Head, and Schofield Barracks opened to receive the 5th Cavalry in 1909. Pearl Harbor's flames ignited World War II, and there has been no looking back since then.

About 32,500 military personnel are stationed in Hawaii (99 percent on O'ahu), with more than 53,000 dependents. This number has slowly but steadily decreased since 1988, when the military was at its greatest strength in the state, and is now lower than at any time since the mid-1950s. The army has the largest contingent with nearly 15,500, followed by the navy at 6,500, marine corps at about 6,000, air force at nearly 5,000, and the coast guard with 1,200 or so. Besides this, 16,000 civilian support personnel account for 65 percent of all federal jobs in Hawaii. The combined services are one of the largest landholders, with more than 238,000 acres, accounting for 6 percent of Hawaiian land. The two major holdings are the 100,000-acre Pohakuloa Training Area on Hawai'i and 81,000 acres on O'ahu, which is a full 21 percent of the island. The army controls 63 percent of the military lands, followed by the navy at 22 percent, the marines with 11 percent, and the remainder goes to the air force and a few small installations to the coast guard.

Agriculture

You'd think that with all the people living on O'ahu, coupled with the constant land development, there'd hardly be any room left for things to grow, but that's not the case. The land is productive, although definitely stressed.

Changing times and attitudes led to a "poi famine" that hit O'ahu in 1967 because very few people were interested in the hard work

PAKALOLO GROWING

In the 1960s and 1970s, mostly *haole* hippies from the Mainland began growing marijuana *(pakalolo)*, usually in the more remote sections of the islands, such as Puna on Hawai'i and around Hana on Maui. They discovered what legitimate planters had known for centuries: Plant a broomstick in Hawaii, treat it right, and it'll grow. *Pakalolo*, after all, is only a weed, and it grows in Hawaii like wildfire. The locals quickly got into the act when they realized that they, too, could grow a "money tree." As a matter of fact, they began resenting the *haole* usurpers, and a quiet and sometimes dangerous feud has been going on ever since. Much is made of the viciousness of the backcountry "growers" of Hawaii as in other areas of the country. There are tales of booby traps and armed patrols guarding plants in the hills, but mostly it's a cat-and-mouse game between the authorities and the growers. If you, as a tourist, are tramping about in the forest and happen upon someone's patch, don't touch anything. Just back off and you'll be OK. Pot has one of the largest monetary turnovers of any crop in the islands and, as such, is now considered a major source of agricultural revenue, albeit illicit and underground.

of farming taro, the source of this staple. Although O'ahu has the smallest average size of farm in the state, it still manages to produce a considerable amount of pineapples and the many products of diversified agriculture and floriculture. Pineapples cover 9,100 acres, with the biggest holdings in the Leilehua Plateau belonging to Dole, a subsidiary of Castle and Cooke. As a result of demand and diversification, O'ahu now also raises a variety of organic greens, freshwater shrimp, coffee, and flowers. Only about 100 acres have been put into coffee, the smallest acreage of any of the islands—on land between Wahiawa and Hale'iwa—but this land produces a respectable 50,000 pounds per year. In the hills, entrepreneurs raise *pakalolo*, or marijuana, which has become one of the state's most productive cash crops. O'ahu is also a huge agricultural consumer, demanding more than four times more vegetables, fruits, meats, and poultry to feed its citizens and visitors than the remainder of the state combined.

Land Ownership
The island of O'ahu is about 600 square miles in size. Although Honolulu County also includes the string of Northwest Islands, only O'ahu is inhabited. This island, smaller than the Big Island and Maui, and only slightly larger than Kaua'i, has nearly three-quarters of the state's population. The federal government owns vast tracts on O'ahu, mostly military bases and military-use areas. Although smaller in area, the state also owns many acres, particularly rugged mountain sections of both the Ko'olau and Wai'anae Ranges. There are two Hawaiian Homelands sections on O'ahu, one in Waimanalo and the other in Nanakuli on the Wai'anae coast. These are just where you might expect them, as many native Hawaiians live in these areas. Of the large landowners, the Bishop Estate, Castle and Cooke, and the James Campbell Estate control the vast majority of land, but the plots of land held by small landowners are larger in size.

The People

Nowhere else on earth can you find such a kaleidoscopic mixture of people as in Hawaii. Every major race is accounted for, and more than 50 ethnic groups are represented throughout the islands, making Hawaii the most racially integrated state in the country. Its population of 1.2 million includes some 85,000 permanently stationed military personnel and their dependents. Until the year 2000, when California's white population fell below 50 percent, Hawaii was the only state where Caucasians were not the majority. About 56 percent of Hawaiian residents were born there, 26 percent were born on the Mainland United States, and 18 percent are foreign-born.

The population of Hawaii has grown steadily in recent times, but it fluctuated wildly in times past. Most European sources gave estimates of between 300,000 and 400,000 for the population of the Hawaiian Islands at the time of Captain Cook's arrival. Some now estimate that number as low as 200,000 or as high as 800,000. In any case, following the arrival of Europeans, the native Hawaiian population declined steadily for a century. In 1876 it ebbed to its lowest, with only 55,000 permanent residents in the islands. This was the era of large sugar plantations; their constant demand for labor and the resulting importation of various peoples from around the world led to Hawaii's racial mix. World War II saw Hawaii's population swell from 400,000 just before the war to 900,000 during the war. Most of the 500,000 military personnel left at war's end, but many returned to settle after getting a taste of island living.

O'ahu Population Figures

Of the 1.2 million people in the islands today, 881,300 live on O'ahu, with slightly less than half of these living in the Honolulu Metropolitan Area, making Honolulu the 11th largest city in the nation. The population is not at all evenly distributed, with O'ahu claiming about 1,470 people per square mile and

Hawai'i barely 37 residents per square mile. Statewide, city dwellers outnumber those living in the country by nine to one. For the island of O'ahu, 96 percent are urban, whereas only 4 percent live rurally. O'ahu's population accounts for 72 percent of the state's population. All these people are on an island comprising only 9 percent of the state's land total. Sections of Waikiki can have a combined population of permanent residents and visitors as high as 90,000 per square mile, making cities like Tokyo, Hong Kong, and New York seem roomy by comparison. The good news is that O'ahu *expects* all these people and knows how to accommodate them comfortably.

More than 400,000 people live in greater Honolulu, the built-up area from 'Aiea to Koko Head. The next most populous urban centers after Honolulu are the Kailua/Kane'ohe area on the Windward side with about 100,000 residents, Mililani and Wahiawa on the Leilehua Plateau with about the same number, followed by Pearl City and Waipahu with a combined total of about 70,000 or so. The strip of towns on the Leeward Coast, including Wai'anae, totals about 40,000 inhabitants. In the last decade, the areas that have had the greatest increase in population are Mililani and 'Ewa.

So where is everybody? Of the major ethnic groups you'll find the Hawaiians clustered around Wai'anae and on the Windward Coast in Waimanalo and near Waiahole; the whites tend to be in Wahiawa, around Koko Head, in Waikiki, and in Kailua/Kane'ohe; those of Japanese ancestry prefer the valleys heading toward the *pali,* including Kalihi, Nu'uanu, and Tantalus; Filipinos live just east of the airport, in downtown Honolulu, and in Wahiawa; the Chinese are in Chinatown and around the Diamond Head area. Of the minor ethnic groups, the highest concentration of blacks is in the army towns around Schofield Barracks; Samoans live along with the Hawaiians in Wai'anae and the Windward coastal towns, although they are most concentrated in downtown Honolulu; Koreans and Vietnamese are scattered here and there, but mostly in Honolulu. There is no ethnic majority on O'ahu. Population numbers include 46 percent Asian, 21 percent Caucasian, 20 percent mixed, 9 percent Hawaiian, and 4 percent other.

THE HAWAIIANS

The study of the native Hawaiians is ultimately a study in tragedy because it nearly ends in their demise as a viable people. When Captain Cook first sighted Hawaii in 1778, there were an estimated 300,000 natives living in relative harmony with their ecological surroundings; within 100 years a scant 50,000 Hawaiians existed almost as wards of the state. Today, although more than 240,000 people claim varying degrees of Hawaiian blood, experts say that fewer than 1,000 are pure Hawaiian, and this is stretching it.

It's easy to see why people of Hawaiian lineage could be bitter over what they have lost, being strangers in their own land now, much like Native Americans. The overwhelming majority of "Hawaiians" are of mixed heritage, and the wisest take the best from all worlds. From the Hawaiian side comes simplicity, love of the land, and acceptance of people. It is the Hawaiian legacy of *aloha* that remains immortal and adds that special elusive quality that *is* Hawaii.

Polynesian Roots

The Polynesians' original stock is muddled and remains an anthropological mystery, but it's believed that they were nomadic wanderers who migrated from both the Indian subcontinent and Southeast Asia through Indonesia, where they learned to sail and navigate on protected waterways. As they migrated they honed their sailing skills until they could take on the Pacific, and as they moved, they absorbed people from other cultures and races until they had coalesced into what we now know as Polynesians.

Abraham Fornander, still considered a major authority on the subject, wrote in his 1885 *An Account of the Polynesian Race* that he believed the Polynesians started as a white (Aryan) race that was heavily influenced by contact with

ALL-PURPOSE *KUKUI*

Reaching heights of 80 feet, the *kukui* (candlenut) was a veritable department store to the Hawaiians, who made use of almost every part of this utilitarian giant. Its nuts, bark, or flowers were ground into potions and salves to be taken as a general tonic, applied to ulcers and cuts as an effective antibiotic, or administered internally as a cure for constipation or asthma attacks. The bark was mixed with water, and the resulting juice was used as a dye in tattooing, tapa-cloth making, and canoe painting, and as a preservative for fishnets. The oily nuts were burned in stone holders as a light source, and they were ground and eaten as a condiment called *'inamona*. Polished nuts took on a beautiful sheen and were strung as lei. Finally, the wood was hollowed into canoes and used as fishnet floats.

the Cushite, Chaldeo-Arabian civilization. He estimated their arrival in Hawaii at A.D. 600, based on Hawaiian genealogical chants. Modern science seems to bear this date out, although it remains skeptical about his other surmises. According to others, the intrepid Polynesians who actually settled Hawaii are believed to have come from the Marquesas Islands, 1,000 miles southeast of Hawaii. The Marquesans were cannibals known for their tenacity and strength, attributes that would serve them well. Tahitians and other islanders arrived several hundred years later, creating a mix even in Polynesian blood.

The Caste System

Hawaiian society was divided into rankings by a strict caste system determined by birth, and from which there was no chance of escaping. The highest rank was the *ali'i*, the chiefs and royalty. The impeccable genealogies of the *ali'i* were traced back to the gods themselves, and the chants (*mo'o ali'i*) were memorized and sung by professionals (called *ku'auhau*), who were themselves *ali'i*. Ranking passed from both father and mother and custom dictated that the first mating of an *ali'i* be with a person of equal status.

A *kahuna* was a highly skilled person whose advice was sought before any major project was undertaken, such as building a house, hollowing a canoe log, or even offering a prayer. The *mo'o kahuna* were the priests of Ku and Lono, and they were in charge of praying and following rituals. They were very powerful *ali'i* and kept strict secrets and laws concerning their various functions.

Besides this priesthood of *kahuna*, there were other *kahuna* who were not *ali'i* but commoners. The two most important were the healers *(kahuna lapa'au)* and the black magicians *(kahuna 'ana'ana)*, who could pray a person to death. The *kahuna lapa'au* had a marvelous pharmacopoeia of herbs and spices that could cure over 250 diseases common to the Hawaiians. The *kahuna 'ana'ana* could be hired to cast a love spell over a person or cause his or her untimely death. They seldom had to send out a reminder of payment!

The common people were called the *maka'ainana*, "the people of land"—the farmers, craftspeople, and fishermen. The land they lived on was owned by the *ali'i*, but they were not bound to it. If the local *ali'i* was cruel or unfair, the *maka'ainana* had the right to leave and reside on another's lands. The *maka'ainana* mostly loved their local *ali'I*, much like a child loves a parent, and the feeling was reciprocal. *Maka'ainana* who lived close to the *ali'i* and could be counted on as warriors in times of trouble were called *kanaka no lua kaua* (a man for the heat of battle). They were treated with greater favor than those who lived in the backcountry, *kanaka no hi'i kua*, whose lesser standing opened them up to discrimination and cruelty. All *maka'ainana* formed extended families called *'ohana* who usually lived on the same section of land, called *ahupua'a*. Those farmers who lived inland would barter their produce with the fishermen who lived on the shore, and thus all shared equally in the bounty of land and sea.

A special group called *kauwa* was an untouchable caste confined to living on reservations. Their origins were obviously Polynesian, but they appeared to be descendants of castaways who had survived and become perhaps the aboriginals of Hawaii before the main migrations. It was *kapu* for anyone to go onto *kauwa* lands; doing so meant instant death. If a human sacrifice was needed, the *kahuna* would simply summon a *kauwa*, who had no recourse but to mutely comply. To this day, to call someone *kauwa*, which now supposedly only means servant, is still considered a fight-provoking insult.

Kapu and Day-to-Day Life

Occasionally there were horrible wars, but mostly the people lived quiet and ordered lives based on a strict caste society and the *kapu* system. Famine was known, but only on a regional level, and the population was kept in check by birth control, crude abortions, and the distasteful practice of infanticide, especially of baby girls. The Hawaiians were absolutely loving and nurturing parents under most circumstances and would even take in *hanai* (an adopted child or oldster), a lovely practice that lingers to this day.

A strict division of labor existed among men and women. Men were the only ones permitted to have anything to do with taro: This foodstuff was so sacred that there were a greater number of *kapu* concerning taro than concerning man himself. Men pounded poi and served it to the women. Men were also the fishermen and the builders of houses, canoes, irrigation ditches, and walls. Women tended to other gardens and shoreline fishing and were responsible for making tapa cloth. The entire family lived in the common house called the *hale noa*.

Certain things were *kapu* between the sexes. Primarily, women could not enter the *mua* (man's eating house), nor could they eat with men. Certain foods, such as pork, coconut, red fish, and bananas were forbidden to women, and it was *kapu* for a man to have intercourse before going fishing, engaging in battle, or attending a religious ceremony. Young boys lived with the women until they underwent a circumcision rite called *pule ipu*. After this was performed, they were required to keep the *kapu* of men. A true Hawaiian settlement required a minimum of five huts: the men's eating hut, women's menstruation hut, women's eating hut, communal sleeping hut, and prayer hut. Without these five separate structures, Hawaiian society could not happen because the *i'a kapu* (forbidden eating between men and women) rules could not be observed.

Ali'i could also declare a *kapu* and often did so. Certain lands or fishing areas were temporarily made *kapu* so that they could revitalize. Even today, it is *kapu* for anyone to remove all the *'opihi* (a type of limpet) from a rock. The great King Kamehameha I even placed a *kapu* on the body of his notoriously unfaithful child bride, Ka'ahumanu. It didn't work! The greatest *kapu (kapu moe)* was afforded to the highest-ranking *ali'i:* anyone coming into their presence had to prostrate themselves. Lesser-ranking *ali'i* were afforded the *kapu noho:* Lessers had to sit or kneel in their presence. Commoners could not let their shadows fall on an *ali'i*, nor enter an *ali'i's* house except through a special door. Breaking a *kapu* meant immediate death.

The Causes of Decline

Less than 100 years after Captain Cook's arrival, King Kalakaua found himself with roughly 48,000 Hawaiian subjects. Wherever the king went, he would beseech his people, *"Ho'oulu lahui"*—"Increase the race"—but it was already too late. It was as if nature had turned her back on these once proud people. Many of their marriages were barren; in 1874, when only 1,400 children were born, a full 75 percent died in infancy. The Hawaiians could do little as their race nearly faded from existence.

The ecological system of Hawaii has always been exceptionally fragile, and this included its people. When the first whites arrived, they found a great people who were large, strong, and virile. But when it came to fighting off the most minor diseases, the Hawaiians proved as delicate as hothouse flowers. By the time the

missionaries came in 1820, they estimated the native population at only 140,000, less than half of what it had been only 40 years since initial contact! In the next 50 years measles, mumps, influenza, and tuberculosis further ravaged the people. Furthermore, Hawaiian men were excellent sailors, and it's estimated that during the whaling years at least 25 percent of all able-bodied Hawaiian men sailed away, never to return.

But the coup de grâce that really ended the Hawaiian race, as such, was that all racial newcomers to the islands were attracted to the Hawaiians and the Hawaiians were in turn attracted to them. With so many interracial marriages, the Hawaiians nearly bred themselves out of existence. By 1910, there were still twice as many full-blooded Hawaiians as mixed-bloods, but by 1940 mixed-blood Hawaiians were the fastest growing group, and full-blooded the fastest declining.

Hawaiians Today

Many of the Hawaiians who moved to the cities became more and more disenfranchised. Their folk society stressed openness and a giving nature but downplayed the individual and ownership of private property. These cultural traits made them easy targets for the users and schemers until they finally became either apathetic or angry. Most surveys reveal that although Hawaiians number only 13 percent of the population, they account for almost 50 percent of the financially destitute families and about half of all arrests and illegitimate births. Ni'ihau, a privately owned island, is home to about 160 pure-blooded Hawaiians, representing the largest concentration of them, per capita, in the islands. The Robinson family, which owns the island, restricts visitors to invited guests only.

The second largest concentration is on Moloka'i, where 2,700 Hawaiians, living mostly on 40-acre *kuleana* of Hawaiian Home Lands, make up 40 percent of that island's population. The majority of mixed-blood Hawaiians, 240,000 or so, live on O'ahu, where they are particularly strong in the hotel and entertainment fields. People of Hawaiian extraction are still a delight to meet, and anyone so lucky as to befriend one long regards this friendship as the highlight of his or her travels. The Hawaiians have always given their *aloha* freely to all the people of the world, and we must acknowledge this precious gift.

THE CHINESE

Next to Americans, the Chinese are the oldest migrant group in Hawaii, and their influence has far outshone their meager numbers. They brought to Hawaii, along with their individuality, Confucianism, Taoism, and Buddhism, although many have long since become Christians. The Chinese population at 56,000 makes up only 5 percent of the state's total, and the vast majority reside on O'ahu. As an ethnic group they account for the highest per capita income, and a disproportionate number of professionals.

The First Chinese

No one knows his name, but an unknown Chinese immigrant is credited with being the first person in Hawaii to refine sugar. This Asian wanderer tried his hand at crude refining on Lana'i in 1802. Fifty years later the sugar plantations desperately needed workers, and the first Chinese brought to Hawaii under the newly passed Masters and Servants Act were 195 unskilled laborers from Xiamen (Amoy) who arrived in 1852. These conscripts were contracted for three to five years and given $3 per month plus room and board. This was for 12 hours per day, six days per week, and even in 1852 these wages were the pits. The Chinese almost always left the plantations the minute their contracts expired. They went into business for themselves and promptly monopolized the restaurant and small shop trades.

The Chinese Niche

Although many people in Hawaii considered all Chinese ethnically the same, they were actually quite different. The majority came from Guangdong Province in southern China. They were two distinct ethnic groups: the Punti made up 75 percent of the immigrants, and the Hakka made up the remainder. In China, they remained separate from each other, never mixing; in Hawaii, they mixed out of necessity. For one thing, hardly any Chinese women came over at first, and the ones who followed were at a premium and gladly accepted as wives, regardless of ethnic background. The Chinese were also one of the first groups who willingly intermarried with the Hawaiians, from whom they gained a reputation for being exceptionally caring spouses.

The Chinese accepted the social order and kept a low profile. For example, during the turbulent labor movements of the 1930s and 1940s in Hawaii, the Chinese community produced not one labor leader, radical intellectual, or left-wing politician. When Hawaii became a state, one of the two senators elected was Hiram Fong, a racially mixed Chinese. Since statehood, the Chinese community has carried on business as usual as they continue to rise both economically and socially.

THE JAPANESE

Most scholars believe that (inevitably) a few Japanese castaways floated to Hawaii long before Captain Cook arrived and might have introduced the iron with which the islanders seemed to be familiar before the white explorers arrived. The first official arrivals from Japan were ambassadors sent by the Japanese shogun to negotiate in Washington, D.C.; they stopped en route at Honolulu in March 1860. But it was as plantation workers that the Japanese were brought en masse to the islands. A small group arrived in 1868, and mass migration started in 1885.

In 1886, because of famine, the Japanese government allowed farmers, mainly from southern Honshu, Kyushu, and Okinawa, to emigrate. Among these were members of Japan's little-talked-about untouchable caste, called *eta* or *burakumin* in Japan and *chorinbo* in Hawaii. They gratefully seized this opportunity to better their lot, an impossibility in Japan. The first Japanese migrants were almost all men. Between 1897 and 1908 migration was steady, with about 70 percent of the immigrants being men. By 1900 there were more than 60,000 Japanese in the islands, constituting the largest ethnic group.

AJAs, Americans of Japanese Ancestry

Parents of most Japanese children born before World War II were *issei* (first generation), who considered themselves apart from other Americans and clung to the notion of "we Japanese." Their children, the *nisei* or second generation, were a different matter altogether. In one generation they had become Americans, and they put into practice the high Japanese virtues of obligation, duty, and loyalty to the homeland, but that homeland was now unquestionably the United States. After Pearl Harbor was bombed, the FBI kept close tabs on the Japanese community, and the menace of the "enemy within" prompted the decision to place Hawaii under martial law for the duration of the war. It has since been noted that not a single charge of espionage or sabotage was ever reported against the Japanese community in Hawaii during the war.

AJAs as GIs

Although the Japanese had formed a battalion during World War I, they were insulted by being considered unacceptable as American soldiers in World War II. Some Japanese-Americans volunteered to serve in labor battalions, and because of their flawless work and loyalty, it was decided to put out a call for a few hundred volunteers to form a combat unit. Over 10,000 signed up! AJAs formed two distinguished units in World War II: the 100th Infantry Battalion and later the 442nd Regimental Combat Team. They landed in Italy at Salerno and even fought from Guadalcanal to Okinawa. They distinguished themselves by becoming the most decorated unit in American military history.

The AJAs Return

Many returning AJAs took advantage of the GI Bill and received college educations. The "Big Five" corporations for the first time accepted former AJA officers as executives, and the old order was changed. Many Japanese became involved with Hawaiian politics, and the first elected to Congress was Daniel Inouye, who had lost an arm fighting in World War II. Hawaii's onetime governor, George Ariyoshi, elected in 1974, was the country's first Japanese-American to reach such a high office.

There are now 290,000 people in Hawaii of Japanese ancestry (another 100,000 of mixed Japanese blood), nearly one-quarter of the state's population. They are the least likely of any ethnic group in Hawaii to marry outside of their group—especially the men—and they enjoy a higher-than-average standard of living.

CAUCASIANS

White people have a distinction separating them from all other ethnic groups in Hawaii: They are lumped together as one. A person can be anything from a Protestant Norwegian dockworker to a Greek Orthodox shipping tycoon, but if his or her skin is white, in Hawaii, he or she is a *haole*. What's more, a person could have arrived at Waikiki from Missoula, Montana, in the last 24 hours, or his or her *kama'aina* family can go back five generations, but again, if a person is white, he or she is a *haole*.

The word *haole* has a floating connotation that depends upon the spirit in which it's used. It can mean everything from a derisive "honky" or "cracker" to nothing more than "white person." The exact Hawaiian meaning is clouded, but some say it meant "a man of no background" because white men couldn't chant a genealogical *kanaenae* telling the Hawaiians who they were. The word eventually evolved to mean foreign white man and today, simply, white person.

White History

Next to Hawaiians themselves, white people have the oldest stake in Hawaii. They've been there as settlers in earnest since the missionaries of the 1820s and were established long before any other migrant group. From the 19th century until statehood, old *haole* families owned and controlled mostly everything, and although they were generally benevolent, philanthropic, and paternalistic, they were also racist. Many *kamaʻaina* families made up the boards of the "Big Five" corporations or owned huge plantations and formed an inner social circle that was closed to the outside. Many managed to find mates from among close family acquaintances.

Their paternalism, which they accepted with grave responsibility, at first extended only to the Hawaiians, who saw them as replacing their own *aliʻi*. Asians were considered primarily instruments of production. These supremacist attitudes tended to drag on in Hawaii until recent times. They are today responsible for the sometimes sour relations between white and nonwhite people in the islands. Today, all white people are resented to a certain degree because of these past acts, even though they personally were in no way involved.

White Plantation Workers

In the 1880s the white landowners looked around and felt surrounded and outnumbered by Asians, so they tried to import white people for plantation work. None of their schemes seemed to work out. Europeans were accustomed to a much higher wage scale and better living conditions than were provided on the plantations. Although only workers and not considered the equals of the ruling elite, they still were expected to act like a special class. They were treated preferentially, which meant higher wages for the same jobs performed by Asians. Some of the imported workers included 600 Scandinavians in 1881; 1,400 Germans 1881–1885; 400 Poles 1897–1898; and 2,400 Russians 1909–1912. Many proved troublesome, like the Poles and Russians who staged strikes after only months on the job. Many quickly moved to the Mainland. A contingency of Scots, who first came as mule-skinners, did become successful plantation managers and supervisors. The Germans and Scandinavians were well received and climbed the social ladder rapidly, becoming professionals and skilled workers.

The Depression years, not as economically bad in Hawaii as in the continental United States, brought many Mainland whites seeking opportunity, mostly from the South and the West. These new people tended to be even more racist toward brown-skinned people and Asians than the *kamaʻaina haole,* and they made matters worse. They also competed more intensely for jobs. The racial tension generated during this period came to a head in 1932 with the infamous Massie Rape Case, in which four local men were falsely accused of raping the wife of a naval officer. The five were finally acquitted, but Thomas Massie and his mother-in-law, with the assistance of several others, killed one of the boys. Found guilty at their trial, these whites served just one hour for the murder, and this is considered one of the greatest miscarriages of justice in American history.

The Portuguese

The last time anyone looked, Portugal was still attached to the European continent, but for some anomalous reason the Portuguese weren't considered *haole* in Hawaii for the longest time. About 12,000 arrived between 1878 and 1887, and another 6,000 came between 1906 and 1913. Accompanied during this period by 8,000 Spanish, they were considered one and the same. Most of the Portuguese were illiterate peasants from Madeira and the Azores, and the Spanish hailed from Andalusia. They were very well received, and because they were white but not *haole* they made a perfect "buffer" ethnic group. Committed to staying in Hawaii, they rose to be skilled workers—the *luna* class on the plantations. However, they deemphasized education and became racist toward Asians, regarding them as a threat to their job security.

By 1920, the 27,000 Portuguese made up 11 percent of the population. After that they tended to blend with the other ethnic groups and weren't counted separately. Portuguese men tended to marry within their ethnic group, but a good portion of Portuguese women married other white men and became closer to the *haole* group, whereas another large portion chose Hawaiian mates and grew further away. Although they didn't originate pidgin English, the unique melodious quality of their native tongue did give pidgin that certain lilt it has today. Also, the ukulele was closely patterned after the *cavaquinho,* a Portuguese stringed folk instrument.

The White Population

Today Caucasians make up the largest group in the islands at about 25 percent of the population. With mixed white blood, that number jumps to nearly 40 percent. They are spread evenly throughout Kaua'i, O'ahu, Maui, and the Big Island, with much smaller percentages on Moloka'i and Lana'i. On O'ahu, there are heavy concentrations in Waikiki, Kailua/Kane'ohe, and around Pearl City. In terms of pure numbers, the white population is the fastest growing in the islands because most people resettling in Hawaii are white Americans predominantly from the West Coast.

FILIPINOS AND OTHERS

The Filipinos who came to Hawaii brought high hopes of amassing personal fortunes and returning home as rich heroes, but for most it was a dream that never came true. Filipinos had been American nationals ever since the Spanish-American War of 1898, and as such weren't subject to immigration laws that curtailed the importation of other Asian workers at the turn of the 20th century. The first to arrive were 15 families in 1906, but a large number came in 1924 as strikebreakers. The majority were illiterate peasants called Ilocanos from the northern Philippines, with about 10 percent Visayans from the central cities. The Visayans were not as hardworking or thrifty but were much more sophisticated. From the first, Filipinos were looked down upon by all the other immigrant groups and were considered particularly uncouth by the Japanese. The value they placed on education was the least of any group, and even by 1930 only about half could speak rudimentary English, the majority remaining illiterate. They were billeted in the worst housing, performed the most menial jobs, and were the last hired and first fired.

One big difference between Filipinos and other groups was that the men brought no Filipino women to marry, so they clung to the idea of returning home. In 1930 there were 30,000 men and only 360 women. Many of these terribly lonely bachelors would feast and drink on weekends and engage in their gruesome but exciting pastime of cockfighting on Sundays. When some did manage to find wives, their mates were inevitably part Hawaiian. Filipino workers continued to be imported, although sporadically, until 1946, so even today, there are still plenty of old Filipino bachelors who never managed to get home.

The Filipinos constitute 14 percent of Hawaii's population, some 170,000 individuals, with almost 75 percent living on O'ahu. Some 275,000 are of mixed Filipino blood. Many visitors to Hawaii mistake Filipinos for Hawaiians because of their dark skin, and this is a minor irritant to both groups. For the most part, these people are hardworking, dependable laborers who do tough work for little recognition. They remain low on the social totem pole and have not yet organized politically to stand up for their rights.

Other Groups

About 10 percent of Hawaii's population is a conglomerate of small ethnic groups. Of these, one of the largest and fastest growing is Koreans, with 25,000 people. About 8,000 Koreans came to Hawaii from 1903 until 1905, when their own government halted emigration. During the same period about 6,000 Puerto Ricans arrived, and today about 30,000 consider themselves a Puerto Rican mix. There were also two attempts made in the 1800s to import other Polynesians to strengthen the dying Hawaiian race, but they were failures. In 1869 only 126 central Polynesian natives could be lured to Hawaii, and from 1878 to 1885, 2,500 Gilbert Islanders arrived. Both groups became immediately disenchanted with Hawaii. They pined for their own islands and departed for home as soon as possible.

Today, however, 16,000 Samoans have settled in Hawaii, and with more on the way they are one of the fastest-growing minorities in the state. For inexplicable reasons, Samoans and native Hawaiians get along extremely poorly and have the worst racial tensions and animosity of any groups. The Samoans ostensibly should represent the archetypal Polynesians that the Hawaiians are seeking, but it doesn't work that way. Samoans are criticized by Hawaiians for their hot tempers, lingering feuds, and petty jealousies. They're clannish and often are the butt of "dumb" jokes. This racism seems especially ridiculous, but that's the way it is.

Just to add a bit more exotic spice to the stew, there are about 22,000 blacks, 3,500 Native American Indians, 4,000 Tongans, 7,000 other Pacific Islanders, and 8,000 Vietnamese living on the islands.

Culture

RELIGION

The Lord saw fit to keep His island paradise secret from humanity for a few million years, but once we finally arrived we were awfully thankful. Hawaii sometimes seems like a floating tabernacle; everywhere you look there's a church, temple, shrine, or *heiau*. The islands are either a very holy place or there's a powerful lot of sinning going on that would require so many houses of prayer. Actually, it's just America's "right to worship" concept fully employed in microcosm. All of the peoples who came to Hawaii brought their own forms of devotion. The Polynesian Hawaiians praised the primordial creators, Wakea and Papa, from whom their pantheon of animist gods sprang. To a modern world, these old gods would never do. Unfortunately for the old gods, there were too many of them, and belief in them was looked upon as superstition, the folly of semicivilized pagans. So the famous missionaries of the 1820s brought Congregational Christianity and the "true path" to heaven.

Inconveniently, the Catholics, Mormons, Reformed Mormons, Adventists, Episcopalians, Unitarians, Christian Scientists, Lutherans, Baptists, Jehovah's Witnesses, Salvation Army, and every other major and minor denomination of Christianity that followed in their wake brought their own brand of enlightenment and never quite agreed with each other. Chinese and Japanese immigrants established major sects of Buddhism, Confucianism, Taoism, and Shintoism. Allah is praised, the Torah is chanted in Jewish synagogues, and nirvana is available at a variety of Hindu temples. If the spirit moves you, a Hare Krishna devotee will be glad to point you in the right direction and give you a "free" flower for only a dollar or two. If the world is still too much with you, you might find peace at a Church of Scientology, or meditate at a Kundalini yoga institute, or perhaps find relief at a local assembly of Baha'i. Anyway, rejoice, because in Hawaii you'll find not only paradise but perhaps also salvation.

Hawaiian Beliefs

The Polynesian Hawaiians worshiped nature. They saw its forces manifested in a multiplicity of forms to which they ascribed godlike powers, and they based daily life on this animistic philosophy. Handpicked and specially trained storytellers chanted the exploits of the gods. These ancient tales, kept alive in a special oral tradition called *mo'olelo*, were recited only by day. Entranced listeners encircled the chanter; in respect for the gods and in fear of their wrath, they were forbidden to move once the tale was begun. This was serious business, during which a person's life could be at stake. It was not like the telling of *ka'ao*, which were simple fictions, tall tales, and yarns of ancient heroes related for amusement and to pass the long nights. Any object, animate or inanimate, could be a god. All could be infused with *mana*, especially a dead body or a respected ancestor.

'*Ohana* had personal family gods called '*aumakua* on whom they called in times of danger or strife. There were children of gods called *kupua* who were thought to live among humans and were distinguished either for their beauty and strength or for their ugliness and terror. It was told that processions of dead *ali'i*, called "Marchers of the Night," wandered through the land of the living, and unless you were properly protected it could mean death if they looked upon you. There were simple ghosts known as *akua lapu* who merely frightened people. Forests, waterfalls, trees, springs, and a thousand forms of nature were the manifestations of *akua li'i*, "little spirits" who could be invoked at any time for help or protection. It made no difference who or what you were in old Hawaii; the gods were ever present, and they took a direct and active role in your life.

Behind all of these beliefs was an innate sense of natural balance and order. It could be interpreted as positive-negative, yin-yang, life-death, light-dark, whatever, but the main idea was that everything had its opposite. The time of darkness when only the gods lived was *po*. When the great gods descended to the earth and created light, this was *ao* and humanity was born. All of these *mo'olelo* are part of *The Kumulipo,* the great chant that records the Hawaiian version of creation. From the time the gods descended and touched the earth at Ku Moku on Lana'i, the genealogies were kept. Unlike the Bible, these included the noble families of female as well as male *ali'i.*

Heiau and Idols

A *heiau* is a Hawaiian temple. The basic *heiau* was a masterfully built and fitted rectangular stone wall that varied in size from about as big as a basketball court to as big as a football field. Once the restraining outer walls were built, the interior was backfilled with smaller stones and the top dressing was expertly laid and then rolled, perhaps with a log, to form a pavement-like surface. All that remains of Hawaii's many *heiau* are the stone platforms or walls. The buildings on them, made from perishable wood, leaves, and grass, have long since disappeared.

© ROBERT NILSEN

Set deep in Makaha Valley, Kane'aki Heiau is the best preserved and semi-restored *heiau* on the island. Here, one gets a feel for what this religious site must have looked like when it was used by priests of ancient Hawaii.

THE STRIFES OF MAUI

Of all the heroes and mythological figures of Polynesia, Maui is the best known. His "strifes" are like the great Greek epics, and they make excellent tales of courage and action that elders loved to relate to youngsters around the evening fire. Maui was abandoned by his mother, Hina of Fire, when he was an infant. She wrapped him in her hair and cast him upon the sea, where she expected him to die, but he lived and returned home to become her favorite. She knew then that he was a born hero and had strength far beyond that of ordinary mortals. His first exploit was to lift the sky. In those days the sky hung so low that humans had to crawl around on all fours. A seductive young woman approached Maui and asked him to use his great strength to lift the sky. In fine heroic fashion, the big boy agreed, if the beautiful woman would euphemistically "give him a drink from her gourd." He then obliged her by lifting the sky, and he might even have made the earth move for her once or twice.

The territory of humanity was small at that time. Maui decided that more land was needed, so he conspired to "fish up islands." He descended into the land of the dead and petitioned an ancestress to fashion him a hook from her jawbone. She obliged and created the mythical hook, *Manai ikalani*. Maui then secured a sacred 'alae bird, which he intended to use for bait, and bid his brothers to paddle him far out to sea. When he arrived at the deepest spot, he lowered *Manai ikalani*, baited with the sacred bird, and his sister, Hina of the Sea, placed it into the mouth of "Old One Tooth," who held the land fast to the bottom of the waters. Maui then exhorted his brothers to row but warned them not to look back. They strained at the oars with all their might, and slowly a great landmass arose. One brother, overcome by curiosity, looked back, and when he did so, the land shattered into all of the islands of Polynesia.

Maui still desired to serve humanity. People were without fire, the secret of which was held by the sacred 'alae birds, who learned it from Maui's far-distant mother. Hina of Fire gave Maui her burning fingernails, but he oafishly kept dropping them into streams until all had fizzled out and he had totally irritated his generous progenitor. She pursued him, trying to burn him to a cinder; Maui chanted for rain to put out her scorching fires. When she saw that they were being quenched, she hid her fire in the bark of special trees and informed the mud hens where they could be found, but first made them promise never to tell humans. Maui knew of this and captured a mud hen, threatening to wring its scrawny, traitorous neck unless it gave up the secret. The bird tried trickery and told Maui first to rub together the stems of sugarcane, then banana, and even taro. None worked, and Maui's determined rubbing is why these plants have hollow roots today.

Finally, with Maui's hands tightening around the mud hen's gizzard, the bird confessed that fire could be found in the *hau* tree and also the sandalwood, which Maui named 'iliaha (fire bark) in its honor. He then rubbed all the feathers off the mud hen's head for being so deceitful, which is why their crowns are featherless today.

Maui's greatest deed, however, was in snaring the sun and exacting a promise that it would go slower across the heavens. The people complained that there were not enough daylight hours to fish or farm. Maui's mother could not dry her tapa cloth because the sun rose and set so quickly. She asked her son to help. Maui went to his blind grandmother, who lived on the slopes of Haleakala and was responsible for cooking the sun's bananas, which he ate every day in passing. She told him to personally weave 16 strong ropes with nooses from his sister's hair. Some say these came from her head, but other versions insist that it was no doubt Hina's pubic hair that had the power to hold the sun god. Maui positioned himself with the rope, and as each of the 16 rays of the sun came across Haleakala, he snared them until the sun was defenseless and had to bargain for his life. Maui agreed to free him if he promised to go more slowly. From that time forward the sun agreed to move slowly, and Haleakala (The House of the Sun) became his home.

Some *heiau* were dreaded temples where human sacrifices were made. Tradition says that this barbaric custom began at Waha'ula Heiau on the Big Island in the 12th century and was introduced by a ferocious Tahitian priest named Pa'ao. Other *heiau*, such as Pu'uhonua o Honaunau, also on the Big Island, were temples of refuge where the weak, widowed, orphaned, and vanquished could find safety and sanctuary.

The Hawaiian people worshiped gods who took the form of idols fashioned from wood, feathers, or stone. The eyes were made from shells, and until these were inlaid, the idol was dormant. The hair used was often human hair, and the arms and legs were usually flexed. The mouth was either gaping or formed a wide figure-eight lying on its side, and more likely than not was lined with glistening dog teeth. Small figures made of woven basketry were expertly covered with feathers. Red and yellow feathers were favorites taken from specific birds by men whose only work was to roam the forests in search of them.

Ghosts

The Hawaiians had countless superstitions and ghost legends, but two of the more interesting involve astral travel of the soul and the Marchers of the Night. The soul, *'uhane,* was considered by Hawaiians to be totally free and independent of its body, *kino.* The soul could separate, leaving the body asleep or drowsy. This disincorporated soul *(hihi'o)* could visit people and was considered quite different from a *lapu,* an ordinary spirit of a dead person. A *kahuna* could immediately recognize if a person's *'uhane* had left the body, and a special wreath was placed on the head to protect him or her and to facilitate reentry.

If confronted by an apparition, one could test to see if it was indeed dead or still alive by placing leaves of an *'ape* plant on the ground. If the leaves tore when they were walked on, the spirit was merely human, but if they remained intact it was a ghost. Or you could sneak up and startle the vision, and if it disappeared it was a ghost. Also, if no reflection of the face appeared when it drank water from an offered calabash, it was a ghost. Unfortunately, there were no instructions to follow once you had determined that you indeed had a ghost on your hands. Maybe it was better not to know! Some people would sprinkle salt and water around their houses, but this kept away evil spirits, not ghosts.

There are also many stories of *kahuna* restoring a soul to a dead body. First they had to catch it and keep it in a gourd. They then placed beautiful tapa and fragrant flowers and herbs around the body to make it more enticing. Slowly, they would coax the soul out of the gourd until it reentered the body through the big toe.

Death Marchers

One inexplicable phenomenon that many people attest to is *ka huaka'i o ka po,* Marchers of the Night. This march of the dead is fatal if you gaze on it, unless one of the marchers happens to be a friendly ancestor who will protect you. The peak time for the march is 7:30 P.M.– 2 A.M. The marchers can be dead *ali'i* and warriors, the gods, or the lesser *'aumakua.* When the *'aumakua* march there is usually chanting and music. *Ali'i* marches are more somber. The entire procession, lit by torches, often stops at the house of a relative and might even carry him or her away. When the gods march, there is often thunder, lightning, and heavy seas. The sky is lit with torches, and they walk six abreast, three gods and three goddesses. If you get in the way of a march, remove your clothing and prostrate yourself. If the marching gods or *'aumakua* happen to be ones to which you prayed, you might be spared. If it's a march of the *ali'i,* you might make it if you lie face upward and feign death. If you *do* see a death march, the last thing you'll worry about is lying naked on the ground and looking ridiculous.

Missionaries

In Hawaii, it's taken for granted that "missionaries" refers to the small and determined band of Congregationalists who arrived aboard the brig *Thaddeus* in 1820, and the follow-up groups called companies, or "packets," that reinforced them. They were sent from Boston by the American Board of Commissioners for Foreign Missions (ABCFM), which learned of the supposed sad and godless plight of the Hawaiian people through returning sailors and especially through the few Hawaiians who had come to America to study.

The person most instrumental in bringing the missionaries to Hawaii was a young man named Henry Opukaha'ia. He was an orphan befriended by a ship's captain and taken to New England, where he studied theology. Obsessed with the desire to return home and save his people from certain damnation, Opukaha'ia wrote accounts of life in Hawaii that were published and widely read. These accounts were directly responsible for the formation of the Pioneer Company to the Sandwich Islands Missions in 1819. Unfortunately, Opukaha'ia died in New England from typhus the year before they left.

The first missionaries had the straightforward task of bringing the Hawaiians out of paganism and into Christianity and civilization. They met with terrible hostility—not from the natives, but from the sea captains and traders who were very happy with the open debauchery and wanton whoremongering that was status quo in the Hawaii of 1820. Many direct confrontations between these two factions even included the cannonading of missionaries' homes by American sea captains, who were denied the customary visits of island women, thanks to meddlesome "do-gooders." The most memorable of these incidents involved "Mad Jack" Percival, the captain of the USS *Dolphin,* who bombed a church in Lahaina to show his rancor. In actuality, the truth of the situation was much closer to the sentiments of James Jarves, who wrote: "The missionary was a far more useful and agreeable man than his Catholicism would indicate; and the trader was not so bad a man as the missionary would make him out to be." The missionaries' primary aim might have been conversion, but the most fortuitous by-product was education, which raised the consciousness of every Hawaiian, regardless of religious affiliation. In 40 short years Hawaii was considered a civilized nation well on

its way into the modern world, and the American Board of Missions officially ended its support in 1863.

Non-Christians

By the late 1800s, both Shintoism and Buddhism, brought by the Japanese and Chinese, were firmly established in Hawaii. The first official Buddhist temple was Hongpa Hongwanji, established on O'ahu in 1889. All the denominations of Buddhism account for 17 percent of the island's religious total, and there are about 50,000 Shintoists. The Hindu religion has perhaps 2,000 adherents, and roughly 10,000 Jewish people live throughout Hawaii. The largest number of people in Hawaii (300,000) remain unaffiliated, and about 10,000 people are in new religious movements and lesser-known faiths such as Baha'i and Unitarianism.

LANGUAGE

Hawaii is part of the United States and people speak English there, but that's not the whole story. If you turn on the TV to catch the evening news, you'll hear "Walter Cronkite" English, unless of course you happen to tune in to a Japanese-language broadcast designed for tourists from that country. You can easily pick up a Chinese-language newspaper or groove to the music on a Filipino radio station, but let's not confuse the issue. All of your needs and requests at airports, car rental agencies, restaurants, hotels, or wherever you happen to travel will be completely understood, as well as answered, in English. However, when you happen to overhear islanders speaking, what they're saying will sound somewhat familiar, but you won't be able to pick up all the words, and the beat and melody of the language will be noticeably different.

Hawaii—like New England, the deep South, and the Midwest—has its own unmistakable linguistic regionalism. The many ethnic people who make up Hawaii have enriched the English spoken there with words, expressions, and subtle shades of meaning that are commonly used and understood throughout the islands. The greatest influence on the English spoken here has come from the Hawaiian language, and words such

THE ALPHABET.

VOWELS.

Names.	SOUND.	
	Ex. in Eng.	Ex. in Hawaii.
A a ---â	as in *father*,	la—sun.
E e --- a	— *tele*,	hemo—cast off.
I i --- e	— *marine*,	marie—quiet.
O o --- o	— *over*,	ono—sweet.
U u --- oo	—*rule*,	nui—large.

CONSONANTS.	Names.	CONSONANTS.	Names.
B b	be	**N n**	nu
D d	de	**P p**	pi
H h	he	**R r**	ro
K k	ke	**T t**	ti
L l	la	**V v**	vi
M m	mu	**W w**	we

The following are used in spelling foreign words:

F f	fe	S s	se
G g	ge	Y y	yi

The cover page of the first Hawaiian primer shows the phonetic rendering of the ancient Hawaiian language before five of the consonants were dropped.

as aloha, hula, lu'au, and lei are familiarly used and understood by most Americans.

Other migrant peoples, especially the Chinese, Japanese, and Portuguese, influenced the local dialect to such an extent that the simplified plantation lingo they spoke has become known as "pidgin." A fun and enriching part of the island experience is picking up a few words of Hawaiian and pidgin. English is the official language of the state, business, education, and perhaps even the mind, but pidgin is the language of the people, the emotions, and life, while Hawaiian (also an official language of the state, but used "only as provided by law") remains the language of the heart and the soul.

Note: Many Hawaiian words are commonly used in English, appear in English dictionaries, and therefore would ordinarily be subject to the rules of English grammar. The Hawaiian language, however, does not pluralize nouns by adding an "s"; the singular and plural are differentiated in context. For purposes of this book, and to highlight the Hawaiian culture, the Hawaiian style of pluralization will be followed for common Hawaiian words. The following are some examples of plural Hawaiian nouns treated this way in this book: *haole* (not *haoles*), *kahuna*, *lei*, *lu'au*, and *nene*.

Pidgin

The dictionary definition of pidgin is "a simplified language with a rudimentary grammar used as a means of communication between people speaking different languages." Hawaiian pidgin is a little more complicated than that. It had its roots during the plantation days of the 19th century when white owners and *luna* (foremen) had to communicate with recently arrived Chinese, Japanese, and Portuguese laborers. It evolved as a simple language of the here and now, primarily concerned with the necessary functions of working, eating, and sleeping. It has an economical noun-verb-object structure (although not necessarily in that order).

Hawaiian words make up most of pidgin's non-English vocabulary, but it includes a good smattering of Chinese, Japanese, and Samoan as well. The distinctive rising inflection is provided by the melodious Mediterranean lilt of the Portuguese. Pidgin is not a stagnant language. It's kept alive by hip new words introduced by cool people or especially by slang words introduced by teenagers. It's a colorful English, like "jive" spoken by American blacks, and is as regionally unique as the speech of Cajuns from Louisiana's bayous. *Maka'ainana* of all socioethnic backgrounds can at least understand pidgin. Most islanders are proud of it, but some consider it a low-class jargon. The Hawaiian House of Representatives has given pidgin an official sanction, and most people feel that it adds a real local style and should be preserved.

Pidgin, if not spoken at home, is first learned in the schoolyard, where all students, regardless of background, are exposed to it. The pidgin spoken by young people today is "fo' real" different from that of their parents. It's no longer only plantation talk but has moved to the streets and picked up some sophistication. At one time there was an academic movement to exterminate it, but that idea died away with the same thinking that insisted on making left-handed people write with their right hands. It is strange, however, that pidgin has become the unofficial language of Hawaii's grassroots movement, when it actually began as a white owners' language that was used to supplant Hawaiian and all other languages brought to the islands.

Although hip young *haole* use pidgin all the time, it has gained the connotation of being the language of the nonwhite locals and is part of the "us against them" way of thinking. All local people, *haole* or not, do consider pidgin their own island language and don't really like it when it's used by *malihini* (newcomers). If you're in the islands long enough, you don't have to bother learning pidgin; it'll learn you. There's a book sold all over the islands called *Pidgin to da Max,* written by (you guessed it) a *haole* from Nebraska named Doug Simonson. You might not be able to understand what's being said by locals speaking pidgin (that's usually the idea), but you should be able to *feel* what's being meant.

Hawaiian

The Hawaiian language sways like a palm tree in a gentle wind. Its words are as melodious as a love song. Linguists say that you can learn a lot about people through their language: When you hear Hawaiian you think of gentleness and love, and it's hard to imagine the ferocious side so evident in Hawaii's past. With its many Polynesian root words easily traced to Indonesian and Malay, Hawaiian is obviously from this same stock. The Hawaiian spoken today is very different from old Hawaiian. Its greatest metamorphosis occurred when the missionaries began to write it down in the 1820s, but in the last couple of decades there has been a movement to reestablish the Hawaiian language. Not only are courses in it offered at the University of Hawai'i, but there is also a successful elementary school immer-

sion program in the state, some books are being printed in it, and more and more musicians are performing it. Many scholars have put forth translations of Hawaiian, but there are endless, volatile disagreements in the academic sector about the real meanings of Hawaiian words. Hawaiian is, by and large, no longer spoken as a language except on Ni'ihau and in Hawaiian-language immersion classes and in the families of those students; the closest tourists will come to it is in place names, street names, and words that have become part of common usage, such as aloha and *mahalo.* A few old Hawaiians still speak it at home, and there are sermons in Hawaiian at some local churches. Kawaiaha'o Church in downtown Honolulu is the most famous of these, but each island has its own.

Thanks to the missionaries, the Hawaiian language is rendered phonetically using only 12 letters. They are the five vowels, a-e-i-o-u, sounded as they are in Italian, and seven consonants, h-k-l-m-n-p-w, sounded exactly as they are in English. Sometimes "w" is pronounced as "v," but this only occurs in the middle of a word and always follows a vowel. A consonant is always followed by a vowel, forming two-letter syllables, but vowels are often found in pairs or even triplets. A slight oddity about Hawaiian is the glottal stop called *'okina.* This is an abrupt break in sound in the middle of a word, such as "oh-oh" in English, and is denoted with a reverse apostrophe ('). A good example is *ali'i* or, even better, the O'ahu town of Ha'iku, which actually means Abrupt Break.

Pronunciation Key

For those unfamiliar with the sounds of Italian or other Romance languages, the vowels are sounded as follows:

A—pronounced as in "ah" (that feels good!). For example, *tapa* is "tah-pah."

E—short "e" is "eh," as in "pen" or "dent" (thus *hale* is "hah-leh"). Long "e" sounds like "ay" as in "sway" or "day." For example, the Hawaiian goose *(nene)* is a "nay-nay," not a "nee-nee."

I—pronounced "ee" as in "see" or "we" (thus *pali* is pronounced "pah-lee").

O—pronounced as in "no" or "oh," such as "oh-noh" (ono).

U—pronounced "oo" as in "do" or "stew"; for example, "kah-poo" *(kapu).*

Diphthongs

Eight vowel pairs are known as "diphthongs" (ae-ai-ao-au-ei-eu-oi-ou). These are the sounds made by gliding from one vowel to another within a syllable. The stress is placed on the first vowel. In English, examples would be **soil** and **bail.** Common examples in Hawaiian are lei and *heiau.*

Stress

The best way to learn which syllables are stressed in Hawaiian is by listening closely. It becomes obvious after a while. There are also some vowel sounds that are held longer than others; these can occur at the beginning of a word, such as the first "a" in *"aina,"* or in the middle of a word, like the first "a" in *lanai.* Again, it's a matter of tuning your ear and paying attention.

When written, these stressed vowels, called *kahako,* occur with a macron, or short line, over them. Stressed vowels with marks are not written as such in this book.

No one is going to give you a hard time if you mispronounce a word. It's good, however, to pay close attention to the pronunciation of street and place names because many Hawaiian words sound alike; a misplaced vowel here or there could be the difference between getting to where you want to go and getting lost.

ARTS OF OLD HAWAII

Because everything in old Hawaii had to be fashioned by hand, almost every object was either a genuine work of art or the product of a highly refined craft. With the "civilizing" of the natives, most of the old ways disappeared, including the old arts and crafts. Most authentic Hawaiian art by master craftsmen exists only in museums, but with the resurgence of Hawaiian roots, many old arts are being revitalized, and their legacy lives on in a few artists who have become proficient in them.

Magnificent Canoes

The most respected artisans in old Hawaii were the canoe makers. With little more than a stone adze and a pump drill, they built canoes that could carry 200 people and last for generations—sleek, well proportioned, and infinitely seaworthy. The main hull was usually a gigantic koa log, and the gunwale planks were minutely drilled and sewn to the sides with sennit rope. Apprenticeships lasted for years, and a young man knew that he had graduated when one day he was nonchalantly asked to sit down and eat with the master builders. Small family-sized canoes with outriggers were used for fishing and perhaps carried a spear rack; large oceangoing double-hulled canoes were used for migration and warfare. On these, the giant logs had been adzed to about two inches thick. A mainsail woven from pandanus was mounted on a central platform, and the boat was steered by two long paddles. The hull was dyed with plant juices and charcoal, and the entire village helped launch the canoe in a ceremony called "drinking the sea."

Carving

Wood was a primary material used by Hawaiian craftsmen. They almost exclusively used koa because of its density, strength, and natural luster. It was turned into canoes, woodware, calabashes, and furniture for the *ali'i.* Temple idols were another major product of wood carving. A variety of stone artifacts were also turned out, including poi pounders, mirrors, fish sinkers, and small idols.

Weaving

Hawaiians became the best basket makers and mat weavers in all of Polynesia. *Ulana* (woven mats) were made from *lau hala* (pandanus) leaves. Once split, the spine was removed and the leaves stored in large rolls. When needed they were soaked, pounded, and then fashioned into various floor coverings and sleeping mats. Intricate geometrical patterns were woven in, and the edges were rolled and well fashioned. Coconut palms were not used to make mats in

ARTS MUSINGS

Referring to Hawaii as paradise is about as hackneyed as you can get, but when you specify artists' paradise, it's the absolute truth. Something about the place evokes art (or at least personal expression). The islands are like a magnet: They not only draw artists to them, but they draw art *from* the artists.

The inspiration comes from the astounding natural surroundings. The land is so beautiful yet so raw; the ocean's power and rhythm are primal and ever-present; the riotous colors of flowers and fruit leap from the deep-green jungle background. Crystal water beads and pale mists turn the mountains into mystic temples, while rainbows ride the crests of waves. The stunning variety of faces begging to be rendered appears as if all the world sent delegations to the islands – and in most cases it did! Inspiration is everywhere, as is art, good or bad.

Sometimes the artwork is overpowering in itself; sometimes it is overwhelming in its sheer volume. There is hardly a shop in Hawaii that doesn't sell some item that falls into the general category of art. You can find everything from carved monkey-face coconut shells to true masterpieces on canvas. The Polynesian Hawaiians were master craftspeople, and their legacy still lives in a wide variety of wood carvings, weavings, featherwork, and tapa cloth. The hula is art in swaying motion, and the true form is rigorously studied and taken seriously. Everywhere you go, slack key balladeers and ukulele players perform the melodious sounds of island music, and the soft twang of Hawaii's own steel guitars spills from many lounges.

old Hawaii, but a wide variety of basketry was made from the aerial root *'ie'ie*. The shapes varied according to use. Some baskets were tall and narrow, some were cones, others were flat like trays, and many were woven around gourds and calabashes.

Featherwork

This highly refined art was practiced only on the islands of Tahiti, New Zealand, and Hawaii, but the fashioning of feather helmets and idols was unique to Hawaii. Favorite colors were red and yellow, which came only in a very limited supply from a small number of birds such as the *'o'o, 'i'iwi, mamo,* and *'apapane.* Professional bird hunters in old Hawaii paid their taxes to *ali'i* in prized feathers. The feathers were fastened to a woven net of *olona* cord and made into helmets, idols, and beautiful flowing capes and cloaks. These resplendent garments were made and worn only by men, especially during battle, when a fine cloak became a great trophy of war. Featherwork was also employed in the making of *kahili* and lei, which were highly prized by the noble *ali'i* women.

Lei Making

Any flower or blossom can be strung into a lei, but the most common are orchids or the lovely smelling plumeria. Lei, like babies, are all beautiful, but special lei are highly prized by those who know what to look for. Of the different stringing styles, the most common is *kui*—stringing the flower through the middle or side. Most "airport-quality" lei are of this type. The *humuhumu* style, reserved for making flat lei, is made by sewing flowers and ferns to a *ti,* banana, or sometimes *hala* leaf. A *humuhumu* lei makes an excellent hatband. *Wili* is the winding together of greenery, ferns, and flowers into short, bouquet-type lengths. The most traditional form is *hili,* which requires no stringing at all but involves braiding fragrant ferns and leaves such as *maile.* If flowers are interwoven, the *hili* becomes the *haku* style, the most difficult and most beautiful type of lei.

Every major island is symbolized by its own lei made from a distinctive flower, shell, or fern. Each island has its own official color as well, although it doesn't necessarily correspond to the color of the island's lei. O'ahu, "The Gathering Place," is symbolized by yellow,

O'AHU ARTS AND CULTURE INFORMATION

Arts With Aloha (www.artswithaloha.com). An association of major arts and cultural organizations in Honolulu that provides quick and easy information about its member organizations through a printed brochure and website.

Bishop Museum (1525 Bernice St., Honolulu, HI 96817, 808/847-3511, www.bishop.hawaii.org). The world's *best* museum covering Hawaii and Polynesia. Exhibits, galleries, archives, demonstrations of Hawaiian crafts, and a planetarium.

Hawai'i Craftsmen (P.O. Box 22145, Honolulu, HI 96823, 808/596-8128, www.hawaiicraftsmen.org). Increases awareness of Hawaiian crafts through programs, exhibitions, workshops, lectures, and demonstrations.

Honolulu Academy of Arts (900 S. Beretania St., Honolulu, HI 96814, 808/532-8701, www.honoluluacademy.org). Collects, preserves, and exhibits works of fine art. Offers public art education programs related to its collections. Also offers tours, classes, lectures, films, and publications.

Mayor's Office of Culture and the Arts (530 S. King St., Rm. 404, Honolulu, HI 96813, 808/523-4674, www.co.honolulu.hi.us/moca). The City and County of Honolulu's official organ for visual and performing arts information islandwide.

Pacific Handcrafters Guild (P.O. Box 29389, Honolulu, HI 96820-1789 or 808/254-6788, www.alternative-hawaii.com/profiles/crafters/phg.htm). Focuses on developing and preserving handicrafts and fine arts of all mediums. The guild sponsors four major crafts fairs annually.

State Foundation on Culture and the Arts (250 Hotel St., 2nd Floor, Honolulu, HI 96813, 808/586-0300, www.hawaii.gov/sfca). Begun by state legislature in 1965 to preserve and promote Hawaii's diverse cultural, artistic, and historical heritage. Manages grants, maintains programs in folk arts and art in public places, and runs the Hawaii State Art Museum.

the color of the tropical sun. Its flower is the delicate *'ilima,* which resembles hibiscus and ranges in color from pastel yellow to a burnt orange. The blooms are about as large as a silver dollar, and lei made from *'ilima* were at one time reserved only for the *ali'i,* designating them as a royal flower.

Tapa Cloth
Tapa, cloth made from tree bark, was common throughout Polynesia and was a woman's art. A few trees such as the *wauke* and *mamaki* produced the best cloth, but a variety of other types of bark could be utilized. First the raw bark was pounded into a feltlike pulp and beaten together to form strips (the beaters had distinctive patterns that helped make the cloth supple). The cloth was then decorated by stamping (a form of block printing) and dyed

with natural colors from plants and sea animals in shades of gray, purple, pink, and red. They were even painted with natural brushes made from pandanus fruit, with an overall gray color made from charcoal. The tapa cloth was sewn together to make bed coverings, and fragrant flowers and herbs were either sewn or pounded in to produce a permanent fragrance. Tapa cloth is still available today, but the Hawaiian methods have been lost, and most tapa comes from other areas of Polynesia.

ARTS TO BUY
Alohawear
Wild Hawaiian shirts or bright mu'umu'u, especially when worn on the Mainland, have the magical effect of making the wearer feel as if they're in Hawaii, while at the same time eliciting spontaneous smiles from passersby.

MUSEUMS AND GALLERIES OF O'AHU

Bishop Museum (1525 Bernice St., Honolulu, 808/847-3511, www.bishopmuseum.org, open daily 9 A.M.–5 P.M.). The best collection in the world on Polynesia in general and Hawaii specifically. A true cultural treat that should not be missed. A small adjunct museum is located at the Hilton Hawaiian Village in Waikiki.

The Contemporary Museum (2411 Makiki Heights Dr., Honolulu, 808/526-0232, www.tcmhi.org, open Tues.–Sat. 10 A.M.–4 P.M., Sun. noon–4 P.M.). The focus is on exhibitions, not collections, although there are permanent displays. Changing exhibits reflect different themes in contemporary art.

Damien Museum (130 Ohua Ave., Waikiki, open weekdays 9 A.M.–3 P.M.), at Saint Augustine Catholic Church, displays photographs, papers, artifacts, and mementos of the legendary Father Damien who helped leprosy patients on Moloka'i.

Hawaii Maritime Center (808/536-6373, open daily except Christmas 8:30 A.M.–5 P.M.) is at Pier 7, Honolulu Harbor. A museum chronicling the exploration and exploitation of Hawaii by the seafarers who have come to its shores. Visit the famous double-hulled canoe *Hokule'a* and the tall-masted *Falls of Clyde*.

Hawaii's Plantation Village (94-695 Waipahu St., Waipahu, 808/677-0110, www.hawaiiplantationvillage.org, open Mon.–Sat. 9 A.M.–3 P.M.). An open-air museum portraying sugar plantation life and the ethnic mix of plantation workers with restored buildings and memorabilia. While the village is open for guided tours only, the galleries in the main building can be seen on your own.

Hawaii State Art Museum (250 Hotel St., Honolulu, 808/586-0304, open Tues.–Sat. 10 A.M.–4 P.M.). Galleries showcase art by Hawaii residents. Open galleries with some guided tours.

Honolulu Academy of Arts (900 S. Beretania St., Honolulu, 808/532-8701, open Tues.–Sat. 10 A.M.–4:30 P.M., Sun. 1-5 P.M.). Collects, preserves, and exhibits works of art, classic and modern, with a strong emphasis on Asian art. Permanent and special exhibitions, with tours, classes, lectures, and films. Across from the Academy of Arts, the affiliated **Academy Art Center at Linekona** displays student artwork, mostly of a contemporary Hawaiian nature.

'Iolani Palace ('Iolani Palace Grounds, Honolulu, 808/522-0832, www.iolanipalace.org). The only royal palace in the United States. Vintage artwork and antiques. Guided and non-guided tours offered.

Honolulu Police Department's Law Enforcement Museum (801 Beretania St., Honolulu, 808/529-3351, open weekdays 9 A.M.–3 P.M.). Located at the city police headquarters, this museum takes a broad look at the history of law enforcement in the state.

King's Guard Museum (131 Kai'ulani Ave., 808/944-6855, open daily 5:30-10 P.M.). Honors an organization paying homage to the king's royal guards from the days of King Kalakaua. Small display of artifacts.

Mission Houses Museum (553 S. King St., Honolulu, 808/531-0481, www.missionhouses.org, open Tues.–Sat.). Two homes, a printing house, and a library make up this early mission compound. Guided tours only. Excellent.

North Shore Surf and Cultural Museum (808/637-8888, Hale'iwa). A down-to-earth collection of surfing memorabilia and surfing life on the North Shore.

Pacific Aviation Museum (Pearl Harbor, 808/690-0169, www.pacificaviationmuseum. org, open daily 9:30 A.M.-4:30 P.M.). Focuses on aviation history, before, during, and after World War II.

Queen Emma Summer Palace (2913 Pali Hwy., Honolulu, 808/595-3167, www.daughtersof-hawaii.org, open daily 9 A.M.-4 P.M., except major holidays). Restored historic home, built about 1848. Furniture and mementos of Queen Emma and her family. Some items belong to other members of the royal family.

Queen's Medical Center Historical Room (1301 Punchbowl St., Honolulu, 808/547-4397, open weekdays 8:30 A.M.-3:30 P.M.). Free exhibits display the history of the Queen's Medical Center (founded 1859) and the history of medicine in Hawaii.

Tennent Art Foundation Gallery (201-203 Prospect St., Honolulu, 808/531-1987, open Tues.-Sat. 10 A.M.-noon, Sun. 2-4 P.M.). Private gallery showing works of Madge Tennent, one of Hawaii's most prolific and esteemed painters.

Tropic Lightning Museum (808/655-0438, open Tues.-Sat. 10 A.M.-4 P.M. except federal holidays) is located directly up from Macomb Gate on Schofield Barracks. Military museum on the history of Schofield Barracks Army Base and the 25th Infantry Division.

University of Hawai'i Art Gallery (808/956-6888, www.hawaii.edu/artgallery). This Department of Art gallery showcases faculty, student, and traveling exhibitions. Open during the academic year only, Mon.-Fri. 10:30 A.M.-4 P.M. and Sunday noon-4 P.M. Also open on the university campus are an Art Department adjunct gallery on the third floor of the student center, the **John Young Museum of Art** at Krauss Hall, the **East-West Center Gallery** at the John Burns Hall.

U.S. Army Museum of Hawaii (808/438-2821, Fort DeRussy, Waikiki, open Tues.-Sun. 10 A.M.-4:15 P.M.). Covers military history of Hawaii from the time of Kamehameha I to the activities of the U.S. Army in East Asia and the Pacific islands.

USS *Arizona* Memorial (Pearl Harbor, 808/422-2771, www.nps.gov/usar, open daily except Thanksgiving, Christmas, and New Year's Day 7:30 A.M.-5 P.M.). Navy launches take you to the sleek 184-foot white concrete structure that spans the sunken USS *Arizona*. No reservations, no fee: entrance is first-come, first-served. Visitors center offers graphic materials and film, reflecting events of the Pearl Harbor attack. A must-see.

USS *Bowfin* Submarine Museum (Pearl Harbor, 808/423-1341, www.bowfin.org, open daily except Thanksgiving, Christmas, and New Year's Day 8 A.M.-5 P.M.). Self-guided tours of this fully restored World War II submarine offer insight into the underwater war. Fascinating. Next door to Arizona Memorial.

USS *Missouri* (Pearl Harbor, 808/423-2263, www.ussmissouri.org, open 9 A.M.-5 P.M. daily). It was on this refurbished World War II ship that the documents ending war hostilities were signed. A fitting counterpoint to the USS *Arizona*, the destruction of which pushed the United States into the war.

Maybe it's the colors, or perhaps it's just the vibe that signifies "party time" or "hang loose," but nothing says Hawaii like alohawear. There are more than a dozen fabric houses in Hawaii turning out distinctive patterns, and many dozens of factories create their own personalized designs. These factories often have attached retail outlets, but in any case you can find hundreds of shops selling alohawear. Aloha shirts were the brilliant idea of a Chinese merchant in Honolulu, who used to hand-tailor them and sell them to the tourists who arrived by ship in the glory days before World War II. They were an instant success. Muʻumuʻu or "Mother Hubbards" were the idea of missionaries, who were appalled by Hawaiian women running about au naturel and insisted on covering their new Christian converts from head to foot. Now the roles are reversed, and it's the Mainlanders who come to Hawaii and immediately strip down to as little clothing as possible.

At one time alohawear was exclusively made of cotton or from manmade, natural fiber-based rayon, and these materials are still the best for any tropical clothing. Beware, however: Polyester has crept into the market! No material could possibly be worse for the island climate, so when buying your alohawear, make sure to check the label for material content. On the bright side, silk is also used and makes a good material, but is a bit heavy for some. Muʻumuʻu now come in various styles and can be worn for the entire spectrum of social occasions in Hawaii. Aloha shirts are basically cut the same as always, but the patterns have undergone changes, and apart from the original flowers and ferns, modern shirts might depict an island scene in the manner of a silk-screen painting. A basic good-quality muʻumuʻu or aloha shirt is guaranteed to be worth its price in good times and happy smiles.

The connoisseur might want to purchase *The Hawaiian Shirt, Its Art and History,* by R. Thomas Steele. It's illustrated with more than 150 shirts that are now considered works of art by collectors the world over. Other newer books with the same dedication to quality are *The Aloha Shirt: Spirit of the Islands* by Dale Hope and **The Art of the Aloha Shirt** by Brown and Arthur.

Scrimshaw

This art of etching and carving on bone and ivory has become an island tradition handed down from the times of the old whaling ships. Although scrimshaw can be found throughout Hawaii, the center remains in the old whaling capital of Lahaina. There along Front Street are a few shops specializing in scrimshaw. Today, pieces are carved on fossilized walrus ivory that is gathered by Inuit and shipped to Hawaii. It comes in a variety of shades from pure white to mocha, depending on the mineral content of the earth in which it was buried. Elephant ivory or whale bone is no longer used because of ecological considerations, but there is a "gray market" in Pacific walrus tusks. Inuit can legally hunt the walrus. They then make a few minimal scratches on the tusks, which technically qualifies them to be "Native American art" and free of most governmental restrictions. The tusks are then sent to Hawaii as art objects, but the superficial scratches are immediately removed and the ivory is reworked by artisans. Scrimshaw is made into everything from belt buckles to delicate earrings and even into coffee-table centerpieces. Prices go from a few dollars up to thousands and can be found in limited quantities in some galleries and fine art shops around the island.

Wood Carvings

While the carving and fashioning of old traditional items has by and large disappeared, lathe-turning of wooden bowls and the creation of wooden furniture from native woods is alive and strong. Old Hawaiians used koa almost exclusively because of its density, strength, and natural luster, but koa is becoming increasingly scarce. Costly *milo* and monkeypod, as well as a host of other native woods, are also excellent for turnings and household items and have largely replaced koa. These modern wooden objects are available at numerous shops and galleries. Countless inexpensive carved items are sold at variety stores, such as little hula girls or salad servers, but most of these are imported from Asia or the Philippines.

Weaving

The tradition of weaving has survived in Hawaii but is not strong. Older experienced weavers are dying and few younger ones are showing interest in continuing the craft. The time-tested material of *lau hala* is still best, although much is now made from coconut fronds. *Lau hala* is traditional Hawaiian weaving from the leaves *(lau)* of the pandanus *(hala)* tree. These leaves vary greatly in length, with the largest over six feet, and they have a thorny spine that must be removed before they can be worked. The color ranges from light tan to dark brown. The leaves are cut into strips one-eighth to one inch wide and are then employed in weaving. Any variety of items can be made or at least covered in *lau hala*. It makes great purses, mats, baskets, and table mats. You can still purchase items from bags to a woven hat, and all share the desirable qualities of strength, lightness, and ventilation.

Woven into a hat, it's absolutely superb but should not be confused with a palm-frond hat. A *lau hala* hat is amazingly supple and will pop back into shape even when squashed. A good one is expensive and will last for years with proper care. All *lau hala* should be given a light application of mineral oil on a monthly basis, especially if it's exposed to the sun. For flat items, iron over a damp cloth and keep purses and baskets stuffed with paper when not in use. Palm fronds are also widely used in weaving. They, too, are a great natural raw material, but not as good as *lau hala*. Almost any woven item, such as a beach bag woven from palm, makes a good authentic yet inexpensive gift or souvenir.

Quilts

Along with the gospel and the will to educate, the early missionaries brought skills and machines to sew. Aside from wanting to cover the naked bodies of their new converts, many taught the Hawaiians how to quilt together small pieces of material into designs for the bed.

Quilting styles and patterns varied over the years and generally shifted from designs familiar to New Englanders to those more pleasing to Hawaiian eyes, and a number of standard patterns include leaves, fruits, and flowers of the islands. Most Hawaiian-design quilts for sale in the islands today are made in the Philippines under the direction of Hawaiian designers. Because of labor costs, they are far less expensive than any quilt actually made in Hawaii.

Paintings

One thing is for sure: like the rest of the Hawaiian Islands, O'ahu draws painters—multitudes of painters. Captivated by the island's beauty, color, natural features, and living things, these artists interpret what they see and sense in a dizzying display from realism to expressionism. From immense *pali* cliffs to the tiniest flower petals, and humble workers' homes to the faces of the island people, they are all portrayed. Color, movement, and feeling are captured, and the essence of Hawaii is the result. Galleries and shops around the island display local artists' work, but there is a concentration of galleries in Waikiki and on the North Shore in Hale'iwa. Well-known artists charge a handsome fee for their work, but you can find some exceptional work for affordable prices hidden here and there among the rest.

Gift Items

Jewelry is always an appreciated gift, especially if it's distinctive, and Hawaii has some of the most original. The sea provides the basic raw materials of pink, gold, and black coral that are as beautiful and fascinating as gemstones. Harvesting coral is very dangerous work. The Lahaina beds off Maui have one of the best black coral lodes in the islands, but unlike reef coral, these trees grow at depths bordering the outer limits of a scuba diver's capabilities. Only the best can dive 180 feet after the black coral, and about one diver per year dies in pursuit of it. Conservationists have placed great pressure on the harvesters of these deep corals, and the state of Hawaii has placed strict limits and guidelines on the firms and divers involved.

Pink coral has long been treasured by humans. The Greeks considered it a talisman for good health, and there's even evidence that it has been coveted since the Stone Age. Coral jewelry is for sale at many shops throughout Hawaii, and the value comes from the color of the coral and the workmanship.

Puka shells (with small, naturally occurring holes) and *'opihi* shells are also made into jewelry. These items are often inexpensive, yet they are authentic and are great purchases for the price.

Hawaii also produces some unique food items appreciated by most people. Jars of macadamia nuts and butters are great gifts, as are tins of rich, gourmet-quality Kona coffee. Guava, pineapple, passion fruit, and mango are often gift-boxed into assortments of jams, jellies, and spicy chutneys. And for that special person in your life, you can bring home island fragrances in bars of soap and bottles of perfumes and colognes in the exotic odors of gardenia, plumeria, and even ginger. All of these items are reasonably priced, lightweight, and easy to carry.

HULA

The hula is more than an ethnic dance; it is the soul of Hawaii expressed in motion. It began as a form of worship during religious ceremonies and was danced only by highly trained men. It gradually evolved into a form of entertainment, but in no regard was it sexual. The hula was the opera, theater, and lecture hall of the islands all rolled into one. It was history portrayed in the performing arts. In the beginning an androgynous deity named Laka descended to earth and taught men how to dance the hula. In time the male aspect of Laka departed for the heavens, but the female aspect remained. The female Laka set up her own special hula *heiau* at Ha'ena on the Na Pali coast of Kaua'i, where it still exists. As time went on women were allowed to learn the hula. Scholars surmise that

Hula dancers perform at hotels, lu'au, shopping centers, and many other venues around the island.

© J.D. BISIGNANI

men became too busy wresting a living from the land to maintain the art form.

Men did retain a type of hula for themselves called *lua*. This was a form of martial art employed in hand-to-hand combat that evolved into a ritualized warfare dance called *hula ku'i*. During the 19th century, the hula almost vanished because the missionaries considered it vile and heathen. King Kalakaua is generally regarded as having saved it during the late 1800s, when he formed his own troupe and encouraged the dancers to learn the old hula. Many of the original dances were forgotten, but some were retained and are performed to this day. Although professional dancers were highly trained, everyone took part in the hula. *Ali'i*, commoners, young, and old all danced.

Hula is art in swaying motion, and the true form is studied rigorously and taken seriously. Today, hula *halau* (schools) are active on every island, teaching hula and keeping the old ways and culture alive. (Ancient hula is called *hula kahiko,* and modern renditions are known as *hula auana.*) Performers still spend years perfecting their techniques. They show off their accomplishments during the fierce competition of the Merrie Monarch Festival in Hilo every April. The winning *halau* is praised and recognized throughout the islands.

Hawaiian hula was never performed in grass skirts; tapa or *ti*-leaf skirts were worn. Grass skirts came to Hawaii from the Gilbert Islands, so if you see grass or cellophane skirts in a hula revue, it's not traditional. Almost every major resort offering entertainment or a lu'au also offers a revue. Most times, young island beauties accompanied by proficient local musicians put on a floor show for the tourists. It'll be fun, but it won't be traditional.

A hula dancer has to learn how to control every part of his or her body, including the facial expressions, which help set the mood. The hands are extremely important and provide instant background scenery. For example, if the hands are thrust outward in an aggressive manner, this can be a battle; if they sway gently overhead, they refer to the gods or to creation; they can easily symbolize rain, clouds, sun, sea, or moon. Watch the hands to get the gist of the story, but as one wise guy said, "You watch the parts you like, and I'll watch the parts I like." The motion of swaying hips can denote a long walk, a canoe ride, or sexual intercourse. Foot motion can portray a battle, a walk, or any kind of conveyance. The overall effect is multidirectional synchronized movement. The correct chanting of the *mele* is an integral part of the performance. These story chants, accompanied by musical instruments, make the hula very much like opera; it is especially similar in the way the tale unfolds.

THAT GOOD OLD ISLAND MUSIC

The missionaries usually take a beating when it's recounted how much Hawaiian culture they destroyed while "civilizing" the natives. However, they seem to have done one thing right. They introduced the Hawaiians to the diatonic musical scale and immediately opened a door to latent and superbly harmonious talent. Before the missionaries, the Hawaiians knew little about melody. Although sonorous, their *mele* were repetitive chants in which the emphasis was placed on historical accuracy and not on "making music." The Hawaiians, in short, didn't *sing*. But within a few years of the missionaries' arrival, they were belting out good old Christian hymns, and one of their favorite pastimes became group and individual singing.

Early in the 1800s, Spanish *vaqueros* from California were imported to teach the Hawaiians how to be cowboys. With them came guitars and moody ballads. The Hawaiian *paniolos* (cowboys) quickly learned how to punch cows and croon away the long, lonely nights on the range. Immigrants who came along a little later in the 19th century, especially from Portugal, helped create a Hawaiian-style music. Their biggest influence was a small, four-stringed instrument called a *braga* or *cavaquinho*. One owned by Augusto Dias was the prototype of a homegrown Hawaiian instrument that became known as the ukulele. Jumping flea, the translation of ukulele, is an appropriate name devised by the Hawaiians when they saw how

CHANTS

Until the 1820s, when New England missionaries began a phonetic rendering of the Hawaiian language, the past was kept vividly alive only by the sonorous voices of special *kahuna* who chanted the sacred *mele*. The chants were beautiful flowing word pictures that captured the essence of every aspect of life. These *mele* praised the land *(mele 'aina)*, royalty *(mele ali'i)*, and life's tender aspects *(mele aloha)*. Chants were dedicated to friendship, hardship, and favorite children. Entire villages sometimes joined together to compose a *mele* – every word was chosen carefully, and the wise old *kahuna* would decide if the words were lucky or unlucky. Some *mele* were bawdy or funny on the surface but contained secret meanings, often bitingly sarcastic, which ridiculed an inept or cruel leader. The most important chants took listeners back into the dim past before people lived in Hawaii. From these genealogies *(koihonua)* the *ali'i* derived the right to rule because these chants went back to the gods Wakea and Papa from whom the *ali'i* were directly descended.

Today, the art of chanting continues but in a manner that is, perhaps, less strict but still serious; it is generally used for cultural events, meetings, and ceremonies where the importance is beyond question. Often the *kahuna* dresses in traditional Hawaiian garb and his resonant voice still casts a spell upon listeners like similar voices have done for generations. Chants also appear on some modern Hawaiian music CDs, so this ancient form is getting a wider hearing.

nimble the fingers were as they jumped over the strings.

King Kalakaua (The Merrie Monarch) and Queen Lili'uokalani were both patrons of the arts who furthered the Hawaiian musical identity at the turn of the 20th century. Kalakaua revived the hula and was also a gifted lyricist and balladeer. He wrote the words to "Hawaii Pono'i," which became the anthem of the nation of Hawaii and later the state anthem. Lili'uokalani wrote the hauntingly beautiful "Aloha O'e," which is often pointed to as the "spirit of Hawaii" in music. Detractors say that its melody is extremely close to that of the old Christian hymn, "Rock Beside the Sea," but the lyrics are so beautiful and perfectly fitted that this doesn't matter.

Just before Kalakaua's reign, a Prussian bandmaster, Captain Henry Berger, was invited to head the fledgling Royal Hawaiian Band, which he turned into a very respectable orchestra lauded by many visitors to the islands. Berger was open-minded and learned to love Hawaiian music. He collaborated with Kalakaua and other island musicians to incorporate their music into a Western format. He headed the band for 43 years, until 1915, and was instrumental in making music a serious pursuit of talented Hawaiians.

Popular Hawaiian Music

Hawaiian music has a unique twang, a special feeling that says the same thing to everyone who hears it: "Relax, sit back in the moonlight, watch the swaying palms as the surf sings a lullaby." This special sound is epitomized by the bouncy ukulele, the falsettos of Hawaiian crooners, and the smooth ring of the steel or Hawaiian guitar. The steel guitar is a variation originated by Joseph Kekuku in the 1890s. Stories abound of how Joseph Kekuku devised this instrument; the most popular versions say that Joe dropped his comb or pocketknife on his guitar strings and liked what he heard. Driven by the faint rhythm of an inner sound, he went to the machine shop at the Kamehameha School and turned out a steel bar for sliding over the strings. To complete the sound he changed the catgut strings to steel and raised them so they wouldn't hit the frets. Voila! Hawaiian music as the world knows it today.

The first melodious strains of **slack-key**

guitar *(ki ho'alu)* can be traced back to the time of Kamehameha III and the *vaqueros* from California. The Spanish had their way of tuning the guitar and played difficult and aggressive music that did not sit well with Hawaiians, who were much more gentle and casual in their manners.

Hawaiians soon became adept at making their own music. At first, one person played the melody, but it lacked fullness. There was no body to the sound. So, as one *paniolo* fooled with the melody, another soon learned to play bass, which added depth. But, players were often alone, and by experimenting they learned that they could get the right hand going with the melody and at the same time play the bass note with the thumb to improve the sound. Singers also learned that they could "open tune" the guitar to match their rich voices.

Hawaiians believed knowledge was sacred, and what is sacred should be treated with utmost respect, which meant keeping it secret, except from sincere apprentices. Guitar playing became a personal art form whose secrets were closely guarded, handed down only to family members, and only to those who showed ability and determination. When old-time slack-key guitar players were done strumming, they loosened all the strings so no one could figure out how they had their guitars tuned. If they were playing, and some interested folks came by who weren't part of the family, the Hawaiians stopped what they were doing, put their guitars down, and put their feet across the strings to wait for the folks to go away. As time went on, more and more Hawaiians began to play slack-key, and a common repertoire emerged.

Accomplished musicians could easily figure out the simple songs, once they had figured out how the family had tuned the guitar. One of the most popular tunings was the "open G." Old Hawaiian folks called it the "taro patch tune." Different songs came out, and if you were in the family and were interested in the guitar, your elders took the time to sit down and teach you. The way they taught was straightforward—and a test of your sincerity at the same time. The old master would start to

play. He just wanted you to listen and get a feel for the music—nothing more than that. You brought your guitar and *listened*. When you felt it, you played it, and the knowledge was transferred. Today, only a handful of slack-key guitar players know how to play the classic tunes classically. The best-known and perhaps greatest slack-key player was Gabby Pahinui, with The Sons of Hawaii. When he passed away he left many recordings behind. A slack-key master still singing and playing is Raymond Kane. Not one of his students is from his own family; most are *haole* musicians trying to preserve the classical method of playing.

Hawaiian music received its biggest boost from a remarkable radio program known as *Hawaii Calls*. This program sent out its music from the Banyan Court of Waikiki's Moana Hotel from 1935 until 1975. At its peak in the mid-1950s, it was syndicated on more than 700 radio stations throughout the world. Ironically, Japanese pilots heading for Pearl Harbor tuned in island music as a signal beam. Some internationally famous classic tunes came out of the 1940s and 1950s. Jack Pitman composed "Beyond the Reef" in 1948; more than 300 artists have recorded it, and it has sold more than 12 million records. Other million-sellers include "Sweet Leilani," "Lovely Hula Hands," "The Cross-eyed Mayor of Kaunakakai," and "The Hawaiian Wedding Song."

By the 1960s, Hawaiian music began to die. Just too corny and light for those turbulent years, it belonged to the older generation and the good times that followed World War II. One man was instrumental in keeping Hawaiian music alive during this period. Don Ho, with his "Tiny Bubbles," became the token Hawaiian musician of the 1960s and early 1970s. He's persevered long enough to become a legend in his own time, and his Polynesian Extravaganza at the Hilton Hawaiian Village packed visitors in until the early 1990s. Al Harrington, "The South Pacific Man," had another Honolulu revue that drew large crowds until his retirement. Of this type of entertainment, perhaps the most Hawaiian was Danny Kaleikini, who entertained his audience with dances, Hawaiian anecdotes, and tunes on the traditional Hawaiian nose flute.

The Beat Goes On

Beginning in the mid-1970s, islanders began to assert their cultural identity. One of the unifying factors was the coming of age of Hawaiian music. It graduated from the "little grass shack" novelty tune and began to include sophisticated jazz, rock, and contemporary rhythms. Accomplished musicians whose roots were in traditional island music began to highlight their tunes with this distinctive sound. The best embellish their arrangements with ukuleles, steel guitars, and traditional percussion and melodic instruments. Some excellent modern recording artists have become island institutions. The local people say that you know the Hawaiian harmonies are good if they give you "chicken skin."

Each year special music awards, **Na Hoku Hanohano,** or Hoku for short, are given to distinguished island musicians. The following are some of the Hoku winners considered by their contemporaries to be among the best in Hawaii: Barney Isaacs and George Kuo, Na Leo Pilimihana, Robi Kahakalau, Keali'i Reichel, Darren Benitez, Sonny Kamahele, Ledward Kaapana, Hapa, Israel Kamakawiwio'ole, and Amy Hanaiali'i. If they're playing while you're in Hawaii, don't miss them. Some, unfortunately, are no longer among the living, but their recorded music can still be appreciated.

Past Hoku winners who have become renowned performers include the Brothers Cazimero, who are blessed with beautiful harmonic voices; Krush, highly regarded for their contemporary sounds; The Peter Moon Band, fantastic performers with a strong traditional sound; Henry Kapono, formerly of Kapono and Cecilio; and The Beamer Brothers. Others include Loyal Garner, Del Beazley, Bryan Kessler and Me No Hoa Aloha, George Kahumoku, Jr., Olomana, Genoa Keawe, and Irmagard Aluli.

Those with access to the Internet can check out the Hawaiian music scene at one of the following: Hawaiian Music Island (www.mele.com), Nahenahenet (www.nahenahe .net). and Hawaiian Music Guide (www.hawaii-music.com). While they are not the only Hawaiian music websites, they are a good place to start. For listening to Hawaiian music on the Internet, try Kaua'i Community Radio (http://kkcr.org).

FESTIVALS, HOLIDAYS, AND EVENTS

In addition to all the American national holidays, Hawaii celebrates its own festivals, pageants, ethnic fairs, and a multitude of specialized exhibits. They occur throughout the year, some particular to only one island or locality; others, such as the Aloha Festivals and Lei Day, are celebrated on all of the islands. Check local newspapers and the free island magazines for dates. Some of the smaller local happenings are semi-spontaneous, so there's no *exact* date when they're held. These are some of the most rewarding events because they provide the best times to have fun with the local people.

O'ahu has more festivities and events than all of the other islands, and these are great social opportunities for meeting people. Everyone is welcome to join in the fun, and the events are usually either free or nominally priced. There's no better way to enjoy yourself while vacationing than by joining in with a local party or happening. Island-specific information is also available on the Web; check the calendar listing at the Hawaii Visitors Bureau (HVB) website (http:// calendar.gohawaii.com), the Hawaii vacation planner website (www.bestplaceshawaii.com/ calendar), or the State Foundation of Culture and the Arts calendar (www.state.hi.us/sfca), which features arts and cultural events, activities, and programs.

January

The **Queen Emma Museum Open House** is on January 2, Queen Emma's birthday, when the public is invited to visit her summer home and view a well-preserved collection of her personal belongings.

The **Narcissus Festival** in Honolulu's Chinatown starts with the parade and festivities of Chinese New Year, with lion dances in the street, fireworks, a beauty pageant, and a coronation ball.

The annual **Hula Bowl** (www.hulabowl hawaii.com) takes place at Aloha Stadium to the rousing cheers of football fans.

February

The **NFL Pro Bowl** (www.nfl.com/probowl) at Aloha Stadium in Honolulu, is an annual all-star football game offering the best from both conferences.

The annual **Cherry Blossom Festival** in Honolulu begins in February and lasts through late March. Events include Japanese cultural shows, tea ceremony, flower arranging, musical events, queen pageant and coronation ball. Check newspapers and free tourist magazines for dates and times of various Japanese cultural events. This festival has been held continuously since 1949.

March

Enjoy the kites at the annual **O'ahu Kite Festival** at Kapi'olani Park.

The annual three-day **Honolulu Festival** (www.honolulufestival.com) takes place at various locations around town, with local and international activities promoting cultural understanding.

April

Easter Sunday brings the Sunrise Service at the National Memorial Cemetery of the Pacific, in Punchbowl Crater, Honolulu.

The **Annual Hawaii Invitational International Music Festival,** held at the Kapi'olani Bandstand in Waikiki, is a grand and lively music competition of groups from all over the islands and the Mainland. This festival is a music lover's smorgasbord offering everything from symphony to swing and all in between.

Wesak, or **Buddha Day,** is on the Sunday closest to April 8 and celebrates the birthday of Gautama Buddha. Ornate offerings of tropical flowers are made at temples throughout Hawaii. Great sunrise ceremonies are held at Kapi'olani Park in Honolulu. Mainly Japanese

in their best *kimono* attend this celebration. A flower festival pageant and dance programs are also held in all island temples.

May

May 1, or May Day in some parts of the world, is **Lei Day** in Hawaii, where red is only one of the profusion of colors seen when everyone dons their flower garlands. Festivities abound throughout Hawaii with special goings-on at Kapi'olani Park in Waikiki.

The **Brothers Cazimero Annual May Day Concert** is one of the most anticipated musical events of the year. These musicians perform at the Waikiki Shell in the evening, as they have done for a quarter of a century.

On **Memorial Day,** special military services are held in Honolulu, at the National Memorial Cemetery of the Pacific at Punchbowl, on the last Monday in May.

The **Hawaii State Fair** is held at the Aloha Stadium parking lot on four weekends in May and June. There is a small admission charge and plenty of rides and booths.

June

King Kamehameha Celebration, June 11, is a Hawaii state holiday honoring Kamehameha the Great, Hawaii's first and greatest universal king. A lei-draping ceremony at the King Kamehameha statue and parades complete with floats and pageantry featuring a *ho'olaule'a* (street party) in Waikiki center take place around the Civic Center in downtown Honolulu. In addition, the **Annual King Kamehameha Hula Competition** is held at the Blaisdell Center.

The **Taste of Honolulu** brings together food from some 30 restaurant and wine vendors plus big-name local entertainment for this weekend-long festivity at the Honolulu Civic Center.

The **Annual Pan-Pacific Festival–Matsuri** (www.pan-pacific-festival.com) brings dances and festivities, parades and performances, music, and arts and crafts in Honolulu at Kapi'olani Park and other locations. It's a show of Japanese culture in Hawaii. Also, *bon odori,* the Japanese festival of departed souls, features dances and candle-lighting ceremonies at numerous Buddhist temples throughout the islands. These festivities change yearly and can be held anytime from late June to early August.

July

Typical Fourth of July celebrations and fireworks take place along Waikiki Beach, Aloha Tower Marketplace, Marine Corps Base Hawaii in Kaneʻohe, and at other locations around the islands. Check with newspaper listings for up-to-the-minute details.

The **Prince Lot Hula Festival** (www.mgf-hawaii.com) is a great chance for visitors to see authentic and noncompetitive hula from some of the finest hula *halau* in the islands. The festival also includes gift and craft sales, quilts, demonstrations, and food vendors. This is a free annual event held at the beautiful Moanalua Gardens in Honolulu.

At the **Queen Liliʻuokalani Keiki Hula Competition,** held at Blaisdell Center in Honolulu, children ages 6–12 compete in a hula contest. Caution: Terminal Cuteness.

The **Annual Ukulele Festival** is held on the last Sunday of the month at Kapiʻolani Park Bandstand in Waikiki. Hundreds of ukulele players from throughout the islands put on a very entertaining show.

The **Hawaii State Farm Fair** (www.hawaii statefarmfair.org) brings agricultural exhibits, down-home cooking, entertainment, a petting zoo, and produce for four weekends at a site in Kapolei.

August

The annual **Dragon Boat Races** provide fun entertainment for all at the Ala Moana Beach Park.

The annual daylong **Hawaiian Slack Key Guitar Festival** is held at the Kapiʻolani Park Bandstand in Waikiki (www.hawaiians lackkeyguitarfestivals.com).

Hawaii celebrates **Admission Day** as a state holiday on the third Friday of the month. Hawaii was admitted as the 50th state of the Union on August 21, 1959.

September

Aloha Festivals (www.alohafestivals.com) celebrate Hawaii's own intangible quality, *aloha*. There are parades, luʻau, historical pageants, balls, and various other entertainment on all islands. The spirit of *aloha* is infectious, and all are welcomed to join in. Check local papers and tourist literature for happenings near you. Downtown parades attract thousands. The savory smells of ethnic foods fill the air from a multitude of stands, and the Honolulu Symphony performs at the Blaisdell Center, while free concerts are given at the Waikiki Shell. More than 300 planned activities take place at various locations on all islands. This is the state's largest multiethnic event.

For the Molokaʻi to Oʻahu **Na Wahine O Ke Kai** Canoe Race, women in Hawaiian-style canoes race from a remote beach on Molokaʻi to Fort DeRussy Beach in Honolulu. In transit they must navigate the rough Kaiwi Channel.

October

For the **Molokaʻi Hoe Outrigger Canoe Race,** men navigate Hawaiian-style canoes across the rough Kaiwi Channel from a Molokaʻi beach to Fort DeRussy Beach in Honolulu.

At the free **Annual Honolulu Orchid Show and Plant Sale,** Hawaii's copious and glorious flowers are displayed in the Blaisdell Center Exhibition Hall, Honolulu.

The annual **Hawaii International Film Festival** (www.hiff.org) is a two-week event showing the best art films from the East, West, and Oceania at more than two dozen locations on all islands.

November

The **Mission Houses Museum Holiday Craft Fair** offers quality items by Hawaii's top craftspeople in an open-air bazaar.

The **Triple Crown of Surfing** (www.triple crownofsurfing.com) consists of the Hawaiian Pro, the World Cup of Surfing, and the Pipeline Masters. The best surfers in the world come to the best surfing beaches on Oʻahu. Wave action determines sites except for the Masters, which is always held at

Even Santa and Mrs. Claus take a little time to enjoy the balmy year-end weather in Hawaii.

Banzai Pipeline on the North Shore of Oʻahu. Big money and national TV coverage make this event spectacular.

The annual **World Invitational Hula Festival** (www.worldhula.com) is held at the Waikiki Shell for participants from several countries. Individual, female, male, and combined events are held.

For music aficionados, the **Hawaii International Jazz Festival** (www.hawaiijazz.com) offers great music from island and international musicians at the Hawaii Theatre and/or other venues around town. Over the years, this festival had moved around from month to month.

December

Every **December 7** in the early afternoon at Punchbowl, the National Cemetery of the Pacific, there is a commemoration of the attacks at Pearl Harbor.

The **Pacific Handcrafters Guild, Winter Fair,** in Thomas Square, Honolulu, is a chance to see the "state of the arts" all in one local-ity—the best by the best. This fair is perfect for early and unique Christmas shopping. Ethnic foods are also offered at various stalls. This guild (808/254-6788) also holds spring, summer, and fall fairs at Thomas Square and other shows periodically around town.

The annual **Honolulu Marathon** (www .honolulumarathon.org) is an institution in marathon races and one of the best-attended and most prestigious races in the country. Top athletes from around the world turn out to compete.

The annual **Honolulu City Lights** festival starts off the Christmas season with the lighting of a Christmas tree at City Hall, followed by an electric light parade and other entertainment.

The **Annual Rainbow Classic** is an invitational tournament of National Collegiate Athletic Association basketball teams held at the University of Hawaiʻi, Manoa.

The **Hawaii Bowl** and **Oʻahu Bowl** are two postseason collegiate football games played at Aloha Stadium—one on Christmas Eve Day, the other in January.

ESSENTIALS

Sports and Recreation

Even on such a heavily populated island as O'ahu, you can still enjoy the great outdoors. In fact, everyone seems to encourage you to get out and partake of what the island has to offer. There are plenty of opportunities for organized recreational tours, but you can easily go it alone and arrange your own outings. For many visitors, the water will be the biggest draw, and surfing, snorkeling, sailboarding, kayaking, and sailing are those activities that create the most interest. For others, land- and air-based activities like golfing, hiking, biking, and helicopter and glider rides will be the ticket. What follows is a sampling of the many great recreational activities O'ahu has to offer. More specific information on a wider variety of activities is located in the travel chapters.

BEACHES

As O'ahu is the second oldest of the major Hawaiian Islands, it's had plenty of time to create wonderful beaches. Great beaches are found on all sides of the island: Some are best known as family-friendly spots or snorkel sites, others are especially known for boogie boarding or sailboarding, and still others are renowned

© ROBERT NILSEN

as world-class surfing locations. Generally speaking, beaches and shorelines on the north and west have high surf conditions and strong ocean currents during winter—so use extreme caution—and those on the south and east experience some high surf during summer. All beaches are open to the public. Most are accessed through beach parks, but some access is over private property.

There are 18 beaches on Oʻahu that have lifeguards on duty during summer and during weekends the rest of the year. At some beaches, flags will warn you of ocean conditions. A yellow flag means use caution. A half-yellow, half-red sign signifies caution because of strong winds. A red flag indicates hazardous water conditions—beach closed, no swimming. In addition, yellow and black signs are sometimes posted at certain beaches to indicate other warnings: dangerous shore break, high surf spot, strong currents, presence of jellyfish, or beach closed. For more information, see the Oʻahu lifeguard and beach safety website (www.aloha.com/~lifeguards).

South Shore Beaches

Generally, these are great family beaches with lots of sand and relatively gentle water that are best during fall, winter, and spring. Summer brings higher waves. The two closest to the city are **Ala Moana Beach** and **Waikiki Beach.** Both can become crowded, but there is generally enough room for everyone. Whereas Waikiki Beach is the haunt of tourists, Ala Moana Beach is where the citizens of Honolulu head for a fun day at the beach with family. Both have all amenities for a great day, restrooms and picnic areas, and good sand bottoms and coral. Farther east is **Hanauma Bay Beach,** set inside the protective arms of a seaside crater. As part of a nature preserve, it is perhaps the best snorkeling spot in the state, with lots of coral and little sand. Beyond that is **Sandy Beach,** a popular spot with surfers and boogie boarders. The water at this beach has plenty of power, so check with the lifeguard here about conditions before entering. Also, box jellyfish seem to like this area and can be found here often. Stay out of the water it they're around.

East Shore Beaches

Many believe that the best overall beaches in the state are on Oʻahu's Windward Coast. Each has a broad expanse of sand backed by trees, drops off gently, and is good for swimming, sailboarding, kitesurfing, and kayaking, as the area gets fairly consistent trade winds for the vast majority of the year. Good beach facilities accompany these beaches, and they have easy access. They are **Waimanalo Beach** and **Bellows Beach** in Waimanalo and **Kailua Beach** in Kailua. Because it has favorable trade winds for much of the year and a reasonably large calm area inside the reef, Kailua Beach has become known as the major sailboarding location on Oʻahu and one of the two best known in the state. A bit more secluded and with no lifeguards or other amenities is **Lanikai Beach** just south of Kailua Beach. Not only is it gentle and safe, but the golden sand and aquamarine water of Lanikai Beach are also offset by the green mounds of the two small offshore islands, the deep blue of the sea beyond, and the lighter blue of the sky above. It is the most picture-perfect and typically tropical of Hawaiian beaches. Farther up the coast, beaches are overall less spectacular for swimming and more conducive to snorkeling, reef fishing, and other such activities. However, this coast is periodically affected by blue jellyfish, so stay out of the water when there are reports of them around.

North Shore Beaches

North Shore Oʻahu beaches are known for their surf—and rightly so—because some of the best surfing conditions in the world manifest themselves along this shoreline during winter. Every year, several surfing competitions are held at these beaches for amateurs and professionals, locals and international surfers. **Sunset, Chukka,** and **Waimea Bay,** are perhaps the best known, but many others, like **Haleʻiwa Aliʻi Beach** and **Mokuleʻia Beach,** are also known locally for great surf. The waves along this shore are wonderful for surfers, but for those who don't ride the board, this coastline still provides great thrills in just watching the power of the ocean.

Winter is the time for surf, but during summer the water calms down and the North Shore beaches, which tend to have more sand at this time, become fine for swimming.

West Shore Beaches

The Wai'anae Coast beaches are much less frequented than those closer to Honolulu and Waikiki. Although they too can be great for swimming when the waves are not rolling in, the beaches on this coast are perhaps best known for the surf, which can come either summer or winter. **Kahe Point** and **Tracks Beach** at the south end and **Makaha Beach** at the north end are surfers' havens. The best for swimming are **Nanakuli, Ma'ili,** and **Poka'i.** With its adjacent beach park, Poka'i is the most protected, and the sand there slides gently into the calm water. The most remote beach is on Yokohama Bay at the entrance to Ka'ena Point State Park. This is the place to come for seclusion, sun, and quiet beach walking time, but much of the year the water is too rough to enter safely. Generally, this Leeward side is drier and warmer than the rest of the island.

SCUBA

If you think O'ahu is beautiful above the sea, wait until you explore below. The warm tropical waters and coral growth make it a fascinating haven for reef fish and aquatic plantlife. You'll soon discover that Hawaiian waters are remarkably clear, with excellent visibility. Fish in every fathomable color parade by. Lavender clusters of coral, red-and-gold coral trees, and more than 1,500 different types of shells carpet the ocean floor. In some spots, like Hanauma Bay, the fish are so accustomed to humans that they'll come looking for you. In other spots, lurking moray eels add the special zest of danger. Sharks and barracuda pose less danger than scraping your knee on the coral or being driven against the rocks by a heavy swell. There are also enormous but harmless sea bass and a profusion of sea turtles. All this awaits below Hawaii's waters.

O'ahu has particularly generous underwater vistas open to anyone donning a mask and fins. Snorkel and dive sites, varying in difficulty and challenge, are accessible from the island. Sites can be totally hospitable, good for families and first-time snorkelers who want an exciting but safe frolic; or they can be accessible only to the experienced diver. Several dive shops on the island offer equipment for rent or purchase and can arrange dive boats and instruction at all levels. There are dozens of well-known dive sites around the island, with many of these clustered along the Wai'anae coast, the eastern half of the North Shore, and the southeastern corner of the island. Some features of note include drop-offs, walls, sea caves, arches, and sunken ships and planes.

Scuba divers must show certification cards to rent gear from local shops, fill tanks, or go on a charter dive. Exceptions are made for basic, guided introductory dives. Plenty of outstanding scuba instructors will give you lessons toward certification, and they're especially reasonable because of the stiff competition. Prices vary, but you can take a three- to five-day semiprivate certification course, including all equipment, for $350–450 (instruction book, dive tables, and logbook are sometimes an extra charge).

Divers who are unaccustomed to Hawaiian waters should not dive alone regardless of their experience. Most opt for dive tours to special dive grounds that are guaranteed to please. These tours also vary, but for an *accompanied* double-tank boat dive, expect to spend around $90–100. Most introductory dives for first-time divers are in the $125 range. Shore dives run slightly less and are often one-tank dives. During winter, shore diving is not recommended because of the "mud line" that tends to obscure visibility close to shore. Some dive companies also offer special charter dives, night dives, and photography dives. Most companies pick you up at your hotel, take you to the site, and return you home. Basic equipment rental costs $30–50 for the day, and most times you'll only need the top of a wet suit.

SNORKELING

Scuba diving takes expensive special equipment, skills, and athletic ability. Snorkeling in comparison is much simpler and enjoyable

REEF FISH

Achilles tang

red-lipped parrotfish

moorish idol

Hawaiian lionfish

lagoon *humu*

manini

blue-spotted cowfish

bluestripe butterflyfish

Potter's angelfish

threadfin butterflyfish

trumpetfish

saddleback wrasse

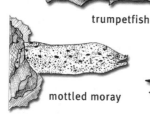
mottled moray

manta ray

uhu

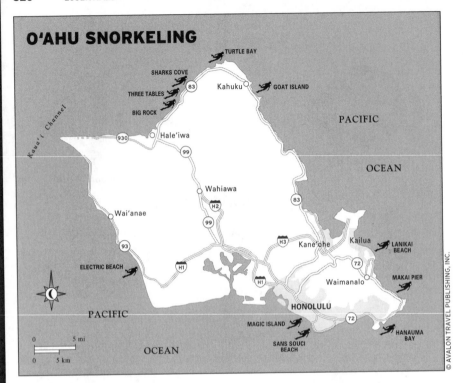

O'AHU SNORKELING

to anyone who can swim. In about 15 minutes you can be taught the fundamentals of snorkeling, but you really don't need formal instructions. Other snorkelers or dive shop attendants can tell you enough to get you started. Because you can breathe without lifting your head, you get great propulsion from the fins and hardly ever need to use your arms. You can go for much greater distances and spend longer periods in the water than if you were swimming. Experienced snorkelers make an art of this sport, and you too can see and do amazing things with a mask, snorkel, and flippers. Don't, however, get a false sense of invincibility and exceed your limitations.

Although there are countless places to snorkel around the island, several are easily accessible to visitors. Perhaps the best spot right at Waikiki is Sans Souci Beach or the area right in front of the Natatorium. Magic Island at Ala

Moana Beach Park is also good and appropriate for kids. Going a little farther around the coast brings you to Hanauma Bay, perhaps the best, and certainly the most popular, spot on the island. Along the Windward Shore, Makai Pier, Lanikai Beach with its offshore island, and Goat Island at Malaekahana Park offer good options. Shark's Cove and Three Tables at Waimea town and Big Rock at Waimea Bay are good, but only when there's no surf. More protected is Turtle Bay and the adjacent Kuilima Cove. On the Leeward side, try Electric Beach at Kahe Point, which is just at the start of the road up the Wai'anae coast.

Those interested can buy or rent equipment in most dive shops and at snorkel and water sports stores around the island. Sometimes condos and hotels have snorkeling equipment free for their guests, but if you have to rent it, don't get it from a hotel or condo; go to a shop where it's much cheaper. Expect to spend $3.50–8 per day for mask, fins, and snorkel. Many charter boats will take you out snorkeling or diving, most often on two- to four-hour trips. Prices range $75–95 but are usually less expensive at Waikiki. Also, hotel activity desks can arrange these excursions for no extra charge. Do yourself a favor and wash all the sand off rented equipment. Most shops irritatingly penalize you by adding an extra fee if you don't. Underwater camera rentals are now normal at most shops and go for around $15 including film (24–27 shots), but not developing. Happy diving!

SURFING

Surfing is a sport indigenous to Hawaii. When the white man first arrived, he was astonished to see natives paddling out to meet the ships on long carved boards, then gracefully riding them into shore on wave crests. The Hawaiians called surfing *he'enalu* (slide on a wave). The newcomers were fascinated by this sport, recording it on engravings and woodcuts marveled at around the world. Meanwhile, the Polynesians left records of surfing as petroglyphs and in *mele* of surfing exploits of times past. A local Waikiki beach boy by the name of Duke Kahanamoku won a treasure box full of gold medals for swimming at the Olympic Games of 1912, and thereafter he became a celebrity who toured the Mainland and introduced surfing to the modern world. Surfing later became a lifestyle, spread far and wide by surf movies and the songs of the Beach Boys in the 1960s. Now surfing is a sport enjoyed around the world, complete with championships, movies, magazines, and advanced board technology. The sport of surfing is still male-dominated, but women champions have been around for years.

It takes years of practice to become good, but with determination, good swimming ability, and a sense of balance, you can learn the fundamentals in a short time. At surf shops all around the island you can rent a board for reasonable prices and sign up for surfing lessons. The boards of the ancient *ali'i* were up to 20

BOOGIE BOARDING

If surfing is a bit too much for you, try a boogie board (or body board) – a foam or hard-shell board about three feet long that you lie on from the waist up. You can get tremendous rides on these boards with the help of flippers for maneuverability. You can learn to ride in minutes, and it's much faster, easier, and more thrilling than bodysurfing. Boogie boards are for sale all over the island and are relatively cheap; many water sports shops rent them. The most highly acclaimed boogie-boarding beach on O'ahu is Sandy Beach (with Makapu'u Beach not far behind). It also has the dubious distinction of being the most dangerous beach in Hawaii, with more drownings, broken backs, and broken necks than anywhere in the state. Waikiki is tame and excellent for boogie boarding, Bellows Beach serves the beginner well, Waimanalo Beach is more for the intermediate boarder, and Kailua Beach has a good break at its northern end.

feet long and weighed more than 150 pounds, but today's board is made from ultralight foam plastic covered in fiberglass. They may be as short as six feet long and weigh 12 pounds or up to 10 feet long and a bit heavier. Innovations occur every day in surfing, but one is the changeable skeg or rudder allowing you to surf in variable conditions.

The most famous surfing beaches in the world are Waimea Bay, Sunset Beach, and Banzai Pipeline on North Shore O'ahu. Every year the nationally televised pro-tour Triple Crown of Surfing is held along the North Shore from late October to early December, and prize money is substantial. In addition, several amateur surfing events also take place around the island.

Surf conditions on O'ahu are perfect for rank beginners up to the best in the world. Waikiki's surf is predictable most of the year, and usually just right to start on, whereas the

O'AHU GOLF COURSES

COURSE	STATUS	PAR	YARDS	FEES†	CART	CLUBS
Ala Wai Golf Course 404 Kapahulu Ave. Honolulu; 808/733-7387 or 808/296-2000 www.honolulu.gov/des/ golf/alawai.htm	Municipal	70	5,861	$42	$16	$25
Bayview Golf Park 45-285 Kane'ohe Bay Dr. Kane'ohe; 808/247-0451	Public	60	3,399	$62/73	incl.	$20
Coral Creek Golf Course 91-1111 Geiger Rd. 'Ewa Beach; 808/441-4653 or 888/868-3387 www.coralcreekgolfhawaii.com	Public	72	6,480	$130	incl.	$40
New Ewa Beach Golf Course 91-050 Fort Weaver Rd. 'Ewa Beach; 808/689-8351	Public	72	6,541	$135	incl.	$40
Ewa Village Golf Course 91-1760 Park Row St. –Ewa Beach; 808/681-0220 or 808/296-2000 www.honolulu.gov/des/golf/ ewa.htm	Municipal	73	6,455	$42	$16	$25
Hawaii Country Club 94-1211 Kunia Rd. Wahiawa; 808/621-5654 www.hawaiicc.com	Public	72	5,910	$55/65	incl.	$30
Hawaii Kai Golf Course Championship Course Executive Course 8902 Kalaniana'ole Hwy. Honolulu; 808/395-2358 www.hawaiikaigolf.com	Public Public	72 55	6,614 2,386	$100/110 $37/42	incl. incl.	$30 $15
Hawaii Prince Golf Club 91-1200 Fort Weaver Rd. 'Ewa Beach; 808/944-4567 www.princeresortshawaii.com/ waikiki-oahu-golf.php	Resort	36***	3,350*	$140**	incl.	$40

COURSE	STATUS	PAR	YARDS	FEES†	CART	CLUBS
Kahuku Golf Course Kahuku; 808/293-5842 www.honolulu.gov/des/ golf/kahuku.htm	Municipal	35*	2,699	$10	$4	$12
Kalakaua Golf Course USAG-HI Bldg. 2104 Schofield Barracks Wahiawa; 808/655-9833	Military	72	6,186	$26	$9	$8
Kapolei Golf Course 91-701 Farrington Hwy. Kapolei; 808/674-2227 or 877/674-2225	Semiprivate	72	6,586	$130/140	incl.	$45
Ko Olina Golf Club 92-1220 Ali'inui Dr. Kapolei; 808/676-5300 www.koolinagolf.com	Resort	72	6,867	$170	incl.	$50
Ko'olau Golf Course 45-550 Kionaole Rd. Kane'ohe; 808/236-4653 www.koolaugolfclub.com	Semiprivate	72	6,797	$135	incl.	$45
Leilehua Golf Course USAG-HI Bldg. 6505 Schofield Barracks Wahiawa; 808/655-4563	Military	72	6,521	$32	$8	$12
Luana Hills Country Club 770 Auloa Rd. Kailua; 808/262-2139 www.luanahills.com	Semiprivate	72	6,164	$125	incl.	$45
Makaha Resort Golf Club 84-626 Makaha Valley Rd. Wai'anae; 808/695-7520 www.makaharesort.net/ golf.asp	Resort	72	7,077	$85-160	incl.	$40
Makaha Valley Country Club 84-627 Makaha Valley Rd. Wai'anae; 808/695-7111 www.makahavalleycc.com	Public	71	6,369	$80	incl.	$30

continued on next page

O'AHU GOLF COURSES (cont'd)

COURSE	STATUS	PAR	YARDS	FEES†	CART	CLUBS
Mililani Golf Club 95-176 Kuahelani Ave. Mililani; 808/623-2222 www.mililanigolf.com	Semiprivate	72	6,455	$99	incl.	$35
Moanalua Golf Club 1250 Ala Aolani St. Honolulu; 808/839-2411 www.moanaluagolfclub.com	Semiprivate	36*	2,972	$25/30	$16	No
Olomana Golf Links 41-1801 Kalaniana'ole Hwy. Waimanalo; 808/259-7926 www.olomanagolflinks.com	Public	72	6,326	$80	incl.	$35
Pali Golf Course 45-050 Kamehameha Hwy. Kane'ohe; 08/266-7612 or 808/296-2000 www.honolulu.gov/des/golf/ pali.htm	Municipal	72	6,524	$42	$16	$20
Pearl Country Club 98-535 Kaonohi St. 'Aiea; 808/487-3802 www.pearlcc.com	Semiprivate	72	6,232	$65/70	incl.	$30
Royal Kunia Country Club 94-1509 Anonui St. Waipahu; 808/688-9222 www.royalkuniacc.com	Public	72	6,002	$110/120	$50	

North Shore has some of the most formidable surfing conditions on earth. Makaha Beach in Wai'anae is perhaps the best all-around surfing beach, frequented by "living legends" in this most graceful sport. *Never* surf without asking a local or lifeguard about conditions, and remember that "a fool and his surfboard, and maybe his life, are soon parted."

GOLF

With 38 (and counting) public, private, municipal, and military golf courses scattered around such a relatively small island, it's a wonder that it doesn't rain golf balls. These courses range from modest nine-holers to world-class courses whose tournaments attract the biggest names in golf today. Prices range from $10 per round up to $175. An added attraction of playing O'ahu's courses is that you get to walk around on some of the most spectacular and manicured pieces of real estate on the island. Some afford sweeping views of the coast, like the **Ko Olina Golf Club,** whereas others, like the **Pali Golf Course,** have a lovely mountain backdrop, or, like Waikiki's **Ala Wai Golf Course,** are sur-

COURSE	STATUS	PAR	YARDS	FEES†	CART	CLUBS
Ted Makalena Golf Course 93-059 Waipio PointAccess Rd. Waipahu; 808/675-6052 or 808/296-2000 www.honolulu.gov/des/golf/makalena.htm	Municipal	71	5,976	$42	$16	$15
Turtle Bay Resort Arnold Palmer Course	Resort	72	6,795	$175	incl.	$45
George Fazio Course 57-049 Kamehameha Hwy. Kahuku; 808/293-8574 www.turtlebayresort.com/golf/golf.asp	Resort	72	6,535	$155	incl.	$45
Waikele Golf Course 94-200 Paioa Place Waipahu; 808/676-9000 www.golfwaikele.com	Semiprivate	72	6,261	$125	incl.	$30
West Lock Golf Course 91-1126 Okupe St. 'Ewa Beach; 808/675-6076 or 808/296-2000 www.honolulu.gov/des/golf/westloch.htm	Municipal	72	6,335	$42	$16	$15

* = 9 holes, ** = 18 holes, *** = 27 holes (par 36 per 9), † = weekday/weekend rates

rounded by city spread. The Ala Wai Golf Course also must be one of the busiest courses in the country, as some 500 rounds of golf are played there daily! In 1994, the PGA rated the **Ko'olau Golf Course** the toughest course in the United States. Tough or easy, flat or full of definition, O'ahu provides ample opportunity and variety for any golfer.

Municipal and public courses are open to everyone. Resort courses cater to the public as well as to resort guests. Semiprivate courses set aside most of their time for members but do have specified days and times when they are open to the public. Private courses are strictly for members only and their guests. Military personnel and dependents, Department of Defense personnel, and those who have access to military bases are welcome to golf at the military courses. Some are also open to the public. If you wish to golf at other than municipal or public courses, be sure to call ahead to verify accessibility. Only golf courses open to the (civilian) public are listed in the accompanying chart.

Most golf courses offer lessons. Many have driving ranges, some lighted. Virtually all have

pro shops and clubhouses with restaurants and lounges or snack shops. Greens fees listed in the chart are for non-Hawaii residents and for civilians at military courses. Many courses offer reduced *kama'aina* rates, special time rates, twilight hour rates, and summer specials. Be sure to ask about these rates because they often afford substantial savings. On the other hand, some courses charge higher fees for non-U.S. residents. Military courses charge different greens fees for civilians than for military personnel, and the military fees might differ depending on rank.

For ease of use of municipal golf courses, the City and County of Honolulu has an automated tee time reservation and information system (808/296-2000) to make or check your reservation or to have your inquiry answered.

For printed information on golf in Hawaii, pick up a copy of the newspaper-format

Hawai'i Golf News and Travel or *Guide to Golf: Hawaiian Islands.*

Some tipping is the norm. A $1 tip to the bag drop attendant is customary, $2 if a bag boy takes your bags from the car, and a few bucks extra if he cleans your clubs for you.

CAMPING

Few people equate visiting O'ahu with camping. The two seem mutually exclusive, especially when you focus on the mystique of Waikiki and the dominance of a major city like Honolulu. But between state, county, and private campgrounds, you have about 20 spots to choose from all over the island. Camping on O'ahu, however, is a little different from camping on the Neighbor Islands, which are simply more amenable to camping. In an island state, they're considered "the woods, the sticks, the backcountry," and camping seems more acceptable there. On Oʻahu they keep a close eye on the campgrounds, enforcing the rules, controlling the situation. The campgrounds are patrolled, adding a measure of strictness along with a measure of security.

Most campgrounds have pavilions, fireplaces, toilets, and running water, but usually no individual electrical hookups. Drinking water is available, but brackish water may be used for flushing toilets and for showers, so read all signs regarding water. Cooking fires are allowed in established fire pits, but no wood is provided. Charcoal is a good idea, but a camp stove is better. Women, especially, should never hike or camp alone, and everyone should take precautions against theft.

State Parks

Oʻahu boasts 21 state parks, recreation areas, waysides, and monuments. Less than half offer a beach for day use or shoreline access, but most have some combination of walking paths, scenic vistas, cultural sites, picnic areas, toilets, showers, and pavilions. Included in these state properties are three *heiau*, **ʻIolani Palace,** the **Royal Mausoleum,** and **Diamond Head.** Of the total parks, three are registered National Historical Landmarks and one is a National Natural Landmark.

Oʻahu state parks close their gates and parking lots at night. Those *not* offering camping are open 7 A.M.–7:45 P.M. from April 1 to Labor Day, closing during the remainder of the year at 6:45 P.M.

Four state parks currently offer tent camping: **Sand Island State Recreation Area,** just a few minutes from downtown Honolulu; **Keaiwa Heiau State Recreation Area,** in the interior on the heights above ʻAiea; **Malaekahana State Recreation Area,** one mile north of Laʻie on the Windward Coast; and **Kahana Valley State Park** between Punaluʻu and Kaʻaʻawa on the Windward Coast.

To camp at Sand Island, Keaiwa Heiau, or Kahana Valley State Park, you must acquire a permit from the Department of Land and Natural Resources, Division of State Parks (P.O. Box 621, 1151 Punchbowl St., Room 310, Ho-

nolulu, HI 96809, 808/587-0300, open weekdays 8 A.M.–3:30 P.M.). Camping fees are $5 per campsite for every night of use. Oʻahu campsite **permit reservations** can be made only 30 days before the first day of camping, but *must* be made at least one week in advance. Write for a permit application form. Information needed includes your name, address, phone number, names and identification numbers of all persons older than 18 years of age in your party, type of permit requested, duration of your stay, and specific dates requested. The permits can be picked up on arrival with proof of identification.

Camping is allowed *only* from 8 A.M. Friday to 8 A.M. Wednesday (parks are closed all day Wednesday and Thursday for camping, but other activities are OK), with the shutdown, supposedly, for regrowth. Camping on Sand Island State Recreation Area only is Friday through Monday. Camping is allowed for only five consecutive days in any one month, and don't forget a parking permit for your vehicle, which must remain within the locked park gates at night. Aloohaaa!

The park service offers special cultural and arts programs at Kahana Valley State Park and talks and guided tours weekdays at the Royal Mausoleum. Tours and other services at ʻIolani Palace are provided by the nonprofit Friends of ʻIolani Palace.

County Parks

There are nearly 300 county parks on the island of Oʻahu. The city and county of Honolulu has opened 15 (these change periodically) of its 62 beach parks around the island to tent camping, and most allow trailers and RVs. A free permit is required, and camping is allowed only from Friday at 8 A.M. until the following Wednesday at 8 A.M., at which time your campsite must be vacated (no camping Wednesday and Thursday evenings). A few of these parks have camping only on the weekends, and one allows it only during summer months, so be sure to ask for particulars. These campsites are also at a premium, but you can write for reservations and pick up your permits

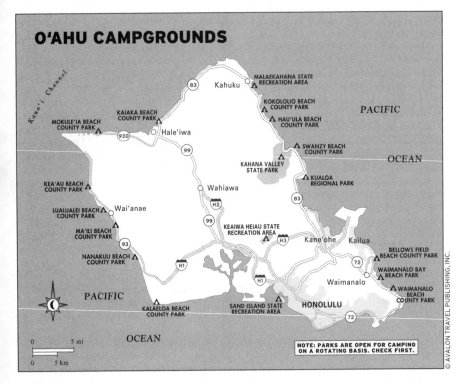

O'AHU CAMPGROUNDS

Kaua'i Channel

Kahuku

MALAEKAHANA STATE
RECREATION AREA

KOKOLOLIO BEACH
COUNTY PARK

PACIFIC

KAIAKA BEACH
COUNTY PARK

HAU'ULA BEACH
COUNTY PARK

MOKULE'IA BEACH
COUNTY PARK

Hale'iwa

OCEAN

SWANZY BEACH
COUNTY PARK

KAHANA VALLEY
STATE PARK

Wahiawa

KUALOA
REGIONAL PARK

KEA'AU BEACH
COUNTY PARK

Wai'anae

LUALUALEI BEACH
COUNTY PARK

KEAIWA HEIAU STATE
RECREATION AREA

MA'ILI BEACH
COUNTY PARK

Kane'ohe   Kailua

BELLOWS FIELD
BEACH COUNTY PARK

NANAKULI BEACH
COUNTY PARK

WAIMANALO BAY
BEACH PARK

Waimanalo

WAIMANALO
BEACH
COUNTY PARK

PACIFIC

KALAELOA BEACH
COUNTY PARK

SAND ISLAND STATE
RECREATION AREA

HONOLULU

OCEAN

0   5 mi

0   5 km

NOTE: PARKS ARE OPEN FOR CAMPING
ON A ROTATING BASIS. CHECK FIRST.

© AVALON TRAVEL PUBLISHING, INC.

on arrival with proper identification. Requests can be made no sooner than two Fridays before your requested camping dates. For information and reservations, write or visit City and County of Honolulu, Department of Parks and Recreation, Permit Section (650 S. King St., Honolulu, HI 96813, 808/523-4525, open weekdays 8 A.M.–4 P.M.). This office is in the Municipal Building, down the street from City Hall. Permits are also available from the satellite city halls around the island—hours vary.

Note: All of the beach parks are closed during designated months (they differ from park to park) throughout the year. This is supposedly for cleaning, but also to reduce the possibility of squatters moving in. Make sure, if you're reserving far in advance, that the park will be open when you arrive. Don't count on the Parks and Recreation Department to inform you!

HIKING

The best way to leave the crowds of tourists behind and become intimate with the beauty of O'ahu is to hike it. Although the Neighbor Islands receive fewer visitors, a higher percentage of people hike them than O'ahu. Don't get the impression that you'll have the island to yourself, but you will be amazed at how open and lovely this crowded island can be. Some cultural and social hikes can be taken without leaving the city, like a stroll through Waikiki and a historical walking tour of downtown Honolulu and Chinatown. But others—some mere jaunts, others quite strenuous—are well worth the time and effort.

Remember that much of O'ahu is privately owned, and you must have permission to cross this land or you may be open to prosecution. Private property is usually marked by signs. Another source that might stomp your hiking plans with their jungle boots is the military. A full 21 percent of O'ahu belongs to Uncle Sam, and he isn't always thrilled when you decide to play in his backyard. Always check and obey any posted signs to avert trouble.

O'ahu has more than 80 maintained trails. Some of the most accessible are in the hills behind Honolulu in the Makiki/Tantalus area. The far side of the Ko'olau Range above Kailua holds other hiking trails that are also easy to reach. Others farther to the north are more remote and less frequented. See the individual travel chapters for specific trails open to the public.

Hike with someone to share the experience. It's also safest. At the least, let someone know where you are going and when you plan to be back; supply an itinerary and your expected route, and then stick to it.

Stay on designated trails. This not only preserves O'ahu's fragile environment, but it also keeps you out of dangerous areas. Occasionally, trails will be closed for maintenance, so stay off these routes. Many trails are well maintained, but trailhead markers are sometimes missing. The trails can be muddy, which can make them treacherously slippery. Buy and use a trail map.

Wear comfortable clothing. Shorts and a T-shirt will suffice on many trails, but long pants and long-sleeve shirts are better where it's rainy and overgrown. Bring a windbreaker or raingear because it can rain and blow at any time. Wear sturdy walking or hiking shoes that you don't mind getting wet and muddy, which is almost guaranteed on some trails. Some very wet spots and stream crossings may be better done in tabi or other water shoes. Your clothes may become permanently stained with mud, providing a wonderful memento of your trip. Officials and others often ask hikers to pick clinging seeds off their clothes when coming out at the trailhead and to wash off boots so as not to unintentionally transport seeds to nonnative areas.

Always bring food because you cannot, in most cases, forage from the land. Carry plenty of drinking water, at least two quarts per day.

Heat can cause your body to lose water and salt. If you become woozy or weak, rest, take in salt, and drink water as you need it. Remember: It takes much more water to restore a dehydrated person than to stay hydrated as you go; take small, frequent sips. No matter how clean it looks, water in most streams is biologically polluted and will give you bad stomach problems if you drink it without purifying it first; either boil it or treat it with tablets. For your part, please don't use the streams as a toilet.

Use sunscreen: The sun can be intense and UV rays go through clouds. Bring and use mosquito lotion; even in paradise these pesky bugs abound. Do not litter. Carry a dedicated trash bag and pack out all your garbage.

Some trails are used by hunters of wild boar, deer, or game birds. It's best not to use these trails during hunting season, but if you do hike in hunting areas during hunting season, wear brightly colored or reflective clothing. Forest reserve trails often have check-in stations at trailheads. Hikers and hunters must sign a logbook, especially if they intend to camp. The comments by previous hikers are worth reading for up-to-the-minute information on trail conditions.

Twilight is short in the islands, and night sets in rapidly. In June, sunrise is around 6 A.M. and sunset 7 P.M.; in December, these occur at 7 A.M. and 6 P.M. If you become lost, find an open spot and stay put; at night, stay as dry as you can. If you must continue, walk on ridges and avoid the gulches, which have more obstacles and make it harder for rescuers to spot you. Do not light a fire. Some forest areas can be very dry, and fire could spread easily. Fog is only encountered at the 1,500- to 5,000-foot level, but be careful of disorientation.

Generally, stay within your limits, be careful, and enjoy yourself.

Hiking Groups and Resources

The **Department of Land and Natural Resources,** Division of Forestry and Wildlife (1151 Punchbowl St., Room 325, Honolulu, 808/587-0058) is helpful in providing trail maps, accessibility information, hunting and fishing regulations, and general forest rules. This office is in the Kalanimoku Hale state office building across from the State Capitol. Many of the public-access trails on O'ahu are part of the state's Na Ala Hele Trail System (www.hawaiitrails.org). See also the private Backyard O'ahu website (www.backyardoahu.com) for specific trail information.

The **Hawaiian Trail and Mountain Club** (P.O. Box 2238, Honolulu, HI 96804, 808/674-1459, http://htmclub.org) meets behind 'Iolani Palace on most Saturdays and Sundays at 8 A.M.; free for members and $2 for nonmembers. The hikes are announced on the group's Internet site and in the *Honolulu Star Bulletin.*

The **Sierra Club, Hawaii Chapter** (1040 Richards St., Honolulu, 808/538-6616, www.hi.sierraclub.org) organizes weekend hikes, $1 members and $5 nonmembers. Ask about its useful booklet *Hiking Softly in Hawai'i* ($5), which gives general information about hiking in Hawaii; preparation, etiquette, and precautions; a brief chart of major trails on each island, along with their physical characteristics; and other sources of information.

The **Hawaii Audubon Society** (850 Richards Street, Suite 505, Honolulu, 808/528-1432, www.hawaiiaudubon.com) runs periodic bird-watching excursions

Since 1995, the ecotour operator **Oahu Nature Tours** (808/924-2473 or 800/861-6018, natureguide@oahunaturetours.com, www.oahunaturetours.com) has offered daily hiking tours that focus on native birds and plants and the island's natural wonders. Over a dozen tour options are available, and these can be combined for multiday touring. The two-hour Diamond Head Crater Sunrise Adventure is offered twice each morning for $24. Two different daily waterfall tours run $42 apiece, and a Natural Highlights of O'ahu tour is $37. Rainforest, valley, and another coastal tours go on various days of the week for $39–47. Conducted by owner Michael Walther or one of his knowledgeable guides, each tour is an environmental education experience as well as a fun outing. This is a first-class operation, and all tours are well worth the time and money.

You will not be disappointed. Transportation and all equipment are provided. Call for departure times.

Mauka Makai Excursions (350 Ward Ave., Honolulu, 808/593-3525 or 866/896-0596, www.hawaiianecotours.net) offers several eco-friendly drive and hiking tours around the island that focus on cultural history and places of archaeological importance. Full- and half-day trips take you to North Shore or Windward O'ahu sites. Trips run $50–80 adults, $10–20 less for kids 6–17 years old.

For well-written and detailed **hiking guides** complete with maps, check out *Oahu Trails,* by Kathy Morey; *Hiking Oahu,* by Robert Smith; *The Hiker's Guide to O'ahu,* by Stuart M. Ball, Jr., and *Hawaiian Hiking Trails,* by Craig Chisholm. Two helpful camping books are *Hawaii: A Camping Guide,* by George Cagala, and Richard McMahon's *Camping Hawaii.*

BICYCLING

Pedaling around O'ahu can be both fascinating and frustrating. The roads are well paved, but the shoulders are often torn up. Traffic in and around Honolulu is horrifying, and the only way to avoid it is to leave very early in the morning. Many, but not all, of the city buses have been equipped with bike racks, so it's easier than before to get your bike from one part of the city to another or out of town. Once you leave the city, traffic, especially on the secondary interior roads, isn't too bad. Unfortunately, all of the coastal roads are heavily trafficked. If you rent a bicycle, you're better off getting a **cruiser** or **mountain bike** (instead of a delicate road bike), which will allow for the sometimes-poor road conditions and open up the possibilities of off-road biking. Even experienced mountain bikers should be careful on O'ahu trails, which are often extremely muddy and rutted.

Pedaling around Waikiki, although congested, is usually safe and a fun way to see the sights. Always use a helmet, lock your bike, and take your bike bag. For longer rides, bring sunglasses, use bike gloves, and wear appropriate bike shoes. If possible, have a bike pump, extra tube, and repair kit with you. Bring plenty of water and some snacks. Take a map, but get information from a bike shop about the kind of riding you want to do before you head out.

You can take your bike with you interisland by plane, but it will cost about $25 one-way. Bikes must be packed in a box or hard case, supplied by the owner. Handlebars must be turned sideways and the pedals removed or turned in. Bikes go space available only, which is usually not a problem, except perhaps during bicycle competitions. In addition, a release of liability for damage must be signed before the airline will accept the bike.

Getting your bike to Hawaii from the Mainland or another country will depend on which airline you take. Some will accept bicycles as baggage traveling with you (approximate additional charge of $50 from the Mainland U.S.) if the bikes are properly broken down and boxed in a bicycle box, while others will only take them as air freight, in which case the rates are exorbitant. Check with the airlines well before you plan to go or explore the possibility of shipping your bike through a package delivery service like UPS or FedEx, which will probably charge $60–100 one way and take about one week.

For general information on biking in Hawaii, contact **Hawaii Bicycling League** (808/735-5756, www.hbl.org). This nonprofit organization promotes biking as recreation, sport, and transportation, as well as encourages safe biking practices, conducts biking education, and advocates for biking issues. It publishes a monthly newsletter, *Spoke-n-Words,* filled with news of the organization's business, its bicycle safety program for kids, and rides that are open to the public, as well as current bicycle issues and sponsored bicycle competitions throughout the state. Group rides for all levels of abilities are sponsored almost every weekend, and nonmembers are welcome. If you are a bicycle rider living on the islands or simply want a subscription to the newsletter, look into a membership. For mountain biking and trail information on all the major islands, pick up a copy of *Mountain Biking the Hawaiian Islands* by John Alford.

For additional information, have a look at the *Bicycle Regulations and Illustrated Safety Tips* booklet put out by the Department of Transportation Services, City and County of Honolulu, written for the island of Oʻahu. Pick up a copy at city hall or any satellite city hall or most bike shops. From the Neighbor Islands or if coming from outside the state, write or call for a copy from the Bicycle Coordinator (711 Kapiʻolani Blvd., Ste. 1200, Honolulu, HI 96813, 808/527-5044). Also informative for rules of the road and commonsense biking tips is the *Rights and Responsibilities for Hawaiʻi's Bicyclists* booklet. This booklet and the state's *Bike Oahu* bicycle route map (www.state. hi.us/dot/highways/bike) are available free from the State Bicycle/Pedestrian Coordinator (808/692-7675) and may be available at city halls and tourist offices.

LAND TOURS

Guided land tours are much more of a luxury than a necessity on Oʻahu. Because of the relatively cheap rental cars and excellent bus system, you spend a lot of money for a narration and to be spared the hassle of driving. If you've come in a group and don't intend to rent a car, they may be worth it. Sea cruises and air tours are equally luxurious but provide glimpses of this beautiful island that you'd normally miss.

If you're going to take a land tour, you must have the right attitude, or it'll be a disaster. Your tour leader, usually driving the van or bus, is equal parts instructor, comedian, and cheerleader. There's enough "corn" in his or her jokes to impress an Iowa hog. On the tour, you're expected to become part of one big happy family, and most important, to be a good sport. Most guides are quite knowledgeable about Oʻahu and its history, and they honestly try to do a good job. But they've done it a million times before, and their performance can be as stale as week-old bread. The larger the tour vehicle and the shorter the miles covered, the worse it is likely to be. If you still want a tour, take a full-day jaunt in a small van: You get to know the other people and the guide, who'll tend to

AIR TOURS

When you soar above O'ahu, you realize just how beautiful this island actually is. Considering that the better part of a million people live in this relatively small space, it's amazing just how much undeveloped land still exists in the interior and even along some coastal stretches. All air tour companies are licensed and regulated for safety, and you have several options when it comes to taking to the air. The majority of helicopter tours and the only seaplane on the island leave from the ocean side of the Honolulu International Airport. The only other helicopter company operating on O'ahu has its base at the Turtle Bay Resort on the northernmost tip of the island. Dillingham airfield in Waialua is the only other location on O'ahu for air tours. There you'll find companies doing the more exhilarating glider and biplane rides, as well as parachute drops.

give you a more in-depth presentation. Tips are cheerfully accepted. Also, be aware that some tours get kickbacks from stores and restaurants they take you to, where you don't always get the best bargains. Most companies offer free hotel pickup and delivery. Lunch or dinner is not included unless specified, but if the tour includes a major tourist spot, admission is usually included.

About half a dozen different tours offered by most companies are variations on the same theme, and the cost is fairly uniform. One of the more popular is a **circle-island tour,** including numerous stops around Waikiki, the Windward Coast, the North Shore, and the center of the island. These usually run about $60, substantially less for children. An afternoon and evening Polynesian Cultural Center tour, including admission and dinner show, costs close to $75. Tours to the sights of Pearl Harbor run about $50, and those to Diamond Head and downtown sights run around $30.

Some reputable companies include **Polynesian Adventure Tours** (808/833-

3000 or 800/622-3011, www.polyad.com), **Roberts Hawaii** (808/954-8652 or 866/898-2519, www.robertshawaii.com), **E Noa Tours** (808/591-2561 or 800/824-8804, www.enoa.com), **Discovering Hawaii Tours** (808/737-3700 or 800/946-4432, www.discoverhawaiitours.com), and **Superstar Hawaii Transit Service** (808/841-7827, www.superstarhawaii.com).

Offering tours mostly focused on the Pearl Harbor area is **Home of the Brave Tours** (808/396-8112, www.pearlharborhq.com). Its Pearl Harbor Victory Tour runs Mon.–Fri. 6 A.M.–2 P.M. for $89 per adult, $79 for children 2–11, seniors over age 55, and military personnel, excluding lunch costs, and takes in the USS Arizona Memorial, several of the nearby military installations, Punchbowl National Cemetery, and downtown sights.

As an alternate, you can come carrying your copy of *Tour Talk O'ahu* (877/585-7499, www.tourtalkhawaii.com), a self-guided driving audio tour for a "go at your own pace" trip. This handy kit comes with an informational booklet and either a CD or cassette for use in your rental car. Order well before you leave for Hawaii.

FISHING
Deep-Sea Fishing

O'ahu has some of the most exciting and productive "blue waters" in all of the world. Here, you can find a sportfishing fleet made up of skippers and crews who are experienced professional anglers. Most game-fishing boats work the waters on the calmer Leeward sides of the islands. Some skippers, carrying anglers who are accustomed to the sea, will also work the much rougher Windward Coasts and island channels where the fish bite just as well. The most advanced marine technology, available on many boats, sends out sonar beeps searching for fish. On deck, the crew and anglers scan the horizon in the age-old Hawaiian tradition, searching for clusters of seabirds feeding on baitfish pursued to the surface by the huge and aggressive game fish.

One of the most famous fishing spots in Ha-

GAME FISH

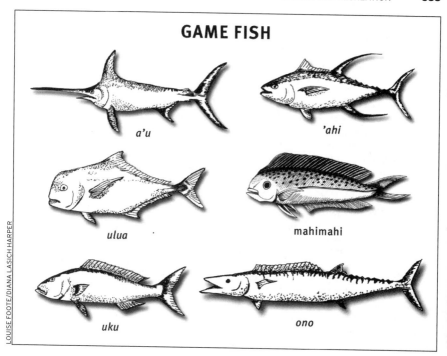

a'u

'ahi

ulua

mahimahi

uku

ono

LOUISE FOOTE/DIANA LASICH HARPER

waii is **Penguin Banks** off the west coast of Moloka'i and the south coast of O'ahu. The waters of the "Chicken Farm" at the southern tip of the Penguin Banks are great for trolling for marlin and mahimahi. The calm waters off the Wai'anae coast, from Barbers Point to Ka'ena Point, yield marlin and 'ahi.

The most thrilling **game fish** in Hawaiian waters is marlin, generically known as billfish or a'u to the locals. The king of them is the blue marlin, with record catches of more than 1,000 pounds. These are known as granders. The mightiest caught in the waters off O'ahu was a record breaker at 1,805 pounds. There are also striped marlin and sailfish, which often weigh more than 200 pounds. The best times for marlin are during spring, summer, and fall. The fishing tapers off in January and picks up again by late February. "Blues" can be caught year-round, but, oddly enough, when they stop biting it seems as though the striped marlin pick up. Second to the marlin are tuna.

'Ahi (yellowfin tuna) are caught in Hawaiian waters at depths of 100–1,000 fathoms. They can weigh 300 pounds, but 25–100 pounds is common. There's also aku (skipjack tuna) and the delicious ono, which average 20–40 pounds. Mahimahi, with its high prominent forehead and long dorsal fin, is another strong-fighting, deep-water game fish abundant in Hawaii. These delicious fish can weigh up to 70 pounds.

Charter Boats

The charter boats of Hawaii come in all shapes and sizes, but they are all manned by professional, competent crews and captains who intimately know Hawaiian waters. You can hire a boat for a private or share charter, staying out for four, six, or eight hours, but 12-hour trips are not unheard of. Some captains like to go for longer runs because there is a better chance of a catch and they can get farther into the water; some now do *only* private charters.

Boat size varies, but six anglers per midsize boat is about average. Although some provide it, be sure to bring food and drink for the day; no bananas, please—they're bad luck. Deepsea fishing on a share basis costs approximately $150 per half day (four hours) or $190 for a full day, per person. On a private charter, expect $700 per half day or up to $975 for a full day, although the rates on the Waiʻanae Coast are usually less. No fishing licenses are required. All tackle is carried on the boats and is part of the service. It is customary for the crew to be given any fish that are caught, but naturally this doesn't apply to trophy fish; the crew is also glad to cut off some steaks and fillets for your personal enjoyment.

While a few boats each tie up at the Waiʻanae Harbor on the Leeward Coast, Haleʻiwa Harbor on the North Shore, and Heʻeia Kea Harbor in Kaneʻohe, the majority of Oʻahu's fleet moors at **Kewalo Basin** just outside Honolulu Harbor along Ala Moana Boulevard. The boat harbor is a sight in itself, and if you're contemplating a fishing trip, it's best to head down there before your desired trip and yarn with the captains and returning fishermen. This way you can get a feel for a charter to best suit you.

Freshwater Fishing

Because of Hawaii's unique geology, only a handful of reservoirs and rivers are good for inland fishing. The state maintains two public freshwater fishing areas on Oʻahu. The **Wahiawa Public Fishing Area** is 300 acres of fishable waters in and around the town of Wahiawa. It's basically an irrigation reservoir used to hold water for cane fields. Species regularly caught here are largemouth and smallmouth bass, sunfish, channel catfish, *tucunare,* oscar, carp, snakehead, and Chinese catfish. The other area is the **Nuʻuanu Reservoir no. 4,** a 25-acre restricted watershed above Honolulu in the Koʻolau Mountains. It's open for fishing only three times

per year in May, August, and November. Fish caught here are Chinese catfish.

Hawaii has only one native freshwater game fish, the *ʻoʻopu.* This goby is an oddball with fused ventral fins. They grow to be 12 inches and are found on all islands. Introduced species include largemouth and smallmouth bass, bluegills, catfish, *tucunare,* oscar, carp, and tilapia. The *tucunare* is a tough, fighting, good-tasting game fish introduced from South America, similar to the oscar from the same region. Both have been compared to bass but are of a different family. The tilapia is from Africa and has become common in Hawaii's irrigation ditches. It is a "mouth breeder," and the young will take refuge in their parents' protective jaws even a few weeks after hatching. The eel-like snakehead inhabits the reservoirs and is a great fighter. The channel catfish can grow to more than 20 pounds; it bites best after sundown. Or go for carp: With its broad tail and tremendous strength, it's the poor man's game fish. All of these species are best caught with light spinning tackle or with a bamboo pole and a trusty old worm. The catch limit of eight species of freshwater fish is regulated.

A **Freshwater Game Fishing license** is good for one year: July 1–June 30. Licenses cost $25 for nonresidents, $10 for seven-day tourist use, $20 for 30-day tourist use; $5 for residents older than age 15 and active duty military personnel, their spouses, and dependents older than age 15; $3 for children ages 9–15; free to senior citizens and children younger than age nine when accompanied by an adult with a license. You can pick up a license at sporting goods stores or at the Division of Aquatic Resources (1151 Punchbowl St., Honolulu, HI 96813, 808/587-0100). Be sure to ask for the *Hawaii Fishing Regulations* and *Freshwater Fishing in Hawaii* booklets. Fishing is usually allowed in most State Forest Reserve Areas. Owners' permission must be obtained to fish on private property.

Getting There

With the number of visitors each year approaching seven million—and another several hundred thousand just passing through—the state of Hawaii is one of the easiest places in the world to get to...by plane. Before planning a trip to and around the islands, be sure to contact the airlines directly, view the airlines' Internet sites, check well-established Internet travel sites, go through your travel agent for the most current information on routes and flying times, or seek out charter companies as they offer attractive alternatives. Familiarize yourself with the alternatives at your disposal so you can make an informed travel selection.

BY AIR
Flights to O'ahu

The old adage of "all roads leading to Rome" applies almost perfectly to O'ahu, although instead of being cobblestones, they're sea lanes and air routes. Except for the cruise ships that still dock at Honolulu Harbor, and the few direct flights to the outer islands, all other passengers to and from Hawaii are routed through Honolulu International Airport. These flights include direct flights to the Neighbor Islands, which means stopping over at Honolulu International and continuing on the same plane, or more likely changing to an interisland carrier whose fare is included in the original price of the flight.

Visas

Entering Hawaii is like entering anywhere else in the United States. Foreign nationals must have a current passport and most must have a proper visa, an ongoing or return air ticket, and sufficient funds for the proposed stay in Hawaii. A visa application can be made at any U.S. embassy or consular office outside the United States and must include a properly filled out application form, two photos 1.5 inches square, and a nonrefundable fee of $100. Canadians do not need a visa but must have a passport. Visitors from 28 countries do not need a visa to enter the United States for 90 days or less. This list is amended periodically, so be sure to check in your country of origin to determine whether you need a visa for U.S. entry.

Agricultural Inspection

Everyone visiting Hawaii must fill out a *Plants and Animals Declaration Form* and present it to an airline flight attendant or the appropriate official upon arrival in the state. Anyone carrying any of the listed items must have those items inspected by an agricultural inspection agent at the airport. These items include but are not limited to fruits, vegetables, plants, seeds, and soil, as well as live insects, seafood, snakes, and amphibians. For additional information on just what is prohibited, contact any U.S. Customs Office or check with an embassy or consulate in foreign countries.

Remember that before you leave Hawaii for the Mainland, all of your bags are again subject to an agricultural inspection, a usually painless procedure taking only a minute or two. To facilitate your departure, leave all bags unlocked and untaped until after inspection. There are no restrictions on beach sand from below the high-water line, coconuts, cooked foods, dried flower arrangements, fresh flower lei, pineapples, certified pest-free plants and cuttings, and seashells. However, papaya must be treated before departure. Some other restricted items are berries, fresh gardenias, jade vines, live insects and snails, cotton, plants in soil, soil itself, and sugarcane. Raw sugarcane is acceptable, however, if it is cut between the nodes, has the outer covering peeled off, is split into fourths, and is commercially prepackaged. For any questions pertaining to plants that you want to take to the Mainland, call the Agricultural Quarantine Inspection office (808/861-8490) in Honolulu.

Foreign countries may have different agricultural inspection requirements for flights from Hawaii (or other points in the United States) to those countries. Be sure to check with the proper foreign authorities for specifics.

Pets and Quarantine

Hawaii has a very rigid pet quarantine policy designed to keep rabies and other Mainland diseases from reaching the state. All domestic pets are subject to **120 days' quarantine** (a 30-day quarantine or a newer five-day-or-less quarantine is allowed by meeting certain pre-arrival and post-arrival requirements—inquire), and this includes substantial fees for boarding. Unless you are contemplating a move to Hawaii, it is not feasible to take pets. For complete information, contact the Department of Agriculture, Animal Quarantine Division (99-951 Halawa Valley St., 'Aiea, HI 96701, 808/483-7151) in Honolulu.

Honolulu International Airport

This international airport is one of the busiest in the entire country, with hundreds of flights to and from cities around the world arriving and departing daily. In a routine year, more than 20 million passengers use this facility. The three terminals (directions given as you face the main entranceway) are the main terminal, accommodating all international and Mainland flights; the interisland terminal, a separate building at the far right end of the main terminal, handling flights between the islands by Hawaiian Airlines and Aloha Airlines; and the commuter terminal, farther to the right side, taking care of the commuter and smaller interisland air carriers.

From both levels of the airport, you can board taxis and TheBus to downtown Honolulu and Waikiki. The ground level outside, on the runway side of the building, has two gardens, a wonderful place to spend some time in the sun if you have a long layover or must wait for a flight. Shuttles also service the commuter terminal, which lies only a few minutes' walk beyond the interisland terminal. This terminal has ticket counters for Island Air, go!, Pacific Wings, and Mokulele airlines, and pickup stops for the inter-terminal shuttle and rental car shuttles. Departures are at the

far end, and arrivals are closest to the Interisland Terminal.

Call (808/836-6413) for general airport information and arrival and departure information or see the airport's arrival/departure Internet site (www.ehawaiigov.org/hnlflights). There are more than one dozen tourist **information booths** at various places around the main and interisland terminals, but they are not always staffed.

Airport Transportation

The free **Wiki-Wiki Shuttle** takes you between the terminals and arrival/departure gates. There are three color-coded lines that service the terminals. From arrival gates, all shuttles make stops at the baggage claim areas, but not all run to every section of the airport. Check with the signs outside the arrival/departure gates for specific route information. Transfer time between the main and interisland terminals is only about 10 minutes.

Some **rental car agencies** have booths on the ground floor of the main and interisland terminals; others have courtesy phones in the baggage areas. Many have lot offices in the parking area outside the main terminal, while some have off-site lots. Rental car shuttles stop outside the baggage claim area of the terminals to pick you up and take you to the nearby facility.

If you're driving to the airport to pick up or drop off someone, you should know about **parking.** If you want to park on the second level of the parking garage for departures, you must take the elevator either up to the fourth floor or down to ground level, and from there cross the pedestrian bridge. There's no way to get across on levels two and three. Parking is $1 for the first half hour, $1 for each additional hour, or $10 maximum for a 24-hour period.

Public transportation to downtown Honolulu, especially Waikiki, is abundant. Moreover, some hotels have courtesy phones near the baggage claim area; if you're staying there, they'll send a van to fetch you. Current charges for taxis, vans, TheBus, and limousine service are posted just outside the baggage

If you have time before your departure, spend a little time in one of the airport's gardens as a final memory of a warm and tropical Hawaii.

claim area, so you won't have to worry about being overcharged.

Only **taxis** that contract with the airport can pick up at the terminal. All others can drop off there but are allowed to pick up only outside the terminal (for example, at a rental car office). From the terminal to Waikiki costs about $35–40, not counting bags. Splitting the fare with other passengers can save money. Shuttles and motorcoaches leave from the central island in the roadway just outside the baggage claim. They charge about $9 one-way ($15 round-trip) to Waikiki, but a wait of up to 25 minutes for one is not out of the ordinary.

You can take **TheBus** (no. 19 or no. 20) to Waikiki via the Ala Moana terminal, from which you can get buses all over the island. If you're heading north, transfer to bus nos. 52 or 55 at the Ala Moana terminal; for the university, transfer to bus no. 6. TheBus only costs $2, but you are allowed only baggage that you can hold on your lap without infringing on other riders. Drivers are sticklers on this point.

DOMESTIC CARRIERS

The following are the major domestic carriers to and from Hawaii. The majority of flights, by all carriers, land at Honolulu International Airport, with the remainder going directly to Kaua'i, Maui, and Hawai'i.

Hawaiian Airlines

Hawaiian Airlines (800/882-8811 in Hawaii, 800/367-5320 Mainland and Canada, www.hawaiianair.com) operates daily direct flights from Los Angeles, San Francisco, Sacramento, San Jose, and San Diego, California; Las Vegas; Phoenix; Seattle; and Portland to Honolulu, with flights also between Maui and Seattle, Portland, and San Diego. Scheduled flights to the South Pacific run between Honolulu and Pago Pago, Samoa; to Papeete, Tahiti; and to Sydney, Australia. Hawaiian Airlines has expanded its service to the West Coast over the past few years, so there may very well be additional (or changed) destinations and service in the future. Hawaiian Airlines offers special discount deals with Dollar rental cars and select major island hotels.

Aloha Airlines
Aloha Airlines (800/367-5250 Hawaii, Mainland, and Canada, www.alohaairlines.com) flies between Honolulu and Oakland and Orange County, California. The Oakland flights carry on to Las Vegas and Orange County flights connect to Sacramento and Reno. Aloha also flies between Maui and Sacramento, Oakland, Orange County, and San Diego, California. These Oakland flights go on to Las Vegas and the Orange County flights connect to either Sacramento or Reno. During summer, the schedule may be expanded. Like Hawaiian, Aloha Airlines has been expanding its West Coast operation, so greater variety and some change will undoubtedly be in store in the future.

United Airlines
Since its first island flight in 1947, United Airlines (800/241-6522, www.united.com) has been top dog in flights to Hawaii. United's Mainland routes connect more than 100 cities to Honolulu. The main gateway cities of San Francisco and Los Angeles have direct flights to Honolulu, with additional flights from Denver and Chicago; flights from all other cities connect through these cities. United also offers direct flights to Maui, Kona, and Kaua'i from San Francisco and Los Angeles. Continuing through Honolulu, United flights go to Tokyo (Narita) and Osaka (Kansai), where connections can be made for other Asian cities. United offers numerous travel packages to all the islands. United partners with Aloha Airlines and deals with Hertz Rent A Car. United is the "big guy" and intends to stay that way. Its packages are hard to beat.

American Airlines
American Airlines (800/433-7300, www.aa.com) offers direct flights to Honolulu from Los Angeles, San Francisco, Dallas/Fort Worth, and Chicago. It also flies daily from its main hubs to Maui, Kona, and Kaua'i. American does not fly to points in Asia or other Pacific destinations from Hawaii. American partners with Hawaiian Airlines.

Continental Airlines
Continental Airlines (800/523-3273, www.continental.com) flights from all Mainland cities to Honolulu connect via Los Angeles, Newark, and Houston. Also available are direct flights from Honolulu to Guam and Nagoya, Japan, from where flights run to numerous other Asian and Pacific cities and islands. Continental partners with Hawaiian Airlines.

Northwest Airlines
Northwest (800/225-2525, www.nwa.com) flies into Honolulu from Los Angeles, Seattle, Portland, San Francisco (via Seattle), and Minneapolis. There are onward nonstop flights to Narita and Osaka in Japan, from where all other Asian destinations are connected.

Delta Air Lines
In 1985, Delta Air Lines (800/221-1212, www.delta.com) entered the Hawaiian market; when it bought out Western Airlines its share became even bigger. Delta has nonstop flights to Honolulu from Los Angeles, Minneapolis, Portland, San Francisco, Salt Lake City, and Atlanta; nonstop flights between Maui and Los Angeles, Salt Lake City, and Houston; and a flight from Seattle to Kona.

ATA Airlines
ATA Airlines (800/435-9282, www.ata.com) flies into Honolulu from Los Angeles, Las Vegas, Oakland and Ontario, California, and Phoenix, with nonstop service to Maui, Hilo, Kona, and Lihue, principally from Oakland.

FOREIGN CARRIERS
The following carriers operate throughout Asia and Oceania but have no U.S. flying rights. This means that for you to vacation in Hawaii using one of these carriers, your flight must originate or terminate in a foreign city. You can have a stopover in Honolulu with a connecting flight to a Neighbor Island.

Air Canada
Nonstop Air Canada (888/247-2262, www.aircanada.ca) flights from Canada originate in Vancouver.

WestJet
Westjet (888/937-8538, www.westjet.com) also flies from Vancouver to both Honolulu and Kahului, Maui, each a couple times per week.

Air New Zealand
Air New Zealand (800/262-1234 Mainland, 800/663-5494 Canada, www.airnewzealand.com) flights link New Zealand, Australia, and numerous South Pacific islands to Honolulu.

Japan Air Lines
The Japanese are the second-largest group, next to Americans, to visit Hawaii. Japan Air Lines (JAL) (800/525-3663, www.jal.co.jp/en) flights to Honolulu originate in Tokyo (Narita), Nagoya, Osaka (Kansai), and Fukuoka. In addition, there are flights between Tokyo (Narita) and Kona on the Big Island.

Qantas
Qantas' (800/227-4500, www.qantas.com.au) daily flights connect Sydney and Melbourne, Australia, with Honolulu.

China Airlines
Routes to Honolulu with China Airlines (800/227-5118, www.china-airlines.com) are only from Taipei and Tokyo. Connections are available in Taipei to most Asian capitals.

Korean Air
Korean Air (800/438-5000, www.koreanair.com) offers flights direct between Honolulu and Seoul, with connections there to many Asian cities.

Air Pacific
Air Pacific (808/227-4446, www.airpacific.com) offers once-weekly nonstop flights between Nadi (Fiji) and Honolulu.

Philippine Airlines
Three times weekly, Philippine Airlines (808/435-7725, www.philippineairlines.com) offers nonstop flights between Honolulu and Manila.

TRAVEL COMPANIES
Many tour companies advertise packages to Hawaii in large-city newspapers every week. They offer very reasonable airfares, car rentals, and accommodations. Without trying, you can get round-trip airfare from the West Coast and a week in Hawaii for $600–700 using one of these companies, with prices invariably more expensive during summer. The following companies offer great deals and most have excellent reputations. This list is by no means exhaustive.

Pleasant Hawaiian Holidays
A California-based company specializing in Hawaii, Pleasant Hawaiian Holidays (800/742-9244, www.pleasantholidays.com) makes arrangements for flights, accommodations, and transportation only. For flights, it primarily uses American Trans Air but also uses select commercial airlines and regularly scheduled flights. Aside from the air connection, Pleasant Hawaiian offers a choice of accommodation levels from budget to luxury, a fly/drive option if you have your own accommodation, and numerous perks, like a flower lei, first morning orientation, service desks at hotels, and coupons and gift certificates. Pleasant Hawaiian is easy to work with and stands behind its services. A deposit is required after booking and there is a time frame for full payment that depends upon when you make your reservation. Fees are assessed for changing particulars after booking, so apprise yourself of all financial particulars. Most major travel agents work with Pleasant Hawaiian, but you can also contact the company directly.

SunTrips
This California-based tour company (800/786-8747, www.suntrips.com) runs flights to the four major islands of Hawaii from Oakland, Portland, Seattle, and Denver. It offers flight,

accommodation, and/or car rental packages that match any for affordability. Most of its flights use Ryan International or North American airlines. Your price will depend upon your choice of accommodations and type of car. Using both charter and commercial air carriers, SunTrips does not offer assigned seating until you get to the airport. They recommend you get there two hours in advance, and they ain't kidding! This is the price you pay for getting such inexpensive air travel. SunTrips financial regulations are similar to those at Pleasant Hawaiian; be sure to inquire.

STA Travel

STA Travel (800/781-4040 or visit www.sta travel.com) is a full-service travel agency specializing in student travel, regardless of age. Those under 26 do not have to be full-time students to get special fares. Through STA, bona fide students can get an International Student Identification Card (ISIC), which often gets you discount fares and fees, and anyone can get a Hostelling International card. Older independent travelers can avail themselves of services; although they are ineligible for student fares, STA works hard to find discounted or budget rates. Many tickets issued by STA are flexible, allowing changes with no penalty, and are open-ended for travel up to one year. Aside from airfares, STA also books accommodations and packages. STA has some 300 offices around the world. STA also maintains Travel Help, a service available at all offices designed to solve all types of problems that may arise while traveling. STA is an established travel agency with an excellent and well-deserved reputation.

Other Similar Companies

Several other companies offer similar package options from the Mainland to Hawaii. Try the following: **Happy Vacations** (831/461-0113 or 800/877-4277, fax 831/461-1604, www.happy-vacations.com), an older and reputable company that gives good service and stands by its policies. **Creative Leisure International** (707/778-1800 or 800/413/1000, fax 707/778-1223, www.creativeleisure.com) utilizes United Airlines. Some airlines offer great package deals that are hard to beat. United Vacations (888/854-3899, www.unitedvacations.com) by United Airlines is one.

Getting Around

Touring O'ahu is especially easy because almost every normal mode of conveyance is readily available. You can rent anything from a moped to a limo, and the competition is stiff, which helps keep prices down. A few differences separate O'ahu from the other islands. To begin with, O'ahu has a model public transportation system called TheBus, which is not only efficient but also inexpensive. O'ahu is also the only island that has a true expressway system, although along with it comes rush hour and traffic jams. A large part of O'ahu's business is processing people, even if it's only to send them on to another island! The agencies operating these businesses on the island are masters at moving people down the road. With the huge volume of tourists that visit every year, it's amazing how smoothly it works. The following is a cross section of what's available. Have fun!

BY AIR

The only effective way for most visitors to travel between the Hawaiian Islands is by air. Luckily, Hawaii has excellent air transportation that boasts one of the industry's safest flight records. All interisland flights have a no-smoking regulation. Items restricted on flights from the Mainland and from overseas are also restricted on flights within the state. Baggage allowances are the same as anywhere, except that due to space constraints, carry-on luggage on the smaller propeller planes may be limited in number and size. The longest di-

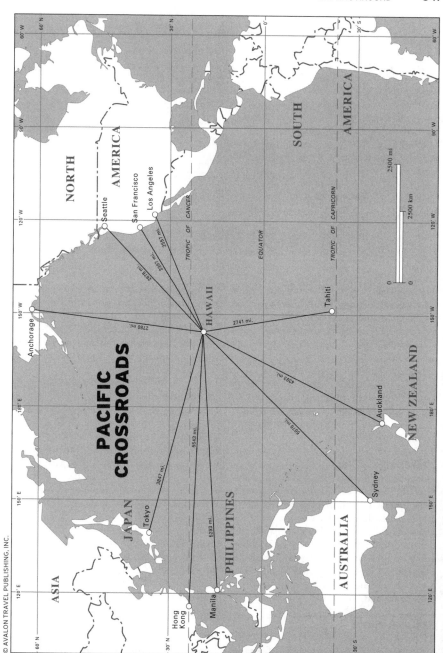

PACIFIC CROSSROADS

NORTH AMERICA

SOUTH AMERICA

Seattle
San Francisco
Los Angeles

2457 mi.
2878 mi.

TROPIC OF CANCER

EQUATOR

Tahiti

TROPIC OF CAPRICORN

Anchorage
2780 mi.

HAWAII
2741 mi.

4383 mi.

Auckland

NEW ZEALAND

5543 mi.

5070 mi.

Sydney

AUSTRALIA

Tokyo
3847 mi.

JAPAN

ASIA

PHILIPPINES

5293 mi.

Manila

Hong Kong

2500 mi

2500 km

© AVALON TRAVEL PUBLISHING, INC.

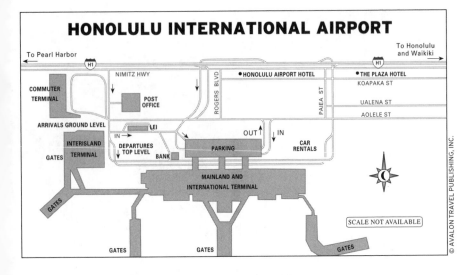

rect interisland flight in the state, 263 miles, is between Lihuʻe and Kona. Following that, it's 214 miles and 45 minutes from Honolulu to Hilo. All others are shorter, but connections will add time. Interisland carriers offer competitive prices.

Note: Although every effort has been made for up-to-date accuracy, remember that schedules are constantly changing. The following should be used only as a point of reference. Please call the airlines or check websites listed for their latest schedules.

Hawaiian Airlines

Hawaiian Airlines (808/838-1555 on Oʻahu, 800/367-5320 Mainland and Canada, www.hawaiianair.com) offers flights from Honolulu to all major Hawaiian cities. From Honolulu to Kauaʻi, nearly a dozen and a half nonstop flights run 5:30 A.M.–9 P.M. There are about as many flights each day to Kahului, Maui, with a dozen or so a day each to Hilo, Kona, and Kapalua, Maui, with a few fewer to both Lanaʻi and Molokaiʻi.

Aloha Airlines

Aloha Airlines (808/484-1111 on Oʻahu, 800/367-5250 Mainland and Canada, www.alohaairlines.com) connects Honolulu to Kauaʻi, Maui, and both Kona and Hilo on the Big Island of Hawaii. Routes from Honolulu to Kauaʻi run about once an hour 7 A.M.–6 P.M. The schedule is much the same for flights to Maui, with only a few fewer flights each day to Kona and Hilo.

Island Air

Island Air (808/484-2222 on Oʻahu, 800/323-3345 Mainland, www.islandair.com), connects Honolulu with the small airports at Kapalua-West Maui, Lanaʻi, and Hoʻolehua on Molokaʻi, as well as to the larger cities of Kahului, Kona, Hilo, and Lihuʻe. About half the flights are on jet aircraft and half on Dash-8 turboprop airplanes.

go!

In 2006, Mesa Airlines decided to get into the Hawaiian market and started the airline called **go!** (888/435-9462, www.iflygo.com), with a few basic routes and ultra-cheap interisland rates of $39. Using Honolulu as a hub, go! flies to Lihuʻe, Kahului, Kona, and Hilo.

Pacific Wings

A local and reputable company operating nine-

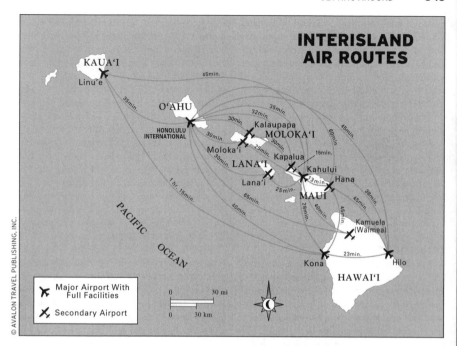

INTERISLAND AIR ROUTES

KAUA'I
Linu'e

45min.
35min.
O'AHU
HONOLULU
INTERNATIONAL
32min.
35min.
30min.
Kalaupapa
MOLOKA'I
30min.
25min.
Moloka'i
Kapalua
15min.
45min.
60min.
LANA'I
Kahului
Hana
Lana'i
73min.
25min.
MAUI
Kamuela
(Waimea)
65min.
40min.
38min.
45min.
28min.
40min.
45min.
1 hr. 15min.
PACIFIC
OCEAN
23min.
Kona
Hilo
HAWAI'I

✈ Major Airport With
  Full Facilities

✗ Secondary Airport

0   30 mi
0   30 km

© AVALON TRAVEL PUBLISHING, INC.

seat, single-engine turboprop, Cessna 208-B planes, Pacific Wings (808/873-0877 or 888/575-4546, www.pacificwings.com) does the pickup routes. They connect Honolulu nonstop with Hana and Kapalua-West Maui on Maui, Lana'i, and Moloka'i, as well as Kamuela, Kona, and Hilo on the Big Island. Pacific Wings services all the commercial airports in the state, large and small, except for those on Kaua'i. Pacific Wings uses the commuter terminal at the Honolulu Airport.

Charter Airlines

If you've got the bucks or just need to go when there's no regularly scheduled flight, try one of the following for islandwide service: **Paragon Air** (808/244-3356 or 800/428-1231 Mainland, www.paragon-air.com), **Mokulele Airlines** (808/326-7070 or 866/260-7070, www.mokuleleairlines.com), or **Air Links Hawaii** (808/871-7529 or 800/496-7529, www.airlinkshawaii.com). Generally, the aircraft used are 8–10-passenger Piper Chieftain or simi-

lar aircraft. These airlines all offer a variety of air tours in addition to their charter services.

BY SHIP
Interisland Cruise Ships

In December 2001, Norwegian Cruise Lines, a subsidiary of Star Cruises PLC of Malaysia, began running a weekly seven-day round-trip cruise that went throughout the Hawaiian Islands with a leg down to Fanning Island, in the Republic of Kiribati, and back. Now under the name NCL America (888/625-4292, www.ncl.com), it offers 10- and 11-day Hawaii and Fanning Island trips on its *Norwegian Wind* and *Norwegian Sun* ships. In addition, the 1,900-passenger *Pride of Aloha* and 2,100-passenger *Pride of America* (newly christened in June 2005) make seven-day roundtrip cruises to the four main islands, making stops at Nawiliwili Harbor on Kaua'i, Honolulu on O'ahu, Kahului on Maui, and both Kona and Hilo on the Big Island. From summer 2006, the new 2,400-passenger *Pride of Hawaii* was added to the fleet for these Hawaii-only routes. The itineraries of these ships differ somewhat, with some spending more time in port and others more time at sea. All the ships begin their journey at Honolulu; however, you may also start your trip on Maui for interisland routes. For specific information on routes, itineraries, and pricing, contact the company directly or work through a travel agent.

Also in 2001, following the terrorist attacks on the Mainland and a dramatic dip in numbers of travelers to the Hawaiian Islands, American Hawaii Cruises stopped all interisland cruise service within the Hawaiian Islands. This company had operated seven-day cruises to four of the islands for years.

Interisland Ferry

While this ferry has not started service as of this writing, the following information is as up-to-date as possible concerning the proposed ferry service and will be of interest to those who desire an alternate way of getting between the islands that does not involve air travel. This ferry service harkens back to the days before airline service when the *only* way between islands was by boat.

With a scheduled start in summer of 2007, the **Hawaii Superferry** (877/443-3779, www.hawaii superferry.com) is set to provide daily ferry service between Honolulu and both Maui and Kaua'i. The large double-hull catamaran ferries will carry both passengers and vehicles, so it will now be possible to take a vehicle from one island to another without having to ship it by barge. Service to either Maui or Kaua'i should take about three hours. Passenger prices are set at $50 and $60 per person for off-peak and peak sailings, with a discount for Internet bookings. Various additional fees will be charged for vehicles and bicycles. Service to Kawaihae on the Big Island of Hawai'i is set to start in 2009.

BY LAND
Car Rental

Rental car options on O'ahu are as numerous as anywhere in the country, from a subcompact to a full-size luxury land yacht, and renting a car is the best way to see the island if you're going to be there for a limited time. The most common rentals seem to be compact cars and midsize sedans, but convertibles and 4WD jeeps are becoming very popular, and some vans and SUVs are also available. Nearly all have automatic transmissions and air conditioning. Generally, you must be 21 years old, although some agencies will rent to 18-year-olds, whereas others require you to be 25 for certain vehicles. Those ages 21–24 will usually be charged an extra fee, which may be significant. You must possess a valid driver's license; licenses from most countries are accepted, but if you are not American, get an International Driver's License to be safe. You should also have a major credit card in your name.

If you're arriving during the peak seasons of Christmas, Easter, or summer, absolutely reserve your car in advance. If you're going during off-peak, you stand a chance of getting the car you want at a price you like once you land on the island. To be on the safe side, and for your own peace of mind, it's generally best to book ahead.

All major rental car companies in Hawaii use flat-rate pricing, which provides a fixed daily rate and unlimited mileage. Most car companies, local and national, offer special rates and deals, like AAA discounts. These deals are common, but don't expect rental companies to let you know about them. Make sure to inquire. The basic rates aren't your only charges, however. On top of the actual rental fee, you may pay an airport access fee, airport concession fee, state tax, and a road tax surcharge—in total, an additional 25–30 percent! For cars not rented at the airports, you'll realize a savings of about 7.5 percent because some of the taxes cannot be charged.

Most companies have child seats available for rent on a daily basis, $5–10 a day or $40–50 maximum, and can install right- or left-hand controls for handicapped drivers. Agencies generally require 48–72 hours advance notice to install hand controls.

Car Rental Agencies

All of the following national companies have locations both at the Honolulu International Air-

DRIVING TIPS

Wear your seat belt – it's the law! Police keep an eye out for miscreants and often ticket those who do not use their restraints. Not wearing a seat belt is a primary offense in Hawaii, meaning officers can pull you over for not wearing a seat belt even if you are not breaking any other laws. Protect your small children as you would at home with car seats. Either bring one from home or rent one from a rental car company.

Mile markers alongside roads are great for pinpointing sights and beaches. The lower number on these small signs is the highway number, so you can always make sure that you're on the right road.

In most cases, you'll get only one key for your rental car. Don't lose it or lock it inside. If you do lock it inside the vehicle, call AAA (or other auto emergency service you might have) for assistance. Failing that, a local locksmith can open your car for a fee or the rental car agency can send out a second key by taxi, but both of these options can get quite pricey.

Many people on the roads in Hawaii are tourists and can be unsure about where they're going. Slow down, be aware, and drive defensively.

In Hawaii, drivers don't generally honk their horns except to say hello or in an emergency. It's considered rude, and honking to hurry someone might earn you a knuckle sandwich. Hawaiian drivers reflect the climate: They're relaxed and polite. Often on small roads, they'll brake to let you turn left when they're coming at you. They may assume you'll do the same, so be ready, after a perfunctory turn signal from another driver, for him or her to turn across your lane. The more rural the area,

the more apt this is to happen. Don't expect it in the large cities.

The H-1 and H-2 freeways throw many Mainlanders a Polynesian screwball. Accustomed to driving on superhighways, Mainlanders assume that these are the same. They're not. O'ahu's superhighways are much more twisted, turned, and convoluted than most Mainland counterparts. Subliminally they look like a normal freeway, except that they've been tied into a Hawaiian knot. There are split-offs, crossroads, and exits in the middle of the exits. Stay alert and don't be lulled into complacency. On the other hand, H-3 is fairly straight as it passes through the mountain between Honolulu and Kane'ohe.

Respect Do Not Enter and Private Property signs – *Kapu* means the same thing.

Car rental companies state that their cars are not to be driven off paved roads – read your policy. This seems absolutely ridiculous for four-wheel drive (4WD) vehicles but may be true nonetheless. When a road is signed for 4WD only, assume that that's the case for a good reason.

Speed limits change periodically along the highways, particularly when they pass through small towns. Police routinely check the speed of traffic with radar equipment. Be aware of this so you don't go home with more than a suntan.

The State Department of Transportation has installed solar-powered emergency call boxes on O'ahu highways that are linked directly to an emergency response network. These boxes dot major roadways. Look for a yellow box on a tall pole topped by a small solar panel and blue light.

port and at one or more locations in Waikiki. The local phone numbers list the main airport location first, followed by the Waikiki location phone numbers.

One of the best national firms with an excellent reputation for service and prices is **Dollar Rent A Car** (808/944-1544 or 808/952-4264 or 800/800-4000 worldwide, www.dollar

car.com). Dollar rents mostly Chrysler vehicles: sedans, Jeeps, convertibles, and 4WDs. They have great weekly rates, and all major credit cards are accepted.

Alamo (808/833-4585 or 808/947-6112 or 800/327-9633, www.goalamo.com) has good weekly rates and rents mostly GM cars.

National Car Rental (808/831-3800 or

808/973-7200 or 800/227-7368 worldwide, www.nationalcar.com) features GM cars and accepts all major credit cards.

Avis (808/834-5536 or 808/971-3700 or 800/331-1212 nationwide, www.avis.com) features late-model GM cars as well as most imports and convertibles. Avis manages the Sears auto rental network.

Budget (808/836-1700 or 808/921-5808 or 800/527-0700 worldwide, www.budget.com) offers competitive rates on late-model Ford and Lincoln-Mercury cars and specialty vehicles.

Hertz (808/831-3500 or 808/971-3535 or 800/654-3011 worldwide, www.hertz.com) is competitively priced with many fly/drive deals. Hertz features Ford vehicles.

Enterprise (808/836-2213 or 808/922-0090 or 800/736-8222 nationwide, www.enterprise.com) rents all types of vehicles at decent rates.

Thrifty (808/831-2279 or 808/971-2660 or 800/847-4389 worldwide, www.thrifty.com) uses Chrysler vehicles.

Motorcycles and Mopeds

Driving a motorcycle can be liberating and exhilarating, yet motorcycle drivers are more vulnerable than drivers of cars and trucks. Enjoy your ride, but be very aware of traffic conditions. Drive safely and defensively. Although helmets are not required in the state, all rental agencies offer them; eye protection is a must. To rent you must be at least 18 years old—at least 23 for some motorcycle rental companies—and have a valid motorcycle endorsement on your driver's license. Payment is usually by a credit card in your name, but some will accept cash payments. All rentals will require a stiff security deposit of $500–3,500 on your credit card for each rental, depending upon the type of bike you rent.

There are numerous moped rental shops in and around Waikiki. Although prices vary, generally you'll be looking at about $30 for up to four hours, $40 for an eight-hour day, or $50 for a 24-hour period, often with a $100 deposit. Mopeds fall into the same vehicle category as bicycles, so become aware of all ap-

propriate rules and regulations before you rent and ride.

TheBus

If Dorothy and her mates had TheBus to get them down the Yellow Brick Road, she might have chosen to stay in Oz and forget about Kansas. TheBus, TheBus, ThewonderfulBus is the always-coming, go-everywhere friend of the budget traveler. Operated by O'ahu Transit Services, Inc. (OTS), TheBus could serve as a model of efficiency and economy in any city of the world. What makes it more amazing is that it all came together by chance, beginning as an emergency service in 1971. Aside from crisscrossing the city, these coaches go up and down both the Windward and Leeward Coasts, through the interior, while passing through all towns in between, and most often stopping near the best sights.

Route signs and numbers are located on the front of the bus and near the bus doors. The **fare** is only $2 adults, $1 students ages 6–17; kids under six who can sit on a parent's lap aren't charged at all. The exact fare is paid upon entering, as drivers cannot make change. A four-day unlimited-use pass is available for $20 from ABC Stores. The adult monthly bus pass, good at any time and on all routes, is $40, but be aware that they are good only from the first to the last day of every month. If you buy a pass in midmonth, or even later, it's still full price. A student monthly pass is $20. Passes for senior citizens and disabled passengers are also issued for a reasonable fee. Seniors (65 or older) must furnish proof of age and will be given the pass within a few minutes of having an ID photo taken. Monthly passes are available at **TheBus Pass Office** (open Mon.–Fri. 7:30 A.M.–4 P.M., 811 Middle St., Honolulu, 808/848-4444, www.thebus.org). Bus no. 1 Kalihi stops within a few feet of TheBus Pass Office.

One free **transfer** is issued upon request when entering TheBus, but you can only use them for ongoing travel in the same direction, on a different line. They are also timed and dated, good for approximately two hours.

Only baggage that can be placed under the

seat or on one's lap is permitted; baby strollers that fold up are allowed. Seeing-eye dogs and other similar service animals can accompany a passenger, but all other animals must be in a carrier that fits under the seat or on the lap. No smoking is allowed, and eating or drinking is not permitted. Please use radios or similar devices with headphones only.

Some buses are now equipped with bike racks, which makes it easier to get around town or out of town without having to jostle with all the traffic. Bike racks carry two bikes only. First, let the bus driver know that you wish to load your bike. Then pull down to unfold the rack, if it isn't down already, and securely set the bike wheels into the slots. Pull up on the securing arm to lock your bike in, then board. When leaving the bus, be sure to let the driver know that you want to unload your bike, or it may continue without you. For additional instructions, consult the *How to Use the New Bike Rack for Buses* booklet, available from TheBus office.

There are about 80 routes in the system. Get full **route and schedule information** by calling 808/848-5555, 5:30 A.M.–10 P.M. or by visiting the information booth at the Ala Moana Terminal and satellite city halls, where you can pick up fliers and maps. For recorded general information and attractions along the routes, call 808/296-1818 and follow the directions. For other issues, contact TheBus lost and found office (808/848-4444) or Customer Service (808/848-4500). One inexpensive guide to major bus routes and attractions is *TheBus Map and Guide Book*. It's available in most bookstores and sundries shops for around $5.

Taxis

The law says that taxis are not allowed to cruise around looking for fares, so you can't hail them. But they do and you can, and most police officers have more important things to do than monitor cabs. Your best bet is to summon one from your hotel or a restaurant. All are radio-dispatched, and they're usually there in a flash. The fares, posted on the taxi doors, are set by law and are fair but still expensive for the budget traveler. The rates do change, but expect about $2.80 for the flag fall, and then $0.30 for each additional one-eighth mile. From the airport to Waikiki is about $35, although luggage costs extra. Most cab drivers are quite good, but you may pause to consider if your cab sports the bumper sticker "Caution! I drive like you do!"

Of the many taxi companies, some with good reputations are **Charley's Taxi** (808/531-1333 or 808/955-2211), **City Taxi** (808/524-2121), and **The Cab** (808/422-2222). If you need some special attention like a Rolls-Royce limo, try **Cloud 9 Limousines** (808/524-7999). It is one of about 50 limo services on the island.

Tips For Travelers

ACCOMMODATIONS

The innkeepers of Oʻahu would be personally embarrassed if you couldn't find adequate lodging on their island. So long as Oʻahu has to suffer the "slings and arrows" of development gone wild, at least you can find all kinds, qualities, and prices of places in which to spend your vacation. Of the more than 73,000 rooms available in Hawaii, 35,000 are on Oʻahu, with 29,000 of them in Waikiki alone! Some accommodations are living landmarks, historic mementos of the days when only millionaires came by ship to Oʻahu, dallying as if it were their own private hideaway. When the jumbo jets began arriving in the early 1960s, Oʻahu, especially Waikiki, began to build frantically. The result was hotel skyscrapers that grew faster than bamboo in a rainforest. These monoliths, which offered the "average family" a place to stay, marked a tremendous change in social status of visitors to Oʻahu. The runaway building continued unabated for two decades, until the city politicians, supported by the hotelkeepers, cried "Enough!" and the activity finally slowed. Now a great deal of money is being put into refurbishing and remodeling what's already been built. Visitors can find breathtakingly beautiful hotels that are the best in the land next door to more humble inns that can satisfy most anyone's taste and pocketbook. On Oʻahu, you may not get your own private beach with swaying palms and hula girls, but it's easy and affordable to visit one of the world's most exotic and premier vacation destinations.

Central Honolulu has one fine business hotel. Some upscale hotels around Ala Moana put you near the beach but away from the heavy activity of Waikiki. For those passing

© ROBERT NILSEN

While the vast majority of hotels on Oʻahu are in Waikiki, a few, such as the JW Marriott Ihilani Resort, pictured here, are at other striking locations around the island.

through, a few no-nonsense hotels are located near the airport. For those looking for less expensive accommodations, the city has a handful of YMCAs, YWCAs, and youth hostels.

The remainder of the island, outside Waikiki, was mostly ignored as far as resort development was concerned, except for the venerable Turtle Bay Resort on the North Shore, the new and luxurious JW Marriott Ihilani Resort in 'Ewa, and the remodeled and more humble Makaha Resort and Golf Club on the Wai'anae coast. In the interior towns and along the other coasts, you won't find a hotel room, only a handful of inns, condos, vacation rentals, and bed-and-breakfasts. To round things out, O'ahu also offers a smattering of places to pitch a tent at both state and county campgrounds.

Hotels

While some hotels have a single basic rate throughout the year, most have a tiered pricing policy based on times of the year. This often translates as regular- and value-season rates (which may be referred to differently at different hotels), and some also include holiday rates. While the difference between "high season" and "low season" is less distinct than it used to be, Hawaii's **peak season** still runs from just before Christmas until after Easter, and then again throughout the summer, when rooms are at a premium. Value-season rates, when rooms are easier to come by, are often about 10 percent below the regular rate.

In Hawaiian hotels you always pay more for a good **view.** Terms vary slightly, but usually "oceanfront" means your room faces the ocean and your view is mostly unimpeded. "Oceanview" is slightly more vague. It could be a decent view or it could require standing on the dresser and craning your neck to catch a tiny slice of the sea sandwiched between two skyscrapers. "Garden view" means just that, and "mountain view" may mean that you have a view of a mountain or simply that you have a view away from the ocean. Rooms with garden view or mountain view are the least expensive, then oceanview, with oceanfront rooms commanding the highest rates. Suites are invariably

larger and more expensive, and these usually get the best locations and views.

Note: Prices listed are based on a standard published rate, double occupancy, without taxes or other charges added, unless otherwise noted.

Condominiums

The main qualitative difference between a condo and a hotel is in amenities. At a condo, you're more on your own. You're temporarily renting an apartment, so there won't be any bellhops and rarely a bar, restaurant, or lounge on the premises, although many times you'll find a sundries store. Condos can be studios (one big room), but mostly they are one- or multiple-bedroom affairs with a complete kitchen. Reasonable housekeeping items should be provided. All have sufficient amenities, but remember that the furnishings provided are all up to the owner. Maid service might be included on a limited basis (for example, once weekly), or you might have to pay extra for it. Swimming pools are common, and depending on the "theme" of the condo, you can find saunas, weight rooms, hot tubs, and tennis courts.

Condos usually require a minimum stay, most often three days, but seven is also commonplace, and during peak season two weeks isn't unheard of. Generally speaking, studios can sleep two, a one-bedroom place will sleep four, two-bedroom units will sleep six, and three-bedroom units will sleep eight. Most have a sleeper couch in the sitting room that folds out into a bed. You can find clean, decent condos for as little as $450 per week, all the way up to exclusive apartments for more than $2,000. Most fall into the $700–1,000 range per week. The method of paying for and reserving a condo is just about the same as for a hotel. However, requirements for deposits, final payments, and cancellation charges are much stiffer than in hotels. Make absolutely sure you fully understand all of these requirements when you make your reservations.

The real advantage of condos is for families, friends who want to share, and especially people on long-term stays, for which you will always get a special rate. The kitchen facilities save a great deal on dining costs, and it's common to find units with their own washers and dryers. To sweeten the deal, many condo companies offer coupons that can save you money on food, gifts, and activities at local establishments. Parking space is ample for guests, and like hotels, plenty of stay/drive deals are offered.

Vacation Rentals

Vacation rentals are homes or cottages that are rented to visitors, usually for a week or longer. Sometimes shorter rentals can be arranged. These rentals come with all the amenities of condo units, but they are usually freestanding homes. As with condos, meals are not part of the option. Although vacation rentals can in most cases be rented directly from the owner, perhaps the best way to locate a vacation rental, at least for the first time that you visit the island, is through a rental/real estate agent. Everything from simple beach homes to luxurious hideaways are put into the hands of rental agents, who all have Internet sites. The agents have descriptions of the properties and terms of the rental contracts, and many will furnish photographs. Be aware that some places, although not all, have outgoing cleaning fees in addition to the rental rate. When contacting an agency, be as specific as possible about your needs, length of stay, desired location, and how much you're willing to spend. Be aware that during high season, rentals are at a premium; if you're slow to inquire, there may be slim pickin's.

Bed-And-Breakfast Inns

Lodging in private homes called bed-and-breakfast (B&B) inns is becoming increasingly fashionable throughout the United States, and Hawaii is no exception, with about 100,000 B&B guests yearly. O'ahu has more than 50 legally registered B&Bs, with many more than those taking guests anyway.

The primary feature of bed-and-breakfasts is that every one is privately owned and therefore unique. The range of B&Bs is as wide, but most fall into the broad middle living standard in America. Still, the lifestyles of B&B hosts differ, so it's prudent to choose a host family with whom one's lifestyle is compatible if at all possible.

Unlike at a hotel or condo, you'll usually be staying *with* a host (usually a family), although your room will be private, with private baths and separate entrances quite common. Many B&Bs now also offer separate cottages, and some homes do not have live-in hosts, but the unifying feature is that breakfast is provided. Meals vary as much as B&B styles. They range from a full-blown, sit-down affair with home-cooked meals at a prescribed time to a plate of fruit and pastries with a bottle of juice left in a room refrigerator for you to have whenever you want.

You can make arrangements directly or you might want to go through an agency which acts as a go-between, matching host and guest. Agencies have a description of each B&B they rent for, its general location, the fees charged, and a good idea of the lifestyle of your host family. What the agency will want to know from you is where you want to stay, what type of place you're looking for, the price range you're willing to pay, arrival and departure dates, and other items that will help them match you with a place. (Are you single? Do you have children? Do you smoke?) You, of course, can do all the legwork yourself, but these people know their territory and guarantee their work. They also inspect each B&B and make sure that each has a license and insurance to operate. Most can also arrange discount car rental and interisland airfares for you.

Make all your arrangements well in advance. You might be lucky and find a place that has an opening on short notice, but give yourself four weeks as a minimum. For holiday travel, three to six months' lead time would not be imprudent. Expect a minimum-stay requirement (three days is common). As with condos, B&Bs have different requirements for making and holding reservations and for payment. Most will hold a room with a credit card deposit or check covering a certain percentage of the total expected bill. Be aware, however, that some B&Bs do not accept credit cards or personal checks, so you must pay in cash, traveler's checks, or money orders. Always inquire about the method of payment when making your initial inquiries.

A top-notch B&B agency is **Bed and Breakfast Hawaii** (P.O. Box 449, Kapaʻa, HI 96746, 808/822-7771 or 800/733-1632, reservations@bandb-hawaii.com, www.bandb-hawaii.com), operated by Evelyn Warner and Al Davis. They've been running this service since 1978, and their reputation is excellent. One of the most experienced agencies, **Bed and Breakfast Honolulu** (Statewide) (3242 Kaohinanai Dr., Honolulu, HI 96817, 808/595-7533 or 800/288-4666, fax 808/595-2030, rainbow@hawaiibnb.com, www.hawaiibnb.com), owned and operated by Mary Lee and Gene Bridges, began in 1982. Since then, they've become masters at finding visitors the perfect accommodations to match their desires, needs, and pocketbooks. **All Island Bed and Breakfast** (808/263-2342 or 800/542-0344, inquires@all-islands.com, www.all-islands.com) can match your needs with numerous homes throughout the state. **Hawaii's Best Bed and Breakfast** (P.O. Box 485, Laupahoehoe, HI 96764, 808/962-0100 or 800/262-9912, fax 808/962-6360, reservations@bestbnb.com, http://bestbnb.com) has listings all over the state.

Both **Pacific Hawaii Reservations** (571 Pauku St., Kailua, HI 96734, 808/262-8133, fax 808/262-5030, pir@aloha.net, www.oahu-hawaii-vacation.com) and **Affordable Paradise Bed and Breakfast** (332 Kuʻukama St., Kailua, HI 96734, 808/261-1693, info@affordable-paradise.com, www.affordable-paradise.com) are located on the Windward side of Oʻahu but handle B&Bs throughout the state.

Hostels

Hostels are the cheapest accommodations on the island, but the amenities will likely not be up to the standards of many visitors. Hostels generally cater to (mostly young) Mainland and foreign travelers, those with onward or return tickets, and therefore usually do not have local, long-term residents. Oʻahu has several reasonably priced hostels, a half dozen within a Frisbee toss of the beach in Waikiki, one near the university, and a couple more along the North Shore.

ALTERNATIVE WAYS TO THE ISLANDS
Educational Trips

Elderhostel Hawaii offers short-term educational programs on five of the Hawaiian islands. Different programs focus on history, culture, cuisine, and the environment in association with one of the colleges or universities on the islands. Most programs use hotels for accommodations. For information, contact Elderhostel (11 Avenue de Lafayette, Boston, MA 02111-1746 or 800/454-5678; www.elderhostel.org).

TRAVELERS WITH DISABILITIES

A person with disabilities can have a wonderful time on Oʻahu; all that's needed is a little planning. The key for a smooth trip is to make as many arrangements ahead of time as possible. Tell the transportation companies and hotels you'll be dealing with the nature of your handicap in advance so they can make arrangements to accommodate you. Bring your medical records and notify medical establishments of your arrival if you'll be needing their services. Travel with a friend or make arrangements for an aide on arrival. Bring your own wheelchair if possible and let airlines know if it is battery-powered. Boarding interisland carriers sometimes requires steps. They'll board wheelchairs early on special lifts, but they must know you're coming. Most hotels and restaurants accommodate persons with disabilities, but always call ahead just to make sure.

Information

The state Commission on Persons with Disabilities was designed with the express purpose of aiding disabled people. It is a source of invaluable information and distributes self-help booklets, which are published jointly by the Disability and Communication Access Board and the Hawaii Centers for Independent Living. Any person with disabilities heading to Hawaii should write first or visit the office of the Hawaii Centers for Independent Living (414 Kuwili St., #102, Honolulu, HI 96817, 808/522-5400, www.hcil.org). Additional information is available on the Disability and Communication Access Board website (www.hawaii.gov/health/dcab/home).

O'ahu Services

At Honolulu International Airport, parking spaces are on the fourth floor of the parking garage near each pedestrian bridge and on each level near the elevators at the interisland terminal. Several of the Wiki-Wiki Shuttles at the airport have lifts for wheelchairs, and there is an on-demand van shuttle service for transportation between locations within the airport facility. O'ahu's public transit system, TheBus, operates most buses with lift capability, but most van transportation and taxis have steps.

For getting around, the City of Honolulu offers a curb-to-curb service for disabled persons; call **Handi-Van** (808/456-5555). You must make arrangements at least a day in advance or up to seven days in advance. A private special taxi company operating all over the island is **Handi-Cabs of the Pacific** (808/848-4500); **The Cab** (808/422-2222) taxi service also has wheelchair accessible vans. Most of the large **rental car companies** can put hand controls (right or left) on their cars, but some restrict these controls to a certain size or type of vehicle. They generally require prior arrangements, one or two days at least, preferably when making your advance reservation. Rates are comparable with standard rental cars.

Access Aloha Travel (414 Kuwili St., #101, Honolulu, 808/545-1143 or 800/480-1143, http://accessalohatravel.com) rents wheelchair lift-equipped vans on O'ahu for $200 per day or $723 per week; monthly rentals are also possible. This is a full-service travel agency and a good source of information on traveling with disabilities.

Valid out-of-state **handicapped parking** **placards** may be used throughout the state of Hawaii. Passes for disabled but ambulatory persons using **TheBus** cost $10. Check at TheBus Pass Office (811 Middle St., Honolulu, 808/848-4500; open Mon.–Fri. 7:30 A.M.–3:30 P.M.)

For **medical equipment rental,** see the following establishments for all kinds of apparatus: **Apria Healthcare** (98-720 Kuahao Pl., Pearl City, 808/485-0178, www.apria.com), **C. R. Newton Co.** (1575 S. Beretania St., Ste. 101, Honolulu, 808/949-8389 or 800/545-2078, www.crnewton.com), and **Hawaiian Islands Medical** (841 Pohukaina St., Ste. 8, Honolulu, 808/597-8087 or 866/246-4633, www.himed.net).

PREVENTING THEFT

From the minute you sit behind the wheel of your rental car, you'll be warned not to leave valuables unattended and to lock up your car tighter than a drum. Signs warning about theft at most major tourist attractions help fuel your paranoia. Many hotel and condo rooms offer safes so you can lock your valuables away and relax while getting sunburned. The majority of theft in Hawaii is of the "sneak thief" variety. If you leave your hotel door unlocked, a camera sitting on the seat of your rental car, or valuables on your beach towel, you'll be inviting a very obliging thief to pad away with your stuff. You have to take precautions, but nothing like those employed in rougher areas of the world—just normal American precautions. Hawaii's reputation is much worse than the reality. Besides, Hawaiians are still among the friendliest, most giving, and understanding people on earth.

If you must walk alone at night, stay on the main streets in well-lit areas. Always lock your hotel door and windows and place valuable jewelry in the hotel safe. When you leave your hotel for the beach, there is absolutely no reason to carry all your travelers checks, credit cards, or a big wad of money. Just take what you'll need for drinks and lunch. If you're uptight about leaving money in your beach bag, stick it in your bathing suit. American money is just as negotiable when damp. Don't leave your camera on the beach unattended. While sightseeing in your shiny new rental car, which immediately brands you as a tourist, again, don't take more than what you'll need for the day. Many people lock valuables away in the trunk, but remember that most good car thieves can jimmy it open as quickly as you can open it with your key.

Campers face special problems because their entire camp is open to thievery. Most campgrounds don't have any real security, but who, after all, wants to fence an old tent or a used sleeping bag? Many tents have zippers that can be secured with a small padlock. In the end, you must just take what precautions you can and trust the goodness of others.

Health and Conduct

In a survey published some years ago by *Science Digest,* Hawaii was cited as the healthiest state in the United States in which to live. Indeed, Hawaiian citizens live longer than anywhere else in America. Their average lifespan is 80 years. Lifestyle, heredity, and diet help with these figures, but Hawaii is still an oasis in the middle of the ocean, and germs just have a tougher time getting there. There are no cases of malaria, cholera, or yellow fever. Because of a strict quarantine law, rabies is also nonexistent. On the other hand, tooth decay, perhaps because of the wide use of sugar and the enzymes present in certain tropical fruits, as well as the fact that fluoride is not added to the water supply, is 30 percent above the national average. With the perfect weather, a multitude of fresh-air activities, soothing negative ionization from the sea, and a generally relaxed and carefree lifestyle, everyone seems to feel better in the islands. Hawaii is just what the doctor ordered: a beautiful, natural health spa. That's one of the main drawing cards. The food and water are perfectly safe, and the air quality is the best in the country.

Handling the Sun

Don't become a victim of your own exuberance. People can't wait to strip down and lie on the sand like beached whales, but the tropical sun will burn you to a cinder if you're silly. The burning rays come through more easily in Hawaii because of the sun's angle, and you don't feel them as much because

there's always a cool breeze. The worst part of the day is 11 A.M.–3 P.M. O'ahu lies about 21.5 degrees north latitude, not even close to the equator, but it's still over 1,000 miles south of sunny southern California beaches. You'll just have to force yourself to go slowly. Don't worry; you'll be able to flaunt your best souvenir, your golden Hawaiian tan, to your green-with-envy friends when you get home. It's better than showing them a boiled lobster body with peeling skin! If your skin is snowflake white, 15 minutes per side on the first day is plenty. Increase by 15-minute intervals every day, which will allow you a full hour per side by the fourth day. Have faith: This is enough to give you a start on a deep golden, uniform tan. If you lie out on the beach or are simply out in the sun during the day, if you're off hiking or kayaking, or have rented a convertible car (an unexpected culprit for sunburn), use sunblock lotion that has greater strength than you use at home—most people recommend SPF 25 or higher—and reapply every couple of hours. If you do burn, try taking aspirin as quickly as you can. No one knows exactly what it does, but it seems to provide some relief. Alternately, apply a cold compress or aloe juice, but be careful with aloe because it may stain clothing.

Whether out on the beach, hiking in the mountains, or just strolling around town, be very aware of dehydration. The sun and wind tend to sap your energy and your store of liquid. Bottled water in various sizes is readily available in all parts of Hawaii. Be sure to carry

HAWAIIAN FOLK MEDICINE AND COMMON CURATIVE PLANTS

Hawaiian folk medicine is well developed, and its cures for common ailments have been used effectively for centuries. Hawaiian *kahuna* were highly regarded for their medicinal skills, and Hawaiians were by far some of the healthiest people in the world until the coming of the Europeans. Many folk remedies and cures are used to this day; what's more, they work. Many of the common plants and fruits you'll encounter provide some of the best remedies. When roots and seeds and special exotic plants are used, the preparation of the medicine is as painstaking as in a modern pharmacy. These prescriptions are exact and take an expert to prepare. They should never be prepared or administered by an amateur.

Arrowroot, for diarrhea, is a powerful narcotic used in rituals and medicines. **Kava** *(Piper methisticum),* also called *'awa,* is chewed and the juice is spat into a container for fermenting. Used as a medicine for urinary tract infections, rheumatism, and asthma, it also induces sleep and cures headaches. A poultice for wounds is made from the skins of ripe **bananas.** Peelings have a powerful antibiotic quality and contain vitamins A, B, and C, phosphorous, calcium, and iron. The nectar from the plant was fed to babies as a vitamin juice. **Breadfruit** sap is used for healing cuts and as a moisturizing lotion. **Coconut** is used to make moisturizing oil, and the juice can be chewed, spat into the hand, and used as a shampoo. **Guava** is a source of vitamins A, B, and C. **Hibiscus** has been used as a laxative. *Kukui* nut oil makes a gargle for sore throats and a laxative, plus the flowers are used to cure diarrhea. *Noni,* an unappetizing handgrenade-shaped fruit that you wouldn't want to eat unless you had to, reduces tumors, diabetes, and high blood pressure, and the juice is good for diarrhea. **Sugarcane** sweetens many concoctions, and the juice of toasted cane was a tonic for sick babies. **Sweet potato** is used as a tonic during pregnancy and juiced as a gargle for phlegm. **Tamarind** is a natural laxative and contains the most acid and sugar of any fruit on earth. **Taro** has been used for lung infections and thrush and as a suppository. **Yams** are good for coughs, vomiting, constipation, and appendicitis.

some with you or stop at a store or restaurant for a fill-'er-up.

Don't forget about your head and eyes. Use your sunglasses and wear a brimmed hat. Some people lay a towel over their neck and shoulders when hiking; others will stick a scarf under their hat and let it drape down over their shoulders to provide some protection.

Haole Rot

A peculiar condition caused by the sun is referred to locally as *haole* rot. It's called this because it supposedly affects only white people, but you'll notice some dark-skinned people with the same condition. Basically, the skin becomes mottled with white spots that refuse to tan. You get a blotchy effect, mostly on the shoulders and back. Dermatologists have a fancy name for it, and they'll give you a fancy prescription with a fancy price tag to cure it. It's common knowledge throughout the islands that Selsun Blue shampoo has an ingredient that stops the white mottling effect. Just wash your hair with it and then make sure to rub the lather over the affected areas, and it should clear up.

Bugs

Everyone, in varying degrees, has an aversion to vermin and creepy crawlers. Hawaii isn't infested with a wide variety, but it does have its share. Mosquitoes were unknown in the islands until their larvae stowed away in the water barrels of the *Wellington* in 1826 and were introduced at Lahaina. They bred in the tropical climate and rapidly spread to all the islands.

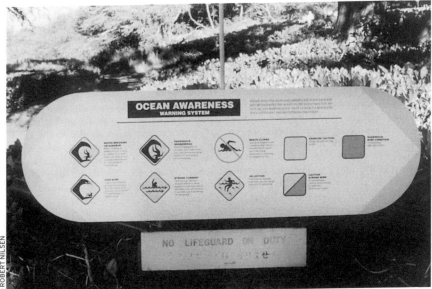

© ROBERT NILSEN

Most popular Hawaiian beaches have ocean awareness signs posted – pay heed.

They are a particular nuisance in the rainforests. Be prepared, and bring a natural repellent like citronella oil, available in most health stores on the islands, or a commercial product available in grocery and drugstores. Campers will be happy to have mosquito coils to burn at night as well.

Cockroaches are very democratic insects. They hassle all strata of society equally. They breed well in Hawaii, and most hotels are at war with them, trying desperately to keep them from being spotted by guests. One comforting thought is that in Hawaii they aren't a sign of filth or dirty housekeeping. They love the climate like everyone else, and it's a real problem keeping them under control.

WATER SAFETY

Hawaii has one very sad claim to fame: More people drown here than anywhere else in the world. Moreover, every year there are dozens of swimming victims with broken necks and backs or with injuries from boogie boarding and snorkeling accidents. These statistics

shouldn't keep you out of the sea, because it is indeed beautiful—benevolent in most cases—and a major reason to go to Hawaii. But if you're foolish, the sea will bounce you like a basketball and suck you away for good. The best remedy is to avoid situations you can't handle. Don't let anyone dare you into a situation that makes you uncomfortable. Macho men who know nothing about the power of the sea will be tumbled into dolls in short order. Ask lifeguards or beach attendants about conditions, and follow their advice. If local people refuse to go in, there's a good reason. Even experts get in trouble in Hawaiian waters. Some beaches are as gentle as lambs, whereas others, especially on the North Coast during the winter months, are frothing giants.

While beachcombing, or especially when walking out on rocks, never turn your back to the sea. Be aware of undertows (the waves drawing back into the sea), which can knock you off your feet. Before entering the water, study it for rocks, breakers, and reefs. Look for ocean currents, especially those within reefs that can cause riptides when the water washes out a channel. Observe the water well before you enter. Note where others are swimming or snorkeling and go there. When snorkeling, wear a T-shirt. It may save your back from major sunburn. Don't swim alone if possible, and obey all warning signs. Come in *before* you get tired.

When the wind comes up, get out. Stay out of water during periods of high surf. High surf often creates riptides that can pull you out to sea. Riptides are powerful currents, like rivers in the sea that can drag you out. Mostly they peter out not too far from shore, and you can often see their choppy waters on the surface. If you get caught in a "rip," don't fight to swim directly against it; you'll lose and only exhaust yourself. Swim diagonally across it, while going along with it, and try to stay parallel to the shore until you are out of the strong pull.

When bodysurfing, never ride straight in; come to shore at a 45-degree angle. Remember, waves come in sets. Little ones can be followed by giants, so watch the action awhile instead of plunging right in. Standard procedure is to duck under a breaking wave. You can survive even thunderous oceans using this technique. Don't try to swim through a heavy froth, and never turn your back and let it smash you.

Stay off of coral. Standing on coral damages it, as does breaking it with your hands, and it might give you a nasty infection.

Leave the fish, turtles, and seals alone. Fish should never be encouraged to feed from humans. Green sea turtles and seals are endangered species, and stiff fines can be levied on those who knowingly disturb them. Have a great time looking, but give them space.

Hawaiians want to entertain you, and they want you to be safe. The county, for its part, doesn't put up ocean conditions signs at beaches to waste money. They're there for your safety. Pay heed. The last rule is, "If in doubt, stay out."

Sharks

Sharks live in all the oceans of the world. Most mind their own business and stay away from shore. Hawaiian sharks are well fed—on fish—and don't usually bother with unsavory humans. If you encounter a shark, don't panic! Never thrash around because this will trigger their attack instinct. If they come close, scream loudly.

Portuguese man-of-wars and other jellyfish put out long, floating tentacles that sting if they touch you. It seems that many floating jellyfish are blown into shore by winds on the eighth, ninth, and 10th days after the full moon. Don't wash the sting off with freshwater because this will only aggravate it. Locals will use hot salt water to take away the sting, as well as alcohol (the drinking or rubbing kind), aftershave lotion, or meat tenderizer (MSG), but lifeguards use common household vinegar. After rinsing, soak with a wet towel. Antihistamine may also bring relief. Expect to start to feel better in about a half hour.

Coral can give you a nasty cut, and it's known for causing infections because it's a living organism. Wash the cut immediately and apply an antiseptic. Keep it clean and covered, and watch for infection. With coral cuts, it's best to have a professional look at it.

Poisonous sea urchins, such as the lacquer-black *wana,* can be beautiful creatures. They are found in shallow tidepools and will hurt you if you step on them. Their spines will break off, enter your foot, and burn like blazes. There are cures. Soaking a couple of times in vinegar for half an hour or so should stop the burning. If vinegar is not available, the Hawaiian method is urine. It might seem ignominious to have someone pee on your foot, but it should put the fire out. The spines will disintegrate in a few days although they could be removed, and there are generally no long-term effects.

Hawaiian reefs also have their share of moray eels. These creatures are ferocious in appearance but will never initiate an attack. You'll have to poke around in their holes while snorkeling or scuba diving to get them to attack. Sometimes this is inadvertent on the diver's part, so be careful where you stick your hand while underwater.

Present in streams, ponds, and muddy soil, leptospirosis is a *freshwater-borne* bacteria, deposited by the urine of infected animals. From two to 20 days after the bacteria enter the body, there is a *sudden* onset of fever accompanied by chills, sweats, headache, and sometimes vomiting and diarrhea. Preventive measures include staying out of freshwater sources and mud where cattle and other animals wade and drink, not swimming in freshwater if you have an open cut, and not drinking stream water. Although not always the case, leptospirosis may be fatal if left untreated.

MEDICAL SERVICES
Full-service **hospitals** include **The Queen's Medical Center** (1301 Punchbowl St., Honolulu, 808/538-9011), **St. Francis Medical Center** (2230 Liliha St., Honolulu, 808/547-6011), and **Straub Clinic and Hospital** (888 S. King St., Honolulu, 808/522-4000) in Honolulu; **Castle Medical Center** (640 Ulukahiki St., 808/263-5500) in Kailua; and **Wahiawa General Hospital** (128 Lehua St., 808/621-8411) in Wahiawa.

For medical clinics and pharmacies, see the *Waikiki* chapter. For chiropractors, acupuncturists, and alternative health care providers, please refer to the Yellow Pages.

Information and Services

MONEY AND FINANCES
Currency
U.S. currency is among the drabbest in the world. It's all the same size, with little variation in color; those unfamiliar with it should spend some time getting acquainted so they don't make costly mistakes. U.S. coinage in use is $.01 (penny), $.05 (nickel), $.10 (dime), $.25 (quarter), $.50 (half dollar), and $1 (uncommon); paper currency is $1, $2 (uncommon), $5, $10, $20, $50, $100. Bills larger than $100 are not in common usage. Since 1996, new designs have been issued for the $100, $50, $20, $10, and $5 bills. Both the old and new bills are accepted as valid currency.

Banks
Full-service bank hours are generally Monday–Thursday 8:30 A.M.–4 P.M. and Friday until 6 P.M. There are no weekend hours, and weekday hours will be a bit longer at counters in grocery stores and other outlets. All main towns on O'ahu have one or more banks. Virtually all branch banks have automated teller machines (ATMs) for 24-hour service, and these can be found at some shopping centers and other venues around the island. ATMs work only when the Hawaiian bank you use is on an affiliate network with your home bank. Of most value to travelers, banks sell and cash travelers checks, give cash advances on credit cards, and exchange and sell foreign currency (sometimes with a fee). Major banks on O'ahu are American Savings Bank, Bank of Hawaii, Central Pacific Bank, and First Hawaiian Bank; each has numerous branch offices throughout the island.

Travelers Checks
Travelers checks are accepted throughout Hawaii at hotels, restaurants, rental car agencies, and in most stores and shops. However, to be readily acceptable they should be in U.S. currency. Some larger hotels that frequently have Japanese and Canadian guests will accept their currency. Banks accept foreign-currency travelers checks, but it'll mean an extra trip and inconvenience. It's best to get most of your travelers checks in $20 or $50 denominations; anything larger will be hard to cash in shops and boutiques, although not in hotels.

Credit Cards
More and more business is transacted in Hawaii using credit cards. Almost every form of accommodation, shop, restaurant, and amusement accepts them. For renting a car they're almost a

must. With credit card insurance readily available, they're as safe as travelers checks and even more convenient. Write down the numbers of your cards in case they're stolen, and keep the numbers separate from the wallet. Don't rely on credit cards completely because some establishments—some bed and breakfasts, for example—won't accept them or perhaps won't accept the kind that you carry.

Taxes

Hawaii does not have a state sales tax, but it does have a general excise tax of about 4 percent, and this will be added to most sales transactions and services. In addition, there is an accommodations tax of 7.25 percent, so approximately 11.4 percent will be added to your hotel bill when you check out.

COMMUNICATION AND MEDIA
Post Offices

There are more than a dozen post offices in Honolulu (800/275-8777), and one in each of the major towns on the island. The normal business hours for window service at many of these are Monday–Friday 8:30 A.M.–4:30 P.M. and Saturday 9 A.M.–1 P.M., although some branch offices have slightly different hours. The main post office in downtown Honolulu (3600 Aolele St.), located next to the King Kamehameha statue has window hours Monday–Friday 7:30 A.M.–8 P.M. and Saturday 8 A.M.–4 P.M. The Waikiki branch (330 Saratoga Rd.) has window hours Monday–Friday 8 A.M.–4:30 P.M., Saturday 9 A.M.–1 P.M.

Telephone

The telephone system on the main islands is modern and comparable to any system on the Mainland. For land lines, any phone call to a number on that island is a **local call;** it's **long distance** when dialing to another island or beyond the state. With standard long distance service, long-distance rates go down at 5 P.M. and again at 11 P.M. until 8 A.M. the next morning. Rates are cheapest from Friday at 5 P.M. until Monday at 8 A.M. Many long-distance companies have moved to a flat rate per minute fee

structure, however, so check with your accommodation. Local calls from public telephones cost $.50. Emergency calls are always free. Public telephones are found at hotels, street booths, restaurants, most public buildings, and some beach parks. It is common to have a phone in most hotel rooms and condominiums, although a service charge is often collected, even on local calls. You can direct dial from Hawaii to the Mainland and more than 160 foreign countries. Undersea cables and satellite communications ensure top-quality phone service. Toll-free calls are preceded by 800/, 888/, 877/, or 866/; there is no charge to the calling party. Many are listed in this book.

Cell (mobile) phone reception is generally very good throughout the state of Hawaii. However, as anywhere, you will find pockets where reception is poor or nonexistent.

For directory assistance, dial: 411 (local), 1-555-1212 (interisland), 1-(area code)/555-1212 (Mainland), 1-800/555-1212 (toll-free).

The area code for all the islands of Hawaii is 808.

Newspapers

Besides special-interest Chinese, Japanese, Korean, Filipino, and military newspapers, two major dailies are published on O'ahu. The *Honolulu Advertiser* (www.honoluluadvertiser.com) is the morning paper, and the *Honolulu Star-Bulletin* (www.starbulletin.com) is the evening paper. They combine to make a Sunday paper. On Friday, the Advertiser runs a TGIF entertainment and arts section that's great for finding out what's happening around town. These two papers run $0.50 daily or $1.75 on Sunday. The alternative free press *Honolulu Weekly* (www.honoluluweekly.com) adds a different perspective to the mix. Aside from feature articles on pertinent local issues, it does a calendar of local arts and events. Free tabloids like the *Waikiki Beach Press* and *Waikiki News* offer entertainment calendars and feature stories of general interest to visitors. Other weekly or monthly free papers that you might see around the island include the *Downtown Planet, Oahu Island News,* the *Midweek Islander* with emphasis on the Windward Coast, the *North Shore News,* and the *Ka Leo O Hawai'i,* the University of Hawai'i at Manoa campus newspaper.

Libraries

There are 23 public libraries on O'ahu, and these include the Hawaii State Library (478 S. King St., 808/586-3500), located next to 'Iolani Palace in downtown Honolulu, the Waikiki-Kapahulu Library (400 Kapahulu, 808/733-8488), and the Kailua Library (239 Ku'ulei Rd., 808/266-9911). Library cards are available free for Hawaii state residents and military personnel stationed in Hawaii, \$25 for nonresidents (valid for five years), and \$10 for up to three months for visitors. The library system offers numerous services, including reference information (808/586-3621) during library hours. Business hours for each library differ, so check with the one you want to visit. Brochures listing hours and other general information are available at all libraries and online. For additional information, see the Hawaii State Public Library System website (www.librarieshawaii.org).

TOURIST INFORMATION
Hawaii Visitors Bureau

The Hawaii Visitors Bureau or HVB (www.gohawaii.com) is a top-notch organization providing help and information to all of Hawaii's visitors. Anyone contemplating a trip to Hawaii should visit a nearby office or check its website for specific information that might be required. The HVB's advice and excellent brochures on virtually every facet of living in, visiting, or simply enjoying Hawaii are free. The material offered is too voluminous to list, but for basics, request individual island brochures, maps, and vacation planners (also on the Web at www.hshawaii.com).

HVB Offices Statewide

Statewide offices include **HVB Administrative Office** (Waikiki Business Plaza, 2270 Kalakaua Ave., Ste. 801, Honolulu, 808/923-1811), **O'ahu Visitors Bureau** (733 Bishop St., Ste. 1872, Honolulu, 808/524-0722 or

The "HVB Warrior" is posted alongside the roadway, marking sites of cultural and historical importance.

877/525-6242, www.visit-oahu.com), **Maui Visitors Bureau** (1727 Wili Pa Loop, Wailuku, 808/244-3530 or 800/525-6284, www.visitmaui.com), **Kaua'i Visitors Bureau** (4334 Rice St., Ste. 101, Lihu'e, 808/245-3971 or 800/262-1400, www.kauaidiscovery.com), **Big Island HVB, Hilo Branch** (250 Keawe St., Hilo, 808/961-5797 or 800/648-2441, www.bigisland.org), and **Big Island HVB, Kona Branch** (250 Waikoloa Beach Dr., Ste. B15, Waikoloa, 808/886-1655).

Additional online information pertaining to the City and County of Honolulu can be found at the official county website (www.co.honolulu.hi.us).

Free Tourist Literature

Don't miss out on the free tourist literature available at all major hotels, shopping malls, the airport, and stands along Waikiki's streets. They all contain up-to-the-minute information on what's happening and a treasure trove of free or reduced-price coupons for various attractions and services. Always featured are events, shopping tips, dining and entertainment, and sightseeing. The main ones are *This Week Oahu,* the best and most complete, *Spotlight Oahu Gold,* with good sections on dining and sightseeing, and the smaller *Activities and Attractions Oahu.* Heavy on sightseeing attractions and activities, *101 Things To Do: Oahu* also has maps, advertising, and some coupons. *Oahu Drive Guide,* handed out by all the major rental car agencies, has some excellent tips and orientation maps. It is especially useful to get you started from the airport.

Maps

Aside from the simple maps in the ubiquitous free tourist literature, the Oʻahu Visitors Bureau and other organizations put out folding pocket maps of the island that are available free at the airport and tourist brochure racks around the island. Various Honolulu City and County street maps are available at the various bookstores around the island. Perhaps the best and most detailed of the island maps is the University of Hawaiʻi Press reference map, *Map of Oʻahu, The Gathering Place.* This map can also be found at gift and sundries shops around the island. Other useful and detailed maps of the island are the Rand NcNally *Oʻahu, Honolulu* map and the AAA *Honolulu Hawaii* map. If you are looking for detail, the best street map atlas of Oʻahu is a spiral-bound publication by Phears Mapbooks called *The Oʻahu Mapbook,* also available at bookshops around the island.

LOCAL RESOURCES
Emergencies

For **police, fire, or ambulance** anywhere on Oʻahu, dial **911.** For **nonemergency police** assistance and information, call 808/529-3111.

Civil Defense: In case of natural disaster such as hurricanes or tsunamis on Oʻahu, call 808/523-4121 or 733-4300.

The **Coast Guard Search and Rescue** can be reached at 800/552-6458.

Sex Abuse Treatment Center Hotline: Call 808/524-7273 for cases involving sexual assault or rape crisis.

Weather, Marine Report, and Time of Day

For recorded information on local island weather, call 808/973-4381; for marine conditions, phone 808/973-4382; and for the surf report, call 808/973-4383. For surf information on the Internet, check www.highsurfwarning.com. For time of day, call 808/643-8463.

Consumer Protection and Tourist Complaints

If you encounter problems with accommodations, bad service, or downright rip-offs, try the following: **The Chamber of Commerce of Hawaii** (808/545-4300), **Office of Consumer Protection** (808/587-3222, www.hawaii.gov/dcca/ocp), or the **Better Business Bureau** (808/536-6956).

Auto Service

AAA (1130 Nimitz Hwy. Suite A170, 808/736-2886, Mon.–Wed. and Fri. 9 A.M.–5 P.M., Thurs. 9 A.M.–7 P.M., Sat. 9 A.M.–2 P.M.) has an Oʻahu office in the Nimitz Center, just west of Hilo Hattie. Stop here for maps, Triptik maps, the Hawaii Tourbook, as well as other AAA information and travel agency services.

WEIGHTS AND MEASURES

Hawaii, like all of the United States, employs the "English method" of measuring weights and distances. Basically, dry weights are in ounces and pounds; liquid measures are in ounces, quarts, and gallons; and distances are measured in inches, feet, yards, and miles. The metric system is known but is not in general use.

Electricity

The same electrical current is in use in Hawaii as on the U.S. Mainland and is uniform throughout the islands. The system functions on 110 volts, 60 cycles of alternating current (AC); type A (two-pin) and type B (three-pin) plugs are used. Appliances from Japan will work, but there is some danger of burnout, whereas those requiring the normal European current of 220 volts, as well as those using other types of plugs, will not work.

Time Zones

There is no daylight saving time in Hawaii. When daylight saving time is not observed on the Mainland, Hawaii is two hours behind the West Coast, four hours behind the Midwest, five hours behind the East Coast, and 11 hours behind Germany; add one hour to these times during daylight saving time months. Hawaii, being just east of the International Date Line, is almost a full day behind most Asian and Oceanian cities. Hours behind these countries and cities are: Japan, 19 hours; Singapore, 18 hours; Sydney, 20 hours; New Zealand, 22 hours; Fiji, 22 hours.

RESOURCES

Glossary

HAWAIIAN

The following list gives you a "taste" of Hawaiian and provides a basic vocabulary of words in common usage that you are likely to hear. Becoming familiar with them is not a strict necessity, but they will definitely enhance your experience and make talking with local people more congenial. Many islanders spice their speech with certain words and you too can use them just as soon as you feel comfortable. You might even discover some Hawaiian words that are so perfectly expressive they'll become regular parts of your vocabulary. Many Hawaiian words have been absorbed into the English language and are found in English dictionaries. The definitions given are not exhaustive, but are generally considered the most common.

'a'a rough clinker lava. 'A'a has become the correct geological term to describe this type of lava found anywhere in the world.

'ae yes

ahupua'a pie-shaped land divisions running from mountain to sea that were governed by *konohiki*, local *ali'i* who owed their allegiance to a reigning chief

aikane friend; pal; buddy

'aina land; the binding spirit to all Hawaiians. Love of the land is paramount in traditional Hawaiian beliefs.

akamai smart; clever; wise

akua a god, or simply "divine"

ali'i a Hawaiian chief or noble

aloha the most common greeting in the islands; can mean both hello and good-bye, welcome and farewell. It can also mean romantic love, affection, or best wishes.

anuenue rainbow

'a'ole no

'aumakua a personal or family god, often an ancestral spirit

auwe alas; ouch! When a great chief or loved one died, it was a traditional wail of mourning.

'awa, also known as *kava,* a mildly intoxicating traditional drink made from the juice of chewed *'awa* root, spat into a bowl, and used in religious ceremonies

halakahiki pineapple

halau school, as in hula school

hale house or building; often combined with other words to name a specific place, such as Haleakala (House of the Sun), or Hale Pa'i at Lahainaluna, meaning Printing House

hana work; *pau hana* means end of work or quitting time

hanai literally "to feed." Part of the true aloha spirit. A *hanai* is a permanent guest or an adopted family member, usually an old person or a child. This is an enduring cultural phenomenon in Hawaii, in which a child from one family (perhaps that of a brother or sister, and quite often one's grandchild) is raised as one's own without formal adoption.

haole a word that at one time meant foreigner, but now means a white person or Caucasian

hapa half, as in a mixed-blooded person being referred to as *hapa haole*

hapai pregnant; used by all ethnic groups when a *keiki* is on the way

haupia a coconut custard dessert often served at a lu'au

he'enalu surfing

heiau A platform made of skillfully fitted rocks,

upon which temporary structures were built as temples and offerings made to the gods.

holomu'u an ankle-length dress that is much more fitted than a mu'umu'u, and which is often worn on formal occasions

hono bay, as in Honolulu (Sheltered Bay)

honu green sea turtle; endangered

ho'oilo traditional Hawaiian winter that began in November

ho'olaule'a any happy event, but especially a family outing or picnic

ho'omalimali sweet talk; flattery

huhu angry; irritated

hui a group; meeting; society. Often used to refer to Chinese businesspeople or family members who pool their money to get businesses started.

hukilau traditional shoreline fish-gathering in which everyone lends a hand to *huki* (pull) the huge net. Anyone taking part shares in the *lau* (food). It is much more like a party than hard work, and if you're lucky you'll be able to take part in one.

hula a native Hawaiian dance in which the rhythm of the islands is captured by swaying hips and stories told by lyrically moving hands. A *halau* is a group or school of hula.

huli huli barbecue, as in *huli huli* chicken

i'a fish in general. *I'a maka* is raw fish.

imu underground oven filled with hot rocks and used for baking. The main cooking method featured at a lu'au, used to steam-bake pork and other succulent dishes. The tending of the *imu* was traditionally for men only.

ipo sweetheart; lover; girl- or boyfriend

kahili a tall pole topped with feathers, resembling a huge feather duster. It was used by an *ali'i* to announce his or her presence.

kahuna priest; sorcerer; doctor; skillful person. In old Hawaii *kahuna* had tremendous power, which they used for both good and evil. The *kahuna ana'ana* was a feared individual who practiced "black magic" and could pray a person to death, while the *kahuna lapa'au* was a medical practitioner bringing aid and comfort to the people.

kai the sea. Many businesses and hotels employ *kai* as part of their name.

kalua means roasted underground in an *imu*. A favorite island food is *kalua* pork.

kama'aina a child of the land; an old-timer; a longtime island resident of any ethnic background; a resident of Hawaii or native son or daughter. Hotels and airlines often offer discounts called *kama'aina* rates to anyone who can prove island residency.

kanaka man or commoner; later used to distinguish a Hawaiian from other races. Tone of voice can make it a derisive expression.

kane means man, but actually used to signify a relationship such as husband or boyfriend. Written on a lavatory door it means men's room.

kapu forbidden; taboo; keep out; do not touch

kaukau slang word meaning food, chow, or grub. Some of the best food in Hawaii comes from the *kaukau* wagons, trucks that sell plate lunches and other morsels.

kauwa a landless, untouchable caste once confined to living on reservations. Members of this caste were often used as human sacrifices at *heiau*. Calling someone *kauwa* is still a grave insult.

kava see *'awa*

keiki child or children; used by all ethnic groups. "Have you hugged your *keiki* today?"

kiawe an algaroba tree from South America commonly found in Hawaii along the shore. It grows a nasty long thorn that can easily puncture a tire. Legend has it that the trees were introduced to the islands by a misguided missionary who hoped the thorns would coerce natives into wearing shoes. Actually, they are good for fuel, as fodder for hogs and cattle, and for reforestation, none of which you'll appreciate if you step on one of the thorns or flatten a tire on your rental car!

ko'ala any food that has been broiled or barbecued

kokua help. As in "Your *kokua* is needed to keep Hawaii free from litter."

kolohe rascal

kona wind a muggy subtropical wind that blows from the south and hits the Leeward side of the islands. It usually brings sticky hot weather and one of the few times when air-conditioning will be appreciated.

konane a traditional Hawaiian game, similar to checkers, played with pebbles on a large flat stone used as a board

ko'olau Windward side of the island

kukui a candlenut tree whose pods are polished and then strung together to make a beautiful lei. Traditionally the oil-rich nuts were strung on the rib of a coconut leaf and used as a candle.

kuleana home site; the old homestead; small farms. Especially used to describe the small spreads on Hawaiian Homelands on Moloka'i.

Kumulipo ancient Hawaiian genealogical chant that records the pantheon of gods, creation, and the beginning of humankind

kupuna a grandparent or old-timer; usually means someone who has gained wisdom. The statewide school system now invites *kupuna* to talk to the children about the old ways and methods.

la the sun. Often combined with other words to be more descriptive, such as *La*haina (Merciless Sun) or Haleaka*la* (House of the Sun).

lanai veranda or porch. You'll pay more for a hotel room if it has a lanai with an ocean view.

lani sky or the heavens

lau hala traditional Hawaiian weaving of mats, hats, etc., from the prepared fronds of the pandanus (screw pine)

lei a traditional garland of flowers or vines. One of Hawaii's most beautiful customs. Given at any auspicious occasion, but especially when arriving or leaving Hawaii.

lele the stone altar at a *heiau*

limu edible seaweed of various types. Gathered from the shoreline, it makes an excellent salad. It's used to garnish many island dishes and is a favorite at lu'au.

lolo crazy, as in "*lolo buggah*" (stupid or crazy guy)

lomi lomi traditional Hawaiian massage; also, raw salmon made into a vinegared salad with chopped onion and spices

lua the toilet; the head; the bathroom

luakini a human-sacrifice temple. Introduced to Hawaii in the 13th century at Waha'ula Heiau on the Big Island.

lu'au a Hawaiian feast featuring poi, *imu*-baked pork, and other traditional foods. Good ones provide some of the best gastronomic delights in the world.

luna foreman or overseer in the plantation fields. They were often mounted on horseback and were renowned for either their fairness or their cruelty. Representing the middle class, they served as a buffer between plantation workers and white plantation owners.

mahalo thank you. *Mahalo nui* means "big thanks" or "thank you very much."

mahele division. The Great Mahele of 1848 changed Hawaii forever when the traditional common lands were broken up into privately owned plots.

mahimahi a favorite eating fish. Often called dolphin fish, but a mahimahi is a true fish, not a cetacean.

mahu a homosexual; often used derisively

maile a fragrant vine used in traditional lei. It looks ordinary but smells delightful.

maka'ainana a commoner; a person "belonging" to the *'aina* (land), who supported the *ali'i* by fishing and farming and as a warrior

makai toward the sea; used by most islanders when giving directions

make dead; deceased

malihini a newcomer; a tenderfoot; a recent arrival

malo the native Hawaiian loincloth. Never worn anymore except at festivals or pageants.

mana power from the spirit world; innate energy of all things animate or inanimate; the grace of god. Mana could be passed on from one person to another, or even stolen. Great care was taken to protect the *ali'i* from having their *mana* defiled. Commoners were required to lie flat on the ground and cover their faces whenever a great *ali'i* approached. *Kahuna* were often employed in the regaining or transference of *mana*.

manini stingy; tight; a Hawaiianized word taken from the name of Don Francisco *Marin,* who was instrumental in bringing many fruits and plants to Hawaii. He was known for never sharing any of the bounty from his substantial gardens on Vineyard Street in Honolulu; therefore, his name came to mean stingy.

manuahi free; gratis; extra

mauka toward the mountains; used by most islanders when giving directions

mauna mountain. Often combined with other words to be more descriptive, such as Mauna Kea (White Mountain)

mele a song or chant in the Hawaiian oral tradition that records the history and genealogies of the *ali'i*

Menehune the legendary "little people" of Hawaii. Like leprechauns, they are said to shun humans and possess magical powers.

moa chicken; fowl

moana the ocean; the sea. Many businesses and hotels as well as places have *moana* as part of their name.

moe sleep

mo'olelo ancient tales kept alive by the oral tradition and recited only by day

mu'umu'u a "Mother Hubbard," an ankle-length dress with a high neckline introduced by the missionaries to cover the nakedness of the Hawaiians. It has become fashionable attire for almost any occasion in Hawaii.

nani beautiful

nui big; great; large; as in *mahalo nui* (thank you very much)

'ohana a family; the fundamental social division; extended family. Now often used to denote a social organization with grassroots overtones.

'okolehau literally "iron bottom"; traditional booze made from *ti* root. *'Okole* means "rear end" and *hau* means "iron," which was descriptive of the huge blubber pots in which *'okolehau* was made. Also, if you drink too much it'll surely knock you on your *'okole.*

oli chant not done to a musical accompaniment

'ono delicious; delightful; the best.

'opihi a shellfish or limpet that clings to rocks and is gathered as one of the islands' favorite *pu pu*. Custom dictates that you never remove all of the *'opihi* from a rock; some are always left to grow for future generations.

'opu belly; stomach

pahoehoe smooth, ropy lava that looks like burnt pancake batter. It is now the correct geological term used to describe this type of lava found anywhere in the world.

pakalolo "crazy smoke"; grass; smoke; dope; marijuana

pake a Chinese person. Can be derisive, depending on the tone in which it is used. It is a bastardization of the Chinese word meaning uncle.

pali a cliff; precipice. Hawaii's geology makes them quite common. The most famous are the *pali* of Oahu where a major battle was fought.

paniolo a Hawaiian cowboy. Derived from the Spanish *español*. The first cowboys brought to Hawaii during the early 19th century were Mexicans from California.

papale hat. Except for the feathered helmets of the *ali'i* warriors of old Hawaii, hats were generally not worn. However, once the islanders saw their practical uses and how fashionable they were, they began weaving them from various materials and quickly became experts at manufacture and design.

pa'u long split skirt often worn by women when horseback riding. In the 1800s, an island treat was watching *pa'u* riders in their beautiful dresses at Kapi'olani Park in Honolulu. The tradition is carried on today at many of Hawaii's rodeos.

pau finished; done; completed. Often combined into *pau hana,* which means end of work or quitting time.

pilau stink; bad smell; stench

pilikia trouble of any kind, big or small; bad times

poi a glutinous paste made from the pounded corm of taro, which ferments slightly and has a light sour taste. Purplish in color, it's a staple at lu'au, where it is called "one-, two-, or three-finger" poi, depending upon its thickness.

pono righteous or excellent

pua flower

puka a hole of any size. *Puka* is used by all island residents, whether talking about a pinhole in a rubber boat or a tunnel through a mountain.

punalua a traditional practice, before the missionaries arrived, of sharing mates. Western seamen took advantage of it, leading to the spread of contagious venereal diseases and eventual rapid decline of the Hawaiian people.

pune'e bed; narrow couch. Used by all ethnic

groups. To recline on a *pune'e* on a breezy lanai is a true island treat.

pu pu an appetizer; a snack; hors d'oeuvres; can be anything from cheese and crackers to sushi. Oftentimes, bars or nightclubs offer them free.

pupule crazy; nuts; out of your mind

pu'u hill, as in Pu'u 'Ula'ula (Red Hill)

tapa a traditional paper cloth made from beaten bark. Intricate designs were stamped in using beaters, and natural dyes added color. The tradition was lost for many years but is now making a comeback, providing some of the most beautiful folk art in the islands. Also called Kapa.

taro the staple of old Hawaii. A plant with a distinctive broad leaf that produces a starchy root. It was brought by the first Polynesians and was grown on magnificently irrigated plantations. According to the oral tradition, the life-giving properties of taro hold mystical significance for Hawaiians, since it was created by the gods at about the same time as humans.

ti a broad-leafed plant that was used for many purposes, from plates to hula skirts. Especially used to wrap religious offerings presented at the *heiau*.

tutu grandmother; granny; older woman. Used by all as a term of respect and endearment.

ukulele *uku* means "flea" and *lele* means "jumping," so literally "jumping flea" — the way the Hawaiians perceived the quick finger movements used on the banjo-like Portuguese folk instrument called a *cavaquinho*. The ukulele quickly became synonymous with the islands.

wahine young woman; female; girl; wife. Used by all ethnic groups. When written on a lavatory door it means women's room.

wai freshwater; drinking water

wela hot. *Wela kahao* is a "hot time" or "making whoopee."

wiki quickly; fast; in a hurry. Often seen as *wiki wiki* (very fast), as in Wiki Wiki Messenger Service.

Useful Phrases

Aloha ahiahi Good evening
Aloha au ia 'oe I love you
Aloha kakahiaka Good morning
Aloha nui loa much love; fondest regards

E komo mai please come in; enter; welcome
Hau'oli la hanau Happy birthday
Hau'oli makahiki hou Happy New Year
Mele kalikimaka Merry Christmas
'Okole maluna bottoms up; salute; cheers; kampai

PIDGIN

The following are a few commonly used words and expressions that should give you an idea of pidgin. It really can't be written properly, merely approximated, but for now, *"Study da' kine an' bimbye it be mo' bettah, brah! OK? Lesgo."*

an' den and then? big deal; so what's next?

auntie respected elderly woman

bad ass very good

bimbye after a while; by and by. "Bimbye, you learn pidgin."

blalah brother, but actually only refers to a large, heavy-set, good-natured Hawaiian man

brah all the bros in Hawaii are brahs; brother; pal. Used to call someone's attention. One of the most common words even among people who are not acquainted. After a fill-up at a gas station, a person would say "Tanks, brah."

chicken skin goose bumps

cockaroach steal; rip off. If you really want to find out what *cockaroach* means, just leave your camera on your beach blanket when you take a little dip.

da' kine a catchall word of many meanings that epitomizes the essence of pidgin. *Da' kine* is a euphemism for pidgin and is substituted whenever the speaker is at a loss for a word or just wants to generalize. It can mean you know? watchamacallit; of that type.

geev um give it to them; give them hell; go for it. Can be used as an encouragement. If a surfer is riding a great wave, the people on the beach might yell, "Geev um, brah!"

grinds food

hana ho again. Especially after a concert the audience shouts "hana ho" (one more!).

hele on let's get going

howzit? as in "howzit, brah?" what's happening? how's it going? The most common greeting, used in place of the more formal "How do you do?"

huhu angry! "You put the make on the wrong da' kine wahine, brah, and you in da' kine trouble if you get one big Hawaiian blalah plenty huhu."

lesgo let's go! do it!

li'dis an' li'dat like this or that; a catch-all grouping especially if you want to avoid details; like, ya' know?

lolo buggah stupid or crazy guy (person). Words to a tropical island song go, "I want to find the lolo who stole my pakalolo."

mo' bettah better, real good! great idea. An island sentiment used to be, "mo' bettah you *come* Hawaii." Now it has subtly changed to "mo' bettah you *visit* Hawaii."

pakalolo literally "crazy smoke"; marijuana; grass; reefer

pakiki head stubborn; bull-headed

pau a Hawaiian word meaning finished; done; over and done with. *Pau hana* means end of work or quitting time. Once used by plantation workers, now used by everyone.

seestah sister, female

shaka hand wave where only the thumb and baby finger stick out, meaning thank you, all right!

sleepah slippers, flip-flops, zori

stink face (or stink eye) basically frowning at someone; using facial expression to show displeasure. Hard looks. What you'll get if you give local people a hard time.

swell head burned up; angry

talk story spinning yarns; shooting the breeze; throwing the bull; a rap session. If you're lucky enough to be around to hear *kupuna* (elders) "talk story," you can hear some fantastic tales in the tradition of old Hawaii.

tanks, brah thanks, thank you

to da max all the way

waddascoops what's the scoop? what's up? what's happening?

Suggested Reading

Many publishers print books on Hawaii. Following are a few that focus on Hawaiian topics: **University of Hawai'i Press** (www.uhpress .hawaii.edu) has the best overall general list of titles on Hawaii. The **Bishop Museum Press** (www.bishopmuseum.org/press) puts out many scholarly works on Hawaiiana, as does **Kamehameha Schools Press** (http://kspress .ksbe.edu). Also good, with a more general-interest list, are **Bess Press** (www.besspress .com), **Mutual Publishing** (www.mutual publishing.com), and **Petroglyph Press** (www .basicallybooks.com). In addition, a website specifically oriented toward books on Hawaii, Hawaiian music, and other things Hawaiian is **Hawaii Books** (www.hawaiibooks.com).

ASTRONOMY

Bryan, E.H. *Stars over Hawaii.* Hilo, HI: Petroglyph Press, 1977. An introduction to astronomy, with information about the constellations and charts featuring the stars filling the night sky in Hawaii, by month. An excellent primer.

Rhoads, Samuel. *The Sky Tonight—A Guided Tour of the Stars over Hawaii.* Honolulu: Bishop Museum, 1993. Four pages per month of star charts—one each for the horizon in every cardinal direction. Exceptional!

COOKING

Alexander, Agnes. *How to Use Hawaiian Fruit.* Hilo, HI: Petroglyph Press, 1984. A slim volume of recipes using delicious and different Hawaiian fruits.

Beeman, Judy, and Martin Beeman. *Joys of Hawaiian Cooking.* Hilo, HI: Petroglyph Press, 1977. A collection of favorite recipes from Big Island chefs.

Choy, Sam. *Cooking from the Heart with Sam Choy.* Honolulu: Mutual Publishing, 1995.

This beautiful, hand-bound cookbook contains many color photos by Douglas Peebles.

Fukuda, Sachi. *Pupus, An Island Tradition.* Honolulu: Bess Press, 1995.

Margah, Irish, and Elvira Monroe. *Hawaii, Cooking with Aloha.* San Carlos, CA: Wide World, 1984. Island recipes, as well as hints on decor.

Rizzuto, Shirley. *Fish Dishes of the Pacific— from the Fishwife.* Honolulu: Hawaii Fishing News, 1986. Features recipes using all the fish commonly caught in Hawaiian waters (husband Jim Rizzuto is the author of *Fishing, Hawaiian Style*).

CULTURE

Buck, Peter. *Arts and Crafts of Hawaii.* Honolulu, Bishop Museum Press, 1957. The most definitive work on traditional Hawaiian crafts from household use to religious significance.

Cox, J. Halley, and Edward Stasack. *Hawaiian Petroglyphs.* Honolulu: Bishop Museum Press, 1970. The most thorough examination of petroglyph sites throughout the islands.

Dudley, Michael Kioni. *Man, Gods, and Nature.* Honolulu: Na Kane O Ka Malo Press, 1990. An examination of the philosophical underpinnings of Hawaiian beliefs and their interconnected reality.

Gutmanis, June. *Kahuna La'au Lapa'au,* Honolulu: Island Heritage, rev. ed. 2001. Text on Hawaiian herbal medicines: diseases, treatments, and medicinal plants, with illustrations.

Handy, E. S., and Elizabeth Handy. *Native Planters in Old Hawaii.* Honolulu: Bishop Museum Press, 1972. A superbly written, easily understood scholarly work on the intimate relationship of precontact Hawaiians and the 'aina (land). Much more than its title implies, this book should be read by anyone seriously interested in Polynesian Hawaii.

Hartwell, Jay. *Na Mamo: Hawaiian People Today*. Honolulu: 'Ai Pohaku Press, 1996. Profiles 12 people practicing Hawaiian traditions in the modern world.

Kamehameha Schools Press. *Life in Early Hawai'i: The Ahupua'a*. 3rd ed. Honolulu: Kamehameha Schools Press, 1994. Written for schoolchildren to better understand the basic organization of old Hawaiian land use and its function, this slim volume is a good primer for people of any age who wish to understand this fundamental societal fixture.

Kirch, Patrick V. *Feathered Gods and Fishhooks: An Introduction to Hawaiian Archaeology and Prehistory*. Honolulu: University of Hawai'i Press, 1997. This scholarly, lavishly illustrated, yet very readable book gives new insight into the development of precontact Hawaiian civilization. It focuses on the sites and major settlements of old Hawai'i and chronicles the main cultural developments while weaving in the social climate that contributed to change. A very worthwhile read.

McBride, Likeke. *Petroglyphs of Hawaii*. Hilo, HI: Petroglyph Press, 1997. A revised and updated guide to petroglyphs found in the Hawaiian Islands. A basic introduction to these old Hawaiian picture stories.

McBride, L. R. *Practical Folk Medicine of Hawaii*. Hilo, HI: Petroglyph Press, 1975. An illustrated guide to Hawaii's medicinal plants as used by the *kahuna lapa'au* (medical healers). Includes a thorough section on ailments, diagnosis, and the proper folk remedy. Illustrated by the author, a renowned botanical researcher and former ranger at Hawai'i Volcanoes National Park.

FAUNA

Boom, Robert. *Hawaiian Seashells*. Honolulu: Waikiki Aquarium, 1972. Photos by Jerry Kringle. A collection of 137 seashells found in Hawaiian waters, featuring many found nowhere else on earth. Broken into categories with accompanying text including common and scientific names, physical descriptions, and likely habitats. A must-read for shell collectors.

Carpenter, Blyth, and Russell Carpenter. *Fish Watching in Hawaii*. San Mateo, CA: Natural World Press, 1981. A color guide to many of the reef fish found in Hawaii and often spotted by snorkelers. If you're interested in the fish you'll be looking at, this guide will be very helpful.

Fielding, Ann, and Ed Robinson. *An Underwater Guide to Hawai'i*. Honolulu: University of Hawai'i Press, 1987. If you've ever had a desire to snorkel/scuba the living reef waters of Hawaii and to be familiar with what you're seeing, get this small but fact-packed book. The amazing array of marinelife found throughout the archipelago is captured in glossy photos with accompanying informative text. Both the scientific and common names of specimens are given. This book will enrich your underwater experience and serve as an easily understood reference guide for many years.

Goodson, Gar. *The Many-Splendored Fishes of Hawaii*. Stanford, CA: Stanford University Press, 1985. This small but thorough fish-watchers' book includes entries on some deep-sea fish.

Hawaiian Audubon Society. *Hawaii's Birds*. 5th ed. Honolulu: Hawaii Audubon Society, 1997. Excellent bird book, giving description, range, voice, and habits of the more than 100 species. Slim volume; good for carrying while hiking.

Hobson, Edmund, and E. H. Chave. *Hawaiian Reef Animals*. Honolulu: University of Hawai'i Press, 1987. Colorful photos and descriptions of the fish, invertebrates, turtles, and seals that call Hawaiian reefs their home.

Kay, Alison, and Olive Schoenberg-Dole. *Shells of Hawai'i*. Honolulu: University of Hawai'i

Press, 1991. Color photos and tips on where to look.

Mahaney, Casey. *Hawaiian Reef Fish, The Identification Book.* Planet Ocean Publishing, 1993. A spiral-bound reference work featuring many color photos and descriptions of common reef fish found in Hawaiian waters.

Nickerson, Roy. *Brother Whale, A Pacific Whalewatcher's Log.* San Francisco: Chronicle Books, 1977. Introduces the average person to the life of earth's greatest mammals. Provides historical accounts, photos, and tips on whale-watching. Well-written, descriptive, and the best "first time" book on whales.

Pratt, Douglas. *A Field Guide to the Birds of Hawaii and the Tropical Pacific.* Princeton, NJ: Princeton University Press, 1987. Useful field guide for novice and expert bird-watchers, covering Hawaii as well as other Pacific Island groups.

Pratt, Douglas. *A Pocket Guide to Hawaii's Birds.* Honolulu: Mutual Publishing, 1996. A condensed version of Pratt's larger work with a focus on bird's of the state.

Tomich, P. Quentin. *Mammals in Hawai'i.* Honolulu: Bishop Museum Press, 1986. Quintessential scholarly text on all mammal species in Hawaii, with description of distribution and historical references. Lengthy bibliography.

van Riper, Charles, and Sandra van Riper. *A Field Guide to the Mammals of Hawaii.* Honolulu: Oriental Publishing. A guide to the surprising number of mammals introduced into Hawaii. Full-color pages document description, uses, tendencies, and habitat. Small and thin, this book makes a worthwhile addition to any serious hiker's backpack.

FLORA

Kepler, Angela. *Hawaiian Heritage Plants.* Honolulu: University of Hawai'i Press, 1998. A treatise on 32 utilitarian plants used by the early Hawaiians.

Kepler, Angela. *Hawai'i's Floral Splendor.* Honolulu: Mutual Publishing, 1997. A general reference to flowers of Hawaii.

Kepler, Angela. *Tropicals of Hawaii.* Honolulu: Mutual Publishing, 1989. This small-format book features many color photos of nonnative flowers.

Kuck, Lorraine, and Richard Togg. *Hawaiian Flowers and Flowering Trees.* Rutland, VT: Tuttle, 1960. A classic, although out-of-print, field guide to tropical and subtropical flora illustrated in watercolor. Succinct descriptions of Hawaiian plants and flowers with a brief history of their places of origin and their introduction to Hawaii.

Merrill, Elmer. *Plant Life of the Pacific World.* Rutland, VT: Tuttle, 1983. This is the definitive book for anyone planning a botanical tour to the entire Pacific Basin. Originally published in the 1930s, it remains a tremendous work, worth tracking down through out-of-print book services.

Miyano, Leland. *Hawai'i, A Floral Paradise.* Honolulu: Mutual Publishing, 1995. Photographed by Douglas Peebles, this large-format book is filled with informative text and beautiful color shots of tropical flowers commonly seen in Hawaii.

Miyano, Leland. *A Pocket Guide to Hawai'i's Flowers.* Honolulu: Mutual Publishing, 2001. A small guide to readily seen flowers in the state. Good for the backpack or back pocket.

Sohmer, S. H., and R. Gustafson. *Plants and Flowers of Hawai'i.* Honolulu: University of Hawai'i Press, 1987. The authors cover the vegetation zones of Hawaii, from mountains to coast, introducing you to the wide and varied floral biology of the islands. They give a good introduction to the history and unique evolution of Hawaiian plantlife. Beautiful color plates are accompanied by clear and concise plant descriptions, with the scientific and common Hawaiian names listed.

Teho, Fortunato. *Plants of Hawaii—How to Grow Them.* Hilo, HI: Petroglyph Press, 1992. A small but useful book for those who want their backyards to bloom into tropical paradises.

Wagner, Warren L., Derral R. Herbst, and H. S. Sohner. *Manual of the Flowering Plants of Hawai'i,* revised edition, vol. 2. Honolulu: University of Hawai'i Press in association with Bishop Museum Press, 1999. Considered the bible of Hawaii's botanical world.

Valier, Kathy. *Ferns of Hawaii.* Honolulu: University of Hawai'i Press, 1995. One of the few books that treat the state's ferns as a single subject.

HEALTH

Gutmanis, June. *Kahuna La'au Lapa'au,* revised edition. Honolulu: Island Heritage, 2001. Text on Hawaiian herbal medicines: diseases, treatments, and medicinal plants, with illustrations.

McBride, L. R. *Practical Folk Medicine of Hawaii.* Hilo, HI: Petroglyph Press, 1975. An illustrated guide to Hawaii's medicinal plants as used by the *kahuna lapa'au* (medical healers). Includes a thorough section on ailments, diagnosis, and the proper folk remedy. Illustrated by the author, a renowned botanical researcher and former ranger at Hawaii Volcanoes National Park.

Wilkerson, James A., M.D., ed. *Medicine for Mountaineering and Other Wilderness.* 4th ed. Seattle: The Mountaineers, 1992. Don't let the title fool you. Although the book focuses on specific health problems that may be encountered while mountaineering, it is the best first-aid and general health guide available today. Written by doctors for the layperson to use until help arrives, it is jam-packed with easily understandable techniques and procedures. For those planning extended hikes, it is a must.

HISTORY

Apple, Russell A. *Trails: From Steppingstones to Kerbstones.* Honolulu: Bishop Museum Press, 1965. This "Special Publication #53" is a special-interest archaeological survey focusing on trails, roadways, footpaths, and highways and how they were designed and maintained throughout the years. Many royal highways from precontact Hawaii are cited.

Ashdown, Inez MacPhee. *Recollections of Kaho'olawe.* Honolulu: Topgallant Publishing, 1979. The tortured story of the lonely island of Kaho'olawe by a member of the family who owned the island until it was turned into a military bombing target during World War II. This is a first-person account of life on the island and is rife with myths, legends, and historical facts about Kaho'olawe.

Ashdown, Inez MacPhee. *Ke Alaloa o Maui.* Wailuku, HI: Kama'aina Historians Inc., 1971. A compilation of the history and legends connected to sites on the island of Maui. Ashdown was at one time a "lady in waiting" for Queen Lili'uokalani and was later proclaimed Maui's Historian Emeritus.

Barnes, Phil. *A Concise History of the Hawaiian Islands.* Hilo, HI: Petroglyph Press, 1999. An easy-to-read examination of the main currents of Hawaiian history and its major players, focusing on the important factors in shaping the social, economic, and political trends of the islands.

Cameron, Roderick. *The Golden Haze.* New York: World Publishing, 1964. An account of Captain James Cook's voyages of discovery throughout the South Seas. Uses original diaries and journals for an "on-the-spot" reconstruction of this great seafaring adventure.

Cooper, George and Gavan Daws. *Land and Power in Hawaii, The Democratic Years.* Honolulu: University of Hawai'i Press, 1990. An examination of how power and land development went hand in hand during the heyday of the Democratically-controlled state government following statehood.

Cordy, Ross. *Exalted Sits the Chief.* Honolulu, Mutual Publishing, 2000. An in-depth examination from archeological and cultural records of the ancient Hawaiian civilization up until the coming of the Western explorers.

Daws, Gavan. *Shoal of Time, A History of the Hawaiian Islands.* Honolulu: University of Hawai'i Press, 1974. A highly readable history of Hawaii dating from its "discovery" by the Western world to its acceptance as the 50th state. Good insight into the psychological makeup of influential characters who helped form Hawaii's past.

Dorrance, William H., and Francis S. Morgan. *Sugar Islands: The 165-Year Story of Sugar in Hawai'i.* Honolulu: Mutual Publishing, 2000. An overall sketch of the sugar industry in Hawaii from inception to decline, with data on many individual plantations and mills around the islands. Definitely a story from the industry's point of view.

Fornander, Abraham. *An Account of the Polynesian Race; Its Origins and Migrations, and the Ancient History of the Hawaiian People to the Times of Kamehameha I.* Rutland, VT: C.E. Tuttle Co., 1969. This is a reprint of a three-volume opus originally published 1878–1885. It is still one of the best sources of information on Hawaiian myth and legend.

Free, David. *Vignettes of Old Hawaii.* Honolulu: Crossroads Press, 1994. A collection of short essays on a variety of subjects.

Fuchs, Lawrence. *Hawaii Pono.* Honolulu: Bess Press, 1961. A detailed, scholarly work presenting an overview of Hawaii's history, based upon ethnic and sociological interpretations. Encompasses most socioethnological groups from native Hawaiians to modern entrepreneurs. This book is a must for obtaining some social historical background.

Ii, John Papa. *Fragments of Hawaiian History.* Honolulu: Bishop Museum, 1959. Hawaii's history under Kamehameha I as told by a Hawaiian who actually experienced it.

Joesting, Edward. *Hawaii: An Uncommon History.* New York: W.W. Norton Co., 1978. A truly uncommon history told in a series of vignettes relating to the lives and personalities of the first Caucasians in Hawaii, Hawaiian nobility, sea captains, writers, and adventurers. Brings history to life. Absolutely excellent!

Kamakau, S. M. *Ruling Chiefs of Hawaii,* revised edition. Honolulu: Kamehameha Schools Press, 1992. A history of Hawaii from the legendary leader 'Umi to the mid-Kamehameha Dynasty, from oral tales and a Hawaiian perspective.

Kamakau, S. M. *The People of Old.* Honolulu, Bishop Museum Press, 1964. Essays on traditional cultural practices of the Hawaii people, by one of Hawaii's first scholars. Also *The Works of the People of Old* and *Tales and Traditions of the People of Old.*

Kurisu, Yasushi. *Sugar Town, Hawaiian Plantation Days Remembered.* Honolulu: Watermark Publishing, 1995. Reminiscences of life growing up on sugar plantations on the Hamakua Coast of the Big Island. Features many old photos.

Lili'uokalani. *Hawaii's Story by Hawaii's Queen,* reprint. Honolulu: Mutual Publishing, 1990. Originally written in 1898, this moving personal account recounts Hawaii's inevitable move from monarchy to U.S. Territory by its last queen, Lili'uokalani. The facts can be found in other histories, but none provides the emotion or point of view expressed by Hawaii's deposed monarch. This is a must-read to get the whole picture.

Nickerson, Roy. *Lahaina, Royal Capital of Hawaii.* Honolulu: Hawaiian Service, 1978. The story of Lahaina from whaling days to present, spiced with ample photographs.

Tabrah, Ruth M. *Ni'ihau: The Last Hawaiian Island.* Kailua, Hawaii: Press Pacifica, 1987. Sympathetic history of the privately owned island of Ni'ihau.

Takaki, Ronald. *Pau Hana: Plantation Life and Labor in Hawaii.* Honolulu: University of Hawai'i Press, 1983. The story of immigrant labor and the sugar industry in Hawaii until the 1920s from the worker's perspective.

INTRODUCTORY

Brown, DeSoto and Linda Boynton Arthur. *The Art of the Aloha Shirt.* Honolulu, Island Heritage Publishing, 2002.

Carroll, Rick, and Marcie Carroll, eds. *Hawai'i: True Stories of the Island Spirit.* San Francisco: Travelers' Tales, Inc., 1999. A collection of stories by a variety of authors that were chosen to elicit the essence of Hawaii and Hawaiian experiences. A great read.

Cohen, David, and Rick Smolan. *A Day in the Life of Hawaii.* New York: Workman, 1984. On December 2, 1983, 50 of the world's top photojournalists were invited to Hawaii to photograph the variety of daily life on the islands. The photos are excellently reproduced and accompanied by a minimum of text.

Day, A. G., and C. Stroven. *A Hawaiian Reader,* reprint. Honolulu: Mutual Publishing, 1984. A poignant compilation of essays, diary entries, and fictitious writings originally published in 1959 that takes you from the death of Captain Cook through the "statehood services."

Department of Geography, University of Hawai'i, Hilo. *Atlas of Hawai'i.* 3rd ed. Honolulu: University of Hawai'i Press, 1998. Much more than an atlas filled with reference maps, this book also contains commentary on the natural environment, culture, and sociology; a gazetteer; and statistical tables. Actually a mini-encyclopedia on Hawaii.

Hope, Dale. *The Aloha Shirt.* Honolulu: Beyond Words Publishing, 2000.

Michener, James A. *Hawaii.* New York: Random House, 1959. Michener's fictionalized historical novel has done more to inform *and* misinform readers about Hawaii than any other book ever written. A great tale with plenty of local color and information, but read it for pleasure, not facts.

Piercy, LaRue. *Hawaii This and That.* Honolulu: Mutual Publishing, 1994. Illustrated by Scot Ebanez. A 60-page book filled with one-sentence facts and oddities about all manner of things Hawaiian. Informative, amazing, and fun to read.

Steele, R. Thomas: *The Hawaiian Shirt: Its Art and History.* New York: Abbeville Press, 1984.

LANGUAGE

Elbert, Samuel. *Spoken Hawaiian.* Honolulu: University of Hawai'i Press, 1970. Progressive conversational lessons.

Elbert, Samuel, and Mary Pukui. *Hawaiian Dictionary.* Honolulu: University of Hawai'i Press, 1986. The best dictionary available on the Hawaiian language. The *Pocket Hawaiian Dictionary* is a less expensive, condensed version of this dictionary and adequate for most travelers with a general interest in the language.

Pukui, Mary Kawena, Samuel Elbert, and Esther T. Mookini. *Place Names of Hawaii.* Honolulu: University of Hawai'i Press, 1974. The most current and comprehensive listing of Hawaiian and foreign place names in the state, giving pronunciation, spelling, meaning, and location.

Schutz, Albert J. *All About Hawaiian.* Honolulu: University of Hawai'i Press, 1995. A brief primer on Hawaiian pronunciation, grammar, and vocabulary. A solid introduction.

Schutz, Albert J. *Voices of Eden, A History of Hawaiian Language Studies*. Honolulu, University of Hawai'i Press, 1994. Broad scholarly treatment.

MYTHOLOGY, LEGEND, AND LITERATURE

Beckwith, Martha. *Hawaiian Mythology*, reprint. Honolulu: University of Hawai'i Press, 1976. Over 60 years after its original printing in 1940, this work remains the definitive text on Hawaiian mythology. Beckwith compiled this book from many sources, giving exhaustive cross-references to genealogies and legends expressed in the oral tradition. If you are only going to read one book on Hawaii's folklore, this should be it.

Beckwith, Martha. *The Kumulipo*, reprint. Honolulu: University of Hawai'i Press, 1972. Translation of the Hawaiian creation chant, originally published in 1951.

Colum, Padraic. *Legends of Hawaii*. New Haven, CT: Yale University Press, 1937. Selected legends of old Hawaii, reinterpreted but closely based on the originals.

Elbert, S. H., ed. *Hawaiian Antiquities and Folklore*. Honolulu: University of Hawai'i Press, 1959. Illustrated by Jean Charlot. A selection of the main legends from Abraham Fornander's great work, *An Account of the Polynesian Race*.

Emerson, Nathaniel B. *Unwritten Literature of Hawaii, The Sacred Songs of the Hula*. Honolulu, 'Ai Pohaku Press, 1997. Reprint of the 1909 Bulletin 38 of the Bureau of American Ethnology, Smithsonian Institution. Hawaiian songs and interpretive descriptions for the layman.

Kalakaua, His Hawaiian Majesty, King David. *The Legends and Myths of Hawaii*. Edited by R. M. Daggett, with a foreword by Glen Grant. Honolulu: Mutual Publishing, 1990. Originally published in 1888, Hawaii's own King Kalakaua draws upon his scholarly and formidable knowledge of the classic oral tradition to bring alive ancient tales from pre-contact Hawaii. A powerful yet somewhat Victorian voice from Hawaii's past speaks clearly and boldly, especially about the intimate role of pre-Christian religion in the lives of the Hawaiian people.

Melville, Leinanai. *Children of the Rainbow*. Wheaton, IL: Theosophical Publishing, 1969. A book on higher spiritual consciousness attuned to nature, which was the basic belief of pre-Christian Hawaii. The appendix contains illustrations of mystical symbols used by the *kahuna*. An enlightening book in many ways.

Pukui, Mary Kawena, and Caroline Curtis. *Hawaii Island Legends*. Honolulu: The Kamehameha Schools Press, 1996. Hawaiian tales and legends for pre-teens.

Pukui, Mary Kawena. *'Olelo No'eau, Hawaiian Proverbs & Poetical Sayings*. Honolulu, Bishop Museum Press, 1983.

Pukui, Mary Kawena, and Caroline Curtis. *Tales of the Menehune*. Honolulu: The Kamehameha Schools Press, 1960. Compilation of legends relating to Hawaii's "little people."

Pukui, Mary Kawena, and Caroline Curtis. *The Waters of Kane and other Hawaiian Legends*. Honolulu: The Kamehameha Schools Press, 1994. More tales and legends for the pre-teens.

Thrum, Thomas. *Hawaiian Folk Tales*, reprint. Chicago: McClurg and Co., 1950. A collection of Hawaiian tales originally printed in 1907 from the oral tradition as told to the author from various sources.

Westervelt, W. D. *Hawaiian Legends of Volcanoes*, reprint. Boston: Ellis Press, 1991. A small book originally printed in 1916 concerning the volcanic legends of Hawaii and how they related to the fledgling field of volcanism in the early 1900s. The vintage photos alone are worth a look.

NATURAL SCIENCES AND GEOGRAPHY

Carlquist, Sherwin. *Hawaii: A Natural History.* National Tropical Botanical Garden, 1984. General and thorough account of Hawaii's natural history. Lots of pictures.

Clark, John. *Beaches of O'ahu.* Honolulu: University of Hawai'i Press, 1997. Definitive guide to beaches, including many off the beaten path. Features maps and black-and-white photos. Also *Beaches of the Big Island, Beaches of Kaua'i and Ni'ihau,* and *Beaches of Maui County.*

Hazlett, Richard, and Donald Hyndman. *Roadside Geology of Hawai'i.* Missoula, MT: Mountain Press Publishing, 1996. Begins with a general discussion of the geology of the Hawaiian Islands, followed by a road guide to the individual islands offering descriptions of easily seen features. A great book to have in the car as you tour the islands.

Hubbard, Douglass, and Gordon Macdonald. *Volcanoes of the National Parks of Hawaii,* reprint. Volcanoes, HI: Hawaii Natural History Association, 1989. The volcanology of Hawaii, documenting the major lava flows and their geological effect on the state; originally printed in 1982.

Kay, E. Alison, comp. *A Natural History of the Hawaiian Islands.* Honolulu: University of Hawai'i Press, 1994. A selection of concise articles by experts in the fields of volcanism, oceanography, meteorology, and biology. An excellent reference source.

Macdonald, Gorden, Agatin Abbott, and Frank Peterson. *Volcanoes in the Sea, The Geology of Hawaii.* Honolulu: University of Hawai'i Press, 1983. The best reference to Hawaiian geology. Well explained for easy understanding. Illustrated.

Ziegler, Alan C., *Hawaiian Natural History, Ecology, and Evolution.* Honolulu: University of Hawai'i Press, 2002. An overview of Hawaiian natural history with treatment of ecology and evolution in that process.

PERIODICALS

Hawaii Magazine. This magazine covers the Hawaiian islands like a tropical breeze. Feature articles on all aspects of life in the islands, with special departments on travel, events, exhibits, and restaurant reviews. Up-to-the-minute information, and a fine read.

POLITICAL SCIENCE

Bell, Roger. *Last Among Equals: Hawaiian Statehood and American Politics.* Honolulu: University of Hawai'i Press, 1984. Documents Hawaii's long and rocky road to statehood, tracing political partisanship, racism, and social change.

SPORTS AND RECREATION

Alford, John, D. *Mountain Biking the Hawaiian Islands.* Ohana Publishing, 1997. Good off-road biking guide to the main Hawaiian islands.

Ambrose, Greg. *Surfer's Guide to Hawai'i.* Honolulu: Bess Press, 1991. Island-by-island guide to surfing spots.

Ball, Stuart. *The Hiker's Guide to the Hawaiian Islands.* Honolulu: University of Hawai'i Press, 2000. This excellent guide includes 44 hikes on each of the four main islands. Ball has also written *The Hiker's Guide to O'ahu.*

Cagala, George. *Hawaii: A Camping Guide.* Boston: Hunter Publishing, 1994. Useful.

Chisholm, Craig. *Hawaiian Hiking Trails.* Lake Oswego, OR: Fernglen Press, 1999. Also *Oahu Hiking Trails, Kaua'i Hiking Trails,* and *Hawaii, The Big Island, Hiking Trails.*

Cisco, Dan. *Hawai'i Sports.* Honolulu: University of Hawai'i Press, 1999. A compendium of popular and little-known sporting events and figures, with facts, tidbits, and statistical information. Go here first for a general overview.

Finney, Ben, and James D. Houston. *Surfing, A History of the Ancient Hawaiian Sport.* Los Angeles: Pomegranate, 1996. Features many early etchings and old photos of Hawaiian surfers practicing their native sport.

Lueras, Leonard. *Surfing, the Ultimate Pleasure.* Honolulu: Emphasis International, 1984. One of the most brilliant books ever written on surfing. Also *Surfing Hawaii: The Ultimate Guide to the World's Most Challenging Waves.*

McMahon, Richard. *Camping Hawai'i: A Complete Guide.* Honolulu: University of Hawai'i Press, 1997. This book has all you need to know about camping in Hawaii, with descriptions of different campsites.

Morey, Kathy. *Oahu Trails.* Berkeley, CA: Wilderness Press, 2003. Morey's books are specialized, detailed hiker's guides to Hawaii's outdoors. Complete with useful maps, historical references, official procedures, and plants and animals encountered along the way. If you're focused on hiking, these are the best guides to take along. *Maui Trails, Kauai Trails,* and *Hawaii Trails* are also available.

Smith, Robert. *Hawaii's Best Hiking Trails.* Kula, Maui, HI: Hawaiian Outdoor Adventures, 2003. Other guides by this author include *Hiking Oahu, Hiking Maui, Hiking Hawaii,* and *Hiking Kauai.*

Sutherland, Audrey. *Paddling Hawai'i,* revised edition. Honolulu: University of Hawai'i Press, 1998. All you need to know about sea kayaking in Hawaiian waters.

Thorne, Chuck. *The Divers' Guide to Maui.* Hana, Hawaii: Maui Dive Guide, 2001. The best practical guide to dive sites on Maui.

Internet Resources

The following websites have information about Oʻahu and the state of Hawaii that may be useful in preparation for a trip to the islands and for general interest.

www.co.honolulu.hi.us

The official website of the City and County of Honolulu. Includes, among other items, information on city government, county data access, visitor information, and information on business and economic development.

www.gohawaii.com

This official site of the Hawaii Visitors and Convention Bureau, the state-run tourism organization, has information about all the major Hawaiian islands: transportation, accommodations, eating, activities, shopping, Hawaiian products, an events calendar, a travel planner, and a resource guide for a host of topics, as well as information about meetings, conventions, and the organization itself.

www.visit-oahu.com

The official site of the Oʻahu Visitors Bureau, a branch of the Hawaii Visitors and Convention Bureau, has much the same information as the previous website but specific to the island of Oʻahu. A very useful resource.

www.bestplaceshawaii.com

Produced and maintained by H&S Publishing, this first-rate commercial site has general and specific information about all major Hawaiian islands, a vacation planner, and suggestions for things to do and places to see. This is a great place to start a search for tourist information about the state or any of its major islands. One of dozens of sites on the Internet with a focus on Hawaii tourism-related information.

www.alternative-hawaii.com

Alternative source for eco-friendly general information and links to specific businesses, with some cultural, historical, and events information.

www.hawaiiecotourism.org

Official Hawaii Ecotourism Association website. Lists goals, members, and activities and provides links to member organizations and related ecotourism groups.

http://calendar.gohawaii.com

For events of all sorts happening throughout the state, visit the calendar of events listing on the Hawaii Visitors Bureau website. Information can be accessed by island, date, or type.

www.state.hi.us/sfca

This site of the State Foundation of Culture and the Arts features a calendar of arts and cultural events, activities, and programs held throughout the state. Information is available by island and type.

www.hawaiianair.com
www.alohaairlines.com

www.pacificwings.com

www.iflygo.com

These websites for Hawaiian Airlines, Aloha Airlines, Pacific Wings, and go! list virtually all regularly scheduled commercial air links throughout the state.

www.mele.com

Check out the Hawaiian music scene at Hawaiian Music Island, one of the largest music websites that focuses on Hawaiian music, books, and videos related to Hawaiian music and culture, concert schedules, Hawaiian music awards, and links to music companies and musicians. Others with broad listings and general-interest information are Nahenahenet, **www.mauicast.net/nahenahe,** and Hawaiian Music Guide, **www.hawaii-music.com.**

www.uhpress.hawaii.edu

The University of Hawaiʻi Press website has the best overall list of titles for books published on Hawaiian themes and topics. Other publishers to check for substantial lists of books on Hawaiiana are the Bishop Museum Press, **www.bishopmuseum.org/press;** Kamehameha Schools Press, **http://kspress.ksbe.edu;** Bess Press, **www.besspress.com;** Mutual Publishing, **www.mutualpublishing.com;** and Petroglyph Press, **www.basicallybooks.com.**

www.hawaiimuseums.org

This site is dedicated to the promotion of museums and cultural attractions in the state of Hawaii with links to member sites on each of the islands. A member organization.

www.bishopmuseum.org

Site of the premier ethnological and cultural museum dedicated to Hawaiian people, their culture, and cultural artifacts.

www.starbulletin.com
www.honoluluadvertiser.com

Websites for Hawaii's two main English-language dailies, the *Honolulu Star-Bulletin* and the *Honolulu Advertiser,* both published in Honolulu. Both have a concentration of news coverage about Oʻahu but also cover major news from the Neighbor Islands.

www.honoluluweekly.com

Site of Honolulu's principal alternative weekly newspaper. For years, this paper has given local residents news with a different slant and often carries stories that the major newspapers do not print. Strong on local coverage with a conscience.

www.oha.org

Official site for the state-mandated organization that deals with native Hawaii-related affairs.

www.reinstated.org

Site of Reinstated Hawaiian Government, one of the organizations of native Hawaiians who are advocating for sovereignty and independence. While there are many independent native Hawaiian rights organizations pushing for various degrees of sovereignty or independence for native Hawaiian people, some others are listed below: Kingdom of Hawaii, **www.freehawaii.org;** (another) Kingdom of Hawaii, **www.pixi.com/~kingdom;** Hawaiian Independence, **www.hawaii-nation.org;** and the Hawaiian Kingdom, **www.hawaiiankingdom.org.**

Index

www.moon.com

For helpful advice on planning a trip, visit www.moon.com for the **TRAVEL PLANNER** and get access to useful travel strategies and valuable information about great places to visit. When you travel with Moon, expect an experience that is uncommon and truly unique.

MAP SYMBOLS

▨	Expressway	◖	Highlight	✗	Airfield	⚑	Golf Course
▨	Primary Road	○	City/Town	✈	Airport	P	Parking Area
▨	Secondary Road	◉	State Capital	▲	Mountain	⬟	Archaeological Site
▨	Unpaved Road	◈	National Capital	✛	Unique Natural Feature	▮	Church
------	Trail	★	Point of Interest			▮	Gas Station
....	Ferry	•	Accommodation	≷	Waterfall	⊙	Glacier
─┼─┼─	Railroad	▼	Restaurant/Bar	⚱	Park	▨	Mangrove
▨	Pedestrian Walkway	■	Other Location	⊓	Trailhead	▨	Reef
▨	Stairs	Λ	Campground	⚐	Skiing Area	▨	Swamp

CONVERSION TABLES

$°C = (°F - 32) / 1.8$
$°F = (°C × 1.8) + 32$
1 inch = 2.54 centimeters (cm)
1 foot = 0.304 meters (m)
1 yard = 0.914 meters
1 mile = 1.6093 kilometers (km)
1 km = 0.6214 miles
1 fathom = 1.8288 m
1 chain = 20.1168 m
1 furlong = 201.168 m
1 acre = 0.4047 hectares
1 sq km = 100 hectares
1 sq mile = 2.59 square km
1 ounce = 28.35 grams
1 pound = 0.4536 kilograms
1 short ton = 0.90718 metric ton
1 short ton = 2,000 pounds
1 long ton = 1.016 metric tons
1 long ton = 2,240 pounds
1 metric ton = 1,000 kilograms
1 quart = 0.94635 liters
1 US gallon = 3.7854 liters
1 Imperial gallon = 4.5459 liters
1 nautical mile = 1.852 km

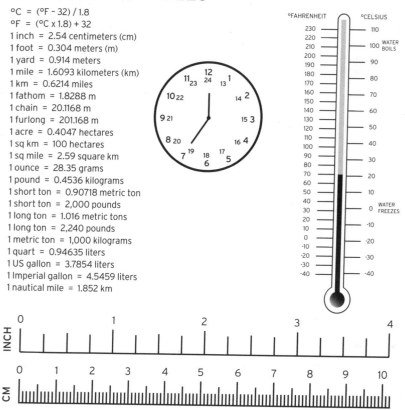

MOON O'AHU

Avalon Travel Publishing
a member of the Perseus Book Group
1400 65th Street, Suite 250
Emeryville, CA 94608, USA
www.moon.com

Editor: Shaharazade Husain
Series Manager: Kathryn Ettinger
Acquisitions Manager: Rebecca K. Browning
Copy Editor: Valerie Sellers Blanton
Graphics Coordinator: Tabitha Lahr
Production Coordinator: Tabitha Lahr
Map Editor: Albert Angulo
Cartographer: Chris Markiewicz, Kat Bennett
Cartography Director: Mike Morgenfeld
Indexer: Judy Hunt

ISBN-10: 1-56691-958-4
ISBN-13: 978-1-56691-958-6
ISSN: 1534-0511

Printing History
1st Edition–1990
6th edition–September 2007
5 4 3 2 1

KEEPING CURRENT

If you have a favorite gem you'd like to see included in the next edition, or see anything
that needs updating, clarification, or correction, please drop us a line. Send your
comments via email to feedback@moon.com, or use the address above.